Classic 1000
Beginners' Recipes

Classic 1000
Beginners' Recipes
Carolyn Humphries

foulsham
LONDON • NEW YORK • TORONTO • SYDNEY

foulsham

The Oriel, Thames Valley Court, 183-187 Bath Road,
Slough, Berkshire, SL1 4AA, England

ISBN 978-0-572-02967-8

Cover photograph by Peter Howard Smith

Photographs by Carol and Terry Pastor

With thanks to the following companies for providing items for the photographs.

For all tiled backgrounds: Smith and Wareham Ltd, Tile Merchants, Unit 2 Autopark,
Eastgate Street, Bury St Edmunds, Suffolk, IP33 1YQ. Tel: 01284 704188/7.
Website: www.smithandwareham.co.uk.

For silver-anodised, easy-release muffin tins and bakeware: Alan Silverwood Ltd, Quality
Bakeware, Ledsam House, Ledsam Street, Birmingham, B16 8DN. Tel: 0121 454
3571. Fax: 0121 454 6749. E-mail: Mike@alansilverwood.co.uk.

For the preparation of the recipes: The Kitchen Machine from the Kitchen Hardware
Professional Range by Morphy Richards (model 48980). Tel: 01709 582402.
Website: www.morphyrichards.co.uk.

Printed in Great Britain by Printwise (Haverhill) Ltd, Haverhill

Contents

Introduction

Do you wish you could cook but don't know where to begin? Perhaps you're just leaving home for the first time and have never had to cook before. Or perhaps you've just decided you're fed up with cook–chill supermarket 'specials' and would like to create your own masterpieces for a change.

However, watching chefs on TV or in trendy restaurants showing off their dexterity – tossing food in pans, chopping vegetables and whisking vigorously with a speed and sleight of hand that would put a conjurer to shame – could well make you feel you're not up to the task. But home-cooking doesn't have to be like that to get fantastic results. It can be simple, as well as healthy, cheap and delicious. And the smug feeling of cooking your supper from scratch and enjoying every mouthful is phenomenal.

With *Classic 1000 Beginners' Recipes,* you'll learn basic cooking skills (no flashy stuff!) as well as general culinary knowledge, and with the help of the straightforward, step-by-step instructions you'll be able to turn out delicious results even at your first attempt. No jargon, no fuss, just down-to-earth cooking at your fingertips. Whatever your age, from school kid to retired bank manager, this book will become a cookery bible to be dipped into at will or used every single day.

Basic food hygiene

First things first: a hygienic cook is a healthy cook – so please bear the following in mind when you are cooking.

- Always wash your hands before preparing food.
- Always wash and dry fresh produce before use.
- Don't lick your fingers.
- Don't keep tasting and stirring with the same spoon. Use a clean spoon every time you taste the food.
- Never use the same cloth to wipe down a chopping board you have been using for cutting up meat, for instance, then to wipe down your work surfaces – you will simply spread germs from one surface to another.

- Always wash your cloths well in hot, soapy water and, ideally, use an anti-bacterial kitchen cleaner on all surfaces too.
- Always transfer leftovers to a clean container and cover with a lid, clingfilm (plastic wrap) or foil. Leave until completely cold, then store in the fridge. Never put any warm food in the fridge.
- Don't put raw and cooked meat on the same shelf in the fridge. Store raw meat on the bottom shelf, so it can't drip over other foods.
- Keep all perishable foods wrapped separately. Don't overfill the fridge or it will remain too warm.
- When reheating food, always make sure it is piping hot throughout, never just lukewarm (see page 21, Reheating cooked foods and Cooking from frozen).
- Never reheat previously cooked food more than once.
- Never re-freeze foods that have defrosted unless you cook them first.

Useful equipment

You can't really even start to cook without a few basic essentials: a frying pan (skillet), spoons, sharp knives, chopping board, scissors, measuring jug, mixing bowl and saucepans. Once you have these, look at the list below and work up from that. You'll find that the more you enjoy cooking, the more equipment you are likely to need. And the more equipment you have, the more you'll enjoy cooking!

Baking (cookie) sheet
Baking tins (pans) – square or rectangular, various sizes
Beater, electric – hand-held
Biscuit (cookie) cutters – fluted and plain in different sizes
Blender or food processor
Cake tins (pans) – deep, loose-bottomed, different sizes, round and/or square
Carving knife and fork
Casserole dishes (Dutch ovens) – have at least one flameproof one for use on top of the stove
Chopping boards – have several different sizes, or shapes or colours, so that they are easily identifiable, and use one for raw

meat; one for strong smelling foods like onions; one for fruit and
  vegetables; and one for bread
Colander – preferably metal, for draining cooked vegetables etc.
Draining spoon
Fish slice
Fluted flan dish (pie pan)
Frying pan (skillet) – 1 medium or large and 1 omelette pan (non-
  stick is a good idea)
Grater – a round or square one with a top handle is better than a
  flat one
Kitchen scissors
Loaf tins (pans) – 450 g/1 lb and 900 g/2 lb
Measuring jug
Measuring spoons
Ovenproof dishes – various sizes, oval or round and rectangular or
  square, including at least one with a lip for pies
Palette knife
Pastry brush
Piping (pastry) bag with a large plain and a star tube (tip)
Potato masher
Potato peeler
Ramekin dishes (custard cups)
Ring tin (pan), about 1.2 litres/2 pts/6 cups
Rolling pin – not vital as a clean bottle will do instead
Roasting tins (baking pans) – 1 large and 1 small
Sandwich tins (pans) – 18 cm/7 in, plus other sizes if liked
Saucepans – at least 1 small, 1 medium and 1 large with lids
Scales
Sharp knives – at least 1 small (for vegetables) and 1 large (for
  cutting up meat) and a bread knife with a serrated edge
Sieve (strainer) – metal or nylon with a fine mesh for making purées
  and straining foods
Skewers – metal for holding raw joints and poultry together; metal
  or wooden for kebabs
Soufflé dish – 15 cm/6 in or 18 cm/7 in diameter
Spatula – for scraping out mixing bowls
Swiss roll tin (jelly roll pan)

Tartlet tins (patty pans)

Whisk – a wire one is best for making sauces, a balloon one for egg whites and cream.

Wire cooling rack

Wooden spoons

Nifty gadgets

None of these is essential but any or all of them make life a lot easier for a keen cook.

Apple corer

Basting spoon with a lip on the side

Boning knife

Canelling knife – for paring off strips of rind from citrus fruit, cucumber, etc.

Cherry stoner

Citrus juicer – I like old-fashioned, wooden, hand-held ones

Double saucepan

Egg pricker – to pierce the end of an egg before boiling, which prevents the shell from cracking

Electric can opener

Fish kettle – a large metal container with a trivet and lid for cooking large, whole fish

Garlic press

Grapefruit knife

Hand-held blender

Herb chopper

Jar opener

Knife sharpener – I like the hand-held sort with two sets of blades you draw the knife across, but you may prefer an electric one or a sharpening steel

Mandolin, for thinly slicing vegetables (not necessary if you have a blade on your grater or food processor)

Meat cleaver

Meat mallet

Melon baller

Mincer (grinder) – not necessary if you have a food processor

Mouli grater
Nutmeg grater
Olive oil can with narrow pouring spout
Pastry (paste) wheel
Pepper mill
Pestle and mortar
Pie funnel – alternatively, you can use an upturned egg cup
Pizza wheel
Poultry shears
Pressure cooker
Salad crisper and shaker
Soup ladle
Spaghetti tongs – the chrome ones with teeth are best
Springform cake tin (pan)
Steamer – the chrome, collapsible sort that fits any saucepan
Toasted sandwich maker – one that cuts and seals the sandwiches
    in halves
Universal cooking thermometer, for sugar, oil, etc.

Useful ingredients

It is a good idea to keep your storecupboard well stocked with
basic ingredients. Use the list below as a guide.

Packets and bottles

Baking powder
Bicarbonate of soda (baking soda)
Cocoa (unsweetened chocolate) powder
Dried herbs – mixed, basil, chives, oregano, thyme, mint and sage
Dried milk (non-fat dry milk)
Dried, minced onion and dried red and green (bell) peppers – not
    vital but great for brightening up rice or pasta and they keep for
    ages
Drinking (sweetened) chocolate powder
Flour – plain (all-purpose), self-raising (self-rising) and wholemeal
Garlic purée (paste) – useful if you can't be bothered to crush
    cloves. Use about 1 cm/½ in per garlic clove or to taste
Honey – clear

Horseradish relish, sauce or cream
Instant coffee
Lemon juice – not vital but a bottle will keep in the fridge for ages
Marmalade
Marmite or other yeast extract
Mayonnaise
Mustard – made English, Dijon and wholegrain
Oil – sunflower and olive, plus a speciality one, such as sesame or walnut
Pasta – dried macaroni and/or other shapes, spaghetti and lasagne sheets, plus stuffed tortellini
Pepper – black peppercorns in a mill and ground white
Preserves – redcurrant jelly (clear conserve) and cranberry sauce
Rice – long-grain, preferably basmati
Salt
Sugar – caster (superfine), granulated, icing (confectioners'), light and dark brown
Spices – ground cayenne and/or chilli powder, cinnamon, ginger, cumin, coriander (cilantro), mixed (apple-pie) spice and grated nutmeg
Stock cubes – vegetable, chicken and beef
Table sauces – ketchup (catsup), brown, Worcestershire, Tabasco, chilli and soy
Tomato purée (paste) – tubes keep best
Vinegar – red or white wine, or cider, plus balsamic and malt

Canny cans

Baked beans
Corned beef and/or ham
Custard
Fish – mackerel, pilchards or sardines, tuna (check the label for 'dolphin friendly')
Fruits – any favourites (pineapple is particularly useful in cooking)
Pulses – red kidney beans, butter (lima) beans, cannellini beans, lentils, etc.
Rice pudding
Soups – condensed mushroom, chicken, tomato (ideal for sauces)

Tomatoes – chopped tomatoes are good for quick sauces
Vegetables – sweetcorn (corn), peas, carrots, green beans,
  mushrooms

Perishables

Bread – loaves, rolls, pitta bread, naan, etc. (store in the freezer and
  take out when required)
Butter and/or margarine – I buy just a reduced-fat olive oil spread,
  suitable for cooking as well as spreading, plus a hard block
  margarine for making pastry (paste)
Cheese – Cheddar and grated Parmesan, plus others as you need
Eggs – medium for cooking, large for boiling
Fresh fruit – apples, bananas, lemons
Fresh vegetables – potatoes, onions, carrots, mushrooms, salad
  stuffs
Frozen prawns (shrimp)
Frozen vegetables – peas, beans, etc.
Milk – keep a carton in the freezer so you won't run out (remember
  that it takes ages to thaw and will need a good shake once
  defrosted)
Plain yoghurt – for sauces and dressings; also for breakfast with
  cereal or for dessert with honey or fruit

Cheats for clever cooks

There are many storecupboard ingredients that are an instant boon
for busy cooks.

Sauces

Any of the following can be used to make a quick sauce:
  Canned, condensed soups
  Passata (sieved tomatoes)
  Creamed mushrooms
  Creamed sweetcorn (corn)
  Canned vegetables, drained and puréed, then thinned with a
    little of the liquid or a little milk
  Garlic and herb soft cheese, melted and thinned with milk
  Soft cheese with black peppercorns, melted and thinned with milk

Mars bar (or other speciality chocolate bar), melted and thinned with milk

Canned fruit, puréed and sieved (strained) if necessary to remove pips

Instant drinking (sweetened) chocolate powder, blended to a smooth paste with milk or water, then cooked, stirring until hot and thinned to the desired consistency with more milk or water

Coatings

To add texture and/or flavour, dip foods such as chops or fish fillets in beaten egg or milk and then one of the following:

Stuffing mix

Crushed cornflakes or bran flakes

Chopped nuts and crushed Weetabix

Crushed Shredded Wheat

Rolled oats, flavoured with herbs or spices (if liked)

Toppings

To finish off savoury dishes before baking or grilling (broiling):

Leftover cooked potatoes, sliced and scattered with small pieces of butter or margarine or mashed with a little milk and butter or margarine

Grated cheese and/or crushed cornflakes or bran flakes

Crushed Weetabix moistened with a little melted butter or margarine

Sliced buttered bread, cut into triangles or cubes

Rolled oats, moistened with a little melted butter or margarine and flavoured with herbs or spices

For sweet dishes:

Crushed Weetabix, moistened with a little melted butter or margarine and sweetened with sugar or honey

Rolled oats, moistened with a little melted butter or margarine, sweetened with sugar or honey and flavoured with cinnamon, nutmeg or mixed (apple pie) spice

Cubes or triangles of buttered bread, sprinkled with light brown sugar

Halved scones (biscuits), buttered and sprinkled with sugar

Thickeners

Use any of these to add extra body to soups, sauces or casseroles
Crumbled Weetabix
Instant oat cereal
Instant mashed potato powder

Planning a meal

Every day, it is important to get a healthy balanced diet, by eating foods from the different food groups in the correct proportions. To help you plan your meals, follow these rules:

- The largest part of every meal and snack should come from starchy foods, such as cereals, potatoes, yams, bread, pasta and rice. These give you energy, fibre, vitamins and minerals.
- Add to the starchy part a small portion of foods rich in protein, vitamins and minerals, such as meat, fish, eggs, nuts, pulses, cheese, milk or other dairy produce.
- Accompany these with lots of fruit and vegetables to give you extra fibre and vitamins and minerals not contained in the other foods.
- Add only a very limited amount of sugar and fat, whether it's in the form of butter, margarine, cream or oil. Also keep to a minimum any foods containing large quantities of sugar and fats, such as cakes, pastries, biscuits (cookies), fried (sautéed) foods, jams (conserves) and relishes, sweets, chocolates and alcohol. These foods will give you warmth and energy, it's true, but if eaten in excess they will make you fat, as they pile on extra calories you don't need.

When you're deciding what to cook, think about what the finished meal will look and taste like. Aim for variety.

Colours and textures are important as well as a healthy balance of ingredients. For instance, you wouldn't want to serve steamed white fish with mashed potatoes and butter (lima) beans. The meal would look unappetisingly pale and taste bland. But if you served the fish with potatoes cooked in their skins, a tomato sauce and French (green) beans, the overall colours and flavours would be much more appealing. In the same way, if you are serving, say, roast pork with apple sauce for a main course, avoid an apple-based dessert.

Remember, too, that expensive foods are not necessarily better for you. For example, mackerel, which is very inexpensive, is just as good for you as a swordfish steak and nibbling asparagus won't make you fitter than eating cabbage! The cheaper cuts of meat are as nutritious as the best steak. The only difference is that the cheaper ones may have more fat, which should be removed before cooking, and the meat will need longer, slower cooking.

But beware of some so-called economy ranges of convenience foods. Cheap minced (ground) meat, for instance, will have a large proportion of fat and the meat content will be of dubious quality. They may also include some added soya protein (this will be clearly stated). Cheap sausages will also have lots of fat and rusk (a bulk filler) and a low proportion of lean meat. Cheap fish fingers and other similar products made with minced fish or meat rather than pure fillet can contain any part of the creature, and so may be of dubious quality.

Basic cooking skills

Most cookery books assume that you can prepare everything straight off without ever having done it before – not this one. This section offers you a step-by-step picture guide to the basic skills.

To chop an onion

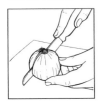 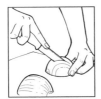 

1   Cut the point off the top of the onion. Pull off all the outer skin leaving the root intact (this will help stop you crying). Cut the onion in half lengthways through the root.
2   Hold one half at a time between your thumb and fingers, flat side down on the chopping board, and cut at intervals from the root end to the tip.
3   Now cut across the first set of cuts. Discard the root end.

To slice an onion

1   Don't peel it. Hold the onion firmly between your thumb and middle finger, with the root end in your hand.
2   Cut into fairly thin slices, starting at the tip end. When you get to the root, discard it.
3   Peel off the brown outer layer and the next layer, if it seems tough, from each slice.
4   Separate the slices into rings.

To prepare and slice (bell) peppers into rings

1 Cut off the stalk end of the pepper.
2 Pull out the core, seeds and any white pith.
3 Tap the pepper, cut side down, on the chopping board to remove any loose seeds.
4 Cut the pepper into rings.

To prepare and slice or dice (bell) peppers

1 Cut the pepper in half lengthways.
2 Pull out the stalk, core, seeds and any white pith from both halves.
3 Tap the pepper, cut sides down, on the chopping board to remove any loose seeds.
4 Holding the pepper cut sides up, cut it into slices. To dice, keep holding the slices together and cut across them. You can vary the width of the slices and the dice as you wish.

To skin tomatoes and other fruit

1 Put the fruit in a bowl and cover with boiling water.
2 Leave to stand for 30 seconds, then drain.
3 Rinse in cold water then peel off the skin with your fingers.

To dice vegetables

1   Peel thinly with a potato peeler or sharp knife, if necessary.
2   Cut lengthways, once for carrots and parsnips, three or four
    times for round vegetables such as potatoes.
3   Hold between your thumb and middle finger and cut into strips.
4   Turn the vegetable, still holding it firmly, and cut across the first
    cuts. For larger dice, make the cuts wider apart. For smaller dice,
    make them closer together.

To chop fresh parsley and other herbs

Good chefs chop their herbs with a sharp knife on a chopping
board, but this is much easier.
1   Leave parsley on its stalks (the stalks have a lot of flavour), but
    for other herbs, pull the leaves off the stalks unless they are very
    small and tender.
2   Put the herbs in a cup.
3   Snip with scissors, as finely as you wish.
4   For chives, hold the bunch in your hand as you snip, letting the
    pieces drop into the cup or directly on to the food to be
    garnished.

To prepare spring onions (scallions) and leeks

Spring onions and leeks are used in many recipes instead of onions.
1 Trim off the ends of the green tops and cut off the root ends.
2 Peel off the tough, damaged, outer leaves and discard.
3 For leeks, slit down through the green end to the white part.
  Wash well under cold running water, to remove grit.
4 Chop diagonally into slices or leave whole as required.

To separate an egg

The authentic chef's way involves juggling with the egg shells but this method is far less tricky! Have a saucer, an egg cup and a small bowl handy.
1 Crack the shell of the egg by tapping in the middle sharply with a knife.
2 Gently pull the two halves of the shell apart over the saucer so the contents fall on the saucer.
3 Invert an egg cup over the yolk. Hold firmly. Pick up the saucer and drain off the white into the small bowl.

Reheating cooked foods from the fridge or freezer

Follow these tips for reheating conventionally or use a microwave oven, following your manufacturer's instructions.

- Cooked food should be reheated only once.
- Always make sure it is piping hot right through, never just warm.
- To check that a dish is hot through, insert a knife down through the centre, wait 5 seconds and remove. The blade should feel burning hot. If not, heat a little longer.
- To make sure foods don't dry out while reheating, either cover or wrap them in foil (not if microwaving!), cover in sauce or gravy or steam over a pan of hot water.

Cooking from frozen

Some foods can be cooked from frozen – and some can't. The following tips will help you to get the best results every time.

- Fruit, vegetables and fish cook very well from frozen.
- Ready-prepared meals and convenience foods like pizzas, sausages and burgers are often labelled: 'Best cooked from frozen'. If so, follow the manufacturer's instructions.
- Home-frozen dishes are best thawed first, ideally in the fridge overnight, or otherwise, covered, at room temperature. If thawing at room temperature, cook as soon as possible after thawing.
- Never cook joints of meat or any kind of poultry from frozen. Thaw as for home-frozen dishes (see above).
- It is possible to cook chops or steaks from frozen, although it is preferable to defrost them first. After quickly browning, cook at a more gentle heat than you would use for thawed meat, and for longer. Make sure they are cooked right through before serving.
- Minced (ground) meat can be cooked from frozen. If in a lump, scrape the browned meat away from the block as it cooks and break up the lump as soon as possible. Make sure every grain is no longer pink before adding the remaining ingredients.
- To speed up the thawing of poultry or meat, immerse the wrapped product in cold water and change the water frequently. Never put it in hot water.
- Don't refreeze thawed food unless you cook it through first.

Glossary of terms

In this book I have tried to avoid all the jargon, using good, plain English instead. But some 'foodie' terms are inevitable, so if in doubt, you can check below. And once you're an old hand at all this, and want to become more adventurous, other books will use all these technical terms, so I thought it worth putting them in.

Al dente – An Italian term, meaning 'to the tooth', widely used to describe the texture of pasta, rice or vegetables cooked until just tender but still with some 'bite'.

Antipasto – The Italian equivalent of hors d'oeuvres. A starter course, often consisting of delicatessen meats, seafood, salads or vegetables marinated in olive oil.

Au gratin – Dishes that are precooked (usually), topped with sauce, then breadcrumbs and grated cheese, and browned under the grill (broiler).

Bake – To cook uncovered in the oven.

Bake blind – To cook a pastry case (pie shell) before filling. The dish is lined with pastry (paste), then filled with crumpled foil or a sheet of greaseproof (waxed) paper and topped with a good layer of dried or ceramic baking beans to keep the pastry in place during cooking.

Bard – To cover lean meat or poultry with strips of fat pork or bacon to stop it drying out during cooking.

Baste – To spoon the cooking fat, juices or marinade over food as it cooks to keep it moist.

Beat – To mix ingredients together in a circular motion with a wooden spoon, wire whisk or electric beaters to incorporate air to make the mixture light and fluffy. The same technique is also used to make smooth batters and sauces. To beat an egg for glazing or binding, break it into a cup and stir briskly with a fork until the yolk and white are well blended.

Bind – To add eggs, milk, cream or a sauce to dry ingredients to hold them together.

Blanch – To plunge foods in boiling water briefly. May be used to loosen the skin of nuts, fruit or vegetables so it can be removed easily, or to remove any bitter or strong flavour from foods, especially from vegetables or salty meats, or to kill enzymes and preserve the colour of vegetables prior to freezing.

Blend – To stir wet and dry ingredients together thoroughly until smooth.

Boil – To cook in liquid at a temperature of at least 100°C/212°F.

Bouquet garni – Traditionally a bunch of fresh herbs tied together and added to a stew or casserole during cooking, then removed before serving. Dried bouquet garni sachets are a convenient alternative.

Braise – To brown the foods in hot fat, then cook slowly (often on a bed of vegetables, called a mirepoix), in a minimum of liquid in a tightly covered container.

Brine – A strong solution of salt and water used for pickling and preserving.

Broiling – American term for grilling.

Brown – To sear the outside of meat quickly in a little hot fat or a non-stick pan to seal in the juices.

Bruise – To crush lightly, to bring out the flavour.

Carve – To cut joints of meat or poultry into slices with a knife.

Casserole dish (Dutch oven) – An ovenproof or flameproof cooking pot with a lid, used to slow-cook fish meat and/or vegetables in liquid.

Chill – To cool food in the fridge to make it very cold before serving. Note: Hot or warm food should always be allowed to cool to room temperature before placing in the fridge.

Chop – To cut ingredients into small pieces with a sharp knife.

Clarify – To clean fat, butter in particular, of any residue. The fat is melted, then the clear liquid poured off for use and the residue is discarded.

Coat – To cover food completely with seasoned flour, egg and breadcrumbs, batter or a sauce.

Coulis – A French term that literally means a sauce – nowadays usually a purée, often of fruit.

Crimp – To decorate the pastry (paste) edge of a pie by pinching all round between your finger and thumb.

Cream – To beat together, using a wooden spoon or an electric beater, until light and fluffy. Usually refers to butter or margarine and sugar.

Croûtes – Pieces of bread, fried (sautéed) in butter or oil until crisp, drained on kitchen paper (paper towels) and used as a garnish or as a base for other foods.

Croûtons – Small cubes of bread, fried (sautéed) in butter or oil until crisp, drained on kitchen paper (paper towels) and used to garnish soups and salads.

Curdle – To separate into solids and liquids as a result of overheating or the addition of acids. This happens to milk, cream and egg dishes when boiled or when excess lemon juice or vinegar is added. Creamed butter or margarine and sugar also curdle when too much egg is added all at once.

Cure – To preserve meat or fish by drying, salting or smoking.

Decorate – To add ingredients to the top or sides of sweet dishes before serving to make them look more attractive. *See also* Garnish.

Deep-fry – To cook food by immersing it in hot oil. For most foods, 190°C/375°F is the correct temperature. To test the oil is hot enough, drop in a cube of day-old bread; it should brown in 30 seconds.

Dice – To cut food into small cubes.

Dilute – To add water or other liquid to make the flavour less strong.

Dissolve – To mix a soluble substance such as salt, sugar or gelatine with liquid until there are no grains left. This is particularly important with gelatine. If you can still see tiny jelly-like granules in the liquid, the finished dish will have unpleasant, gelatinous lumps in it.

Dot – To put small pieces of an ingredient, usually butter or margarine, all over the surface of a dish before cooking.

Dough – Flour, milk or water and/or egg mixed together, usually with fat, to form a pliable mixture which can be kneaded, shaped or rolled.

Drain – To remove the liquid from food either by placing in a colander or sieve (strainer) or by lifting the food out with a draining spoon and leaving it to finish draining on kitchen paper (paper towels), if necessary.

Dredge – To sprinkle food liberally with flour or sugar.

Drizzle – To trickle liquids such as oil, syrup, melted butter or sauce over the surface of food.

Dry-fry – To cook foods in their own fat in a non-stick frying pan (skillet) without the addition of extra oil or other fat.

Dry ingredients – Grainy or powdery ingredients such as flour, sugar, spices, etc. Not moist foods, such as fat, eggs, syrups, jams (conserves) or sauces, even though they are not actually liquid.

Dust – To sprinkle lightly with flour, sugar, spices or other seasoning.

Emulsion – A mixture, such as mayonnaise, where the oil is held in suspension to form a smooth, glossy mass.

Ferment – The action of live yeast with moisture and sugar in a recipe.

Fillet – The leanest, most tender cuts of all meats – the undercut of the sirloin of beef; a cut taken from the fleshy part of the buttocks of pork; the 'eye' of meat in the thick end of the neck or loin of lamb; also, the boned flesh of fish and the boned breasts of poultry.

Flake – To separate cooked fish into individual flakes using a fork.

Flambé – To toss food in a shallow pan in flaming brandy or other spirit until the flames die down.

Flute – To decorate a pie by marking at regular intervals the edge of the pastry (paste) all round with a series of small cuts made with the back of a knife (usually about 1 cm/½ in apart for savoury pies, 5 mm/¼ in apart for sweet ones).

Fold in – To incorporate one ingredient or mixture gently into another, using a metal spoon in a cutting and turning 'figure of eight' movement, so as not to spoil the texture.

Frosting – To coat the rim of a glass or individual fruits in beaten egg white, then caster (superfine) sugar. Also an American term for icing.

Fry (sauté) – To cook food quickly over direct heat in a little oil, butter or other fat.

Garnish – To decorate a savoury dish before serving.

Glaze – A shiny finish given to some foods before baking by brushing with beaten egg, cream, yoghurt or milk. Foods may also be glazed after cooking by brushing with sugar syrup, aspic or sweet jelly (jello) or melted preserves such as redcurrant jelly (clear conserve). Also refers to a sticky, shiny finish given to meat, poultry, vegetables or fruit by cooking them in a reduced, clear sauce.

Goujons – Small thin strips of meat or fish, usually coated in egg and crumbs or batter and fried (sautéed) until crisp.

Grate – To shred into small pieces. The fine mesh of a grater is used for nutmeg and onion; the medium mesh for citrus rind, ginger, cheese, chocolate and breadcrumbs; the coarse side for cheese, chocolate, vegetables and fat such as animal suet.

Hand-hot – When liquid feels hot to the touch but not unbearably so.

Hors d'oeuvres – A French term for the first course of a meal; may be hot or cold.

Hull – To remove the green central calyx from strawberries, raspberries, tomatoes, etc.

Icing (frosting) – A sugary coating for cakes or biscuits (cookies).

Infuse – To steep herbs, spices or other flavourings in water or other liquid to extract the flavour. The ingredients are discarded before the liquid is used.

Joint – A large piece of meat that is cooked and cut into slices for serving. Also, to cut poultry or game into pieces at the joints.

Jus – French term for flavoured cooking juices, served as a sauce.

Kebab – Meat, poultry, fish, vegetables or fruit grilled (broiled) on a skewer.

Knead – To push and stretch a dough with the heel of your hand. For pastry (paste), the kneading should be brief and gentle, just to remove the cracks. For yeast dough, it should be much firmer and take several minutes, until the dough is smooth and elastic.

Knock back (punch down) – To punch a risen yeast dough with your knuckles to knock out the air and return it to its original size. This makes it more elastic, ready to knead and shape before allowing it to rise again.

Knock up – To slash the top and bottom edges of a pie crust gently together with the back of a knife, to seal them.

Lardons – Tiny pieces of fat pork or bacon, cooked until crisp and served in a salad. Also strips of fat, threaded through the surface of meat with a special needle to keep it moist during roasting.

Macedoine – A mixture of sliced or diced fruits or vegetables.

Macerate – To steep food in spirits, liqueurs, wine, fruit juice and/or sugar syrup and then serve in the liquid.

Marinade – A mixture of liquids and flavourings, used to soak raw foods to add flavour and to tenderise them before cooking. Often spooned over food during cooking; any remainder may be made into a sauce to serve with the cooked dish. *See also* Baste.

Marinate – To soak foods in a marinade (see above).

Mash – To use a fork or potato masher to squash and beat cooked or soft foods to a pulp.

Medallion – Small, round cut of tender meat, fish or pâté.

Mirepoix – A bed of sweated vegetables on which food is braised.

Mix – To stir ingredients together until combined.

Noisette – A best end of neck of lamb cutlet, boned and tied in a round.

Parboil – To part-cook in boiling water. The food is then finished by cooking another way, for example parboiled potatoes may then be roasted.

Pare – To remove a thin layer of outer skin.

Peel – To remove the skin of fruit and vegetables.

Pipe – To force soft mixtures such as icing (frosting), whipped cream, mashed potato, choux pastry (paste), biscuit (cookie) dough, melted chocolate or redcurrant jelly (clear conserve) through a plain or shaped tube (tip) fitted to a piping (pastry) bag.

Pith – The white layer between the rind and flesh of citrus fruit.

Poach – To cook gently in hot, but not boiling, liquid (just enough to cover the food), until softly cooked.

Prove – To put yeast dough in a warm place to rise until doubled in bulk.

Pulses – Dried peas, beans and lentils.

Purée – To pass fruit or vegetables through a fine sieve (strainer) or process in a blender or food processor to make a smooth pulp.

Reduce – To boil cooking juices or a sauce rapidly so that it evaporates, thickens and concentrates the flavour.

Rind – The tough skin of bacon or pork. Also, the oily, coloured skin of citrus fruit.

Rise – To expand and puff up. The effect of heat on certain dishes with a lot of air incorporated, such as soufflés, puff and choux pastry (paste), Yorkshire pudding, breads and scones (biscuits).

Roast – To cook in the oven in fat or oil.

Roll out – To flatten and spread out dough with the help of a rolling pin.

Rub in – To incorporate fat into flour by working it gently between your thumb and fingertips and letting it drop back into the bowl until the mixture looks like breadcrumbs.

Sauté – *see* Fry

Scald – To bring milk or cream to just below boiling point (when tiny bubbles rise to the surface) before use in a recipe.

Scrape – To scratch with a knife to remove the skin from young vegetables, the scales of fish, etc., without damaging the flesh.

Sear – To brown meat or poultry quickly over a high heat to seal in the juices before finishing cooking at a lower temperature.

Seasoned flour – Flour to which a little salt and pepper have been added. Used to dust meat, poultry, fish or vegetables before frying (sautéing).

Seasoning – Usually salt and pepper (preferably freshly ground) but it can include other flavourings such as chilli powder, Tabasco sauce, etc.

Score – To make shallow cuts with a sharp knife at regular intervals over the surface of meats such as steaks, to tenderise them before grilling (broiling) or frying (sautéing); also over the rind of pork to allow it to 'crackle' when roasted.

Shallow-fry – To cook food in about 5 mm/¼ in hot oil in a frying pan (skillet).

Sift – To pass flour, icing (confectioners') sugar or other powders through a sieve (strainer), using a wooden spoon, or through a flour sifter, to remove the lumps.

Sieve (strain) – To push soft ingredients such as raspberries, through a wire- or nylon-meshed sieve (strainer), using a wooden spoon, to remove lumps or seeds.

Simmer – To cook gently in liquid kept just below boiling point, so that only occasional bubbles rise to the surface.

Skim – To spoon off the fat or scum from the surface of a soup, stew, casserole or gravy. Floating fat can also be skimmed by laying a sheet of kitchen paper (paper towel) lightly on the surface until the fat is absorbed. This may need to be repeated with several sheets.

Skin – To remove the outer layer of a food before use. For whole fish, it is often easiest to skin the fish after it has been cooked. Poultry and game may be skinned when raw, using a knife to help if necessary. *See also* Blanch *and* Peel.

Soft dropping consistency – A texture best illustrated by lifting a spoonful of the mixture out of the bowl: it should drop softly off the spoon when tilted.

Steam – To cook in water vapour rising from boiling liquid. The food may be suspended in a special steamer or a covered colander over a pan of simmering water. Alternatively, it may be placed in a well-covered basin inside a pan containing enough boiling water to come halfway up the sides of the basin; the pan is then covered while the food is steamed. It may be necessary to top up the boiling water during cooking. It is important that the food does not actually come into contact with the boiling water when steaming.

Stew – To cook food slowly in liquid, or its own juice, on top of the stove.

Stir-fry – To cook small, even-sized pieces of food quickly in a little oil or other fat in a wok or frying pan (skillet), lifting and stirring over a high heat.

Strain – To remove solids from liquid through a sieve (strainer), retaining the liquid for further use.

Sweat – To soften vegetables by cooking gently in fat in a covered pan.

Toss – To turn foods over to coat them in a marinade, sauce, dressing or melted butter by gently lifting them slightly, using a spoon and fork or salad servers, and letting them drop back in the bowl or pan. Also to turn a pancake by tossing it into the air so it turns over and is caught again in the pan to cook the other side.

Truss – To tie up a joint or bird with string to keep it in a neat shape for cooking.

Whip –To stir rapidly or beat using a fork, wire whisk or electric beater, in order to incorporate air quickly into ingredients like cream.

Whisk – To use a wire whisk or electric beater, usually to add air to egg white or egg and sugar mixtures. Also to remove the lumps from a sauce, gravy, etc., during cooking.

Zest – The oily, coloured rind of citrus fruit.

Notes on the recipes

- Most recipes serve four people. It is easy to halve or quarter the quantities if cooking for one or two. Alternatively, make the full amount according to the recipe, and store the remainder in the fridge or freezer for another day.
- Read through the recipe and assemble all your ingredients before you start to cook.
- All ingredients are given in imperial, metric and American measures. Follow one set only in a recipe. American terms are given in brackets.
- All spoon measures are level: 1 tsp=5 ml; 1 tbsp=15 ml
- Eggs are medium unless otherwise stated.
- Always wash, peel, core and seed, if necessary, fresh produce before use.
- Seasoning and the use of strongly flavoured ingredients such as garlic or chillies are very much a matter of personal taste. Adjust to suit your own palate.
- Always use fresh herbs unless dried are specifically called for. If you wish to substitute dried for fresh, use only half the quantity or less, as they are very pungent. Frozen, chopped varieties have a better colour and flavour than the dried ones if fresh have been called for.
- All can sizes are approximate as they vary from brand to brand. For example, if I call for a 400 g/14 oz/large can of tomatoes and yours is a 397 g can, that's fine.
- I have given the choice of butter or margarine in many of the recipes. Use a different spread if you prefer but check that it is suitable for general cooking, not just for spreading (some turn watery when heated). Note that in some cases, for example when making shortbread, only butter will give the best flavour.
- Cooking times are approximate and should be used as a guide only. Always check food is piping hot and cooked through before serving.
- In some recipes I call for yeast extract. This is the generic term for spreads like Marmite or Vegemite.

- Where plain rice or pasta is called for as an accompaniment, I have given a measured quantity. However, when plain vegetables are suggested, such as new potatoes or broccoli, the amount you use is up to your personal taste and appetite.
- Where mayonnaise is called for, I do not recommend trying to make your own. Instead I suggest you buy a good-quality, ready-made one – I prefer those made with olive oil.
- When serving custard, I always use ready-made – I prefer the low-fat variety that comes in a carton. Delicious fresh custard sauces are also available in the chiller cabinet of your local supermarket. You can, of course, make your own, using custard powder or an instant mix – just follow the instructions on the packet or see my recipe for Cheat's Custard, page 384.

Starters

This chapter contains every sort of starter or hors d'oeuvres you're ever likely to want to make. They're all very simple to prepare but are designed to impress. The key to this is presentation: it is important always to make a meal look attractive, especially when cooking for other people. Starters in particular should look really tempting to whet the appetite. Remember, however, this course should be literally a taster – don't make the portions too big or you'll spoil everyone's enjoyment of the fantastic main course that's to follow!

If a recipe calls for hot bread, rolls, etc either warm them very briefly in the microwave or pop them in a preheated oven at 200°C/400°F/gas mark 6 for a few minutes just before serving.

Crostini Napolitana

SERVES 4

4 canned anchovy fillets
45 ml/3 tbsp milk
1 garlic clove, halved
15 ml/1 tbsp pine nuts
5 ml/1 tsp lemon juice
45 ml/3 tbsp olive oil
4 thick diagonal slices of ciabatta
    bread
4 ripe tomatoes, sliced
Freshly ground black pepper
8 fresh basil leaves, torn, to garnish

1 Soak the anchovies in the milk for
15 minutes, then drain.
2 With the machine running, drop
them in a blender or food processor
with the garlic, pine nuts and lemon
juice. Stop and scrape down the sides,
then run the machine again and trickle
in 30 ml/2 tbsp of the olive oil to form a
paste.
3 Preheat the grill (broiler). Brush one
side of the bread slices with the
remaining oil. Grill (broil) this side until
toasted.
4 Turn the bread over and spread with
the paste. Top with the tomatoes and
a good grinding of pepper. Grill again
until the tomatoes are soft and the
paste is bubbling.
5 Scatter the basil over and serve.

Crostini with Olives and Mushrooms

*You can use your food processor to
chop the mushrooms, too.*

SERVES 4

8 diagonal slices from a French stick
1 large garlic clove, halved
175 g/6 oz chestnut mushrooms, finely
    chopped
30 ml/2 tbsp olive oil
15 ml/1 tbsp dry vermouth
Freshly ground black pepper
50 g/2 oz stoned (pitted) black olives
5 ml/1 tsp lemon juice
15 ml/1 tbsp chopped fresh basil

1 Preheat the oven to 180°C/350°F/
gas mark 4. Put the slices of bread on
a baking (cookie) sheet and rub with
the cut garlic clove.
2 Bake the bread in the oven for
20 minutes until crisp and golden.
3 Crush the garlic and put it in a
saucepan with the mushrooms, half the
oil, the vermouth and a good grinding
of pepper. Cook over a moderate heat,
stirring for 5 minutes.
4 Meanwhile, put the olives and lemon
juice in a blender or food processor and
chop as finely as possible, stopping and
scraping down the sides of the machine
as necessary until they form a rough
paste.
5 Spread the olive paste on the bread
and top with the mushrooms. Sprinkle
with the basil and serve straight away.

Peach and Parma Ham Crostini

SERVES 4

2 peaches, halved and stoned (pitted)

8 diagonal slices of ciabatta bread

30 ml/2 tbsp olive oil

4 wafer-thin slices of Parma ham, halved widthways

175 g/6 oz Mozzarella cheese, thinly sliced

8 fresh basil leaves, torn

A few lollo rosso leaves

A little French Dressing (see page 337)

1 Preheat the grill (broiler). Cut each peach half into four slices and place on foil on the grill rack.

2 Brush the slices of bread with the olive oil and place on the foil.

3 Grill (broil) on one side until the bread is toasted. Turn over and top each with a slice of ham, then cheese and finally the basil. Top each with two slices of peach and cook until the cheese is beginning to melt.

4 Transfer to plates and add a garnish of lollo rosso leaves with a little French Dressing spooned over.

Antipasto Speciality

SERVES 6

6 thin slices of Milano salami

6 thin slices of Parma ham

6 thin slices of Mortadella sausage

6 thin slices of Bresaola (cured beef)

6 fresh figs

1 small galia or ogen melon

12 black and 12 green olives

45 ml/3 tbsp olive oil

Freshly ground black pepper

1 lemon, cut into small wedges

Focaccia with sun-dried tomatoes, to serve

1 Arrange the meats attractively on six individual plates.

2 Quarter the figs and arrange in a starburst pattern in the centre of each plate.

3 Halve the melon and remove the seeds. Cut each half into six slices. Cut off the rind.

4 Cut the slices into chunks and arrange around the edge of each plate.

5 Scatter the olives over, trickle olive oil over and add some freshly ground black pepper. Put a lemon wedge on each plate and serve with the focaccia with sun-dried tomatoes.

Parma Ham and Melon Antipasto

SERVES 6

12 thin slices of Parma ham
1 small honeydew melon, peeled,
seeded and cut into 6 wedges
6 stoned (pitted) black olives, sliced
6 stuffed green olives, sliced

1 Arrange the ham slices attractively on six small plates with a wedge of melon to one side of each.
2 Scatter the olive slices over and serve chilled.

Italian Egg Salad

SERVES 4

4 eggs
4 beefsteak tomatoes, each cut into
6 slices
2 x 125 g/4½ oz buffalo Mozzarella
cheeses, each cut into 6 slices
12 stoned (pitted) black olives
8 basil leaves, torn
30 ml/2 tbsp olive oil
15 ml/1 tbsp red wine vinegar
Freshly ground black pepper

1 Hard-boil (hard-cook) the eggs (see page 76). Once cooked, place immediately in a bowl of cold water to cool, then shell and slice.
2 Arrange the slices of tomato, egg and cheese overlapping each other attractively on four plates. Scatter the olives and basil over.
3 Trickle the oil and vinegar over the salads and sprinkle with pepper. Serve.

Chorizo with Churrasco Salsa

In Spain you can buy the salsa in bottles, but I haven't found a good one here yet.

SERVES 4

60 ml/4 tbsp olive oil
30 ml/2 tbsp sweet sherry
20 ml/4 tsp white wine vinegar
5 ml/1 tsp lemon juice
1 shallot, very finely chopped
1 garlic clove, crushed
30 ml/2 tbsp finely chopped fresh
parsley
10 ml/2 tsp chopped fresh oregano
A good pinch of chilli powder
Salt and freshly ground black pepper
350 g/12 oz chorizo sausage
Fresh crusty bread, to serve

1 Using a fork, whisk 45 ml/3 tbsp of the oil together with all the remaining ingredients except the sausages. Cover and leave to allow the flavours to develop.
2 Preheat the grill (broiler). Grill (broil) the sausages for 2–3 minutes on each side until hot through and sizzling. Cut into chunks.
3 Place on plates, whisk the salsa again and pour over. Serve with lots of crusty bread to mop up the juices.

English Cheese Pâté

SERVES 4

100 g/4 oz/1 cup Cheddar cheese, grated

100 g/4 oz/1 cup Stilton cheese, crumbled

25 g/1 oz/2 tbsp butter or margarine, softened

45 ml/3 tbsp medium-dry sherry

A pinch of ground mace

Salt and freshly ground black pepper

Hot toast or crackers, to serve

1 Put all the ingredients in a bowl and stir briskly with a wooden spoon until the mixture forms a paste.

2 Press the pâté into a small pot and chill until ready to serve with hot toast or crackers.

Golden Camembert with Cranberry Sauce

SERVES 4

4 individual Camembert portions, chilled

1 large egg, beaten

40 g/1½ oz/¾ cup fresh white breadcrumbs

Oil, for deep-frying

Mixed salad leaves, to garnish

60 ml/4 tbsp cranberry sauce

Warm French bread, to serve

1 Dip the cheeses in beaten egg, then breadcrumbs. Repeat so they are thoroughly coated. Chill for 30 minutes.

2 Heat the oil in a saucepan, deep frying pan (skillet) or deep-fat fryer to 190°C/ 375°F or until a cube of day-old bread browns in 30 seconds. Add the cheeses and cook for about 2 minutes until golden and crisp.

3 Drain on kitchen paper (paper towels). Place on serving plates, garnish with salad leaves and add a spoonful of cranberry sauce to the side of each. Serve straight away with French bread.

Hazelnut, Cheese and Olive Roll

SERVES 6

225 g/8 oz/2 cups Cheddar cheese, grated

25 g/1 oz stuffed olives, chopped

3 hard-boiled (hard-cooked) eggs (see page 76), chopped

2.5 ml/½ tsp Dijon mustard

30 ml/2 tbsp single (light) cream

30 ml/2 tbsp mayonnaise

30 ml/2 tbsp snipped fresh chives

Salt and freshly ground black pepper

45 ml/3 tbsp toasted chopped hazelnuts (filberts)

A few lettuce leaves

Wedges of tomato and slices of cucumber, to garnish

Crackers or crisp toast, to serve

1 Mix all the ingredients except the nuts and lettuce in a bowl until well blended, stirring briskly with a wooden spoon.

2 Shape into a roll on a sheet of greaseproof (waxed) paper or non-stick baking parchment, roll up firmly and chill for 2 hours. Unwrap and roll in the chopped nuts.

3 Cut into slices and arrange on the lettuce leaves. Garnish with tomato wedges and cucumber slices before serving with crackers or crisp toast.

Grilled Camembert Tomatoes

SERVES 4

4 large tomatoes, halved

225 g/8 oz Camembert, cut into small dice

50 g/2 oz/1 cup fresh white breadcrumbs

15 ml/1 tbsp snipped fresh chives

Freshly ground black pepper

A few lettuce leaves

60 ml/4 tbsp balsamic vinegar

1 Scoop the seeds out of the tomatoes with a spoon and discard.

2 Put the tomato 'shells' in a flameproof dish.

3 Mix the cheese with the breadcrumbs, chives and some pepper and spoon into the tomatoes.

4 Preheat the grill (broiler). Remove the grill rack and place the dish in the pan. Grill (broil) for about 4 minutes until the cheese melts and bubbles and the tops are golden.

5 Arrange a few lettuce leaves on each of four plates. Put two halves of tomato on top and spoon the balsamic vinegar over. Serve straight away.

Savoury Smothered Pears

SERVES 4

4 ripe pears

A few lettuce leaves

1 quantity of Blue Cheese Mayonnaise (see page 339)

15 ml/1 tbsp milk

10 ml/2 tsp chopped fresh tarragon

Paprika, to garnish

1 Peel, halve and core the pears. Lay each one, rounded side up, on a bed of lettuce on a plate.

2 Thin the mayonnaise with the milk and stir in the tarragon. Spoon the dressing over the pears and sprinkle with paprika. Chill until ready to serve.

Portuguese Stuffed Pears

SERVES 4

100 g/4 oz smooth chicken liver pâté

15 ml/1 tbsp port

4 eating (dessert) pears, peeled, halved and cored

A few lettuce leaves

175 g/6 oz/¾ cup medium-fat soft cheese

45 ml/3 tbsp mayonnaise

15 ml/1 tbsp milk

Salt and white pepper

50 g/2 oz stoned (pitted) black olives, chopped

50 g/2 oz stoned green olives, chopped

Hot wholemeal rolls, to serve

1 In a bowl, mash the pâté and port with a fork until smooth.

2 Spoon into the cavities of the pears and place, rounded sides up, on lettuce leaves on four plates, so that the filling is hidden underneath.

3 Whisk the cheese with the mayonnaise and milk, season to taste and spoon over the pears.

4 Mix the olives together and scatter over the dressing. Serve with hot wholemeal rolls.

Nutty Stuffed Peaches

SERVES 4

175 g/6 oz/¾ cup cottage cheese with
  chives
2 celery sticks, finely chopped
30 ml/2 tbsp chopped walnuts, plus 8
  halves, to garnish
30 ml/2 tbsp mayonnaise
Salt and freshly ground black pepper
8 canned peach halves, drained
A few lettuce leaves

1 Mix the cheese with the celery and
chopped walnuts. Stir in the
mayonnaise and season to taste.
2 Pile into the peach halves and place
on lettuce leaves on four plates.
Garnish with the walnut halves and
chill before serving.

Pacific Ham and Pineapple

SERVES 6

75 g/3 oz/⅓ cup long-grain rice
50 g/2 oz/1 cup frozen peas
30 ml/2 tbsp olive oil
10 ml/2 tsp lemon juice
5 ml/1 tsp soy sauce
2 spring onions (scallions), finely
  chopped
225 g/8 oz/2 cups diced cooked ham
225 g/8 oz/1 small can of pineapple
  chunks in natural juice, drained,
  reserving the juice
12 stoned (pitted) black olives
30 ml/2 tbsp mayonnaise

1 Cook the rice according to the packet
directions (or see page 294), adding the
peas halfway through cooking. Drain in
a colander, rinse with cold water and
drain again.

2 Whisk the oil, lemon juice, soy sauce
and spring onions together in a bowl.
Add the rice, mix well and divide
between six small plates.
3 Mix the ham and pineapple together
with the mayonnaise. Slice six of the
olives and stir in. Thin the mixture with
a little of the pineapple juice, if
necessary. Pile on to the rice and
garnish each with an olive.

Pâté and Horseradish Dip

SERVES 4

100 g/4 oz/½ cup medium-fat soft
  cheese
60 ml/4 tbsp single (light) cream
15 ml/1 tbsp horseradish relish
100 g/4 oz smooth chicken liver pâté
A little milk
Salt and freshly ground black pepper
3 stuffed olives, sliced, to garnish
Carrot, cucumber and red (bell)
  pepper sticks, to serve

1 Mix the cheese, cream, horseradish
and pâté in a bowl until smooth,
stirring briskly with a wooden spoon.
2 Thin with milk to a soft consistency
that will drop easily off a spoon but is
not runny. Season to taste.
3 Turn into four small bowls. Garnish
with a few sliced olives and serve with
a pile of carrot, cucumber and red
pepper sticks to dip in.

Coarse Pork Pâté

SERVES 6

450 g/1 lb pig's liver
100 g/4 oz fat bacon pieces
225 g/8 oz belly pork
1 small onion
1 cooking (tart) apple
150 ml/¼ pt/⅔ cup water
Salt and freshly ground black pepper
1.5 ml/¼ tsp ground mace
2.5 ml/½ tsp dried sage
75 g/3 oz/⅓ cup butter
Wedges of lemon and hot toast
    triangles, to serve

1 Cut the liver into chunky pieces.
2 Cut off any rind on the bacon and pork and cut out any bones. Cut into chunks.
3 Peel and quarter the onion.
4 Cut the apple into quarters. Cut off the peel, then cut out the cores.
5 Pass the liver, then the bacon, then the apple and finally the onion through a mincer (grinder) or, with the machine running, drop the ingredients a piece at a time into a food processor until chopped. Pull out of the mixture any stringy bits of bacon or pork fat that you can't cut up, and discard them.
6 Tip the mixture into a saucepan and add all the remaining ingredients except the butter.
7 Cook, stirring occasionally, over a moderate heat for 30 minutes until the mixture is cooked through.
8 Taste and add a little more salt and pepper if liked.

9 Tip into an attractive dish and smooth the surface. Leave until cold.
10 Melt the butter in a saucepan. Pour over the top of the pâté and chill until firm.
11 Serve with lemon wedges to squeeze over and hot toast triangles.

Soft Chicken Liver Pâté with Celery

SERVES 4

200 g/7 oz chicken livers
25 g/1 oz/2 tbsp butter or margarine
1 small onion, chopped
15 ml/1 tbsp lemon juice
200 g/7 oz/scant 1 cup medium-fat
    soft cheese
30 ml/2 tbsp chopped fresh parsley
Celery sticks, cut into matchsticks,
    to serve

1 Cut the livers into small pieces, trimming off any stringy bits.
2 Melt the butter or margarine in a saucepan over a fairly high heat. Add the onion and fry (sauté) for 3 minutes until lightly golden. Add the chicken livers and cook for 4–5 minutes, stirring, until no liquid remains.
3 Purée in a blender or food processor. Tip into a bowl and leave to cool for 5 minutes, then mix in the lemon juice, cheese and parsley, stirring briskly with a wooden spoon until completely blended.
4 Spoon into four small pots, cover and chill.
5 To serve, place a pot of pâté on each of four small plates, and surround with plenty of celery matchsticks.

Potted Duck with Stilton and Redcurrants

1 duck breast with skin
50 g/2 oz/½ cup white Stilton cheese, crumbled
50 g/2 oz/¼ cup unsalted (sweet) butter
15 ml/1 tbsp mayonnaise
Salt and freshly ground black pepper
4 small sprigs of redcurrants
Oatcakes (see page 401), to serve

1 Preheat the grill (broiler). Place the duck breast under the grill and grill (broil) for about 20 minutes, until cooked through and the skin is well browned and crisp.
2 Remove the skin and cut the duck into pieces.
3 Put the duck, cheese, butter and mayonnaise in a blender or food processor. Run the machine until the mixture forms a paste, stopping the machine and scraping down the sides if necessary. Season to taste.
4 Spoon the duck mixture into a small dish and chill. When ready to serve, spoon on to four small plates. Lay a sprig of redcurrants to the side of each and serve with oatcakes.

Hot Chicken Livers, Bacon and Spinach

225 g/8 oz chicken livers
25 g/1 oz/2 tbsp butter or margarine
4 rashers (slices) of streaky bacon, rinded and diced
A pinch of dried sage
Salt and freshly ground black pepper
350 g/12 oz leaf spinach, well-washed
Crusty bread, to serve

1 Cut the livers into small pieces, trimming off any stringy bits.
2 Melt the butter or margarine in a frying pan (skillet) over a fairly high heat. Add the chicken livers and bacon with the sage and fry (sauté) for 5 minutes, stirring, until just cooked and still pink. Season with salt and pepper.
3 Meanwhile, put the wet spinach in a saucepan with no extra water. Sprinkle with a little salt. Cover and cook over a high heat for 5 minutes until tender. Drain in a colander and chop with scissors.
4 Spoon the spinach on to warm plates. Spoon the chicken livers on top. Serve with crusty bread.

Warm Chicken Livers with Raspberries

SERVES 6

450 g/1 lb chicken livers
25 g/1 oz/2 tbsp butter or margarine
Salt and freshly ground black pepper
175 g/6 oz raspberries
15 ml/1 tbsp port
175 g/6 oz mixed salad leaves
30 ml/2 tbsp raspberry vinegar
15 ml/1 tbsp olive oil
5 ml/1 tsp wholegrain mustard

1 Trim the chicken livers of any stringy bits and cut them into bite-sized pieces. Heat the butter or margarine in a non-stick frying pan (skillet) over a fairly high heat. Add the chicken livers and a little seasoning and stir-fry for 4–5 minutes until just cooked but still soft. Remove from the pan and keep warm.
2 Add the raspberries and port to the pan juices, cover with a lid, turn down the heat to fairly low and cook gently for 1 minute.
3 Meanwhile, arrange the salad leaves on individual plates. Whisk together the vinegar, oil and mustard, season with salt and pepper in a bowl and spoon over the salad. Top with the chicken livers and spoon over the raspberries and their juices. Serve warm.

Warm Chicken Liver, Pancetta and Rocket Salad

SERVES 4

225 g/8 oz chicken livers
50 g/2 oz pancetta or pancetta arrotolata, diced
60 ml/4 tbsp olive oil
1.5 ml/¼ tsp dried sage
1 garlic clove, crushed
Salt and freshly ground black pepper
100 g/4 oz rocket leaves
30 ml/2 tbsp balsamic vinegar
15 ml/1 tbsp snipped fresh chives
Crusty bread, to serve

1 Trim the chicken livers of any stringy bits and cut them into bite-sized pieces.
2 Dry-fry the pancetta until crisp and brown over a high heat in a frying pan (skillet). Drain on kitchen paper (paper towels).
3 Heat the oil in the same pan. Add the chicken livers with the sage and garlic and fry (sauté) for 5 minutes, stirring, until just cooked and still pink. Season with salt and pepper.
4 Put the rocket on four plates.
5 Lift the livers out of the pan with a draining spoon and place on the rocket.
6 Add the balsamic vinegar to the juices in the pan with a good grinding of pepper. Heat through and add the chives. Spoon this liquid over the livers, top with the bacon and serve with crusty bread.

Gambas a la Plancha

You can make this with cooked prawns (shrimp) but the flavour won't be quite as good. Make sure you provide finger bowls when you serve these!

SERVES 4

24 raw unpeeled tiger prawns (jumbo shrimp)
Salt
A little olive oil
Wedges of lemon

1 Sprinkle the prawns with salt.
2 Brush a griddle or heavy-based frying pan (skillet) with oil and set over a high heat.
3 When really hot, add the prawns and cook for 2–3 minutes, turning occasionally, until pink and piping hot. Serve straight away with lemon wedges.

Tiger Prawns with Garlic Butter

You'll certainly need finger bowls with this dish – and crusty bread to mop up the butter.

SERVES 4

24 raw unpeeled tiger prawns (jumbo shrimp)
Salt
100 g/4 oz/½ cup unsalted (sweet) butter
2 small garlic cloves, crushed
30 ml/2 tbsp chopped fresh parsley
Wedges of lemon, to garnish

1 Sprinkle the prawns with salt. Melt 15 g/½ oz/1 tbsp of the butter in a heavy-based frying pan (skillet) over a high heat.

2 Add the prawns and cook for 2–3 minutes, turning occasionally, until just pink.
3 Add the remaining butter, the garlic and parsley and allow to sizzle until melted. Turn the prawns over in the butter, then pile on to warm plates, spoon the butter over and garnish with lemon wedges.

Seafood Cocktail

SERVES 6

1 small iceberg lettuce, shredded
170 g/6 oz/1 small can of white crabmeat, drained
250 g/9 oz/1 medium can of mussels in brine, drained
185 g/6½ oz/1 small can of tuna, drained
175 g/6 oz cooked peeled prawns (shrimp)
6 celery sticks, chopped
90 ml/6 tbsp olive oil
45 ml/3 tbsp white wine vinegar
15 ml/1 tbsp chopped fresh parsley
15 ml/1 tbsp chopped fresh thyme
Salt and freshly ground black pepper
5 ml/1 tsp caster (superfine) sugar

1 Divide the lettuce between six glass sundae dishes or large wine goblets.
2 Mix all the fish together in a bowl with the celery.
3 Whisk the remaining ingredients together in a small bowl and pour over the fish mixture. Lift and stir gently until well blended, then pile on the lettuce.

Artichoke and Prawn Cocktail

SERVES 4

425 g/15 oz/1 large can of artichoke
  hearts, drained and roughly
  chopped
175 g/6 oz cooked peeled prawns
  (shrimp)
45 ml/3 tbsp olive oil
15 ml/1 tbsp white wine vinegar
Salt and freshly ground black pepper
150 ml/¼ pt/⅔ cup soured (dairy sour)
  cream
50 g/2 oz/1 small jar of Danish lumpfish
  roe

1 Mix the artichokes and prawns
together in a bowl. Sprinkle over the oil,
vinegar and some salt and pepper and
lift and stir gently until well blended.
2 Spoon into four wine goblets. Top
each with a good spoonful of soured
cream and chill.
3 Just before serving, garnish with a
spoonful of lumpfish roe.

Prawn Cocktail

SERVES 4

60 ml/4 tbsp mayonnaise
30 ml/2 tbsp single (light) cream
15 ml/1 tbsp tomato ketchup (catsup)
A few drops of Tabasco sauce
5 ml/1 tsp Worcestershire sauce
Freshly ground black pepper
½ round lettuce, shredded
175 g/6 oz cooked peeled prawns
  (shrimp), drained on kitchen paper
  (paper towels)
4 slices of lemon and a little paprika,
  to garnish
Brown bread and butter, to serve

1 Mix the mayonnaise in a small bowl
with the cream, ketchup, Tabasco and
Worcestershire sauces and a good
grinding of pepper.
2 Divide the lettuce between four wine
goblets.
3 Top with the prawns and then the
sauce.
4 Make a cut from the centre to one
edge of each lemon slice and hang one
over the rim of each glass. Sprinkle the
sauce with paprika and serve with
brown bread and butter.

Tuna Cocktail

SERVES 4

Prepare as for Prawn Cocktail but use
a 185 g/6½ oz/small can of tuna,
drained, instead of the prawns (shrimp).
Garnish each with a cooked, unpeeled
prawn hung over the side of each glass
as well as the lemon and paprika.

Tuna and Mushroom Cocktail

SERVES 6

Prepare as for Tuna Cocktail but add
50 g/2 oz thinly sliced baby button
mushrooms to the sauce.

Potted Shrimps

This is the traditional way of serving these little crustaceans. When they are set firm in their pots, you can loosen the edges all round and turn them out on to a bed of lettuce. Alternatively, simply serve them in the pots.

SERVES 4

225 g/8 oz/1 cup unsalted (sweet) butter
450 g/1 lb cooked peeled shrimps
1.5 ml/¼ tsp ground mace
A few drops of Tabasco sauce
Salt and freshly ground black pepper
Crusty bread, to serve

1 Put half the butter in a saucepan and melt over a moderate heat. Add the shrimps and cook gently, turning them in the butter, for 2 minutes until hot through. Season with the mace, a few drops of Tabasco sauce and salt and pepper.
2 Pack into four small pots. Melt the remaining butter and pour over the surfaces.
3 Leave to cool, then chill until firm. Serve with crusty bread.

Potted Prawns

SERVES 4

Prepare as for Potted Shrimps but use cooked, peeled prawns (shrimp), instead of the smaller shrimps.

Kipper Pâté

SERVES 6

4 kipper fillets
225 g/8 oz/1 cup unsalted (sweet) butter
Juice of 1 small lemon
Salt and freshly ground black pepper
Thin white toast, to serve

1 Put the fish in a saucepan with just enough water to cover. Bring to the boil, reduce the heat until just bubbling round the edges, cover and cook gently for about 6 minutes or until the fish flakes easily with a fork. Remove from the water.
2 Remove the skin and any remaining bones.
3 Place the fish in a blender or food processor with half the butter and half the lemon juice. Run the machine until the mixture forms a paste. Season to taste and add more of the lemon juice, if liked.
4 Pack the pâté into a small pot and chill, then serve with toast.

Smoked Haddock Pâté

SERVES 6

Prepare as for Kipper Pâté but use 350 g/12 oz smoked haddock fillet instead of kippers.

Smoked Trout Pâté

SERVES 6

Prepare as for Kipper Pâté (page 45). There is no need to cook the fish first, however: simply remove the skin, then place in a blender or food processor and continue as before, adding 5 ml/ 1 tsp grated horseradish or horseradish relish to the mixture.

Smoked Mackerel Pâté

SERVES 6

Prepare as for Smoked Trout Pâté but use smoked mackerel instead of smoked trout.

Sardine Pâté Crispers

SERVES 4

120 g/4½ oz/1 small can of sardines in oil, drained
40 g/1½ oz/3 tbsp butter or margarine, softened
75 ml/5 tbsp plain yoghurt
2.5 ml/½ tsp lemon juice
A few drops of Tabasco sauce
Salt and freshly ground black pepper
1 small onion, thinly sliced and separated into rings
15 ml/1 tbsp chopped fresh parsley
8 rye crispbreads, to serve

1 Put all the ingredients except the onion and parsley in a blender or food processor and run the machine until smooth, stopping and scraping down the sides if necessary.
2 Spread the pâté thickly on the crispbreads and top with the onion rings and parsley. Serve straight away.

Smoked Salmon Pâté

SERVES 6

Prepare as for Smoked Trout Pâté but use smoked salmon trimmings instead of smoked trout. There is no need to skin, simply place the pieces in a blender or food processor and continue as before.

Pilchard Pots

This also makes a delicious sandwich filling, with slices of tomato, cucumber or some shredded lettuce.

SERVES 4

425 g/15 oz/1 large can of pilchards in tomato sauce
30 ml/2 tbsp mayonnaise
15 ml/1 tbsp tomato purée (paste)
90 ml/6 tbsp plain yoghurt
5 ml/1 tsp red wine vinegar
1.5 ml/¼ tsp cayenne
15 ml/1 tbsp snipped fresh chives, to garnish
Toast, to serve

1 Empty the pilchards into a bowl and mash thoroughly (including the bones) with a fork.
2 Add the remaining ingredients and stir briskly with a wooden spoon until well blended.
3 Spoon the mixture into ramekin dishes (custard cups) and chill, if time allows, until ready to serve.
4 Sprinkle the tops with snipped chives and serve with toast.

Seviche

This dish is made with raw fish, which is 'cooked' and tenderised by the lemon juice. Turbot is probably best for this recipe, but any white fish will do, as long as it is very fresh. If you're not sure how to seed chillies, see Fiery Mussel Spaghettini, page 134.

SERVES 4

450 g/1 lb firm white fish fillet, skinned and cubed
1 onion, thinly sliced into rings
1 green (bell) pepper, diced
1 green chilli, seeded and chopped
Salt and freshly ground black pepper
75 ml/5 tbsp fresh lime or lemon juice
A few lettuce leaves and 15 ml/1 tbsp chopped fresh parsley, to garnish

1 Put the fish in a shallow dish. Add the onion, green pepper and chilli and season with salt and pepper.
2 Add the lime or lemon juice, mix gently until well coated and chill for 2 hours or until the fish turns pure white, as if it's cooked.
3 Spoon the fish mixture on to a bed of lettuce leaves and sprinkle with chopped parsley before serving.

Blinis with Smoked Salmon

You can make your own mock 'blinis' if you prefer. Use the recipe for Plain Drop Scones on page 399 but make larger ones – about 12 instead of the 24 small ones.

SERVES 4–6

12 ready-made blinis
200 g/7 oz/scant 1 cup cream cheese
100 g/4 oz/1 cup smoked salmon pieces, finely chopped
1 bunch of spring onions (scallions), finely chopped
4 wedges of lemon
4 sprigs of parsley

1 Wrap the blinis in kitchen paper (paper towels), place on a plate and warm briefly in the microwave or over a pan of boiling water.
2 To serve, arrange them on individual plates with a spoonful of cream cheese, a spoonful of salmon, a small pile of chopped spring onion, a lemon wedge and a sprig of parsley.

Blinis with Caviar

SERVES 4–6

Prepare as for Blinis with Smoked Salmon but omit the salmon and substitute 100 g/4 oz/1 small jar of Danish lumpfish roe (or better-quality caviar if you can afford it) instead. Use soured (dairy sour) cream instead of cream cheese and continue as before.

Blinis with Egg and Caviar

SERVES 4-6

Prepare as for Blinis with Smoked Salmon (see page 47) but use half the quantity of lumpfish roe and add one hard-boiled (hard-cooked) egg (see page 76), sliced, per person. Substitute mayonnaise for the soured (dairy sour) cream, then continue as before.

Avocado with Prawns

SERVES 4

2 ripe avocados
A little lemon juice
100 g/4 oz cooked peeled prawns (shrimp)
45 ml/3 tbsp mayonnaise
15 ml/2 tbsp tomato ketchup (catsup)
2.5 ml/½ tsp Worcestershire sauce
A few drops of Tabasco sauce
Salt and freshly ground black pepper
Wedges of lemon and sprigs of parsley, to garnish

1 Halve the avocados and discard the stones (pits). Brush the cut surfaces with lemon juice to prevent browning and place in individual dishes.
2 Put the prawns in the hollows.
3 Mix the remaining ingredients together in a bowl and spoon over. Garnish with lemon wedges and sprigs of parsley before serving.

Crab and Avocado Cream

To make twists of lemon, make a cut from the centre to the edge of each slice, then twist the points away from each other. Lay the twists on the top of the food as a garnish. You can do the same thing with slices of cucumber.

SERVES 6

2 ripe avocados, halved and stoned (pitted)
15 ml/1 tbsp lemon juice
2 x 40 g/1½ oz/small cans of dressed crab
1 small red (bell) pepper, chopped
1 small green pepper, chopped
30 ml/2 tbsp mayonnaise
A few drops of Tabasco sauce
60 ml/4 tbsp crème fraîche
Salt and freshly ground black pepper
Twists of lemon and 30 ml/2 tbsp chopped fresh parsley, to garnish
Wholemeal toast, to serve

1 Scoop the avocado flesh into a bowl and mash with the lemon juice, using a fork.
2 Mix in the crab, stirring briskly with a wooden spoon, then stir in the peppers, mayonnaise and Tabasco sauce, to taste.
3 Gently stir in the crème fraîche and season to taste.
4 Spoon the mixture into small pots. Garnish with twists of lemon and chopped parsley and serve with wholemeal toast.

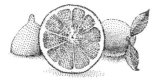

Moules à la Marinière

These are really very easy. If you have time, when you get the mussels home, tip them into a large bowl, cover with cold water and sprinkle a small handful of porridge oats or oatmeal over the surface. Leave them for an hour or two. This will help to clean them.

SERVES 4

1.75 kg/4 lb mussels in their shells
40 g/1½ oz/3 tbsp butter or margarine
1 large onion, finely chopped
1 celery stick, finely chopped
250 ml/8 fl oz/1 cup white wine
120 ml/4 fl oz/½ cup water
Freshly ground black pepper
30 ml/2 tbsp chopped fresh parsley
French bread, to serve

1 Scrub the mussels with a small, clean brush or pan scourer, and scrape off any barnacles with a knife.

2 Discard any that are broken and any that are open and won't close when sharply tapped with the knife. Pull off the 'beards' (the threads hanging down from the shells).

3 Melt the butter or margarine in a large saucepan and add the onion and celery. Cover and cook over a gentle heat for 3 minutes until softened but not browned.

4 Add the mussels, wine and water and a good grinding of pepper. Cover, turn up the heat and cook for about 5 minutes, shaking the pan occasionally until the mussels open. Discard any that remain closed.

5 Pile the mussels into large, warm bowls with their cooking juices and sprinkle with parsley.

6 Serve with French bread to mop up the juices and remember to put a large empty dish on the table for the empty shells.

Piri Piri Prawns

If you're not sure how to seed chillies, see Fiery Mussel Spaghettini, page 134.

SERVES 4

24 raw peeled tiger prawns (jumbo shrimp), tails left on
1 green chilli, seeded and chopped
2.5 ml/½ tsp salt
Juice of 1 lime
Olive oil, for shallow-frying
Wedges of lime, to garnish

1 Place the prawns in a shallow dish. Mix the chilli with the salt and lime juice and sprinkle over, stir well to coat and leave to marinate for 1 hour.

2 Heat the oil in a large frying pan (skillet). Add the prawns and cook, stirring, over a high heat for 2–3 minutes until pink. Do not overcook.

3 Spoon the prawns on to warm plates and garnish with lime wedges.

Oysters au Naturel

Oysters look so impressive, yet they couldn't be easier to prepare! Some people like to add a dash of Tabasco sauce before eating, for an extra kick.

SERVES 4

24 oysters in their shells
Cracked ice
Wedges of lemon
Sprigs of parsley
Thinly sliced brown bread and butter,
    to serve

1 Shuck (open) the oysters in the following way: hold one firmly in one hand protected with a cloth or oven glove. Insert a sharp pointed knife between the two shells, near the hinge. Pushing against the hinge, twist the knife until the hinge breaks.

2 Gently open the oyster, taking care not to spill the juice, and loosen it from its shell. Repeat until they are all opened.

3 Lay the oysters in their half shells on a bed of crushed ice. Garnish with lemon wedges and sprigs of parsley and serve with thin slices of brown bread and butter.

Grilled Oysters with Cream

SERVES 4

16 oysters in their shells
Freshly ground black pepper
90 ml/6 tbsp double (heavy) cream
90 ml/6 tbsp freshly grated Parmesan
    cheese

1 Shuck (open) the oysters (see Oysters au Naturel, above), taking care not to spill the juice.

2 Preheat the grill (broiler). Remove the grill rack and put the oysters in their half shells in the grill pan.

3 Grill (broil) for 2–3 minutes until sizzling. Top each with a spoonful of cream and cheese and return to the grill until just bubbling. Serve at once.

Crispy Fish Goujons

SERVES 4–6

450 g/1 lb whiting, cod or haddock
    fillets, skinned
30 ml/2 tbsp plain (all-purpose) flour
Salt and freshly ground black pepper
2 eggs, beaten
100 g/4 oz/2 cups fresh white
    breadcrumbs
Oil, for deep-frying
Sprigs of parsley and wedges of lemon,
    to garnish
Piquant Dip (see page 340), to serve

1 Cut the fish into strips 5 cm/2 in long and about 1 cm/½ in wide.

2 Mix the flour with a little salt and pepper in a dish. Add the fish and mix gently to coat.

3 Put the eggs in one shallow dish and the breadcrumbs in another. Dip the fish in the beaten egg, then the breadcrumbs to coat completely.

4 Heat the oil in a saucepan or deep-fat fryer to 190°C/375°F or until a cube of day-old bread browns in 30 seconds. Deep-fry for about 2–3 minutes until golden brown, then drain on kitchen paper (paper towels).

5 Pile on warm plates, garnish with parsley and lemon wedges and serve with the Piquant Dip.

Italian Creamed Mussels

Make sure you use mussels preserved in brine, not vinegar, for this dish.

SERVES 6

15 g/½ oz/1 tbsp butter or margarine
1 onion, finely chopped
1 garlic clove, crushed
2 x 250 g/9 oz/medium cans of mussels in brine
2 sun-dried tomatoes in oil, drained and chopped
150 ml/¼ pt/⅔ cup dry vermouth
150 ml/¼ pt/⅔ cup water
15 ml/1 tbsp cornflour (cornstarch)
150 ml/¼ pt/⅔ cup single (light) cream
Freshly ground black pepper
30 ml/2 tbsp chopped fresh parsley
Hot ciabatta bread, to serve

1 Melt the butter or margarine in a saucepan over a moderate heat. Add the onion and garlic and fry (sauté) for 2 minutes, stirring, until softened but not browned.
2 Drain one of the cans of mussels and add them to the onion. Add the second can, including its juice. Add the tomatoes and vermouth.
3 Mix the water with the cornflour in a cup and stir into the mixture. Turn up the heat, bring to the boil and cook for 1 minute, stirring until thickened.
4 Stir in the cream and season to taste. Do not allow to boil again. Add the parsley. Spoon into warm bowls and serve with hot ciabatta bread.

Tuna Dip

SERVES 4–6

185 g/6½ oz/1 small can of tuna, drained
60 ml/4 tbsp mayonnaise
45 ml/3 tbsp plain yoghurt
15 ml/1 tbsp tomato ketchup (catsup)
5 ml/1 tsp lemon juice
1.5 ml/¼ tsp chilli powder
Tortilla chips, to serve

1 Put all the ingredients in a bowl and stir briskly with a wooden spoon until well blended.
2 Spoon into small pots. Put the pots on individual plates and surround with tortilla chips.

Tuna and Bean Dip

SERVES 6

425 g/15 oz/1 large can of cannellini beans, drained
1 garlic clove, crushed
85 g/3½ oz/1 very small can of tuna, drained
30 ml/2 tbsp sunflower oil
15 ml/1 tbsp lemon juice
A good pinch of cayenne
15 ml/1 tbsp chopped fresh parsley, to garnish
Pitta bread, cut into fingers, to serve

1 Put all the ingredients in a blender or food processor and run the machine until smooth, stopping and scraping down the sides if necessary.
2 Spoon on to plates, garnish with parsley and serve with pitta bread fingers.

Tuna Cheese

See Crab and Avocado Cream (page 48) for how to make lemon twists.

SERVES 4–6

185 g/6½ oz/1 small can of tuna, drained
200 g/7 oz/scant 1 cup medium-fat soft cheese
15 ml/1 tbsp lemon juice
1.5 ml/¼ tsp cayenne
Salt and freshly ground black pepper
15 ml/1 tbsp chopped fresh parsley
Mixed salad leaves and twists of lemon, to garnish
Hot toast, to serve

1 Put the tuna and cheese in a bowl and stir briskly with a wooden spoon until well blended. Add the remaining ingredients, again stirring briskly.
2 Shape into a roll on a sheet of greaseproof (waxed) paper or non-stick baking parchment. Wrap and chill for at least 1 hour.
3 Cut the roll into 12 slices. Arrange on four or six plates and garnish with salad leaves and twists of lemon. Serve with hot toast.

Luxury Salmon Pâté

SERVES 6

200 g/7 oz/1 small can of red salmon, drained and black skin removed
75 g/3 oz/⅓ cup unsalted (sweet) butter, melted
150 ml/¼ pt/⅔ cup crème fraîche
5 ml/1 tsp anchovy essence (extract)
5 ml/1 tsp lemon juice
A good pinch of cayenne
Salt and freshly ground black pepper
3 eggs
6 large round lettuce leaves
2 red onions, thinly sliced and separated into rings
30 ml/2 tbsp chopped fresh parsley
Hot toast, to serve

1 Put the salmon, including the bones, in a blender or food processor. Run the machine, then gradually blend in the melted butter.
2 Add the crème fraîche, anchovy essence, lemon juice, cayenne and a little salt and pepper and run the machine again until well blended. Spoon into a pot and chill until ready to serve.
3 Meanwhile, hard-boil (hard-cook) the eggs (see page 76). Once cooked, immediately put into a bowl of cold water to cool, then shell and slice.
4 Spoon the pâté on to the lettuce leaves arranged on individual plates. Top with egg slices and onion rings and sprinkle with chopped parsley. Serve with toast.

Scallop Tartlets with Pesto

*You can use the recipe for Simple
Pesto Sauce on page 336 if you
want to make your own.*

SERVES 6

1 sheet of ready-rolled puff pastry
    (paste)
1 egg, beaten
45 ml/3 tbsp ready-made pesto
1 ripe tomato, skinned and cut into
    6 slices
6 shelled scallops with their coral
45 ml/3 tbsp Pernod
45 ml/3 tbsp crème fraîche
A few mixed salad leaves, to garnish

1 Preheat the oven to 200°C/400°F/
gas mark 6. Rinse a baking (cookie)
sheet with water and leave damp.
2 Cut six rounds out of the pastry using
a 7.5 cm/3 in cutter. Place on the
dampened baking sheet and brush
with beaten egg to glaze. Bake in the
oven for 10–15 minutes until puffy and
golden.
3 Spread with the pesto and top each
with a slice of tomato. Keep warm in a
low oven.
4 Meanwhile, heat the oil in a frying
pan (skillet). Add the scallops and fry
(sauté) over a fairly high heat for
2 minutes on each side until just cooked
through. Add the Pernod and bring to
the boil. Stir in the crème fraîche and
season to taste.
5 Put the pastry rounds on warm
plates. Top each with a scallop and
spoon the pan juices over. Garnish each
plate with a few mixed salad leaves
and serve warm.

Bagna Cauda

*The very cold vegetables in this
recipe make a wonderful contrast,
dipped into the hot fishy oil. Have
some breadsticks on the table for
dipping, too.*

SERVES 4

1 fennel bulb, trimmed and cut into
    strips
2 carrots, cut into strips
1 red (bell) pepper, cut into strips
1 green or yellow pepper, cut into strips
¼ large cucumber, cut into strips
2 celery sticks, cut into strips
150 ml/¼ pt/⅔ cup olive oil
3 garlic cloves, crushed
2 x 50 g/2 oz/small cans of anchovies
50 g/2 oz/¼ cup unsalted (sweet)
    butter, cut into small pieces

1 Chill the prepared vegetables for at
least 1 hour before serving.
2 Put the oil and garlic in saucepan.
Drain the anchovy oil into the pan.
Chop the fish finely and add to the pan.
3 Cook, stirring, over a fairly low heat,
for 5 minutes until the fish have 'melted'
into the oil.
4 Stir in the butter, a piece at a time,
stirring briskly with a wooden spoon
until the mixture is glistening.
5 Spoon into four small pots on
individual plates, and arrange the
vegetables around. Serve straight
away.

Majorcan Squid

If the squid are sold with tentacles, chop these, discarding the hard bases, and add to the pan.

SERVES 4

450 g/1 lb cleaned baby squid tubes
120 ml/4 fl oz/½ cup olive oil
2 garlic cloves, crushed
1 lemon
Salt and freshly ground black pepper
30 ml/2 tbsp chopped fresh parsley
Crusty bread, to serve

1 Slice the squid into rings.
2 Heat the oil in a large frying pan (skillet). Add the squid and garlic and fry (sauté), stirring, over a fairly high heat for 2 minutes until turning opaque.
3 Cover the pan, turn down the heat to low and continue cooking gently for 10 minutes until the squid are really tender and turning slightly pink.
4 Squeeze the lemon into the pan and add some salt and pepper and the parsley. Stir to mix together, then spoon into shallow bowls and serve with crusty bread to mop up the juices.

Spicy Crab Pots

SERVES 4

200 g/7 oz/scant 1 cup medium-fat soft cheese
30 ml/2 tbsp crème fraîche
1.5 ml/¼ tsp chilli powder
15 ml/1 tbsp tomato ketchup (catsup)
170 g/6 oz/1 small can of white crabmeat, drained
Lemon juice
Salt and freshly ground black pepper
¼ cucumber, finely chopped
Pretzels, to serve

1 Using a fork, mash the cheese with the crème fraîche in a bowl until smooth.
2 Stir in the chilli, tomato ketchup and crab. Add lemon juice, salt and pepper to taste.
3 Spoon the mixture into small pots and chill until ready to serve.
4 Cover each with a layer of finely chopped cucumber and serve surrounded by pretzels.

Creamy Baked Garlic Mushrooms

To peel mushrooms, pull away the thin outer layer in strips, starting from the outer edge, all round.

SERVES 4

8–12 large, flat mushrooms
25 g/1 oz/2 tbsp butter or margarine
2 large garlic cloves, very finely
   chopped
Salt and freshly ground black pepper
1 wineglass of dry white wine
150 ml/¼ pt/⅔ cup double (heavy)
   cream
30 ml/2 tbsp chopped fresh parsley
Hot French bread, to serve

1 Preheat the oven to 190°C/375°F/ gas mark 5.

2 Peel the mushrooms, cut off the stalks, and chop them.

3 Grease a large, shallow baking tin (pan) with the butter or margarine. Lay the mushrooms in it and sprinkle the chopped stalks over.

4 Sprinkle the garlic over and season lightly.

5 Pour in the wine. Cover with foil and bake in the oven for 20 minutes.

6 Carefully transfer the mushrooms to warm plates. Stir the cream into the juices and bring just to the boil over a high heat. Taste and re-season. Pour over the mushrooms and sprinkle with parsley before serving with hot French bread.

Potted Garlic Mushrooms

SERVES 4

100 g/4 oz/½ cup butter or margarine
1 onion, chopped
450 g/1 lb open mushrooms, peeled
   (see left) and sliced
15 ml/1 tbsp chopped fresh parsley
1 large garlic clove, crushed
Salt and freshly ground black pepper
Hot toast, to serve

1 Melt half the butter or margarine in a saucepan. Add the onion and fry (sauté) over a fairly high heat for 2 minutes, stirring.

2 Stir in the mushrooms, parsley and garlic and season lightly. Cover, turn down the heat to fairly low and cook gently for 10 minutes, stirring occasionally, until the mushrooms are really tender and the juices have run.

3 Spoon the mixture into a blender or food processor and run the machine briefly to chop the mushrooms and onion finely, but do not purée. Taste and re-season if necessary.

4 Spoon into four ramekin dishes (custard cups) and level the surfaces. Leave to cool, then chill until firm.

5 Melt the remaining butter or margarine and pour over the mushroom mixture. Chill until firm. Serve with hot toast.

Avocado Sorrento

SERVES 4

2 ripe avocados
120 ml/4 fl oz/½ cup passata (sieved tomatoes)
5 ml/1 tsp dried oregano
Salt and freshly ground black pepper
100 g/4 oz Mozzarella cheese, thinly sliced

1 Halve the avocados, remove the stones (pits), then peel off the skins. It is best to use your fingers to avoid damaging the flesh, but if the avocados aren't quite ripe you will have to cut away the skins with a knife.
2 Cut the flesh into slices and place in four individual, shallow, flameproof dishes.
3 Spoon over the passata, sprinkle with the oregano and season lightly.
4 Lay the Mozzarella on top.
5 Preheat the grill (broiler). Remove the grill rack and lay the dishes in the pan, then grill (broil) until the cheese melts and bubbles. Do not overheat or the avocado may become bitter and the cheese will go rubbery! Serve straight away.

Baked Avocados with Prawns

SERVES 4

2 ripe avocados
5 ml/1 tsp lemon juice
2 spring onions (scallions), finely chopped
75 g/3 oz/⅓ cup garlic and herb soft cheese
100 g/4 oz cooked peeled prawns (shrimp)
Salt and freshly ground black pepper
A few drops of Tabasco sauce
15 g/½ oz/1 tbsp butter or margarine
25 g/1 oz/½ cup fresh white breadcrumbs
15 ml/1 tbsp grated Parmesan cheese

1 Preheat the oven to 200°C/400°F/ gas mark 6.
2 Halve the avocados, remove the stones (pits) and scoop the flesh into a bowl. Reserve the shells. Mash the flesh well with the lemon juice, using a fork.
3 Stir in the spring onions, soft cheese and prawns. Season to taste with salt, pepper and Tabasco sauce.
4 Spoon this mixture back into the shells and place in a shallow baking dish. Melt the butter or margarine in a small saucepan, stir in the breadcrumbs and Parmesan cheese and spoon over the filling.
5 Bake in the oven for about 10–15 minutes until the tops are golden brown and the filling piping hot. Serve straight away.

Mediterranean Aubergines

This is my version of Melanzane alla Parmigiana, a delicious hot Italian dish.

SERVES 4

90 ml/6 tbsp olive oil

1 large aubergine (eggplant), sliced

Salt and freshly ground black pepper

120 ml/4 fl oz/½ cup passata (sieved tomatoes)

5 ml/1 tsp dried basil

100 g/4 oz Mozzarella cheese, thinly sliced

30 ml/2 tbsp grated Parmesan cheese

1 Heat the oil in a frying pan (skillet). Fry (sauté) the aubergine slices over a high heat until golden on both sides. Drain on kitchen paper (paper towels), then arrange in four individual gratin dishes. Sprinkle with salt and pepper.

2 Spoon the passata over the aubergines and sprinkle with the basil. Top with the Mozzarella, then the Parmesan.

3 Preheat the grill (broiler). Remove the grill rack and place the dishes in the grill pan. Grill (broil) until the cheese melts and bubbles. Serve straight away.

Aubergine Dip with Crudités

This can be made in advance and kept in a covered container in the fridge. It's also great spread on toast.

SERVES 4

1 large aubergine (eggplant)

1 spring onion (scallion), very finely chopped

1 small garlic clove, crushed

2 large ripe tomatoes, skinned, seeded and chopped

45 ml/3 tbsp olive oil

Lemon juice, to taste

Salt and freshly ground black pepper

15 ml/1 tbsp chopped fresh parsley

2 carrots, cut into matchsticks

¼ cucumber, cut into matchsticks

1 red (bell) pepper, cut into thin strips

16 whole tiny button mushrooms

1 Preheat the grill (broiler). Grill (broil) the aubergine for about 15 minutes, turning occasionally, until the skin blackens and the flesh feels soft when squeezed.

2 When cool enough to handle, peel off the skin and discard, then chop the flesh finely and place in a bowl.

3 Add the spring onion, garlic and tomatoes and mix well.

4 Add the oil, a drop or two at a time, stirring briskly with a wooden spoon after each addition, until the mixture is glistening but still quite thick. Add lemon juice, salt and pepper to taste.

5 Spoon the mixture into small pots and sprinkle with parsley. Chill until ready to serve. Arrange the prepared vegetables around and serve very cold.

Walnut and Sesame Dip

This dish looks particularly good if you use (bell) peppers of different colours – red, green, yellow and orange. To toast sesame seeds, put them in a frying pan (skillet) and stir over a moderate heat for 1–2 minutes until golden.

SERVES 4

1 large garlic clove
25 g/1 oz/¼ cup walnut pieces
1 slice of white bread
15 ml/1 tbsp sesame seeds, toasted
6 fresh basil leaves
15 ml/1 tbsp lemon juice
175 ml/6 fl oz/¾ cup mayonnaise
120 ml/4 fl oz/½ cup crème fraîche
Salt and freshly ground black pepper
4 peppers, halved and sliced

1 Put the garlic, walnuts, bread, sesame seeds, basil and lemon juice in a blender or food processor. Run the machine until the mixture forms a paste, stopping the machine and scraping down the sides.

2 Add the mayonnaise and crème fraîche and run the machine until smooth.

3 Season to taste, then spoon into small bowls, cover and chill until ready to serve with the pepper dippers.

Soups

Soups make wonderful, warming starters, but are best before a fairly light main course or they can be a bit too filling.

Alternatively, they can be served as main courses themselves, for lunch or supper, accompanied by some crusty bread or warm rolls.

I have included a recipe for home-made stock in this chaper – the basis of any good soup. Of course, you can always use stock cubes dissolved in water, as I've indicated in the recipes, but do try home-made sometimes. It tastes much better and is full of goodness.

Home-made Stock

This recipe can be used as the basis for any soup, but also for gravy, or any other recipe that calls for chicken or meat stock.

MAKES ABOUT 900 ML/1½ PTS/3¾ CUPS

1 cooked chicken or turkey carcass or bone from the Sunday joint
1 onion
1 bay leaf
1 carrot, cut into chunks
Salt and freshly ground black pepper

1 Break up the carcass or separate the bone at the joint (if there is one) and put the pieces in a saucepan with the onion, bay leaf, carrot and enough water to cover. Add a little salt and pepper.

2 Put the pan over a high heat until the water is boiling. Skim off any scum from the surface with a draining spoon and discard.

3 Reduce the heat until the liquid is just bubbling gently, cover with a lid and cook for 2 hours. Strain the stock through a colander into a large bowl. Leave until cold, then chill or freeze in two or three quantities for use as required.

Cream of Chicken and Tarragon Soup

SERVES 4

1 onion, grated
15 g/½ oz/1 tbsp butter or margarine
300 ml/½ pt/1¼ cups chicken stock, made with 1 stock cube
100 g/4 oz/1 cup cooked chicken, very finely chopped
15 ml/1 tbsp chopped fresh tarragon
30 ml/2 tbsp plain (all-purpose) flour
300 ml/½ pt/1¼ cups milk
45 ml/3 tbsp double (heavy) cream
Salt and freshly ground black pepper

1 Put the onion and butter or margarine in a saucepan. Cook over a moderate heat, stirring, for 2 minutes until softened but not browned.

2 Add the stock, chopped chicken and tarragon. Turn up the heat and cook until boiling. Turn down the heat until gently bubbling around the edges and cook gently for 5 minutes, stirring occasionally.

3 Mix the flour with 60 ml/4 tbsp of the milk in a small bowl or cup until smooth. Stir into the saucepan with the remaining milk.

4 Cook over a high heat, stirring, until boiling and thickened, then turn down the heat again and cook for 2 minutes, stirring all the time.

5 Stir in 30 ml/2 tbsp of the cream and heat again briefly. Taste and season.

6 Ladle into warm bowls. Use a teaspoon to spoon a small swirl of the remaining cream in the centre of each bowl of soup. It will float on the surface. Serve straight away.

Creamy Chicken and Vegetable Soup

You can use any quantity of whatever vegetables you may have left over from a previous meal. However, avoid roasted potatoes or parsnips, as they don't have a very good flavour. Pick any last scraps of chicken off the carcass before making this soup and use the meat for sandwiches.

MAKES ABOUT 900 ML/1½ PTS/3¾ CUPS

1 roast chicken carcass

900 ml/1½ pts/3¾ cups water

1 bay leaf

1 chicken stock cube

Salt and freshly ground black pepper

100 g/4 oz cooked leftover vegetables

60 ml/4 tbsp dried milk powder (non-fat dry milk)

30 ml/2 tbsp plain (all-purpose) flour

1 Break the carcass into pieces and place in a saucepan.

2 Cover with the water, add the bay leaf, stock cube and some salt and pepper.

3 Bring to the boil over a high heat, then turn down the heat so it is bubbling gently around the edges. Cover with a lid and cook for 1 hour.

4 Put a colander over a large bowl. Tip the contents of the saucepan into the colander so the liquid drips through. Rinse out the saucepan, and then tip the liquid back into the pan. Throw away the carcass.

5 Add the vegetables to the liquid. Cook, boiling gently, for 5 minutes.

6 Pour everything into a blender or food processor with the dried milk powder and flour. Run the machine until the mixture is smooth, then pour it back into the saucepan.

7 Cook, stirring over a high heat until boiling, then turn down the heat and cook for a further 2 minutes, stirring. Taste and re-season if necessary. Pour into bowls and serve.

Chicken Noodle Soup

SERVES 4

900 ml/1½ pts/3¾ cups chicken stock, made with 2 stock cubes

1 bay leaf

1 onion, halved

1 small skinless chicken breast

50 g/2 oz vermicelli, broken into small pieces, or soup pasta

Salt and freshly ground black pepper

15 ml/1 tbsp chopped fresh parsley

1 Put everything except the parsley in a saucepan over a high heat.

2 Cook until the mixture is boiling, stirring once or twice. Turn down the heat until gently bubbling around the edges. Cook for 10 minutes until the chicken and pasta are really tender.

3 Lift the chicken out of the pan with a draining spoon and cut into very small pieces.

4 Lift out the onion and bay leaf and discard. Return the chopped chicken to the pan and season to taste with salt and pepper, then heat through.

5 Ladle into warm soup bowls and sprinkle with chopped parsley before serving.

Almond Chicken Soup

This soup is even better made with home-made stock (see page 60) instead of the cubes.

SERVES 6

100 g/4 oz/1 cup ground almonds

1.2 litres/2 pts/5 cups hot chicken stock, made with 2 stock cubes

Salt and freshly ground white pepper

100 g/4 oz/1 cup finely chopped cooked chicken

50 g/2 oz/¼ cup long-grain rice

150 ml/¼ pt/⅔ cup double (heavy) cream

15 ml/1 tbsp chopped fresh parsley, to garnish

1 Put the almonds in a saucepan. Add about 300 ml/½ pt/1¼ cups of the hot stock, whisking all the time until the mixture is smooth. Whisk in the remaining stock and a little salt and pepper.

2 Bring to the boil over a high heat, reduce the heat until bubbling gently around the edges and cook for 20 minutes.

3 Add the chicken and rice and cook for a further 10 minutes. Stir in the cream and heat through. Taste and re-season if necessary. Serve straight away, garnished with chopped parsley.

Chicken and Corn Chowder

SERVES 4

1 chicken portion

450 ml/¾ pt/2 cups water

1 bunch of spring onions (scallions), chopped

2 potatoes, finely diced

Salt and freshly ground black pepper

320 g/12 oz/1 large can of sweetcorn (corn)

300 ml/½ pt/1¼ cups milk

30 ml/2 tbsp chopped fresh parsley

1 Put the chicken portion in a pan with the water. Bring to the boil over a high heat, then reduce the heat until gently bubbling around the edges, part-cover and cook for 45 minutes. Remove from the heat.

2 Carefully lift out the chicken, remove all meat from the bones, chop and reserve.

3 Add the spring onions, potatoes and some salt and pepper to the chicken stock, return to a fairly high heat and cook for 10 minutes. Add the chicken, sweetcorn and milk and heat through for 2 minutes.

4 Stir in the parsley and season with more pepper, if liked. Ladle into bowls and serve hot.

Quick Scottish Chicken Soup

SERVES 4–6

2 x 295 g/10½ oz/medium cans of
  condensed cream of chicken soup
About 600 ml/1 pt/2½ cups milk
45 ml/3 tbsp Scotch whisky
60 ml/4 tbsp single (light) cream
15 ml/1 tbsp chopped fresh parsley

1 Empty the soup into a pan and add
two canfuls of milk.
2 Whisk in the whisky and heat
through over a fairly high heat until
piping hot but not boiling. Ladle into
warm bowls.
3 Add a spoonful of cream to each
and sprinkle with chopped parsley.

Sherried Chicken and Pasta Soup

SERVES 4

1 small skinless chicken breast, cut into
  thin strips about 2.5 cm/1 in long
900 ml/1½ pts/3¾ cups chicken stock,
  made with 2 stock cubes
4 spring onions (scallions), chopped
100 g/4 oz small button mushrooms,
  sliced
50 g/2 oz soup pasta shapes
1 bouquet garni sachet
Salt and freshly ground black pepper
60 ml/4 tbsp medium-dry sherry

1 Put all the ingredients except the
sherry in a saucepan. Bring to the boil
over a high heat, reduce the heat until
gently bubbling around the edges and
cook for 10 minutes.
2 Stir in the sherry, taste and re-season
if necessary. Ladle into warm bowls
and serve hot.

Oriental Chicken and Sweetcorn Soup

SERVES 6

900 ml/1½ pts/3¾ cups chicken stock,
  made with 2 stock cubes
2 thin slices of fresh root ginger
1 garlic clove, halved
320 g/12 oz/1 medium can of sweetcorn
  (corn)
100 g/4 oz/1 cup finely chopped
  cooked chicken
30 ml/2 tbsp dry sherry
15 ml/1 tbsp light soy sauce
1 spring onion (scallion), very finely
  chopped
15 ml/1 tbsp cornflour (cornstarch)
30 ml/2 tbsp water
Salt and white pepper

1 Put the stock in a saucepan with the
ginger and garlic. Bring to the boil over
a high heat, then reduce the heat until
gently bubbling around the edges,
cover and cook for 5 minutes.
2 Remove the ginger and garlic with a
draining spoon and discard. Add all the
remaining ingredients except the
cornflour, water and seasoning. Bring to
the boil over a high heat again, reduce
the heat as before and cook gently for
3 minutes.
3 Mix the cornflour with the water in a
cup and stir into the soup. Cook over a
high heat, stirring until slightly
thickened, then cook for a further
minute. Season to taste with salt and
pepper and add a little extra soy sauce
if liked. Ladle into warm bowls and
serve.

Cheese and Broccoli Potage

Try this with Camembert, Cheddar or even blue cheese for a change. You can also substitute cauliflower for the broccoli.

SERVES 4

15 g/½ oz/1 tbsp butter or margarine
1 large onion, chopped
2 large potatoes, diced
1 litre/1¾ pts/4¼ cups chicken or vegetable stock, made with 2 stock cubes
Salt and freshly ground black pepper
100 g/4 oz Brie, chopped
100 g/4 oz raw or cooked broccoli, chopped
30 ml/2 tbsp milk or double (heavy) cream

1 Melt the butter or margarine in a saucepan over a moderate heat. Add the onion and potato and fry (sauté) for 2 minutes until slightly softened but not browned, stirring all the time with a wooden spoon.

2 Add the stock and sprinkle in a little salt and pepper.

3 Turn up the heat until the soup boils, then turn it down again until gently bubbling around the edges and cook for 20 minutes.

4 Add the cheese and broccoli and stir well. Cook for a further 5 minutes, stirring occasionally.

5 Pour the soup into a blender or food processor with the milk or cream. Run the machine until smooth, then tip back into the saucepan. Taste and add more salt and pepper if necessary.

6 Heat through over a gentle heat just until the first bubbles appear. Ladle the soup into bowls and serve.

Farmhouse Potage

Use a chicken stock cube if you have no home-made stock.

SERVES 6

25 g/1 oz/2 tbsp butter or margarine
2 leeks, well-washed, trimmed and thinly sliced
2 carrots, finely chopped
2 potatoes, diced
600 ml/1 pt/2½ cups home-made stock (see page 60)
400 g/14 oz/1 large can of chopped tomatoes
400 g/14 oz/1 large can of baked beans
100 g/4 oz/1 cup chopped cooked chicken or turkey
5 ml/1 tsp dried oregano
Salt and freshly ground black pepper
Grated cheese, to serve

1 Melt the butter or margarine in a saucepan over a fairly high heat. Add the leeks, carrots and potatoes and fry (sauté) for 2 minutes, stirring.

2 Add the stock, bring to the boil, then reduce the heat until gently bubbling around the edges and cook for 15 minutes.

3 Add the remaining ingredients and heat rapidly until boiling, then turn down the heat again as before and cook for a further 10 minutes. Taste and re-season if necessary. Ladle into warm bowls and serve with grated cheese to sprinkle over.

Photograph opposite: **Warm Chicken Liver, Pancetta and Rocket Salad (see page 42)**

Stilton and Celery Soup

This is a good way of using up the outer sticks of a head of celery and the end of a piece of Stilton or any other blue cheese.

SERVES 4

2 celery sticks, chopped

1 onion, chopped

1 potato, diced

1 litre/1¾ pts/4¼ cups chicken or vegetable stock, made with 2 stock cubes

100 g/4 oz Stilton cheese

Salt and freshly ground black pepper

15 ml/1 tbsp cornflour (cornstarch)

30 ml/2 tbsp milk or single (light) cream

30 ml/2 tbsp chopped fresh parsley or a few celery leaves, to garnish

1 Put the celery, onion and potato in a saucepan and add the stock.

2 Heat rapidly until boiling. Turn down the heat until bubbling gently around the edges and cook for 30 minutes.

3 Cut off any rind from the cheese and cut it into small pieces. Put it in a blender or food processor, pour in the soup and add seasoning to taste.

4 Run the machine until the mixture is smooth.

5 Put a sieve (strainer) over the rinsed-out saucepan and pour the soup into the sieve, stirring with a wooden spoon to help it pass through. Any fibrous bits of celery will be left in the sieve. You can omit this stage if you don't mind the odd stringy bit in your soup!

6 Blend the cornflour with the milk or single cream. Stir into the pan, bring to the boil over a high heat and cook for 1 minute, stirring all the time.

7 Taste the soup and re-season if necessary. Ladle into bowls and sprinkle with the chopped parsley or celery leaves.

Cheese, Celery and Corn Chowder

SERVES 4

295 g/10½ oz/1 medium can of condensed celery soup

About 300 ml/½ pt/1¼ cups milk

200 g/7 oz/1 small can of sweetcorn (corn)

100 g/4 oz/1 cup Cheddar cheese, grated

Freshly ground black pepper

1 Empty the celery soup into a saucepan.

2 Add a canful of milk.

3 Stir in the contents of the can of sweetcorn, including the liquid.

4 Heat through, stirring over a fairly high heat.

5 When small bubbles are appearing around the edges, add the cheese and heat, stirring, until it has melted.

6 Thin with a little more milk, if liked, and heat through again. Season the soup to taste with pepper and ladle into warm bowls.

Photograph opposite:
Mighty Minestrone (see page 69)

French Onion Soup

SERVES 4

3 large onions, thinly sliced
25 g/1 oz/2 tbsp butter or margarine
10 ml/2 tsp light brown sugar
1 litre/1¾ pts/4¼ cups beef stock, made
    with 2 stock cubes
Salt and freshly ground black pepper
4 slices of French bread
50 g/2 oz/½ cup Gruyère (Swiss) cheese,
    grated

1 Put the onions in a saucepan with the butter or margarine. Cook, stirring, for 5 minutes until turning golden.
2 Sprinkle in the sugar and continue to cook, stirring over a fairly gentle heat for about 10 minutes until the onions are a rich brown. Do not allow to burn.
3 Add the stock and some salt and pepper. Turn up the heat until the soup boils, then turn it down to fairly low, part-cover with a lid and cook gently for 20 minutes.
4 Meanwhile, preheat the grill (broiler) and toast the bread on both sides. Top with the cheese, then grill (broil) again until the cheese melts.
5 Spoon the soup into four warm bowls. Float a piece of cheesy bread on each and serve.

Carrot and Cumin Soup

SERVES 4

40 g/1½ oz/3 tbsp butter or margarine
450 g/1 lb carrots, sliced
2 potatoes, chopped
1 onion, chopped
2.5 ml/½ tsp ground cumin
600 ml/1 pt/2½ cups chicken stock,
    made with 1 stock cube
1 bay leaf
A pinch of cayenne
Salt and freshly ground black pepper
150 ml/¼ pt/⅔ cup milk
2 slices of bread, cubed
30 ml/2 tbsp sunflower oil
1 garlic clove, halved

1 Melt 25 g/1 oz/2 tbsp of the butter or margarine in a saucepan. Add the carrots, potatoes and onion and fry (sauté) over a fairly high heat for 2 minutes, stirring. Stir in the cumin and cook for 1 minute.
2 Add the stock, bay leaf, cayenne and a little salt and pepper. Bring to the boil, reduce the heat until gently bubbling around the edges and cook for 20 minutes. Discard the bay leaf.
3 Purée the soup in a blender or food processor and return to the saucepan. Stir in the milk, taste and re-season if necessary.
4 Meanwhile, heat the remaining butter or margarine and the oil in a frying pan (skillet), and fry the bread cubes with the garlic over a fairly high heat, stirring and turning until golden. Drain on kitchen paper (paper towels) and discard the garlic.
5 Ladle the soup into bowls and sprinkle with the croûtons.

The Easiest Sweetcorn Soup

SERVES 4

A knob of butter or margarine
1 onion, chopped
4 potatoes, sliced
320 g/12 oz/1 medium can of sweetcorn (corn)
900 ml/1½ pts/3¾ cups chicken or vegetable stock, made with 2 stock cubes
Salt and freshly ground black pepper

1 Melt the butter or margarine in a saucepan and add the onion. Cook over a fairly high heat for 2 minutes, stirring until the onion softens and is just turning pale golden.
2 Add the remaining ingredients and heat until boiling.
3 Turn down the heat until bubbling gently around the edges, part-cover the pan and cook for 20 minutes.
4 Either mash the potatoes into the liquid with a potato masher or tip the mixture into a blender or food processor and run the machine until smooth. Taste and re-season if necessary. Reheat in the saucepan and serve hot.

Cheese and Sweetcorn Soup

SERVES 4

Make exactly as The Easiest Sweetcorn Soup, but add 50 g/2 oz/½ cup grated Cheddar cheese to the blended soup and stir to melt before serving.

Clam Bisque

SERVES 4

15 g/½ oz/1 tbsp butter or margarine
1 onion, finely chopped
30 ml/2 tbsp cornflour (cornstarch)
300 ml/½ pt/1¼ cups chicken stock, made with 1 stock cube
300 ml/½ pt/1¼ cups milk
300 g/11 oz/1 medium can of minced clams
5 ml/1 tsp celery salt
Freshly ground black pepper
30 ml/2 tbsp double (heavy) cream
15 ml/1 tbsp chopped fresh parsley

1 Melt the butter or margarine in a saucepan over a moderate heat. Add the onion and cook for 2 minutes, stirring until softened but not browned.
2 Remove from the heat and stir in the cornflour. Then gradually blend in the stock and milk.
3 Return to a high heat, stir all the time until boiling, then cook for 1 further minute.
4 Stir in the minced clams with their liquid and season to taste with the celery salt and pepper. Stir in the cream.
5 Turn down the heat to moderate and heat through again but don't allow to boil.
6 Ladle into warm bowls and sprinkle with chopped parsley.

Gazpacho

SERVES 4

1 slice of white bread
150 ml/¼ pt/⅔ cup water
400 g/14 oz/1 large can of chopped tomatoes
½ small onion, quartered
1 green (bell) pepper, quartered
1 small garlic clove, crushed
15 ml/1 tbsp white wine vinegar
15 ml/1 tbsp olive oil
15 ml/1 tbsp lemon juice
A good pinch of caster (superfine) sugar
Salt and freshly ground black pepper
5 cm/2 in piece of cucumber, finely chopped

1 Soak the bread and water in a bowl, then tip them into a blender or food processor.
2 Add all the remaining ingredients except the cucumber and run the machine until smooth.
3 Tip into a bowl or jug and chill until required. Serve in small bowls sprinkled with the chopped cucumber.

Triple Tomato Soup

SERVES 4

295 g/10½ oz/1 medium can of condensed tomato soup
400 g/14 oz/1 large can of chopped tomatoes
425 g/15 oz/1 large can of haricot (navy) beans, drained
2 sun-dried tomatoes, finely chopped
2.5 ml/½ tsp dried basil

1 Empty the can of condensed tomato soup into a saucepan.
2 Add one canful of water, whisking with a wire whisk.
3 Stir in the chopped tomatoes and beans.
4 Stir in the sun-dried tomatoes and the basil.
5 Heat through until almost boiling. Ladle into bowls and serve.

Green Velvet Soup

SERVES 4

1 onion, chopped
1 potato, finely chopped
225 g/8 oz/2 cups frozen broad (fava) beans
225 g/8 oz frozen spinach, thawed
900 ml/1½ pts/3¾ cups vegetable or chicken stock, made with 2 stock cubes
Salt and freshly ground black pepper
A little grated nutmeg
60 ml/4 tbsp plain yoghurt

1 Put all the ingredients except the nutmeg and yoghurt in a saucepan. Bring to the boil over a high heat, then reduce the heat until gently bubbling around the edges, part-cover and cook for 10 minutes until everything is tender.
2 Purée the soup in a blender or food processor and return to the pan. Add salt, pepper and nutmeg to taste. Reheat.
3 Ladle into warm bowls and add a spoonful of yoghurt to each. Serve hot.

Rich Tomato Soup

25 g/1 oz/2 tbsp butter or margarine

1 onion, chopped

2 carrots, chopped

1 celery stick, chopped

40 g/1½ oz/3 tbsp plain (all-purpose) flour

1.2 litres/2 pts/5 cups chicken stock, made with 2 stock cubes

1 small garlic clove, crushed

700 g/1½ lb tomatoes, skinned and chopped

15 ml/1 tbsp tomato purée (paste)

15 ml/1 tbsp caster (superfine) sugar

Salt and freshly ground black pepper

150 ml/¼ pt/⅔ cup single (light) cream

30 ml/2 tbsp chopped fresh basil

1 Melt the butter or margarine in a saucepan. Fry (sauté) the onion, carrots and celery over a fairly high heat for 3 minutes, stirring, until softened but not browned.

2 Stir the flour into the vegetables and cook for 1 minute.

3 Remove from the heat and stir in the stock. Add all the remaining ingredients except the cream. Heat rapidly until boiling, then reduce the heat until gently bubbling around the edges and cook for 45 minutes.

4 Purée the soup in a blender or food processor, then tip the soup into a sieve (strainer) over the pan and push through with a wooden spoon.

5 Stir in the cream and heat through over a moderate heat, stirring, but do not allow to boil. Taste and re-season if necessary. Ladle into warm bowls, sprinkle with basil and serve hot.

Mighty Minestrone

15 g/½ oz/1 tbsp butter or margarine

1 large onion, halved and thinly sliced

2 carrots, chopped

1 turnip, chopped

400 g/14 oz/1 large can of chopped tomatoes

1 bay leaf

2 chicken or vegetable stock cubes

1 peperami stick, chopped, or 50 g/2 oz sliced pepperoni (optional)

50 g/2 oz short-cut macaroni

425 g/15 oz/1 large can of haricot (navy) beans, drained

¼ small green cabbage, shredded

Salt and freshly ground black pepper

1 Melt the butter or margarine in a large saucepan over a fairly high heat. Add the onion, carrots and turnip and fry (sauté) for 3 minutes, stirring.

2 Stir in the tomatoes. Fill the can with water and add. Repeat with a second canful of water.

3 Add the bay leaf and stock cubes, bring to the boil, reduce the heat until gently bubbling around the edges and cook for 30 minutes.

4 Discard the bay leaf and add the remaining ingredients. Bring back to the boil, reduce the heat and cook gently for a further 10–15 minutes until everything is really tender. Taste and re-season if necessary.

Chilled Tomato Soup

SERVES 4

600 ml/1 pt/2½ cups passata (sieved tomatoes)
150 ml/¼ pt/⅔ cup vegetable stock, made with ½ stock cube
15 ml/1 tbsp red wine vinegar
15 ml/1 tbsp olive oil
45 ml/3 tbsp crème fraîche
5 ml/1 tsp dried basil
A good pinch of caster (superfine) sugar
Salt and freshly ground black pepper

1 Whisk all the ingredients together in a bowl until thoroughly blended, seasoning to taste with salt and pepper.
2 Chill for at least 1 hour before serving.

Crunchy Mushroom Soup

SERVES 4

295 g/10½ oz/1 medium can of condensed mushroom soup
About 300 ml/½ pt/1¼ cups milk
170 g/6 oz/1 small can of sliced mushrooms, drained
2 slices of wholemeal bread
Butter or margarine, for spreading
75 g/3 oz/¾ cup Cheddar cheese, grated

1 Empty the soup into the pan.
2 Stir in a canful of milk.
3 Add the mushrooms to the pan. Heat through, stirring.
4 Meanwhile, preheat the grill (broiler) and toast the bread on both sides. Spread one side with butter or margarine and cover with the cheese. Grill (broil) until melted. Cut into dice.
5 Ladle the soup into bowls, top with the toasted cheese and serve.

Crab and Potato Bisque

SERVES 4–6

25 g/1 oz/2 tbsp butter or margarine
1 large potato, coarsely grated
1 carrot, coarsely grated
1 small onion, grated
40 g/1½ oz/1 very small can of dressed crab
45 ml/3 tbsp plain (all-purpose) flour
900 ml/1½ pts/3¾ cups fish, chicken or vegetable stock, made with 2 stock cubes
5 ml/1 tsp celery salt
15 ml/1 tbsp brandy
150 ml/¼ pt/⅔ cup milk
150 ml/¼ pt/⅔ cup single (light) cream
170 g/6 oz/1 small can of white crabmeat
30 ml/2 tbsp chopped fresh parsley

1 Melt the butter or margarine in a saucepan over a moderate heat.
2 Add the potato, carrot and onion. Stir, then turn down the heat, cover and cook very gently for 2 minutes until softened but not browned.
3 Stir the dressed crab and flour into the pan and cook for 1 minute, stirring all the time.
4 Remove from the heat and stir in the stock, a little at a time, stirring well after each addition.
5 Place over a high heat and cook, stirring, until boiling. Turn down the heat until very gently bubbling around the edges and cook for 10 minutes, stirring occasionally.
6 Stir in all the remaining ingredients except the parsley and heat through. Ladle into bowls and sprinkle with parsley before serving.

Chinese Hot and Sour Soup

SERVES 4

30 ml/2 tbsp sunflower oil

8 button mushrooms, thinly sliced

30 ml/2 tbsp pure orange juice

30 ml/2 tbsp light soy sauce

15 ml/1 tbsp clear honey

30 ml/2 tbsp red wine vinegar

100 g/4 oz/1 cup chopped cooked
chicken

1.2 litres/2 pts/5 cups chicken stock,
made with 2 stock cubes

2 spring onions (scallions), finely
chopped

1 Heat the oil in a saucepan over a
fairly high heat. Add the mushrooms
and stir-fry for 1 minute.
2 Add all the remaining ingredients
except the spring onions. Bring to the
boil, then turn down the heat until
gently bubbling around the edges and
cook for 5 minutes. Add the spring
onions, cook for 1 further minute and
serve.

Thai Noodle Soup

SERVES 4

1.2 litres/2 pts/5 cups chicken stock,
made with 2 stock cubes

1 stalk of lemon grass, finely chopped

15 ml/1 tbsp soy sauce

100 g/4 oz vermicelli, broken into pieces

1 Put the stock in a saucepan with the
lemon grass and soy sauce. Heat over
a high heat until the stock is boiling.
2 Add the vermicelli to the stock.
Continue to boil for 5 minutes.
3 Ladle into warm bowls and serve.

Creamy Mushroom Soup

SERVES 4

50 g/2 oz/¼ cup butter or margarine

225 g/8 oz small button mushrooms,
finely chopped

45 ml/3 tbsp plain (all-purpose) flour

600 ml/1 pt/2½ cups chicken stock,
made with 1 stock cube

150 ml/¼ pt/⅔ cup milk

1 bay leaf

45 ml/3 tbsp single (light) cream

Salt and freshly ground black pepper

15 ml/1 tbsp chopped fresh parsley, to
garnish

1 Put the butter or margarine in a
saucepan, add the mushrooms and fry
(sauté) over a moderate heat for
2 minutes, stirring until softened but not
browned.
2 Stir the flour into the pan and cook
for 2 minutes, stirring.
3 Remove from the heat and
gradually stir in the stock and milk.
Return to the heat and bring to the
boil, stirring over a high heat. Add the
bay leaf.
4 Reduce the heat until bubbling
gently around the edges, part-cover
the pan and cook for 10 minutes.
Discard the bay leaf. Remove from the
heat and stir 30 ml/2 tbsp of the cream
into the soup. Season to taste.
5 Ladle into warm bowls, then, using a
teaspoon, top each with a swirl of the
remaining cream. Sprinkle with parsley
and serve.

Monday Scotch Broth

If you have a food processor, you can chop the onion in it, then put on the grating attachment and prepare all the other vegetables.

SERVES 4

1 roast lamb bone from the Sunday joint
A handful of pearl barley
1 onion, finely chopped
1 carrot, coarsely grated
1 potato, coarsely grated
1 turnip, coarsely grated
900 ml/1½ pts/3¾ cups water
1 bouquet garni sachet
1 chicken or lamb stock cube
Salt and freshly ground black pepper

1 Place the lamb bone in a saucepan.
2 Add the pearl barley, onion, carrot, potato and turnip.
3 Add the water, bouquet garni sachet, stock cube and some salt and pepper.
4 Heat rapidly until the water boils, then reduce the heat until the liquid is just bubbling gently around the edges, rest the lid on the pan so it doesn't seal the top completely, and cook for 1½ hours.
5 Carefully lift the lamb bone and bouquet garni sachet out of the pan with a draining spoon. Cut any meat off the bone, cut into small pieces and return to the pan. Taste and re-season.
6 Heat through again and serve.

Lentil and Tomato Soup with Cardamom

SERVES 4

10 ml/2 tsp olive oil
1 onion, chopped
100 g/4 oz/⅔ cup red lentils
600 ml/1 pt/2½ cups tomato juice
300 ml/½ pt/1¼ cups chicken or vegetable stock, made with 1 stock cube
15 ml/1 tbsp tomato purée (paste)
3 cardamom pods, split
Salt and freshly ground black pepper
30 ml/2 tbsp plain yoghurt and 15 ml/ 1 tbsp chopped fresh coriander (cilantro), to garnish

1 Heat the oil in a saucepan over a moderate heat. Add the onion and fry (sauté) for 2 minutes, stirring, until softened but not browned.
2 Add the remaining ingredients. Turn up the heat, bring to the boil, reduce the heat until bubbling gently around the edges and cook for about 30 minutes until the lentils are completely soft. Discard the cardamom pods.
3 Taste the soup and re-season if necessary. Ladle into warm bowls and garnish each with a small spoonful of yoghurt and a sprinkling of chopped coriander.

Sausage Soup

SERVES 4

25 g/1 oz/2 tbsp butter or margarine

4 thick pork sausages, cut into small
chunks

2 onions, thinly sliced

900 ml/1½ pts/3¾ cups beef stock,
made with 1 stock cube

5 ml/1 tsp Dijon mustard

1.5 ml/¼ tsp dried sage

Salt and freshly ground black pepper

100 g/4 oz/1 cup Cheddar cheese,
grated

Crusty bread, to serve

1 Melt the butter or margarine in a
large saucepan, over a fairly high heat,
then add the sausages and onions and
brown, stirring for 3–4 minutes.

2 Add the stock, mustard, sage and
seasoning, bring to the boil, reduce the
heat until gently bubbling around the
edges and cook for 20 minutes.

3 Stir in the cheese until melted and
serve piping hot with crusty bread.

Greek Meatball Soup

SERVES 4

175 g/6 oz minced (ground) lamb

100 g/4 oz/½ cup long-grain rice

1 small egg, beaten

15 ml/1 tbsp chopped fresh parsley

5 ml/1 tsp dried oregano

Salt and freshly ground black pepper

A little plain (all-purpose) flour

1.2 litres/2 pts/5 cups lamb stock, made
with 2 stock cubes

2 eggs

Juice of 1 large lemon

1 Mix the lamb with the rice, egg,
parsley, oregano and a little salt and
pepper. Shape into small balls and roll
in the flour.

2 Bring the stock to the boil over a
high heat. Add the meatballs, turn
down the heat until gently bubbling
round the edges and cook for 15
minutes. Remove from the heat.

3 Whisk the eggs and lemon juice
together in a bowl with a wire whisk.
Whisk in a little of the lamb stock. Pour
back into the mixture and stir gently.
Ladle into bowls and serve.

Bortsch

This soup is also delicious chilled.

SERVES 4

2 celery sticks, coarsely grated,
discarding the strings

2 carrots, coarsely grated

1 small onion, grated

3 cooked beetroot (red beets), coarsely
grated

900 ml/1½ pts/3¾ cups beef stock,
made with 2 stock cubes

15 ml/1 tbsp red wine vinegar

Salt and freshly ground black pepper

60 ml/4 tbsp soured (dairy sour) cream

1 Put the grated vegetables in a
saucepan with the stock, vinegar and
some salt and pepper.

2 Heat rapidly until boiling.

3 Turn down the heat until gently
bubbling around the edges, then part-
cover the pan with a lid and cook for
20 minutes. Re-season if necessary.

4 Ladle into warm bowls and top each
with a spoonful of soured (dairy sour)
cream before serving.

Green Pea and Bacon Soup

SERVES 4

4 rashers (slices) of unsmoked streaky
  bacon, rinded and diced
1 small onion, chopped
15 g/½ oz/1 tbsp butter or margarine
350 g/12 oz/3 cups frozen peas
600 ml/1 pt/2½ cups chicken or ham
  stock, made with 1 stock cube
Salt and freshly ground black pepper
15 ml/1 tbsp plain (all-purpose) flour
75 ml/5 tbsp milk
A pinch of grated nutmeg

1 Put two of the bacon rashers in a
pan with the onion and butter or
margarine, over a moderate heat. Fry
(sauté) for 3 minutes, stirring until
softened but not browned.
2 Add the peas, stock and a little salt
and pepper. Bring to the boil, reduce
the heat until gently bubbling around
the edges, part-cover and cook for
10 minutes.
3 Purée the soup in a blender or food
processor.
4 Meanwhile, dry-fry the remaining
bacon in the saucepan until crisp. Lift
out with a draining spoon and drain on
kitchen paper (paper towels).
5 Stir the flour into the fat in the
saucepan, then gradually stir in the
milk until smooth. Return the purée to
the pan and stir well, then bring to the
boil over a high heat and cook, stirring
for 2 minutes.
6 Add the nutmeg, taste and re-season
if necessary. Ladle into warm bowls
and sprinkle with the crisp bacon.

Chilli Winter Warmer

SERVES 4

100 g/4 oz minced (ground) beef
2 onions, finely chopped
2 carrots, finely chopped
2.5 ml/½ tsp chilli powder
15 ml/1 tbsp tomato purée (paste)
900 ml/1½ pts/3¾ cups beef stock,
  made with 2 stock cubes
5 ml/1 tsp yeast extract
2.5 ml/½ tsp dried oregano
Salt and freshly ground black pepper
100 g/4 oz soup pasta shapes
15 ml/1 tbsp cornflour (cornstarch)
30 ml/2 tbsp water
15 ml/1 tbsp chopped fresh parsley

1 Put the beef, onions and carrots in a
large saucepan and cook over a fairly
high heat, stirring, until the grains of
meat are separate and no longer pink.
2 Add everything except the pasta,
cornflour, water and parsley. Bring to
the boil, stirring over a high heat, then
reduce the heat until gently bubbling
around the edges and cook for
20 minutes, stirring occasionally.
3 Add the pasta and cook for a further
10 minutes.
4 Mix the cornflour with the water in a
cup. Stir into the soup, turn up the heat
and bring back to the boil. Continue to
cook, stirring, for 1 minute. Season to
taste. Serve hot, garnished with
chopped parsley.

Snacks and Light Meals

Eggs probably reign as the most common ingredient in quick snacks, but there's more to this section than egg sandwiches and scrambled eggs on toast. There are fabulous ideas for all sorts of hot and cold snacks from wraps, pizzas and quiches to ... yes, sandwiches – but extra special ones, of course. Many are ideal for taking for packed lunches, others are best enjoyed in the comfort of your own home!

Boiled Eggs

ALLOW 1 EGG PER PERSON

Soft-boiled: Everyone has their own different method. Mine works well, but don't try to cook more than six at once. It's a good idea to have the eggs at room temperature before you start, especially if you don't have an egg pricker, as they are less likely to crack when boiled.

1 If you have an egg-pricker, prick the wider end of the eggs.

2 Place in a saucepan just large enough to hold the eggs in a single layer.

3 Add just enough cold water to cover them. Put on a lid and heat until boiling.

4 As soon as the water is bubbling, start to time the eggs. Cook them for 3½ minutes, then immediately lift the eggs out of the water with a draining spoon and place in egg cups.

5 Tap the tops gently with a spoon to prevent further cooking.

Hard-boiled (hard-cooked):

Prepare as for soft-boiled but cook for 7 minutes. If serving cold, drain off the boiling water and cover with cold water to prevent a black ring forming round the yolk. Leave until cold before shelling. To shell, tap the egg on a work surface. Roll it, pressing gently with your hand until the shell is cracked all over, then peel it all off.

Fried Eggs

ALLOW 1–2 EGGS PER PERSON

1 Melt just enough butter, margarine or oil in a heavy-based or non-stick frying pan (skillet) to cover the base.

2 Break the eggs, one at a time, into a cup, then gently slide into the pan.

3 When the whites are nearly set, tilt the pan slightly and spoon the hot fat over the eggs (this is called 'basting') as they cook.

4 Cook until the whites are just firm but the yolk is still soft. If you like crispy edges, cook over a fairly high heat (but be careful of the fat spluttering). If you like them soft, use a lower heat.

5 Remove from the pan with a fish slice to allow the fat to drain off, then transfer to warm plates.

Poached Eggs (1)

This is the traditional method, which produces soft, delicate eggs.

ALLOW 1–2 EGGS PER PERSON

1 Put about 2.5 cm/1 in water in a heavy-based frying pan (skillet) and add 15 ml/1 tbsp lemon juice.

2 Bring to the boil, then reduce the heat until the water is just bubbling round the edges.

3 Break the eggs, one at a time, into a cup, then gently slide into the water.

4 Cover with a lid and poach for about 3 minutes for soft-cooked eggs, 4–5 minutes for firm ones.

Poached Eggs (2)

If you have an egg-poacher, use this method.

ALLOW 1–2 EGGS PER PERSON

1 Half-fill the pan with water and put a knob of butter or margarine in each egg-holder.

2 Heat until the water is boiling.

3 Break an egg into each holder and season with salt and pepper.

4 Cover with the lid and cook for 2–4 minutes until cooked to your liking.

5 Carefully, loosen the eggs round the edges with a round-bladed knife before sliding them out.

Eggs Benedict

SERVES 1–2

1 quantity of Fast Hollandaise Sauce (see page 330)
2 slices of bread
Butter or margarine, for spreading
2 eggs
2 slices of ham

1 Make the Hollandaise sauce.

2 Cut as large a round as possible from each slice of bread. Spread on both sides with butter or margarine and fry (sauté) until golden on both sides.

3 Meanwhile, poach the eggs (see left and above).

4 Preheat the grill (broiler). Cut the ham to fit the fried bread, set on top of the bread and place on plates.

5 Top with the poached eggs, then spoon the Hollandaise sauce over. Place under the hot grill for 1–2 minutes to brown lightly.

Eggs Florentine

SERVES 1–2

225 g/8 oz spinach
15 ml/1 tbsp double (heavy) cream
A little grated nutmeg
Salt and freshly ground black pepper
1 quantity of Cheese Sauce (see page 329)
2 eggs

1 Wash the spinach and put it in a saucepan with no extra water. Cover and cook over a moderate heat for 5 minutes until tender. Drain thoroughly and tip back into the pan. Snip with scissors to chop, then stir in the cream, a little nutmeg, and salt and pepper to taste. Heat through. Spoon the spinach into one or two individual dishes.

2 Make the cheese sauce.

3 Poach the eggs (see page 76 and left). Preheat the grill (broiler).

4 Put an egg on each bed of spinach and spoon the sauce over. Place under the grill for about 2 minutes to brown the top lightly. Serve immediately.

Scrambled Eggs

ALLOW 2 EGGS PER PERSON

1 Break the eggs in a pan with 15 ml/ 1 tbsp milk or cream per egg and a small knob of butter or margarine. Season lightly.

2 Cook over a gentle heat, stirring all the time, until the mixture is just set but still creamy. Do not allow to boil or the mixture will curdle.

Microwave Scrambled Eggs

ALLOW 2 EGGS PER PERSON

1 Prepare as for the recipe on page 77, using a non-metallic bowl.
2 Microwave on High for about 45 seconds per egg, stirring every 30 seconds until almost set.
3 Leave to stand for 2 minutes to complete cooking.

Smoked Salmon with Scrambled Egg

SERVES 4

8 eggs
30 ml/2 tbsp milk
A good knob of butter or margarine, plus extra for spreading
100 g/4 oz smoked salmon trimmings
4 large slices of wholemeal toast, buttered
Sprigs of parsley

1 Beat the eggs in a pan with the milk.
2 Add the butter or margarine and very little salt and lots of pepper.
3 Cook over a very gentle heat, stirring all the time, until the egg mixture sets but is still creamy.
4 Break up the salmon and stir in just long enough to heat through. Put the toast on plates, pile the egg mixture on top, garnish with parsley and serve hot.

Kippers with Scrambled Egg

SERVES 4

Prepare as for Smoked Salmon with Scrambled Egg but cook two boil-in-the-bag kippers as directed on the packet. Drain and cut into pieces. Add to the eggs as before and serve.

Plain Omelette

Make one omelette at a time.

ALLOW 2–3 EGGS PER PERSON

1 Beat the eggs in a bowl with a little salt and pepper and 15 ml/1 tbsp water.
2 Melt a small knob of butter in an omelette pan over a moderate heat.
3 Add the egg mixture. Cook, lifting the mixture as it sets to let the runny, uncooked egg trickle underneath, until the base is golden brown and the omelette is just set but creamy on top.
4 Fold the omelette in half, then slide out on to a warm plate.

Cheese Omelette

ALLOW 2–3 EGGS PER PERSON

Prepare as for Plain Omelette but scatter 25 g/1 oz/¼ cup grated Cheddar cheese, over half the omelette when about half-set, or stir it into the eggs before cooking.

Mushroom Omelette

ALLOW 2–3 EGGS PER PERSON

Prepare as for Plain Omelette but stew 50 g/2 oz sliced mushrooms in a little water, then scatter them over half the just-cooked omelette before folding and sliding on to a plate.

Ham Omelette

ALLOW 2–3 EGGS PER PERSON

Prepare as for Plain Omelette but sprinkle 30 ml/2 tbsp chopped ham over the surface when the omelette is almost cooked. Cook for a minute or two longer before folding and sliding on to a plate.

Chicken Omelette

ALLOW 2–3 EGGS PER PERSON

Prepare as for Plain Omelette but scatter with 30 ml/2 tbsp chopped, cooked chicken and a pinch of dried thyme when the omelette is almost cooked. Cook for a minute or two longer, then fold and slide on to a plate.

Tomato Omelette

ALLOW 2–3 EGGS PER PERSON

Prepare as for Plain Omelette but arrange a sliced tomato over one half of the omelette when it is almost cooked. Cook for a minute or two longer to heat through, sprinkle with a few chopped fresh basil leaves, fold and slide on to a plate.

Herb Omelette

ALLOW 2–3 EGGS PER PERSON

Prepare as for Plain Omelette but scatter 15 ml/1 tbsp of any mixed, chopped, fresh herbs (parsley, thyme and basil are good) over half the almost-cooked omelette. Sprinkle with a few drops of soy sauce. Cook for a minute or two longer, fold and slide on to a plate.

Soufflé Omelette

To make a filled soufflé omelette, use any of the fillings listed left. Either fold into the egg mixture before cooking or spread over the browned omelette, quickly heat under the grill (broiler), then fold and serve.

ALLOW 2–3 EGGS PER PERSON

1 Separate the eggs.

2 Stir the yolks with a pinch of salt and pepper and 30 ml/2 tbsp water until blended.

3 Whisk the egg whites until stiff with an electric or balloon whisk, then add the yolk mixture and stir very gently with a metal spoon.

4 Heat a knob of butter or margarine in an omelette pan over a moderate heat. Add the egg mixture.

5 Cook until the base of the omelette is golden brown. Meanwhile, preheat the grill (broiler).

6 Place the pan under the grill and cook for 2–3 minutes until the omelette is risen and golden on top.

7 Fold in half and slide on to a plate.

Sweet Soufflé Omelette

ALLOW 2–3 EGGS PER PERSON

Prepare as for Soufflé Omelette but omit the salt and pepper and whisk 15 ml/1 tbsp caster (superfine) sugar into the whisked egg whites. When cooked, spread with a little warm jam (conserve) or fruit purée, then fold and serve. Dust with a little sifted icing (confectioners') sugar before serving.

The Easiest Cheese Soufflé

So you thought soufflés were for experienced cooks only ... Not any more – this absolutely-no-skill version is the lightest and most delicious I've ever made!

SERVES 4

A little butter or margarine, for greasing
100 g/4 oz/½ cup Cheddar cheese spread
30 ml/2 tbsp milk
30 ml/2 tbsp plain (all-purpose) flour
1.5 ml/¼ tsp made English mustard
30 ml/2 tbsp grated Parmesan cheese
Salt and freshly ground black pepper
2 eggs, separated

1 Preheat the oven to 190°C/375°F/ gas mark 5. Grease four individual ramekin dishes (custard cups) or a 15 cm/6 in soufflé dish.

2 Put all the ingredients except the egg whites in a bowl and mix with a wooden spoon until well blended.

3 Whisk the egg whites until stiff with an electric or balloon whisk and stir gently into the mixture with a metal spoon.

4 Spoon into the prepared ramekins or larger dish and bake in the oven – 15 minutes for individual ones and 25 minutes for a large soufflé – until well risen, golden and just set. Serve straight away.

Baked Eggs

ALLOW 1–2 EGGS PER PERSON

1 Preheat the oven to 180°C/350°F/ gas mark 4. Lightly butter one ramekin dish (custard cup) for each egg you intend to cook.

2 Break an egg into each dish. Season lightly.

3 Add 15 ml/1 tbsp double (heavy) cream to each.

4 Stand the dishes in a shallow baking tin (pan) with enough hot water to come halfway up the sides of the dishes.

5 Cook in the oven for 8–10 minutes.

Microwave Baked Eggs

ALLOW 1–2 EGGS PER PERSON

1 Prepare as above but prick the yolk twice with a cocktail stick (toothpick).

2 Cook on High (100 per cent power) for 1–1½ minutes per egg (depending on the output of your microwave) and leave to stand for 2 minutes. For a firmer egg, cook for 30 seconds more per egg.

Baked Eggs with Ham

ALLOW 1–2 EGGS PER PERSON

Prepare as Baked Eggs, using either method, but put 15 ml/1 tbsp chopped ham in the base of each dish before adding the egg.

Baked Eggs with Asparagus

ALLOW 1–2 EGGS PER PERSON

Prepare as Baked Eggs, using either method, but spread 15 ml/1 tbsp chopped, cooked asparagus in each dish before adding the egg.

Baked Eggs with Tomatoes

ALLOW 1–2 EGGS PER PERSON

Prepare as Baked Eggs, using either method, but put a skinned, chopped tomato in the base of each dish and sprinkle each with two chopped fresh basil leaves before adding the egg.

Swiss Baked Eggs

ALLOW 1–2 EGGS PER PERSON

Prepare as Baked Eggs, using either method, but put 15 ml/1 tbsp grated Gruyère or Emmental (Swiss) cheese in the base of each dish before adding the egg.

Piperade

SERVES 2

15 g/½ oz/1 tbsp butter or margarine
15 ml/1 tbsp olive oil
2 onions, sliced
1 green (bell) pepper, sliced
1 red pepper, sliced
4 ripe tomatoes, roughly chopped
1 garlic clove, crushed
4 eggs, beaten
Salt and freshly ground black pepper

1 Heat the butter or margarine and oil in a large frying pan (skillet).
2 Add the onion, peppers, tomato and garlic and cook, stirring over a moderate heat, for 5 minutes until soft. Turn down the heat.
3 Add the eggs and some salt and pepper and cook over a gentle heat, stirring until just set. Do not allow to boil. Serve straight from the pan.

Greek Pittas

SERVES 4

4 pitta breads
225 g/8 oz taramasalata
A little shredded lettuce
15 ml/1 tbsp sliced stoned (pitted) black olives
¼ lemon
Freshly ground black pepper
15 ml/1 tbsp olive oil

1 Warm the pittas under the grill (broiler) or briefly in the microwave. Cut into halves widthways and gently open to form pockets.
2 Fill with the taramasalata, some shredded lettuce and the olives. Add a squeeze of lemon, a good grinding of pepper and a trickle of olive oil.

Tuna Crunchy Corn Pittas

SERVES 4

185 g/6½ oz/1 small can of tuna, drained
200 g/7 oz/1 small can of sweetcorn (corn), drained
15 ml/1 tbsp pine nuts
1 celery stick, finely chopped
30 ml/2 tbsp tomato relish
4 sesame seed pitta breads

1 Mix all the ingredients except the pitta breads together.
2 Warm the pittas under the grill (broiler) or briefly in the microwave. Cut into halves and open each half to form a pocket.
3 Spoon the filling in the pockets and serve.

Mushroom and Onion Quiche

Use any variety of savoury filling you like. Try ham and tomato or tuna and sweetcorn (corn). As a guide to quantities, you need enough ingredients to almost half-fill the flan case (pie shell). You can make your own shortcrust pastry (basic pie crust), using the recipe on page 391, if you prefer.

SERVES 4

225 g/8 oz shortcrust pastry, thawed if frozen
100 g/4 oz button mushrooms, sliced
1 onion, sliced
15 ml/1 tbsp sunflower oil
2.5 ml/½ tsp dried oregano
50 g/2 oz/½ cup Cheddar cheese, grated
Salt and freshly ground black pepper
300 ml/½ pt/1¼ cups milk, or milk and single (light) cream, mixed
2 eggs

1 Roll out the pastry (paste) to slightly larger than a 20 cm/8 in flan dish (pie pan). Lay the pastry in the dish and press gently into the corners and up the sides. Trim the top, level with the dish, using a small, sharp knife. Prick the base with a fork. Place on a baking (cookie) sheet.
2 Preheat the oven to 190°C/375°F/ gas mark 5. Fry (sauté) the mushrooms and onion in the oil for 3 minutes, stirring, until softened.
3 Turn into the flan case, sprinkle with the oregano and top with the cheese.
4 Beat the milk or milk and cream together with the eggs and season with some salt and pepper.

5 Pour into the flan and bake in the oven for about 30 minutes until the filling is set and golden brown. Serve hot or cold.

Scotch Eggs

SERVES 4

4 hard-boiled (hard-cooked) eggs (see page 76)
30 ml/2 tbsp plain (all-purpose) flour
225 g/8 oz pork sausagemeat
5 ml/1 tsp dried onion granules
1 egg, beaten
75 g/3 oz/1½ cups fresh white or wholemeal breadcrumbs
Oil, for deep-frying

1 Shell the eggs and roll them in the flour.
2 Divide the sausagemeat into four pieces. Flatten each to a round.
3 Dust with the onion granules, then shape each piece round an egg to cover it completely.
4 Put the egg and breadcrumbs on separate plates. Roll the balls in beaten egg, then in the breadcrumbs. Chill for 30 minutes.
5 Heat the oil in a large saucepan or deep-fat fryer to 190°C/375°F or until a cube of day-old bread browns in 30 seconds. Add the eggs and cook for about 6 minutes until they are golden brown and crisp and the sausage is cooked through. Drain on kitchen paper (paper towels). Serve warm or cold.

Beany Pitta Bites

SERVES 2–4

400 g/14 oz/1 large can of baked beans
   with pork sausages
1 Weetabix
4 pitta breads
2 tomatoes, sliced
50 g/2 oz/½ cup Cheddar cheese,
   grated

1 Heat the beans in a saucepan.
2 Crumble in the Weetabix and stir
until thickened.
3 Warm the pittas under the grill
(broiler) or briefly in the microwave.
Open each along the edge.
4 Line with tomato slices and cheese.
Spoon in the bean mixture and serve
straight away.

Quick Chinese Chicken Pittas

SERVES 4

175 g/6 oz/1½ cups chopped cooked
   chicken
425 g/15 oz/1 large can of stir-fry
   vegetables, rinsed and drained
15 ml/1 tbsp medium-dry sherry
15 ml/1 tbsp soy sauce
10 ml/2 tsp toasted sesame seeds
4 sesame seed pitta breads

1 Put the chicken, vegetables, sherry
and soy sauce in a saucepan and heat
through, stirring, until piping hot.
2 Sprinkle in the sesame seeds.
3 Warm the pitta breads under the grill
(broiler) or briefly in the microwave.
4 Cut into halves and gently open up
to form pockets. Fill with the chicken
mixture and serve straight away.

Smoked Oyster Cottage Pittas

Use smoked mussels, if you prefer.

SERVES 4

25 g/1 oz/2 tbsp butter or margarine
1 small onion, finely chopped
100 g/4 oz/1 small can of smoked
   oysters
225 g/8 oz/1 cup cottage cheese with
   chives
2 tomatoes, finely chopped
Salt and freshly ground black pepper
4 pitta breads
Shredded lettuce, to garnish

1 Melt the butter or margarine in a
saucepan over a moderate heat and
add the onion. Fry (sauté), stirring, for
5 minutes.
2 Stir in the oysters, cheese and
tomatoes and season to taste. Heat
through, gently.
3 Meanwhile, grill (broil) the pittas
briefly until they start to puff up, or
heat briefly in the microwave. Make a
slit along one edge of each to form a
pocket. Spoon in the warm cheese
mixture, add some shredded lettuce
and serve straight away.

Spicy Sardine and Bean Pittas

SERVES 4

120 g/4½ oz/1 small can of sardines in
tomato sauce
1 small garlic clove, crushed
1.5 ml/¼ tsp chilli powder
225 g/8 oz/1 small can of butter (lima)
beans, drained and mashed with a
fork
Salt and freshly ground black pepper
4 wholemeal pitta breads
Shredded lettuce and slices of
cucumber, to garnish

1 Mash the sardines, preferably
including the bones. Add the garlic, chilli
powder and mashed beans and season
to taste.
2 Warm the pittas under the grill
(broiler) or heat briefly in the
microwave. Make a slit along one side
of each to form a pocket. Spoon in the
sardine mixture and add some
shredded lettuce and cucumber slices.

Curried Chicken and Peach Pittas

SERVES 4

5 ml/1 tsp curry paste
30 ml/2 tbsp crème fraîche
Salt and freshly ground black pepper
100 g/4 oz/1 cup chopped cooked
chicken
225 g/8 oz/1 small can of peach slices,
drained and chopped
15 ml/1 tbsp chopped fresh coriander
(cilantro)
4 garlic pitta breads
4 crisp lettuce leaves

1 Mix the curry paste and crème fraîche
together with a little salt and pepper.
Stir in the chicken, peaches and
coriander.
2 Warm the pitta breads under the grill
(broiler) or heat briefly in the
microwave.
3 Make a slit along one side of each
pitta and open up to form a pocket.
Line each with a crisp lettuce leaf, then
fill with the curried chicken and peach
mixture.

Mustard, Chicken, Carrot and Courgette Pittas

SERVES 4

60 ml/4 tbsp olive oil
30 ml/2 tbsp black mustard seeds
1 large carrot, coarsely grated
1 large courgette (zucchini), coarsely
grated
175 g/6 oz/1½ cups chopped cooked
chicken
Lemon juice, to taste
Salt and freshly ground black pepper
4 pitta breads

1 Heat the oil in a large saucepan. Add
the mustard seeds and cook until the
seeds 'pop'.
2 Add the carrot, courgette and
chicken. Stir over a moderate heat until
piping hot. Add lemon juice and season
with salt and pepper.
3 Warm the pitta breads under the grill
(broiler) or briefly in the microwave.
4 Gently cut a slit along one side of
each bread. Open up to form a
pocket. Spoon in the chicken mixture
and serve straight away.

Prawn and Chilli Mayo Wraps

SERVES 4

60 ml/4 tbsp mayonnaise
15 ml/1 tbsp chilli relish
175 g/6 oz cooked peeled prawns
(shrimp)
2 tomatoes, chopped
5 ml/2 in piece of cucumber, chopped
4 flour tortillas
A few lettuce leaves, shredded

1 Mix the mayonnaise with the relish.
2 Stir in the prawns, tomatoes and cucumber.
3 Sprinkle the tortillas with lettuce. Spread on the prawn mixture, fold in the sides, then fold over to form filled pockets.

Bagels from Pompeii

SERVES 4

30 ml/2 tbsp tomato purée (paste)
5 ml/1 tsp water
2 bagels, split in half and toasted
50 g/2 oz/½ cup Mozzarella cheese, grated
4 cherry tomatoes, sliced
50 g/2 oz/1 small can of anchovies, drained
8 fresh basil leaves, chopped

1 Preheat the grill (broiler). Toast the bagels. Mix the tomato purée with the water and spread over the cut sides of the bagels. Sprinkle the cheese over.
2 Arrange the slices of tomato on top, then lay the anchovies over in a criss-cross pattern. Sprinkle with the basil.
3 Grill (broil) until the cheese melts and bubbles and serve straight away.

Smoked Mackerel and Soft Cheese Bagels

SERVES 2

2 smoked mackerel fillets
2 bagels, split in half
30 ml/2 tbsp medium-fat soft cheese
10 ml/2 tsp horseradish relish
A little lemon juice
Freshly ground black pepper
Salad cress, to garnish

1 Cut the smoked mackerel fillets into small pieces, discarding the skin if liked.
2 Spread the halved bagels with the soft cheese. Top with a spreading of horseradish relish, then the mackerel.
3 Sprinkle with lemon juice and add a good grinding of pepper. Top with salad cress and serve.

Chilli Bean Wraps

SERVES 4

425 g/15 oz/1 large can of red kidney beans, drained
15 ml/1 tbsp chilli relish
1 green (bell) pepper, chopped
2.5 cm/1 in piece of cucumber, chopped
2 tomatoes, chopped
Salt and freshly ground black pepper
4 flour tortillas
1 wedge of iceberg lettuce, shredded
60 ml/4 tbsp soured (dairy sour) cream

1 Halve a quarter of the beans, mash the rest with a fork and stir in all the remaining ingredients except the tortillas, lettuce and soured cream.
2 Spread the tortillas with the bean mixture.
3 Top with the lettuce, then the soured cream. Roll up and serve.

Prawn and Avocado Coolers

SERVES 4

8 slices of granary bread
Butter or margarine, for spreading
30 ml/2 tbsp mayonnaise
100 g/4 oz cooked peeled prawns
   (shrimp)
1 ripe avocado, halved, peeled, stoned
   (pitted) and thinly sliced
5 ml/1 tsp lemon juice
Freshly ground black pepper

1 Spread one side of each slice of bread
with a little butter or margarine.
2 Top four slices with mayonnaise, then
the prawns. Mix the slices of avocado
with the lemon juice and arrange on
the prawns. Season well with pepper.
3 Top with the other slices or bread, cut
into quarters, and serve.

Crunchy Salmon Tartare Sandwiches

To make tartare sauce, see page 336.

SERVES 4

75 g/3 oz/⅓ cup butter or margarine
100 g/4 oz/1 small can of pink salmon,
   drained and skin removed
30 ml/2 tbsp tartare sauce
Salt and freshly ground black pepper
30 ml/2 tbsp pine nuts
8 slices of wholemeal bread

1 Mash the butter or margarine with a
fork, then mash in the fish, discarding
the bones, if liked.
2 Stir in the tartare sauce, seasoning
and pine nuts. Spread over the slices of
bread and sandwich together in pairs.
Cut into triangles and serve.

Smoked Mackerel, Orange and Fromage Frais Deckers

SERVES 4

1 smoked mackerel fillet, skinned
60 ml/4 tbsp fromage frais
Freshly ground black pepper
300 g/11 oz/1 medium can of mandarin
   oranges, drained
8 slices of granary bread
Butter or margarine, for spreading
30 ml/2 tbsp salad cress

1 Mash the mackerel, discarding any
bones. Work in the fromage frais and
season with pepper.
2 Drain the oranges thoroughly on
kitchen paper (paper towels).
3 Spread the bread with a little butter
or margarine. Top four slices with the
mackerel mixture. Top with the
oranges, then a sprinkling of cress.
Cover with the remaining buttered
bread, cut into quarters and serve.

Egg, Cress and Prawn Sandwiches

SERVES 4

2 hard-boiled (hard-cooked) eggs, chopped (see page 76)
15 ml/1 tbsp mayonnaise
75 g/3 oz cooked peeled prawns (shrimp)
Freshly ground black pepper
8 slices of granary bread
Butter or margarine, for spreading
½ punnet of salad cress

1 Shell the eggs and, using a fork, mash in a bowl with the mayonnaise.
2 Stir the prawns and some pepper into the egg mixture.
3 Spread the bread with the butter or margarine. Spread half the slices with the egg mixture. Top with the cress, then the other slices. Cut into halves and serve.

Smoked Salmon and Soft Cheese Sandwiches

SERVES 4

100 g/4 oz/½ cup medium-fat soft cheese
8 slices of brown bread
4 small slices of smoked salmon
Freshly ground black pepper
A little lemon juice

1 Spread the cheese on the bread.
2 Top four slices of bread with the salmon slices. Season with pepper and top with a sprinkling of lemon juice.
3 Cover with the remaining slices of bread. Cut off the crusts, if liked. Cut into triangles and serve.

Curried Chicken and Fresh Mango Sandwiches

SERVES 4

8 slices of wholemeal bread
Butter or margarine, for spreading
1 small fresh mango, peeled
30 ml/2 tbsp mayonnaise
10 ml/2 tsp curry paste
100 g/4 oz/1 cup chopped cooked chicken
Salt and freshly ground black pepper

1 Spread one side of each slice of bread with butter or margarine.
2 Cut all the flesh off the mango and chop.
3 Mix the mayonnaise with the curry paste. Stir in the chicken and mango. Season to taste.
4 Spread on four slices of the bread and top with the remaining slices. Cut into quarters and serve.

Chicken, Red Pepper and Chilli Sarnies

SERVES 4

8 slices of white bread
100 g/4 oz/½ cup medium-fat soft cheese
100 g/4 oz/1 cup diced cooked chicken
1 red (bell) pepper, thinly sliced
1 red onion, thinly sliced
Chilli relish, to taste

1 Spread one side of each slice of bread with soft cheese.
2 Top four of the slices with the chicken, pepper and onion slices.
3 Spread the remaining slices of bread with relish. Invert on to the chicken mixture. Press down lightly. Cut into quarters and serve.

BLTs

If you like crispy bacon, use streaky rashers (slices) instead of back – you will need 12, as they are smaller.

SERVES 4

8 rashers (slices) of back bacon
8 slices of wholemeal bread, buttered
45 ml/3 tbsp mayonnaise
4 small tomatoes, sliced
4–8 crisp lettuce leaves
Freshly ground black pepper

1 Grill (broil) the bacon until cooked to your liking.
2 Spread four of the buttered bread slices with the mayonnaise. Top with slices of tomato, then the lettuce.
3 Lay the hot bacon on top, add a good grinding of pepper, then cover with the remaining buttered bread.
4 Cut into halves and serve.

Bacon, Tomato and Mussel Sandwiches

SERVES 4

15 ml/1 tbsp olive oil
4 rashers (slices) of smoked back bacon
2 tomatoes, sliced
250 g/9 oz/1 medium can of mussels in brine, drained
8 slices of wholemeal bread
45 ml/3 tbsp mayonnaise
A little shredded lettuce

1 Heat the oil in a frying pan (skillet). Add the bacon and fry (sauté) for 2 minutes on each side until cooked through and lightly golden. Remove from the pan and keep warm.
2 Add the tomato slices and mussels and cook for 1–2 minutes until hot.

3 Spread the bread with the mayonnaise. Cover four slices with a little shredded lettuce. Top each with a bacon rasher, then a quarter of the tomato and mussel mixture. Add a good grinding of pepper and top with the other slices of bread. Cut into halves and serve while still warm.

Chicken Maryland Sandwich

Delicatessen sliced chicken breast is very good for this.

SERVES 2

A little butter or margarine
4 slices of granary bread
30 ml/2 tbsp corn relish
2 slices of cooked chicken breast
1 banana, sliced
2.5 ml/½ tsp ground cumin
2.5 ml/½ tsp onion granules
1.5 ml/¼ tsp dried thyme
Salt and freshly ground black pepper

1 Preheat the grill (broiler) or sandwich toaster. Thinly spread butter or margarine on one side of each slice of bread. Spread two slices with the corn relish, on the unbuttered sides, and top with the chicken.
2 Mash the banana in a bowl with a fork and spread over.
3 Mix the cumin, onion granules, thyme and a little salt and pepper together and sprinkle over. Top with the remaining bread slices, buttered sides up. Grill (broil) or cook in the sandwich maker until golden on both sides or fry (sauté) in a frying pan (skillet).
4 Cut into halves and serve.

Toasted Baked Bean and Cheese Sandwiches

SERVES 4

8 slices of bread, buttered
20 ml/4 tsp brown table sauce
400 g/14 oz/1 large can of baked beans
50 g/2 oz/½ cup Cheddar cheese, grated

1 Preheat the grill (broiler) or sandwich toaster. Lay four slices of the bread, buttered side down, on a board.
2 Spread lightly with the brown sauce. Stir the beans, then divide among the centres of the sandwiches and spread out all round, not too near the edges. If the tomato sauce is very runny, don't add too much. Sprinkle on the cheese.
3 Top with the remaining bread slices, buttered sides up. Place on the grill rack with a cooling rack pressed firmly over the top. Grill (broil) until the tops are golden brown. With oven-gloved hands, invert the grill rack so the cooling rack is on the bottom and return to the grill to toast the other sides. Alternatively, cook in the sandwich toaster in the normal way. They may also be fried (sautéed) in a frying pan (skillet) – press down firmly from time to time with a fish slice, until the base is golden, then carefully turn over, and brown the other sides.

Toasted Turkey, Cranberry and Mayo Sandwiches

SERVES 4

8 slices of granary bread, buttered
175 g/6 oz/1½ cups chopped cooked turkey
15 ml/1 tbsp cranberry sauce
30 ml/2 tbsp mayonnaise
Salt and freshly ground black pepper

1 Preheat the grill (broiler) or sandwich toaster. Put four of the slices of the bread, buttered sides down, on a board.
2 Mix the turkey, cranberry and mayonnaise with a little salt and pepper in a bowl and spread over the bread.
3 Top with the remaining slices, buttered sides up. Cook as for Toasted Baked Bean and Cheese Sandwiches.

Croque Monsieur

SERVES 2

4 slices of white bread
Butter or margarine, for spreading
2 slices of ham
2 slices of Cheddar or Gruyère (Swiss) cheese

1 Preheat the grill (broiler) or sandwich toaster. Spread the bread with the butter or margarine on one side only.
2 Sandwich together, buttered sides out, with the ham and cheese slices inside.
3 Cook as for Toasted Baked Bean and Cheese Sandwiches.

Toasted Curried Chicken Sandwiches

SERVES 4

8 slices of wholemeal bread, buttered
20 ml/4 tsp mango or peach chutney
175 g/6 oz/1½ cups chopped cooked
 chicken
45 ml/3 tbsp mayonnaise
5–10 ml/1–2 tsp curry paste
Salt and freshly ground black pepper

1 Preheat the grill (broiler) or sandwich toaster. Put four slices of bread, buttered sides down, on a board. Spread with the chutney.
2 Mix the chicken with the mayonnaise and curry paste to taste in a bowl. Season lightly.
3 Spread over the bread, not quite to the edges.
4 Top with the remaining slices, buttered sides up. Cook as for Toasted Baked Bean and Cheese Sandwiches.

Golden Melties

SERVES 2

4 slices of white bread
Butter or margarine, for spreading
30 ml/2 tbsp corn relish
2 slices of Cheddar or Gruyère (Swiss)
 cheese

1 Preheat the grill (broiler) or sandwich toaster. Spread the bread with the butter or margarine on one side only.
2 Sandwich together, buttered sides out, with the corn relish and cheese inside.
3 Cook as for Toasted Baked Bean and Cheese Sandwiches (page 89).

Pâté Fingers

SERVES 4

1 egg
100 g/4 oz smooth chicken liver pâté
15 ml/1 tbsp brandy
4 slices of wholemeal bread
Butter or margarine, for spreading
A little paprika

1 Hard-boil (hard-cook) the egg (see page 76) and once cooked, immediately place in a bowl of cold water to cool. Shell and chop.
2 Put the pâté in a bowl, add the brandy and chopped egg and stir briskly with a wooden spoon until well blended.
3 Toast the bread and spread with a little butter or margarine. Spread the pâté over and cut each into three fingers. Sprinkle with a little paprika before serving.

Hot Pastrami on Rye

SERVES 4

8 slices of dark rye bread
100 g/4 oz/½ cup medium-fat soft
    cheese
15 ml/1 tbsp horseradish relish
8 slices of pastrami
15 ml/1 tbsp sunflower oil
Freshly ground black pepper
8 gherkins (cornichons), halved
    lengthways

1 Preheat the grill (broiler). Toast the bread slices on one side.
2 Mash the cheese and horseradish together and spread over the untoasted sides. Place on plates.
3 Place the pastrami on foil on the grill rack. Brush with oil and grill (broil) until just beginning to sizzle.
4 Quickly place on top of the cheese, sprinkle with pepper and top each with a halved gherkin. Serve straight away.

Everyday Rarebit

SERVES 2

175 g/6 oz/1½ cups Cheddar cheese,
    grated
5 ml/1 tsp made English mustard
30 ml/2 tbsp apple juice
2 slices of toast

1 Put everything except the toast in a small pan and heat, stirring, until melted and blended.
2 Spoon on to the toast and serve straight away.

Somerset Rarebit

SERVES 2

Prepare as for Everyday Rarebit but substitute cider for the apple juice. Peel, core and slice an eating apple and place on the toast. Spoon the cheese mixture over and serve.

Welsh Rarebit

SERVES 2

15 g/½ oz/1 tbsp butter or margarine
15 ml/1 tbsp plain (all-purpose) flour
100 g/4 oz/1 cup Cheddar cheese,
    grated
A pinch of salt
A little cayenne
1.5 ml/¼ tsp made English mustard
30 ml/2 tbsp beer
A few drops of Worcestershire sauce
2 slices of bread

1 Blend all the ingredients except the bread in a small saucepan. Heat gently, stirring all the time until thick and bubbling.
2 Preheat the grill (broiler). Toast the bread on both sides. Spread the cheese mixture over and return to the grill until golden and bubbling. Serve hot.

Buck Rarebit

SERVES 1–2

Prepare as for Welsh Rarebit but top each with a poached egg (see page 76), before serving.

Hot Salmon Special

SERVES 2–4

200 g/7 oz/1 small can of pink or red salmon
30 ml/2 tbsp mayonnaise
10 ml/2 tsp capers, chopped
2.5 cm/1 in piece of cucumber, chopped
4 slices of wholemeal bread
Butter or margarine, for spreading
50 g/2 oz/½ cup Mozzarella cheese, grated
Freshly ground black pepper

1 Drain the fish, discard any skin and mash well. Remove the bones if you like but they are very good for you!
2 Mix in the mayonnaise, capers and cucumber. Preheat the grill (broiler).
3 Toast the bread on both sides. Leave on the grill (broiler) rack. Spread one side with butter or margarine, then top with the salmon mixture.
4 Sprinkle the cheese over and add a good grinding of pepper. Grill (broil) under a moderate heat until the cheese melts and bubbles. Serve straight away.

Cheese Blushers

SERVES 4

100 g/4 oz/1 cup Wensleydale cheese, crumbled
45 ml/3 tbsp mayonnaise
4 croissants, split
1 small red onion, thinly sliced
2–3 cooked baby beetroot (red beets), thinly sliced
Freshly ground black pepper

1 Mash the cheese with the mayonnaise and spread in the croissants.
2 Fill with the onion and beetroot slices and add a good grinding of pepper.

Sardine Special on Toast

SERVES 2

2 slices of wholemeal bread
15 g/½ oz/1 tbsp butter or margarine, softened
10 ml/2 tsp horseradish relish
120 g/4½ oz/1 small can of sardines, drained
A dash of lemon juice
Freshly ground black pepper
15 ml/1 tbsp chopped fresh parsley

1 Preheat the grill (broiler) and toast the bread on both sides.
2 Mash the butter or margarine with the horseradish in a small bowl and spread on the toast.
3 Top the toast with the sardines and return to the grill to heat through. Sprinkle with lemon juice, pepper and parsley and serve straight away.

Swiss Cheese Toasts

SERVES 4

4 slices of wholemeal bread
Butter or margarine, for spreading
30 ml/2 tbsp tomato purée (paste)
4 slices of ham
225 g/8 oz/1 small can of pineapple
slices, drained
4 slices of Gruyère or Emmental (Swiss)
cheese
1 tomato, cut into 4 slices
2.5 ml/½ tsp dried basil

1 Preheat the grill (broiler) and toast
the bread on one side only.
2 Butter the untoasted sides and place
on the grill rack.
3 Spread with the tomato purée, then
top with the slices of ham, pineapple
and cheese.
4 Put a slice of tomato on top of each
and sprinkle with dried basil. Grill (broil)
until the cheese melts and bubbles.
Serve hot.

Melting Crescents

SERVES 2

2 croissants
2 thin slices of smoked cooked ham
2 slices of Gruyère or Emmental (Swiss)
cheese
Tomato slices, to garnish

1 Preheat the grill (broiler). Split the
croissants along one side.
2 Fold the slices of ham and tuck into
the croissants with the cheese slices.
3 Grill (broil) under a moderate heat
until the cheese melts, turning once.
4 Serve garnished with tomato slices.

Gooey Salami and Mushroom Crescents

SERVES 2–4

4 croissants
170 g/6 oz/1 small can of creamed
mushrooms
4 thin slices of Milano salami, halved
8 fresh basil leaves, torn
4 thin slices of Mozzarella cheese

1 Preheat the grill (broiler). Split the
croissants along one edge.
2 Spread the mushroom mixture in
each. Top with the halved slices of
salami and add the basil and cheese.
3 Grill (broil) under a moderate heat,
turning once until hot and the cheese
melts. Serve straight away.

Parma Crescents

SERVES 2

2 croissants
2 slices of Parma ham
1 tomato, thinly sliced
About 8 shavings of Parmesan cheese,
pared from a block with a potato
peeler
A good pinch of dried oregano
Freshly ground black pepper

1 Preheat the grill (broiler). Split the
croissants and fill each with a slice of
ham and half a sliced tomato.
2 Push in the Parmesan shavings and
sprinkle oregano and pepper inside.
3 Grill (broil) under a moderate heat
until hot through and the croissants are
crisp, turning once.

Italian Lunch

SERVES 4

1 large ciabatta loaf, cut into 4 chunks

8 slices of Italian salami

1 beefsteak tomato, cut into 8 thin slices

4 sun-dried tomatoes in oil, drained and chopped

12 fresh basil leaves, torn

60 ml/4 tbsp olive oil

Freshly ground black pepper

1 Split the chunks of bread along one side and gently open up slightly.

2 Lay the salami in the bread. Top with the tomato slices.

3 Scatter the chopped sun-dried tomatoes and basil over. Trickle the olive oil on top of the tomatoes and add a good grinding of black pepper.

Minted Curried Lamb Naans

SERVES 4

4 small garlic and coriander (cilantro) naan breads

20 ml/4 tsp curry paste

5 cm/2 in piece of cucumber, very thinly sliced

45 ml/3 tbsp thick plain yoghurt

5 ml/1 tsp dried mint

Salt and freshly ground black pepper

175 g/6 oz/1½ cups diced cooked lamb

1 Grill (broil) the naan breads briefly to warm, then place on plates and spread with the curry paste.

2 Lay the cucumber slices on top.

3 Mix the remaining ingredients together.

4 Spoon the yoghurt mixture on top and serve.

Pan-roasted Vegetable Ciabattas

SERVES 4

30 ml/2 tbsp olive oil

1 red (bell) pepper, sliced

1 green pepper, sliced

1 yellow pepper, sliced

1 red onion, sliced

2 sun-dried tomatoes in oil, drained and chopped

Salt and freshly ground black pepper

4 thick diagonal slices of ciabatta bread

15 ml/1 tbsp sun-dried tomato oil from the jar

8 fresh basil leaves, torn

1 Heat the olive oil in a large frying pan (skillet). Add the peppers and onion and fry (sauté), stirring, for abut 4 minutes until softened but still with a little 'bite'.

2 Add the sun-dried tomatoes and some salt and pepper and mix thoroughly.

3 Meanwhile, toast the bread on one side only.

4 Place, untoasted sides up, on warm plates. Trickle the sun-dried tomato oil over.

5 Pile the pepper mixture on top, scatter the basil over and serve.

Greek Salad Seedies

Use the bread you pull out of the rolls for breadcrumbs.

SERVES 4

½ small iceberg lettuce, finely shredded
1 tomato, chopped
5 cm/2 in piece of cucumber, chopped
15 ml/1 tbsp sliced stoned (pitted) black
    olives
½ small onion, thinly sliced
75 g/3 oz/¾ cup Feta cheese, crumbled
2.5 ml/½ tsp dried oregano
30 ml/2 tbsp olive oil
15 ml/1 tbsp red wine vinegar
Salt and freshly ground black pepper
4 large seeded rolls

1 Put everything except the rolls in a large bowl and turn the mixture over with a spoon and fork.
2 Cut a slice off the top of each roll. Pull out most of the soft bread inside to leave a shell.
3 Pack the salad into each roll and top with the lids. Serve straight away.

Fragrant Chicken and Pesto Baguettes

You can use the recipe for Simple Pesto Sauce (see page 336) if you prefer to make your own.

SERVES 4

4 small baguettes
Butter or margarine, for spreading
4 large crisp lettuce leaves
60 ml/4 tbsp ready-made pesto
90 ml/6 tbsp mayonnaise
275 g/10 oz/2½ cups chopped cooked
    chicken
60 ml/4 tbsp pine nuts, toasted

1 Split the baguettes along one side. Spread inside with butter or margarine.
2 Line with the lettuce leaves.
3 Mix the pesto with the mayonnaise in a bowl with a wooden spoon and stir in the chicken. Spread inside the baguettes and sprinkle with the pine nuts.

Pâté Crunch Baguettes

SERVES 4

4 small baguettes
100 g/4 oz smooth chicken liver pâté
100 g/4 oz/½ cup medium-fat soft
    cheese
15 ml/1 tbsp sunflower seeds
1 celery stick, finely chopped
5 cm/2 in piece of cucumber, sliced
2 tomatoes, sliced
Mustard and cress, to garnish

1 Cut along one edge of each baguette.
2 Mash the liver pâté, soft cheese, sunflower seeds and celery together in a bowl with a fork and spread in the baguettes.
3 Fill with slices of cucumber and tomato and garnish with mustard and cress.

Cheese and Parma Ham Panini

If you have a hinged electric grill (broiler) or flat sandwich toaster (not the sort that divides the sandwiches), use this instead of flattening before grilling (broiling).

SERVES 4

4 small part-baked baguettes
30 ml/2 tbsp olive oil
4 thin slices of Parma ham
4 slices of Emmental (Swiss) cheese

1 Preheat the grill. Split the baguettes and open out slightly.
2 Trickle the olive oil in each.
3 Lay a slice of ham and cheese in each.
4 Place between two boards and press down hard to flatten the baguettes.
5 Grill under a moderate heat until toasted and golden on both sides.

Chicken and Spinach Panini

You can buy ready-made tomato and basil pasta sauce in a jar.

SERVES 4

4 small part-baked baguettes
60 ml/4 tbsp tomato and basil pasta sauce
16 baby spinach leaves
2 cooked chicken breasts, cut into strips
20 ml/4 tsp grated Parmesan cheese
Freshly ground black pepper

1 Preheat the grill (broiler). Split the baguettes and open out slightly.
2 Spread the insides with the pasta sauce.

3 Lay the spinach leaves on top, then the chicken pieces.
4 Sprinkle with the Parmesan and season with pepper.
5 Place between two boards and press down firmly to flatten the baguettes.
6 Grill (broil) under a moderate heat until golden on both sides and hot through.

Smoked Salmon and Ricotta Panini

SERVES 4

4 small part-baked ciabatta rolls
100 g/4 oz/½ cup medium-fat soft cheese
4 slices of smoked salmon
4 radicchio leaves
1 spring onion (scallion), finely chopped
Freshly ground black pepper
30 ml/2 tbsp olive oil

1 Preheat the grill (broiler). Split the ciabatta rolls, not quite right through, and open out slightly.
2 Spread with the cheese.
3 Top with the salmon, folding it to fit, then add the radicchio leaves and sprinkle with the spring onion and pepper, to taste.
4 Place between two boards and press down firmly to flatten.
5 Brush with olive oil and grill (broil) under a moderate heat until golden on both sides.

Photograph opposite: **Chilli Bean Wraps (see page 85)**

Perfect Pizza Marguerita

You can add any extra pizza toppings you like before adding the cheese.

SERVES 4

275 g/10 oz/1 packet of pizza base mix
45 ml/3 tbsp tomato purée (paste)
2.5 ml/½ tsp dried oregano
4 ripe tomatoes, sliced
30 ml/2 tbsp olive oil
Freshly ground black pepper
100 g/4 oz Mozzarella cheese, sliced
8 fresh basil leaves, torn
A few black olives

1 Make up the pizza base mix as directed on the packet. Preheat the oven to 220°C/425°F/gas mark 7.
2 Roll out to a thin round, about 23 cm/9 in in diameter, and place on an oiled baking (cookie) sheet.
3 Spread with the tomato purée and sprinkle with the oregano.
4 Top the purée with the tomato slices and trickle half the oil over the surface. Add a good grinding of pepper.
5 Bake in the oven for 10 minutes. Top with the cheese, trickle the remaining oil over and scatter the basil and olives over. Bake for a further 10 minutes or until golden round the edges and the cheese has melted and is bubbling. Serve hot.

Quick Pan Pizza

Add other toppings of your choice before adding the cheese, if you like.

SERVES 1–2

100 g/4 oz/1 cup self-raising (self-rising) flour
A pinch of salt
45 ml/3 tbsp sunflower or olive oil
About 60 ml/4 tbsp water
225 g/8 oz/1 small can of chopped tomatoes, drained
1.5 ml/¼ tsp dried oregano
50 g/2 oz/½ cup Cheddar cheese, grated

1 Mix the flour and salt in a bowl. Add 30 ml/2 tbsp of the oil and mix with enough cold water to form a soft but not sticky dough.
2 Squeeze gently on a lightly floured surface to form a ball and roll out to a round the size of a medium frying pan (skillet).
3 Heat the remaining oil in the frying pan and add the dough. Cook for 3 minutes until golden brown underneath.
4 Turn over and top with the tomatoes, oregano and cheese. Cook for 2–3 minutes. Meanwhile, preheat the grill (broiler).
5 Transfer the pan to the grill and cook for about 3 minutes or until the cheese melts and bubbles. Serve hot.

Photograph opposite: **Gingered Salmon with Mixed Vegetable Stir-fry (see page 111)**

Neapolitan Pizza Rolls

You can heat these in the microwave: leave unwrapped and put them in a microwave-safe dish with a lid. Microwave for 2 minutes, rearrange and cook a little longer, depending on the output of your microwave. Do not overcook or they will be tough.

SERVES 4

4 soft rolls
225 g/8 oz/1 small can of chopped
   tomatoes, drained thoroughly
5 ml/1 tsp dried basil
50 g/2 oz/1 small can of anchovy fillets
100 g/4 oz/1 cup Mozzarella or
   Cheddar cheese, grated

1 Cut a shallow slit in the top of each roll, not quite removing the slice. Pull out some of the soft centre, leaving a thick wall of crust.
2 Spoon in the tomatoes, sprinkle with the basil, then roll up the anchovies and add these with the cheese. Wrap each roll in foil and steam in a steamer or a colander, covered with a lid over a pan of simmering water, for 10 minutes until the cheese is melted. Alternatively, cook in a preheated oven at 220°C/425°F/ gas mark 7 for 10 minutes.

Prawn Pizza Rolls

SERVES 4

Prepare exactly as for Neapolitan Pizza Rolls but substitute 50 g/2 oz cooked, peeled prawns (shrimp) for the anchovies and use dried oregano instead of basil.

Swiss Cheese Fondue

SERVES 4

1 garlic clove, halved
15 ml/1 tbsp cornflour (cornstarch)
15 ml/1 tbsp water
300 ml/½ pt/1¼ cups white wine
30 ml/2 tbsp kirsch
5 ml/1 tsp lemon juice
225 g/8 oz/2 cups Emmental or
   Gruyère (Swiss) cheese, grated
225 g/8 oz/2 cups Cheddar cheese,
   grated
25 g/1 oz/2 tbsp butter or margarine
Salt and freshly ground black pepper
A good pinch of grated nutmeg
Cubes of French bread, to serve

1 Rub the halved garlic clove round the inside of a fondue pot or a saucepan, then discard.
2 Mix the cornflour with the water in the pot. Stir in the remaining ingredients with a wooden spoon.
3 Heat over a fairly low heat, stirring all the time, until the cheese melts and the mixture is smooth and glossy. Taste and re-season if necessary. Do not allow to boil.
4 When serving, provide forks to dip the pieces of bread into the fondue.

Cosa Nostra

SERVES 2

275 g/10 oz/1 packet of pizza base mix
2 tomatoes, chopped
1 canned pimiento cap, chopped
A few cooked French (green) beans,
    cut into small pieces
1 slice of ham, diced
5 ml/1 tsp capers
1.5 ml/¼ tsp dried oregano
60 ml/4 tbsp grated Mozzarella cheese
Salt and freshly ground black pepper
A little olive oil
200 ml/7 fl oz/scant 1 cup passata
    (sieved tomatoes)
A good pinch of dried basil
30 ml/2 tbsp grated Parmesan cheese

1 Make up the pizza base mix
according to the packet directions.
Preheat the oven to 200°C/400°F/
gas mark 6.
2 Cut the dough into halves and roll
out each half to a fairly thin round.
3 Divide the tomatoes, pimiento, beans,
ham, capers, oregano and Mozzarella
between the centres of the rounds.
Season lightly.
4 Brush the edges with water and
draw the dough up over the filling to
cover completely. Press the edges
together to seal.
5 Place, sealed sides down, on a lightly
oiled baking (cookie) sheet.
6 Brush with olive oil. Bake in the oven
for about 20 minutes until golden
brown and cooked through.

7 Meanwhile, heat the passata with
the basil in a saucepan. Transfer the
stuffed pizzas to warm plates. Spoon
the sauce over the centre and sprinkle
with Parmesan cheese before serving.

Tofu Cakes

SERVES 4

150 g/5 oz firm tofu, drained and finely
    chopped
1 large potato, finely grated
1 small onion, grated
30 ml/2 tbsp chopped fresh parsley
30 ml/2 tbsp sunflower oil, plus extra
    for frying (sautéing)
Salt and freshly ground black pepper
75 ml/3 oz/¾ cup self-raising (self-
    rising) wholemeal flour
150 ml/¼ pt/⅔ cup milk
Sweet pickle or tomato ketchup
    (catsup), to serve

1 Mix all the ingredients except the milk
together in a bowl.
2 Whisk in the milk, a little at a time,
using a wire whisk, to form a batter.
3 Heat a little oil a large, heavy-based
frying pan (skillet) over a fairly high
heat and drop in spoonfuls of the
batter.
4 Fry (sauté) for about 3 minutes on
each side until cooked through and
golden brown. Drain on kitchen paper
(paper towels). Keep warm while
cooking the remainder.
5 Serve hot with pickle or tomato
ketchup.

Hot Chilli Dogs

SERVES 4

25 g/1 oz/2 tbsp butter or margarine
1 large onion, chopped
1 green (bell) pepper, thinly sliced
425 g/15 oz/1 large can of hot dog
 sausages
8 finger rolls
45 ml/3 tbsp chilli relish

1 Melt the butter or margarine in a
small saucepan over a moderate heat.
Add the onion and pepper and fry
(sauté) for 2 minutes, stirring. Cover,
reduce the heat and cook gently for
5 minutes or until the onion and
pepper are tender.
2 Meanwhile, heat the hot dogs
according to the instructions on the can.
3 Split the rolls and spread one cut
surface with chilli relish. Spoon the onion
and pepper mixture on top. Add a hot
dog to each and serve at once.

Cheesy Stuffed Jackets

SERVES 4

4 large potatoes, scrubbed
25 g/1 oz/2 tbsp butter or margarine
225 g/8 oz/1 cup medium-fat soft
 cheese
100 g/4 oz/1 cup Cheddar cheese,
 grated
15 ml/1 tbsp chopped fresh parsley
Salt and freshly ground black pepper

1 Prick the potatoes all over. Boil in
water for about 20 minutes or until
tender; alternatively, bake in a
preheated oven at 180°C/350°F/
gas mark 4 for 1½ hours or until tender
when squeezed. They may also be

cooked in the microwave: wrap in
kitchen paper (paper towels) and
microwave on High for about
4 minutes per potato until soft when
squeezed.
2 Halve the cooked potatoes and
scoop out most of the flesh into a bowl.
Using a fork, mash with the butter or
margarine, the cheeses and parsley.
Add salt and pepper to taste.
3 Preheat the grill (broiler). Pack the
potato mixture back into the shells.
Place on the grill and grill (broil) for
about 5 minutes until hot and golden.

Pimiento and Anchovy Jackets with Mozzarella

SERVES 4

Prepare as for Cheesy Stuffed Jackets
but omit the Cheddar cheese and add
a 200 g/7 oz/small can of pimientos,
drained and diced. Then drain a 50 g/
2 oz/small can of anchovies and soak in
a little milk for 10 minutes. Drain again,
chop and add to the mixture. After
packing back in the shells, top each half
of potato with 10 ml/2 tsp grated
Mozzarella cheese, then grill (broil) and
garnish with a few torn basil leaves.

Blue Cheese and Celery Jackets

SERVES 4

Prepare as for Cheesy Stuffed Jackets
but use crumbled blue cheese instead
of the Cheddar and add two finely
chopped celery sticks. Once grilled
(broiled), top each with a spoonful of
plain Greek-style yoghurt.

Sardine Jackets

SERVES 4

Prepare as for Cheesy Stuffed Jackets (page 100) but substitute a 120 g/ 4½ oz/small can of sardines, drained and mashed, for the Cheddar cheese and add lemon juice to taste.

Ham and Sun-dried Tomato Jackets

SERVES 4

Prepare as for Cheesy Stuffed Jackets (page 100) but omit the Cheddar cheese and add 50 g/2 oz/½ cup cooked, diced, smoked ham, two drained sun-dried tomatoes, finely chopped, and 10 ml/2 tsp chopped fresh basil.

Smoked Mackerel Jackets with Horseradish Mayonnaise

SERVES 4

Prepare as for Cheesy Stuffed Jackets (page 100) but substitute one smoked mackerel fillet, skinned and flaked, for the Cheddar cheese. Mix 30 ml/2 tbsp mayonnaise with 10 ml/2 tsp horseradish relish and add a good grinding of pepper. Spoon this on top of the grilled (broiled) jackets before serving.

Tuna Mayonnaise Jackets

SERVES 4

4 large potatoes, scrubbed
25 g/1 oz/2 tbsp butter or margarine
185 g/6½ oz/1 small can of tuna, drained
45 ml/3 tbsp mayonnaise
15 ml/1 tbsp snipped fresh chives
Salt and freshly ground black pepper

1 Cook the potatoes as for Cheesy Stuffed Jackets (page 100).
2 Halve and scoop out most of the potato into a bowl. Using a fork, mash in the butter or margarine, tuna, half the mayonnaise, the chives and a little salt and pepper.
3 Preheat the grill (broiler). Pack the potato mixture back into the shells and grill (broil) for about 5 minutes until hot and lightly golden. Top with the remaining mayonnaise and serve.

Prawn Cocktail Jackets

SERVES 4

4 large potatoes, scrubbed

4 knobs of butter or margarine

45 ml/3 tbsp mayonnaise

15 ml/1 tbsp tomato ketchup (catsup)

5 ml/1 tsp Worcestershire sauce

5 ml/1 tsp soy sauce

A few drops of Tabasco

Salt and freshly ground black pepper

175 g/6 oz cooked peeled prawns (shrimp)

A little paprika and a few wedges of lemon, to garnish

1 Cook the potatoes in the oven or microwave as in Cheesy Stuffed Jackets (page 100).

2 Make a cross cut into the top of each one, squeeze gently and add a knob of butter or margarine.

3 Meanwhile, mix the mayonnaise with the ketchup, Worcestershire, soy and Tabasco sauces. Season to taste, then stir in the prawns.

4 Spoon this mixture on top of the hot, cooked potatoes. Garnish with a sprinkling of paprika and lemon wedges.

Luxury Smoked Salmon and Crème Fraîche Jackets

SERVES 4

Prepare as for Prawn Cocktail Jackets but after cutting and squeezing the potatoes and adding the butter or margarine, top each with a good spoonful of smoked salmon trimmings, a dollop of crème fraîche, a squeeze of lemon juice and a generous grinding of black pepper.

American-style Fish Fingers

You can buy processed cheese slices and ready-made tartare sauce, if you prefer!

SERVES 2

8 fish fingers

2 soft baps

2 slices of Cheddar cheese

30 ml/2 tbsp Tartare Sauce (see page 336)

A little shredded lettuce

1 Preheat the grill (broiler) and grill (broil) the fish fingers.

2 Split the rolls and lay the fish fingers on the bottom halves on the grill rack.

3 Top the fish with the cheese and place under the hot grill to melt the cheese. Remove from the grill.

4 Add the tartare sauce, top with a little shredded lettuce and then the lids of the rolls.

Fish Finger Fingers

SERVES 2

20 g/¾ oz/1½ tbsp butter or margarine
15 ml/1 tbsp tomato ketchup (catsup)
5 ml/1 tsp capers, chopped
6 fish fingers
2 slices of wholemeal bread

1 Preheat the grill (broiler). Mash the butter or margarine with the tomato ketchup and capers in a small bowl.
2 Grill (broil) the fish fingers and the bread on both sides until the fish is cooked and the bread is golden. Remove the bread if it is ready before the fish.
3 Spread the toast with the butter mixture. Cut each slice into three fingers. Top each with a fish finger and serve.

Chilli Fingers

SERVES 4

4 small baguettes, split
Butter or margarine, for spreading
30 ml/2 tbsp tomato chutney
30 ml/2 tbsp mayonnaise
Hot chilli sauce, to taste
10 fish fingers
A little shredded lettuce

1 Split the baguettes and spread with butter or margarine.
2 Mix the tomato chutney with the mayonnaise in a bowl and pep up with hot chilli sauce to taste.
3 Grill (broil) or fry (sauté) the fish fingers. Divide between the baguettes. Top with the spicy mayonnaise and push in some shredded lettuce. Serve while still hot.

Fried Fish Sangers

SERVES 4

4 fresh or frozen breaded cod or
   haddock fillets
30 ml/2 tbsp tomato ketchup (catsup)
25 g/1 oz/2 tbsp butter or margarine,
   softened
8 thick slices of crusty white bread
A little lemon juice
Salt and freshly ground black pepper

1 Fry (sauté) or grill (broil) the fish fillets according to the packet instructions.
2 Meanwhile, mash the ketchup into the butter or margarine in a small bowl with a fork. Spread on the bread.
3 Put one slice on each of four individual plates. Top each with a cooked fish fillet, sprinkle with lemon juice, salt and pepper and top with the remaining slices of tomato buttered bread. Cut into halves and serve hot.

Fish and Chip Butties

SERVES 4

4 fresh or frozen breaded cod or
   haddock fillets
2 handfuls of oven chips
8 slices of white bread
Butter or margarine, for spreading
Tomato ketchup (catsup) and malt
   vinegar, to serve
Salt and freshly ground black pepper

1 Preheat the grill (broiler). Fry (sauté)
the fish fillets as directed on the packet
and grill (broil) the oven chips until
golden, turning occasionally.
2 Spread the bread lightly with butter
or margarine. Put four slices on plates.
3 Spread a little ketchup over the four
slices, if liked.
4 Lay the fish and chips on top and
sprinkle with vinegar, salt and pepper
to taste.
5 Cover with the remaining bread
slices. Cut into halves and serve.

Butter Bean Bake

For vegetarians, simply omit the ham.

SERVES 2

1 quantity of Cheese Sauce (see page
   329)
425 g/15 oz/1 large can of butter (lima)
   beans, drained
A pinch of dried mixed herbs
A pinch of cayenne
100 g/4 oz/1 cup diced cooked ham
30 ml/2 tbsp crushed cornflakes

1 Preheat the oven to 190°C/375°F/
gas mark 5. Make the cheese sauce.

2 Put the butter beans in a shallow
dish. Add the herbs, cayenne and ham
and stir.
3 Pour over the cheese sauce and
sprinkle with the crushed cornflakes.
4 Bake in the oven for about
25 minutes or until golden and hot
through.

Spicy Potato Cakes

SERVES 4

2 fairly large potatoes, coarsely grated
1 small onion, grated
2.5 ml/½ tsp garam masala
1.5 ml/¼ tsp chilli powder
10 ml/2 tsp plain (all-purpose) flour
Salt and freshly ground black pepper
1 large egg, beaten
45 ml/3 tbsp sunflower oil
Shredded lettuce and mango chutney,
   to serve

1 Mix the potato with the onion and
spices. Add the flour and a little salt
and pepper. Mix with the beaten egg,
to bind.
2 Heat the oil in a frying pan (skillet).
Add spoonfuls of the mixture and fry
(sauté) over a fairly high heat for
about 3 minutes until golden brown
underneath, pressing down lightly with
a fish slice.
3 Turn over and cook the other sides
for 2–3 minutes until golden brown and
cooked through. Drain on kitchen
paper (paper towels).
4 Serve on a bed of shredded lettuce
with mango chutney.

Tuna Mornay

SERVES 2–4

40 g/1½ oz/3 tbsp butter or margarine

2 onions, thinly sliced

20 g/¾ oz/3 tbsp plain (all-purpose) flour

300 ml/½ pt/1¼ cups milk

Salt and freshly ground black pepper

50 g/2 oz/½ cup Cheddar cheese, grated

185 g/6½ oz/1 small can of tuna, drained

Crusty bread, to serve

1 Melt the butter or margarine in a saucepan. Add the onions and cook, stirring over a fairly high heat, for 3 minutes until softened.

2 Stir the flour into the pan and cook for 1 minute. Remove from the heat and gradually stir in the milk, seasoning and half the cheese. Return to the heat, bring to the boil and cook for 2 minutes, stirring.

3 Preheat the grill (broiler).

4 Tip the tuna into a flameproof dish and break up with a fork. Pour the sauce over and sprinkle with the remaining cheese.

5 Cook under the grill for about 6 minutes until golden, bubbling and hot through. Serve with crusty bread.

Tuna and Egg Mornay

SERVES 2–4

Prepare as for Tuna Mornay but add two sliced hard-boiled (hard-cooked) eggs (see page 76) on top of the tuna before pouring on the sauce. Cover loosely with foil and heat for a few minutes until piping hot.

Spiced Banana and Corn Toppers

SERVES 4

5 eggs

2 bananas, thickly sliced

50 g/2 oz/1 cup fresh white breadcrumbs

1.5 ml/¼ tsp chilli powder

2.5 ml/½ tsp pimenton or paprika

A little sunflower oil

200 g/7 oz/1 small can of sweetcorn (corn) with (bell) peppers

30 ml/2 tbsp mayonnaise

4 slices of granary bread, toasted

4 red or green pepper rings, to garnish

1 Whisk one of the eggs in a bowl with a wire whisk or fork. Add the bananas and stir to coat. Mix the breadcrumbs with the spices on a plate. Dip the banana pieces in to coat completely.

2 Heat a little oil in a frying pan (skillet) and fry (sauté) the bananas over a fairly high heat, turning occasionally, for about 3 minutes until golden. Drain on kitchen paper (paper towels) and keep warm.

3 Heat the sweetcorn in a saucepan and stir in the mayonnaise.

4 Meanwhile, fry the remaining eggs in a little more oil until cooked to your liking (see page 76).

5 Put a slice of toast on each of four plates. Top with the sweetcorn, then the bananas and finally the eggs. Garnish each with a pepper ring and serve hot.

Fish and Seafood

Fish and other seafood are great to eat at any time. They are excellent sources of protein, vitamins A and D and also fish oils, which, unlike meat fat, are now considered to be good for you as they are high in polyunsaturated Omega-3 fatty acids, thought to help prevent heart disease.

All fish and seafood are quick and easy to cook – particularly rewarding for novice cooks. The most important tip is, never overcook it.

I have included suggestions for vegetable accompaniments for most of the dishes in this chapter together with explanations as to when to cook them. You will find instructions on how to prepare and cook individual vegetables on pages 291–92.

To skin fish fillets

1 Place the fillet on a board, skin-side down.
2 Make a small cut between the flesh and skin at one end.
3 Hold the flap of skin firmly between your finger and thumb (dip
   your fingers in salt first to help you to grip), then ease the flesh
   away from the skin, with a large, sharp knife, pulling the skin as
   you go. It should come away fairly easily.

To bone whole fish such as mackerel

1 Cut off the head and tail and trim off the fins with scissors.
2 Open out the cleaned fish and lay it skin-side up on a board.
3 Run your thumb firmly up and down the backbone several times.
4 Turn the fish over and lift off the backbone and any loose bones.

Simple Pan Swordfish

Put the potatoes on to cook before you start preparing the fish. Put the beans on as soon as you have put the fish in the pan.

SERVES 4

4 swordfish steaks, about 175 g/6 oz each
Salt and freshly ground black pepper
5 ml/1 tsp dried oregano
25 g/1 oz/2 tbsp butter or margarine
30 ml/2 tbsp chopped fresh parsley
Wedges of lemon and sprigs of parsley, to garnish
Baby new potatoes and French (green) beans, to serve

1 Pull the skin off the swordfish, then season lightly with salt and pepper and the oregano.
2 Heat the butter or margarine in a large frying pan (skillet). Add the fish and fry (sauté) for 3–4 minutes on each side until cooked through and golden.
3 Sprinkle with parsley, then, using a fish slice, transfer to warm plates and spoon the juices over. Garnish with wedges of lemon and sprigs of parsley and serve with the baby new potatoes and French beans.

Trout with Cashew Nuts

Put the potatoes on to cook before cooking the trout. Cook the mangetout (snow peas) while the trout is cooking.

SERVES 4

4 cleaned trout, heads removed if liked
Salt and freshly ground black pepper
75 g/3 oz/⅓ cup butter or margarine
50 g/2 oz/½ cup raw cashew nuts
15 ml/1 tbsp lemon juice
30 ml/2 tbsp chopped fresh parsley
New potatoes and mangetout, to serve

1 Wipe the fish inside and out with kitchen paper (paper towels). Make several slashes on each side. Season with salt and pepper
2 Heat the butter or margarine in a large frying pan (skillet).
3 Add the fish and fry (sauté) over a high heat for 3–4 minutes until golden brown underneath.
4 Turn over using a fish slice and add the nuts. Fry for a further 3 minutes until golden and cooked through.
5 Carefully transfer to warm plates, leaving the nuts in the pan.
6 Add the lemon juice and parsley to the pan with a little more salt and pepper. Heat through, stirring. Spoon over the fish and serve hot with the new potatoes and mangetout.

Trout with Lemon and Tarragon

SERVES 4

4 cleaned trout, heads removed if liked

120 ml/4 fl oz/½ cup dry white wine

1 small lemon, thinly sliced

1 small onion, finely chopped

15 ml/1 tbsp chopped fresh tarragon

30 ml/2 tbsp chopped fresh parsley

Salt and freshly ground black pepper

150 ml/¼ pt/⅔ cup double (heavy) cream

Super Creamed Potatoes (see page 298) and broccoli, to serve

1 Lay the fish in a large frying pan (skillet) and pour the wine over. Cover with the slices of lemon, the onion, the tarragon and half the parsley. Season lightly, bring to the boil, then cover, turn down the heat to fairly low and cook for 10 minutes until the trout are tender and cooked through. Meanwhile, make the Super Creamed Potatoes.

2 Carefully transfer the fish to warm plates using a fish slice and keep warm. Start to cook the broccoli.

3 Turn up the heat under the frying pan and boil the cooking liquid for 2–3 minutes until reduced by half. Stir in the cream and cook for 2 minutes. Season to taste.

4 Spoon the sauce over the fish, sprinkle with the remaining parsley and serve with the creamed potatoes and broccoli.

Welsh Trout with Bacon

SERVES 4

2 leeks, thinly sliced

1 turnip, coarsely grated

25 g/1 oz/ 2 tbsp butter or margarine, plus a little for greasing

4 cleaned trout, heads removed if liked

12 rashers (slices) of streaky bacon, rinded

Freshly ground black pepper

30 ml/2 tbsp chopped fresh parsley

Mashed Potatoes (see page 298), to serve

1 Preheat the oven to 180°C/350°F/ gas mark 4.

2 Cook the leeks and turnip gently in the butter or margarine in a saucepan for about 5 minutes, stirring until softened.

3 Rinse the trout under cold water. Dry on kitchen paper (paper towels). Push some of the cooked vegetables inside the cavity of each, then wrap each in three rashers of bacon. Lay in a lightly buttered roasting tin (pan). Season with lots of pepper.

4 Cover with foil and bake in the oven for about 20 minutes, removing the foil after 10 minutes to brown the bacon. Meanwhile, cook and mash the potatoes.

5 Using a fish slice, transfer the fish to warm dishes. Sprinkle with parsley and serve with the mashed potatoes.

Soy Salmon

SERVES 4

450 g/1 lb salmon fillet, skinned (see page 107)

Freshly ground black pepper

30 ml/2 tbsp soy sauce

10 ml/2 tsp Worcestershire sauce

15 ml/1 tbsp lemon juice

50 g/2 oz/½ cup plain (all-purpose) flour

2 eggs, beaten

100 g/4 oz/2 cups fresh white breadcrumbs

5 ml/1 tsp dried onion granules

Oil, for deep-frying

250 g/9 oz/1 packet of Chinese egg noodles

Ginger Dipping Sauce (see page 341), to serve

1 Cut the fish into strips 2.5 cm/1 in wide and place in a shallow dish. Season with pepper.

2 Mix the soy sauce with the Worcestershire sauce and lemon juice. Pour over the fish and mix gently with your hands until well coated. Leave to marinate for 1 hour.

3 Put the flour, eggs and breadcrumbs on separate plates. Add the onion granules to the breadcrumbs. Dip the pieces in the flour, then the eggs, and then the breadcrumb mix.

4 Heat the oil in a large saucepan or deep-fat fryer to 190°C/375°F or until a cube of day-old bread browns in 30 seconds. Gently drop in the fish and cook for about 4 minutes until crisp and golden brown. Drain on kitchen paper (paper towels).

5 Meanwhile, cook the Chinese egg noodles according to the packet directions and make the Ginger Dipping Sauce. Pour the sauce into individual small bowls. Drain the noodles. Put the fish on warm plates with the noodles and serve with the bowls of Ginger Dipping Sauce.

Trout with Almonds

This is lovely served with lots of warm French bread and a well-dressed green salad. Make the salad before cooking the trout. Warm the bread in a fairly hot oven for about 3 minutes before serving.

SERVES 4

4 cleaned trout, heads removed if liked

Salt and freshly ground black pepper

25 g/1 oz/2 tbsp butter or margarine

30 ml/2 tbsp toasted flaked (slivered) almonds

A dash of lemon juice

15 ml/1 tbsp chopped fresh parsley

1 Slash the trout in several places on each side with a sharp knife, then season with salt and pepper.

2 Heat the butter or margarine in a large frying pan (skillet), then add the fish and fry (sauté) for 4–5 minutes on each side until golden brown and cooked through. Sprinkle with the almonds and lemon juice to taste.

3 Transfer to warm plates with a fish slice and spoon the juices over. Sprinkle with parsley and serve.

Gingered Salmon with Mixed Vegetable Stir-fry

SERVES 4

30 ml/2 tbsp sunflower oil
1 small garlic clove, crushed
15 ml/1 tbsp chopped fresh root ginger
100 g/4 oz broccoli, cut into tiny florets
1 large carrot, cut into thin matchsticks
100 g/4 oz baby corn cobs
100 g/4 oz mangetout (snow peas)
¼ small red cabbage, very finely shredded
50 g/2 oz button mushrooms, thinly sliced
50 g/2 oz/1 cup beansprouts
15 ml/1 tbsp soy sauce
4 pieces of salmon fillet, about 175 g/ 6 oz each
10 ml/2 tsp lemon juice
Salt and freshly ground black pepper
1 bunch of spring onions (scallions), finely chopped
15 ml/1 tbsp chopped fresh coriander (cilantro)
5 ml/1 tsp sesame oil

1 Heat half the oil in a wok or large frying pan (skillet). Add the garlic and 5 ml/1 tsp of the ginger and cook for 10 seconds.
2 Add the broccoli, carrot, corn cobs, mangetout, cabbage, mushrooms and beansprouts. Cook, stirring and turning for 6 minutes, then stir in the soy sauce.
3 At the same time, preheat the grill (broiler) and place the salmon on foil on the grill rack. Sprinkle with lemon juice, salt and pepper. Grill (broil) for about 6 minutes until tender. Spoon the vegetables on to warm plates. Put the salmon on top and keep warm.

4 Heat the remaining sunflower oil and ginger, the spring onions, coriander and sesame oil in a small saucepan with a good grinding of pepper. When bubbling, spoon over the salmon and serve.

Salmon with Cucumber and Dill

Cook the potatoes before you start cooking the fish, then finish off the salad while the fish is cooking in the sauce.

SERVES 4

50 g/2 oz/¼ cup unsalted (sweet) butter
4 salmon tail fillets, about 175 g/6 oz each
Salt and freshly ground black pepper
½ cucumber, peeled and finely diced
300 ml/½ pt/1¼ cups soured (dairy sour) cream
5 ml/1 tsp dried dill (dill weed)
A good pinch of caster (superfine) sugar
Hot Potato Salad (see page 309), to serve

1 Heat the butter in a large frying pan (skillet). Add the salmon, skin-sides up, and fry (sauté) over a fairly high heat for 1½ minutes. Carefully turn over with a fish slice and fry for a further 1½ minutes.
2 Season well. Add the cucumber, soured cream, dill and sugar. When bubbling, turn down the heat, cover and cook gently for 5 minutes. Serve straight from the pan with the potato salad.

Pan Salmon with Rocket

Start cooking the potatoes before you cook the salmon.

SERVES 4

25 g/1 oz/2 tbsp unsalted (sweet) butter

4 salmon tail fillets, about 175 g/6 oz each

30 ml/2 tbsp brandy

60 ml/4 tbsp crème fraîche

Salt and freshly ground black pepper

A good pinch of caster (superfine) sugar

50 g/2 oz rocket leaves

Wedges of lime, to garnish

Sauté Potatoes (see page 296), to serve

1 Melt the butter in a frying pan (skillet). Add the salmon, skin-sides up, and fry (sauté) for 3 minutes over a fairly high heat. Carefully turn over with a fish slice and continue to fry for about 3 minutes until tender and just cooked through. Remove from the pan with the fish slice and keep warm.

2 Pour the brandy into the pan and ignite. When the flames die down, stir in the crème fraîche, some salt and pepper and the sugar. Put the rocket on four warm plates. Top with a salmon fillet and spoon a little sauce over each. Garnish with wedges of lime and serve with the sauté potatoes.

Grilled Salmon with Tomatoes and Green Hollandaise

Make the salad in advance and put the potatoes on to cook before cooking the salmon.

SERVES 4

4 salmon tail fillets, about 175 g/6 oz each

8 tomatoes, halved

Salt and freshly ground black pepper

60 ml/4 tbsp olive oil

30 ml/2 tbsp balsamic vinegar

1 quantity of Green Hollandaise (see page 330)

New potatoes and a Green Salad (see page 308), to serve

1 Preheat the grill (broiler).

2 Put the salmon on foil on the grill rack and surround with the tomatoes. Season lightly, trickle all over with the olive oil and sprinkle the tomatoes with the balsamic vinegar.

3 Grill (broil) for about 5–6 minutes until the salmon and tomatoes are cooked through. Do not overcook and do not turn over.

4 Meanwhile, make the Green Hollandaise.

5 Carefully transfer the tomatoes to four warm plates and lay a piece of salmon on top of each. Spoon a little of the sauce over the fish and serve with the new potatoes and green salad.

Grilled Cod with Wholegrain Mustard

I don't normally recommend heating the oven just to cook potatoes, but these wedges do go so well with this dish. You can always use the hot oven to warm a pudding, perhaps a ready-made pie or even some canned rice pudding, tipped into an ovenproof dish and covered with foil, at the same time. Put the potato wedges in the oven first and start cooking the fish when you turn the wedges. Boil the peas while the fish is cooking.

SERVES 4

4 pieces of cod fillet, about 175 g/6 oz each

50 g/2 oz/¼ cup butter or margarine

30 ml/2 tbsp wholegrain mustard

15 ml/1 tbsp chopped fresh parsley

5 ml/1 tsp light brown sugar

Salt and freshly ground black pepper

Wedges of lemon, to garnish

Garlic Potato Wedges (see page 295) and peas, to serve

1 Preheat the grill (broiler).

2 Lay the cod on foil on the grill rack, skin-sides up. Dot with 15 g/½ oz/1 tbsp of the butter or margarine and grill (broil) for 3 minutes.

3 Turn the fish over. Mash the remaining butter or margarine with the mustard, parsley, sugar and a little salt and pepper. Spread over the flesh and grill for about 4–5 minutes until sizzling, golden and cooked through.

4 Using a fish slice, transfer to warm plates, garnish with wedges of lemon and serve with the potato wedges and peas.

Mackerel with Chickpeas

SERVES 4

4 cleaned mackerel

Salt and freshly ground black pepper

425 g/15 oz/1 large can of chickpeas (garbanzos), drained

60 ml/4 tbsp passata (sieved tomatoes)

15 ml/1 tbsp tomato purée (paste)

45 ml/3 tbsp dry white wine

5 ml/1 tsp caster (superfine) sugar

1 large garlic clove, crushed

5 ml/1 tsp dried thyme

15 ml/1 tbsp chopped fresh parsley

Wedges of lemon, to garnish

Crusty French bread, to serve

1 Preheat the grill (broiler).

2 Make several slashes on both sides of the mackerel, then season with salt and pepper.

3 Grill (broil) for about 5 minutes on each side until cooked through and golden brown.

4 Meanwhile, put the chickpeas in a saucepan with the remaining ingredients. Bring to the boil over a high heat and cook for about 4 minutes until the chickpeas are bathed in sauce. Season to taste.

5 Spoon the chickpeas on to warm plates and top with the mackerel. Garnish with wedges of lemon and serve with lots of crusty French bread.

Spiced Mackerel with Lemon and Coriander

If you're not sure how to seed the chilli, see Fiery Mussel Spaghettini, page 134.

SERVES 4

Finely grated rind and juice of 1 lemon
60 ml/4 tbsp chopped fresh coriander (cilantro)
1 green chilli, seeded and finely chopped
4 cleaned mackerel, heads removed and boned (see page 107)
Salt and freshly ground black pepper
30 ml/2 tbsp sunflower oil
Tomato Butter (see page 342) and plain potatoes, to serve

1 Mix the lemon rind and juice with the coriander and chilli.
2 Make several slashes on each side of the fish. Lay the fish in a large, shallow dish and sprinkle with the lemon mixture and some salt and pepper. Leave to marinate for 30 minutes. Meanwhile, make the tomato butter and put the potatoes on to cook.
3 Preheat the grill (broiler).
4 Fold the boned halves of the fish together, back to their original shape, and lay them on foil on the grill rack. Brush with oil and grill (broil) for 4 minutes until the skin is golden and crispy. Turn over with a fish slice, brush with a little more oil and grill for a further 3 minutes or until cooked through.
5 Transfer to warm plates and serve with the tomato butter and plain potatoes.

Tuna Steaks with Garlic and Coriander

SERVES 4

4 tuna steaks, about 175 g/6 oz each
Salt and freshly ground black pepper
60 ml/4 tbsp olive oil
Juice of 1 lemon
5 ml/1 tsp ground cumin
2 garlic cloves, finely chopped
60 ml/4 tbsp chopped fresh coriander (cilantro)
Crusty French bread and a Green Salad (see page 308), to serve

1 Wipe the fish, place in a shallow dish and season lightly with salt and pepper.
2 Whisk half the oil with the lemon juice and cumin in a bowl, with a wire whisk, and pour over. Sprinkle with the chopped garlic and coriander. Turn to coat completely. Leave to marinate for 30 minutes. Meanwhile, make the green salad.
3 Heat the remaining oil in a frying pan (skillet). Lift the fish out of the marinade, add to the hot pan and cook for about 3 minutes on each side until just cooked through. Do not overcook.
4 Carefully transfer the fish to warm plates. Pour any remaining marinade into the pan and heat through. Pour over the fish and serve with crusty bread and the salad.

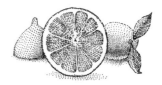

Spanish Tuna Steaks

Pimenton is a smoky-flavoured paprika from Spain, available in good supermarkets. You can use sweet paprika instead but the flavour won't be so good. Start cooking the potatoes first and put the beans on to cook as soon as you have added the tuna to the frying pan (skillet).

SERVES 4

60 ml/4 tbsp olive oil
25 g/1 oz/2 tbsp butter or margarine
4 tuna steaks, about 175 g/6 oz each
Salt and freshly ground black pepper
5 ml/1 tsp pimenton
30 ml/2 tbsp chopped fresh parsley
1 large garlic clove, chopped
1 lemon
Sauté Potatoes (see page 296) and
    French (green) beans, to serve

1 Heat the oil and butter or margarine in a large frying pan. Add the tuna and sprinkle with salt and pepper and half the pimenton. Fry (sauté) for 3 minutes.

2 Turn the fish over, using a fish slice, season with more salt and pepper and the remaining pimenton. Sprinkle with the parsley and garlic and cook for a further 3 minutes.

3 Cut the lemon in half and squeeze the juice from one half into the pan. Cut the other half into wedges.

4 Transfer the fish and the juices to warm plates, using a fish slice. Garnish with the lemon wedges and serve with the sauté potatoes and French beans.

Thai Grilled Lemon Sole

To bruise the lemon grass, crush it lightly with a meat mallet or heavy weight, just enough to release the flavour.

SERVES 4

4 lemon sole fillets
2.5 ml/½ tsp coarse sea salt
Juice of 2 limes
1 stalk of lemon grass, bruised
3 fresh basil leaves, torn
225 g/8 oz/1 cup Thai fragrant rice
1 red (bell) pepper, finely diced
1 green pepper, finely diced
90 ml/6 tbsp light brown sugar
Wedges of lime, to garnish

1 Lay the fish fillets in a shallow dish. Sprinkle with coarse sea salt. Sprinkle the lime juice over and add the lemon grass and basil. Leave to marinate for 1 hour. Remove the basil and lemon grass.

2 Meanwhile, cook the rice according to the packet directions (or see page 294), adding the peppers for the last 5 minutes' cooking time. Drain in a colander. Put 2.5 cm/1 in water in the saucepan and sit the colander on top. Cover the rice with the saucepan lid and keep warm over a very gentle heat until ready to serve.

3 Preheat the grill (broiler).

4 Lay the fillets on foil on a grill rack. Sprinkle the sugar over. Grill (broil) for about 5 minutes until tender and the sugar has caramelised.

5 Spoon the rice and peppers on to warm plates, top with the fish and garnish with wedges of lime.

Plaice Mornay

Put the potatoes and carrots on to cook before you cook the fish. Finish the potato dish while the plaice browns under the grill (broiler).

SERVES 4

4 plaice fillets, dark skin removed (see page 107)
300 ml/½ pt/1¼ cups milk
30 ml/2 tbsp cornflour (cornstarch)
50 g/2 oz/½ cup strong Cheddar cheese, grated
5 ml/1 tsp Dijon mustard
Salt and freshly ground black pepper
Potato and Leek Mash (see page 298) and carrots, to serve

1 Cut the fish into strips, place in a saucepan and add all but 30 ml/2 tbsp of the milk. Bring to the boil, reduce the heat and cook gently for 5 minutes or until the fish is tender. Carefully lift the fish out of the pan and place in a shallow, flameproof dish.
2 Put the cornflour in a cup and mix with the remaining milk. Add to the pan, bring to the boil and cook for 1 minute, stirring until thickened and smooth. Stir in three-quarters of the cheese, the mustard and seasoning to taste. Pour over the fish.
3 Preheat the grill.
4 Sprinkle the remaining cheese over the dish and brown under the grill for about 3 minutes. Serve with the Potato and Leek Mash and carrots.

Smoked Haddock Mornay

SERVES 4

Prepare as for Plaice Mornay but substitute smoked haddock for the plaice and serve with Super Creamed Potatoes (see page 298) and spinach.

Cod Provençal

SERVES 4

15 ml/1 tbsp olive oil
1 large onion, finely chopped
1 large garlic clove, crushed
1 green (bell) pepper, diced
400 g/14 oz/1 large can of chopped tomatoes
15 ml/1 tbsp tomato purée (paste)
30 ml/2 tbsp white or red wine
450 g/1 lb cod fillet, skinned (see page 107) and cubed
Salt and freshly ground black pepper
30 ml/2 tbsp sliced stuffed olives
225 g/8 oz/1 cup long-grain rice

1 Heat the oil in a saucepan. Add the onion, garlic and green pepper and cook gently for 3 minutes, stirring.
2 Add the tomatoes, tomato purée and wine. Bring to the boil, reduce the heat until bubbling gently round the edges and cook for 5 minutes.
3 Add the fish and a little salt and pepper and continue cooking for about 5 minutes or until the fish is tender. Stir in the olives.
4 Meanwhile, cook the rice according to the packet directions (or see page 294). Drain in a colander.
5 Spoon the rice on to warm plates. Top with the fish mixture and serve.

Tuna and Vegetable Cheese

Use cooked frozen vegetables if you have no leftovers.

SERVES 4

1 quantity of Cheese Sauce
(see page 329)

350 g/12 oz cooked leftover
vegetables, chopped

185 g/6½ oz/1 small can of tuna,
drained

25 g/1 oz/¼ cup Cheddar cheese,
grated

30 ml/2 tbsp cornflakes, crushed

3 tomatoes, sliced

1 Make up the cheese sauce.

2 Mix in the vegetables and tuna and heat through for about 3 minutes until piping hot.

3 Spoon the hot mixture into a flameproof serving dish.

4 Sprinkle with the Cheddar cheese and the crushed cornflakes.

5 Arrange the tomato slices around the top.

6 Preheat the grill (broiler). Remove the grill rack and place the dish in the grill pan. Cook until golden and bubbling. Serve hot.

Speedy Seaside Crumble

SERVES 4

75 g/3 oz/¾ cup plain (all-purpose)
flour

A pinch of salt

40 g/1½ oz/3 tbsp soft tub margarine

50 g/2 oz/½ cup Cheddar cheese,
grated

450 g/1 lb white fish fillets, skinned (see
page 107) and diced

100 g/4 oz frozen diced mixed
vegetables

295 g/10½ oz/1 medium can of
condensed celery soup

5 ml/1 tsp dried chives or 15 ml/1 tbsp
fresh snipped chives

1 Preheat the oven to 200°C/400°F/ gas mark 6.

2 Put the flour and salt in a bowl and mash in the margarine with a fork until crumbly. Stir in the cheese.

3 Put the fish in an ovenproof dish. Add the vegetables, then spoon the soup over.

4 Sprinkle with the chives and then the cheese crumble. Bake in the oven for 30 minutes or until golden and cooked through. Serve hot.

Hake Dolcelatte

SERVES 4

75 g/3 oz/⅓ cup butter or margarine
4 hake fillets, about 175 g/6 oz each, skinned (see page 107)
10 ml/2 tsp lemon juice
225 g/8 oz Dolcelatte or other creamy blue cheese
60 ml/4 tbsp single (light) cream
15 ml/1 tbsp chopped fresh parsley
Salt and freshly ground black pepper
Ciabatta bread and a Green Salad (see page 308), to serve

1 Preheat the grill (broiler). Use a little of the butter or margarine to grease a large piece of foil and place on the grill rack.
2 Lay the hake, skinned sides up, on the foil. Top with a third of the remaining butter or margarine, cut into small pieces, and sprinkle with lemon juice.
3 Grill (broil) for 5 minutes until almost cooked. Carefully turn over, using a fish slice.
4 While the fish is cooking, mash the remaining butter or margarine with the Dolcelatte, cream, parsley and season with a little salt and lots of pepper.
5 Spread this mixture over the fish and grill for a further 5 minutes or until the cheese has melted and is turning golden brown.
6 Make the salad. Serve the fish with the salad and ciabatta bread.

Hake in Asparagus Cream Sauce

SERVES 4

225 g/8 oz/1 cup long-grain rice
1 onion, finely chopped
15 g/½ oz/1 tbsp butter or margarine
295 g/10½ oz/1 medium can of condensed asparagus soup
4 pieces of hake fillet, about 175 g/6 oz each
150 ml/¼ pt/⅔ cup crème fraîche
425 g/15 oz/1 large can of cut asparagus
Freshly ground black pepper
Paprika, to garnish

1 Cook the rice according to the packet directions (or see page 294). Drain in a colander. Put 2.5 cm/1 in water in the saucepan and sit the colander on top. Cover the rice with the saucepan lid and keep warm over a very gentle heat until ready to serve.
2 Meanwhile, fry (sauté) the onion in the butter or margarine in a flameproof casserole (Dutch oven) until softened but not browned. Stir in the soup.
3 Add the fish, cover and cook gently for about 8 minutes or until the fish is tender.
4 Carefully lift the fish out on to warm plates. Stir the crème fraîche and asparagus into the sauce and heat through. Season with pepper and spoon over the fish.
5 Pile the rice to one side and sprinkle with paprika before serving.

Smoked Cod and Egg Bake

Make this with any smoked fish.

SERVES 4

3 eggs
40 g/1½ oz/3 tbsp butter or margarine
450 g/1 lb smoked cod, skinned (see
    page 107) and cut into neat pieces
20 g/¾ oz/3 tbsp plain (all-purpose)
    flour
300 ml/½ pt/1¼ cups milk
75 g/3 oz/¾ cup Cheddar cheese, grated
Salt and freshly ground black pepper
25 g/1 oz/½ cup fresh white
    breadcrumbs
Baked Tomatoes with Basil
    (see page 306), to serve

1 Hard-boil (hard-cook) the eggs (see
page 76).
2 Grease a shallow 1.2 litre/2 pt/5 cup
ovenproof dish with a little butter or
margarine. Lay the fish in the dish.
3 Preheat the oven to 190°C/375°F/
gas mark 5.
4 Mix the flour with a little of the milk
in a saucepan, using a wire whisk. Add
the remaining milk and 20 g/¾ oz/
1½ tbsp of the remaining butter or
margarine. Bring to the boil and cook
for 2 minutes, whisking all the time until
thick and smooth. Stir in the cheese and
season to taste.
5 Shell the eggs, slice and arrange over
the fish and top with the sauce.
6 Sprinkle with the breadcrumbs and
bake in the oven for 45 minutes until
golden and the fish is cooked through.
While it is cooking, prepare the Baked
Tomatoes with Basil and cook in the
oven at the same time. Serve the cod
and eggs with the tomatoes.

Smoked Cod and Egg Florentine

SERVES 4

Prepare as for Smoked Cod and Egg
Bake, but put a layer of 350 g/12 oz
chopped, thawed if frozen, spinach in
the base of the dish before adding the
fish.

Golden-topped Ratatouille with Cod

SERVES 4

4 fillets of cod, about 175 g/6 oz each
390 g/14 oz/1 large can of ratatouille
15 ml/1 tbsp red wine
75 g/3 oz/¾ cup Cheddar cheese,
    grated
Crusty bread, to serve

1 Preheat the oven to 190°C/375°F/
gas mark 5.
2 Lay the cod in a single layer in a
large, shallow, ovenproof dish.
3 Mix the ratatouille with the wine and
spoon over. Top with the cheese and
bake in the oven for 20 minutes or until
golden and bubbling and the fish is
cooked through.
4 Serve straight away with crusty
bread.

Royal Hake Bake

SERVES 4

4 large waxy potatoes, scrubbed and
diced
12 button (pearl) onions, peeled but
left whole
25 g/1 oz/2 tbsp butter or margarine
450 g/1 lb hake fillets, skinned (see
page 107)
Juice of ½ small lemon
Salt and freshly ground black pepper
300 ml/½ pt /1¼ cups mayonnaise
2 spring onions (scallions), finely
chopped
30 ml/2 tbsp chopped fresh parsley

1 Boil the potatoes and onions in lightly
salted water for about 5 minutes until
just tender. Drain in a colander, return
to the pan, add the butter or
margarine and stir until coated.
2 Preheat the oven to 190°C/375°F/
gas mark 5.
3 Lay the fish down the centre of a
shallow, ovenproof dish. Arrange the
potatoes and onions down both sides.
4 Sprinkle the fish with the lemon and
a good grinding of salt and pepper.
Spoon the mayonnaise over the fish.
Sprinkle the potatoes and onions with
the spring onions.
5 Bake in the oven for about
30 minutes until the fish is tender and
the top is lightly golden. Serve
garnished with chopped parsley.

Fireside Fish Pot

SERVES 4

25 g/1 oz/2 tbsp butter or margarine
1 onion, sliced
1 carrot, thinly sliced
2 large potatoes, diced
¼ small cabbage, shredded
400 g/14 oz/1 large can of chopped
tomatoes
300 ml/½ pt/1¼ cups chicken or fish
stock, made with 1 stock cube
225 g/8 oz white fish fillet, cubed
225 g/8 oz smoked haddock fillet,
skinned (see page 107) and cubed
Salt and freshly ground black pepper
Snipped fresh chives, to garnish

1 Melt the butter or margarine in a
very large saucepan. Add the
prepared fresh vegetables and cook,
stirring, for 5 minutes.
2 Add the tomatoes and stock. Bring
to the boil over a high heat, reduce the
heat to fairly low, cover with a lid and
cook gently for 15 minutes.
3 Add the fish, re-cover and continue
to cook for a further 5 minutes until the
fish and vegetables are tender. Season
to taste.
4 Ladle into warm bowls and serve
sprinkled with snipped chives.

Family Fish Pie

If you decide to make this in advance, leave it to cool completely before storing it in the fridge. To reheat, bake in a preheated oven at 190°C/375°F/gas mark 5 for about 35 minutes until golden brown and piping hot throughout.

SERVES 4

700 g/1½ lb potatoes, cut into bite-sized pieces

325 ml/11 fl oz/1⅓ cups milk

75 g/3 oz/¾ cup Cheddar cheese, grated

100 g/4 oz button mushrooms, sliced

225 g/8 oz frozen mixed vegetables

450 g/1 lb white fish fillet

Salt and freshly ground black pepper

45 ml/3 tbsp plain (all-purpose) flour

30 ml/2 tbsp chopped fresh parsley

1 Put the potatoes in a saucepan. Add just enough water to cover and bring to the boil over a high heat. Boil for about 10 minutes, until really tender.

2 Drain in a colander, return to the pan and mash with 25 ml/1½ tbsp of the milk and half the cheese.

3 Meanwhile, put the mushrooms in a saucepan with the vegetables, fish and 300 ml/½ pt/1¼ cups of the remaining milk. Season with salt and pepper. Bring to the boil over a high heat, reduce the heat, part-cover and cook gently for 8–10 minutes until the fish and vegetables are tender.

4 Carefully lift the fish out of the saucepan. Remove any skin and bones and break up the fish into chunky pieces.

5 Blend the flour with the remaining milk until smooth. Stir into the saucepan with the parsley, bring to the boil over a high heat and cook for 2 minutes, stirring until thickened. Stir the fish into the sauce. Taste and add more salt and pepper, if liked.

6 Spoon the mixture into a flameproof serving dish. Spoon the cheesy potato on top and spread out very gently with a fork. Sprinkle with the remaining cheese. If serving immediately, grill (broil) for about 5 minutes until golden and piping hot.

Spiced Tuna and Beans

SERVES 4

400 g/14 oz/1 large can of chopped tomatoes

1 garlic clove, crushed

2 x 425 g/15 oz/large cans of mixed pulses, drained

185 g/6½ oz/1 small can of tuna, drained and flaked

1.5 ml/¼ tsp chilli powder

Salt and freshly ground black pepper

10 ml/2 tsp red wine vinegar

2.5 ml/½ tsp caster (superfine) sugar

30 ml/2 tbsp snipped fresh chives

1 Put everything except half the chives into a saucepan. Bring to the boil over a high heat, stirring, turn down the heat to moderate and cook for 4 minutes.

2 Stir the mixture and season to taste if necessary, then spoon into warm bowls, sprinkle with the remaining chives and serve with crusty bread.

Simple Sardine Bake

SERVES 4

2 x 120 g/4½ oz/small cans of sardines
in oil, drained
Salt and freshly ground black pepper
45 ml/3 tbsp olive oil
15 ml/1 tbsp chopped fresh parsley
15 ml/1 tbsp snipped fresh chives
15 ml/1 tbsp chopped fresh thyme
45 ml/3 tbsp chopped capers
6 large tomatoes, thinly sliced
25 g/1 oz/½ cup fresh white
breadcrumbs
15 ml/1 tbsp grated Parmesan cheese

1 Preheat the oven to 180°C/350°F/
gas mark 4.
2 Lay the fish in a shallow ovenproof
dish. Season lightly and trickle 15 ml/
1 tbsp of the oil over.
3 Mix all the herbs with the capers and
scatter over the top with the tomatoes.
4 Mix together the breadcrumbs and
cheese and sprinkle over.
5 Trickle the remaining oil over the
surface. Bake in the oven for about
25 minutes until golden and bubbling.

Satisfying Tuna Bake

SERVES 4

Prepare as for Simple Sardine Bake but
substitute a 185 g/6½ oz/small can of
tuna for the sardines. Use chopped
gherkins (cornichons) instead of the
capers and top with 50 g/2 oz/½ cup
grated Cheddar cheese, mixed with the
breadcrumbs.

Potty Fish Supper

SERVES 4

600 ml/1 pt/ 2½ cups fish or chicken
stock, made with 1 stock cube
5 ml/1 tsp anchovy essence (extract)
100 g/4 oz/1 cup conchiglie or other
pasta shapes
2 carrots, diced
100 g/4 oz French (green) beans, cut
into short lengths
350 g/12 oz white fish fillet, skinned
(see page 107) and cut into chunks
400 g/14 oz/1 large can of chopped
tomatoes
5 ml/1 tsp dried basil
Salt and freshly ground black pepper
Crusty bread, to serve

1 Put the stock in a saucepan with the
anchovy essence, pasta and carrots.
Bring to the boil and boil over a fairly
high heat for 7 minutes.
2 Add all the remaining ingredients,
bring back to the boil, and cook for
5–8 minutes or until the pasta,
vegetables and fish are tender. Taste
and re-season if necessary.
3 Serve with lots of crusty bread.

Storecupboard Fish Supper

It's a good idea to keep some fish fillets in the freezer for a quick and appetising meal.

SERVES 4

400 g/14 oz/1 large can of chopped tomatoes

275 g/10 oz/1 medium can of new potatoes, drained and quartered

275 g/10 oz/1 medium can of baby carrots, drained

275 g/10 oz/1 medium can of garden peas, drained

300 ml/½ pt/1¼ cups fish, vegetable or chicken stock, made with 1 stock cube

5 ml/1 tsp anchovy essence (extract)

15 ml/1 tbsp tomato purée (paste)

A pinch of caster (superfine) sugar

Salt and freshly ground black pepper

350 g/12 oz frozen white fish fillets, thawed, skinned (see page 107) and cut into small chunks

15 ml/1 tbsp chopped fresh parsley, to garnish

1 Put all the ingredients except the fish in a large saucepan. Heat rapidly until boiling. Turn down the heat to moderate and cook for 3 minutes.

2 Add the fish, heat until the mixture is bubbling again, then continue to cook for 5 minutes or until the fish is cooked and will break easily with the point of a knife.

3 Taste the sauce and re-season if necessary. Ladle into warm bowls and sprinkle with parsley before serving.

Oriental Seafood Hot-pot

SERVES 6

350 g/12 oz white fish fillet, skinned and cut into strips

4 mackerel fillets, skinned (see page 107) and cut into strips

6 raw peeled king prawns (jumbo shrimp)

6 shelled scallops, sliced

4 cleaned baby squid, cut into rings

1.2 litres/2 pts/5 cups chicken stock, made with 2 stock cubes

5 ml/1 tsp chopped fresh root ginger

4 spring onions (scallions), chopped

50 g/2 oz cellophane noodles, soaked in warm water for 5 minutes

450 g/1 lb spring cabbage, shredded

Hoisin sauce, to taste

1 Place the fish, stock, ginger and spring onions in a large, flameproof casserole dish (Dutch oven). Bring to the boil, reduce the heat until bubbling round the edges, then cover and cook gently for 5 minutes.

2 Add all the remaining ingredients except the hoisin sauce, heat until bubbling again, then cook for 5–10 minutes until the fish and cabbage are tender. Stir in a little hoisin sauce (add it 5 ml/1 tsp at a time, as it's quite strong, and keep tasting until it's right for you).

3 Serve ladled into warm bowls.

Oriental Tuna Casserole

SERVES 6

100 g/4 oz Chinese egg noodles

2 x 185 g/6½ oz/small cans of tuna, drained

295 g/10½ oz/1 medium can of condensed mushroom soup

60 ml/4 tbsp water

15 ml/1 tbsp soy sauce

2 celery sticks, chopped

100 g/4 oz/1 cup cashew nuts

4 spring onions (scallions), chopped

100 g/4 oz button mushrooms, quartered

1 Preheat the oven to 190°C/375°F/ gas mark 5.

2 Cook the noodles according to the packet directions. Drain.

3 Mix the noodles with all the remaining ingredients in an ovenproof dish.

4 Bake in the oven for about 40 minutes until golden and bubbling.

Chinese Prawn Fried Rice

SERVES 4–6

225 g/8 oz/1 cup long-grain rice

30 ml/2 tbsp sunflower oil

½ bunch of spring onions (scallions), chopped

100 g/4 oz mushrooms, chopped

1 small red (bell) pepper, chopped

1 small green pepper, chopped

100 g/4 oz cooked peeled prawns (shrimp)

100 g/4 oz/1 cup diced cooked ham

2.5 ml/½ tsp ground ginger

1.5 ml/¼ tsp cayenne

Salt

1 Cook the rice according to the packet directions (or see page 294). Drain in a colander.

2 Heat the oil in a large frying pan (skillet) or wok. Add the onions, mushrooms and peppers. Fry (sauté) for 2 minutes, stirring.

3 Add the cooked rice and fry, stirring, for 3 minutes.

4 Add the remaining ingredients and cook, stirring, for about 4 minutes, until piping hot.

Quick Paella

SERVES 4

120 g/4½ oz/1 packet of savoury vegetable rice

5 ml/1 tsp ground turmeric

450 ml/¾ pt/2 cups boiling water

100 g/4 oz/1 cup diced cooked chicken

250 g/9 oz/1 medium can of mussels in brine, drained

100 g/4 oz cooked peeled prawns (shrimp)

15 ml/1 tbsp chopped fresh parsley

1 Put the rice, turmeric and water in a large frying pan (skillet). Bring to the boil, turn down the heat to fairly low and simmer for 12 minutes.

2 Add all the remaining ingredients, cover and simmer gently for a further 8 minutes until all the liquid has been absorbed and the rice is tender.

3 Fluff up with a fork and sprinkle with chopped fresh parsley before serving.

One-pot Kedgeree

This is traditionally served for breakfast, but is equally good for lunch or supper.

SERVES 4

3 eggs, scrubbed under cold running
    water
225 g/8 oz/1 cup long-grain rice
Salt
5 ml/1 tsp ground turmeric
225 g/8 oz smoked haddock fillet
100 g/4 oz/1 cup frozen peas
2.5 ml/½ tsp ground cumin
45 ml/3 tbsp chopped fresh parsley
45 ml/3 tbsp single (light) cream
Freshly ground black pepper

1 Put the eggs in a large saucepan of water. Bring to the boil.

2 Add the rice, a pinch of salt and the turmeric. Stir well, then cook over a high heat for 5 minutes. Add the fish and peas and cook for a further 5 minutes or until the rice and fish are tender.

3 Lift out the eggs and fish. Put the eggs in a bowl of cold water. Drain the rice in a colander and return to the pan. Stir in the cumin.

4 Remove the skin from the fish and break the flesh into chunks. Add to the rice.

5 Shell the eggs and cut into chunks. Add to the rice.

6 Add the parsley, cream and lots of pepper. Stir gently over a fairly low heat until piping hot. Pile on warm plates and serve.

White Fish Kedgeree

SERVES 4

Prepare as for One-pot Kedgeree but use plain white haddock, cod or hake instead of the smoked fish.

Cheesy Prawns on Rice

SERVES 4

225 g/8 oz cooked peeled prawns (shrimp)
295 g/10½ oz/1 medium can of
    condensed mushroom soup
15 ml/1 tbsp tomato ketchup (catsup)
50 g/2 oz/1 cup fresh white
    breadcrumbs
100 g/4 oz/1 cup Cheddar cheese,
    grated
225 g/8 oz/1 cup long-grain rice
225 g/8 oz broccoli, cut into tiny florets
50 g/2 oz/½ cup toasted flaked
    (slivered) almonds

1 Preheat the oven at 200°C/400°F/ gas mark 6.

2 Mix the prawns with the soup, ketchup, half the breadcrumbs and half the cheese in a shallow, ovenproof serving dish.

3 Sprinkle with the remaining breadcrumbs and cheese. Bake in the oven for 20–25 minutes until golden and bubbling.

4 Meanwhile, cook the rice according to the packet directions (or see page 294). Add the broccoli for the last 6 minutes of cooking time.

5 Drain in a colander and stir in the almonds.

6 Serve the rice mixture with the prawns.

Spiced Tomato Prawns

SERVES 4

225 g/8 oz/1 cup wild rice mix
1 large onion, finely chopped
1 garlic clove, crushed
45 ml/3 tbsp olive oil
10 ml/2 tsp curry paste
250 ml/8 fl oz/1 cup passata (sieved
    tomatoes)
10 ml/2 tsp tomato purée (paste)
Salt and freshly ground black pepper
45 ml/3 tbsp tomato chutney
45 ml/3 tbsp cornflour (cornstarch)
450 g/1 lb raw peeled tiger prawns
    (jumbo shrimp)
Oil, for deep-frying

1 Cook the rice according to the packet
directions (or see page 294). Drain in a
colander. Put 2.5 cm/1 in water in the
saucepan and sit the colander on top.
Cover the rice with the saucepan lid
and keep warm over a very gentle
heat until ready to serve.
2 Fry (sauté) the onion and garlic in
the olive oil in a saucepan for
3 minutes, until lightly golden. Stir in the
curry paste and cook for 1 minute.
3 Add the passata, tomato purée and
a little salt and pepper. Heat rapidly
until boiling, then turn down the heat
to fairly low and cook for 5 minutes.
Remove from the heat and stir in the
chutney.
4 Meanwhile, put the cornflour in a
shallow dish with a little salt and
pepper. Add the prawns and turn over
in the cornflour until completely coated.
5 Heat the oil for deep-frying in a large
saucepan or deep-fat fryer to
190°C/375°F or until a cube of day-old

bread browns in 30 seconds. Cook the
prawns for 2–3 minutes until golden.
Drain on kitchen paper (paper towels).
6 Spoon the rice mix on to warm
plates. Pile the prawns on top and
spoon the sauce over. Serve straight
away.

Prawn Sag

SERVES 4

30 ml/2 tbsp sunflower oil
2 onions, halved and thinly sliced
1 garlic clove, crushed
10 ml/2 tsp mild curry paste
60 ml/4 tbsp chopped fresh coriander
    (cilantro)
1 large tomato, finely chopped
Salt
5 ml/1 tsp caster (superfine) sugar
175 g/6 oz frozen leaf spinach, thawed
225 g/8 oz cooked peeled prawns
    (shrimp)
4 cooked potatoes, cut into small
    chunks
Naan bread, to serve

1 Heat the oil in a saucepan and
fry (sauté) the onions and garlic for
3 minutes, stirring.
2 Add the curry paste, coriander and
tomato and season lightly with salt.
Cook, stirring, for 1 minute.
3 Add the sugar, spinach, prawns and
potatoes and stir well. Cook until the
mixture bubbles, then turn down the
heat, cover with a lid and cook gently
for 5 minutes. Serve with naan bread.

Scampi Provençal

SERVES 4

30 ml/2 tbsp olive oil
2 large onions, sliced
2 green (bell) peppers, diced
1 garlic clove, crushed
400 g/14 oz/1 large can of chopped
   tomatoes
15 ml/1 tbsp tomato purée (paste)
5 ml/1 tsp dried mixed herbs
5 ml/1 tsp anchovy essence (extract)
350 g/12 oz raw shelled scampi
Salt and freshly ground black pepper
12 stoned (pitted) black olives, halved
225 g/8 oz/1 cup wild rice mix

1 Heat the oil in a saucepan, then add
the onions, peppers and garlic and fry
(sauté) over a high heat for 3 minutes,
stirring all the time.
2 Add the tomatoes, tomato purée,
herbs and anchovy essence. Bring to
the boil, turn down the heat to
moderate and allow to bubble for
about 5 minutes, stirring occasionally,
until pulpy.
3 Add the scampi and cook, stirring, for
a further 5 minutes. Season to taste
and stir in the olives.
4 Meanwhile, cook the rice according
to the packet directions (or see page
294). Drain.
5 Spoon the rice mix on to warm
plates, top with the scampi and serve
very hot.

Fish and Mushroom Curry

SERVES 4

225 g/8 oz/1 cup long-grain rice
295 g/10½ oz/1 medium can of
   condensed mushroom soup
90 ml/6 tbsp water
30 ml/2 tbsp tomato purée (paste)
1 garlic clove, crushed
5 ml/1 tsp dried onion granules
15 ml/1 tbsp curry paste
5 ml/1 tsp garam masala
30 ml/2 tbsp mango chutney
50 g/2 oz creamed coconut, cut into
   pieces
50 g/2 oz mushrooms, sliced
450 g/1 lb chunky white fish fillet,
   skinned (see page 107) and cut into
   large cubes
A few coriander (cilantro) leaves, to
   garnish

1 Cook the rice according to the packet
directions (or see page 294). Drain in a
colander.
2 Meanwhile, put all the remaining
ingredients except the mushrooms and
fish in a saucepan.
3 Cook over a moderate heat, stirring
to blend, until the coconut melts.
4 When bubbling gently, add the
mushrooms and the fish and stir very
gently so everything is coated in the
sauce. Wait until the mixture bubbles
again.
5 Cover with a lid, turn down the
heat to fairly low and cook for about
5 minutes or until the fish is tender.
6 Spoon the rice on to warm plates.
Add the curried fish, garnish with
coriander leaves and serve.

Prawn Jalfrezi

If you don't know how to seed chillies, see Fiery Mussel Spaghettini, page 134. Cook lots of poppadoms in advance (see page 317) and pile on a plate to serve with the Jalfrezi.

SERVES 4

225 g/8 oz/1 cup long-grain rice

350 g/12 oz raw peeled tiger prawns (jumbo shrimp)

100 g/4 oz button mushrooms, quartered

1 garlic clove, crushed

5 ml/1 tsp chilli powder

5 ml/1 tsp ground ginger

25 g/1 oz/2 tbsp butter or margarine

1 onion, very finely chopped

30 ml/2 tbsp curry paste

2 green (bell) peppers, cut into thin strips

30 ml/2 tbsp water

4 mild green chillies, seeded and chopped

60 ml/4 tbsp chopped fresh coriander (cilantro)

Salt and caster (superfine) sugar, to taste

Poppadoms, to serve

1 Cook the rice according to the packet directions (or see page 294). Drain in a colander. Put 2.5 cm/1 in water in the saucepan and sit the colander on top. Cover the rice with the saucepan lid and keep warm over a very gentle heat until ready to serve.

2 Put the prawns and mushrooms in a shallow dish and sprinkle with the garlic, chilli powder and the ginger.

3 Heat the butter or margarine in a large frying pan (skillet) over a fairly high heat. Add the onion and fry (sauté), stirring, for 2 minutes. Add the curry paste, prawns mushrooms and peppers and stir-fry for 3 minutes.

4 Add the measured water, the chillies and coriander and cook gently for 2 minutes. Season with salt and sugar.

5 Top the rice with the prawns and serve with poppadoms.

Smokies Supper

SERVES 4

100 g/4 oz/½ cup wild rice mix

1 onion, chopped

50 g/2 oz/¼ cup butter or margarine

275 g/10 oz smoked trout fillets, skinned (see page 107) and broken into small pieces

4 large tomatoes, skinned, seeded and chopped

2.5 ml/½ tsp dried mixed herbs

Juice of 1 lemon

Salt and freshly ground black pepper

225 g/8 oz/2 cups Cheddar cheese, grated

1 Preheat the oven to 200°C/400°F/ gas mark 6.

2 Cook the wild rice mix according to the packet directions (or see page 294). Drain in a colander.

3 Fry (sauté) the onion in the butter or margarine for 2 minutes, stirring. Remove from the heat.

4 Stir in the rice and remaining ingredients, using only half the cheese. Pack into four ovenproof dishes and sprinkle with the remaining cheese. Bake in the oven for about 20 minutes until bubbling and golden on top.

Cheat's Prawn Dhansak

SERVES 4

225 g/8 oz/1 cup long-grain rice

2.5 ml/½ tsp ground turmeric

3 cardamom pods, split (optional)

425 g/15 oz/1 large can of green lentils, drained

1 garlic clove, crushed

385 g/13½ oz/1 large can of curry cook-in sauce

350 g/12 oz cooked peeled prawns (shrimp)

2 hard-boiled (hard-cooked) eggs (see page 76), sliced

2 bananas, sliced and mixed with a little lemon juice

2 tomatoes, sliced

¼ cucumber, sliced

Minted Yoghurt and Cucumber (see page 340), to serve

1 Cook the rice according to the packet directions (or see page 294), adding the turmeric and cardamom pods, if using, to the water. Drain.

2 Meanwhile, put the lentils, garlic, curry sauce and prawns in a saucepan. Cook over a moderate heat, stirring, for 5 minutes. Make the Minted Yoghurt and Cucumber.

3 Spoon the rice in a ring on each of four warm plates. Spoon the prawns and sauce in the centres. Arrange all the sliced ingredients attractively around the edges. Serve with the Minted Yoghurt and Cucumber.

Crispy Spiced Prawns

SERVES 4

15 ml/1 tbsp grated fresh root ginger

2 garlic cloves, crushed

5 ml/1 tsp ground turmeric

2.5 ml/½ tsp chilli powder

5 ml/1 tsp garam masala

5 ml/1 tsp ground cumin

15 ml/1 tbsp lemon juice

450 g/1 lb raw peeled tiger prawns (jumbo shrimp)

50 g/2 oz/½ cup rice flour

Oil, for deep-frying

Quick Pilau Rice (see page 314) and Minted Yoghurt and Cucumber (see page 340), to serve

1 Put the ginger, garlic and ground spices in a container with a lid and mix with the lemon juice to form a paste.

2 Stir in the prawns until well coated, cover and marinate for 30 minutes. Meanwhile, cook the rice and prepare the Minted Yoghurt and Cucumber.

3 Put the rice flour in a shallow dish. Coat the prawns in this, adding a little more flour, if necessary.

4 Heat the oil in a large saucepan or deep-fat fryer to 190°C/375°F or until a cube of day-old bread browns in 30 seconds. Cook the prawns, a few at a time, for about 3 minutes until crisp and golden. Drain on kitchen paper (paper towels). Keep warm while cooking the remainder.

5 Serve with the Quick Pilau Rice and Minted Yoghurt with Cucumber.

Tandoori Fish with Tomato and Coriander Rice

SERVES 4

450 g/1 lb any white fish fillet
150 ml/¼ pt/⅔ cup plain yoghurt
15 ml/1 tbsp lemon juice
5 ml/1 tsp ground cumin
5 ml/1 tsp ground coriander (cilantro)
2.5 ml/½ tsp chilli powder
2.5 ml/½ tsp ground turmeric
A good pinch of salt
175 g/6 oz/¾ cup basmati rice, rinsed
400 g/14 oz/1 large can of chopped tomatoes
300 ml/½ pt/1¼ cups water
30 ml/2 tbsp chopped fresh coriander
2 tomatoes, chopped
5 cm/2 in piece of cucumber, chopped
Poppadoms (see page 317), to serve

1 Cut the fish into four pieces. Place in a shallow, ovenproof dish, in one layer.
2 Mix the yoghurt, lemon juice, spices and salt together and pour over the fish. Turn the fillets to coat completely, cover and marinate for 2 hours.
3 Preheat the oven to 180°C/350°F/gas mark 4. Cook the fish in the oven for 20 minutes, spooning the cooking juices over occasionally.
4 As soon as you put the fish in the oven to cook, put the rice in a saucepan with the tomatoes and water. Bring to the boil over a high heat, reduce the heat to low, cover and cook gently for 20 minutes until the rice is tender and has absorbed the liquid. Cook as many poppadoms as you like to make a stack.
5 When the rice is cooked, stir in the coriander and season to taste.
6 Spoon the rice on to warm plates and top with the fish. Sprinkle with the chopped tomato and cucumber and serve with the stack of poppadoms.

Riviera Cod and Rice

SERVES 4

15 ml/1 tbsp olive oil
1 onion, chopped
2 garlic cloves, crushed
1 red (bell) pepper, sliced
600 ml/1 pt/2½ cups passata (sieved tomatoes)
15 ml/1 tbsp tomato purée (paste)
150 ml/¼ pt/⅔ cup water
225 g/8 oz/1 cup long-grain rice
Salt and freshly ground black pepper
450 g/1 lb cod fillet, skinned (see page 107) and cubed
30 ml/2 tbsp chopped fresh parsley and a few green olives, to garnish

1 Heat the oil in a saucepan. Add the onion, garlic and pepper and fry (sauté), stirring, for 2 minutes.
2 Stir in the passata, tomato purée, water, rice and a little salt and pepper. Bring to the boil over a high heat, then cover, turn down the heat to moderate and cook, stirring occasionally, for 10 minutes.
3 Add the fish and, if the mixture is getting dry, a little more water. Season with salt and pepper and cook for a further 5 minutes until all the liquid has been absorbed and the rice and fish are cooked. Serve sprinkled with chopped parsley and a few green olives.

Prawn Pilau

175 g/6 oz/¾ cup long-grain rice
Salt
25 g/1 oz/¼ cup flaked (slivered)
　　almonds
15 g/½ oz/1 tbsp butter or margarine
2 onions, thinly sliced
1 large tomato, chopped
1 green (bell) pepper, chopped
50 g/2 oz/⅓ cup sultanas (golden
　　raisins)
2.5 ml/½ tsp curry powder
A good pinch of ground turmeric
225 g/8 oz cooked peeled prawns
　　(shrimp)
Freshly ground black pepper

1 Cook the rice according to the packet directions (or see page 294). Drain in a colander, rinse with boiling water and drain again.
2 Put the almonds in a large non-stick frying pan (skillet) and cook over a fairly high heat, stirring all the time, until lightly browned. Remove from the pan and reserve.
3 Heat the butter or margarine in the same pan and fry (sauté) the onion for 3 minutes, stirring, until lightly golden.
4 Add the tomato, pepper, sultanas and spices and fry for 1 minute.
5 Stir in the rice and prawns, turn down the heat and stir gently for 5 minutes. Season with pepper and serve very hot.

Okra and Prawn Pilaf

1 onion, chopped
4 rashers (slices) of streaky bacon,
　　rinded and diced
15 ml/1 tbsp sunflower or olive oil
225 g/8 oz okra (ladies' fingers), sliced
225 g/8 oz/1 cup long-grain rice
5 ml/1 tsp ground cumin
600 ml/1 pt/2½ cups water
1 chicken stock cube
Salt and freshly ground black pepper
225 g/8 oz raw peeled prawns (shrimp)
15 ml/1 tbsp chopped fresh parsley
　　(optional)

1 In a large saucepan, fry (sauté) the onion and bacon in the oil for 2 minutes, stirring.
2 Stir in the okra, rice and cumin and cook, stirring, for about 1 minute until everything is glistening in the oil.
3 Add all the remaining ingredients except the prawns, cover and cook over a fairly gentle heat for about 15 minutes.
4 Add the prawns, then cover and cook for a further 5 minutes or until the rice is tender and has absorbed the liquid. Taste and re-season if necessary.
5 Sprinkle with chopped fresh parsley, if using, and serve straight from the pot.

Cod Ragu

SERVES 4–6

1 onion, chopped
1 garlic clove, crushed
15 ml/1 tbsp olive oil
100 g/4 oz button mushrooms, sliced
400 g/14 oz/1 large can of chopped
    tomatoes
15 ml/1 tbsp tomato purée (paste)
50 g/2 oz/½ cup frozen peas
15 ml/1 tbsp chopped fresh basil
Salt and freshly ground black pepper
450 g/1 lb cod fillet, skinned (see page
    107) and cubed
350 g/12 oz pappardelle
A few fresh basil leaves, to garnish
50 g/2 oz/½ cup Cheddar cheese,
    grated

1 Fry (sauté) the onion and garlic in the oil in a saucepan over a fairly high heat for 2 minutes until softened but not browned.

2 Add all the remaining ingredients except the cod, pasta, whole basil leaves and cheese. Bring to the boil over a high heat, reduce the heat to moderate until gently bubbling and cook for 5 minutes until pulpy, stirring occasionally.

3 Add the fish and cook for a further 5 minutes, stirring gently occasionally, until the fish is cooked.

4 Meanwhile, cook the pappardelle according to the packet directions (or see page 293). Drain in a colander.

5 Pile on to a warm serving dish, spoon the fish mixture over, garnish with a few basil leaves and serve with the grated cheese.

Salmon Macaroni

SERVES 4

25 g/1 oz/¼ cup plain (all-purpose)
    flour
300 ml/½ pt/1¼ cups milk
25 g/1 oz/2 tbsp butter or margarine
200 g/7oz/1 small can of pink or red
    salmon
5 ml/1 tsp anchovy essence (extract)
15 ml/1 tbsp tomato ketchup (catsup)
Salt and freshly ground black pepper
225 g/8 oz short-cut macaroni
100 g/4 oz/1 cup Cheddar cheese,
    grated
Wedges of lemon, to garnish

1 Whisk the flour with the milk in a saucepan until smooth, using a wire whisk. Add the butter or margarine. Bring to the boil over a high heat and cook for 2 minutes, stirring with the whisk all the time.

2 Discard the skin from the fish and the bones, if liked (but they are very good for you!). Stir into the sauce with the juice from the can. Add the anchovy essence, ketchup and salt and pepper to taste.

3 Meanwhile, cook the macaroni according to the packet directions (or see page 293). Drain in a colander and stir into the fish sauce.

4 Preheat the grill (broiler). Spoon the fish mixture into a flameproof dish.

5 Sprinkle the cheese over and brown under the grill for 3–4 minutes. Garnish with wedges of lemon before serving.

Quick Curried Prawn and Pasta Supper

SERVES 4

225 g/8 oz pasta shapes

295 g/10½ oz/1 medium can of condensed cream of chicken soup

15 ml/1 tbsp curry paste

225 g/8 oz cooked peeled prawns

15 ml/1 tbsp chopped fresh coriander (cilantro) or parsley

50 g/2 oz/1 cup fresh white breadcrumbs

15 g/½ oz/1 tbsp butter, melted

1 Cook the pasta according to the packet directions (or see page 293).
2 Drain, then return to the pan and add all the remaining ingredients except the breadcrumbs and butter. Heat gently, stirring, until piping hot and well mixed.
3 Spoon into a flameproof dish. Preheat the grill (broiler).
4 Mix the crumbs with the butter and sprinkle over. Grill (broil) for 4–5 minutes until crisp and golden. Serve straight away.

Quick Cod and Macaroni Casserole

SERVES 4

175 g/6 oz quick-cook macaroni

15 g/½ oz/1 tbsp butter or margarine, for greasing

450 g/1 lb cod fillet, skinned (see page 107) and diced

300 ml/½ pt/1¼ cups milk

425 g/15 oz/1 large can of crab bisque

Salt and freshly ground black pepper

30 ml/2 tbsp chopped fresh parsley

Crusty bread, to serve

1 Preheat the oven to 180°C/350°F/ gas mark 4.
2 Put the dry pasta in the base of a well-greased casserole (Dutch oven). Put the fish in a layer over the top.
3 Blend the remaining ingredients together in a bowl with a wooden spoon and pour over.
4 Cover with a lid. Bake in the oven for about 50 minutes until the pasta is cooked. Serve with crusty bread.

Tagliatelle alla Rustica

SERVES 4

2 garlic cloves, crushed

90 ml/6 tbsp olive oil

50 g/2 oz/1 small can of anchovies, chopped, reserving the oil

5 ml/1 tsp dried oregano

45 ml/3 tbsp roughly chopped fresh parsley

Salt and freshly ground black pepper

225 g/8 oz tagliatelle

Thin slivers of fresh Parmesan cheese, to garnish

1 Fry (sauté) the garlic in the oil until golden brown. Remove from the heat and add the anchovies and their oil. Return to the heat and cook gently, stirring, until the anchovies form a paste.
2 Stir in the oregano, parsley, a very little salt and lots of black pepper.
3 Meanwhile, cook the tagliatelle according to the packet directions (or see page 293). Drain and return to the pan.
4 Add the sauce, and lift and stir gently to coat well, heating gently all the time. Serve garnished with thin slivers of Parmesan.

Rigatoni with Tuna and Sweetcorn

SERVES 4

225 g/8 oz rigatoni

1 quantity of Cheese Sauce (see page 329)

185 g/6½ oz/1 small can of tuna, drained

200 g/7 oz/1 small can of sweetcorn (corn), drained

Salt and freshly ground black pepper

Paprika and 30 ml/2 tbsp chopped fresh parsley, to garnish

1 Cook the pasta according to the packet directions (or see page 293). Drain in a colander and return to the saucepan.

2 Meanwhile, make the cheese sauce and stir the tuna and sweetcorn into it. Heat through over a moderate heat, stirring all the time. Season to taste.

3 Add to the cooked pasta and stir gently over a fairly low heat until piping hot and well mixed.

4 Spoon on to warm plates. Sprinkle with paprika and parsley and serve.

Fiery Mussel Spaghettini

The seeds are the hottest part of chillies, so don't leave them in unless you like searingly spicy food. To seed chillies, split them lengthways and scoop out the seeds with the point of a knife. Discard the seeds straight away. Wash your hands well.

SERVES 4

30 ml/2 tbsp olive oil

1 onion, finely chopped

1 garlic clove, crushed

1–2 red chillies, seeded and chopped

200 g/7 oz/1 small can of pimientos, drained and chopped

400 g/14 oz/1 large can of chopped tomatoes

15 ml/1 tbsp tomato purée (paste)

250 g/9 oz/1 medium can of mussels in brine, drained

Salt and freshly ground black pepper

350 g/12 oz spaghettini

1 Heat the oil in a saucepan. Add the onion and garlic and cook over a moderate heat for 2 minutes, stirring, until softened but not browned.

2 Add the chillies, pimientos, tomatoes and tomato purée. Bring to the boil, reduce the heat to moderate and cook gently for 5 minutes until pulpy.

3 Stir in the mussels. Season to taste and heat through gently until piping hot.

4 Meanwhile, cook the spaghettini according to the packet directions (or see page 293). Drain in a colander and return to the pan.

5 Add the mussel mixture and lift and stir gently over a low heat until well mixed. Pile on warm plates and serve.

Tuscany Macaroni

SERVES 4

250 ml/8 fl oz/1 cup olive oil
100 ml/3½ fl oz/scant ½ cup lemon juice
2 garlic cloves, crushed
425 g/15 oz/1 large can of black-eye beans, drained
30 ml/2 tbsp chopped fresh parsley
185 g/6½ oz/1 small can of tuna, drained
Salt and freshly ground black pepper
175 g/6 oz short-cut macaroni
A few black olives
30 ml/2 tbsp snipped fresh chives

1 Mix the oil, lemon juice, garlic, beans and parsley together in a saucepan. Cook over a fairly gentle heat for 5 minutes, stirring occasionally, until hot.
2 Gently stir in the tuna and a little salt and pepper and heat through, taking care not to break up the tuna chunks.
3 Meanwhile, cook the macaroni according to the packet directions (or see page 293). Drain in a colander.
4 Add to the sauce. Heat gently, lifting and stirring all the time. Serve garnished with a few black olives and the snipped chives.

Fishy Pasta Grill

SERVES 4

225 g/8 oz pasta shapes
225 g/8 oz/1 medium can of pilchards in tomato sauce, mashed
30 ml/2 tbsp olive oil
30 ml/2 tbsp snipped fresh chives
A good squeeze of lemon juice
60 ml/4 tbsp passata (sieved tomatoes)
Salt and freshly ground black pepper
75 g/3 oz/¾ cup Cheddar cheese, grated
2 tomatoes, sliced

1 Cook the pasta according to the packet directions (or see page 293). Drain in a colander and return to the saucepan.
2 Add all the remaining ingredients except the cheese and sliced tomatoes. Heat gently, lifting and stirring until well combined. Season to taste. Add a little more passata to moisten if necessary.
3 Preheat the grill (broiler). Spoon the mixture into a flameproof dish. Cover with the grated cheese and arrange the tomato slices around the top.
4 Grill (broil) for 3–4 minutes or until the cheese melts and bubbles. Serve straight away.

Vermicelli with Smoked Salmon and Broccoli

This sounds grand but smoked salmon trimmings are not expensive and a few go a long way. It is also delicious made with pappardelle – thick ribbon pasta – instead of vermicelli, but you will need to cook the pasta for about 7 minutes before adding the broccoli.

SERVES 4

225 g/8 oz vermicelli
175 g/6 oz broccoli, cut into tiny florets
175 g/6 oz smoked salmon trimmings
150 ml/¼ pt/⅔ cup single (light) cream
2 eggs
Salt and freshly ground black pepper
30 ml/2 tbsp chopped fresh parsley
A dash of lemon juice
60 ml/4 tbsp grated Parmesan cheese, to garnish

1 Bring a large pan of lightly salted water to the boil. Add the vermicelli and broccoli and, when boiling again, cook for 5 minutes until just tender. Drain thoroughly in a colander and return to the saucepan.
2 Break up the salmon and add to the pan.
3 Using a wire whisk or a fork, mix the cream and eggs together with some salt and lots of pepper until well blended. Add to the pan.
4 Cook, stirring gently, over a low heat until the mixture is piping hot. Do not allow to boil or the mixture will curdle.
5 Stir in the parsley and add lemon juice and a little more salt and pepper to taste.

6 Pile on warm plates and serve sprinkled with grated Parmesan cheese.

Spaghetti with Clams

SERVES 4

350 g/12 oz spaghetti
1 large onion, finely chopped
1 large garlic clove, crushed
15 g/½ oz/1 tbsp butter or margarine
400 g/14 oz/1 large can of chopped tomatoes
15 ml/1 tbsp tomato purée (paste)
2 x 295 g/10½ oz/medium cans of baby clams, drained
Salt and freshly ground black pepper
15 ml/1 tbsp chopped fresh parsley
A Green Salad (see page 308), to serve

1 Cook the spaghetti according to the packet directions (or see page 293). Drain in a colander and return to the pan.
2 Meanwhile, fry (sauté) the onion and garlic in the butter or margarine in a saucepan over a moderate heat for 2 minutes, stirring, until softened but not browned.
3 Add the tomatoes and tomato purée. Bring to the boil, then reduce the heat to moderate and cook for 5 minutes until pulpy. Meanwhile, make the salad.
4 Stir in the clams and season with salt and pepper. Heat for 2 minutes.
5 Add to the spaghetti and lift and stir gently over a low heat until well mixed. Pile on warm plates and sprinkle with chopped fresh parsley before serving with the green salad.

Chinese-style Prawns with Cucumber

SERVES 4

1 cucumber, diced
50 g/2 oz/¼ cup butter or margarine
175 g/6 oz button mushrooms, sliced
15 ml/1 tbsp plain (all-purpose) flour
150 ml/¼ pt/⅔ cup chicken stock, made
    with ½ stock cube
15 ml/1 tbsp medium-dry sherry
5 ml/1 tsp grated fresh root ginger
90 ml/6 tbsp single (light) cream
175 g/6 oz cooked peeled prawns
    (shrimp)
Salt and freshly ground black pepper
250 g/9 oz/1 packet of Chinese egg
    noodles

1 Bring a saucepan of lightly salted water to the boil. Add the cucumber, bring back to the boil and cook for 3 minutes. Drain in a colander, rinse with cold water and drain again.
2 Melt the butter or margarine in the same saucepan over a moderate heat. Add the mushrooms and cook for 2 minutes, stirring. Add the cucumber, cover and cook for a further 3 minutes.
3 Stir in the flour, then the stock, sherry, ginger and cream. Turn up the heat until boiling and cook for 2 minutes, stirring.
4 Add the prawns, heat through until piping hot and season to taste.
5 Meanwhile, cook the noodles according to the packet directions (or see page 293). Drain and pile into warm bowls. Spoon the prawn mixture over and serve.

Creamy Crab and Butter Bean Creation

SERVES 4

225 g/8 oz/1 cup long-grain rice
60 ml/4 tbsp water
100 g/4 oz button mushrooms, sliced
225 g/8 oz crab sticks, diced
425 g/15 oz/1 large can of butter (lima)
    beans, drained
425 g/15 oz/1 large can of crab bisque
Salt and freshly ground black pepper
30 ml/2 tbsp single (light) cream
30 ml/2 tbsp chopped fresh parsley
Lemon juice, to taste
Wedges of lemon, to garnish

1 Cook the rice according to the packet directions (or see page 294). Drain in a colander. Put about 2.5 cm/1 in water in the saucepan and sit the colander on top. Cover the rice with the saucepan lid and keep warm over a very gentle heat until ready to serve.
2 In a separate pan, put the measured water and the mushrooms, cover and cook for 3 minutes. Remove the lid, turn up the heat and cook until the water has evaporated, stirring frequently.
3 Add the crab sticks, butter·beans, soup, a little salt and pepper, the cream and parsley and heat through gently, stirring. Sharpen with lemon juice to taste.
4 Spoon the rice on warm plates and spread out to form nests. Spoon the crab mixture in the centres and serve hot, garnished with a lemon wedge on each plate.

Salmon Parcels

SERVES 4

4 small salmon tail fillets, skinned (see page 107)
4 large sheets of filo pastry (paste), thawed if frozen
50 g/2 oz/¼ cup butter or margarine, melted
4 cup mushrooms, sliced
1 large tomato, chopped
5 ml/1 tsp dried oregano
Salt and freshly ground black pepper
120 ml/4 fl oz/½ cup passata (sieved tomatoes)
New potatoes and French (green) beans, to serve

1 Preheat the oven to 190°C/375°F/ gas mark 5.
2 Put a sheet of filo pastry on a board and brush with a little of the melted butter or margarine. Fold in half to form a square and brush again.
3 Top with a quarter of the mushroom slices and chopped tomato and sprinkle with some of the oregano. Add a portion of salmon and season well.
4 Draw the pastry up over the fish, pinching it together to form a pouch. Lightly grease a baking (cookie) sheet with a little of the remaining butter or margarine and place the pouch on the sheet. Repeat with the remaining pastry sheets and filling.
5 Bake in the oven for about 15 minutes until golden brown and the fish is tender.
6 Meanwhile, cook the potatoes and beans. Heat the passata in a small saucepan, then spoon on to warm plates.

7 Carefully lift the parcels off the sheet with a fish slice and place in the centres of the plates. Serve with the new potatoes and French beans.

Fish, Pea and Potato Fry

SERVES 4

15 g/½ oz/1 tbsp butter or margarine
15 ml/1 tbsp sunflower oil
450 g/1 lb potatoes, coarsely grated
Salt and freshly ground black pepper
350 g/12 oz cod fillet, skinned (see page 107) and cubed, discarding any bones
195 g/10½ oz/1 medium can of garden peas, drained
300 ml/½ pt/1¼ cups passata (sieved tomatoes)
A good pinch of caster (superfine) sugar
Carrots Vichy (see page 304), to serve

1 Melt the butter or margarine in a heavy-based frying pan (skillet) over a moderate heat and add the oil. Add half the potatoes and press down well. Sprinkle with salt and pepper.
2 Scatter the fish and peas over the top, then add the remaining potatoes. Press down well again. Season lightly. Cover with foil or a lid and cook over a fairly gentle heat for 30 minutes until cooked through and the base is golden brown.
3 Meanwhile, cook the Carrots Vichy and heat the passata with the sugar.
4 Turn the fish cake out on to a warm plate. Serve cut into wedges with the passata and carrots.

Smoked Haddock Rosti

SERVES 4

Prepare as for Fish, Pea and Potato Fry, but substitute smoked haddock for the cod. Instead of the peas, add 225 g/8 oz frozen chopped spinach – thaw it and drain it very well first and sprinkle with a pinch of grated nutmeg. Flavour the passata with 2.5 ml/½ tsp dried mixed herbs.

Salmon and Cucumber Puffs

SERVES 4

7.5 cm/3 in piece of cucumber, finely chopped

Salt

425 g/15 oz/1 large can of pink or red salmon, drained

350 g/12 oz puff pastry (paste), thawed if frozen

5 ml/1 tsp dried dill (dill weed)

Freshly ground black pepper

A little milk, for glazing

170 g/6 oz/1 small can of creamed mushrooms

Wedges of lemon and sprigs of parsley, to garnish (optional)

New potatoes and peas, to serve

1 Put the cucumber in a colander and sprinkle with salt. Leave to stand for 15 minutes. Rinse under cold running water, then pat dry on kitchen paper (paper towels).

2 Preheat the oven to 200°C/400°F/ gas mark 6. Rinse a baking (cookie) sheet with cold water and leave damp.

3 Empty the fish into a shallow dish. Split into four portions, discarding the black skin and bones (if liked).

4 Cut the pastry into quarters and roll out each to a thin square. Trim. Divide the cucumber between the centres of the pastry and sprinkle with dill and pepper. Top with the fish. Brush the edges with water and fold over the fish to cover completely. Invert on to the dampened baking sheet. Make leaves out of the trimmings. Brush the parcels with milk, put the leaves in place and brush again.

5 Cook in the oven for 15 minutes until puffy and golden brown.

6 Meanwhile, cook the potatoes and peas. Put the mushrooms in a saucepan with 15 ml/1 tbsp milk. Heat, stirring, until bubbling.

7 Using a fish slice, transfer the puffs to warm plates and put a spoonful of the mushroom mixture to one side of each. Garnish the plates with wedges of lemon and sprigs of parsley, if using, and serve with the new potatoes and peas.

Spicy Prawn Fajitas

*If you don't know how to seed
chillies, see Fiery Mussel Spaghettini,
page 134.*

SERVES 4

30 ml/2 tbsp olive oil
1 red onion, chopped
1 large garlic clove, crushed
100 g/4 oz button mushrooms, sliced
1 red chilli, seeded and chopped
400 g/14 oz/1 large can of chopped
    tomatoes
30 ml/2 tbsp tomato purée (paste)
5 ml/1 tsp caster (superfine) sugar
Salt and freshly ground black pepper
225 g/8 oz raw peeled tiger prawns
    (jumbo shrimp)
8 large flour tortillas
¼ iceberg lettuce, finely shredded
5 cm/2 in piece of cucumber, finely
    chopped
1 small red (bell) pepper, finely
    chopped
150 ml/¼ pt/⅔ cup soured (dairy sour)
    cream

1 Heat the oil in a saucepan and fry
(sauté) the onion, garlic and mushrooms
over a moderate heat for 3 minutes,
stirring, until softened but not browned.
2 Add the chilli, tomatoes, tomato
purée, sugar and a little salt and
pepper, bring to the boil and boil fairly
rapidly for about 5 minutes, stirring
occasionally, until really thick and
pulpy.
3 Add the prawns and continue to
bubble until the prawns are pink. Taste
and re-season if necessary.
4 Meanwhile, warm the tortillas
according to the packet directions.

5 Divide the lettuce, cucumber and
pepper between the tortillas. Top with
the prawns and spoon a little soured
cream over. Roll up and serve.

Seaside Pancakes

SERVES 4

1 quantity of Simple Pancakes (see
    page 392)
15 g/½ oz/1 tbsp butter or margarine
225 g/8 oz cod fillet, skinned (see page
    107) and cut into small dice
295 g/10½ oz/1 medium can of
    condensed mushroom soup
200 g/7 oz/1 small can of sweetcorn
    (corn) with (bell) peppers, drained
Freshly ground black pepper
75 g/3 oz/¾ cup Cheddar cheese,
    grated
Slices of cucumber, to garnish

1 Make the pancakes. Keep warm
while making the filling.
2 Melt the butter or margarine in a
saucepan over a moderate heat. Add
the fish and cook, stirring gently, for
about 4 minutes until just cooked.
3 Stir in the soup, gently, with the
drained sweetcorn and black pepper
to taste. Heat through until bubbling.
4 Preheat the grill (broiler).
5 Use the mixture to fill the pancakes,
roll up and place in a flameproof
serving dish. Sprinkle with the cheese
and grill (broil) for about 4 minutes
until golden and bubbling. Garnish with
cucumber slices before serving.

Smoked Trout Rosti

SERVES 4

25 g/1 oz/2 tbsp butter or margarine
450 g/1 lb potatoes, grated
Salt and freshly ground black pepper
225 g/8 oz smoked trout, cut into small pieces
100 g/4 oz button mushrooms, thinly sliced
15 ml/1 tbsp chopped fresh parsley
Grated rind of ½ lemon
300 ml/½ pt/1¼ cups passata (sieved tomatoes)
5 ml/1 tsp chopped fresh basil
Wedges of lemon (use the ungrated half of the lemon), to garnish
A Green Salad (see page 308), to serve

1 Melt the butter or margarine in a frying pan (skillet) over a moderate heat. Add half the potatoes and press down well, then season with salt and pepper.
2 Add the fish in an even layer and sprinkle with the mushrooms, parsley, lemon rind and a little more seasoning. Top with the remaining potatoes, press down well again and season lightly.
3 Cover with foil or a lid and cook over a fairly gentle heat for 30 minutes until cooked through and the base is golden brown.
4 Meanwhile, make the green salad.
5 Heat the passata with the basil in a small saucepan. Turn the fish cake out on to a warmed serving plate. Garnish with wedges of lemon and serve cut into quarters with the tomato sauce and salad.

Mackerel in Oatmeal with Horseradish Mayonnaise

You can also cook herrings in this way but get your fishmonger to remove the scales for you. Put the potatoes on before you start preparing the mackerel. Cook the peas, while the mackerel is cooking.

SERVES 4

4 cleaned mackerel, boned (see page 107)
Salt and freshly ground black pepper
100 g/4 oz/1 cup fine or medium oatmeal
50 g/2 oz/¼ cup butter or margarine
30 ml/2 tbsp olive oil
60 ml/4 tbsp mayonnaise
10 ml/2 tsp horseradish relish
Wedges of lemon, to garnish
Plain potatoes and peas, to serve

1 Season the mackerel with salt and pepper and coat thoroughly in the oatmeal, pressing it into the surface with your fingers.
2 Heat the butter or margarine and oil over a fairly high heat in a large frying pan (skillet) and fry (sauté) the fish for 5 minutes on each side until crisp, golden and cooked through. Drain on kitchen paper (paper towels) and transfer to warm plates.
3 Mix the mayonnaise with the horseradish and season to taste. Put a spoonful to the side of each mackerel and garnish the plates with a wedge of lemon. Serve with plain potatoes and peas.

Mackerel in Millet

SERVES 4

4 cleaned mackerel, boned (see page
    107) and heads removed
75 g/3 oz/¾ cup millet flakes
30 ml/2 tbsp chopped fresh thyme
5 ml/1 tsp paprika
Salt and freshly ground black pepper
1 egg, beaten
60 ml/4 tbsp sunflower oil
Wedges of lemon and sprigs of parsley,
    to garnish
Potato and Parsnip Mash (see page
    298) and Baked Tomatoes with
    Basil (see page 306), to serve

1 Preheat the oven to 190°C/375°F/
gas mark 5.
2 Rinse the fish and dry on kitchen
paper (paper towels).
3 Mix the millet with the thyme,
paprika and a little salt and pepper.
Dip the fish in the beaten egg, then the
millet mixture, to coat completely.
4 Brush a baking (cookie) sheet with
some of the oil. Add the fish, skin-sides
down. Trickle the remaining oil all over
the fish.
5 Bake on a shelf near the top of the
oven for about 25 minutes until golden
and cooked through. While it is
cooking, cook the mash and the Baked
Tomatoes with Basil.
6 Pile the cooked mash on warm
plates. Top each pile with a mackerel,
using a fish slice to transfer them from
the baking sheet. Garnish with wedges
of lemon and parsley and serve with
the baked tomatoes.

Mackerel with Mushrooms and Tomatoes

*Start cooking the potatoes before
you cook the fish.*

SERVES 4

4 cleaned mackerel
25 g/1 oz/2 tbsp butter or margarine
1 garlic clove, crushed
4 tomatoes, skinned and chopped
100 g/4 oz button mushrooms, sliced
15 ml/1 tbsp chopped fresh parsley
15 ml/1 tbsp snipped fresh chives
5 ml/1 tsp tomato purée (paste)
A good pinch of caster (superfine)
    sugar
Salt and freshly ground black pepper
Plain potatoes, to serve

1 Slash the fish several times on each
side with a sharp knife.
2 Heat the butter or margarine in a
large frying pan (skillet). Add the fish
and brown over a fairly high heat for
2 minutes on each side.
3 Add the tomatoes and mushrooms,
cover the pan, turn down the heat to
moderate and cook for a further
5–8 minutes until the fish is cooked and
the tomatoes are pulpy.
4 Lift the fish out of the pan with a fish
slice and keep warm.
5 Add the herbs, tomato purée, sugar
and some salt and pepper to the pan.
Continue to cook, stirring, for 2 minutes.
Spoon over the fish and serve with
plain potatoes.

Curried Fish Croquettes

1 large potato, peeled and cut into small chunks

50 g/2 oz/¼ cup long-grain rice

350 g/12 oz white fish fillet

1 small onion, grated

10 ml/2 tsp curry powder

10 ml/2 tsp mango chutney

Salt and freshly ground black pepper

1 egg, beaten

25 g/1 oz/½ cup fresh white breadcrumbs

Oil, for deep-frying

Wedges of lemon, to garnish

A large Mixed Salad (see page 308), to serve

1 Half-fill a saucepan with water and boil. Add the potatoes, rice and then the fish. Cook gently for 10 minutes until tender. Meanwhile, make the salad.

2 Lift the fish out. Pull off the skin and remove any bones.

3 Drain the potatoes and rice and return to the pan. Add the fish and mash well together.

4 Add the onion, curry powder, chutney and salt and pepper to taste.

5 Shape into eight small rolls. Put the egg and breadcrumbs on separate plates. Dip the rolls in the egg, then the breadcrumbs, to coat completely.

6 Heat oil in a large saucepan or deep-fat fryer to 190°C/375°F or until a cube of day-old bread browns in 30 seconds. Cook the fish rolls for 3–4 minutes until golden brown.

7 Drain on kitchen paper (paper towels) and serve garnished with wedges of lemon with the salad.

Cod Roe Fritters

Cook the potatoes and peas before you cook the fritters. Keep the potatoes warm in a low oven. Refresh the peas by pouring boiling water over them just before serving.

2 x 200 g/7 oz/small cans of pressed cod's roe

50 g/2 oz/½ cup wholemeal flour

Salt and freshly ground black pepper

1.5 ml/¼ tsp cayenne

30 ml/2 tbsp chopped fresh parsley

Sunflower oil, for shallow-frying

Wedges of lemon and sprigs of parsley, to garnish

Sauté Potatoes (see page 296) and peas, to serve

1 Slice each can of roe into six slices.

2 Mix the flour with some salt and pepper, the cayenne and parsley and use to coat the slices.

3 Heat enough oil to cover the base of a frying pan (skillet) and fry (sauté) the slices for about 3 minutes on each side until golden. Drain on kitchen paper (paper towels).

4 Transfer to warm plates. Garnish with wedges of lemon and sprigs of parsley and serve with the sauté potatoes and peas.

Fish and Mushroom Pancakes

SERVES 4

225 g/8 oz smoked or white fish, skinned (see page 107)

100 g/4 oz button mushrooms, sliced

350 ml/12 fl oz/1½ cups milk

45 ml/3 tbsp plain (all-purpose) flour

5 ml/1 tsp lemon juice

30 ml/2 tbsp chopped fresh parsley

Salt and freshly ground black pepper

1 quantity of Simple Pancakes (see page 392)

Wedges of lemon and sprigs of parsley, to garnish

Baby carrots and peas, to serve

1 Make the filling. Put the fish and mushrooms in 300 ml/½ pt/1¼ cups of the milk in a saucepan. Heat rapidly until the milk bubbles. Turn down the heat, then cover and cook gently for about 6 minutes or until the fish is cooked and will break up easily with a fork. Remove from the heat.

2 Lift the fish out of the milk, using a fish slice, and reserve.

3 Blend the flour with the remaining milk in a small bowl, using a wire whisk. Stir into the fish cooking milk in the saucepan. Cook over a high heat, stirring all the time with the whisk, until the mixture thickens and bubbles. Turn down the heat and continue to cook, stirring, for 2 minutes. Remove from the heat. Add the lemon juice, parsley and seasoning to taste.

4 Break up the fish with a fork. Add to the sauce and mix in gently.

5 Make the pancakes, keeping them all warm.

6 Cook the carrots and peas.

7 Heat the fish mixture, stirring gently until piping hot. Divide the mixture among the pancakes, roll up and arrange on warm plates. Garnish with wedges of lemon and sprigs of parsley and serve straight away with the baby carrots and peas.

Tuna, Sweetcorn and Pimiento Pancakes

SERVES 4

1 quantity of Simple Pancakes (see page 392)

1 quantity of Cheese Sauce (see page 329)

185 g/6½ oz/1 small can of tuna, drained

200 g/7 oz/1 small can of sweetcorn (corn), drained

200 g/7 oz/1 small can of pimientos, drained and chopped

30 ml/2 tbsp chopped fresh parsley

50 g/2 oz/½ cup Cheddar cheese, grated

A Tomato and Cucumber Salad (see page 309), to serve

1 Make up the pancakes and keep warm. Preheat the grill (broiler).

2 Make the cheese sauce and stir in the tuna, sweetcorn, pimientos and parsley and heat through.

3 Divide the mixture between the pancakes and roll up. Place in a shallow, flameproof dish.

4 Sprinkle with the grated cheese and place under the grill until golden and bubbling. Meanwhile, make the Tomato and Cucumber Salad and serve with the hot pancakes.

Tuna Fish Cakes

SERVES 4

2 potatoes, cut into chunks
A knob of butter or margarine
185 g/6½ oz/1 small can of tuna,
    drained
15 ml/1 tbsp chopped fresh parsley
Salt and freshly ground black pepper
2 eggs
45 ml/3 tbsp plain (all-purpose) flour
60 ml/4 tbsp dried breadcrumbs
Oil, for shallow-frying
Wedges of lemon and sprigs of parsley,
    to garnish

1 Boil the potatoes. Drain and mash with the butter or margarine.

2 Add the tuna, parsley and salt and pepper to taste and stir briskly with a wooden spoon until well mixed.

3 Break one of the eggs into a cup and beat with a fork. Add to the potato mixture and mix with the wooden spoon until blended in.

4 Divide the mixture into eight equal pieces and shape into small cakes, then roll in the flour.

5 Beat the other egg with a fork in a shallow dish and put the breadcrumbs in another. Dip the cakes in the egg and then in the breadcrumbs to coat completely.

6 Heat about 5 mm/¼ in of oil in a frying pan (skillet) until hot but not smoking. Add the fish cakes and cook for 3 minutes on each side until golden brown. Drain on kitchen paper (paper towels) and serve hot, garnished with wedges of lemon and sprigs of parsley.

White Fish Cakes

SERVES 4

Prepare as for Tuna Fish Cakes but use 225 g/8 oz any raw white fish fillet, skinned (see page 107) and finely chopped, instead of the tuna.

Curried Fish Cakes

SERVES 4

Prepare as for White Fish Cakes but add 10 ml/2 tsp curry paste to the potatoes and serve with mango chutney.

Salmon Fish Cakes

SERVES 4

Prepare as for Tuna Fish Cakes but use a 200 g/7 oz/small can of salmon, drained, skin removed and mashed, instead of the tuna. Remove the bones, if liked, but they are very good for you.

Smoked Haddock Fish Cakes

SERVES 4

Prepare as for Tuna Fish Cakes but substitute 225 g/8 oz smoked haddock fillet, skinned (see page 107) and finely chopped, for the tuna and substitute snipped fresh chives for the parsley.

Smoked Haddock and Cheese Fish Cakes

SERVES 4

Prepare as for Tuna Fish Cakes but use 225 g/8 oz smoked haddock fillet, skinned (see page 107) and finely chopped, instead of the tuna and add 50 g/2 oz/½ cup grated Cheddar cheese to the potato. Omit the butter or margarine.

Egg Foo Yung

SERVES 2

6 eggs
5 ml/1 tsp soy sauce, plus extra for
    serving
Freshly ground black pepper
2 spring onions (scallions), finely
    chopped
30 ml/2 tbsp thawed frozen peas
175 g/6 oz cooked peeled prawns
    (shrimp)
A pinch of Chinese five spice powder
30 ml/2 tbsp sunflower oil

1 Using a fork or wire whisk, mix the eggs in a bowl with the soy sauce and a little pepper. Stir in the spring onions, peas, prawns and spice.
2 Heat the oil in a frying pan (skillet) over a moderate heat. Add the egg mixture and cook, lifting and stirring, until golden brown underneath and almost set.
3 Turn the cooked egg over with a fish slice and cook the other side.
4 Tip out of the pan on to a board. Roll up and transfer to a warm serving dish. Sprinkle with soy sauce and serve cut into slices.

Prawn Omelette

SERVES 1

2 eggs
15 ml/1 tbsp water
Salt and freshly ground black pepper
5 ml/1 tsp butter or margarine
50 g/2 oz cooked peeled prawns
    (shrimp)
15 ml/1 tbsp chopped fresh parsley
10 ml/2 tsp tomato ketchup (catsup)
A few drops of Worcestershire sauce

1 Break the eggs into a bowl, and add the water with a little salt and pepper. Mix briskly with a fork or wire whisk until well blended.
2 Melt the butter or margarine in a small omelette pan over a moderate heat. Add the egg mixture and cook, lifting and stirring gently, until the base is golden and the egg is almost set.
3 Mix the prawns with the parsley, ketchup, and a few drops of Worcestershire sauce. Spoon over half the omelette. Heat through for a few minutes. Sprinkle with a little more Worcestershire sauce. Fold the omelette over the filling. Slide on to a warm plate and serve.

Creamy Prawn Omelette

SERVES 1

Prepare as for Prawn Omelette but mix 15 ml/1 tbsp crème fraîche into the prawn (shrimp) mixture and use snipped fresh chives instead of chopped fresh parsley.

Monkfish and Bacon Kebabs

SERVES 4

450 g/1 lb monkfish, cubed
30 ml/2 tbsp lemon juice
60 ml/4 tbsp olive oil
Salt and freshly ground black pepper
1 garlic clove, chopped
15 ml/1 tbsp chopped fresh parsley
15 ml/1 tbsp chopped fresh basil
4 rashers (slices) of streaky bacon,
    rinded and cut into squares
8 cherry tomatoes
Potato and Celeriac Mash
    (see page 298) and a Green Salad
    (see page 308), to serve

1 Place the fish in a shallow dish. Pour over the lemon juice and oil and add a little salt and pepper, the garlic and herbs. Stir well and leave in the fridge to marinate for 2 hours.

2 Just before the fish has finished marinating, start to cook the Potato and Celeriac Mash. Make the salad.

3 When you are ready to start cooking, preheat the grill (broiler).

4 Thread the monkfish on eight skewers with the bacon and tomatoes. Place on a piece of foil on the grill rack and brush with the marinade. Grill (broil) for 8–10 minutes until cooked through, turning occasionally and brushing with any remaining marinade from time to time.

5 Finish preparing the mash. When the kebabs are cooked, pile the mash on to warm plates.

6 Pull the fish, bacon and tomatoes off the skewers, place on the potato piles and serve with the Green Salad.

Scallops with Bacon

Prepare the salad before you cook the scallops.

SERVES 4

12 shelled scallops
6 rashers (slices) of streaky bacon,
    rinded and halved
1 thick slice of crusty white bread
1 garlic clove, halved
45 ml/3 tbsp olive oil
15 ml/1 tbsp lemon juice
Freshly ground black pepper
Hot Potato Salad (see page 309),
    to serve

1 Halve the scallops and wrap each half in a halved bacon rasher.

2 Rub the bread all over with the garlic, cut into cubes and coat in 15 ml/ 1 tbsp of the oil.

3 Mix the remaining oil and lemon juice together with a good grinding of black pepper and pour over the bacon rolls. Turn to coat in the mixture.

4 Thread the bacon rolls and bread alternately on four kebab skewers.

5 Preheat the grill (broiler).

6 Lay the kebabs on foil on the grill rack. Grill (broil) for 4–5 minutes until the bacon is just cooked and the bread is golden brown, turning and brushing the bacon with any remaining oil and lemon juice during cooking. Serve straight away with the Hot Potato Salad.

Swordfish, Sun-dried Tomato and Courgette Kebabs

SERVES 4

8 sun-dried tomatoes in oil, drained
4 small swordfish steaks, cubed
30 ml/2 tbsp olive oil
15 ml/1 tbsp sun-dried tomato oil
10 ml/2 tsp red wine vinegar
15 ml/1 tbsp chopped fresh basil
A good pinch of caster (superfine) sugar
Salt and freshly ground black pepper
4 small courgettes (zucchini), cut into chunks
Piquant Dip (see page 340) and crusty bread, to serve

1 Put the drained tomatoes and cubed fish in a shallow dish.
2 Whisk the oils, vinegar, basil, sugar and a little salt and pepper together and pour over. Stir well, then leave in the fridge to marinate for 2 hours.
3 Meanwhile, heat a pan of lightly salted water until boiling. Add the courgettes, bring to the boil again, then cook for 3 minutes. Drain in a colander, rinse with cold water and drain again.
4 Preheat the grill (broiler).
5 Thread the fish, tomatoes and courgettes on four metal skewers. Lay on foil on the grill rack and brush with any remaining marinade. Grill (broil) for about 8 minutes, turning and brushing occasionally with any remaining marinade until golden and cooked through. While they are cooking, make the Piquant Dip.
6 Serve the kebabs with the dip and lots of crusty bread.

Prawn and Artichoke Kebabs

Make the Aioli and salad first. When using wooden skewers, always soak them in cold water beforehand to prevent them from burning.

SERVES 4

425 g/15 oz/1 large can of artichoke hearts, drained
16 raw peeled king prawns (jumbo shrimp)
30 ml/2 tbsp olive oil
15 ml/1 tbsp lemon juice
10 ml/2 tsp paprika
Freshly ground black pepper
Wedges of lemon, to garnish
Aioli (see page 341) and a Mixed Salad (see page 308), to serve

1 Halve the artichoke hearts and pat dry on kitchen paper (paper towels).
2 Thread alternately on soaked wooden skewers with the prawns and place on foil on the grill (broiler) rack.
3 Preheat the grill.
4 Whisk the oil and lemon juice together with the paprika and a little black pepper. Brush over the kebabs.
5 Grill (broil) for 4–6 minutes, turning occasionally and brushing with the oil and lemon, until golden and the prawns are cooked through.
6 Garnish with wedges of lemon and serve with the Aioli and the mixed salad.

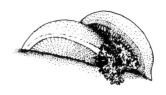

Traditional Fish and Chips

Don't reuse the oil after cooking fish. All other deep-frying oil should be discarded after reheating three times.

SERVES 4

700 g/1½ lb cod or haddock fillet, skinned (see page 107) and cut into 4 equal pieces

100 g/4 oz/1 cup plain (all-purpose) flour

Salt and freshly ground black pepper

1 kg/2¼ lb potatoes

1 large egg white

120 ml/4 fl oz/½ cup tepid water

15 ml/1 tbsp sunflower oil, plus extra for cooking

Vinegar, tomato ketchup (catsup) and peas, to serve

1 Wipe the fish. Mix 25 g/1 oz/¼ cup of the flour with a little salt and pepper in a shallow dish. Dip the fish in the seasoned flour to coat completely.

2 Cut the potatoes into thick slices, then cut each slice into thick fingers. Place in a bowl of cold water.

3 Put the egg white in a clean bowl and whisk until stiff with an electric or balloon whisk.

4 Put the remaining flour in a bowl with a pinch of salt. Add the measured water and oil and whisk with the same whisk until smooth.

5 Add the egg white and mix in gently with a metal spoon.

6 Drain the potatoes and dry on kitchen paper (paper towels).

7 Heat the oil for deep-frying in a large saucepan or deep-fat fryer to 190°C/375°F or until a cube of day-old bread browns in 30 seconds. Add about a quarter of the chips (fries) and

cook for about 3 minutes until softened but not browned. Drain on kitchen paper and cook the remaining chips in the same way.

8 Dip the fish in the batter to coat completely. Reheat the oil and deep-fry for 5–6 minutes until golden brown and cooked through. Drain on kitchen paper and keep warm.

9 Reheat the oil again. Put all the chips back in and cook until crisp and golden. While they are cooking, cook the peas.

10 Drain the chips on kitchen paper. Serve the fish and chips with vinegar, tomato ketchup and the peas.

Squid with Pesto

Use ready-made pesto, if you prefer.

SERVES 4

15 ml/1 tbsp olive oil

16 cleaned baby squid, sliced into rings

1 quantity of Simple Pesto Sauce (see page 336)

1 wineglass of dry white wine

A Tomato and Cucumber Salad (see page 309) and lots of crusty bread, to serve

1 Heat the oil in a frying pan (skillet) over a moderate heat.

2 Add the squid and stir gently for 3 minutes until turning opaque.

3 Add the pesto and wine and let the mixture bubble gently for about 10 minutes, stirring occasionally, until the squid is tender.

4 While it is cooking, make the Tomato and Cucumber Salad.

5 Serve with the squid, together with lots of crusty bread.

Mushroom and Tomato Kebabs

SERVES 4

16 small chestnut mushrooms
60 ml/4 tbsp water
450 g/1 lb thick smoked haddock fillet, skinned (see page 107)
8 rashers (slices) of streaky bacon, rinded and halved
8 large cherry tomatoes
25 g/1 oz/2 tbsp butter or margarine, melted
100 g/4 oz baby spinach leaves
Cheese Dressing (see page 338), to serve

1 Put the mushrooms in a saucepan with the water. Cook over a high heat for 2–3 minutes, stirring, until softened slightly. Drain in a colander.
2 Cut the fish into 16 chunks. Stretch each piece of bacon with the back of a knife and and wrap one around each piece of fish.
3 Thread a tomato on to each of eight skewers. Add the mushrooms and fish rolls alternately to the skewers.
4 Preheat the grill (broiler).
5 Lay the kebabs on foil on the grill rack. Brush with melted butter or margarine and grill (broil), turning occasionally and brushing with more butter or margarine, for about 6 minutes until cooked through.
6 Pile the spinach leaves on plates and spoon the dressing over. Pull the fish rolls, mushrooms and tomatoes off the skewers and pile on top. Serve straight away.

Seafood Gratin

SERVES 4

1 quantity of Béchamel Sauce (see page 330)
450 g/1 lb cod fillet, skinned (see page 107) and cut into strips
100 g/4 oz cooked peeled prawns (shrimp)
295 g/10½ oz/1 small can of clams, drained
50 g/2 oz button mushrooms, thinly sliced
5 ml/1 tsp lemon juice
Salt and freshly ground black pepper
15 ml/1 tbsp chopped fresh parsley
30 ml/2 tbsp freshly grated Parmesan cheese

1 Preheat the oven to 180°C/350°F/ gas mark 4. Make the Béchamel Sauce.
2 Divide the cod, prawns, clams and mushrooms between four individual shallow ovenproof dishes. Sprinkle with the lemon juice, salt, pepper and the parsley. Spoon the sauce over and sprinkle with the cheese.
3 Bake in the oven for 25 minutes or until golden brown and bubbling. Serve hot.

Salade Niçoise

SERVES 4

8 baby new potatoes, scrubbed

3 eggs, scrubbed under cold water

225 g/8 oz French (green) beans, cut into short lengths

8 cherry tomatoes, halved

5 cm/2 in piece of cucumber, diced

1 little gem lettuce, cut into bite-sized pieces

185 g/6½ oz/1 small can of tuna, drained

8 black olives

45 ml/3 tbsp olive oil

15 ml/1 tbsp white wine vinegar

2.5 ml/½ tsp dried mixed herbs

A good pinch of caster (superfine) sugar

2.5 ml/½ tsp Dijon mustard

Salt and freshly ground black pepper

1 small onion, thinly sliced into rings

15 ml/1 tbsp chopped fresh parsley

1 Bring a saucepan of lightly salted water to the boil. Add the potatoes and eggs and cook for 5 minutes. Add the beans and cook for a further 5 minutes or until the vegetables are tender. Lift out the eggs with a draining spoon and place in a bowl of cold water. Drain the vegetables in a colander, rinse with cold water and drain again.

2 Put the potatoes and beans in a large salad bowl with the tomatoes, cucumber, lettuce, tuna and olives.

3 Shell the eggs, cut into quarters and reserve.

4 Whisk together the oil, vinegar, mixed herbs, sugar, mustard and some salt and pepper.

5 Pour over the salad and lift and stir very gently with salad servers or a spoon and fork until the ingredients are all well mixed and coated with the dressing.

6 Scatter the onion rings and eggs on top and sprinkle with the parsley.

Mixed Bean and Sild Salad

Sild are very small sardines.

SERVES 4

425 g/15 oz/1 large can of mixed pulses, drained, rinsed and drained again

2 x 120 g/4½ oz/small cans of sild, drained

1 onion, chopped

200 g/7 oz/1 small can of pimientos, drained and sliced

4 gherkins (cornichons), chopped

30 ml/2 tbsp olive oil

15 ml/1 tbsp red wine vinegar

A pinch of caster (superfine) sugar

Salt and freshly ground black pepper

Crusty bread, to serve

1 Put the pulses in a large salad bowl with the sild, onion, pimientos and gherkins.

2 Put the remaining ingredients in a small bowl. Whisk with a wire whisk until well blended and pour over the salad. Very gently turn the salad over in the dressing to coat completely.

3 Chill for at least 1 hour to allow the flavours to develop.

4 Serve in bowls with crusty bread.

Caesar Salad

SERVES 4

1 garlic clove, halved

2 slices of white bread, cut into small dice

75 ml/5 tbsp olive oil

15 ml/1 tbsp white wine vinegar

15 ml/1 tbsp balsamic vinegar

2.5 ml/½ tsp dried tarragon

2.5 ml/½ tsp caster (superfine) sugar

Salt and freshly ground black pepper

1 egg

15 ml/1 tbsp milk or single (light) cream

15 g/½ oz/1 tbsp butter or margarine

1 cos (romaine) lettuce, cut into bite-sized pieces

50 g/2 oz/1 small can of anchovy fillets, drained and roughly chopped

50 g/2 oz Parmesan cheese, shaved with a potato peeler

1 Rub the garlic clove all round a salad bowl and discard.

2 Fry (sauté) the bread, stirring, in 30 ml/2 tbsp of the oil in a frying pan (skillet) until golden brown. Drain on kitchen paper (paper towels).

3 Whisk the remaining oil with the vinegars, tarragon, sugar and a little salt and pepper.

4 Put the egg in a pan with just enough water to cover. Bring to the boil and boil for 1½ minutes.

5 Lift out and cool under cold running water. Break the egg and scoop into a bowl. Whisk in the cream.

6 Put the lettuce in the salad bowl. Add the dressing, egg and anchovy fillets and lift and stir gently until well mixed. Add the Parmesan cheese and croûtons and serve straight away.

Seafood Pasta Salad

SERVES 4

175 g/6 oz conchiglie (pasta shells)

225 g/8 oz cooked seafood cocktail, thawed if frozen

1 small onion, finely chopped

1 green (bell) pepper, finely chopped

60 ml/4 tbsp olive oil

30 ml/2 tbsp lemon juice

5 ml/1 tsp caster (superfine) sugar

1 garlic clove, crushed

Salt and freshly ground black pepper

Lettuce leaves

1 Cook the pasta according to the packet directions (or see page 293). Drain in a colander, rinse with cold water and drain again. Place in a bowl.

2 Drain the seafood on kitchen paper (paper towels) and add to the pasta with the onion and green pepper.

3 Whisk the oil and lemon juice together with the sugar, garlic and a little salt and pepper.

4 Pour over the salad, lift and stir gently until everything is coated in the dressing and chill until ready to serve on a bed of lettuce.

Smoked Mackerel and Potato Salad

SERVES 4

450 g/1 lb baby new potatoes, scrubbed and halved

A sprig of mint

4 ready-to-eat smoked mackerel fillets, skinned (see page 107) and cut into bite-sized pieces

100 g/4 oz/1 cup shelled fresh or cooked frozen peas

45 ml/3 tbsp mayonnaise

30 ml/2 tbsp sunflower oil

15 ml/1 tbsp lemon juice

10 ml/2 tsp horseradish relish

Salt and freshly ground black pepper

A few lettuce leaves

4 cooked beetroot (red beets), diced, to garnish

1 Boil the potatoes with the mint added to the water. Drain in a colander and tip into a large bowl, discarding the mint.

2 Add the fish and peas and mix gently.

3 Put the mayonnaise, oil, lemon juice, horseradish relish and a little salt and pepper in a small bowl. Whisk with a wire whisk or fork until well blended. Spoon the dressing over the potato mixture. Lift and stir gently with a spoon and fork until everything is lightly coated in dressing.

4 Line four large soup bowls with lettuce leaves and spoon in the potato and fish mixture. Spoon the beetroot round the edge of each bowl of salad and serve.

Devilled Tuna Salad

SERVES 4

45 ml/3 tbsp olive oil

15 ml/1 tbsp red wine vinegar

30 ml/2 tbsp tomato ketchup (catsup)

2.5 ml/½ tsp made English mustard

5 ml/1 tsp Worcestershire sauce

A few drops of Tabasco sauce

5 ml/1 tsp clear honey

185 g/6½ oz/1 small can of tuna, drained

350 g/12 oz flat beans, cut diagonally into 2.5 cm/1 in pieces

¼ cucumber, thinly sliced

50 g/2 oz/1 small can of anchovy fillets, drained and halved lengthways

6 stoned (pitted) olives, halved

1 Put the oil, vinegar, ketchup, mustard, Worcestershire and Tabasco sauces and honey in a bowl and whisk together with a wire whisk until well blended.

2 Stir in the tuna, breaking it up well with a fork. Chill while preparing the remainder of the dish.

3 Bring a pan of lightly salted water to the boil. Add the beans, bring back to the boil and cook for 4 minutes until just tender. Drain in a colander, rinse with cold water and drain again.

4 Put a thin layer of half the beans in the base of a shallow serving dish. Top with half the dressed tuna. Repeat the layers and top with a layer of cucumber slices, then a lattice of anchovies. Garnish with the olives in between the anchovies and chill for at least 1 hour before serving.

Meat Main Courses

In this chapter I explain exactly how to cook every type of meat (the cooking methods also apply to poultry and game). You can also learn the step-by-step method to cooking a complete Sunday lunch plus every sort of meat recipe you'll ever need. I've included good old favourites like Spaghetti Bolognese as well as more adventurous ones such as Beef Wellington and exciting new recipes like Redcurrant Lamb with Rosemary – all made exceptionally easy of course!

There are also suggestions for vegetables and other accompaniments including when to prepare and cook them. Check pages 291–92 for instructions on how to cook individual vegetables.

Meat cooking methods – suitable also for poultry

To grill (broil): Suitable for tender cuts, such as steaks, chops, fillets, kidneys, liver and sausages.

1   Brush the meat with a little oil or dot with butter or margarine. Season lightly.
2   Place under a preheated grill (broiler) and cook until done to your liking, turning the meat over once the first side is browned. The time will depend on the thickness of the meat (see Cook's tips for cooking meat, page 159).

To fry (sauté): Suitable for tender cuts, such as steaks, chops, fillets, kidneys, liver and sausages.

1   Heat a little oil or butter or margarine and oil in a frying pan (skillet).
2   Season the meat and place in the pan. Cook quickly until brown underneath. Turn over and cook the other side until brown.
3   Reduce the heat and continue to cook, until done to your liking. The cooking time will depend on the thickness (see Cook's tips for cooking meat, page 159).

To braise or casserole: Suitable for most meats, including braising or stewing cuts that are diced or in slabs, also chops, kidneys, liver, sausages, steaks, ribs and rashers (slices).

1   Dip the meat in flour mixed with a little salt and pepper, if liked.
2   Heat a little oil in a flameproof casserole (Dutch oven). Add the meat and cook over a high heat, turning it occasionally, until browned all over. Remove from the pan with a draining spoon.
3   Add diced vegetables as appropriate and stir in the hot oil for 2–3 minutes.
4   Replace the meat and add just enough stock or stock and wine to cover the meat. Add a bouquet garni sachet or bay leaf, if liked. Bring to the boil, then cover and transfer to a preheated oven at 160°C/320°F/gas mark 3 for 1½ –2½ hours.
5   Remove the herbs, if used. Taste and season if necessary.

To pot-roast: Suitable for joints and whole birds, especially if not very tender.

1   Prepare the joint by following steps 1–3 as for braising (see page 155).
2   Add just enough stock or stock and wine to cover the vegetables (not the meat).
3   Cover with a tight-fitting lid and cook on top of the stove or in a preheated oven at 160°C/325°F/gas mark 3 for 40 minutes per 450 g/1 lb.

To boil/stew: Suitable for stewing and braising meats, either diced or in slabs, also joints, chops and sausages.

1   Place the joint or pieces of meat in a saucepan or flameproof casserole (Dutch oven) with vegetables, cut into large, chunky pieces and other flavourings of your choice.
2   Add just enough water or stock to cover.
3   Bring to the boil, skim the surface with a draining spoon to remove any scum.
4   Turn down the heat until just small bubbles are rising to the surface round the edges. Cover and cook at a very gentle simmer for up to 1 hour per 450 g/1 lb meat until really tender.
5   Taste and re-season if necessary.

To roast: Suitable for joints but also fattier cuts, such as belly pork rashers or breast of lamb.

1   If using stuffing, spread the stuffing on the side of the meat where the bones were. Roll up and tie with string or secure with skewers.
2   Place the joint in a roasting tin (pan). Stand pork on a rack in the tin. Brush beef or lamb with a little oil. Season lightly.
3   For pork, score the rind by slashing it with a sharp knife at regular intervals all over. Rub the rind with oil and salt. This will help it 'crackle' as it cooks. For chicken or other birds, rub the skin with a little oil and sprinkle with salt.
4   Roast in a preheated oven at 220°C/425°F/gas mark 7 for 10 minutes, then reduce the heat to 190°C/375°F/gas mark 5 for the remaining cooking time.

Roasting times

For rare meat (beef only): Allow 15 minutes per 450 g/1 lb plus 15 minutes over.

For medium (for beef or lamb): Allow 20 minutes per lb plus 20 minutes over. The meat should still be slightly pink in the centre.

For well done (beef, lamb or pork): Allow 30 minutes per lb plus 30 minutes over.

For chicken: Allow 20 minutes per 450 g/1 lb plus 20 minutes over.

Step-by-step to the perfect roast

The tricky thing about any roast dinner is getting everything on the table hot and at the same time. Here is the perfect guide to how to do it. There are separate recipes in the poultry section for roasting different birds. See also the cook's tips on page 159.

1   When cooking a roast, first decide what time you want to eat. Work out how long the meat (or chicken) will take (see Roasting times, above), then add on an extra 45 minutes to allow for preparation time, making the gravy and so on.

2   Calculate how many vegetables you need to prepare – I usually allow four pieces of potato and two pieces of parsnip, an average-sized carrot and a handful of green vegetables for each person.

3   Turn on the oven to 190°C/375°F/gas mark 5. Weigh the meat and calculate the cooking time (see Roasting times, above), then prepare the meat for the oven (see To roast, page 156). Stuff the meat or the neck end of the bird, if liked, using any of the stuffing recipes on pages 321–23.

4   Put 30 ml/2 tbsp oil in a roasting tin (pan) and put on a shelf near the top of the oven.

5   Prepare the potatoes and parsnips for boiling. Cook together for 3 minutes only. Don't prepare the carrots or greens yet.

6   Strain the potatoes and parsnips in a colander over a bowl to save the cooking water for gravy. Remove the roasting tin from the oven and add the part-cooked potatoes and parsnips. Turn over in the oil, then return to the shelf near the top of the oven.

7 Put the meat on the centre shelf and note when it will be cooked (the potatoes can cook for the same amount of time).

8 Make up bread, apple or other sauce if appropriate.

9 Check the potatoes and parsnips and turn over in the oil to brown the other sides.

10 When they are cooked and golden and the meat is nearing the end of its cooking time, prepare and cook the carrots and a green leafy vegetable.

11 Put plates, a carving dish and serving dishes, if using, to warm.

12 Remove the meat from the oven and transfer to a carving dish. Leave to rest while making the gravy.

13 Sprinkle about 45 ml/3 tbsp flour into the roasting tin and stir in with a wire whisk to soak up the fat and juices. Add a little more flour if necessary.

14 Measure about 450 ml/¾ pt/2 cups vegetable cooking water in a measuring jug and gradually stir into the roasting tin until smooth. Put over a fairly high heat and cook, stirring all the time with the whisk, until bubbling, thickened and smooth. Add gravy block or browning and salt to taste. If the gravy seems too thick for your liking, add a little more water.

15 Carve the meat into slices or slice the breast of a chicken, then cut off the limbs where they join the body. Serve with the vegetables, gravy and chosen accompaniments.

Traditional accompaniments to roast meats

Roast beef: English mustard, Yorkshire pudding and horseradish relish or cream

Roast lamb: Mint sauce and/or redcurrant jelly (clear conserve)

Roast pork: Sage and onion stuffing, apple sauce

See also pages 321–27.

Offal

There is much less offal available these days. Delicacies such as sweetbreads, brains and oxtail are not seen as frequently as they used to be. Liver, kidneys and heart are still widely available, however, and are highly nutritious and worth cooking. Heart needs long, slow cooking to tenderise it, but liver and kidneys can be either cooked very quickly or braised in a rich sauce (see individual recipes). Tongue is also a treat for dedicated cooks to prepare but definitely not for beginners! Ready-cooked, pressed tongues are always available at the deli counter.

Cook's tips for cooking meat

- Always brush steaks or chops with oil or melted butter or margarine before grilling (broiling) or the surface will harden.
- To test if a steak or chop is cooked to your liking: once it is browned on both sides, press it gently with your finger. If it still feels very flexible and a little 'wobbly', it will be very rare. If firmer but with a little 'give', it will be medium-rare. If it feels firm to the touch, it will be well done. And if it is hard, it will be dry and over-cooked!
- Snip the rind of pork chops before grilling (broiling) to prevent it curling at the edges.
- To keep chops juicy, resist the temptation to keep prodding with a knife or fork during cooking, or the juices will all run out.
- When serving small Yorkshire puddings with roast beef, I find it best to roast the beef, then remove it from the oven to rest while cooking the Yorkshires. I also move the potatoes to the bottom of the oven. This avoids anything being overcooked. Of course, traditionally a large Yorkshire pud should be baked directly under the meat, so the juices drip down into it.
- If you are daunted by the thought of making your own Yorkshire puddings, cheat and buy ready-made ones, which can be popped in the oven to reheat while you make the gravy (but try my recipe on page 325 first as it is almost foolproof!).
- Prime cuts of young lamb are delicious cooked until just pink and juicy in the centre. Older lamb or mutton is best cooked through.
- Lamb tends to spit in the oven when being roasted, so a roaster baster – a covered roasting tin (pan) – is a good idea.
- Lamb can be fatty, so remove as much visible fat as possible before cooking.
- To get your crackling crisp, score in narrow strips with a sharp knife and rub well with oil, then salt. Always stand a pork joint on a rack in the roasting tin (pan).

- If your crackling turns out soggy, remove and place the rind under a preheated grill (broiler) for a few minutes to puff up. Turn once and take care it does not burn. Alternatively, wrap it in greaseproof (waxed) paper and cook in the microwave for a minute or two until it stops making crackling sounds.
- Liver and kidneys harden very quickly if overcooked so, when browning, fry (sauté) on one side, then turn over and cook only until beads of juice rise to the surface, and remove immediately from the pan.

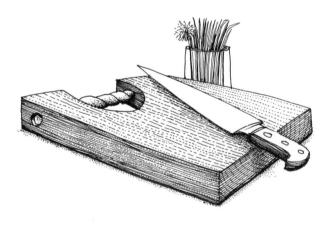

Photograph opposite: Crispy Spiced Prawns (see page 129)

Spaghetti Bolognese

Prepare the garlic bread in advance, and put on to cook about 15 minutes before the meal will be ready. Make the salad while the Bolognese is cooking.

SERVES 4

350 g/12 oz minced (ground) beef
1 large onion, finely chopped
1 carrot, finely chopped
1 garlic clove, crushed
400 g/14 oz/1 large can of chopped
    tomatoes
30 ml/2 tbsp tomato purée (paste)
45 ml/3 tbsp red wine or water
5 ml/1 tsp caster (superfine) sugar
5 ml/1 tsp dried oregano
Salt and freshly ground black pepper
350 g/12 oz spaghetti
A handful of grated Parmesan cheese
Garlic Bread (see page 395) and a
    Green Salad (see page 308), to
    serve

1 Put the beef, onion, carrot and garlic in a saucepan and cook, stirring, over a fairly high heat for about 5 minutes until the meat is brown and all the grains are separate.

2 Add the tomatoes, purée, wine or water, sugar and oregano. Season well. Bring to the boil, stirring. Part-cover, reduce the heat until just bubbling round the edges. Cook gently, stirring occasionally, for 30 minutes until tender and the meat is bathed in a rich sauce

Photograph opposite: **Beef Stir-fry with Chinese Leaves (see page 169)**

3 Meanwhile, cook the spaghetti according to the packet directions (or see page 293). Drain.

4 Pile the spaghetti on warm plates. Top with the Bolognese sauce and sprinkle with Parmesan before serving with the garlic bread and green salad.

Lasagne al Forno

If you like a very saucy lasagne, make double the quantity of cheese sauce for the top. Put the garlic bread in the oven for the last 15 minutes' cooking time and make the salad while it is heating.

SERVES 4

Bolognese sauce (as for Spaghetti
    Bolognese, left)
About 8 sheets of no-need-to-precook
    lasagne
1 quantity of Cheese Sauce
    (see page 329)
Garlic Bread (see page 395) and a
    Green Salad (see page 308),
    to serve

1 Preheat the oven to 190°C/375°F/ gas mark 5.

2 Spoon just a little of the meat sauce into a shallow ovenproof dish, then cover with a layer of lasagne sheets.

3 Layer the meat thinly with lasagne until all the meat is used, finishing with a layer of lasagne.

4 Spoon the cheese sauce over.

5 Bake in the oven for 35 minutes or until golden brown and bubbling and the lasagne feels tender when a knife is inserted down through the centre. Serve hot with the garlic bread and green salad.

Cannelloni al Forno

SERVES 4

Prepare and cook as for Lasagne al Forno (see page 161), but spoon the meat mixture into no-need-to-precook cannelloni tubes. Place in a shallow ovenproof dish and top with the cheese sauce.

Hungarian Goulash

SERVES 4

700 g/1½ lb braising steak
60 ml/4 tbsp plain (all-purpose) flour
Salt and freshly ground black pepper
45 ml/3 tbsp sunflower or olive oil
2 onions, peeled and sliced
2 large carrots, diced
15 ml/1 tbsp paprika
600 ml/1 pt/2½ cups beef stock, made
 with 1 stock cube
30 ml/2 tbsp tomato purée (paste)
5 ml/1 tsp caster (superfine) sugar
3 large potatoes, diced
2 green (bell) peppers, sliced
60 ml/4 tbsp soured (dairy sour) cream
5 ml/1 tsp caraway seeds
5 ml/1 tsp poppy seeds
Crusty bread, to serve

1 Cut any fat and gristle off the meat with a sharp knife and cut the meat into bite-sized pieces.

2 Mix the flour with a little salt and pepper in a plastic bag. Add the meat cubes, hold the top firmly and shake to coat in the flour.

3 Heat half the oil in a flameproof casserole (Dutch oven). Add the onions and carrots and cook, stirring, for 2 minutes over a fairly high heat until the onions are golden. Lift out of the casserole with a draining spoon and reserve.

4 Add the remaining oil to the pan, then add the beef and cook, stirring over a high heat, until browned on all sides. Stir in any flour left in the bag.

5 Return the onions and carrots to the pan and stir in the paprika, stock, tomato purée and sugar. Bring to the boil.

6 Cover with a lid and turn the heat down until the liquid is just bubbling gently round the edges. Stir again, cover and cook for 1½ hours.

7 Stir in the potatoes, peppers and a little more seasoning. Re-cover and simmer for a further 30 minutes or until the beef and vegetables are tender and bathed in a rich sauce.

8 Taste and re-season if necessary. Ladle into warm bowls, top with a spoonful of soured cream and a sprinkling of caraway and poppy seeds. Serve with crusty bread.

Rich Country Beef Casserole

Cook the potatoes at the same time as the casserole. Cook the green vegetable about 10 minutes before the casserole will be ready.

SERVES 4

700 g/1½ lb braising steak, cubed, discarding any fat or gristle
60 ml/4 tbsp plain (all-purpose) flour
Salt and freshly ground black pepper
45 ml/3 tbsp sunflower oil
2 onions, sliced
2 carrots, diced
600 ml/1 pt/2½ cups beef stock, made with 1 stock cube
A little gravy block or browning
1 bay leaf
Jacket-baked Potatoes (see page 296) and a green vegetable, to serve

1 Preheat the oven to 160°C/325°F/ gas mark 3.
2 Put the meat in a plastic bag with the flour and a little salt and pepper. Close tightly and shake well to coat.
3 Heat the oil in a flameproof casserole (Dutch oven) over a fairly high heat. Add the onions and carrots and fry (sauté), stirring, for 2 minutes. Remove from the pan with a draining spoon.
4 Add the beef and fry, stirring, until browned on all sides.
5 Add any flour left in the bag and stir in with the onions and carrots.
6 Pour on the stock and bring to the boil, stirring. Add a little gravy block or browning, a little more seasoning and the bay leaf.

7 Cover and cook in the oven for 2–2½ hours until really tender. Taste and re-season if necessary. Discard the bay leaf.
8 Serve with the jacket-baked potatoes and green vegetable.

Beef Carbonnade

SERVES 4

Prepare as for Rich Country Beef Casserole but use a 330 ml can of brown ale or bitter beer and 250 ml/ 8 fl oz/1 cup beef stock, made with 1 stock cube, instead of the stock in the recipe. To garnish the dish, cut eight slices off a French stick. Toast, then spread with butter or margarine and a little wholegrain mustard. Return to the grill (broiler) until the tops are bubbling and arrange around the top of the dish just before serving.

Beef in Cider with Mushrooms

SERVES 4

Prepare as for Rich Country Beef Casserole, but use half medium-sweet cider and half stock (made with 1 stock cube) instead of the stock in the recipe. Add 100 g/4 oz button mushrooms, 15 ml/1 tbsp tomato purée (paste) and 2.5 ml/½ tsp caster (superfine) sugar after adding the stock.

Steak Strips Sizzle with Crunchy Noodles

SERVES 4

350 g/12 oz thin-cut lean beef steak
15 ml/1 tbsp lemon juice
30 ml/2 tbsp sunflower oil
1 large onion, finely chopped
100 g/4 oz button mushrooms, sliced
175 g/6 oz fresh spinach, well-washed
  and shredded
45 ml/3 tbsp Worcestershire sauce
30 ml/2 tbsp apple juice
30 ml/2 tbsp chopped fresh parsley
225 g/8 oz tagliatelle
25 g/1 oz/2 tbsp butter or margarine
25 g/1 oz/½ cup fresh white
  breadcrumbs
25 g/1 oz/¼ cup chopped mixed nuts

1 Cut the steak into thin strips. Place in a shallow dish and toss in the lemon juice. Leave to stand for at least 2 hours.
2 Heat the oil in a large frying pan (skillet) or wok. Add the onion and cook, stirring over a moderate heat, for 2 minutes to soften. Add the steak and mushrooms and cook, stirring, for 2 minutes.
3 Add the spinach, Worcestershire sauce, apple juice and parsley. Cover with foil or a lid and cook for 3 minutes.
4 Meanwhile, cook the tagliatelle according to the packet instructions (or see page 293). Drain in a colander.
5 Melt the butter or margarine in the pasta saucepan and add the breadcrumbs and nuts. Stir over a fairly high heat until golden. Add the pasta to the pan and stir to coat.

6 Pile the pasta on warm plates. Top with the steak mixture and serve.

Crunchy Beef Pot

This is a complete meal in one dish – ideal when you have very little time.

SERVES 4

3 large potatoes, scrubbed and sliced
2 x 420 g/15 oz/large cans of stewed
  steak in gravy
225 g/8 oz/1 small can of water
  chestnuts, drained and sliced
400 g/14 oz/1 large can of baby carrots,
  drained
295 g/10½ oz/1 medium can of
  condensed mushroom soup
Salt and freshly ground black pepper

1 Preheat the oven to 190°C/375°F/gas mark 5.
2 Put the potatoes in a saucepan with enough lightly salted water to cover. Bring to the boil over a high heat and cook for 3–4 minutes until almost tender but still holding their shape. Drain in a colander.
3 Spoon the stewed steak and its gravy into an ovenproof dish. Gently stir in the water chestnuts. Scatter the carrots over.
4 Spoon half the soup over and spread out gently.
5 Arrange the potatoes in overlapping slices on top.
6 Mix the remaining soup with 45 ml/ 3 tbsp water to make it just pourable. Spread over the surface of the potato.
7 Bake in the oven for about 40 minutes until golden brown on top and piping hot.

Very Slow-cooked Beef in Red Wine

The potatoes are delicious cooked in the oven for the whole of the casserole cooking time. Start to cook the broccoli about 10 minutes before the casserole will be ready.

SERVES 4

700 g/1½ lb diced braising steak
45 ml/3 tbsp plain flour
Salt and freshly ground black pepper
45 ml/3 tbsp sunflower oil
1 large onion, thinly sliced
2 carrots, cut into small dice
300 ml/½ pt/1¼ cups red wine
450 ml/¾ pt/2 cups beef stock, made
  with 1 stock cube
15 ml/1 tbsp brandy
15 ml/1 tbsp tomato purée (paste)
2.5 ml/½ tsp Dijon mustard
5 ml/1 tsp caster (superfine) sugar
1 bouquet garni sachet
175 g/6 oz whole button mushrooms
4 large potatoes, scrubbed
Broccoli, to serve

1 Preheat the oven to 150°C/300°F/gas mark 2.

2 Mix the flour with a little salt and pepper in a plastic bag. Add the meat and shake the bag well to coat the meat in the flour.

3 Heat 15 ml/1 tbsp of the oil in a flameproof casserole (Dutch oven) and fry (sauté) the onion and carrots over a fairly high heat, stirring, for 2 minutes. Remove from the pan with a draining spoon.

4 Add the remaining oil and brown the meat on all sides. Remove from the pan.

5 Add any remaining flour to the pan, then blend in the wine, stock, brandy, tomato purée, mustard and sugar. Season well and return the carrots, onion and meat to the liquid. Bring to the boil and add the bouquet garni and mushrooms.

6 Cover and place in the oven. Prick the potatoes all over and place alongside the casserole.

7 Cook for 4 hours or until the meat is really tender and bathed in a rich sauce. Discard the bouquet garni, taste and re-season if necessary. Serve hot with the jacket potatoes and broccoli.

Rich Weekday Mince with Potatoes

SERVES 4

30 ml/2 tbsp sunflower oil
2 large onions, chopped
450 g/1 lb minced (ground) beef
2 carrots, chopped
45 ml/3 tbsp plain (all-purpose) flour
750 ml/1¼ pts/3 cups beef stock, made with 2 stock cubes
1 bay leaf
Salt and freshly ground black pepper
450 g/1 lb baby new potatoes, scrubbed but left whole
175 g/6 oz/1½ cups frozen peas

1 Preheat the oven to 160°C/325°F/ gas mark 3.

2 Heat the oil in a flameproof casserole (Dutch oven) and fry (sauté) the onions, beef and carrots, stirring, over a fairly high heat for about 5 minutes until the meat is no longer pink and all the grains are separate.

3 Stir in the flour and cook for 1 minute.

4 Blend in the stock and bring to the boil, stirring.

5 Add the bay leaf, seasoning and the vegetables. Cover with the lid and cook in the oven for 2 hours.

6 Discard the bay leaf, stir in the peas and return to the oven for 15 minutes. Taste and re-season if necessary. Ladle into warm soup bowls and serve.

Beef Stroganoff

SERVES 4

2 large onions, sliced
25 g/1 oz/2 tbsp butter or margarine
450 g/1 lb braising steak, cut into thin strips
450 ml/¾ pt/2 cups beef stock, made with 1 stock cube
Salt and freshly ground black pepper
30 ml/2 tbsp plain (all-purpose) flour
30 ml/2 tbsp water
30 ml/2 tbsp tomato purée (paste)
150 ml/¼ pt/⅔ cup crème fraîche
225 g/8 oz/1 cup long-grain rice
A Green Salad (see page 308), to serve

1 Fry (sauté) the onions in the butter or margarine in a flameproof casserole (Dutch oven) for 2 minutes, stirring.

2 Add the steak and fry for a further 2 minutes, stirring.

3 Add the stock and a little salt and pepper. Bring to the boil, cover, reduce the heat and simmer very gently for 1½ hours or until the beef is really tender.

4 Blend the flour with the water. Stir in a little of the hot beef liquid, then stir this into the beef. Bring to the boil, stirring, and cook for 2 minutes.

5 Stir in the tomato purée and crème fraîche. Reheat.

6 Meanwhile, cook the rice according to the packet directions (or see page 294). Drain in a colander. Make the salad. Taste and re-season the beef if necessary. Serve the casserole with the rice and salad.

Steak and Kidney Pudding

To make extra gravy, see Extra Tasty Gravy, page 324.

SERVES 4–6

365 g/12½ oz/generous 3 cups self-raising (self-rising) flour

5 ml/1 tsp mustard powder

Salt

175 g/6 oz/1½ cups shredded (chopped) suet

About 120 ml/4 fl oz/½ cup cold water

A little oil, for greasing

900 g/2 lb diced stewing steak and kidney

Freshly ground black pepper

30 ml/2 tbsp chopped fresh parsley

300 ml/½ pt/1¼ cups beef stock, made with 1 stock cube

Carrots and extra gravy (optional), to serve

1 Reserve 30 ml/2 tbsp of the flour, and sift the rest with the mustard and 5 ml/1 tsp salt into a bowl. Stir in the suet.

2 Add cold water, a little at a time, mixing to form a firm dough.

3 Draw together in a ball. Place on a lightly floured surface and squeeze gently to remove the cracks. Cut off a quarter and roll out the remainder. Lightly grease a 1.2 litre/2 pt/5 cup pudding basin with oil and line with the larger piece of pastry (paste), pressing it firmly but gently into the corners.

4 Mix the reserved flour with salt and pepper and the parsley. Add the meat and kidney, close tightly and shake well.

5 Pack into the basin and pour in the stock. Roll out the small piece of pastry, dampen with water and place on top as a lid.

6 Cover with a double thickness of greaseproof (waxed) paper or foil, with a pleat in the centre, then twist and fold under the rim to secure.

7 Place in a steamer over a pan of boiling water or place on an old saucer in the pan with enough boiling water to come halfway up the sides of the basin. Cover and steam for 4 hours, topping up with boiling water as necessary. Cook the carrots and make extra gravy, if liked, about 20 minutes before the pudding is due to be ready. Serve hot with carrots and extra gravy, if liked.

Simple Beef Curry

SERVES 4

30 ml/2 tbsp plain (all-purpose) flour
Salt and freshly ground black pepper
700 g/1½ lb diced braising steak
45 ml/3 tbsp sunflower oil
2 large onions, chopped
1 garlic clove, crushed
30 ml/2 tbsp mild curry paste
45 ml/3 tbsp mango chutney
450 ml/¾ pt/2 cups beef stock, made
    with 1 stock cube
15 ml/1 tbsp tomato purée (paste)
30 ml/2 tbsp fresh chopped coriander
    (cilantro)
225 g/8 oz/1 cup long-grain rice
30 ml/2 tbsp desiccated (shredded)
    coconut, to garnish

1 Mix the flour with a little salt and
pepper in a plastic bag. Add the meat,
close the bag tightly and shake to coat
the meat in the flour.

2 Heat 30 ml/2 tbsp of the oil in a
flameproof casserole (Dutch oven). Add
the meat and cook over a high heat
until browned on all sides, stirring
frequently. Remove from the pan with
a draining spoon.

3 Add the remaining oil and fry (sauté)
the onions and garlic, for 2 minutes,
stirring, until lightly golden. Add the
curry paste and cook, stirring, for
1 minute. Return the meat to the pan.

4 Add the chutney, stock and tomato
purée. Bring to the boil, stirring all the
time. Turn down the heat very low so
the liquid is just bubbling very gently
around the edges. Cover and cook for
2½ hours, stirring occasionally to prevent
sticking.

5 Season to taste and stir in the
coriander.

6 Meanwhile, cook the rice according
to the packet directions (or see page
294). Drain in a colander, then spoon
on to warm plates. Spoon the curry on
top and sprinkle with coconut.

Corned Beef Hash

*This is a great mid-week supper
when time is short. If you have some
cooked, leftover potatoes, it's even
quicker as you can omit the
10 minutes' cooking with the onions.*

SERVES 4

60 ml/4 tbsp sunflower oil
1 large onion, finely chopped
4 large potatoes, finely diced
350 g/12 oz/1 large can of corned beef,
    diced
400 g/14 oz/1 large can of baked beans
2.5 ml/½ tsp dried oregano
5 ml/1 tsp brown table sauce
Salt and freshly ground black pepper
Crusty bread and a Green Salad (see
    page 308), to serve

1 Heat the oil in a large frying pan
(skillet). Add the onion and potatoes
and cook over a fairly high heat,
stirring, for 2 minutes. Cover with a lid,
turn down the heat to low and cook
gently for 10 minutes, stirring
occasionally.

2 Add the remaining ingredients and
cook, stirring, for 5 minutes, then press
down, and cook for a further 5 minutes
until crispy and golden underneath.
While it is cooking, make the salad.

3 Serve the hash straight from the pan
with crusty bread and the salad.

Beef Stir-fry with Chinese Leaves

Cook the rice before starting to stir-fry, leave it in the pan, then reheat it, stirring over a low heat until piping hot, just before serving. As an alternative, serve the stir-fried beef on fresh Chinese leaves.

SERVES 4

1 small garlic clove, crushed
5 ml/1 tsp dry sherry
5 ml/1 tsp soy sauce
5 ml/1 tsp light brown sugar
5 ml/1 tsp sesame oil
1 egg yolk
350 g/12 oz thin-cut sirloin steak, cut into narrow strips
1 small head of Chinese leaves (stem lettuce)
60 ml/4 tbsp sunflower oil
2.5 ml/½ tsp Chinese five spice powder
30 ml/2 tbsp oyster sauce
30 ml/2 tbsp water
Salt and freshly ground black pepper
Egg Fried Rice (see page 315), to serve

1 Mix the garlic with the sherry, soy sauce, sugar, oil and egg yolk in a shallow dish. Add the beef and stir gently to mix. Leave in the fridge to marinate for 1 hour.

2 Cut off the root from the Chinese leaves and cut the head into eight long wedges.

3 Heat half the sunflower oil in a wok or large frying pan (skillet). Add the Chinese leaves, sprinkle with the five spice powder and fry (sauté) over a high heat for 4–5 minutes, turning once or twice until softened and lightly golden around the edges. Transfer to a shallow serving dish and keep warm.

4 Heat the remaining sunflower oil in the same pan. Add the beef mixture and stir-fry for about 3 minutes until cooked through. Stir in the oyster sauce, water and salt and pepper to taste. Cook, stirring, until thick. Spoon over the Chinese leaves and serve with the Egg Fried Rice.

Corned Beef Fritters

Cook the potatoes before you start the fritters. The peas can be cooked quickly while the fritters are cooking.

SERVES 4

50 g/2 oz/½ cup plain (all-purpose) flour
Salt and freshly ground black pepper
2 eggs, beaten
60 ml/4 tbsp milk
350 g/12 oz/1 large can of corned beef, cut into 8 slices
Oil, for shallow-frying
Tomato relish, Super Creamed Potatoes (see page 298) and peas, to serve

1 Put the flour in a bowl with a little salt and pepper. Add the eggs and milk and beat well.

2 Dip the corned beef in the batter.

3 Heat about 5 mm/¼ in oil in a frying pan (skillet). When hot but not smoking, fry (sauté) the fritters over a fairly high heat for about 3 minutes on each side until golden brown.

4 Drain on kitchen paper (paper towels) and serve with tomato relish, Super Creamed Potatoes and peas.

Creamy Peppered Steaks

For a slightly less rich result, use low-fat crème fraîche instead of double (heavy) cream.

SERVES 4

40 g/1½ oz/3 tbsp butter or margarine
15 ml/1 tbsp olive oil
4 fillet steaks, about 175 g/6 oz each
15 ml/1 tbsp pickled green peppercorns
30 ml/2 tbsp brandy
150 ml/¼ pt/⅔ cup double (heavy) cream
Salt and freshly ground black pepper
225 g/8 oz/1 cup wild rice mix
175 g/6 oz broccoli, cut into small florets

1 Heat the butter or margarine and oil in a frying pan (skillet) and fry (sauté) the steaks over a high heat until golden brown on both sides.
2 Reduce the heat to fairly low and continue to cook for 5–10 minutes, depending on thickness and how well you like your steaks done, turning once or twice. (To check if they are done, see Cook's tips for cooking meat, page 159.) Remove from the pan and keep warm.
3 Add the peppercorns and brandy and ignite. Shake the pan until the flames subside.
4 Stir in the cream and bubble until slightly thickening. Season to taste.
5 Meanwhile, cook the rice according to the packet directions (or see page 294), adding the broccoli after 5 minutes' cooking time. Drain in a colander. Spoon on to plates and top with the steaks. Spoon the sauce over and serve.

Flash-in-the-pan Steaks

Start to cook the potatoes before you begin cooking the steaks.

SERVES 4

4 thin frying steaks, about 100 g/4 oz each
10 ml/2 tsp lemon juice
Freshly ground black pepper
25 g/1 oz/2 tbsp butter or margarine
15 ml/1 tbsp olive oil
1 small onion, finely chopped
15 ml/1 tbsp chopped fresh parsley
5 ml/1 tsp soy sauce
45 ml/3 tbsp Worcestershire sauce
30 ml/2 tbsp crème fraîche
Sauté Potatoes (see page 296) and peas, to serve

1 Put the steaks one at a time in a plastic bag and beat with a meat mallet or rolling pin to tenderise and flatten them. Brush all over with the lemon juice and add a good grinding of pepper to each.
2 Melt the butter or margarine with the oil in a large frying pan (skillet). Add the steaks and cook over a high heat for about 2 minutes on each side until just cooked through. Remove from the pan and keep warm.
3 Add the onion to the pan and cook, stirring, for 1 minute. Add the remaining ingredients and allow to bubble for 1 minute. Spoon over the steaks and serve with the sauté potatoes and peas.

Savoury Beef Pittas

The quantities are not vital for this dish. Use as little or as much beef and mushrooms as you like (or have!) and make up with extra salad to pad out the pockets, if necessary. Very large appetites will eat more pittas. Start cooking the chips (fries) before you make the beef mixture.

SERVES 2–4

1 large onion, finely chopped
8 or more button mushrooms, sliced
25 g/1 oz/2 tbsp butter or margarine
100–175 g/4–6 oz leftover roast beef, cut into very thin strips
60 ml/4 tbsp Worcestershire sauce
5 ml/1 tsp lemon juice
15 ml/1 tbsp water
Salt and freshly ground black pepper
4 pitta breads
Shredded lettuce, sliced tomatoes, sliced cucumber and chips (see page 296), to serve

1 Fry (sauté) the onion and mushrooms in the butter or margarine over a fairly gentle heat, stirring, for 3–4 minutes until softened but not browned.

2 Add the beef and stir just until hot through – don't cook for long or it will toughen.

3 Add the Worcestershire sauce, lemon juice, water and a little salt and pepper.

4 Cook gently, stirring, until the meat is bathed in the juices.

5 Meanwhile, warm the pitta breads in a toaster, under the grill (broiler) or briefly in the microwave. Cut into halves widthways and gently open into pockets.

6 Spoon in the beef mixture and fill with shredded lettuce, tomato and cucumber. Serve straight away.

Beef Steakwiches

Start cooking the chips (fries) before you cook the steak.

SERVES 4

45 ml/3 tbsp horseradish relish
100 g/4 oz/½ cup fromage frais
Salt and freshly ground black pepper
4 frozen minced (ground) beef steaks
A little Worcestershire sauce
4 small baguettes
A little crisp lettuce, shredded
4 tomatoes, thickly sliced
Chips (see page 296), to serve

1 Preheat the grill (broiler). Mix the horseradish with the fromage frais and season to taste with salt and pepper.

2 Place the beef on a grill rack and sprinkle each steak with a dash of Worcestershire sauce. Grill (broil) until browned on one side. Turn over, sprinkle with a little more Worcestershire sauce and grill again until cooked through (check the packet directions).

3 Split the baguettes lengthways and spread with the horseradish mixture. Add some shredded lettuce and the tomato. Cut the steaks in halves lengthways and put in the baguettes. Serve straight away with the chips.

Beef Wellington

I like to serve this with Mushroom Sauce (see page 328). Put the potatoes on about five minutes after you put the Wellington in the oven. The peas can be cooked quickly just before you serve everything.

SERVES 6

700 g/1½ lb beef fillet, in one piece
Salt and freshly ground black pepper
15 g/½ oz/1 tbsp butter or margarine
15 ml/1 tbsp olive oil
1 onion, finely chopped
100 g/4 oz button mushrooms, sliced
15 ml/1 tbsp chopped fresh parsley
225 g/8 oz puff pastry (paste), thawed
    if frozen
100 g/4 oz smooth spreading liver pâté
1 egg, beaten, to glaze
Horseradish relish, new potatoes and
    peas, to serve

1 Season the meat with salt and pepper.

2 Heat the butter or margarine and oil in a frying pan (skillet) and brown the meat quickly on all sides over a high heat, then turn down the heat to moderate and cook, turning occasionally, for 10 minutes. Remove from the pan.

3 Add the onion and mushrooms to the pan and fry (sauté) for 3 minutes until softened. Stir in the parsley and remove from the heat.

4 Preheat the oven to 220°C/425°F/ gas mark 7. Rinse a baking (cookie) sheet with cold water.

5 Roll out the pastry on a lightly floured surface to a square about 2.5 cm/1 in longer than the piece of meat.

6 Spread the pâté down the centre and top with the onion and mushroom mixture. Lay the meat on top.

7 Brush the edges with water and fold the pastry up over the meat to cover completely and fold in the ends to form a parcel.

8 Place, folded-sides down, on the baking sheet and brush the top and sides with beaten egg. Make several small slashes in the top of the pastry.

9 Bake in the oven for 15 minutes, turn down the heat to 190°C/375°F/ gas mark 5 and cook for a further 10 minutes.

10 Meanwhile, cook the new potatoes, then the peas (see note, left). Carefully transfer the beef to a warm serving dish. Garnish with parsley and serve cut into thick slices with the horseradish relish, potatoes and peas.

Big Bite Burgers

The easiest way to mix the burgers is to use your hands! Start cooking the chips (fries) before you grill (broil) the burgers.

SERVES 4

450 g/1 lb minced (ground) steak
1 small onion, finely chopped
5 ml/1 tsp mustard powder
10 ml/2 tsp tomato purée (paste)
10 ml/2 tsp Worcestershire sauce
Salt and freshly ground black pepper
1 egg, beaten
10 ml/2 tsp olive oil
4 seeded burger buns
1 dill-pickled cucumber, sliced
30 ml/2 tbsp tomato relish
A little shredded lettuce
Chips (see page 296), to serve

1 Mix the meat with the onion, mustard powder, tomato purée, Worcestershire sauce and a little salt and pepper in a bowl.
2 Add the egg and mix thoroughly to bind.
3 Shape the mixture into four round balls, then flatten each to form a cake about the diameter of a burger bun.
4 Preheat the grill (broiler).
5 Place the cakes on lightly oiled foil on the grill rack and brush with oil.
6 Grill for about 6 minutes on each side until just cooked through.
7 Place in the buns, top each with a few slices of dill pickle, a little tomato relish and some shredded lettuce and serve with the chips.

Steak au Poivre

Cook the potatoes before you start to cook the steak and keep warm over a very low heat. Add the beans to a pan of boiling water when you start to cook the steaks.

SERVES 4

4 rump or sirloin steaks, about 175 g/ 6 oz each
30 ml/2 tbsp olive oil
10 ml/2 tsp coarsely crushed black peppercorns
25 g/1 oz/2 tbsp butter or margarine
150 ml/¼ pt/⅔ cup beef stock, made with ½ stock cube
Salt
15 ml/1 tbsp brandy
Super Creamed Potatoes (see page 298) and French (green) beans, to serve

1 Rub the steaks with half the oil.
2 Sprinkle both sides with peppercorns.
3 Heat the remaining oil and half the butter or margarine in a large, heavy frying pan (skillet). Add the steaks and cook over a high heat for 2 minutes on each side for rare, 3–4 minutes on each side for medium and 5–6 minutes on each side for well done.
4 Remove from the pan and keep warm.
5 Melt the remaining butter or margarine in the pan. Add the stock, a pinch of salt and the brandy. Bring to the boil and boil for 1–2 minutes until almost half the liquid has evaporated, scraping up any sediment in the base of the pan. Spoon these concentrated juices over the steaks and serve with Super Creamed Potatoes and French beans.

Chilli con Carne

You can make this hotter or milder, to suit your own taste, by adjusting the quantity of chilli powder.

SERVES 4

225 g/8 oz minced (ground) lamb or beef

1 large onion, chopped

5 ml/1 tsp chilli powder

5 ml/1 tsp ground cumin

5 ml/1 tsp dried oregano

450 ml/¾ pt/2 cups passata (sieved tomatoes)

2 x 425 g/15 oz/large cans of red kidney beans, drained

15 ml/1 tbsp tomato purée (paste)

Salt and freshly ground black pepper

225 g/8 oz/1 cup long-grain rice

Shredded lettuce and grated Cheddar cheese, to serve

1 Put the mince and onion in a saucepan and dry-fry, stirring, over a high heat for 5 minutes until the meat is no longer pink and all the grains are separate.

2 Stir the chilli, cumin and oregano into the meat and cook for a further 1 minute.

3 Stir in the passata, beans, tomato purée and a little salt and pepper.

4 Bring to the boil, then turn down the heat until just bubbling round the edges and cook gently for 20 minutes, stirring occasionally.

5 Meanwhile, cook the rice according to the packet directions (or see page 294). Drain and spoon into bowls. Top with the chilli and serve with shredded lettuce and grated Cheddar cheese.

Enchiladas

SERVES 4

1 quantity of Chilli con Carne (see left)

8 large flour tortillas

100 g/4 oz/1 cup Cheddar cheese, grated

Shredded lettuce and chilli relish, to serve

1 Prepare as for Chilli con Carne up to and including step 4. Preheat the oven to 190°C/370°F/gas mark 5.

2 Roll the meat mixture in the tortillas and lay in an ovenproof dish.

3 Sprinkle with the cheese, cover with foil and bake in the oven for 20 minutes.

4 Serve with the shredded lettuce and chilli relish.

Crispy Tacos

SERVES 4

1 quantity of Chilli con Carne (see left)

1 box of crispy corn taco shells

Shredded lettuce, chopped tomato, cucumber and onion, soured (dairy sour) cream and grated Cheddar cheese, to serve

1 Prepare and cook the Chilli con Carne.

2 Warm the tacos as directed on the packet.

3 Fill the tacos with the chilli and top with a little lettuce, chopped tomato, cucumber and onion, a small spoonful of soured cream and a little grated cheese.

Greek-style Roast Lamb

You can use a small shoulder of lamb instead of the leg, but you'll need to trim off the excess fat before cooking.

SERVES 4

½ leg of lamb, about 1 kg/2¼ lb
1 large garlic clove, cut into slivers
2.5 ml/½ tsp dried oregano
Salt and freshly ground black pepper
8 large potatoes, peeled and halved
450 ml/¾ pt/2 cups lamb or chicken stock, made with 1 stock cube
30 ml/2 tbsp chopped fresh parsley, to garnish
Warm pitta breads and a Village Salad (see page 310), to serve

1 Preheat the oven to 160°C/325°F/ gas mark 3.
2 Put the lamb in a fairly large, flameproof casserole dish (Dutch oven). Lay the garlic slivers over and sprinkle with the oregano and a little salt and pepper.
3 Arrange the halved potatoes around and season lightly. Pour the stock around.
4 Cover and cook in the oven for 3½ hours or until meltingly tender. While it is cooking, make the salad.
5 Transfer the meat and potatoes to a carving dish. Put the casserole on top of the stove and boil the liquid rapidly until slightly reduced (this means it has evaporated and thickened a little). Warm the pitta breads in the oven briefly.
6 Cut all the meat off the bone (it will fall away) and cut into neat pieces. Transfer to warm plates with the potatoes. Spoon the juices over and sprinkle with parsley. Serve with pitta breads and a Village Salad.

No-effort Italian Lamb

SERVES 4

4 large or 8 small lamb chump chops
1 onion, finely chopped
15 ml/1 tbsp olive oil
295 g/10½ oz/1 medium can of condensed tomato soup
2.5 ml/½ tsp dried basil
Salt and freshly ground black pepper
350 g/12 oz tagliatelle
A Green Salad (see page 308), to serve

1 Preheat the oven to 160°C/325°F/ gas mark 3.
2 Brown the chops and onion in the oil in a flameproof casserole (Dutch oven) over a high heat for 2–3 minutes, turning the chops once.
3 Spoon the soup over and sprinkle with the basil and a little salt and pepper. When bubbling, cover and cook in the oven for 1½ hours or until the chops are tender and bathed in sauce.
4 Meanwhile, make the salad, then cook the tagliatelle according to the packet directions (or see page 293). Drain in a colander. Transfer the pasta to warm plates and top with the lamb. Serve with the green salad.

Sticky Oriental Lamb Spare Ribs

SERVES 4

1.25 kg/2½ lb whole breast of lamb
60 ml/4 tbsp red wine vinegar
45 ml/3 tbsp clear honey
30 ml/2 tbsp tomato ketchup (catsup)
15 ml/1 tbsp tomato purée (paste)
15 ml/1 tbsp Worcestershire sauce
15 ml/1 tbsp soy sauce
A few drops of Tabasco sauce
1 garlic clove, crushed
Egg Fried Rice (see page 315) and a
    Beansprout Salad (see page 310), to
    serve

1 Trim as much fat from the lamb as possible, using a sharp knife.
2 With a large, sharp knife, cut between the bones to separate into spare ribs.
3 Place the pieces in a saucepan and cover with water. Add half the vinegar. Cook over a high heat until boiling, then skim off any scum from the surface with a draining spoon. Turn down the heat until just bubbling round the edges, cover with a lid and cook for 1 hour. Drain.
4 Preheat the oven to 200°C/400°F/gas mark 6.
5 Mix the remaining vinegar with the rest of the ingredients in a roasting tin (pan). Add the ribs and turn over until well coated with the sauce.
6 Cook in the oven for 35 minutes until well browned and coated in a sticky glaze, turning over after 15 minutes. While the ribs are cooking, make the Egg Fried Rice and Beansprout Salad.

7 Spoon the rice on to four warm plates. Pile the lamb ribs on top and serve with the salad.

Lamb Steakwiches

Make the salad and put the potatoes on before you start to cook the lamb.

SERVES 4

10 cm/4 in piece of cucumber
10 ml/2 tsp dried mint
120 ml/4 fl oz/½ cup thick plain
    yoghurt
Salt and freshly ground black pepper
4 frozen minced (ground) lamb steaks
4 small baguettes
A little crisp lettuce, shredded
Sauté Potatoes (see page 296) and a
    Tomato, Sweetcorn and Onion
    Salad (see page 312), to serve

1 Grate the cucumber and squeeze out the juice. Mix with the mint, yoghurt and a little salt and pepper and leave to stand while you cook the meat.
2 Grill (broil) the lamb steaks on both sides until cooked through. Cut into halves lengthways.
3 Split the baguettes lengthways and spread with the yoghurt mixture and some shredded lettuce. Add the meat. Serve with the sauté potatoes and Tomato, Sweetcorn and Onion Salad.

Sheesh Kebabs

SERVES 4

1 onion, grated

15 ml/1 tbsp grated fresh root ginger

10 ml/2 tsp ground cinnamon

5 ml/1 tsp ground cumin

2.5 ml/½ tsp chilli powder

450 g/1 lb minced (ground) lamb

10 ml/2 tsp lemon juice

30 ml/2 tbsp plain yoghurt

30 ml/2 tbsp plain (all-purpose) flour, plus extra for dusting

30 ml/2 tbsp chopped fresh coriander (cilantro)

Salt and freshly ground black pepper

225 g/8 oz/1 cup long-grain rice

Wedges of lemon, to garnish

Shredded lettuce, sliced tomatoes, sliced cucumber and mango chutney, to serve

1 Put the onion in a large bowl with the spices and mix to a paste.

2 Add the lamb, lemon juice, yoghurt, flour, coriander, 2.5 ml/½ tsp salt and a good grinding of pepper, then squeeze together until well mixed.

3 Preheat the grill (broiler).

4 With floured hands, divide the mixture into eight pieces and shape each piece into a sausage shape around a skewer. Lay on foil on a grill rack. Grill (broil) for 10 minutes, turning once or twice until golden brown and cooked through.

5 Meanwhile, cook the rice according to the packet directions (or see page 294). Drain. Pile on plates, top with the kebabs, garnish with lemon wedges and serve with lettuce, tomato, cucumber and mango chutney.

Rich Lamb and Bean Hot-pot

SERVES 4

175 g/6 oz/1 cup flageolet beans, soaked overnight in cold water

450 ml/¾ pt/2 cups water

1 lamb or beef stock cube

30 ml/2 tbsp redcurrant jelly (clear conserve)

2 leeks, sliced

2 lamb's kidneys, cored and chopped

8 best end of neck lamb cutlets

Salt and freshly ground black pepper

15 ml/1 tbsp chopped fresh rosemary

700 g/1½ lb potatoes, scrubbed and thinly sliced

15 g/½ oz/1 tbsp butter or margarine

Leaf spinach, to serve

1 Drain the beans and place in a saucepan with the water. Bring to the boil and cook rapidly for 10 minutes. Reduce the heat until just bubbling round the edges, part-cover and cook gently for 1 hour. Stir in the stock and redcurrant jelly until dissolved. Turn into a fairly shallow, 2.25 litre/4 pt/10 cup ovenproof dish.

2 Preheat the oven to 160°C/325°F/ gas mark 3.

3 Add the leeks, kidneys and cutlets to the beans and season with salt, pepper and the rosemary and stir gently to mix.

4 Arrange the potato slices in layers on the top. Scatter with pieces of butter or margarine. Season again, cover with foil and bake in the oven for 1½ hours.

5 Remove the foil and continue cooking for a further 1 hour until tender and golden. Prepare and cook the spinach about 10 minutes before the lamb will be ready.

Mediterranean Lamb Crunch

Make the salad first. Cut as much fat as possible off the lamb when you dice it.

SERVES 4

75 g/3 oz/⅓ cup butter or margarine

2 thick slices of bread, cut into cubes

2 courgettes (zucchini), trimmed and diced

1 aubergine (eggplant), diced, discarding the stalk end

4 cup mushrooms, sliced

175 g/6 oz/1½ cups diced cooked lamb

30 ml/2 tbsp capers, chopped

15 ml/1 tbsp caper vinegar (from the jar)

Salt and freshly ground black pepper

30 ml/2 tbsp plain (all-purpose) flour

300 ml/½ pt/1¼ cups lamb or chicken stock, made with 1 stock cube

2 eggs, beaten

30 ml/2 tbsp chopped fresh parsley

Middle Eastern Coleslaw (see page 311), to serve

1 Melt half the butter or margarine in a saucepan. Remove from the heat. Add the bread and toss to coat completely. Remove from the pan and reserve.

2 Melt the remaining butter or margarine in the same pan over a fairly high heat. Add the courgettes, aubergine and mushrooms and stir well. Cover, turn down the heat to fairly low and cook the vegetables for 5 minutes, stirring occasionally to prevent sticking.

3 Add the lamb, capers, vinegar and a little salt and pepper. Cover and continue to cook for a further 5 minutes, stirring once or twice.

4 Stir in the flour and cook for 1 minute. Remove from the heat, stir in the stock, then heat again until boiling and cook, stirring, for 2 minutes.

5 Remove from the heat once more and stir in the beaten eggs and parsley. Taste and re-season if necessary.

6 Preheat the grill (broiler). Spoon the meat mixture into four individual flameproof dishes and top with the bread cubes. Place under the grill until the top is golden brown. Serve hot with the Middle Eastern Coleslaw.

Redcurrant Lamb with Rosemary

Cook the potatoes before preparing the lamb. Cook the mangetout (snow peas) quickly, while the lamb is cooking.

SERVES 4

350 g/12 oz lamb neck fillet, cut into 12 thin slices

40 g/1½ oz/3 tbsp butter or margarine

1 red onion, finely chopped

1 cooked beetroot (red beet), finely diced

30 ml/2 tbsp chopped fresh rosemary

1 garlic clove, crushed

15 ml/1 tbsp tomato purée (paste)

30 ml/2 tbsp redcurrant jelly (clear conserve)

150 ml/¼ pt/⅔ cup lamb or chicken stock

10 ml/2 tsp red wine vinegar

15 ml/1 tbsp chopped fresh parsley, to garnish

Super Creamed Potatoes (see page 298) and mangetout, to serve

1 Place the lamb slices one at a time in a plastic bag and beat with a rolling pin or meat mallet to flatten.

2 Melt 25 g/1 oz/2 tbsp of the butter or margarine in a frying pan (skillet) and fry (sauté) the lamb over a high heat for about 2 minutes on each side until golden brown and just cooked through. Remove from the pan with a draining spoon and keep warm.

3 Melt the remaining butter or margarine in the pan and fry the onion for 2 minutes until softened slightly.

4 Add the remaining ingredients and stir until the jelly dissolves, then bring to the boil, reduce the heat to moderate and cook, stirring, until slightly thickened. Taste and re-season if necessary.

5 Transfer the lamb to warm plates and pour any juices back into the pan.

6 Stir, then spoon the sauce over the lamb and garnish with chopped parsley. Serve with the Super Creamed Potatoes and mangetout.

Moroccan Lamb

Couscous is really easy to cook and this makes an impressive dish. If you are not sure how to seed chillies, see Fiery Mussel Spaghettini, page 134.

SERVES 4
---

700 g/1½ lb diced stewing lamb

12 button (pearl) onions, peeled but left whole

1 large garlic clove, crushed

1 green chilli, seeded and chopped

1.5 ml/¼ tsp ground cinnamon

1.5 ml/¼ tsp ground ginger

Salt and freshly ground black pepper

900 ml/1½ pts/3¾ cups lamb stock, made with 2 stock cubes

10 ml/2 tsp tomato purée (paste)

100 g/4 oz/⅔ cup no-need-to-soak dried apricots, halved

2 courgettes (zucchini), diced

2 carrots, diced

1 green (bell) pepper, diced

30 ml/2 tbsp chopped fresh coriander (cilantro)

30 ml/2 tbsp chopped fresh parsley

225 g/8 oz/1⅓ cups couscous

1 Put the lamb and onions in a large saucepan with the garlic, chilli, spices, a little salt and pepper, the lamb stock and tomato purée. Bring to the boil, stirring over a high heat. Reduce the heat until just bubbling gently around the edges, then cover and cook gently for 1½ hours, stirring occasionally.

2 Meanwhile, put the couscous in a bowl with just enough boiling water to cover. Leave to stand for 5 minutes, then tip into a steamer or sieve (strainer) that will fit on top of the saucepan without touching the lamb.

3 Add the apricots and vegetables to the lamb mixture with half the herbs. Sit the steamer of couscous on top of the pan, cover and cook for a further 15 minutes.

4 Stir the couscous gently with a fork. If necessary, boil the stew rapidly without a lid, stirring all the time, so that the liquid reduces to a thick sauce. Taste and re-season if necessary.

5 Spoon the couscous on to plates. Spoon the lamb mixture on top and sprinkle with the remaining herbs before serving.

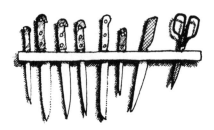

Red-cooked Lamb

SERVES 4

1 kg/2¼ lb diced lamb

2 large garlic cloves, chopped

1 bunch of spring onions (scallions), cut
   into short lengths

2 red (bell) peppers, finely chopped

2.5 cm/1 in piece of fresh root ginger,
   peeled and grated

5 ml/1 tsp Chinese five spice powder

15 ml/1 tbsp tomato purée (paste)

45 ml/3 tbsp dry sherry

75 ml/5 tbsp soy sauce

5 ml/1 tsp Worcestershire sauce

600 ml/1 pt/2½ cups beef stock, made
   with 1 stock cube

50 g/2 oz/¼ cup light brown sugar

225 g/8 oz/1 cup Thai fragrant rice

1 Put the lamb, garlic, spring onions and
one of the peppers in a flameproof
casserole (Dutch oven).

2 Mix together all the remaining
ingredients except the rice and the
remaining pepper and pour over. Stir
well.

3 Cook over a high heat until boiling.
Turn down the heat until just gently
bubbling round the edges. Stir again,
cover with a lid and cook for 1½ hours.

4 Remove the lid, turn up the heat
and cook rapidly for a few minutes,
stirring all the time, until the sauce is
rich and thick.

5 Meanwhile, cook the rice according
to the packet directions (or see page
294). Spoon on to warm plates, top
with the lamb and scatter the
remaining pepper over before serving.

Bramley Lamb Pie

SERVES 4

1 kg/2¼ lb potatoes, thinly sliced

50 g/2 oz/¼ cup butter or margarine

8 small lamb chops

2 onions, thinly sliced

2 cooking (tart) apples, chopped

10 ml/2 tsp light brown sugar

10 ml/2 tsp chopped fresh mint

Salt and freshly ground black pepper

200 ml/7 fl oz/1 cup beef stock, made
   with ½ stock cube

A green vegetable, to serve

1 Put the sliced potatoes in a large
bowl of water to prevent browning.

2 Preheat the oven to 180°C/350°F/
gas mark 4.

3 Melt a quarter of the butter or
margarine in a flameproof casserole
(Dutch oven). Brown the chops on both
sides over a high heat and remove
from the dish.

4 Add the onions and apples and cook
quickly, stirring for 2 minutes. Remove
from the pan and turn off the heat.

5 Drain the potatoes and layer half in
the base of the casserole. Place the
chops on this and spoon the onion and
apple mixture over. Sprinkle with the
sugar, mint, salt and pepper.

6 Put the remaining potatoes in a
layer over the top. Pour on the stock,
then scatter with small pieces of the
remaining butter or margarine.

7 Cook in the oven for 1½ hours until
the potatoes and meat are cooked
through and the top is golden brown.
Cook a green vegetable about
10 minutes before serving with the pie.

Moussaka

There are many variations of this famous dish. This low-fat one is simple but delicious.

SERVES 4

2 aubergines (eggplants), sliced
350 g/12 oz minced (ground) lamb
1 onion, finely chopped
1 garlic clove, crushed
400 g/14 oz/1 large can of chopped
    tomatoes
2.5 ml/½ tsp ground cinnamon
2.5 ml/½ tsp dried oregano
30 ml/2 tbsp chopped fresh parsley
Salt and freshly ground black pepper
1 egg
150 ml/¼ pt/⅔ cup plain yoghurt
50 g/2 oz/½ cup Cheddar cheese,
    grated
A Village Salad (see page 310),
    to serve

1 Bring a saucepan of water to the boil and add a good pinch of salt. Add the aubergine slices and when the water is bubbling again, cook for 4 minutes. Drain in a colander.

2 Meanwhile, put the meat, onion and garlic in a saucepan and cook over a high heat, stirring, until the meat is no longer pink and all the grains are separate.

3 Add the tomatoes, cinnamon, herbs and some salt and pepper and cook over a high heat until boiling. Turn down the heat until the mixture is just bubbling round the edges and continue to cook, stirring occasionally, for 15 minutes. Taste and re-season if necessary.

4 Preheat the oven to 190°C/375°F/ gas mark 5.

5 Layer a third of the aubergines in a 1.5 litre/2½ pt/6 cup ovenproof dish. Spoon half the meat over. Repeat the layers, finishing with a layer of aubergine slices.

6 Break the egg in a bowl and add the yoghurt and little salt and pepper. Stir briskly with a fork or whisk until blended. Pour over the top of the aubergines and sprinkle with the cheese. Bake in the oven for about 40 minutes. Meanwhile, make the salad.

7 When the top of the moussaka is set and golden, serve with the salad.

Hearty Country Casserole

A beef Oxo cube is particularly good for the stock in this recipe.

SERVES 4

4 lamb's hearts

2 turnips, cut into small chunks

1 large onion, sliced

2 large carrots, thickly sliced

10 ml/2 tsp tomato purée (paste)

2.5 ml/½ tsp caster (superfine) sugar

600 ml/1 pt/2½ cups beef stock, made with 1 stock cube

Salt and freshly ground black pepper

1 large bay leaf

4 large potatoes, scrubbed

A little oil

Butter or margarine, to serve

1 Preheat the oven at 160°C/325°F/ gas mark 3.

2 Using scissors, snip off any pipes from the hearts. Cut the hearts in half, then cut the halves into thick slices.

3 Place in a flameproof casserole (Dutch oven) with the turnips, onion and carrots.

4 Mix the tomato purée and sugar into the stock. Pour into the casserole and add a little salt and pepper and the bay leaf.

5 Bring to the boil over a high heat, then cover with the lid and transfer to the oven.

6 Scrub the potatoes and prick all over with a fork. Rub the skins with a little oil and sprinkle with salt. Put on the shelf below the casserole. Cook everything for 3½ hours until the casserole is really tender and bathed in a rich sauce. Discard the bay leaf.

7 Cut a cross in the top of each potato and add a knob of butter or margarine. Serve with the casserole.

Popovers

This is a delicious way of using up a small amount of leftover roast meat. You can use up the gravy too, if there is any, if not see page 324.

SERVES 4

½ quantity of Yorkshire pudding batter (see page 325)

175 g/6 oz/1½ cups diced roast meat

175 g/6 oz diced cooked vegetables

2.5 ml/½ tsp dried oregano

Salt and freshly ground black pepper

45 ml/3 tbsp oil

Plain boiled potatoes, a green vegetable and gravy, to serve

1 Make up the batter. Preheat the oven to 220°C/425°F/gas mark 7.

2 Mix the meat and vegetables with the oregano and a little salt and pepper.

3 Pour the oil into 12 sections of a tartlet tin (patty pan). Heat in the oven until sizzling.

4 Add the meat and vegetables and return to the oven for 2 minutes.

5 Spoon the batter into the tins and cook for about 20 minutes until puffy, crisp and golden. Meanwhile, cook the potatoes and a green vegetable. Heat some gravy.

6 Serve the popovers hot with the potatoes, vegetable and gravy.

Cornish Pasties

*If you want to make your own pastry
(paste), use 1½ quantities of the
recipe on page 391.*

SERVES 4

1 carrot, finely chopped

¼ small swede (rutabaga), finely
   chopped

1 potato, finely chopped

1 small onion, finely chopped

100 g/4 oz/1 cup finely chopped
   cooked lamb

Salt and freshly ground black pepper

2.5 ml/½ tsp dried mixed herbs

350 g/12 oz ready-made shortcrust
   pastry (basic pie crust), thawed if
   frozen

A little oil, for greasing

A little milk, for glazing

Baked beans and brown table sauce,
   to serve

1 Mix the prepared vegetables with the
meat, some salt and pepper and the
herbs.

2 Roll out the pastry and cut into four
18 cm/7 in squares or circles.

3 Spoon the filling into the centre of
each. Add 10 ml/2 tsp water to each.
Brush the edges with water and draw
up over the filling. Press the edges well
together to seal and crimp the edge by
squeezing it across the fold at regular
intervals between your finger and
thumb.

4 Preheat the oven to 200°C/400°F/
gas mark 6. Lightly grease a baking
(cookie) sheet.

5 Transfer the pasties to the baking
sheet. Brush with a little milk to glaze.

6 Bake in the oven for 15 minutes, then
reduce the heat to 180°C/350°F/
gas mark 4 and continue cooking for
30 minutes until the vegetables are
tender and the pastry is golden brown.
About 5 minutes before they are
ready, heat the beans in a saucepan.

7 Serve the pasties hot with the baked
beans and brown table sauce.

Rustic Pan Pork Steaks

Start cooking the potatoes before you cook the pork.

SERVES 4

25 g/1 oz/2 tbsp butter or margarine
4 pork loin steaks
Salt and freshly ground black pepper
2.5 ml/½ tsp dried oregano
100 g/4 oz chestnut mushrooms, sliced
150 ml/¼ pt/⅔ cup chicken stock, made with ½ stock cube
1 large garlic clove, finely chopped
30 ml/2 tbsp chopped fresh parsley
Sauté Potatoes (see page 296) and French (green) beans, to serve

1 Melt the butter or margarine in a frying pan (skillet). Brown the steaks over a high heat for 2 minutes on each side. Season and sprinkle with the oregano.
2 Reduce the heat to moderate and fry (sauté) gently for about 6 minutes, turning once, until cooked through but still juicy. Remove from the pan and keep warm.
3 Add the mushrooms and fry for 2 minutes, stirring. Add the stock, turn up the heat and bring to the boil.
4 Return the pork to the pan, sprinkle the garlic and parsley over, turn down the heat to low, cover and cook gently for 5 minutes. Cook the beans.
5 Transfer the pork and mushrooms to warm plates with a draining spoon. Taste and re-season the liquid if necessary. Bring back to the boil and cook rapidly for 30 seconds, spoon over the pork and serve with the sauté potatoes and French beans.

Pork and Green Pepper Stir-fry with Oyster Sauce

SERVES 4

450 g/1 lb pork stir-fry meat
45 ml/3 tbsp cornflour (cornstarch)
Salt and freshly ground black pepper
45 ml/3 tbsp sunflower oil
1 bunch of spring onions (scallions), cut diagonally into 2.5 cm/1 in lengths
1 green (bell) pepper, cut into thin strips
50 g/2 oz oyster mushrooms, sliced
30 ml/2 tbsp medium-dry sherry
300 ml/½ pt/1¼ cups pork or chicken stock, made with 1 stock cube
15 ml/1 tbsp oyster sauce
A pinch of dried sage
250 g/9 oz/1 packet of Chinese egg noodles

1 Toss the pork in the cornflour, seasoned with a little salt and pepper.
2 Heat the oil in a wok or large frying pan (skillet). Add the spring onions, pepper and mushrooms and stir-fry over a high heat for 3 minutes. Remove from the pan with a draining spoon.
3 Add the pork and stir-fry until browned.
4 Return the vegetables to the pan and add the remaining ingredients. Bring back to the boil, turn down the heat to moderate and cook for about 8 minutes, stirring occasionally, until the pork is tender.
5 Meanwhile, cook the noodles according to the packet directions. Drain and pile in shallow, warm bowls. Spoon the stir-fry on top and serve.

The Easiest Chinese Pork Ribs

If you can't be bothered to grate ginger, you can buy a jar of ready-prepared fresh ginger.

SERVES 4

120 ml/4 fl oz/½ cup soy sauce
10 ml/2 tsp grated fresh root ginger
2 large garlic cloves, crushed
1.5 ml/¼ tsp chilli powder
10 ml/2 tsp Chinese five spice powder
1 kg/2¼ lb Chinese pork spare ribs
90 ml/6 tbsp sunflower oil
60 ml/4 tbsp clear honey
30 ml/2 tbsp water
Egg Fried Rice (see page 315) and a Beansprout Salad (see page 310)

1 Mix together the soy sauce, ginger, garlic and spice powders in a large container with a lid. Add the ribs and turn over to coat completely. Seal the lid and leave to marinate for several hours or preferably overnight in the fridge.
2 Preheat the oven to 180°C/350°F/ gas mark 4.
3 Heat the oil in a large flameproof casserole (Dutch oven). Lift the ribs out of the marinade and fry (sauté) over a high heat, a few at a time, until browned on all sides. Remove each batch while browning the remainder.
4 Put them all back in the pan with the remaining marinade, the honey and water. Cover with a lid and cook in the oven for 2 hours, turning occasionally until really tender. Meanwhile, cook the Egg Fried Rice and make the Beansprout Salad.
5 Serve the ribs hot with the rice and salad.

Pork and Bean Hot-pot

SERVES 4

225 g/8 oz/1½ cups dried black-eyed beans, soaked in cold water overnight
450 ml/¾ pt/2 cups water
1 beef stock cube
15 ml/1 tbsp olive oil
225 g/8 oz diced pork
1 large onion, chopped
2 carrots, diced
2 celery sticks, chopped
225 g/8 oz/1 small can of chopped tomatoes
15 ml/1 tbsp golden (light corn) syrup
2.5 ml/½ tsp dried sage
Salt and freshly ground black pepper
30 ml/2 tbsp snipped fresh chives, to garnish
Crusty bread, to serve

1 Drain the beans and place in a large, flameproof casserole (Dutch oven) with the water. Bring to the boil over a high heat and boil rapidly for 10 minutes.
2 Crumble in the stock cube and stir until dissolved.
3 Preheat the oven to 150°C/300°F/ gas mark 2.
4 While the oven is warming, heat the oil in a frying pan (skillet). Fry (sauté) the pork, onion, carrots and celery over a high heat for 2 minutes, stirring.
5 Add to the beans with the remaining ingredients. Bring back to the boil.
6 Cover and cook in the oven for 4 hours or until the beans are really tender and bathed in a rich sauce.
7 Taste and re-season if necessary. Sprinkle with chives and serve with crusty bread.

Pork Spring Rolls with Egg Fried Rice

SERVES 4

175 g/6 oz pork fillet, cut into very thin strips
15 ml/1 tbsp cornflour (cornstarch)
45 ml/3 tbsp sunflower oil
1 garlic clove, crushed
6 spring onions (scallions), finely chopped
4 mushrooms, thinly sliced
100 g/4 oz/2 cups beansprouts
50 g/2 oz/½ cup frozen peas, thawed
1.5 ml/¼ tsp ground ginger
45 ml/3 tbsp soy sauce
4 sheets of filo pastry (paste), thawed if frozen
Egg Fried Rice (see page 315), to serve

1 Mix the pork with the cornflour.
2 Heat 15 ml/1 tbsp of the oil in a frying pan (skillet) and fry (sauté) the pork over a high heat for 1 minute, stirring. Add all the remaining ingredients except for 15 ml/1 tbsp of the soy sauce and the pastry and stir-fry for 3 minutes. Remove from the heat.
3 Preheat the oven to 190°C/375°F/ gas mark 5.
4 Lay the pastry sheets on a work surface and fold into halves. Divide the pork mixture into four and spoon one in the centre of one edge of each sheet. Fold in the sides, then roll up.
5 Brush a baking (cookie) sheet with a little of the remaining oil and place the rolls on the sheet. Brush with a little more of the oil. Bake in the oven for about 20 minutes until golden brown. While they are baking, cook the rice.
6 Serve the rolls with Egg Fried Rice.

Pork and Prune Kebabs

SERVES 4

350 g/12 oz pork fillet, cut into cubes
100 g/4 oz no-need-to-soak stoned (pitted) prunes
1 red (bell) pepper, cut into large pieces
1 green pepper, cut into large pieces
45 ml/3 tbsp olive oil
15 ml/1 tbsp lemon juice
1 garlic clove, crushed
5 ml/1 tsp ground cumin
Salt and freshly ground black pepper
225 g/8 oz/1 cup wild rice mix
Minted Yoghurt with Cucumber (see page 340), to serve

1 Put the pork, prunes and peppers in a large, shallow dish.
2 Whisk together the oil, lemon juice, garlic, cumin and some salt and pepper. Pour over the meat mixture and stir well to coat. Leave to marinate for at least 2 hours, turning occasionally.
3 Cook the wild rice according to the packet directions (or see page 294). Drain in a colander. Put some water in the saucepan and sit the colander on top. Cover the rice with the saucepan lid and keep warm over a very gentle heat until ready to serve. Make the yoghurt and cucumber.
4 Preheat the grill (broiler). Thread the pork, prunes and peppers alternately on four metal skewers. Place on foil on a grill rack. Grill (broil) for about 8 minutes, turning occasionally and brushing with any remaining marinade until golden and cooked through.
5 Serve with the rice and Minted Yoghurt with Cucumber.

Boston Baked Beans

SERVES 4

225 g/8 oz/1⅓ cups dried haricot (navy) beans, soaked overnight in water
450 ml/¾ pt/2 cups water
1 beef stock cube
15 ml/1 tbsp sunflower oil
350 g/12 oz lean belly pork rashers, rinded and diced, discarding any bones
1 large onion, finely chopped
1 carrot, finely diced
4 tomatoes, skinned and chopped
15 ml/1 tbsp black treacle (molasses)
2.5 ml/½ tsp dried mixed herbs
A few drops of Tabasco sauce
5 ml/1 tsp light brown sugar
Salt and freshly ground black pepper
15 ml/1 tbsp chopped fresh parsley, to garnish
Crusty bread and a green salad (see (page 308), to serve

1 Drain the beans and place in a flameproof casserole (Dutch oven) with the measured water. Bring to the boil over a high heat and boil rapidly for 10 minutes. Stir in the stock cube until dissolved. Preheat the oven to 150°C/300°F/gas mark 2.
2 Meanwhile, heat the oil in a frying pan (skillet). Add the meat, onion and carrot and fry (sauté), stirring, over a high heat for 3 minutes until browned.
3 Tip into the beans and add all the remaining ingredients. Stir well.
4 Cover and cook in the oven for 4 hours or until the beans are soft and bathed in a rich sauce. While they are cooking, make the salad.
5 Taste and re-season the beans if

necessary. Sprinkle with the parsley and serve with crusty bread and the green salad.

Traditional Toad in the Hole

SERVES 4

1 quantity of Yorkshire pudding batter (see page 325)
60 ml/4 tbsp sunflower oil
8 thick pork sausages
Extra Tasty Gravy (see page 324), carrots and a green vegetable, to serve

1 Preheat the oven to 220°C/425°F/gas mark 7.
2 Make up the Yorkshire pudding batter.
3 Put the oil and sausages in a 28 x 18 cm/11 x 7 in shallow baking tin (pan). Cook on a shelf near the top of the oven for about 5 minutes until the oil is sizzling.
4 Pour in the batter and cook in the oven for about 35 minutes or until puffy, golden, crispy round the edges and set in the centre. Meanwhile, make the gravy and cook the vegetables. Serve the 'toad' with gravy, carrots and a green vegetable.

Sage and Onion Sausage Toad with Carrot Gravy

SERVES 4

1 quantity of Yorkshire pudding batter (see page 325)
8 thick pork sausages
30 ml/2 tbsp sunflower oil
3 onions, finely chopped
15 ml/1 tbsp chopped fresh sage
15 g/½ oz/1 tbsp butter or margarine
1 potato, grated
2 large carrots, grated
450 ml/¾ pt/2 cups vegetable or chicken stock
Salt and freshly ground black pepper
1 small bay leaf
Super Creamed Potatoes (see page 298) and peas, to serve

1 Make up the batter. Preheat the oven to 220°C/425°F/gas mark 7.

2 Put the sausages in an 18 x 28 cm/ 7 x 11 in shallow baking tin (pan) with the oil and two of the onions.

3 Heat on a shelf near the top of the oven for about 5 minutes until really sizzling.

4 Pour in the batter and sprinkle with the sage. Return to the oven and cook for about 35–40 minutes until risen, crisp and golden.

5 While it is cooking, melt the butter or margarine in a saucepan. Fry (sauté) the remaining onion, grated potato and carrots over a fairly high heat for 3 minutes, stirring until lightly golden. Start to make the creamed potatoes.

6 Add the stock to the vegetables with a little salt and pepper and the bay leaf. Bring back to the boil, reduce the heat until bubbling gently round the edges and cook for 10 minutes or until really soft. Discard the bay leaf.

7 Purée this mixture in a blender or food processor and return to the pan. Taste and re-season if necessary. Finish the creamed potatoes and cook the peas.

8 Serve the 'toad' with the carrot gravy, Super Creamed Potatoes and peas.

Bratwurst with Chunky Tomato and Sage Sauce

SERVES 4

1 onion, chopped
15 ml/1 tbsp olive oil
400 g/14 oz/1 large can of chopped tomatoes
1 large garlic clove, crushed
5 ml/1 tsp dried sage
2.5 ml/½ tsp made German mustard
Salt and freshly ground black pepper
5 ml/1 tsp light brown sugar
450 g/1 lb bratwurst
Crusty bread, to serve

1 Put the onion and oil in a saucepan and cook, stirring, over a fairly high heat for 2 minutes to soften.

2 Add the tomatoes, garlic, sage, mustard, a little salt and pepper and the sugar. Bring to the boil and cook for 5 minutes, stirring until pulpy.

3 Preheat the grill (broiler). Put the bratwurst on foil on a grill rack. Brush with a little of the tomato mixture.

4 Grill (broil) for 15 minutes, turning and brushing with the sauce mixture until golden and cooked through.

5 Heat the remaining sauce until bubbling again. Serve with the sausages with lots of crusty bread.

Pork Paprikash

If you like sauerkraut, it is very good served hot, sprinkled with caraway seeds, instead of the green salad.

SERVES 4

15 ml/1 tbsp sunflower oil

700 g/1½ lb diced pork

1 large onion, chopped

15 ml/1 tbsp paprika

200 g/7 oz/1 small can of pimientos, drained and cut into strips

150 ml/¼ pt/⅔ chicken stock, made with ½ stock cube

Salt and freshly ground black pepper

5 ml/1 tsp caster (superfine) sugar

350 g/12 oz tagliatelle

30 ml/2 tbsp plain (all-purpose) flour

30 ml/2 tbsp water

45 ml/3 tbsp single (light) cream

15 ml/1 tbsp chopped fresh parsley

A Green Salad (see page 308), to serve

1 Heat the oil in a saucepan, add the pork and brown over a high heat, stirring, for 3 minutes.

2 Add the onion and fry (sauté) for a few minutes until softened, then add the paprika and cook for 30 seconds.

3 Stir in the pimientos, stock, a little salt and pepper and the sugar.

4 Bring to the boil, then reduce the heat until just bubbling round the edges, cover and cook gently for 1 hour or until the pork is really tender.

5 Meanwhile, cook the tagliatelle according to the packet directions (or see page 293). Drain in a colander. Make the salad.

6 When the meat is tender, stir the flour with the water until smooth in a small bowl. Stir into the pan, turn up the heat, bring back to the boil and cook, stirring, for 2 minutes. Stir in the cream.

7 Pile the pasta on to warm plates and spoon the meat mixture over. Sprinkle with the parsley and serve with the green salad.

Ham, Broccoli and Tomato Gratin

SERVES 4

450 g/1 lb broccoli, cut into 8 florets

1 quantity of Cheese Sauce (see page 329)

8 thin slices of ham

150 ml/¼ pt/⅔ cup passata

2.5 ml/½ tsp dried basil

25 g/1 oz/¼ cup Cheddar cheese, grated

30 ml/2 tbsp cornflakes, crushed

1 Pour about 5 cm/2 in lightly salted water into a pan and bring it to the boil over a high heat. Add the broccoli and cook for 4 minutes. Drain in a colander.

2 Make the cheese sauce.

3 Wrap a slice of ham round each floret and arrange in a flameproof serving dish. Preheat the grill (broiler).

4 Spoon the passata over the broccoli and sprinkle with the basil.

5 Pour the cheese sauce over and sprinkle with the cheese and cornflakes.

6 Place under the grill until the top is golden and bubbling. Serve hot.

Monday Sweet and Sour Pork

Use up the Sunday roast in this tasty Oriental-style dish.

SERVES 4

1 quantity of Chunky Sweet and Sour Sauce (see page 332)

1 quantity of Egg Fried Rice (see page 315)

100 g/4 oz/1 cup self-raising (self-rising) flour

5 ml/1 tsp salt

150 ml/¼ pt/⅔ cup cold water

175 g/6 oz piece of roast pork, cut into very small cubes

Oil, for deep-frying

1 Prepare the Chunky Sweet and Sour Sauce first, then make the Egg Fried Rice. Once cooked, it can be reheated just before serving.

2 Mix the flour and salt in a bowl. Gradually stir in the water, using a wire whisk, to form a smooth, coating batter.

3 Add the pork and stir in.

4 Heat the oil for deep-frying in a large saucepan or deep-fat fryer to 190°C/375°F or until a cube of day-old bread browns in 30 seconds.

5 Use a small spoon to drop each coated cube of meat into the hot oil. Cook only half the quantity at a time. Cook for 3–4 minutes, turning every now and then, until brown, puffy and crisp.

6 Remove from the oil with a draining spoon (or remove the basket from the fryer) and drain the crispy balls on kitchen paper (paper towels). Keep warm while cooking the remainder.

7 Reheat the sauce and the rice and serve with the hot pork balls.

Salamagundi

Quantities are not important for this recipe. Simply use as much or as little as you like (or have in the cupboard!) of each ingredient for a colourful and tasty summer meal.

SERVES AS MANY AS YOU WANT

Shredded lettuce

Cooked roast meat (beef, lamb, pork, chicken, turkey or ham), cut into thin strips

Hard-boiled (hard-cooked) eggs (see page 76), cut into quarters

Cooked potatoes, cut into neat pieces, mixed with a little mayonnaise

Cooked peas and carrots, mixed with a little mayonnaise

Cooked French (green) beans

Pickled beetroot (red beets), diced, or whole baby ones

Pickled button (pearl) onions

Tomatoes, cut into wedges

Cucumber, sliced, sprinkled with vinegar and freshly ground black pepper

Canned sweetcorn (corn), drained

Canned pimientos, drained and cut into thin strips

Olives

Olive oil

White wine vinegar

Salt

Chopped fresh parsley

1 Put a bed of shredded lettuce on a large meat platter.

2 Arrange the meats and any of the other ingredients over the lettuce.

3 Trickle oil and vinegar over the surface and season with a little salt and freshly ground black pepper.

4 Sprinkle with chopped parsley.

Taj Mahal Pork

*Make the salad before you prepare
the main course.*

SERVES 4

4 pork chops
10 ml/2 tsp garam masala
30 ml/2 tbsp sunflower oil
425 g/15 oz/1 large can of pease
  pudding
20 ml/1½ tbsp curry paste
30 ml/2 tbsp sultanas (golden raisins)
Salt and freshly ground black pepper
4 individual naan breads
30 ml/2 tbsp desiccated (shredded)
  coconut
Wedges of lemon and sprigs of
  coriander (cilantro), to garnish
Mango chutney and a Mixed Salad
  (see page 308), to serve

1 Sprinkle the chops with the garam
masala. Heat the oil in a large frying
pan (skillet). Add the pork and brown
over a high heat for about 2 minutes
on each side until golden, then turn
down the heat to moderate and
continue to cook for about 3 minutes
on each side until cooked through.
Remove from the pan and keep warm.
2 Empty the pease pudding into the
frying pan and stir in the curry paste,
sultanas and seasoning. Heat through,
stirring gently.
3 Warm the naans under the grill
(broiler) or briefly in the microwave.
Place on warm plates. Spoon the
pease pudding mixture on top and
then put a pork chop on each.
4 Sprinkle the chops with the coconut
and garnish with wedges of lemon and
sprigs of coriander.

5 Serve straight away with mango
chutney and the mixed salad.

Alpine Gammon Grill

*Start cooking the potatoes before
you prepare the rest of the dish.*

SERVES 4

4 gammon steaks
10 ml/2 tsp Dijon mustard
225 g/8 oz/1 small can of pineapple
  slices, drained
30 ml/2 tbsp chopped gherkins
  (cornichons)
4 slices of Emmental (Swiss) cheese
1 tomato, sliced
Sauté Potatoes (see page 296) and
  peas, to serve

1 Preheat the grill (broiler). Snip the
edges of the gammon with scissors.
Place on foil on a grill rack.
2 Grill (broil) the gammon for 4 minutes
on each side. Cook the peas now.
3 Spread each slice of gammon with
Dijon mustard, then top with a slice of
pineapple and place the chopped
gherkins in the holes in the centres. Lay
a slice of cheese over, then a slice of
tomato.
4 Grill until the cheese melts and
bubbles and the fruit is hot. Serve with
the sauté potatoes and peas.

Photograph opposite: **Swiss Baked
Gammon and Potato Cake
(see page 195)**

Baked Smoked Gammon with Seeded Potatoes

Gammon joints, especially fresh ones, are sometimes very salty. To get rid of excess salt, put the joint in a pan of cold water, bring to the boil and then throw the water away.

SERVES 4–6

700 g/1½ lb small potatoes, scrubbed and halved

30 ml/2 tbsp olive oil

Salt

15 ml/1 tbsp sesame seeds

15 ml/1 tbsp caraway seeds

15 ml/1 tbsp poppy seeds

700 g/1½ lb smoked gammon joint (see note above)

300 ml/½ pt/1¼ cups medium-sweet cider

300 ml/½ pt/1¼ cups water

1 bay leaf

100 g/4 oz/1 cup dried apple rings

15 ml/1 tbsp clear honey

15 ml/1 tbsp wholegrain mustard

30 ml/2 tbsp cornflour (cornstarch)

French (green) beans, to serve

1 Preheat the oven to 190°C/375°F/ gas mark 5.

2 Put the potatoes in a roasting tin (pan). Add the oil and mix with your hands until they are coated completely. Sprinkle with salt and the seeds. Place on a shelf near the top of the oven.

3 Put the gammon in a small roasting tin (pan). Pour the cider and water around and add the bay leaf and apple rings.

4 Cover the tin with foil and place below the potatoes in the oven. Cook for 45 minutes. Turn the potatoes over.

5 Remove the foil and pull or cut off any rind from the gammon, then mix the honey and mustard together and spread over the fatty surface of the meat. Return to the oven and roast for a further 15 minutes or until cooked through. While the meat is cooking cook the beans. Transfer the meat and apple rings to a carving dish.

6 Mix the cornflour with 30 ml/2 tbsp water in a small bowl, then stir into the cooking juices. Place over a high heat, bring to the boil and cook for 1 minute, stirring all the time until thickened and fairly clear. Discard the bay leaf.

7 Carve the gammon into slices and serve with the apples, the sauce, the seeded potatoes and French beans.

Photograph opposite: **Chicken and Cranberry Pouches with green beans (see page 214)**

Creamy Ham and Mushroom Risotto

For a Plain Mushroom Risotto, omit the ham and double the quantity of the fungi.

SERVES 4–6

25 g/1 oz/2 tbsp butter or margarine
30 ml/2 tbsp olive oil
1 onion, finely chopped
100 g/4 oz button mushrooms, sliced
450 g/1 lb/2 cups risotto rice
1.5 litres/2½ pts/6 cups hot chicken stock, made with 2 stock cubes
100 g/4 oz/1 cup diced cooked ham
150 ml/¼ pt/⅔ cup single (light) cream
Salt and freshly ground black pepper
30 ml/2 tbsp chopped fresh parsley
Grated Parmesan cheese, to serve

1 Melt the butter or margarine with the oil in a heavy-based saucepan.
2 Add the onion and mushrooms and fry (sauté), stirring, over a moderate heat for 2 minutes.
3 Add the rice and cook, stirring, for 1 minute until glistening.
4 Pour on about 300 ml/½ pt/1¼ cups of the stock and cook gently, stirring occasionally, until the liquid is absorbed.
5 Keep adding the stock and simmering in this way until all the liquid is used and the rice is just tender but creamy. It will take about 20 minutes.
6 Stir the ham and cream into the rice and heat through, stirring. Do not boil. Add salt and pepper, to taste.
7 Pile on warm plates, sprinkle with parsley and serve with grated Parmesan cheese.

Sausage, Sage and Apple Burgers

SERVES 4

1 cooking (tart) apple, peeled, cored and sliced
1 small onion, finely chopped
2.5 ml/½ tsp dried sage
Caster (superfine) sugar
450 g/1 lb pork sausagemeat
15 ml/1 tbsp sunflower oil
60 ml/4 tbsp mayonnaise
Sliced tomato, cucumber and shredded lettuce, to serve
4 burger buns

1 Put the apple, onion, sage and 5 ml/1 tsp sugar in a small, non-stick saucepan. Cook, stirring, over a moderate heat until the apple is pulpy. Sweeten to taste with a little more sugar, if liked. Leave to cool.
2 Divide the sausagemeat into eight pieces. Flatten four pieces and spoon the apple mixture in the centre, keeping away from the edges. Top with the remaining sausagemeat and press the edges well together to seal.
3 Preheat the grill (broiler), if using.
4 Brush the burgers with oil and grill (broil) for about 4–5 minutes on each side until browned and cooked through, or fry (sauté) in the oil. Drain on kitchen paper (paper towels). Put the mayonnaise and a little salad in the burger buns and add the burgers.
5 Serve hot.

Swiss Baked Gammon and Potato Cake

SERVES 4

50 g/2 oz/¼ cup butter or margarine

450 g/1 lb potatoes, scrubbed and very thinly sliced

175 g/6 oz/1½ cups Gruyère (Swiss) cheese, grated

225 g/8 oz/2 cups finely diced cooked gammon

1 garlic clove, crushed

15 ml/1 tbsp chopped fresh parsley

10 ml/2 tsp chopped fresh sage

Salt and freshly ground black pepper

300 ml/½ pt/1¼ cups plain yoghurt

1 egg, beaten

Broccoli, to serve

1 Preheat the oven to 190°C/375°F/ gas mark 5. Grease a 1.2 litre/2½ pt/ 5 cup ovenproof dish with a little of the butter or margarine.

2 Layer the potatoes, cheese, gammon, garlic, parsley, sage and a little salt and pepper in the dish, putting small flakes of the remaining butter or margarine over each layer, and finishing with a layer of cheese.

3 Whisk the yoghurt and egg together and pour over the potatoes. Cover with foil.

4 Bake in the oven for 30 minutes, then remove the foil and bake for a further 30 minutes until the potatoes feel tender when a knife is inserted down through the centre and the top is golden. Meanwhile, cook the broccoli.

5 Serve the cake hot with the broccoli.

Sausage-stuffed Mushrooms

If you don't know how to seed a chilli, see Fiery Mussel Spaghettini, page 134.

SERVES 4

4 large open mushrooms

225 g/8 oz pork sausagemeat

100 g/4 oz/½ cup medium-fat soft cheese

1 small red chilli, seeded and chopped

30 ml/2 tbsp chopped fresh parsley

Freshly ground black pepper

30 ml/2 tbsp sunflower oil

Crusty bread and a Green Salad (see page 308), to serve

1 Peel the mushrooms by pulling off the outer skin in strips from the edge to the centre with your fingers. Remove the stalks and chop them finely.

2 Dry-fry the sausagemeat with the mushroom stalks in a saucepan for about 3 minutes, stirring over a fairly high heat, until cooked through and crumbly. Remove from the heat and stir in the cheese, chilli, parsley and some pepper, using a wooden spoon. Spoon the mixture into the mushroom caps, pressing down well.

3 Heat the oil in a frying pan (skillet) over a moderate heat. Add the mushrooms and fry (sauté) for 5 minutes until golden underneath.

4 Preheat the grill (broiler). Place the pan under the grill and cook for about 5 minutes until bubbling and lightly golden on top. Make the salad. Serve the mushrooms with crusty bread and the salad.

Pytt I Panna

This Swedish dish was originally made with leftover cooked meat but I prefer to make it with sausages.

SERVES 4

4 potatoes, scrubbed
25 g/1 oz/2 tbsp butter or margarine
30 ml/2 tbsp olive oil
1 large onion, thinly sliced
450 g/1 lb pork sausages, cut into chunks
6 rashers (slices) of streaky bacon, rinded and diced
10 ml/2 tsp Worcestershire sauce
Salt and freshly ground black pepper
4 eggs

1 Prick the potatoes and boil in water for about 20 minutes until tender. Alternatively, wrap in kitchen paper (paper towels) and cook in the microwave on High for about 4 minutes per potato. Cut into dice.
2 While the potatoes are cooking, heat half the butter or margarine and half the oil in a large frying pan (skillet). Add the onion, sausages and bacon and fry (sauté) for about 5–6 minutes, stirring over a high heat, until golden brown and cooked through. Remove from the pan with a draining spoon.
3 Add the potatoes to the frying pan. Fry for about 5 minutes, stirring, until golden brown. Return the sausage mixture to the pan and sprinkle over the Worcestershire sauce and some salt and pepper.
4 In a separate frying pan, heat the remaining oil and butter or margarine. Break the eggs one at a time into a cup and slide into the pan. Cook to your liking (see page 76).

5 Spoon the potato mixture on to warm plates and top each portion with a fried egg.

Warming Baltic Stew

SERVES 4

45 ml/3 tbsp olive oil
1 large leek, halved and chopped
1 large garlic clove, crushed
1 large onion, chopped
1 small green cabbage, shredded
1 smoked pork ring, thickly sliced
300 ml/½ pt/1¼ cups pork or chicken stock, made with 1 stock cube
3 large potatoes, cut into small pieces
5 ml/1 tsp dried thyme
Salt and freshly ground black pepper
10 ml/2 tsp poppy seeds
15 ml/1 tbsp snipped fresh chives
Rye bread, to serve

1 Heat the oil in a large saucepan. Add the leek, garlic and onion and fry (sauté) over a fairly high heat, stirring, for 3 minutes.
2 Stir the cabbage into the pot and cook for a further 2 minutes until beginning to soften slightly.
3 Add the remaining ingredients, stir well, turn down the heat until gently bubbling round the edges, cover and cook for 30 minutes until everything is tender.
4 Taste the stew and re-season if necessary. Ladle into warm bowls, sprinkle with the chives and serve with lots of rye bread.

Curried Turnovers

SERVES 4

350 g/12 oz puff pastry, thawed if frozen
1 small onion, finely chopped
1 small eating (dessert) apple, peeled and diced
15 g/½ oz/1 tbsp butter or margarine
25 g/1 oz/¼ cup frozen peas
50 g/2 oz/½ cup chopped cooked roast pork, lamb, chicken or beef
5 ml/1 tsp curry paste
15 ml/1 tbsp desiccated (shredded) coconut
5 ml/1 tsp tomato purée (paste)
15 ml/1 tbsp raisins
10 ml/2 tsp water
A little milk, to glaze
Mango chutney and a Mixed Salad (see page 308), to serve

1 Fry (sauté) the onion and apple in the butter or margarine for 2 minutes, stirring until softened.

2 Stir in all the remaining ingredients except the pastry and simmer for 5 minutes, stirring occasionally. Remove from the heat and leave to cool.

3 Preheat the oven to 200°C/400°F/ gas mark 6. Rinse a baking (cookie) sheet in cold water and leave damp.

4 Cut the pastry into quarters. Roll out each piece to (approximately) 18 cm/ 7 in squares.

5 Divide the filling between the centres. Brush the edges with water and fold the pastry over to form triangles.

6 Pinch the edges well together to seal all round and make a small hole in the top to allow steam to escape. Transfer to the baking sheet. Brush with a little milk to glaze.

7 Bake in the oven for 15–20 minutes until crisp and golden brown. Make the salad while they are cooking.

8 Serve the turnovers warm or cold with mango chutney and the salad.

Kidneys Turbigo

SERVES 4

45 ml/3 tbsp olive oil

2 slices of white bread, cut into triangles

8 lambs' kidneys

40 g/1½ oz/3 tbsp butter or margarine

4 chipolata sausages, each cut into 3 pieces

3 onions, cut into quarters

30 ml/2 tbsp plain (all-purpose) flour

300 ml/½ pt/1¼ cups beef stock, made with 1 stock cube

90 ml/6 tbsp dry white wine

10 ml/2 tsp tomato purée (paste)

15 ml/1 tbsp brandy

2.5 ml/½ tsp dried mixed herbs

Salt and freshly ground black pepper

15 ml/1 tbsp chopped fresh parsley

Super Creamed Potatoes (see page 298) and spring (collard) greens, to serve

1 Heat the oil in a large frying pan (skillet). Add the bread and fry (sauté) over a high heat on both sides until golden brown. Drain on kitchen paper (paper towels) and keep warm until ready to serve.

2 Cut the kidneys into halves, snip the cores out with scissors, then cut into bite-sized pieces.

3 Melt the butter or margarine in the same frying pan. Add the kidneys, sausage pieces and onions and fry, stirring, until golden brown all over. Lift out of the pan with a draining spoon.

4 Stir the flour into the remaining fat and juices in the pan. Remove from the heat and gradually stir in the stock, using a wire whisk to prevent lumps. Stir in the wine, tomato purée, brandy, herbs and some salt and pepper.

5 Return to the heat and bring to the boil, stirring all the time. Return the kidney mixture to the pan and turn down the heat until just bubbling very gently. Cook, stirring occasionally, for 20 minutes. Taste and re-season if necessary. Meanwhile, cook the potatoes and about 10 minutes before everything is ready, prepare and cook the greens.

6 Sprinkle the kidneys with the parsley and serve with the Super Creamed Potatoes and spring greens.

Devilled Kidneys

SERVES 4

225 g/8 oz/1 cup long-grain rice

8 lambs' kidneys

50 g/2 oz/¼ cup butter or margarine

4 rashers (slices) of streaky bacon, rinded and diced

6 cup mushrooms, sliced

5 ml/1 tsp curry paste

5 ml/1 tsp made English mustard

30 ml/2 tbsp tomato purée (paste)

15 ml/1 tbsp light brown sugar

15 ml/1 tbsp Worcestershire sauce

15 ml/1 tbsp water

French (green) beans, to serve

1 Cook the rice according to the packet directions (or see page 294). Drain in a colander. Put some water in the saucepan and sit the colander on top. Cover the rice with the saucepan lid and keep warm over a very gentle heat until ready to serve.
2 Cut the kidneys into halves, snip out the cores with scissors and cut into bite-sized pieces, discarding the skin, if necessary. Put the beans on to cook.
3 Heat the butter or margarine in a large frying pan (skillet) over a fairly high heat. Add the kidneys, bacon and mushrooms and fry (sauté), stirring for 3 minutes.
4 Add the remaining ingredients and cook, stirring, for about 4 minutes until the kidneys are cooked through and bathed in sauce.
5 Spoon the rice on to warm plates and top with the kidneys. Serve with French beans.

Sherried Kidneys with Fresh Sage

Put the potatoes on to boil before you prepare the kidneys and cook the spinach while the kidneys are simmering.

SERVES 4

4 pigs' kidneys

25 g/1 oz/2 tbsp butter or margarine

2 large onions, halved and sliced

100 g/4 oz button mushrooms, sliced

10 ml/2 tsp chopped fresh sage

45 ml/3 tbsp double (heavy) cream

15 ml/1 tbsp medium-dry sherry

Salt and freshly ground black pepper

4 fresh sage leaves and 4 black olives, to garnish

New potatoes and spinach, to serve

1 Halve the kidneys and snip out the cores with scissors. Cut into bite-sized pieces.
2 Melt the butter or margarine in a frying pan (skillet). Add the onions and mushrooms and fry (sauté) over a fairly high heat for 3 minutes.
3 Add the kidneys and fry for 2 minutes, stirring to brown all over.
4 Cover the pan with a lid or foil, turn down the heat to low and cook very gently for 8 minutes until the kidneys are tender.
5 Stir in the chopped sage, the cream and sherry, turn up the heat and allow to bubble for 1 minute. Season to taste.
6 Spoon the kidneys on to warm plates, garnish each with a sage leaf and an olive and serve with the new potatoes and spinach.

Liver and Onion Hot-pot

SERVES 4

450 g/1 lb pig's liver, cut into chunks
30 ml/2 tbsp milk
40 g/1½ oz/3 tbsp butter or margarine
3 large onions, sliced
1 eating (dessert) apple, peeled, cored and sliced
15 ml/1 tbsp plain (all-purpose) flour
450 ml/¾ pt/2 cups chicken stock, made with 1 stock cube
5 ml/1 tsp dried sage
Salt and freshly ground black pepper
450 g/1 lb potatoes, scrubbed and sliced
Broad (fava) beans and baby carrots, to serve

1 Soak the liver in the milk for 15 minutes. Drain.
2 Preheat the oven to 190°C/375°F/ gas mark 5.
3 Heat 25 g/1 oz/2 tbsp of the butter or margarine in a flameproof casserole (Dutch oven). Fry (sauté) the onions over a fairly high heat for 3 minutes, stirring, until lightly golden. Add the liver and fry for 2 minutes.
4 Stir in all the remaining ingredients except the potatoes. Bring to the boil, stirring.
5 Lay the potatoes over the top and scatter with small pieces of the remaining butter or margarine.
6 Cover the casserole with a lid or foil and bake in the oven for 30 minutes. Remove the lid or foil and cook for a further 30 minutes or until cooked through and the top is golden. When almost ready, cook the vegetables and serve with the hot-pot.

Peppered Liver

You can buy crushed peppercorns, but freshly pounded whole ones have much more fragrance. Use a pestle and mortar or improvise with the end of a rolling pin in a small bowl. Cook the potatoes before you start cooking the liver and keep them warm over a very gentle heat. Put the broccoli on to boil as you start cooking the liver.

SERVES 4

15 ml/1 tbsp plain (all-purpose) flour
30 ml/2 tbsp coarsely crushed black peppercorns
350 g/12 oz lamb's liver, cut into very thin slices
25 g/1 oz/2 tbsp butter or margarine
30 ml/2 tbsp olive oil
150 ml/¼ pt/⅔ cup red wine
15 ml/1 tbsp tomato purée (paste)
5 ml/1 tsp caster (superfine) sugar
A pinch of salt
Super Creamed Potatoes (see page 298) and broccoli, to serve

1 Mix the flour and peppercorns and dip the liver in to coat each side.
2 Heat the butter or margarine and oil in a large frying pan (skillet). Fry (sauté) the liver over a high heat on one side to brown. Turn over and cook just until droplets of juice appear on the surface. Remove from the pan immediately and keep warm.
3 Stir the wine, tomato purée, sugar and a little salt into the juices in the pan. Cook, stirring, until bubbling. Thin with a little water, if necessary.
4 Transfer the liver to warm plates. Spoon the juices over and serve hot with the potatoes and broccoli.

Poultry Main Courses

Chicken is probably one of the most versatile foods we have and certainly one of the most popular. In this chapter, you'll find out how to turn it into a wonderful array of dishes, from firm favourites like Chicken Kiev to extravagant creations like Chicken Aubergine and Pine Nut Casserole. There are also some delicious recipes for turkey and duck and you can learn how to roast a pheasant or goose too. Page references for suggested sauces, accompaniments and side dishes are given, plus instructions on when to prepare them, but remember to look in the vegetables section on pages 291–92 for full instructions on how to cook individual vegetables.

To joint a chicken (or other bird)

1   Gently pull one leg away from the body and cut through the skin and flesh down to the joint.
2   Using your hands, break the leg joint, then cut through the remaining flesh and remove the leg portion.
3   Repeat with the other side.
4   Cut down one side of the breastbone, easing the breast meat away from the carcass. Find the wing joint and cut through, then cut away the remaining skin and remove the breast portion. Repeat with the other side. You will now have four large portions.
5   For eight portions, separate the leg and thigh by cutting through the joint and separate the breast and wing by cutting through the wing joint.

Traditional roast poultry

There are lots of recipes in this chapter, explaining how to roast different birds. To learn how to cook a complete roast poultry Sunday lunch, see the step-by-step instructions on pages 157–58 in the Meat Main Meals chapter.

Traditional accompaniments to roast poultry and game

Roast chicken: Parsley and thyme stuffing, bread sauce
Roast turkey: Sausagemeat stuffing or sausage and bacon rolls, parsley and thyme stuffing, bread sauce, cranberry sauce
Roast duck: Sage and onion stuffing, apple sauce
Roast pheasant or other game: Game chips, buttered crumbs, redcurrant jelly (clear conserve)
See also pages 321–27.

Olive-roast Chicken with Garlic and Potatoes

SERVES 4

900 g/2 lb potatoes, scrubbed and cut
   into chunky pieces
1 oven-ready chicken, about 1.5 kg/3 lb
2 garlic cloves, peeled and halved
1 large sprig of rosemary
Salt and freshly ground black pepper
75 ml/5 tbsp olive oil
75 g/3 oz stoned (pitted) green olives
300 ml/½ pt/1¼ cups chicken stock,
   made with 1 stock cube
Mangetout (snow peas), to serve

1 Preheat the oven to 190°C/375°F/
gas mark 5.

2 Put the potatoes in a saucepan with
just enough lightly salted water to
cover them. Bring to the boil over a
high heat and cook for 3 minutes.
Drain in a colander.

3 Remove the giblets from the chicken
if necessary. Pull off any fat around the
inside of the rim of the body cavity.
Wipe inside and out with kitchen paper
(paper towels).

4 Put the two halved garlic cloves
inside the bird with the sprig of

rosemary. Place in a roasting tin (pan).
Season the bird with salt and pepper.
Rub all over the breast with 30 ml/
2 tbsp of the oil.

5 Arrange the potatoes around the
bird and pour the remaining oil over.
Turn the potatoes to coat in the oil.

6 Roast in the oven for 45 minutes.
Turn the potatoes over and scatter
with the olives. Roast for a further
45 minutes or until tender, golden and
the juices from the bird run clear when
the thigh is pierced with a skewer.

7 Just before removing the chicken
from the oven, put the mangetout on
to cook. Transfer the chicken, potatoes
and olives to a warm carving dish and
keep warm.

8 Pour the stock into the tin, and bring
to the boil over a high heat, on top of
the stove, scraping any sediment off the
base of the tin with a spoon. Continue
to boil rapidly for 2–3 minutes until the
liquid has evaporated slightly and the
flavour is concentrated. Season to taste.
Pour into a sauceboat. Carve the
chicken or cut into quarters (see page
202). Serve with the gravy, potatoes
and olives and mangetout.

Butter-roast Chicken and Potatoes

SERVES 4

900 g/2 lb potatoes, cut into chunks
1 oven-ready chicken, about 1.5 kg/3 lb
Salt and freshly ground black pepper
15 ml/1 tbsp plain (all-purpose) flour
75 g/3 oz/⅓ cup butter, softened
1 quantity of Mushroom Sauce (see page 328) and peas, to serve

1 Put the potatoes in a pan and add just enough lightly salted water to cover them. Bring to the boil and cook for 3 minutes. Drain in a colander and return to the pan.

2 With the lid on the pan, give the pan a good shake to roughen the edges of the potatoes.

3 Preheat the oven to 190°C/375°F/ gas mark 5.

4 Remove the giblets from the chicken if necessary. Pull out any fat from inside the rim of the body cavity. Wipe inside and out with kitchen paper (paper towels).

5 Place in a roasting tin (pan). Season with salt and pepper. Sprinkle the breast with flour. Smear all over the breast with 50 g/2 oz/¼ cup of the butter.

6 Arrange the potatoes around the bird. Cut the remaining butter into small flakes and scatter over the potatoes. Roast in the oven for 1½ hours, spooning the fat over the breast occasionally and turning the potatoes over halfway through cooking.

7 Make the sauce and cook the peas. Cut the bird into quarters or carve. Serve with mushroom sauce and peas.

Traditional Roast Turkey

SERVES 10–12

1 oven-ready turkey, about 4.5 kg/10 lb
2 quantities of any stuffing (see pages 321–3)
Sunflower oil or softened butter or margarine
Salt and freshly ground black pepper
Bacon-wrapped Chipolatas (see page 419), Bread Sauce (see page 326), Cranberry Sauce (see page 327), gravy (see page 323), roast potatoes (see page 295), Brussels sprouts and carrots, to serve

1 Preheat the oven to 190°C/375°F/ gas mark 5.

2 Remove the giblets from the bird if necessary. Wipe the turkey inside and out with kitchen paper (paper towels). Make up the chosen stuffing and push it into the neck end. Secure the neck skin with a skewer.

3 Tuck the wing tips under the bird if necessary. Rub the breast with oil or softened butter or margarine. Place upside-down in a roasting tin (pan) and rub oil, butter or margarine over the base of the bird. Season with a little salt. Cover with foil. Prepare the Bacon-wrapped Chipolatas and put on the top shelf of the oven. Put the bird in on a lower shelf.

4 Remove the sausages after about 30 minutes. They can be reheated later.

5 While the sausages and turkey are cooking, prepare the roast potatoes.

6 After the bird has been in the oven for 1½ hours, turn it over and sprinkle with salt. Put the roast potatoes in the top of the oven now. Roast the turkey, uncovered, for a further 1½ hours, during which you can make the sauces.

7 The turkey should now be cooked: check that the skin is golden brown and the juices run clear when the thickest part of the thigh is pierced with a skewer. Transfer to a carving dish and leave to rest for 10 minutes. Meanwhile, put the sausages back in the oven to heat through while you make the gravy and cook the sprouts and carrots.

8 Carve the bird and serve with all the accompaniments.

Traditional Roast Duck

If you don't have any giblet stock, use the same quantity of vegetable water or chicken stock, made with 1 stock cube.

SERVES 4

1 oven-ready duck, about 2 kg/4½ lb
1 small onion
A few fresh sage leaves or 2.5 ml/½ tsp dried sage
Salt and freshly ground black pepper
1 quantity of Sage and Onion Stuffing (see page 321)
1 quantity of Apple Sauce (see page 328)
45 ml/3 tbsp plain (all-purpose) flour
450 ml/¾ pt/2 cups giblet stock (see page 323)
A little gravy block or browning
Roast potatoes (see page 295), peas and carrots

1 Preheat the oven to 220°C/425°F/ gas mark 7.

2 Wipe the duck inside and out with kitchen paper (paper towels). Prick all over with a fork. Put the onion and sage in the body cavity.

3 Place on a rack or small upturned plate in a roasting tin (pan). Sprinkle with salt and pepper. Prepare the potatoes for roasting.

4 Put the potatoes on a shelf at the top of the oven, with the duck on a lower shelf. Make the stuffing and place in a greased, shallow dish beneath the duck, to cook at the same time.

5 Cook for 1 hour, then turn down the heat to 180°C/350°F/gas mark 4 and cook for a further 30 minutes until the duck is really tender and the potatoes are golden.

6 Meanwhile, make the apple sauce.

7 Cook the peas and carrots now. Transfer the duck to a carving dish. Pour off all but 15 ml/1 tbsp of the fat but leave all the juices in the pan. Stir in the flour with a wire whisk and cook, stirring, over a moderate heat for 2 minutes. Remove from the heat and gradually stir in the stock. Return to the heat, bring to the boil and cook for 2 minutes, stirring. Add gravy block or browning and seasoning, to taste.

8 Carve the duck or cut into quarters (see page 202) and serve with all the accompaniments.

Roast Pheasant

If you want a large pheasant, ask for a cock bird. Traditionalists prefer to buy a brace – or pair – of birds. If you do, cook them side by side, using double the quantities of ingredients. The cooking time remains the same.

SERVES 2–4

1 oven-ready pheasant

Salt and freshly ground black pepper

1 whole clove

1 small onion

50 g/2 oz/¼ cup butter or margarine, softened

4 rashers (slices) of streaky bacon

30 ml/2 tbsp plain (all-purpose) flour

Buttered Crumbs (see page 325), Game Chips (see page 326), gravy (see page 323), redcurrant jelly (clear conserve) and broccoli, to serve

1 Preheat the oven to 200°C/400°F/ gas mark 6.

2 Wipe the bird inside and out with kitchen paper (paper towels) and season inside and out.

3 Press the clove into the onion and place inside the bird. Put the bird in a roasting tin (pan) and smear the breast all over with the butter or margarine. Lay the bacon rashers on top.

4 Roast in the oven for 30 minutes. Remove the bacon and spoon the juices and butter or margarine in the tin over the breast. Sprinkle the breast all over with the flour and baste with more butter or margarine. Return to the oven for a further 20–30 minutes until the breast is golden brown.

5 Make the Buttered Crumbs and Game Chips and cook the broccoli. Transfer the pheasant to a serving dish. Make the gravy. Carve the bird and serve with all the accompaniments.

Roast Goose

Goose can be tough, so needs long, slow cooking. if you want to serve it for lunch, you'll have to get up early!

SERVES 8–10

1 oven-ready goose, about 4.5 g/10 lb

2 quantities of Sage and Onion Stuffing (see page 321)

Salt and freshly ground black pepper

25 g/1 oz/2 tbsp butter or margarine

1 chicken stock cube

900 ml/1½ pts/3¾ cups water

Apple Sauce (see page 328), new potatoes, peas and carrots, to serve

1 Preheat the oven to 180°C/350°F/ gas mark 4.

2 Wipe the goose inside and out with kitchen paper (paper towels). Prick all over with a fork.

3 Pack some of the stuffing into the neck end of the goose. Secure with a skewer and place the bird on a rack in a roasting tin (pan). Rub the skin well with salt and pepper. Cover the breast with foil greased with a little of the butter or margarine.

4 Put the remaining stuffing in a shallow, ovenproof dish, greased with a little of the remaining butter or margarine. Cut the last of the butter or margarine into small pieces and scatter over the stuffing surface.

5 Put the goose on the bottom shelf of the oven to roast for 4½–5 hours. After 1 hour, spoon off any fat in the roasting tin. Dissolve the stock cube in the measured water and pour the warmed stock over the bird. Spoon the juices over the breast every 30 minutes, replacing the foil each time. After 2½ hours, remove the foil from the goose and put the dish of stuffing in the oven. Cook for a further 2 –2½ hours until the goose is tender with brown, crispy skin and the stuffing is well browned and cooked through.

6 An hour before the end of the cooking time, make the apple sauce and prepare and cook the vegetables.

7 Transfer the goose to a warm carving dish. Spoon off as much fat as possible from the liquid left in the roasting tin and boil the liquid rapidly until slightly thickened. Taste and re-season if necessary. Carve and serve with the stuffing, gravy, apple sauce, new potatoes, peas and carrots.

Grilled Chicken with Hot Olive Sauce

SERVES 4

45 ml/3 tbsp olive oil
1 onion, finely chopped
2 garlic cloves, crushed
1 green (bell) pepper, chopped
400 g/14 oz/1 large can of chopped
    tomatoes
75 g/3 oz stuffed olives, sliced
2.5 ml/½ tsp cayenne
A few drops of Worcestershire sauce
Salt and freshly ground black pepper
4 chicken portions
225 g/8 oz/1⅓ cups couscous
400 ml/14 fl oz/1¾ cups boiling water

1 Heat 30 ml/2 tbsp of the oil in a saucepan and fry (sauté) the onion, garlic and pepper for 4 minutes over a fairly high heat until soft and golden.

2 Add the tomatoes, olives, cayenne and Worcestershire sauce and season lightly. Bring to the boil, then turn down the heat to moderate and cook for 5 minutes until pulpy. Keep warm.

3 Brush the chicken with the remaining oil. Place on foil on a grill (broiler) rack. Season with salt and pepper and grill (broil) for about 20 minutes, turning often until well browned and cooked through, brushing with oil as necessary.

4 Meanwhile, put the couscous in a saucepan and stir in the boiling water until thoroughly mixed. Leave to stand for 5 minutes, then cook over a low heat for a further 5 minutes until tender and fluffy, stirring frequently.

5 Spoon on to warm plates, top with the chicken and sauce and serve.

Lemon Chicken

SERVES 4

4 skinless chicken breasts
300 ml/½ pt/1¼ cups chicken stock, made with 1 stock cube
Finely grated rind and juice of 1 small lemon
30 ml/2 tbsp clear honey
1 bay leaf
Salt and freshly ground black pepper
225 g/8 oz/1 cup wild rice mix
15 ml/1 tbsp cornflour (cornstarch)
15 ml/1 tbsp cold water
30 ml/2 tbsp double (heavy) cream
30 ml/2 tbsp chopped fresh parsley
Leaf spinach, to serve

1 Put the chicken breasts in a flameproof casserole dish (Dutch oven). Add the stock, lemon rind and juice, honey, bay leaf, salt and lots of pepper. Bring to the boil over a high heat, then reduce the heat to fairly low, cover and cook very gently for 15 minutes.
2 Meanwhile, cook the rice according to the packet directions (or see page 294), then drain in a colander. Cook the spinach.
3 Remove the bay leaf from the casserole, then carefully lift out the chicken breasts.
4 Mix the cornflour with the water in a cup or small bowl. Stir into the cooking juices. Bring to the boil over a high heat and cook for 1 minute, stirring all the time.
5 Stir in the cream. Return the chicken to the sauce and heat through. Sprinkle the parsley over and serve with wild rice mix and leaf spinach.

One-pot Chicken

This is a delicious, moist way of cooking a chicken. The remaining stock can be served as a soup and any leftover chicken is delicious cold. Make some parsley sauce (see page 328) to accompany the finished dish, if liked.

SERVES 4

1 oven-ready chicken, about 1.5 kg/3 lb
10 ml/2 tsp salt
Freshly ground black pepper
600 ml/1 pt/2½ cups water
1 bouquet garni sachet
2 onions, quartered
2 carrots, cut into chunks
2 leeks, well-washed and cut into chunks
1 parsnip, cut into chunks
8–12 fairly small waxy potatoes, scrubbed

1 Remove any giblets from the chicken and pull off any fat from just inside the rim of the body cavity.
2 Place in a large saucepan with the salt, a good grinding of pepper and the bouquet garni sachet. Heat rapidly until boiling. Turn down the heat until just bubbling round the edges, cover with a lid and cook for 30 minutes.
3 Add all the prepared vegetables around the chicken. Bring quickly back to the boil, turn down the heat again, cover and cook gently for 30 minutes until the vegetables and chicken are tender.
4 Lift the bird and vegetables out of the stock. Discard the bouquet garni. Cut the chicken into pieces and serve with the vegetables and a little of the broth.

Cheesy Chicken, Ham and Tomato Grill

SERVES 4

225 g/8 oz tagliatelle
25 g/1 oz/2 tbsp butter or margarine
Freshly ground black pepper
4 skinless chicken breasts
30 ml/2 tbsp sunflower or olive oil
4 slices of lean ham
4 tomatoes, sliced
8 fresh basil leaves, torn
50 g/2 oz/½ cup Mozzarella cheese, grated

1 Cook the pasta according to the packet directions (or see page 293). Drain in a colander and return to the pan. Add the butter or margarine and stir well until every strand is coated. Add a good grinding of pepper.
2 Meanwhile, preheat the grill (broiler).
3 Put the fillets one at a time into a plastic bag and beat with a rolling pin or meat mallet to flatten. Brush with half the oil.
4 Place on foil on the grill rack and grill (broil) for 3 minutes. Turn over, brush with the remaining oil and grill for a further 3 minutes.
5 Top each with a slice of ham, then tomato slices, then the basil. Cover with the cheese and grill for about 2 minutes until the cheese is melted and bubbling.
6 Spoon the buttered pasta on warm plates, add the chicken and serve.

Mild Spiced Chicken and Mushroom Casserole

SERVES 4

25 g/1 oz/2 tbsp butter or margarine
4 chicken portions
1 onion, finely chopped
100 g/4 oz button mushrooms, sliced
15 ml/1 tbsp mild curry paste
295 g/10½ oz/1 medium can of condensed mushroom soup
225 g/8 oz/1 cup long-grain rice
A leafy green vegetable, to serve

1 Preheat the oven to 180°C/350°F/ gas mark 4.
2 Melt the butter or margarine in a flameproof casserole (Dutch oven) over a high heat.
3 Add the chicken and fry (sauté) on all sides until browned. Remove with a draining spoon.
4 Add the onion and mushrooms and fry, stirring, for 3 minutes to soften.
5 Add the curry paste and cook, stirring, for 30 seconds.
6 Stir in the soup until well blended. Add the chicken and spoon the soup mixture over them.
7 Cover the casserole with a lid and cook in the oven for 1¼ hours until tender and bathed in a rich sauce.
8 Meanwhile, cook the rice according to the packet directions (or see page 294) and drain in a colander. Cook a green vegetable. Serve the casserole with the rice and greens.

Coq au Vin

It is traditional to use whole baby onions in this recipe, but you can use a roughly chopped large onion instead.

SERVES 4

5 ml/1 tbsp olive oil

15 g/½ oz/1 tbsp butter or margarine

4 chicken portions

2 rashers (slices) of streaky bacon, rinded and diced

12 button (pearl) onions

45 g/3 tbsp plain (all-purpose) flour

300 ml/½ pt/1¼ cups red wine

150 ml/¼ pt/⅔ cup chicken stock, made with ½ stock cube

100 g/4 oz button mushrooms

Salt and freshly ground black pepper

15 ml/1 tbsp brandy

1 bouquet garni sachet

15 ml/1 tbsp chopped fresh parsley, to garnish

French bread and a Green Salad (see page 308), to serve

1 Preheat the oven to 180°C/350°F/ gas mark 4.

2 Heat the oil with the butter or margarine in a large, flameproof casserole (Dutch oven) over a fairly high heat. Brown the chicken portions on all sides and remove.

3 Add the bacon and onions and cook quickly, stirring, until lightly browned.

4 Add the flour and cook for 1 minute, stirring. Remove from the heat and stir in the wine and stock. Return to the heat and bring to the boil, stirring, then put the chicken back into the casserole and add the mushrooms. Season and add the brandy and bouquet garni.

5 Cover and cook in the oven for 1 hour. Meanwhile, make the salad.

6 When the chicken is cooked, stir gently, remove the bouquet garni sachet, taste and re-season if necessary.

7 Sprinkle with chopped parsley and serve hot with French bread and the green salad.

Chicken and Corn Pasta Bake

SERVES 4

225 g/8 oz pasta shapes

1 quantity of Quick Tomato Sauce (see page 335)

175 g/6 oz/1½ cups roughly chopped cooked chicken

200 g/7 oz/1 small can of sweetcorn (corn)

225 g/8 oz frozen spinach, thawed (optional)

50 g/2 oz/½ cup Cheddar cheese, grated

1 Cook the pasta according to the packet directions (or see page 293). Drain and return to the saucepan. While the pasta is cooking, make the tomato sauce.

2 Preheat the oven to 190°C/375°F/ gas mark 5.

3 Stir the sauce into the pasta with the chicken.

4 Spoon half into an ovenproof serving dish. Top with the sweetcorn and spinach, if using.

5 Top with the remaining pasta and sprinkle with the cheese.

6 Bake in the oven for about 30 minutes or until bubbling and turning golden.

Sherried Chicken Casserole

Prepare the potatoes and cook in the oven at the same time as the casserole.

SERVES 4

30 ml/2 tbsp sunflower oil

4 chicken portions

1 large onion, finely chopped

100 g/4 oz button mushrooms, quartered

15 ml/1 tbsp cornflour (cornstarch)

400 g/14 oz/1 large can of chopped tomatoes

30 ml/2 tbsp medium-dry sherry

Salt and freshly ground black pepper

1 bouquet garni sachet

Jacket-baked Potatoes (see page 296) and peas, to serve

1 Preheat the oven to 180°C/350°F/ gas mark 4.

2 Heat the oil in a flameproof casserole (Dutch oven) over a fairly high heat. Add the chicken portions and cook for about 5 minutes, until browned on all sides. Remove from the pan with a draining spoon.

3 Add the onion and fry (sauté) for 2 minutes, stirring. Add the mushrooms and cook, stirring, for 1 minute. Remove from the heat.

4 Sprinkle in the cornflour and stir well. Stir in the can of tomatoes and the sherry. Bring back to the boil over a high heat, stirring.

5 Return the chicken to the casserole. Season and add the bouquet garni.

6 Cover and cook in the oven for 1½ hours until the chicken is really tender.

7 Just before the end of the cooking time, put the peas on to boil. Stir the cooked casserole gently. Taste and re-season if necessary. Discard the bouquet garni and serve with the jacket-baked potatoes and peas.

Monday Chicken Curry

Warm the naan bread under the grill (broiler) while the chicken is cooking.

SERVES 4

1 onion, chopped

1 garlic clove, crushed

30 ml/2 tbsp sunflower oil

175 g/6 oz button mushrooms, halved

15 ml/1 tbsp curry paste

450 ml/¾ pt/2 cups chicken stock, made with 1 stock cube

100 g/4 oz creamed coconut, cut into pieces

45 ml/3 tbsp raisins

225 g/8 oz/2 cups diced cooked chicken

175 g/6 oz cooked leftover vegetables, chopped if necessary

Salt and freshly ground black pepper

30 ml/2 tbsp chopped fresh coriander (cilantro)

Naan bread, to serve

1 Cook the onion and garlic in the oil in a saucepan for 3 minutes until golden.

2 Add the mushrooms and cook for 1 minute.

3 Add the curry paste and stock. Bring to the boil and stir in the coconut and raisins. Turn down the heat to moderate and cook, stirring, until the coconut dissolves.

4 Add the chicken and vegetables and, when bubbling gently, turn down the heat to low, cover and cook for 10 minutes. Season to taste and stir in the coriander. Serve with naan bread.

Chicken, Aubergine and Pine Nut Casserole

SERVES 4

1 large aubergine (eggplant), sliced
30 ml/2 tbsp olive oil
4 chicken portions
1 onion, finely chopped
50 g/2 oz/½ cup pine nuts
15 ml/1 tbsp tomato purée (paste)
15 ml/1 tbsp lemon juice
300 ml/½ pt/1¼ cups chicken stock, made with 1 stock cube
2.5 ml/½ tsp dried oregano
5 ml/1 tsp clear honey
Salt and freshly ground black pepper
225 g/8 oz/1 cup long-grain rice

1 Preheat the oven to 180°C/350°F/ gas mark 4.
2 Bring a saucepan of water with a good pinch of salt to the boil over a high heat. Add the aubergine slices and cook for 3 minutes or until almost tender. Drain in a colander.
3 Heat the olive oil in a flameproof casserole (Dutch oven). Add the chicken and brown on all sides over a high heat. Remove from the pan with a draining spoon.
4 Fry (sauté) the onion in the casserole for 2 minutes to soften. Add the aubergine and then the remaining ingredients. Bring to the boil, stirring. Return the chicken to the pan and cover. Cook in the oven for 1½ hours until the chicken is really tender.
5 Meanwhile, cook the rice according to the packet directions (or see page 294). Drain in a colander. Serve with the casserole.

Shanghai Rice

SERVES 4

350 g/12 oz/1½ cups long-grain rice
30 ml/2 tbsp sunflower oil
4 eggs, beaten
100 g/4 oz/1 cup diced cooked chicken
175 g/6 oz chopped cooked vegetables
5 cm/2 in piece of cucumber, diced
4 spring onions (scallions) or a small onion, chopped
15 ml/1 tbsp soy sauce
Salt and freshly ground black pepper

1 Cook the rice according to the packet directions (or see page 294). Drain in a colander, rinse with cold water and drain again.
2 Heat half the oil in a large frying pan (skillet) or wok. Add half the egg and fry (sauté), stirring, until just beginning to set. Add the rice, chicken, vegetables, cucumber and onion and cook, stirring, for about 3 minutes until piping hot. Sprinkle in the soy sauce and stir gently.
3 Heat the remaining oil in a small frying pan. Pour in the remaining egg, season with salt and pepper and cook until the underside is set, lifting gently occasionally to allow the uncooked egg to run underneath.
4 Slide out of the pan on to a plate, then tip back in to cook on the underside. Tip out on to the plate again. When cool enough to handle, roll up the omelette and cut it into thin shreds.
5 Spoon the rice on to warm plates and scatter the omelette shreds over the top.

Chicken Maryland

SERVES 6

6 chicken portions
A little milk
90 ml/6 tbsp plain (all-purpose) flour
Salt and freshly ground black pepper
75 g/3 oz/¾ cup dried breadcrumbs
100 g/4 oz/½ cup butter or margarine
45 ml/3 tbsp sunflower oil
4 bananas
175 g/6 oz/¾ cup brown rice
Sprigs of watercress, to garnish
Corn Fritters (see page 308) and a
    Green Salad (see page 308), to
    serve

1 Dip the chicken in milk, then coat in the flour, seasoned with a little salt and pepper, and chill for 30 minutes.
2 Preheat the oven at 190°C/375°F/ gas mark 5.
3 Dip the chicken in the milk again, then coat in the breadcrumbs.
4 Melt 75 g/3 oz/⅓ cup of the butter or margarine with 30 ml/2 tbsp of the oil

in the oven in a large roasting tin (pan). When sizzling, add the chicken and turn over in the fat to coat completely.
5 Bake for 1 hour until golden brown and cooked through. Drain on kitchen paper (paper towels).
6 While the chicken is cooking, halve the bananas. Melt the remaining butter or margarine and oil in a shallow baking tin (pan), add the bananas and turn over in the fat.
7 Place them on the shelf under the chicken and cook for 30 minutes or until tender but still holding their shape (the exact time will depend on the ripeness of the bananas).
8 Cook the rice according to the packet directions (or see page 294) and drain in a colander. While it is cooking, make the Corn Fritters and a green salad.
9 Transfer the chicken and bananas to a large warm platter and garnish with watercress sprigs. Serve with the fritters, rice and salad.

Chicken and Cranberry Pouches

Prepare the side vegetables before you start, then cook them while the chicken is in the oven.

SERVES 4

15 ml/1 tbsp sunflower oil

4 skinless chicken breasts

4 large sheets of filo pastry (paste), thawed if frozen

50 g/2 oz/¼ cup butter or margarine, melted

Salt and freshly ground black pepper

2.5 ml/½ tsp dried thyme

90 ml/6 tbsp cranberry sauce

295 g/10½ oz/1 medium can of condensed cream of mushroom soup

Sprigs of parsley, to garnish

New potatoes and French (green) beans, to serve

1 Heat the oil in a frying pan (skillet). Add the chicken breasts and cook over a high heat for 4 minutes until lightly browned underneath. Turn over and cook for a further 4 minutes until lightly browned on the other side. Remove with a fish slice and leave to cool.

2 Preheat the oven to 190°C/375°F/ gas mark 5.

3 Brush the pastry sheets with some of the butter or margarine. Fold into halves and brush again.

4 Put a cooled chicken breast in the centre of each piece of pastry. Sprinkle with salt and pepper and the thyme. Top each with 10 ml/2 tsp cranberry sauce, then spoon over the soup.

5 Draw the pastry up over the filling and pinch together to form pouches.

Brush a baking (cookie) sheet with a little of the remaining butter or margarine and put the pouches on it.

6 Brush the pastry pouches all over with the remaining butter or margarine and bake in the oven for about 15 minutes or until golden brown and cooked through.

7 Use a fish slice to lift the pouches on to warm plates. Garnish each with a spoonful of the remaining cranberry sauce and a sprig of parsley and serve with new potatoes and beans.

Buttered Chicken with Herbs

Cook the potatoes and make the salad while the chicken is grilling (broiling). For Buttered Garlic Chicken add 1–2 crushed garlic cloves to the butter mixture.

SERVES 4

4 chicken portions

50 g/2 oz/¼ cup butter or margarine, melted

10 ml/2 tsp lemon juice

5 ml/1 tsp dried mixed herbs

Salt and freshly ground black pepper

Sauté Potatoes (see page 296) and a Mixed Salad (see page 308), to serve

1 Preheat the grill (broiler). Place the chicken on foil on the grill rack.

2 Mix the butter or margarine with the lemon juice, herbs and some salt and pepper. Brush all over the chicken.

3 Grill for about 20 minutes, turning several times and brushing with the butter mixture until crisp on the outside, golden brown and cooked through. Serve with the sauté potatoes and salad.

Spicy Mint Chicken

SERVES 4

25 g/1 oz/2 tbsp butter or margarine
45 ml/3 tbsp chopped fresh mint
2.5 ml/½ tsp ground cinnamon
2.5 ml/½ tsp ground cumin
15 ml/1 tbsp lemon juice
10 ml/2 tsp caster (superfine) sugar
4 skinless chicken breasts
1 lemon, sliced, and sprigs of parsley, to garnish
New potatoes and a Mixed Salad (see page 308), to serve

1 Mash the butter or margarine with the mint, spices, lemon juice and sugar in a small bowl with a fork.

2 Preheat the grill (broiler). Place the chicken on foil on a grill (broiler) rack and spread the buttery mixture all over. Put the potatoes on to cook.

3 Grill the chicken for about 6 minutes on each side or until golden brown and cooked through, brushing with the buttery mixture as it melts. Make the salad while it cooks.

4 Garnish with lemon slices and sprigs of parsley and serve with the new potatoes and salad.

Sweet Spiced Chicken with Coriander and Lemon

SERVES 4

Prepare as for Spicy Mint Chicken but substitute chopped fresh coriander (cilantro) for the mint and add the finely grated rind of ½ lemon to the mixture.

Spanish Rice

This tastes similar to paella, but is much easier to make.

SERVES 4

25 g/1 oz/2 tbsp butter or margarine
175 g/6 oz boneless chicken meat, diced
1 small green (bell) pepper, diced
1 small red pepper, diced
1 onion, chopped
225 g/8 oz/1 cup long-grain rice
5 ml/1 tsp ground turmeric or saffron powder
600 ml/1 pt/2½ cups chicken stock, made with 1 stock cube
2 tomatoes, roughly chopped
100 g/4 oz/1 cup frozen peas
100 g/4 oz cooked peeled prawns (shrimp)
Salt and freshly ground black pepper
4 stoned (pitted) black olives, halved
15 ml/1 tbsp chopped fresh parsley

1 Melt the butter or margarine in a large frying pan (skillet). Add the chicken, peppers and onion and fry (sauté) over a moderate heat, stirring, for 4 minutes. Stir in the rice and cook for 1 minute.

2 Add the turmeric or saffron and the stock, turn up the heat and bring to the boil, stirring. Turn down the heat until just bubbling gently round the edges. Cover and cook for 10 minutes.

3 Stir in the tomatoes, peas, prawns and a little salt and pepper. Cover and continue cooking for a further 10 minutes over a low heat until the rice is cooked and has absorbed all the liquid. Stir gently with a fork, spoon on to warm plates and garnish with halved olives and chopped parsley.

South Pacific Chicken

SERVES 4

4 chicken portions
2.5 ml/½ tsp garlic salt
Freshly ground black pepper
30 ml/2 tbsp sunflower oil
300 ml/½ pt/1¼ cups pineapple juice
2 celery sticks, thinly sliced
4 tomatoes, quartered
1 red (bell) pepper, sliced
1 green pepper, sliced
1 green banana, cut into chunks
225 g/8 oz/1 cup long-grain rice
15 ml/1 tbsp soy sauce
15 ml/1 tbsp cornflour (cornstarch)
30 ml/2 tbsp toasted coconut, to
  garnish

1 Wipe the chicken with kitchen paper (paper towels), then season with the garlic salt and some pepper. Heat the oil in a flameproof casserole (Dutch oven) and brown the chicken on all sides over a high heat. Cover the pan, reduce the heat to fairly low and cook gently for 20 minutes.

2 Add the pineapple juice, celery, tomatoes, peppers and banana. Cover and cook gently for 20–25 minutes until the chicken is tender.

3 While the chicken is cooking, cook the rice according to the packet directions (or see page 294). Drain in a colander.

4 Mix the soy sauce and cornflour together in a small cup. Lift the chicken portions out of the casserole and place on the upturned lid. Stir the cornflour mixture into the casserole. Heat until boiling again and cook for 1 minute. Taste and re-season if necessary.

5 Spoon the rice on to warm plates, top with the chicken and spoon the sauce over. Sprinkle with toasted coconut and serve.

Spiced Yoghurt Chicken Kebabs

SERVES 4

60 ml/4 tbsp plain yoghurt
5 ml/1 tsp garam masala
5 ml1 tsp ground cumin
1 garlic clove, crushed
5 ml/1 tsp light brown sugar
Salt and freshly ground black pepper
5 ml/1 tsp lemon juice
350 g/12 oz skinless chicken breasts, cut
  into chunks
Quick Pilau Rice (see page 314), to
  serve
Wedges of lemon and sprigs of
  coriander (cilantro), to garnish

1 Mix together everything but the chicken breasts. Add the chicken and mix well. Leave to marinate for 2 hours. Thread on skewers.

2 Preheat the grill (broiler). Put the rice on to cook.

3 Put the kebabs on foil on the grill rack and grill (broil) for about 8–10 minutes, turning frequently until golden and cooked through.

4 Spoon the rice on warm plates, top with the kebabs and garnish with wedges of lemon and sprigs of coriander.

Stuffed Pot-roast Chicken

SERVES 4–6

1 oven-ready chicken, about 1.5 kg/3 lb
30 ml/2 tbsp fresh wholemeal
  breadcrumbs
100 g/4 oz smooth liver pâté with
  garlic
45 ml/3 tbsp chopped fresh parsley
Salt and freshly ground black pepper
40 g/1½ oz/3 tbsp butter or margarine
100 g/4 oz streaky bacon rashers
  (slices), rinded and diced
2 carrots, diced
2 leeks, well-washed and sliced
450 g/1 lb baby potatoes, scrubbed
  but left whole
15 ml/1 tbsp cornflour (cornstarch)
300 ml/½ pt/1¼ cups chicken stock,
  made with 1 stock cube

1 Wipe the chicken inside and out with kitchen paper (paper towels) and pull out any fat just inside the body cavity. Preheat the oven at 180°C/350°F/ gas mark 4.

2 Mash the breadcrumbs with the pâté and 30 ml/2 tbsp of the parsley and season well. Use to stuff the neck end of the bird and secure with skewers or cocktail sticks (toothpicks).

3 Melt the butter or margarine in a flameproof casserole (Dutch oven) and brown the chicken all over. Remove from the pan.

4 Add the bacon, carrots, leeks and potatoes and toss in the fat. Return the chicken to the pot. Season, then cover and cook in the preheated oven for 1½ hours.

5 Transfer the chicken and vegetables to a carving dish.

6 Blend the cornflour into the cooking juices in the casserole, then gradually blend in the stock. Bring to the boil and cook for 1 minute, stirring. Taste and re-season if necessary.

7 Carve the chicken and serve with the vegetables and sauce.

Oven-fried Chicken and Potatoes with Sour Chive Dip

SERVES 4

45 ml/3 tbsp plain (all-purpose) flour
5 ml/1 tsp curry powder
Salt and freshly ground black pepper
4 chicken portions
75 g/3 oz/⅓ cup butter or margarine
75 ml/5 tbsp sunflower oil
450 g/1 lb potatoes, halved and cut into wedges
1.5 ml/¼ tsp chilli powder
150 ml/¼ pt/⅔ cup plain yoghurt
30 ml/2 tbsp snipped fresh chives
A pinch of garlic salt
A Mixed Salad (see page 308), to serve

1 Preheat the oven to 180°C/350°F/ gas mark 4.

2 Mix the flour with the curry powder and a little salt and pepper in a shallow dish. Add the chicken and turn over in the mixture to coat.

3 Melt 50 g/2 oz/¼ cup of the butter or margarine with 60 ml/4 tbsp of the oil in a large roasting tin (pan) over a moderate heat.

4 Add the chicken, skin-sides down.

5 Melt the remaining butter or margarine and oil in a separate shallow baking tin. Add the potato wedges, season with salt, pepper and the chilli powder and turn in the fat.

6 Put the potatoes on the top shelf of the oven, and the chicken just above the middle. Bake for 25 minutes.

7 Turn the potatoes and chicken over and return to the oven for 25–30 minutes until golden and cooked through.

8 While they are cooking, mix the yoghurt with the chives, garlic salt and a little pepper. Chill until ready to serve. Make the mixed salad.

9 Drain the chicken and potatoes on kitchen paper (paper towels) and serve with the dip and salad.

Winter Chicken Pot

SERVES 4

25 g/1 oz/2 tbsp butter or margarine
8 boneless chicken thighs, skinned
1 onion, sliced
4 carrots, sliced
2 turnips, sliced
100 g/4 oz/generous ½ cup pearl barley
900 ml/1½ pts/3¾ cups chicken stock, made with 2 stock cubes
Salt and freshly ground black pepper
3 potatoes, scrubbed and cut into bite-sized chunks
1 small green cabbage, shredded

1 Melt the butter or margarine in a large saucepan. Add the chicken and brown on all sides over a high heat. Remove from the pan with a draining spoon.

2 Add the onion, carrots and turnips and fry (sauté) for 2 minutes, stirring. Add the barley and stock and return the chicken to the pan. Season to taste. Bring to the boil, reduce the heat until gently bubbling round the edges, part-cover and cook for 45 minutes.

3 Add the potatoes and cabbage, cover and continue cooking for 20 minutes or until everything is tender. Serve in large, open soup bowls.

Quick Italian Chicken Casserole

SERVES 4

4 skinless chicken breasts
4 tomatoes, sliced
295 g/10½ oz/1 medium can of
    condensed cream of tomato soup
2.5 ml/½ tsp dried basil
Freshly ground black pepper
225 g/8 oz tagliatelle
30 ml/2 tbsp olive oil
A Green Salad (see page 308), to serve

1 Put the chicken breasts in a flameproof casserole (Dutch oven). Lay the tomato slices on top and spoon over the soup. Half-fill the soup can with water, and pour over. Add the basil and lots of pepper.
2 Heat rapidly until boiling, then turn down the heat until just gently bubbling round the edges, cover and cook for 20 minutes, moving the chicken around occasionally until cooked through and bathed in a rich tomato sauce.
3 While the chicken is cooking, cook the tagliatelle according to the packet directions (or see page 293) and make the salad. Drain the pasta in a colander and return to the pan. Add the olive oil and a good grinding of pepper and stir gently until every strand is coated in oil.
4 Pile the pasta on warm plates. Top with the chicken and sauce and serve.

Quick French Chicken Casserole

SERVES 4

Prepare as for Quick Italian Chicken Casserole but use cup mushrooms instead of tomatoes and a can of condensed mushroom soup instead of the tomato soup. Add 15 ml/1 tbsp brandy and use dried mixed herbs instead of basil.

Mediterranean Chicken Casserole

SERVES 4

60 ml/4 tbsp olive oil
1 onion, thinly sliced
1 aubergine (eggplant), sliced
1 green (bell) pepper, sliced
2 courgettes (zucchini), sliced
1 large garlic clove, crushed
400 g/14 oz/1 large can of chopped tomatoes
Salt and freshly ground black pepper
1 bouquet garni sachet
250 ml/8 fl oz/1 cup red wine
15 ml/1 tbsp tomato purée (paste)
4 skinless chicken breasts
Plain potatoes and a Green Salad (see page 308), to serve

1 Heat the oil in a large flameproof casserole (Dutch oven). Fry (sauté) the onion, aubergine, green pepper, courgettes and garlic, stirring, for 5 minutes.
2 Add the tomatoes, some salt and pepper, the bouquet garni, wine and tomato purée. Stir well. Push the chicken breasts into the mixture so they are completely covered.
3 Bring to the boil, then turn down the heat until just bubbling around the edges. Cover and cook for 40 minutes.
4 Meanwhile, prepare and cook the potatoes and make the salad.
5 Remove the bouquet garni from the chicken, taste and re-season if necessary. If there is too much liquid, boil rapidly without the lid for a few minutes to evaporate some liquid. Serve with the potatoes and salad.

Spiced Chicken Burgers

SERVES 4

900 g/2 lb minced (ground) chicken
30 ml/2 tbsp chopped fresh parsley
1.5 ml/¼ tsp chilli powder
1.5 ml/¼ tsp ground mace
Salt and freshly ground black pepper
1 egg, beaten
25 g/1 oz/2 tbsp unsalted (sweet) butter
Pizzaiola Sauce (see page 333), Italian Coleslaw (see page 311) and ciabatta bread, to serve

1 Mix the chicken with the parsley, chilli powder, mace and a little salt and pepper.
2 Mix in the beaten egg. Shape into eight small cakes and chill for 30 minutes.
3 Make the Pizzaiola Sauce and coleslaw while the burgers chill. Keep the sauce warm over a gentle heat.
4 Heat the butter in a large, non-stick frying pan (skillet). Fry (sauté) the burgers for about 4 minutes on each side until cooked through and golden brown. Transfer to warm plates. Spoon the Pizzaiola Sauce over and serve with the coleslaw and lots of ciabatta bread.

Chicken Paprika

SERVES 4

50 g/2 oz/¼ cup butter or margarine
2 onions, sliced
4 skinless chicken breasts
30 ml/2 tbsp paprika
400 g/14 oz/1 large can of chopped
  tomatoes
225 g/8 oz/1 small can of pimientos,
  drained and chopped
Salt and freshly ground black pepper
225 g/8 oz tagliatelle
15 ml/1 tbsp caraway seeds
45 ml/3 tbsp thick plain yoghurt
15 ml/1 tbsp chopped fresh parsley, to
  garnish
A Green Salad (see page 308), to serve

1 Melt half the butter or margarine in a
flameproof casserole dish (Dutch oven)
and fry (sauté) the onion over a high
heat, stirring, for 2 minutes.
2 Add the chicken breasts and fry on
each side to brown. Add the paprika,
tomatoes, pimientos and some salt and
pepper. Bring to the boil, reduce the
heat until just bubbling around the
edges, part-cover and cook for
20 minutes, removing the lid after
10 minutes.
3 Meanwhile, cook the tagliatelle
according to the packet directions (or
see page 293). Drain and return to the
pan. Add the remaining butter or
margarine, the caraway seeds and a
good grinding of pepper. Heat gently,
stirring until every strand is coated.
While the pasta is cooking, make the
salad.

4 Remove the chicken from the sauce
and transfer to warm plates. Stir the
yoghurt into the sauce. Taste and re-
season if necessary but do not re-boil
or it will curdle. Spoon over the chicken,
garnish with chopped parsley and
serve with the seeded noodles and a
green salad.

Honey-glazed Chicken

SERVES 4

25 g/1 oz/2 tbsp butter or margarine
4 skinless chicken breasts
120 ml/4 fl oz/½ cup dry vermouth
15 ml/1 tbsp clear honey
Salt and freshly ground black pepper
15 ml/1 tbsp chopped fresh parsley
Super Creamed Potatoes (see page
  298) and French (green) beans, to
  serve

1 Melt the butter or margarine in a
large frying pan (skillet). Brown the
chicken breasts on both sides over a
fairly high heat.
2 Add the vermouth, honey and a little
salt and pepper and cook for about
15–20 minutes until the chicken is
cooked through and stickily glazed,
turning the chicken once or twice
during cooking. Meanwhile, cook the
Super Creamed Potatoes and beans.
3 Add the parsley to the pan and turn
the chicken over once more. Serve with
the potatoes and French beans.

Chicken Gumbo

SERVES 4

15 g/½ oz/1 tbsp butter or margarine

450 g/1 lb skinless chicken meat, cut
into dice

12 button (pearl) onions, peeled but
left whole

1 rasher (slice) of back bacon, rinded
and cut into small dice

5 ml/1 tsp ground turmeric

5 ml/1 tsp ground coriander (cilantro)

2.5 ml/½ tsp chilli powder

225 g/8 oz okra (ladies' fingers),
trimmed

1 red (bell) pepper, sliced

1 green pepper, sliced

225 g/8 oz/1 small can of chopped
tomatoes

15 ml/1 tbsp tomato purée (paste)

1 large bay leaf

2.5 ml/½ tsp dried oregano

600 ml/1 pt/2½ cups chicken stock,
made with 1 stock cube

Salt and freshly ground black pepper

225 g/8 oz/1 cup long-grain rice

15 ml/1 tbsp chopped fresh parsley

1 Melt the butter or margarine in a
large flameproof casserole (Dutch
oven). Add the chicken and brown
over a high heat for 3 minutes, stirring.
Add the onions, bacon and spices and
cook, stirring, for a further 1 minute.

2 Add all the remaining ingredients
except the rice and parsley. Bring to
the boil, reduce the heat, cover and
simmer very gently for 1 hour.

3 Meanwhile, cook the rice according
to the packet directions (or see page
294). Drain in a colander. Put some
water in the saucepan and sit the

colander on top. Cover the rice with
the saucepan lid and keep warm over
a very gentle heat until ready to serve.

4 Remove the bay leaf from the
gumbo, taste and re-season if
necessary. Spoon the rice into warm
bowls, top with the gumbo and
sprinkle with the parsley before serving.

Chicken Fillets with Cognac

*Prepare and cook the potatoes and
leeks and make the salad before you
cook the chicken. Then just finish
mashing the vegetables when the
chicken is cooked.*

SERVES 4

700 g/1½ lb small chicken fillets

30 ml/2 tbsp coarsely crushed black
peppercorns

1.5 ml/¼ tsp salt

50 g/2 oz/¼ cup unsalted (sweet)
butter

2 garlic cloves, crushed

60 ml/4 tbsp cognac

Potato and Leek Mash (see page 298)
and a Mixed Salad (see page 308),
to serve

1 Season the chicken with the crushed
peppercorns and salt.

2 Melt the butter in a large frying pan
(skillet). Add the chicken and garlic and
fry (sauté) for about 8 minutes until
cooked through.

3 Add the cognac to the pan and set
alight. Shake the pan until the flames
subside. Serve straight from the pan
with the mash and salad.

Spiced Chicken Casserole

Cook the potatoes in the oven at the same time as the chicken and make the salad while the casserole and potatoes are cooking.

SERVES 4

30 ml/2 tbsp plain (all-purpose) flour
Salt and freshly ground black pepper
5 ml/1 tsp paprika
4 chicken portions
25 g/1 oz/2 tbsp butter or margarine
5 ml/1 tsp curry powder
295 g/10½ oz/1 medium can of
  condensed celery soup
2 celery sticks, chopped
Wedges of lemon, to garnish
Jacket-baked Potatoes (see page 296)
  and a Green Salad (see page 308),
  to serve

1 Preheat the oven to 180°C/350°F/ gas mark 4.
2 Mix the flour with a little salt and pepper and the paprika in a shallow bowl. Add the chicken and turn to coat it completely.
3 Melt the butter or margarine in a flameproof casserole (Dutch oven). Add the chicken and brown on all sides over a high heat. Remove from the pan. Drain off any excess fat.
4 Sprinkle the curry powder into the casserole and add the condensed soup. Add a little more pepper. Bring to the boil, stirring. Add the chicken and celery, then turn the chicken to coat well with the sauce. Cover and cook in the oven for 1½ hours or until tender. Spoon on to warm plates, garnish with wedges of lemon and serve with the jacket-baked potatoes and salad.

Rich and Creamy Risotto

SERVES 4

15 g/½ oz/1 tbsp unsalted (sweet) butter
1 small onion, finely chopped
100 g/4 oz/1 cup finely diced pancetta
2 skinless chicken breasts, cut into small
  pieces
100 g/4 oz button mushrooms, sliced
450 g/1 lb/2 cups risotto rice
1.5 litres/2½ pts/6 cups hot chicken
  stock, made with 2 stock cubes
120 ml/4 fl oz/½ cup double (heavy)
  cream
Salt and freshly ground black pepper
100 g/4 oz/1 cup Parmesan cheese,
  grated

1 Melt the butter in a flameproof casserole (Dutch oven). Add the onion, pancetta, chicken and mushrooms and fry (sauté) over a fairly high heat for 3 minutes until the onion is golden and the pancetta has lost its pink colour.
2 Stir in the rice and cook for 1 minute. Stir in two ladlefuls of the stock and simmer until it has been absorbed. Repeat, adding a little stock at a time until the rice is just tender and creamy but still has some 'bite' – it should take about 20 minutes.
3 Stir in the cream, season to taste and add the Parmesan. Serve straight away.

Chicken Tetrazzini

SERVES 4

350 g/12 oz spaghetti

25 g/1 oz/2 tbsp unsalted (sweet) butter

1 onion, finely chopped

175 g/6 oz button mushrooms, sliced

1 celeriac (celery root), grated

1 carrot, grated

15 ml/1 tbsp plain (all-purpose) flour

150 ml/¼ pt/⅔ cup chicken stock

150 ml/¼ pt/⅔ cup single (light) cream

225 g/8 oz/2 cups diced cooked chicken

A little milk

50 g/2 oz/½ cup Parmesan cheese, grated

30 ml/2 tbsp flaked (slivered) almonds

15 ml/1 tbsp chopped fresh parsley

1 Cook the spaghetti according to the packet directions (or see page 293). Drain in a colander.

2 Melt the butter in a separate pan. Cook the onion, mushrooms, celeriac and carrot for 4 minutes over a moderate heat, stirring, until softened but not browned. Blend in the flour and cook for 1 minute.

3 Stir in the stock and cream. Bring to the boil and simmer for 2 minutes. Add the chicken and heat through. Stir in the spaghetti and thin with a little milk if necessary.

4 Stir gently over a low heat. Preheat the grill (broiler).

5 Spoon the spaghetti mixture into a flameproof dish. Sprinkle with the Parmesan, almonds and parsley and grill (broil) briefly until bubbling and the almonds are toasted.

Chicken Cordon Bleu

Cook the potatoes and the beans while the chicken is cooking in the stock.

SERVES 4

25 g/1 oz/2 tbsp butter or margarine

30 ml/2 tbsp sunflower oil

4 skinless chicken breasts

15 ml/1 tbsp chopped fresh parsley

4 slices of ham

8 cup mushrooms, sliced

150 ml/¼ pt/⅔ cup chicken stock, made with ½ stock cube

4 slices of Leerdammer or Gruyère (Swiss) cheese

Sauté Potatoes with Garlic (see page 296) and French (green) beans, to serve

1 Heat the butter or margarine and oil in a large frying pan (skillet) over a fairly high heat. Add the chicken and fry (sauté) for 2 minutes on each side to brown.

2 Top each with a little parsley, a slice of ham and the mushrooms. Pour the stock around. Bring to the boil, turn down the heat until gently bubbling around the edges, cover and cook gently for 10 minutes until cooked through.

3 Top each chicken breast with a slice of cheese. Cover and continue cooking for 2–3 minutes until the cheese melts. Transfer the chicken to warm plates.

4 Turn up the heat and boil the liquid rapidly until it reduces and thickens, then spoon over the chicken. Serve straight away with the Sauté Potatoes with Garlic and French beans.

Louisiana Jambalaya

SERVES 4

30 ml/2 tbsp sunflower oil
4 chicken portions
225 g/8 oz smoked pork sausage, sliced
1 onion, chopped
2 celery sticks, chopped
2 garlic cloves, crushed
1 green (bell) pepper, sliced into strips
1 carrot, chopped
750 ml/1¼ pts/3 cups chicken stock,
   made with 2 stock cubes
225 g/8 oz/1 cup long-grain rice
10 ml/2 tsp paprika
15 ml/1 tbsp tomato purée (paste)
A few drops of Tabasco sauce
1 bunch of spring onions (scallions),
   chopped
Salt and freshly ground black pepper

1 Heat the oil in a large flameproof casserole (Dutch oven).

2 Add the chicken and brown on all sides over a high heat. Remove from the pan with a draining spoon. Add the sausage and fry (sauté) for 3 minutes. Remove from the pan with a draining spoon.

3 Add the prepared vegetables and fry for 2–3 minutes, stirring. Return the chicken and sausage to the pan.

4 Add the stock, cover and bring to the boil. Turn down the heat until gently bubbling round the edges and cook for 15 minutes.

5 Add the rice, paprika, tomato purée, a few drops of Tabasco sauce and half the spring onions. Stir well. Turn up the heat and bring back to the boil, then turn it down again, cover and cook gently for a further 15 minutes or until

the rice is tender and has absorbed the liquid. Taste and season if necessary.

6 Sprinkle with the remaining spring onions before serving.

Chicken with Curry Butter

SERVES 4

4 spring onions (scallions), chopped
100 g/4 oz/½ cup unsalted (sweet)
   butter
15 ml/1 tbsp curry paste
5 ml/1 tsp lemon juice
Salt and freshly ground black pepper
4 skinless chicken breasts
225 g/8 oz/1 cup wild rice mix
A Mixed Salad (see page 308), to serve

1 Put the spring onions in a blender or food processor with the butter, curry paste and lemon juice. Run the machine until smooth. Season with salt and pepper and run the machine again.

2 Place the chicken breasts on foil on the grill (broiler) rack. Spread with half the butter mixture and grill (broil) for 8 minutes, brushing frequently with the melted butter. Turn over and spread the other side of the chicken with the remaining curry butter. Grill for a further 8 minutes until sizzling and cooked through, brushing frequently as before.

3 Meanwhile, cook the rice according to the packet directions (or see page 294). Drain in a colander. Make the salad.

4 Spoon the rice on warm plates. Top with the chicken and all the buttery juices and serve with the salad.

Grilled Chicken with Herby Fresh Pasta

Make the salad while the chicken is cooking.

SERVES 4

4 chicken portions
2 garlic cloves, cut into thin slivers
30 ml/2 tbsp olive oil
Salt and freshly ground black pepper
225 g/8 oz fresh pasta
50 g/2 oz/¼ cup unsalted (sweet) butter
50 g/2 oz/½ cup Parmesan cheese, freshly grated
30 ml/2 tbsp chopped fresh basil
30 ml/2 tbsp chopped fresh parsley
Wedges of lemon, to garnish
A Green Salad (see page 308), to serve

1 Preheat the grill (broiler).
2 Gently lift the skin on the chicken and push a few slivers of garlic underneath on each portion.
3 Place on foil on the grill rack and brush all over with oil. Season with salt and pepper. Grill (broil) for 20 minutes, turning occasionally, until cooked through and the skin is crispy, brushing with a little more oil during cooking.
4 Meanwhile, cook the pasta according to the packet directions (or see page 293) but remember, it will take only about 4 minutes until just tender. Drain in a colander and return to the pan.
5 Add the butter, cut into small pieces, lots of freshly ground black pepper, the cheese and herbs, and lift and stir with two forks over a gentle heat until the butter is melted and the pasta is coated in the fragrant herbs.

6 Pile on to warm plates, and top with the chicken. Garnish with wedges of lemon and serve with the salad.

Oven-baked Risotto

SERVES 4

60 ml/4 tbsp olive oil
1 small onion, finely chopped
2 large chicken breasts, cut into chunks
450 g/1 lb/2 cups risotto rice
1.5 litres/2½ pts/6 cups chicken stock, made with 2 stock cubes
Salt and freshly ground black pepper
15 g/½ oz/1 tbsp unsalted (sweet) butter
Quick Tomato Sauce (see page 335) and grated Parmesan cheese, to serve

1 Preheat the oven to 180°C/350°F/ gas mark 4.
2 Heat the oil in a flameproof casserole (Dutch oven) over a fairly high heat. Add the onion and chicken and fry (sauté) for 2 minutes.
3 Stir the rice into the casserole and cook for 1 minute.
4 Stir in the stock, season well and bring to the boil. Cover tightly and bake in the oven for 1 hour. Stir in the butter and re-season if necessary. While the rice is cooking, make the sauce.
5 Serve the risotto with the tomato sauce and grated Parmesan cheese.

Herb-stuffed Chicken Rolls

SERVES 4

40 g/1½ oz/¾ cup fresh white
    breadcrumbs
30 ml/2 tbsp chopped fresh parsley
15 ml/1 tbsp chopped fresh basil
15 ml/1 tbsp chopped fresh thyme
Salt and freshly ground black pepper
1 egg, beaten
4 small skinless chicken breasts
300 ml/½ pt/1¼ cups chicken stock,
    made with 1 stock cube
15 ml/1 tbsp cornflour (cornstarch)
30 ml/2 tbsp single (light) cream
New potatoes and carrots, to serve

1 Mix the breadcrumbs with the herbs, seasoning and beaten egg.

2 Cut each chicken breast in half widthways. Put one at a time in a plastic bag and beat with a rolling pin or meat mallet until flat. Spread the stuffing over each slice and roll up. Secure with cocktail sticks (toothpicks).

3 Place in a flameproof casserole dish (Dutch oven) with the stock. Heat rapidly until boiling, then turn down the heat until just bubbling gently round the edges, cover with a lid and cook for 15 minutes or until cooked through.

4 While the chicken is cooking, prepare and cook the potatoes and carrots.

5 Place the chicken rolls on warm plates and remove the cocktail sticks. Keep warm.

6 Mix the cornflour with the cream and stir into the stock. Bring to the boil and cook, stirring, for 2 minutes. Taste and add more seasoning if necessary. Pour over the chicken and serve with the new potatoes and carrots.

Chicken in Black Bean Sauce

SERVES 4

350 g/12 oz chicken stir-fry meat
10 ml/2 tsp cornflour (cornstarch)
30 ml/2 tbsp black bean sauce
1 large garlic clove, crushed
2.5 cm/1 in piece of fresh root ginger,
    peeled and grated
60 ml/4 tbsp soy sauce
60 ml/4 tbsp medium-dry sherry
45 ml/3 tbsp clear honey
60 ml/4 tbsp sunflower oil
300 ml/½ pt/1¼ cups chicken stock,
    made with 1 stock cube
100 g/4 oz shiitake mushrooms, sliced
225 g/8 oz/1 cup long-grain rice
15 ml/1 tbsp hot chilli sauce
5 cm/2 in piece of cucumber, finely
    chopped, to garnish

1 Mix the chicken with the cornflour, bean sauce, garlic, ginger, soy sauce, sherry and honey in a shallow dish. Cover and leave to marinate for 1 hour.

2 Heat 45 ml/3 tbsp of the oil in a flameproof casserole (Dutch oven). Add the chicken mixture and fry (sauté) over a high heat, stirring, for 3 minutes. Add the stock and mushrooms. Bring to the boil, turn down the heat until gently bubbling round the edges, cover with a lid and cook for 30 minutes.

3 Meanwhile, cook the rice according to the packet directions (or see page 294). Drain.

4 Mix the chilli sauce with the remaining oil. Spoon the rice into warm bowls. Spoon the chicken mixture over. Sprinkle with the chilli sauce and cucumber before serving.

Chinese Chicken with Water Chestnuts

SERVES 4

4 chicken breasts, cut into chunks
15 ml/1 tbsp dry sherry
5 ml/1 tsp light brown sugar
30 ml/2 tbsp sunflower oil
1 bunch of spring onions (scallions),
    diagonally sliced
175 g/6 oz button mushrooms, sliced
225 g/8 oz/1 small can of water
    chestnuts, drained and quartered
600 ml/1 pt/2½ cups chicken stock,
    made with 1 stock cube
15 ml/1 tbsp soy sauce
100 g/4 oz Chinese egg noodles
15 ml/1 tbsp cornflour (cornstarch)
30 ml/2 tbsp water

1 Place the chicken in a shallow dish.
Add the sherry and the sugar. Mix with
your hands until well coated, then
cover and marinate for 2 hours.
2 Preheat the oven to 180°C/350°F/
gas mark 4.
3 Heat the oil in a flameproof casserole
(Dutch oven). Add the chicken and
brown over a high heat on all sides.
Remove from the pan with a draining
spoon.
4 Add the spring onions and
mushrooms and cook, stirring, for
2 minutes. Add the water chestnuts,
stock and soy sauce. Return the chicken
to the pan and bring to the boil. Cover
and cook in the oven for 45 minutes
until the chicken is tender.
5 Meanwhile, cook the noodles
according to the packet directions.
Drain in a colander.

6 Mix the cornflour with the water in a
small cup and stir into the casserole.
Bring to the boil over a high heat and
cook for 2 minutes, stirring. Stir in the
noodles. Serve in warm bowls.

Chicken Teriyaki

SERVES 4

45 ml/3 tbsp soy sauce
30 ml/2 tbsp medium-dry sherry
1 garlic clove, crushed
A good pinch of ground ginger
10 ml/2 tsp clear honey
350 g/12 oz skinless chicken breasts, cut
    into cubes
225 g/8 oz soba noodles
A Beansprout Salad (see page 310),
    to serve

1 Mix the soy sauce with the sherry,
garlic, ginger and honey. Add the diced
chicken and mix well. Leave in a cool
place to marinate for at least 2 hours.
Thread on soaked wooden skewers.
Meanwhile, make the salad.
2 Just before starting to cook the
chicken, put the noodles on to cook
according to the packet directions.
Drain in a colander and sprinkle with
15 ml/1 tbsp of the soy sauce. Lift and
stir with a spoon and fork to mix into
the noodles. Preheat the grill (broiler).
3 Put the chicken on foil on the grill
rack. Grill (broil) for 8–10 minutes,
turning and brushing occasionally with
any remaining marinade, until tender
and cooked through.
4 Pile the noodles on warm plates. Top
with the chicken and serve with the
salad.

Simple Fried Chicken

SERVES 4

4 chicken portions
60 ml/4 tbsp milk
30 ml/2 tbsp plain (all-purpose) flour
Salt and freshly ground black pepper
75 g/3 oz/⅓ cup butter or margarine
30 ml/2 tbsp olive oil
15 ml/1 tbsp lemon juice
30 ml/2 tbsp chopped fresh parsley
Sauté Potatoes (see page 296) and a
    Green Salad (see page 308), to
    serve

1 Dip the chicken in the milk. Mix the
flour with a little salt and pepper on a
plate and turn the chicken in this to
coat completely.
2 Melt half the butter or margarine
and the oil in a large frying pan (skillet).
Fry (sauté) the chicken over a high
heat, turning to brown on all sides.
With the skin-sides up, cover the pan,
reduce the heat to fairly low and cook
gently for about 20 minutes until the
chicken is tender and cooked through.
3 Meanwhile, cook the potatoes and
make the salad.
4 Transfer the chicken to warm plates.
Add the remaining butter or
margarine, lemon juice and parsley to
the frying pan, turn up the heat to
moderate and heat, stirring, until
melted. Season lightly. Spoon over the
chicken and serve straight away with
the potatoes and salad.

Garlic Fried Chicken

SERVES 4

Prepare as for Simple Fried Chicken
but add 1–2 finely chopped garlic cloves
to the browned chicken before
covering and finishing cooking.

Fragrant Fried Chicken

SERVES 4

Prepare as for Simple Fried Chicken
but add 15 ml/1 tbsp chopped fresh basil
and 10 ml/2 tsp chopped fresh sage
with the parsley.

Spicy Fried Chicken

SERVES 4

Prepare as for Simple Fried Chicken
but add 2.5 ml/½ tsp chilli powder to
the seasoned flour and mix a few drops
of Tabasco sauce with the lemon juice.
Serve with tomato or chilli relish on the
side.

Chicken Kiev

SERVES 4

100 g/4 oz/½ cup butter, softened
2 garlic cloves, crushed
30 ml/2 tbsp chopped fresh parsley
Finely grated rind and juice of ½ lemon
Freshly ground black pepper
4 part-boned chicken breasts
25 g/1 oz/¼ cup plain (all-purpose)
   flour
1 egg, beaten
100 g/4 oz/2 cups fresh white
   breadcrumbs
225 g/8 oz/1 cup long-grain rice
175 g/6 oz broccoli, cut into small florets
Oil, for deep-frying

1 Mash the butter with the garlic, parsley, lemon rind and juice and some black pepper in a bowl with a fork. Wrap in non-stick baking parchment or greaseproof (waxed) paper and chill for at least 30 minutes until firm. Cut into four pieces.
2 Make a slit in the side of each chicken breast and push a piece of flavoured butter inside. Secure with wooden cocktail sticks (toothpicks).
3 Put the flour, egg and breadcrumbs on separate plates. Dip in the flour,

then the egg and lastly the breadcrumbs to coat completely. Chill for at least 1 hour.
4 Heat about 2.5 cm/1 in oil in a large, heavy-based frying pan (skillet) until hot but not smoking. Fry (sauté) the chicken over a fairly high heat for 15 minutes, turning once, until crisp, golden and cooked through.
5 As soon as the chicken is cooking, cook the rice according to the packet instructions (or see page 294), adding the broccoli to the water after 5 minutes' cooking time. Drain in a colander.
6 When the chicken is cooked, drain on kitchen paper (paper towels). Remove the cocktail sticks and serve with the rice and broccoli.

Cheesy Chicken Kiev

SERVES 4

Prepare as for Fried Chicken Kiev but mash 75 g/3 oz/⅓ cup garlic and herb soft cheese with 50 g/2 oz/¼ cup butter and omit the garlic, parsley and lemon. Continue as before.

Chicken Liver Brochettes

Cook the potato dish and the salad while the livers are marinating. Keep the potatoes warm over a very low heat.

SERVES 4

8 chicken livers
45 ml/3 tbsp olive oil
Salt and freshly ground black pepper
5 ml/1 tsp lemon juice
2.5 ml/½ tsp dried sage
12 button (pearl) onions, peeled but left whole
4 rashers (slices) of back bacon, rinded and cut into chunks
12 button mushrooms
Potato and Celeriac Mash (see page 298) and a Tomato and Onion Salad (see page 309), to serve

1 Trim any sinews off the livers, using scissors, and cut into halves. Put in a bowl and mix with the oil, a little salt and pepper, the lemon juice and sage. Leave to stand for 30 minutes.
2 Meanwhile, boil the onions in water for 3 minutes. Drain.
3 Thread the livers, onions, bacon and mushrooms on four skewers.
4 Place on foil on a grill (broiler) rack. Grill (broil) for about 6 minutes, turning occasionally and brushing with any remaining marinade, until cooked through.
5 Pile the mash on warm plates and top with the brochettes and any juices. Serve straight away with the salad.

Cheesy Chicken with Sweetcorn

Put the bread in the oven and make the salad before starting to cook the chicken.

SERVES 4

4 skinless chicken breasts
20 g/¾ oz/4 tsp butter or margarine, melted
200 g/7 oz/1 small can of sweetcorn (corn), drained
50 g/2 oz/½ cup Emmental (Swiss) or Cheddar cheese, grated
Sprigs of watercress, to garnish
Garlic Bread (see page 395) and a Mixed Salad (see page 308), to serve

1 Preheat the grill (broiler). Place the chicken breasts one at a time in a plastic bag and beat with a rolling pin or meat mallet to flatten.
2 Brush with the butter or margarine and place on a grill rack. Grill (broil) for 3 minutes on each side. Spoon the sweetcorn over and top with the cheese. Grill under a moderate heat until the cheese is melted and golden.
3 Garnish with watercress and serve straight away with the garlic bread and salad.

Cheat's Chicken Maryland

Put the chips (fries) in the oven before you start preparing the rest of the recipe.

SERVES 4

2 bananas, halved widthways and then lengthways

25 g/1 oz/2 tbsp butter or margarine

4–8 rashers (slices) of streaky bacon, rinded

450 g/1 lb crumb-coated chicken breast pieces

320 g/12 oz/1 medium can of sweetcorn (corn)

Watercress, to garnish

Oven chips, to serve

1 Put the bananas in a small roasting tin (pan) and scatter over small pieces of the butter or margarine. Place on the shelf below the oven chips to cook. Check after 10 minutes, and if they are getting too soft, move to the bottom shelf of the oven.

2 Stretch the bacon rashers with the back of a knife. Cut into halves and roll up. Grill (broil) for about 4 minutes, turning once, until cooked through. Place on a plate, cover with foil and keep warm on the bottom shelf of the oven.

3 Grill the crumb-coated chicken pieces according to the packet directions.

4 Heat the sweetcorn in a saucepan.

5 Put the chicken, bacon and bananas on warm plates, garnish with the watercress and serve with the oven chips and the sweetcorn.

Chicken Mushroom and Tomato Kebabs

You can use the recipe for Simple Pesto Sauce on page 336, if you prefer to make your own.

SERVES 4

350 g/12 oz skinless chicken breasts, cut into chunks

30 ml/2 tbsp olive oil

10 ml/2 tsp balsamic vinegar

1 garlic clove, crushed

Salt and freshly ground black pepper

100 g/4 oz button mushrooms

8 cherry tomatoes

8 basil leaves

350 g/12 oz tagliatelle

45 ml/3 tbsp ready-made pesto

1 Put the chicken in a shallow dish. Add the oil, balsamic vinegar and garlic and season with a little salt and pepper. Mix well and leave to stand for 30 minutes.

2 While you wait, blanch the mushrooms by dropping into boiling water for 1 minute, then draining thoroughly. Cook the pasta according to the packet directions (or see page 293). Drain in a colander, return to the pan and stir in the pesto.

3 Preheat the grill (broiler) and thread the chicken, mushrooms, tomatoes and basil on skewers. Put the kebabs on foil on the grill rack and brush with any remaining marinade. Grill (broil) for about 8–10 minutes, turning once, until the chicken is cooked through.

4 Spoon the tagliatelle on to warm plates and serve with the kebabs placed alongside.

Chicken, Bacon and Corn Kebabs

Put the potatoes on to cook just before you prepare the kebabs. Finish making the potato salad while the kebabs are grilling (broiling).

SERVES 4

350 g/12 oz skinless chicken breasts, cut into chunks

30 ml/2 tbsp olive oil

15 ml/1 tbsp lemon juice

5 ml/1 tsp dried sage

Salt and freshly ground black pepper

2 corn cobs, each cut into 4 chunks

4 rashers (slices) of streaky bacon, rinded

A little melted butter or margarine, for brushing

Hot Potato Salad (see page 309), to serve

1 Put the chicken in a dish, add the oil, lemon juice, sage and a little salt and pepper and mix well.

2 Boil the corn cob pieces for 5 minutes in lightly salted water. While they are cooking, stretch the bacon rashers by scraping with the back of a knife. Cut each in half and roll up each half.

3 Thread the chicken on to skewers, interspersed with the bacon rolls and corn cob pieces. Preheat the grill (broiler).

4 Put the kebabs on foil on the grill rack and grill for about 8–10 minutes, turning and brushing with a little melted butter or margarine until golden and cooked through. Serve with the Hot Potato Salad.

Sweet and Sour Chicken

Make the rice dish before you start cooking the chicken and reheat it just before serving.

SERVES 4

30 ml/2 tbsp sunflower oil

225 g/8 oz chicken stir-fry meat

1 carrot, cut into matchsticks

1 small red (bell) pepper, cut into thin strips

¼ cucumber, cut into matchsticks

430 g/15½ oz/1 large can of pineapple pieces in natural juice

30 ml/2 tbsp tomato purée (paste)

45 ml/3 tbsp soy sauce

2.5 ml/½ tsp ground ginger

60 ml/4 tbsp malt vinegar

10 ml/2 tsp cornflour (cornstarch)

15 ml/1 tbsp water

Egg Fried Rice (see page 315), to serve

1 Heat the oil in a large frying pan (skillet) or wok. Add the chicken and cook, stirring, for 4 minutes over a high heat. Remove from the pan.

2 Add all the remaining ingredients except the cornflour and water and bring to the boil. Turn down the heat to moderate and cook for 5 minutes.

3 Mix the cornflour with the water in a cup and stir into the pan. Heat rapidly until boiling and cook for 1 minute, stirring until thickened and clear. Return the chicken to the pan and heat through.

4 Serve with the Egg Fried Rice.

Chicken Satay

SERVES 4

30 ml/2 tbsp sunflower oil
1 small onion, finely chopped
1 large garlic clove, crushed
30 ml/2 tbsp smooth peanut butter
10 ml/2 tsp lime juice
15 ml/1 tbsp clear honey
15 ml/1 tbsp soy sauce
1.5 ml/¼ tsp chilli powder
120 ml/4 fl oz/½ cup milk
450 g/1 lb skinless chicken breasts, diced
225 g/8 oz/1 cup long-grain rice
A Beansprout Salad (see page 310), to serve

1 Heat the oil in a saucepan. Add the onion and garlic and fry (sauté) over a high heat for 2 minutes, stirring. Stir in all the remaining ingredients except the milk, chicken and rice. Bring to the boil, stirring.
2 Stir in 90 ml/6 tbsp of the milk, reduce the heat to moderate and cook for 2 minutes.
3 Preheat the grill (broiler). Thread the chicken on soaked wooden skewers and place on foil on the grill rack. Brush with a little of the sauce.
4 Grill (broil) for about 8 minutes, turning occasionally, until tender and cooked through. Meanwhile, make the salad and cook the rice according to the packet directions (or see page 294). Drain in a colander.
5 Add the remaining milk to the sauce and heat through, stirring. Spoon the rice on warm plates. Top with the kebabs and spoon the remaining sauce over. Serve with the Beansprout Salad.

Sautéed Chicken and Avocado

A just-ripe avocado should give slightly when gently squeezed in the palm of your hand.

SERVES 4

4 just-ripe avocados
15 ml/1 tbsp lemon juice
15 ml/1 tbsp olive oil
225 g/8 oz chicken stir-fry meat
1 red (bell) pepper, cut into thin strips
1 bunch of spring onions (scallions), cut into short lengths
30 ml/2 tbsp soy sauce
15 ml/1 tbsp medium-dry sherry
A good pinch of ground ginger
Freshly ground black pepper
Lettuce leaves, to garnish
Prawn crackers, to serve

1 Cut the avocados into halves, remove the stones (pits) and scoop out the flesh. Cut the flesh into neat pieces and place in a bowl. Add the lemon juice and stir gently to coat (this will prevent browning).
2 Heat the oil in a frying pan (skillet). Add the chicken, pepper and spring onions and cook, stirring, for 5–7 minutes until the chicken is tender.
3 Add the avocado pieces, the soy sauce, sherry and ginger. Stir gently, turning the mixture over until the avocado is heated through and everything is coated. Season with pepper to taste.
4 Line four bowls with lettuce leaves. Spoon the chicken mixture into each and serve straight away with prawn crackers.

Chunky Chicken Parcels with Cranberry Conserve

SERVES 4

4 sheets of filo pastry (paste), thawed if frozen

50 g/2 oz/¼ cup butter or margarine, melted

425 g/15 oz/1 large can of chunky chicken in white sauce

5 ml/1 tsp dried thyme

60 ml/4 tbsp ready-made cranberry sauce

15 ml/1 tbsp port

Finely grated rind of ½ lemon

Sprigs of parsley, to garnish

New potatoes and French (green) beans, to serve

1 Preheat the oven to 190°C/375°F/ gas mark 5.
2 Brush a sheet of pastry with butter or margarine. Fold in half. Brush again.
3 Put a quarter of the chicken in the centre of the pastry, sprinkle with a quarter of the herbs. Draw the pastry over the filling and squeeze the edges together to form a pouch. Grease a baking (cookie) sheet with a little of the remaining butter or margarine. Transfer the pouch to the baking sheet. Repeat to make four parcels and brush with the remaining butter or margarine.
4 Bake in the oven for about 15 minutes until golden brown.
5 Meanwhile, cook the potatoes and beans. Gently heat the cranberry sauce, port and lemon rind stirring.
6 Transfer the parcels to warm plates. Put a spoonful of cranberry sauce to the side of each, garnish with parsley and serve with new potatoes and French beans.

Chicken Florentine Parcels

SERVES 4

350 g/12 oz puff pasty (paste), thawed if frozen

4 small skinless chicken breasts

350 g/12 oz frozen leaf spinach, thawed and squeezed well to drain

2 tomatoes, skinned and sliced

175 g/6 oz Mozzarella cheese, thinly sliced

A little grated nutmeg

Salt and freshly ground black pepper

1 egg, beaten

A Celeriac and Carrot Salad (see page 312), to serve

1 Preheat the oven to 200°C/400°F/ gas mark 6. Rinse a baking (cookie) sheet in cold water and leave damp.
2 Cut the pastry into four pieces and roll out each one to about a 20 cm/ 8 in square. Place a chicken breast on each. Top with the spinach, then the tomato slices and Mozzarella cheese. Sprinkle with nutmeg, salt and pepper.
3 Brush the edges with beaten egg, then fold over the pastry to form neat parcels. Transfer to the baking sheet, sealed sides down. Make two small slits in the top of each parcel to allow steam to escape. Brush the top and sides with beaten egg.
4 Bake in the oven for 35 minutes until golden and cooked through. While they are cooking, make the salad. Transfer to warm plates and serve hot with the salad.

Deep-fried Chicken Parcels

If you prefer to make your own pastry (paste), use 1½ quantities of the recipe for shortcrust (basic pie crust) on page 391.

SERVES 4–6

375 g/13 oz shortcrust pastry, thawed if frozen
175 g/6 oz/1½ cups chopped cooked chicken
15 ml/1 tbsp mayonnaise
15 ml/1 tbsp corn or tomato relish
Salt and freshly ground black pepper
Oil, for deep-frying
Super Creamed Potatoes (see page 298) and peas, to serve

1 Roll out the pastry to 5 mm/¼ in thick and cut into 12 squares.
2 Mix the chicken with the mayonnaise, relish and salt and pepper to taste in a bowl.
3 Divide the mixture between the centres of the pastry. Brush the edges with water.
4 Fold the pastry over the filling and press the edges well together. Pinch all round between your finger and thumb to decorate and seal firmly. Chill, if time allows, for 30 minutes.
5 Prepare and cook the potatoes while the parcels are chilling.
6 Heat the oil in a saucepan or deep-fat fryer to 190°C/375°F or until a cube of day-old bread browns in 30 seconds. Deep-fry for about 7 minutes until crisp and golden brown. Drain on kitchen paper (paper towels). Cook the peas while the parcels are cooking. Serve the parcels hot with the potatoes and peas.

Tandoori Chicken

SERVES 4

8 small or 4 large chicken portions, skin removed as far as possible
300 ml/½ pt/1¼ cups plain yoghurt
1 small garlic clove, crushed
15 ml/1 tbsp tandoori powder
5 ml/1 tsp chopped fresh coriander (cilantro)
Salt and freshly ground black pepper
Shredded lettuce, sprigs of coriander and wedges of lemon and tomato, to garnish
Quick Pilau Rice (see page 314) and mango chutney or lime pickle, to serve

1 Make several slashes in the flesh of the chicken. Mix the remaining ingredients together in a large, shallow dish. Add the chicken and rub the mixture well into the slits. When well-coated, leave to marinate for at least 3 hours.
2 Preheat the oven to 200°C/400°F/ gas mark 6. Place the chicken in a baking tin (pan). Spoon any remaining marinade over. Cover with foil. Bake in the oven for 45 minutes.
3 Remove the foil from the chicken, pour off any liquid and return to the oven to cook, uncovered, for a further 15 minutes or until well browned and cooked through. Meanwhile, cook the Quick Pilau Rice.
4 Transfer the chicken to warm plates. Garnish with shredded lettuce, coriander leaves and wedges of lemon and tomato, and serve with the rice and mango chutney or lime pickle.

Chicken Bhuna Masala

For seeding chillies, see Fiery Mussel Spaghettini, page 134. Make the yoghurt before you start preparing the chicken. Warm the naan breads under the grill (broiler) just before the chicken is ready.

SERVES 4

15 ml/1 tbsp sunflower oil

25 g/1 oz/2 tbsp butter or margarine

10 ml/2 tsp ground cardamom

1.5 ml/¼ tsp ground cloves

5 ml/1 tsp ground ginger

2.5 ml/½ tsp ground turmeric

2 green chillies, seeded and chopped

2 large onions, finely chopped

1 large garlic clove, crushed

4 skinless chicken breasts

225 g/8 oz/1 small can of chopped tomatoes

Salt and freshly ground black pepper

60 ml/4 tbsp water

30 ml/2 tbsp chopped fresh coriander (cilantro)

Naan breads and Minted Yoghurt and Cucumber (see page 340), to serve

1 Heat the oil and butter or margarine in a large pan over a moderate heat. Add the spices, chillies, onions and garlic and fry (sauté) for 2 minutes, stirring.

2 Add the chicken breasts and cook for 2 minutes on each side.

3 Add all the remaining ingredients except the coriander and heat until boiling, then turn down the heat until just bubbling gently round the edges. Cook for 45 minutes. Taste and re-season if necessary.

4 Sprinkle with coriander and serve with the naan breads and yoghurt.

Oriental Chicken Curry

SERVES 4

100 g/4 oz creamed coconut, cut into chunks

600 ml/1 pt/2½ cups boiling water

45 ml/3 tbsp curry powder

5 ml/1 tsp Chinese five spice powder

10 ml/2 tsp grated fresh root ginger

450 g/1 lb chicken breasts, diced

60 ml/4 tbsp sunflower oil

2 garlic cloves, crushed

Salt

30 ml/2 tbsp chopped fresh coriander (cilantro)

225 g/8 oz/1 cup long-grain rice

1 Put the coconut in a bowl and stir in the boiling water. When dissolved, stir in the spices. Leave to cool. Add the chicken and leave to marinate for 1 hour.

2 Heat the oil in a wok or large frying pan (skillet). Add the garlic and cook, stirring, for 1 minute over a fairly high heat. Lift the chicken out of the marinade and cook, stirring, for 5 minutes.

3 Reduce the heat and add the marinade, then cook over a moderate heat for a further 15–20 minutes, stirring, until cooked through. Season with salt to taste and stir in the coriander.

4 Meanwhile, cook the rice according to the packet directions (or see page 294). Drain in a colander and spoon on warm plates. Top with the curry and serve.

Eastern Apricot Chicken

See Fiery Mussel Spaghettini, page 134, for how to seed a chilli.

SERVES 4

40 g/1½ oz/3 tbsp butter or margarine
1 onion, finely chopped
8 chicken drumsticks
1 garlic clove, crushed
1 green chilli, seeded and finely chopped
5 ml/1 tsp ground cumin
225 g/8 oz/1 small can of chopped tomatoes
175 g/6 oz/1 cup no-need-to-soak dried apricots, halved
Salt and freshly ground black pepper
150 ml/¼ pt/⅔ cup water
A little desiccated (shredded) coconut and chopped fresh coriander (cilantro), to garnish
Naan bread, to serve

1 Melt the butter or margarine in a deep frying pan (skillet). Add the onion and fry (sauté) for 3 minutes over a fairly high heat.
2 Add the chicken and brown on all sides. Remove from the pan.
3 Stir in the garlic and spices. Cook for 1 minute, then add the tomatoes, apricots, seasoning and water. Return the chicken to the pan and season lightly.
4 Turn down the heat to fairly low, cover and cook very gently for 1 hour. Taste and re-season if necessary. Warm the bread under the grill (broiler) just before the chicken is ready.
5 Spoon the chicken into warm bowls, sprinkle with desiccated coconut and coriander and serve with the naan bread.

Chicken Sag

SERVES 4

30 ml/2 tbsp sunflower oil
2 onions, halved and thinly sliced
15 ml/1 tbsp mild curry paste
1 garlic clove, crushed
30 ml/2 tbsp water
60 ml/4 tbsp chopped fresh coriander (cilantro)
1 large tomato, finely chopped
Salt
5 ml/1 tsp caster (superfine) sugar
175 g/6 oz frozen leaf spinach, thawed
225 g/8 oz/2 cups diced cooked chicken
4 cooked potatoes, cut into small chunks
Poppadoms (see page 317), to serve

1 Heat the oil in a saucepan. Fry (sauté) the onions for 3 minutes over a high heat, stirring.
2 Add the curry paste, garlic, water, coriander, and tomato and season lightly with salt. Fry for 1 minute.
3 Add the sugar, spinach, chicken and potatoes, stir well, then cover, turn down the heat to low and cook gently for 5 minutes, stirring occasionally. Cook as many poppadoms as you like and serve them in a stack with the Sag.

Chicken Breasts Masala

SERVES 4

150 ml/¼ pt/⅔ cup plain yoghurt
1 garlic clove, crushed
5 ml/1 tsp ground ginger
5 ml/1 tsp chilli powder
5 ml/1 tsp ground cumin
5 ml/1 tsp garam masala
5 ml/1 tsp salt
5 ml/1 tsp ground black pepper
4 skinless chicken breasts
Lettuce, wedges of tomato and slices
  of cucumber, to garnish
Quick Pilau Rice (see page 314), to
  serve

1 Mix the yoghurt with the garlic, spices, salt and pepper in a shallow dish. Add the chicken, turn over to coat completely, then cover and chill for several hours or overnight.
2 Preheat the oven to 190°C/375°F/ gas mark 5. Remove the chicken from the marinade and place in a single layer in a shallow baking dish. Bake in the oven for about 30 minutes until cooked through, turning once halfway through cooking. Alternatively grill (broil) for about 8 minutes on each side. Meanwhile, cook the rice.
3 Garnish with lettuce, tomato and cucumber and serve on a bed of rice.

Chicken Jalfrezi

If you're not sure how to seed chillies, see Fiery Mussel Spaghettini, page 134.

SERVES 4

225 g/8 oz/1 cup long-grain rice
2 large or 4 small skinless chicken
  breasts, cut into cubes
10 ml/2 tsp garlic powder
5 ml/1 tsp ground ginger
5 ml/1 tsp chilli powder
25 g/1 oz/2 tbsp butter or margarine
1 onion, very finely chopped
30 ml/2 tbsp curry paste
2 green (bell) peppers, cut into thin
  strips
4 mild green chillies, seeded and
  chopped
60 ml/4 tbsp chopped fresh coriander
  (cilantro)
Salt and sugar, to taste

1 Cook the rice according to the packet directions (or see page 294). Drain in a colander.
2 Put the cubed chicken in a shallow dish and sprinkle with the garlic and chilli powders and the ground ginger.
3 Melt the butter or margarine in a large frying pan (skillet) over a high heat. Add the onion and fry (sauté), stirring, for 2 minutes. Add the curry paste, chicken and peppers and stir-fry for 6–8 minutes until the chicken is cooked.
4 Add 30 ml/2 tbsp water, the chillies and coriander to the pan and cook, stirring, for 2 minutes. Season to taste with salt and sugar. Serve on a bed of the rice.

Big and Bounteous Salad

SERVES 6

225 g/8 oz wholewheat pasta shapes

175 g/6 oz cherry tomatoes, halved

1 bunch of spring onions (scallions), chopped

1 green (bell) pepper, diced

200 g/7 oz/1 small can of sweetcorn (corn) drained

1 eating (dessert) apple, cored and diced

175 g/6 oz/1½ cups diced cooked chicken

100 g/4 oz/1 cup diced cooked ham

175 g/6 oz/1½ cups Cheddar cheese, diced

60 ml/4 tbsp olive oil, plus a little extra for serving

25 ml/1½ tbsp lemon juice

5 ml/1 tsp Dijon mustard

A good pinch of salt and pepper

10 ml/2 tsp chopped fresh parsley

1 Cook the pasta according to the packet directions (or see page 293). Drain in a colander, rinse with cold water and drain again. Place in a large salad bowl.

2 Add the tomatoes, spring onions, pepper, sweetcorn, apple, chicken, ham and cheese.

3 Whisk the remaining ingredients together in a bowl with a wire whisk and pour over. Lift and stir the salad gently until well blended. Chill for at least 1 hour to allow the flavours to develop.

Curried Chicken and Pasta Salad

Make the Tomato and Onion Salad while the pasta is cooking.

SERVES 4

225 g/8 oz pasta shapes

225 g/8 oz/2 cups diced cooked chicken

45 ml/3 tbsp mayonnaise

5 ml/1 tsp curry paste

225 g/8 oz/1 small can of curried baked beans

1 green (bell) pepper, diced

A few lettuce leaves

30 ml/2 tbsp coconut flakes

A Tomato and Onion Salad (see page 309), to serve

1 Cook the pasta according to the packet directions (or see page 293). Drain in a colander, rinse with cold water and drain again. Tip into a large bowl.

2 Add the chicken to the pasta. Mix the mayonnaise with the curry paste and baked beans. Add to the pasta with the diced pepper and lift and stir gently.

3 Pile the salad on to lettuce leaves.

4 Dry-fry the coconut in a frying pan (skillet) until golden – be careful as it will burn very easily. Remove from the pan straight away. Scatter over the salad and serve with the Tomato and Onion Salad.

Chicken and Spiced Almond Salad

Put the potatoes on to cook before preparing the chicken salad.

SERVES 4

1 ready-cooked chicken, about
  1.5 kg/3 lb
75 ml/5 tbsp mayonnaise
75 ml/5 tbsp plain yoghurt
15 ml/1 tbsp tomato purée (paste)
5 ml/1 tsp Worcestershire sauce
5 cm/2 in piece of cucumber, chopped
A knob of butter or margarine
50 g/2 oz/½ cup blanched almonds
1.5 ml/¼ tsp chilli powder
1.5 ml/¼ tsp mixed (apple-pie) spice
1.5 ml/¼ tsp chilli powder
Lettuce leaves and wedges of lemon,
  to garnish
New potatoes, to serve

1 Cut the chicken into four portions (see page 202).
Mix the mayonnaise with the yoghurt, tomato purée and Worcestershire sauce in a small bowl. Season lightly. Stir in the cucumber.
2 Melt the butter or margarine in a frying pan (skillet) over a moderate heat. Fry (sauté) the almonds until golden brown. Remove from the heat. Sprinkle with the spices and stir well until coated. Drain on kitchen paper (paper towels).
3 Arrange the lettuce leaves on four plates. Top each with a piece of chicken. Spoon the sauce over, scatter with the almonds and garnish with the wedges of lemon. Serve with the new potatoes.

Apple, Chicken and Walnut Salad

SERVES 4

225 g/8 oz/1 cup long-grain rice
1 large green eating (dessert) apple,
  cored and diced
Juice of 1 lemon
2 celery sticks, chopped
50 g/2 oz/½ cup walnut halves, roughly
  chopped
175 g/6 oz/1½ cups diced cooked
  chicken
30 ml/2 tbsp olive oil
30 ml/2 tbsp mayonnaise
Salt and freshly ground black pepper
15 ml/1 tbsp snipped fresh chives, to
  garnish

1 Cook the rice according to the packet directions (or see page 294). Drain in a colander, rinse with cold water and drain again. Place in a large salad bowl.
2 Mix the apple in a little of the lemon juice to prevent browning. Add to the rice with the celery, nuts and chicken and stir gently until well mixed.
3 Using a wire whisk, whisk the olive oil, remaining lemon juice and mayonnaise together in a small bowl with a little salt and pepper and pour over the salad. Lift and stir gently until completely coated, then spoon into bowls and serve garnished with the chives.

Summer Beach Chicken Salad

SERVES 4

175 g/6 oz/¾ cup long-grain rice

4 rashers (slices) of streaky bacon, rinded and cut into small pieces

2 bananas, cut into chunky slices

15 ml/1 tbsp lemon juice

30 ml/2 tbsp mayonnaise

15 ml/1 tbsp olive oil

225 g/8 oz/2 cups diced cooked chicken

1 green (bell) pepper, diced

200 g/7 oz/1 small can of sweetcorn (corn) with (bell) peppers, drained

Salt and freshly ground black pepper

Lettuce leaves

2 tomatoes, cut into small wedges

1 Cook the rice according to the packet directions (or see page 294). Drain in a colander, rinse with cold water and drain again and place in a large bowl.

2 Dry-fry the bacon in a frying pan (skillet), stirring until crisp and brown. Drain on kitchen paper (paper towels).

3 Mix the banana chunks with the lemon juice. Mix the mayonnaise with the oil to thin it slightly.

4 Add the banana with all the juice to the rice, then the mayonnaise mixture, the chicken, pepper and sweetcorn. Lift and stir gently, turning the ingredients over until thoroughly mixed, adding salt and pepper to taste.

5 Line four individual salad bowls with lettuce leaves. Pile the salad on top, sprinkle with the bacon and garnish with tomato wedges before serving.

Oriental Chicken and Beansprout Salad

SERVES 4

225 g/8 oz/1 medium can of pineapple rings, drained, reserving the juice

100 g/4 oz/2 cups beansprouts

175 g/6 oz/1½ cups diced cooked chicken

1 green (bell) pepper, halved and thinly sliced

1 onion, halved and thinly sliced

15 ml/1 tbsp soy sauce

15 ml/1 tbsp sunflower oil

5 ml/1 tsp tomato purée (paste)

Salt and freshly ground black pepper

A few lettuce leaves

Prawn crackers, to serve

1 Cut the pineapple rings into chunks and mix with the beansprouts, chicken, pepper and onion.

2 Using a wire whisk, mix the pineapple juice in a small bowl with all the remaining ingredients except the lettuce.

3 Pour over the salad, then lift and stir gently until well mixed. Leave to stand for 30 minutes.

4 Line four bowls with lettuce leaves. Spoon in the salad and serve with prawn crackers.

Sunny Chicken Salad

SERVES 4

225 g/8 oz/1 cup long-grain rice
50 g/2 oz/½ cup frozen peas
Salt
225 g/8 oz/1 small can of pineapple
   rings, drained, reserving the juice,
   and cut into small pieces
2 tomatoes, cut into chunks
10 cm/4 in piece of cucumber, cut into
   chunks
1 small green (bell) pepper, diced
175 g/6 oz/1½ cups diced cooked
   chicken
45 ml/3 tbsp mayonnaise
Freshly ground black pepper
Lettuce leaves

1 Cook the rice according to the packet
directions (or see page 294), adding the
peas halfway through cooking. Drain in
a colander, rinse with cold water and
drain again.
2 Place in a bowl and add all the
remaining ingredients except the
lettuce. Lift and stir gently, adding a
little pineapple juice to thin if necessary.
3 Pile on to lettuce leaves and serve.

Savoury Turkey Escalopes

*This recipe also works well with
chicken breasts or slices of pork fillet.*

SERVES 4

4 small turkey steaks, about 175 g/6 oz
   each
85 g/3½ oz/1 small packet of sage and
   onion stuffing mix
1 egg
15 ml/1 tbsp milk
Sunflower oil, for shallow frying
Wedges of lemon and sprigs of parsley
   or sage, to garnish
Puréed Potatoes (see page 299) and
   French (green) beans, to serve

1 Put the turkey steaks one at a time
into a plastic bag and beat with a
rolling pin or meat mallet until
flattened and fairly thin.
2 Put the stuffing mix in a shallow dish
and beat the egg and milk in a
separate dish.
3 Dip the turkey in the beaten egg,
then the stuffing, to coat completely.
4 Heat enough oil to cover the base of
a frying pan (skillet) and fry (sauté) the
escalopes for 3–4 minutes until golden
brown underneath.
5 Turn over and fry the other sides until
cooked through and golden.
6 Drain on kitchen paper (paper
towels). Meanwhile, cook the potatoes
and beans.
7 Garnish with wedges of lemon and
sprigs of parsley or sage and serve with
the puréed potatoes and French beans.

Warming Turkey Casserole

This is a complete meal in one pot – perfect for a fireside supper. For very big appetites, serve some crusty bread to accompany it.

SERVES 4

60 ml/4 tbsp plain (all-purpose) flour
Salt and freshly ground black pepper
450 g/1 lb turkey thigh meat, diced
30 ml/2 tbsp sunflower oil
1 onion, chopped
100 g/4 oz button mushrooms, halved
1 small swede (rutabaga), cut into chunks
2 large carrots, cut into chunks
1 large leek, well-washed and cut into chunks
4 large potatoes, cut into chunks
600 ml/1 pt/2½ cups beef stock, made with 1 stock cube
1 bouquet garni sachet
A little gravy block or browning
15 ml/1 tbsp chopped fresh parsley, to garnish

1 Mix the flour with a little salt and pepper in a plastic bag. Add the turkey, hold the bag closed and shake it to coat all the meat with the flour.

2 Heat the oil in a flameproof casserole (Dutch oven). Add the turkey and onion and cook over a fairly high heat, stirring and turning, until the turkey is lightly coloured all over.

3 Add all the other ingredients with enough gravy block or browning to give a rich, brown colour, then turn down the heat until only just bubbling round the edges.

4 Cover the casserole with a lid and cook for 1½ hours, stirring once or twice to prevent sticking, until everything is really tender.

5 Discard the bouquet garni, stir gently once again, taste and add more salt and pepper if necessary. Serve in warm bowls, sprinkled with parsley.

Three-herb Turkey Casserole

SERVES 4

30 ml/2 tbsp sunflower oil
4 turkey steaks
1 garlic clove, crushed
15 ml/1 tbsp chopped fresh parsley
15 ml/1 tbsp chopped fresh basil
15 ml/1 tbsp chopped fresh oregano
2.5 ml/½ tsp paprika
30 ml/2 tbsp tomato purée (paste)
150 ml/¼ pt/⅔ cup dry white wine
Salt and freshly ground black pepper
225 g/8 oz/1 cup long-grain rice
Broccoli, to serve

1 Preheat the oven to 190°C/375°F/ gas mark 5.

2 Heat the oil in a flameproof casserole (Dutch oven) and fry (sauté) the turkey quickly on both sides to brown.

3 Mix the remaining ingredients together and pour over. Cover and cook in the oven for about 40 minutes until the turkey is tender. Taste and re-season if necessary.

4 Meanwhile, cook the rice according to the packet directions (or see page 294). Cook the broccoli, drain in a colander and serve with the turkey and rice.

Cheat's Kentucky Fried Turkey with Barbecued Beans

Put the chips (fries) in to cook before you cook the turkey.

SERVES 3

6 crumb-coated minced (ground) turkey drumsticks

A little sunflower oil

2.5 ml/½ tsp dried onion granules

2.5 ml/½ tsp ground cumin

2.5 ml/½ tsp dried mixed herbs

2.5 ml/½ tsp salt

A good pinch of white pepper

400 g/14 oz/1 large can of baked beans

15 ml/1 tbsp bottled barbecue or sweet brown sauce

Lettuce leaves, tomato slices, cucumber slices and wedges of lemon, to garnish

Oven chips, to serve

1 Preheat the grill (broiler). Brush the turkey drummers with a little oil. Mix the onion granules, cumin, herbs, salt and pepper together and sprinkle all over the turkey. Place on the grill rack.
2 Grill (broil), according to the packet directions, until golden brown and cooked through, turning once.
3 While they are cooking, put the beans in a saucepan and stir in the sauce. Heat through thoroughly, stirring occasionally.
4 Transfer the turkey to plates and add the beans. Garnish with the salad and wedges of lemon and serve with the oven chips.

Tyrolean Turkey

SERVES 4

25 g/1 oz/2 tbsp butter or margarine

4 turkey steaks

1 onion, finely chopped

1 eating (dessert) apple, peeled, cored and chopped

1 garlic clove, crushed

1 small red cabbage, finely shredded

30 ml/2 tbsp raisins

15 ml/1 tbsp caraway seeds

Salt and freshly ground black pepper

2 large potatoes, thinly sliced

300 ml/½ pt/1¼ cups chicken stock, made with 1 stock cube

1 Preheat the oven to 160°C/325°F/ gas mark 3.
2 Melt the butter or margarine in a flameproof casserole (Dutch oven). Add the turkey and brown quickly on both sides over a high heat. Remove from the pan.
3 Add the onion and apple and fry (sauté), stirring, for 1 minute. Add the garlic and cabbage and cook, stirring, for 2 minutes until the cabbage begins to soften slightly.
4 Add the raisins, caraway seeds and a little salt and pepper. Return the turkey to the pan and top with the potato slices. Pour over the stock and season again lightly with salt and pepper. Cover with a lid or foil and bake in a preheated oven for 1 hour.
5 Remove the lid or foil, turn up the heat to 190°C/375°F/gas mark 5 and cook for a further 30 minutes until the potatoes are turning golden brown. Serve hot.

Turkey with White Wine and Cream

SERVES 4

225 g/8 oz/1 cup long-grain rice

25 g/1 oz/2 tbsp butter or margarine

4 turkey steaks

150 ml/¼ pt/⅔ cup dry white wine

150 ml/¼ pt/⅔ cup chicken stock, made with ½ stock cube

100 g/4 oz button mushrooms, sliced

2.5 ml/½ tsp dried thyme

Salt and freshly ground black pepper

15 ml/1 tbsp cornflour (cornstarch)

15 ml/1 tbsp brandy

60 ml/4 tbsp crème fraîche

15 ml/1 tbsp chopped fresh parsley

Mangetout (snow peas), to serve

1 Cook the rice according to the packet directions (or see page 294). Drain in a colander.

2 Meanwhile, melt the butter or margarine in a large frying pan (skillet). Add the turkey and brown over a fairly high heat on both sides.

3 Add the wine, stock, mushrooms, thyme, salt and pepper.

4 Bring to the boil, turn down the heat until just gently bubbling round the edges, cover and cook for about 8 minutes or until cooked through.

5 Remove the turkey steaks and keep warm. Cook the mangetout.

6 Mix the cornflour with the brandy in a small cup and stir into the pan. Bring to the boil, stirring and boil for 1 minute.

7 Stir the crème fraîche into the sauce and heat through. Taste and re-season.

8 Spoon over the turkey, sprinkle with parsley and serve with the rice and mangetout.

Turkey in Smooth Cider Sauce

Put the potatoes on to cook before you start cooking the turkey. Cook the beans and carrots while the turkey is cooking.

SERVES 4

4 turkey steaks

150 ml/¼ pt/⅔ cup medium-sweet cider

150 ml/¼ pt/⅔ cup chicken stock, made with ½ stock cube

2.5 ml/½ tsp dried basil

2.5 ml/½ tsp dried oregano

Salt and freshly ground black pepper

20 ml/4 tsp cornflour (cornstarch)

30 ml/2 tbsp milk

150 ml/¼ pt/⅔ cup single (light) cream

15 ml/1 tbsp chopped fresh parsley, to garnish

Super Creamed Potatoes (see page 298), runner beans and baby carrots, to serve

1 Place the turkey steaks in a large frying pan (skillet) and add the cider, stock, herbs and a little salt and pepper. Bring to the boil over a high heat, turn down the heat until gently bubbling round the edges, cover and cook for 10–15 minutes until tender. Remove the turkey from the pan with a draining spoon and keep warm.

2 Mix the cornflour with the milk in a small cup. Stir into the pan and bring to the boil, stirring over a high heat. Cook for 1 minute. Stir in the cream, taste and re-season. Heat through.

3 Transfer the turkey to warm plates. Spoon the sauce over, sprinkle with the parsley and serve with the Super Creamed Potatoes, runner beans and baby carrots.

Creamed Turkey Grand Marnier

SERVES 4

Prepare as for Turkey with Smooth Cider Sauce but use 90 ml/6 tbsp dry white wine and 60 ml/4 tbsp Grand Marnier instead of the cider and use crème fraîche instead of the single (light) cream. Garnish with watercress and slices of orange instead of parsley.

Boxing Day Pie

The quantities of stuffing or vegetables don't really matter – just use whatever you have. Put the scrubbed potatoes in the preheated oven before you start preparing the pie so everything will be ready at the same time. Cook the beans while the pie is in the oven.

SERVES 4

225 g/8 oz puff pastry (paste), thawed if frozen

225 g/8 oz/2 cups diced cooked turkey

100 g/4 oz cooked sausagemeat and/or stuffing, cut into pieces

100 g/4 oz cooked leftover vegetables

100 g/4 oz button mushrooms, sliced

295 g/10½ oz/1 medium can of condensed mushrooms soup

45 ml/3 tbsp cranberry sauce

Freshly ground black pepper

Beaten egg or a little single (light) cream, to glaze

Jacket-baked Potatoes (see page 296) and French (green) beans, to serve

1 Preheat the oven to 200°C/400°F/ gas mark 6.

2 Roll out the pastry to a round slightly larger than the top of a 1.2 litre/2 pt/ 5 cup pie dish. Put a pie funnel or eggcup in the centre of the dish.

3 Put the turkey, sausagemeat, stuffing, vegetables and mushrooms in the dish and mix well. Spoon the soup and cranberry sauce over and season with black pepper.

4 Cut a strip off the pastry. Dampen the edge of the dish and lay the strip of pastry round the edge. Lay the pastry lid in position, pressing well to the edge to seal. Pinch all round the edge between your finger and thumb to decorate and seal the top both layers of pastry together.

5 Make a slit in the centre over the pie funnel or eggcup to allow steam to escape. Make leaves out of pastry trimmings, or roll them out and cut into attractive shapes with a pastry cutter, if liked. Brush the pastry lid with beaten egg or cream to glaze. Lay the leaves or shapes in position and brush again.

6 Bake in the oven for about 35 minutes or until puffy, golden brown and piping hot. Serve with jacket-baked potatoes and French beans.

Oriental Duck with Ginger

Make the salad before you start to cook the duck.

SERVES 4

20 g/¾ oz/1½ tbsp butter or margarine

2 large duck breasts

Salt and freshly ground black pepper

150 ml/¼ pt/⅔ cup chicken stock, made with ½ stock cube

30 ml/2 tbsp ginger wine

30 ml/1 tbsp light soy sauce

10 ml/2 tsp cornflour (cornstarch)

250 g/9 oz/1 packet of Chinese egg noodles

30 ml/2 tbsp snipped fresh chives

A Beansprout Salad (see page 310), to serve

1 Heat the butter or margarine in a non-stick frying pan (skillet). Add the duck, season with salt and pepper and fry (sauté) for 8 minutes, then turn, season again and fry for a further 7 minutes until slightly pink in the centre. Cook a little longer if you like it well-done. Remove from the pan and keep warm.

2 Add the stock and ginger wine to the pan and bring to the boil.

3 Mix the soy sauce with the cornflour in a small cup and stir into the pan. Bring to the boil and cook for 2 minutes, stirring until thickened. Taste and re-season if necessary.

4 Meanwhile, cook the noodles according to the packet directions. Drain and stir in the remaining soy sauce. Pile on warm plates.

5 Slice the duck and arrange on top of the noodles with the sauce. Sprinkle with chives and serve with the salad.

Duck with Port and Redcurrants

Prepare the vegetables for serving before you start the duck, then cook them while the duck is cooking.

SERVES 4

20 g/¾ oz/1½ tbsp butter or margarine

2 large duck breasts

Salt and freshly ground black pepper

150 ml/¼ pt/⅔ cup chicken stock, made with ½ stock cube

45 ml/3 tbsp port

15 ml/1 tbsp redcurrant jelly (clear conserve)

15 ml/1 tbsp cornflour (cornstarch)

15 ml/1 tbsp water

50 g/2 oz fresh redcurrants, removed from their stalks

New potatoes and French (green) beans, to serve

1 Heat the butter or margarine in a non-stick frying pan (skillet). Add the duck, season and fry (sauté) over a fairly high heat for 8 minutes.

2 Turn the duck over, season again and fry for a further 7 minutes or until just pink in the centre. Cook a little longer for well-done duck. Remove from the pan and keep warm.

3 Add the stock, port and redcurrant jelly. Heat, stirring, until the jelly dissolves.

4 Mix the cornflour with the water and stir in. Bring to the boil and cook for 2 minutes, stirring. Taste and re-season if necessary. Stir in the redcurrants.

5 Cut the duck into thin slices and arrange on four warm plates. Spoon the sauce over and serve with the new potatoes and French beans.

Blackcurrant Duck

SERVES 4

Prepare as for Duck with Port and Redcurrants but substitute blackcurrant jelly (clear conserve) for the redcurrant and crème de cassis for the port. Add blackcurrants to the sauce instead of redcurrants.

Minted Duck with Peas

SERVES 4

1 oven-ready duck, about 1.75 kg/4 lb
25 g/1 oz/2 tbsp butter or margarine
2 onions, halved and thinly sliced
600 ml/1 pt/2½ cups giblet stock (see page 323) or chicken stock, made with 1 stock cube
Salt and freshly ground black pepper
225 g/8 oz/2 cups frozen peas
15 ml/1 tbsp chopped fresh mint
15 ml/1 tbsp chopped fresh oregano
15 ml/1 tbsp chopped fresh parsley
1.5 ml/¼ tsp grated nutmeg
1 round lettuce, shredded
45 ml/3 tbsp plain (all-purpose) flour
Sprigs of mint, to garnish
Plain potatoes, to serve

1 Remove the giblets from the duck and use for the stock, if liked. Wipe inside and out with kitchen paper (paper towels). Prick all over with a fork.
2 Preheat the oven to 200°C/400°F/ gas mark 6.
3 Melt the butter or margarine in a flameproof casserole (Dutch oven). Add the duck and brown over a fairly high heat on all sides. Remove the duck. Add the onions and cook, stirring, for 2 minutes. Pour off any fat.

4 Return the duck to the casserole. Add the stock and a little salt and pepper. Bring to the boil, cover and transfer to the oven for 30 minutes.
5 Again spoon off any fat. Add all the remaining ingredients except the flour. Turn down the oven to 180°C/350°F/ gas mark 4 and cook for a further 1½ hours. About 30 minutes before the duck is due to be ready, prepare and cook the potatoes.
6 Remove the duck and keep warm. Spoon off any fat. Mix the flour with the water in a small cup. Stir into the casserole, place on top of the stove and cook over a high heat for 3 minutes, stirring. Taste and re-season if necessary.
7 Cut the duck into quarters. Transfer to warm plates. Spoon pea sauce over each portion, garnish with sprigs of mint and serve with the potatoes.

Duck with Orange

Put the potatoes on to cook before you start to make the orange sauce (step 4). Cook the peas while the sauce is cooking.

SERVES 4

1 oven-ready duck, about 1.75 kg/4 lb
2 small onions
Salt
300 ml/½ pt/1¼ cups water
1 chicken stock cube
15 g/½ oz/1 tbsp butter or margarine
5 ml/1 tsp light brown sugar
Thinly pared rind and juice of 1 orange
60 ml/4 tbsp port
Freshly ground black pepper
15 ml/1 tbsp cornflour (cornstarch)
Slices of orange and sprigs of parsley, to garnish
New potatoes and peas, to serve

1 Preheat the oven to 200°C/400°F/ gas mark 6. Remove the giblets from the duck and reserve. Prick all over the skin with a fork. Push one of the onions into the cavity of the duck.

2 Place on a rack in a roasting tin (pan) and sprinkle with salt. Roast in the oven for 1 hour 20 minutes. Turn down the heat to 180°C/350°F/ gas mark 4 and continue to roast for 30 minutes, until crisp, golden and tender.

3 While the duck is cooking, put the giblets in a saucepan with the water and stock cube. Bring to the boil over a high heat, turn down the heat until bubbling gently, cover and cook for 40 minutes. Strain the liquid through a sieve (strainer) into a bowl and reserve.

4 Chop the remaining onion and fry (sauté) in the butter or margarine in a saucepan for about 5 minutes, stirring over a high heat until richly browned, adding the sugar after 3 minutes. Add the orange rind and juice and the strained stock.

5 Bring to the boil, turn down the heat until gently bubbling, then cover and cook for 10 minutes. Remove the orange rind. Stir in the port and season to taste.

6 Mix the cornflour with the water in a small cup and stir in. Bring to the boil and cook for 1 minute.

7 Transfer the duck to a carving dish and cut into portions. Transfer to warm plates.

8 Strain the sauce over, garnish with orange slices and sprigs of parsley and serve with the new potatoes and peas.

Russian Duck

Put the potatoes on to cook before the duck. Make the salad while the duck is cooking. Beetroot (red beets) cooked and pickled in vinegar are not suitable for this recipe.

SERVES 4

50 g/2 oz/¼ cup unsalted (sweet) butter
4 small boneless duck breasts
Salt and freshly ground black pepper
30 ml/2 tbsp orange marmalade
Finely grated rind and juice of 1 small orange
450 g/1 lb cooked beetroot, peeled and diced
30 ml/2 tbsp soured (dairy sour) cream
30 ml/2 tbsp snipped fresh chives
Plain potatoes and a Green Salad (see page 308), to serve

1 Heat half the butter in a frying pan (skillet). Add the duck, season and fry (sauté) for 4–5 minutes on each side over a high heat until tender and still slightly pink in the centre.

2 Meanwhile, heat the remaining butter in a saucepan. Stir in the marmalade, orange rind and juice and stir until melted.

3 Add the beetroot, stir gently and cook over a moderate heat for 5–10 minutes, stirring gently, until the liquid has evaporated.

4 Spoon the beetroot on to warm plates and top with a spoonful of soured cream and a sprinkling of chives. Put the duck breasts to one side and spoon any juices over.

5 Serve with the potatoes and salad.

Warm Duck Salad with Raspberries

SERVES 4

450 g/1 lb baby new potatoes, scrubbed
30 ml/2 tbsp mayonnaise
4 small boneless duck breasts
Salt and freshly ground black pepper
60 ml/4 tbsp olive oil
175 g/6 oz mixed salad leaves
4 cherry tomatoes, quartered
100 g/4 oz/1 cup shelled fresh peas (about 225 g/8 oz unshelled weight)
15 ml/1 tbsp raspberry vinegar
10 ml/2 tsp tomato purée (paste)
45 ml/3 tbsp apple juice
100 g/4 oz raspberries
30 ml/2 tbsp snipped fresh chives

1 Put the potatoes in a pan of salted water. Cover and bring to the boil, then cook for 10–15 minutes until tender. Drain, return to the pan, stir in the mayonnaise and cover.

2 Meanwhile, season the duck with salt and pepper. Heat 30 ml/2 tbsp of the oil in a frying pan (skillet) over a high heat. Add the duck, skin-sides down. Fry (sauté) for about 6 minutes, turn over and cook for a further 6 minutes until just pink in the centre.

3 While the duck is cooking, gently mix the salad leaves, tomatoes, peas and new potatoes and put on plates. Slice the cooked duck breasts diagonally and arrange on top.

4 Add the remaining oil to the pan juices with the vinegar, tomato purée and apple juice. Bring to the boil, stirring until well blended. Season. Spoon over the duck, scatter with raspberries and chives and serve.

Vegetarian Main Courses

Everyone except vegans can enjoy these delicious alternatives to meat, poultry or fish. And even if you are normally a meat-eater, you'll love these colourful and nutritious concoctions for a tasty and exciting change from your usual diet. Many contain cheese, however, so if you are a strict vegetarian, make sure that the brands you use are suitable.

I have included explanations for when to prepare and cook the serving suggestions. For details of cooking techniques for all kinds of individual vegetables, see pages 291–92.

Soya Bean Roast

Use hot or mild curry paste, according to your taste.

SERVES 6

2 x 425 g/15 oz/large cans of soya
    beans, drained
50 g/2 oz/¼ cup butter or margarine,
    plus a little for greasing
45 ml/3 tbsp dried breadcrumbs
1 large onion, finely chopped
1 carrot, grated
1 potato, grated
1 turnip, grated
15 ml/1 tbsp curry paste
30 ml/2 tbsp mango chutney
Salt and freshly ground black pepper
2 eggs, beaten
A Curried Rice Salad (see page 313), to
    serve

1 Empty the soya beans into a bowl and mash with a potato masher.

2 Grease a 900 g/2 lb loaf tin (pan) with a little butter or margarine and sprinkle with the dried breadcrumbs. Preheat the oven to 190°C/375°F/ gas mark 5.

3 Melt the measured butter or margarine in a saucepan over a moderate heat. Add the prepared vegetables and the curry paste and fry (sauté), stirring, for 5 minutes.

4 Stir this mixture into the soya beans with the breadcrumbs and the mango chutney. Season well.

5 Mix in the beaten eggs, then turn the mixture into the prepared tin and smooth the surface.

6 Cover the tin with foil and bake in the oven for 1½ hours until firm to the touch. Cool for 10 minutes, while you

make the salad, then turn the loaf out on to a serving dish.

7 Serve the loaf warm or cold, sliced with the curried rice.

Greek-style Mushrooms with Chickpeas

SERVES 4

60 ml/4 tbsp olive oil
1 large onion, chopped
300 ml/½ pt/1¼ cups dry white wine
1 bay leaf
2.5 ml/½ tsp dried oregano
1 garlic clove, crushed
450 g/1 lb small button mushrooms
400 g/14 oz/1 large can of chopped
    tomatoes
425 g/15 oz/1 large can of chickpeas
    (garbanzos), drained
30 ml/2 tbsp chopped fresh parsley
A Village Salad (see page 310) and
    crusty bread, to serve

1 Heat the oil in a large saucepan. Add the onion and cook over a fairly gentle heat for 3 minutes until softened but not browned, stirring all the time.

2 Add the remaining ingredients and bring to the boil. Turn down the heat until just bubbling gently round the edges and cook for 15 minutes while you make the salad. Leave to cool slightly, then remove the bay leaf.

3 Spoon into bowls, sprinkle with the parsley and serve warm with crusty bread and the Village Salad.

French-style Cannellini Beans

SERVES 4

2 onions, thinly sliced
30 ml/2 tbsp olive oil
1 large garlic clove, crushed
400 g/14 oz/1 large can of chopped
  tomatoes
30 ml/2 tbsp tomato purée (paste)
2.5 ml/½ tsp caster (superfine) sugar
45 ml/3 tbsp dry white wine
5 ml/1 tsp dried herbes de Provence
2 x 425 g/15 oz/large cans of cannellini
  beans, drained
12 stoned (pitted) black olives, halved
30 ml/2 tbsp chopped fresh parsley
225 g/8 oz/1 cup long-grain rice, to
  serve

1 Put the onions and oil in a saucepan
and fry (sauté) for 4 minutes, stirring
until golden.
2 Add the garlic, tomatoes, tomato
purée, sugar, wine and herbs. Cook
over a high heat until the mixture is
boiling, then turn the heat down to
moderate and continue to cook for
5 minutes, stirring occasionally, until
pulpy.
3 Stir in the beans, olives and half the
parsley and cook for a further 5
minutes, stirring.
4 Meanwhile, cook the rice according
to the packet directions (or see page
294). Drain in a colander. Spoon on to
plates, top with the bean mixture and
sprinkle with the remaining parsley.

Greek Chickpea Casserole

SERVES 4

450 g/1 lb spinach, well-washed and
  thick stalks removed
30 ml/2 tbsp olive oil
1 red onion, chopped
1 garlic clove, crushed
50 g/2 oz Greek black olives, halved
  and stoned (pitted)
425 g/15 oz/1 large can of chickpeas
  (garbanzos)
400 g/14 oz/1 large can of chopped
  tomatoes
5 ml/1 tsp dried oregano
100 g/4 oz/1 cup Feta cheese, crumbled
Freshly ground black pepper
120 ml/4 fl oz/½ cup plain Greek
  yoghurt
Daktyla (Greek seeded bread), to
  serve

1 Put the wet spinach in a saucepan
with no extra water. Cover and cook
over a moderate heat for 5 minutes
until tender. Drain in a colander, then
snip with scissors to chop.
2 Meanwhile, in a separate saucepan,
heat the oil and cook the onion and
garlic over a fairly high heat for
2 minutes, stirring. Add the olives,
chickpeas, tomatoes and oregano.
Bring to the boil, then turn down the
heat until gently bubbling round the
edges and cook for 15 minutes, stirring.
3 Stir in the spinach and Feta and add
a good grinding of pepper. Heat
through, stirring, for 2 minutes. Spoon
into warm bowls and top each with a
spoonful of yoghurt. Serve with daktyla
bread.

Spicy Lentil and Mushroom Rissoles

Cook the rice (see page 294) while the lentils are cooking. Keep it warm in a colander, covered with a lid, over a pan of hot water, over a very gentle heat. Make the salad before you fry (sauté) the rissoles. See Fiery Mussel Spaghettini, (page 134), for instructions on seeding chillies.

SERVES 4

225 g/8 oz/1⅓ cups brown lentils, soaked for 2 hours in cold water

1 onion, finely chopped

100 g/4 oz mushrooms, finely chopped

50 g/2 oz/¼ cup butter or margarine

30 ml/2 tbsp chopped fresh coriander (cilantro)

1 fresh green chilli, seeded and chopped

5 ml/1 tsp ground cumin

Salt and freshly ground black pepper

75 g/3 oz/1½ cups fresh wholemeal breadcrumbs

1 egg, beaten

Oil, for shallow-frying

300 ml/½ pt/1¼ cups passata (sieved tomatoes)

5 ml/1 tsp caster (superfine) sugar

30 ml/2 tbsp plain yoghurt

Brown rice and a Green Salad (see page 308), to serve

1 Drain the lentils and place in a saucepan. Cover with water. Bring to the boil and boil rapidly for 10 minutes, reduce the heat, cover and cook gently for about 1 hour or until the lentils are really soft and all the liquid has been absorbed.

2 Meanwhile, fry the onion and mushrooms in the butter or margarine for 2 minutes, stirring.

3 Stir in half the coriander, the chilli, cumin and a little salt and pepper to taste.

4 Blend in the breadcrumbs and mix with the beaten egg to bind. Shape into 16 cakes with floured hands.

5 Heat about 5 mm/¼ in oil in a large frying pan (skillet). When hot, but not smoking, fry the rissoles in two batches until golden brown on each side. Drain on kitchen paper (paper towels).

6 Meanwhile, heat the passata with the remaining coriander, the sugar and salt and pepper to taste.

7 Arrange the rissoles on four warm plates. Spoon the sauce over and add a swirl of the yoghurt. Serve with the brown rice and salad.

Chilli Bean Tacos

SERVES 4

8 taco shells
1 avocado
1 large tomato
30 ml/2 tbsp olive oil
1 onion, finely chopped
425 g/15 oz/1 large can of red kidney
  beans, drained
5 ml/1 tsp hot chilli sauce
100 g/4 oz/½ cup Cheddar cheese,
  grated

1 Separate the taco shells, place on a baking (cookie) sheet and warm in the oven on the lowest setting while making the filling.
2 Halve the avocado, remove the stone (pit), then peel off the skin with your fingers and dice the flesh. Dice the tomato.
3 Heat the oil in a large frying pan (skillet). Add the onion and cook, stirring, over a fairly high heat for 3 minutes. Turn down the heat to moderate.
4 Add the beans and mash with a fork or potato masher.
5 Stir in the avocado, tomato and chilli sauce. Heat through, stirring.
6 Spoon into the taco shells and top with grated cheese before serving.

Scrambled Beans

This is particularly good with focaccia flavoured with sun-dried tomatoes, olives or mushrooms.

SERVES 4

1 round of focaccia bread
50 g/2 oz/¼ cup butter or margarine
45 ml/3 tbsp snipped fresh chives
2 x 425 g/15 oz/large cans of mixed
  pulses, drained
3 eggs, beaten
45 ml/3 tbsp milk
100 g/4 oz/1 cup red Leicester cheese,
  grated
A good pinch of cayenne
Salt and freshly ground black pepper

1 Cut the focaccia horizontally to create four large round slices. Wrap in foil and heat in the oven at 150°C/300°F/gas mark 2 while you prepare the rest of the dish.
2 Melt the butter or margarine in a large non-stick saucepan over a fairly high heat.
3 Add 30 ml/2 tbsp of the chives and all the remaining ingredients, turn down the heat to low and cook, stirring, until the eggs have set. Do not allow the mixture to boil.
4 Transfer the warm bread slices to warm plates. Spoon the scrambled mixture over and sprinkle with the remaining chives.

Photograph opposite: **Warm Duck Salad With Raspberries (see page 251)**

Aubergine, Pea and Lentil Curry

SERVES 4

1 onion, sliced
45 ml/3 tbsp sunflower oil
1 garlic clove, crushed
1 large waxy potato, scrubbed and diced
1 large aubergine (eggplant), diced
5 ml/1 tsp ground cumin
5 ml/1 tsp ground coriander (cilantro)
5 ml/1 tsp ground turmeric
2.5 ml/½ tsp chilli powder
150 ml/¼ pt/⅔ cup vegetable stock, made with ½ stock cube
425 g/15 oz/1 large can of green or brown lentils, drained
225 g/8 oz/2 cups frozen peas
Salt and freshly ground black pepper
150 ml/¼ pt/⅔ cup plain yoghurt
30 ml/2 tbsp chopped fresh coriander
Naan breads, to serve

1 Fry (sauté) the onion, stirring, in the oil over a moderate heat for 2 minutes in a large saucepan. Add the garlic, potato, aubergine and spices and cook, stirring, for 3 minutes.
2 Add the stock, cover with a lid, turn down the heat and cook gently for 15 minutes.
3 Stir in the lentils, peas, some salt and pepper and the yoghurt. Continue to cook gently, uncovered, for a further 15 minutes until everything is tender and bathed in sauce. Warm the naan breads briefly under the grill (broiler).
4 Stir in the fresh coriander, taste and add more salt and pepper if necessary. Serve hot with the naan breads.

Sweet and Sour Beans

Traditional Worcestershire sauce contains anchovies so true veggies will need to buy theirs from a health food shop.

SERVES 4

900 g/2 lb runner beans, stringed and diagonally sliced
250 g/9 oz/1 packet of Chinese egg noodles
50 g/2 oz/¼ cup butter or margarine
100 g/4 oz button mushrooms, sliced
30 ml/2 tbsp Worcestershire sauce
15 ml/1 tbsp soy sauce
30 ml/2 tbsp clear honey
30 ml/2 tbsp red wine vinegar
425 g/15 oz/1 large can of flageolet beans, drained

1 Bring a large pan of water to the boil over a high heat. Add a good pinch of salt, the runner beans and noodles. Bring back to the boil, then cook for 5 minutes until just tender. Drain in a colander.
2 Melt the butter or margarine in the bean saucepan. Add the mushrooms and cook, stirring, for 2 minutes.
3 Add the Worcestershire sauce, soy sauce, honey and vinegar and stir well. Return the runner beans and noodles to the pan and add the flageolets. Cook over a low heat, stirring gently, for 4 minutes until piping hot. Serve in warm bowls.

Photograph opposite: **Corn, Pepper and Camembert Fritters (see page 261)**

Lentil and Cheese Croquettes

Make the tomato sauce while the lentil mixture is cooling. Put the broccoli on to cook while you fry (sauté) the croquettes.

SERVES 4

1 large onion, finely chopped
175 g/6 oz/1 cup red lentils
600 ml/1 pt/2½ cups water
2.5 ml/½ tsp dried mixed herbs
30 ml/2 tbsp chopped fresh parsley
100 g/4 oz/1 cup Cheddar cheese, grated
100 g/4 oz/2 cups fresh wholemeal breadcrumbs
1 egg, separated
Salt and freshly ground black pepper
85 g/3½ oz/1 small packet of parsley and thyme stuffing mix
Oil, for shallow-frying
Quick Tomato Sauce (see page 335) and broccoli, to serve

1 Put the onion, lentils and water in a saucepan. Bring to the boil over a high heat, then turn down the heat until just bubbling gently round the edges. Cook for about 30 minutes or until the lentils are tender and have absorbed all the liquid, stirring frequently to prevent sticking.
2 Stir in the herbs, parsley, cheese, breadcrumbs, egg yolk and some salt and pepper. Tip out into a shallow dish, spread out and leave to cool.
3 Divide into eight equal portions and roll each into a sausage shape.
4 Put the stuffing mix in a shallow dish.
5 Brush the rolls with the egg white, then turn over in the stuffing mix to coat completely.

6 Heat about 5 mm/¼ in oil in a frying pan (skillet). When hot, but not smoking, fry the rolls for 4–5 minutes until golden on all sides. Drain on kitchen paper (paper towels) and serve with the tomato sauce and broccoli.

Rich Cheese Pudding

SERVES 4

170 g/6 oz/1 small can of unsweetened condensed milk
2 eggs, beaten
100 g/4 oz/2 cups fresh white breadcrumbs
100 g/4 oz/1 cup Cheddar cheese, grated
2.5 ml/½ tsp dried oregano
Salt and freshly ground black pepper
A little butter or margarine, for greasing
300 ml/½ pt/1¼ cups passata (sieved tomatoes)
A Green Salad (see page 308), to serve

1 Make the milk up to 300 ml/½ pt/1¼ cups with water.
2 Mix with the eggs, breadcrumbs, 75 g/3 oz/¾ cup of the cheese, the herbs and a little salt and pepper.
3 Lightly grease a 1.2 litre/2 pt/5 cup ovenproof dish.
4 Turn the mixture into the dish and leave to stand for 15 minutes. Meanwhile, preheat the oven to 190°C/375°F/gas mark 5.
5 Sprinkle with the remaining cheese and bake in the oven for about 45 minutes until golden brown, risen and set. While it cooks, warm the passata and make the salad.
6 Serve with the cheese pudding.

Chickpea Goulash

*Add 225 g/8 oz sliced chorizo
sausage or a sliced smoked pork ring
to this dish, if you like, unless you're
a vegetarian, of course!*

SERVES 4

225 g/8 oz/1⅓ cups chickpeas
(garbanzos), soaked overnight in
cold water
1.2 litres/2 pts/5 cups vegetable stock,
made with 2 stock cubes
30 ml/2 tbsp olive oil
1 onion, chopped
1 garlic clove, crushed
2 large carrots, diced
1 celery stick, chopped
2 leeks, well-washed and chopped
100 g/4 oz button mushrooms, sliced
170 g/6 oz/1 small can of pimiento caps,
drained and diced
15 ml/1 tbsp paprika
2.5 ml/½ tsp dried oregano
30 ml/2 tbsp tomato purée (paste)
15 ml/1 tbsp Worcestershire sauce
5 ml/1 tsp light brown sugar
Salt and freshly ground black pepper
60 ml/4 tbsp crème fraîche and 15 ml/
1 tbsp caraway seeds, to garnish

1 Drain the chickpeas and place in a
large saucepan with the stock. Bring to
the boil and boil rapidly for 10 minutes.
2 Meanwhile, preheat the oven to
160°C/325°F/gas mark 3. Heat the oil in
a large, flameproof casserole (Dutch
oven). Fry (sauté) the onion and garlic
over a fairly high heat for 2 minutes.
Add all the remaining ingredients
including the chickpeas and stock. Bring
to the boil, stirring. Remove from the
heat.

3 Cover and cook in the oven for
3½ hours until the chickpeas are really
tender and bathed in a rich sauce.
4 Ladle into warm bowls and serve
topped with a spoonful of crème
fraîche and a sprinkling of caraway
seeds.

Cauliflower Cheese

*This dish can be baked in the oven
instead of grilling (broiling). If you
decide to bake it, preheat the oven at
190°C/375°F/gas mark 5 when you
start to make the sauce.*

SERVES 4

1 cauliflower
5 ml/1 tsp made English mustard
2 quantities of Cheese Sauce
(see page 329)
50 g/2 oz/½ cup Cheddar cheese,
grated
25 g/1 oz/½ cup cornflakes, crushed
3 tomatoes, sliced

1 Cut the cauliflower into small florets.
Cook in boiling, lightly salted water for
4–5 minutes until just tender.
2 Drain and place in a flameproof
serving dish. Make the sauce.
3 Stir the mustard into the sauce and
spoon over the vegetables.
4 Scatter the cheese and cornflakes
over and arrange the sliced tomatoes
round the edge.
5 Place under a preheated grill
(broiler) until the top is golden and
bubbling or bake in a preheated oven
for about 35 minutes.

Broccoli and Tomato Cheese

SERVES 4

Prepare exactly as for Cauliflower Cheese (page 259) but use a large head of broccoli instead. After putting the cooked broccoli in the dish, spoon a 400 g/14 oz/large can of chopped tomatoes over before adding the cheese sauce and omit the tomatoes on the top.

Cheese and Potato Bake

SERVES 4

A knob of butter or margarine, for greasing
700 g/1½ lb potatoes, thinly sliced
1 bunch of spring onions (scallions), chopped
15 ml/1 tbsp chopped fresh parsley
5 ml/1 tsp chopped fresh sage
175 g/6 oz/1½ cups Cheddar cheese, grated
Salt and freshly ground black pepper
300 ml/½ pt/1¼ cups milk
2 eggs, beaten
A Mixed Salad (see page 308), to serve

1 Preheat the oven to 180°C/350°F/ gas mark 4.
2 Grease a 1.5 litre/2½ pt/6 cup ovenproof dish with the butter or margarine.
3 Layer the potatoes with the spring onions, herbs and cheese, sprinkling each layer of potatoes with a little salt and pepper and finishing with a layer of cheese.
4 Whisk the milk and eggs together in a bowl with a wire whisk and pour into the dish.

5 Cover the dish with foil and bake in the oven for 1 hour. Remove the foil and continue cooking for about 15 minutes until golden and the potatoes are tender. Meanwhile, make the salad and serve with the hot potato bake.

Cottage Cheese Loaf

SERVES 4

225 g/8 oz/1 cup cottage cheese
1 small onion, grated
50 g/2 oz/½ cup walnuts, chopped
2.5 ml/½ tsp dried mixed herbs
5 ml/1 tsp made English mustard
100 g/4 oz/2 cups fresh white breadcrumbs
2 eggs, beaten
Salt and freshly ground black pepper
A little oil, for greasing
Pickles and a Mixed Salad (see page 308), to serve

1 Preheat the oven to 180°C/350°F/gas mark 4. Mix the cheese with all the remaining ingredients, seasoning to taste with salt and pepper.
2 Lightly oil a 450 g/1 lb loaf tin (pan). Cut an oblong of non-stick baking parchment the same size as the base and put it in the bottom of the tin. Pour the cheese mixture into the tin and level the surface.
3 Bake in the oven for about 40 minutes or until set. While it is cooking, make the mixed salad.
4 Leave the loaf to cool in the tin for 5 minutes, then turn out, remove the paper and serve hot or cold, cut into slices, with pickles and the salad.

Corn, Pepper and Camembert Fritters

These are also good served with Aioli (see page 341) as a starter for six or as an exciting breakfast, served with fried (sautéed) tomatoes instead of the salad leaves.

SERVES 4

15 ml/1 tbsp sunflower or olive oil, plus extra for shallow-frying
1 red (bell) pepper, chopped
1 leek, well-washed and chopped
1 garlic clove, crushed
75 g/3 oz/⅓ cup plain (all-purpose) flour
A good pinch of salt
15 ml/1 tbsp baking powder
105–120 ml/7–8 tbsp water
200 g/7 oz/1 small can of sweetcorn (corn), drained
100 g/4 oz firm individual Camembert, chilled and cut into small dice
175 g/6 oz mixed salad leaves and French Dressing (see page 337), to serve

1 Heat the oil in a frying pan (skillet) and fry the pepper, leek and garlic, stirring over a fairly high heat, for 2–3 minutes, until lightly golden. Remove the pan from the heat.

2 Mix the flour with the salt and baking powder in a bowl. Stir in enough of the water to form a thick, creamy batter, using a wire whisk. Stir in the pepper mixture with any juices, the sweetcorn and cheese.

3 Wipe out the frying pan with kitchen paper (paper towels), then heat about 5 mm/¼ in oil in the pan. When hot, but not smoking, drop in spoonfuls of the batter. Fry (sauté) for 2–3 minutes until golden brown underneath. Turn over with a fish slice and cook for a further 2 minutes or until golden and crisp. Drain on kitchen paper (paper towels).

4 Pile the salad leaves on plates and spoon the French Dressing over. Set the fritters on top and serve.

Creamed Baked Rice with Cheese

SERVES 4–6

450 g/1 lb/2 cups risotto rice
225 g/8 oz/2 cups Fontina or Cheddar cheese, thinly sliced
25 g/1 oz/2 tbsp unsalted (sweet) butter, cut into small pieces
Salt and freshly ground black pepper
120 ml/4 fl oz/½ cup double (heavy) cream
100 g/4 oz/1 cup grated Parmesan cheese

1 Cook the rice in plenty of boiling, salted water for about 15 minutes until almost tender. Drain thoroughly. Preheat the oven at 180°C/350°F/ gas mark 4.

2 Spread half the rice in a shallow ovenproof dish. Cover with half the Fontina or Cheddar cheese, scatter over the butter and season lightly. Pour over half the cream. Repeat the layers and then top the whole dish with the grated Parmesan.

3 Bake in the preheated oven for about 20 minutes until golden on top.

Vegetable Risotto

SERVES 4

90 ml/6 tbsp olive oil
1 large onion, chopped
1 green (bell) pepper, diced
1 aubergine (eggplant), diced
1 courgette (zucchini), diced
225 g/8 oz/1 cup brown rice
900 ml/1½ pts/3¾ cups vegetable stock,
    made with 2 stock cubes
400 g/14 oz/1 large can of chopped
    tomatoes
5 ml/1 tsp dried basil
Salt and freshly ground black pepper
30 ml/2 tbsp chopped fresh parsley
100 g/4 oz/1 cup Cheddar cheese,
    grated, to serve

1 Heat the oil in a large saucepan and fry (sauté) all the prepared vegetables, stirring over a moderate heat for 5 minutes.
2 Add the rice and stir for 1 minute.
3 Add the remaining ingredients and bring to the boil over a high heat. Stir well, turn down the heat to very low, then cover and cook for 50 minutes without stirring. The rice should be just tender and have absorbed nearly all the liquid.
4 Stir well and serve sprinkled with grated cheese.

Cheesy Dhal

Put the breads to warm briefly under the grill (broiler) when you add the cheese to the dhal.

SERVES 4

25 g/1 oz/2 tbsp butter or margarine
15 ml/1 tbsp sunflower oil
1 onion, chopped
10 ml/2 tsp mild curry paste
275 g/10 oz/1⅓ cups red lentils
600 ml/1 pt/2½ cups vegetable stock,
    made with 1 stock cube
1 bay leaf
Salt and freshly ground black pepper
175 g/6 oz/1½ cups mild Cheddar
    cheese, cubed
15 ml/1 tbsp chopped fresh coriander
    (cilantro)
Garlic and coriander naan breads, to
    serve

1 Heat the butter or margarine and oil in a saucepan. Add the onion and cook, stirring, for 2 minutes.
2 Stir in all the remaining ingredients except the cheese. Cook until bubbling, then turn down the heat, cover and cook gently for 20 minutes, stirring occasionally, until the lentils are tender and have absorbed the liquid.
3 Stir in the cheese and continue to heat until it is just beginning to melt. Spoon the dhal into bowls, sprinkle with the coriander and serve straight away with the naan breads.

Blue Cheese, Egg and Broccoli Saucers

If you make your own shortcrust pastry (basic pie crust), use 1½ quantities of the recipe on page 391.

SERVES 4

350 g/12 oz shortcrust pastry, thawed if frozen

175 g/6 oz broccoli, cut into tiny florets

100 g/4 oz/1 cup blue cheese, crumbled

3 eggs

45 ml/3 tbsp milk, plus extra for glazing

Salt and freshly ground black pepper

Pickles, to serve

1 Preheat the oven to 200°C/400°F/ gas mark 6. Cut the pastry (paste) into eight equal pieces. Roll out each piece to a round, using a saucer as a guide. Use four rounds to line four saucers.

2 Put about 5 cm/2 in water in a medium saucepan and add a pinch of salt. Bring to the boil and cook the broccoli for 3 minutes. Drain in a colander, rinse with cold water and drain again.

3 Divide the broccoli and cheese between the pastry-lined saucers.

4 Whisk the eggs and milk with a little salt and pepper and pour over.

5 Brush the edges with water and place the other pastry rounds on top, pressing round the edges with the prongs of a fork to seal and decorate.

6 Brush with a little milk to glaze and bake in the oven for 15 minutes, then turn down the oven to 160°C/325°F/ gas mark 3 and continue cooking for a further 10–15 minutes until golden and the filling is set. Serve with pickles.

Savoury Soufflé

Ring the changes with different canned soups and appropriate vegetables.

SERVES 4

295 g/10½ oz/1 medium can of condensed asparagus soup

4 eggs, separated

75 g/3 oz/¾ cup Cheddar cheese, grated

295 g/10½ oz/1 medium can of cut asparagus spears, drained

A little butter or margarine, for greasing

Crusty bread and a Mixed Salad (see page 308), to serve

1 Preheat the oven to 200°C/400°F/ gas mark 6. Empty the soup into a bowl and mix in the egg yolks and cheese with a fork.

2 Whisk the egg whites until stiff in a clean bowl with a balloon or electric whisk and stir gently into the mixture with a metal spoon using a figure-of-eight movement.

3 Put the asparagus pieces in a lightly greased 18 cm/7 in soufflé dish. Spoon in the egg mixture.

4 Bake in the oven for about 25 minutes or until risen, golden and just set. While it is cooking, make the salad.

5 Serve the soufflé straight from the oven with crusty bread and the salad.

Quick Fix Vegetable Pie

Use the recipe on page 391 for Fork Shortcrust Pastry, if you wish to make your own.

SERVES 4

225 g/8 oz shortcrust pastry (basic pie crust), thawed if frozen
225 g/8 oz frozen mixed vegetables
400 g/14 oz/1 large can of mushroom soup
5 ml/1 tsp dried oregano
A little milk, for glazing
Baked beans, to serve

1 Preheat the oven to 200°C/400°F/gas mark 6.
2 Cut the pastry (paste) in half. Roll out one half and place in a 20 cm/8 in pie dish. Press gently in position and trim the edges. Put the dish on a baking (cookie) sheet. Roll out the other half ready to use as a lid.
3 Put a pan of water over a high heat. When bubbling, add the vegetables and cook for 3 minutes. Tip into a colander, rinse under cold running water, then drain well again.
4 Tip into the dish and spoon the soup over. Sprinkle with the oregano.
5 Brush the edges of the pastry with water and put the pastry 'lid' in position. Trim the edges and press them well together to seal.
6 Make a hole in the centre to allow steam to escape and brush the surface with a little milk.
7 Bake in the oven for about 30 minutes until golden brown and cooked through. Heat the baked beans in a saucepan and serve with the pie.

Creamy Swiss Cheese Flan

SERVES 4

175 g/6 oz puff pastry (paste), thawed if frozen
175 g/6 oz/1½ cups Gruyère cheese, grated
4 spring onions (scallions), finely chopped
2 eggs
300 ml/½ pt/1¼ cups double (heavy) cream
2.5 ml/½ tsp grated nutmeg
Salt and freshly ground black pepper
A Mixed Salad (see page 308), to serve

1 Preheat the oven to 200°C/400°F/gas mark 6.
2 Roll out the pastry and use to line a 20 cm/8 in flan dish (pie pan). Prick the base with a fork in several places. Put the cheese in the pastry-lined dish and scatter the onions over.
3 Break the eggs in a bowl and whisk in the cream, the nutmeg and a little salt and pepper, using a wire whisk. Pour into the dish.
4 Bake in the oven for about 30 minutes until golden and set. While it is cooking, make a mixed salad. Serve the flan warm with the salad.

Savoury Cheese and Carrot Bread and Butter Pudding

SERVES 4

6 medium slices of white bread
Butter or margarine, for spreading
5 ml/1 tsp yeast extract
2 carrots, coarsely grated
225 g/8 oz/2 cups Cheddar cheese, grated
2 eggs
300 ml/½ pt/1¼ cups milk
1.5 ml/¼ tsp made English mustard
Salt and freshly ground black pepper
A Green Salad (see page 308), to serve

1 Spread the bread thinly with butter or margarine. Spread four of the slices with a scraping of yeast extract. Cut all the slices into triangles.

2 Line a lightly buttered 1.5 litre/2½ pt/ 6 cup ovenproof dish with some of the yeast extract triangles. Sprinkle with half the carrots and half the cheese.

3 Cover with the other yeast extract triangles and then the remaining carrot and cheese. Arrange the plain buttered triangles attractively over the top.

4 Whisk the eggs and milk together with the mustard and a little salt and pepper in a bowl with a whisk.

5 Pour over the bread and leave to soak for 30 minutes. Preheat the oven to 190°C/375°F/gas mark 5. Make the salad.

6 Bake in the oven for about 45 minutes until golden brown and set. Serve warm with the salad.

Tomato, Leek and Basil Gougère

This sounds tricky, but choux pastry (paste) is really very easy!

SERVES 4

25 g/1 oz/2 tbsp butter or margarine, plus a little for greasing
400 g/14 oz/1 large can of tomatoes
4 leeks, well-washed and sliced
15 ml/1 tbsp chopped fresh basil
A pinch of caster (superfine) sugar
Salt and freshly ground black pepper
1 quantity of Choux Pastry (see page 392)
25 g/1 oz/¼ cup Parmesan cheese, grated

1 Melt the butter or margarine in a saucepan over a fairly high heat. Add the tomatoes and leeks and cook for 2 minutes, stirring.

2 Add the basil, sugar and some salt and pepper, turn down the heat fairly low, cover and cook gently for a further 4 minutes.

3 Meanwhile, preheat the oven to 220°C/425°F/gas mark 7 and make the choux pastry.

4 Lightly grease a 23 cm/9 in shallow ovenproof dish with a little butter or margarine. Spoon the pastry round the edge.

5 Spoon the leek mixture into the centre and sprinkle all over with the Parmesan cheese. Bake in the oven for 30 minutes until puffy and golden brown. Serve hot.

Spring Vegetable Pot

SERVES 4

1 large onion, cut into chunks
15 g/½ oz/1 tbsp butter or margarine
2 large potatoes, cut into chunks
3 large carrots, cut into chunks
1 turnip, cut into chunks
2 leeks, well-washed and cut into
    chunks
425 g/15 oz/1 large can of haricot
    (navy) beans, drained
400 g/14 oz/1 large can of chopped
    tomatoes
600 ml/1 pt/2½ cups vegetable stock,
    made with 2 stock cubes
1 bay leaf
Salt and freshly ground black pepper
100 g/4 oz baby corn cobs
100 g/4 oz okra (ladies' fingers),
    trimmed
½ small green cabbage, shredded
Grated Cheddar cheese and crusty
    bread, to serve

1 Fry (sauté) the onion in the butter or
margarine in a large, flameproof
casserole (Dutch oven) for 2 minutes,
stirring over a fairly high heat.
2 Add the prepared root vegetables,
beans, tomatoes, stock and seasoning.
Bring to the boil, reduce the heat until
just bubbling gently round the edges,
then cover and cook gently for
30 minutes.
3 Add the remaining ingredients to the
pan and stir gently. Cover and cook for
a further 20 minutes or until everything
is really tender.
4 Remove the bay leaf and serve in
large, warm bowls, with grated cheese
to sprinkle over and crusty bread.

Veggie Cottage Pie

SERVES 4

450 g/1 lb potatoes, cut into chunks
A knob of butter or margarine
15 ml/1 tbsp milk
350 g/12 oz leftover cooked
    vegetables, finely chopped
2 slices of wholemeal bread, chopped
400 g/14 oz/1 large can of baked beans
10 ml/2 tsp yeast extract
30 ml/2 tbsp boiling water
2.5 ml/½ tsp dried mixed herbs
Salt and freshly ground black pepper
50 g/2 oz/½ cup Cheddar cheese,
    grated
3 tomatoes, sliced

1 Cook and mash the potatoes with
the butter or margarine and milk (see
page 298). Preheat the oven to
200°C/400°F/
gas mark 6.
2 Mix the vegetables with the bread
and beans in a 1.2 litre/2 pt/5 cup
ovenproof serving dish.
3 Blend the yeast extract with the
water and stir in the herbs and
seasoning to taste. Stir into the dish until
thoroughly mixed.
4 Top with the mashed potato, then
the cheese. Arrange the tomatoes
round the edge.
5 Bake in the oven for 35 minutes until
golden brown and piping hot. Serve
hot.

Vegetable Dolmas

This is a great way to use up the outer leaves of a cabbage and any leftover rice.

SERVES 4

8 large cabbage leaves
425 g/15 oz/1 large can of ratatouille
60 ml/4 tbsp cooked long-grain rice
300 ml/½ pt/1¼ cups vegetable stock, made with 1 stock cube
30 ml/2 tbsp tomato purée (paste)
Salt and freshly ground black pepper
Grated Cheddar cheese and crusty bread, to serve

1 Cut a 'V' shape out of the base of each thick, central cabbage leaf stalk.
2 Bring a pan of water to the boil. Drop in the leaves and cook for 3 minutes (this is known as blanching). Drain, rinse with cold water and drain again. Dry on kitchen paper (paper towels).
3 Mix the ratatouille with the rice.
4 Lay a leaf on a board and overlap the two points where the stalk was. Put some of the filling on top. Fold in the sides and roll up.
5 Place in a flameproof casserole (Dutch oven). Repeat with the remaining cabbage leaves and filling.
6 Mix the stock and tomato purée together and pour around the cabbage rolls. Season lightly.
7 Bring to the boil, cover, reduce the heat to low and cook for 20 minutes until the cabbage is tender. Spoon on to warm plates and spoon any juices over. Serve hot, sprinkled with grated cheese, with crusty bread.

Mushroom Stroganoff

SERVES 4

75 g/3 oz/⅓ cup butter or margarine
1 large onion, thinly sliced
1 garlic clove, crushed
1 kg/2¼ lb button mushrooms, halved if large
150 ml/¼ pt/⅔ cups dry white wine
15 ml/1 tbsp cornflour (cornstarch)
30 ml/2 tbsp water
300 ml/½ pt/1¼ cups single (light) cream
A good squeeze of lemon juice
Salt and freshly ground black pepper
30 ml/2 tbsp chopped fresh parsley
225 g/8 oz/1 cup long-grain rice

1 Melt the butter or margarine in a large saucepan.
2 Add the onion and cook over a moderate heat, stirring, for 2 minutes until softened but not browned.
3 Add the garlic, mushrooms and wine, stir, turn down the heat to fairly low, cover and cook for 30 minutes, stirring occasionally.
4 Mix the cornflour with the water and stir into the pan with the cream. Turn up the heat and let the mixture bubble, stirring for 5 minutes.
5 Add lemon juice, salt and pepper to taste and stir in the parsley.
6 Meanwhile, cook the rice according to the packet directions (or see page 294). Spoon the rice on to warm plates and spoon the hot mushroom mixture on top.

Spinach and Sweet Potato Cutlets

SERVES 4

450 g/1 lb frozen chopped spinach, thawed
1 large sweet potato, grated
25 g/1 oz/2 tbsp butter or margarine
30 ml/2 tbsp black mustard seeds
2 eggs
225 g/8 oz/2 cups Halloumi cheese, grated
5 ml/1 tsp dried oregano
Salt and freshly ground black pepper
100 g/4 oz/2 cups fresh white breadcrumbs
A little plain (all-purpose) flour
Oil, for shallow-frying

1 Put the spinach and sweet potato in a saucepan. Cook, stirring, for about 5 minutes. Tip into a colander and press down well with the back of a spoon to extract as much moisture as possible. Tip into a large bowl.

2 Melt the butter or margarine in the same saucepan. Add the mustard seeds and cook over a high heat until they start to 'pop'. Add to the spinach mixture.

3 Break one of the eggs into a small bowl and whisk with a fork or wire whisk. Add to the spinach mixture with the cheese, oregano and some salt and pepper. Mix thoroughly and chill for 30 minutes.

4 Break the remaining egg on to a plate and whisk with a fork. Put the breadcrumbs on a second plate.

5 Dust your hands with flour and shape the mixture into eight wedge-shaped cakes, or cutlets.

6 Dip the cutlets in the egg, then breadcrumbs, to coat completely.

7 Heat about 5 mm/¼ in oil in a large frying pan (skillet) until hot, but not smoking. Add the cutlets and cook for about 3 minutes until golden. Turn over with a fish slice and cook the other sides until golden. Drain on kitchen paper (paper towels) and serve hot.

Fast Stuffed Courgettes

SERVES 4

4 large courgettes (zucchini)
120 g/4½ oz/1 packet of mushroom or vegetable savoury rice
45 ml/3 tbsp olive oil
100 g/4 oz/1 cup Cheddar cheese, grated
120 ml/4 fl oz/½ cup water

1 Preheat the oven at 200°C/400°F/gas mark 6.

2 Cut the ends off the courgettes and cut in half lengthways. Scoop out the seeds using a teaspoon.

3 Heat a large saucepan of water over a high heat until boiling. Add the courgettes, bring back to the boil and cook for 3 minutes. Tip into a colander to drain. Rinse with cold water, then drain again. Place the courgettes in a baking tin (pan).

4 Cook the rice according to the packet directions. Spoon into the courgettes and trickle the oil over the tops. Cover with the cheese.

5 Pour the measured water around the courgettes and bake in the oven for about 20 minutes or until tender and the cheese has melted. Serve hot.

Falafels

If you aren't sure how to seed chillies, see Fiery Mussel Spaghettini (page 134). Make the Minted Yoghurt and Cucumber and the salad before you start making the falafels.

SERVES 4

1 green chilli, seeded

425 g/15 oz/1 large can of chickpeas (garbanzos), drained

1 onion, quartered

1 garlic clove, chopped

5 ml/1 tsp dried mint

5 ml/1 tsp ground cumin

5 ml/1 tsp caraway seeds

90 ml/6 tbsp plain (all-purpose) flour

1 egg

100 g/4 oz/1 cup dried breadcrumbs

Oil, for shallow-frying

4 pitta breads

Minted Yoghurt and Cucumber (see page 340) and a Mixed Salad (see page 308), to serve

1 Put the chilli, chickpeas, onion, garlic, mint, cumin and caraway in a blender or food processor. Run the machine until the mixture forms a paste, stopping and scraping down the sides as necessary.

2 Using lightly floured hands, shape the mixture into eight small cakes.

3 Break the egg on a plate and whisk with a fork. Put the remaining flour on a second plate and the breadcrumbs on a third.

4 Dip the cakes in the flour, then the egg and then the breadcrumbs, to coat completely.

5 Heat about 5 mm/¼ in oil in a large frying pan (skillet) until hot, but not smoking. Add the cakes and cook over a high heat for about 3 minutes on each side until golden brown. Drain on kitchen paper (paper towels).

6 Warm the pitta breads in the toaster, under the grill (broiler) or, briefly, in the microwave. Make a slit along one edge and open to form pockets. Put two falafels in each pitta bread and spoon in some Minted Yoghurt and Cucumber. Serve with the salad.

Tagliatelle with Pesto and Oyster Mushrooms

Make the salad while the pasta is cooking. If you want to make your own pesto, see page 336.

SERVES 4

350 g/12 oz tagliatelle

25 g/1 oz/2 tbsp butter or margarine

100 g/4 oz oyster mushrooms, sliced

1 onion, finely chopped

45 ml/3 tbsp pesto

A Mixed Salad (see page 308), to serve

1 Cook the tagliatelle according to the packet directions (or see page 293). Drain and return to the saucepan.

2 Meanwhile, melt the butter or margarine in a frying pan (skillet), add the mushrooms and onion and cook for 3–4 minutes until soft and lightly golden.

3 Add the pesto and the mushroom mixture to the pasta and lift and stir lightly over a gentle heat until every strand is coated. Pile on to warm plates and serve with the mixed salad.

Roasted Veggies with Couscous

At step 5, check the cooking instructions on the couscous packet as they vary slightly from brand to brand.

SERVES 4

2 large carrots, cut into thick fingers

1 large sweet potato, cut into chunks

2 potatoes, scrubbed and cut into wedges

1 red (bell) pepper, cut into thick strips

1 green pepper, cut into thick strips

1 butternut squash, peeled and cut into chunks

1 garlic clove, chopped

60 ml/4 tbsp olive oil

Salt and freshly ground black pepper

5 ml/1 tsp dried oregano

225 g/8 oz/1⅓ cups couscous

400 ml/14 fl oz/1¾ cups boiling water

25 g/1 oz/2 tbsp butter or margarine

450 ml/¾ pt/2 cups passata (sieved tomatoes)

2.5 ml/½ tsp chilli powder

15 ml/1 tbsp tomato ketchup (catsup)

1 Preheat the oven to 200°C/400°F/ gas mark 6. Put all the prepared vegetables except the garlic in a large saucepan and add just enough water to cover. Bring to the boil over a high heat, then turn down the heat and cook gently for 2 minutes. Drain in a colander, then tip the vegetables back into the saucepan.

2 Add the garlic, oil, some salt and pepper and the oregano. Mix gently with your hands or two spoons, to coat evenly.

3 Tip the coated vegetables into a large roaster bag. Tie the bag with the twist tie and place on a baking (cookie) sheet, spreading out the vegetables inside the bag.

4 Roast the vegetables on a shelf near the top of the oven for 1 hour or until golden and tender.

5 Meanwhile, put the couscous in a saucepan, stir in the boiling water and leave to stand for 5 minutes. Add the butter or margarine and stir over a gentle heat for 5 minutes (or cook according to the packet directions).

6 Meanwhile, put the passata, chilli powder, ketchup and a little salt and pepper in a small ovenproof dish. Cover with a lid or foil and heat in the oven on a shelf below the vegetables.

7 Spoon the couscous on to four warm plates. Pile the roasted vegetables on top and spoon a little of the tomato sauce over.

Cottage Garden Pie

You can use cooked, frozen vegetables if it's more convenient.

SERVES 4

4 potatoes, peeled and cut into chunks

A good knob of butter or margarine

30 ml/2 tbsp milk

350 g/12 oz cooked leftover
vegetables, chopped

400 g/14 oz/1 large can of chopped
tomatoes

425 g/15 oz/1 large can of butter (fava)
beans, drained

75 g/3 oz/1½ cups fresh wholemeal
breadcrumbs

5 ml/1 tsp dried minced onion

10 ml/2 tsp yeast extract

30 ml/2 tbsp boiling water

2.5 ml/½ tsp dried thyme

Salt and freshly ground black pepper

50 g/2 oz/½ cup red Leicester cheese,
grated

1 Boil and mash the potatoes with the butter or margarine and the milk (see page 298).

2 Preheat the oven to 200°C/400°F/ gas mark 6. Mix the chopped vegetables with the tomatoes, beans, breadcrumbs and dried onion in a 1.2 litre/2 pt/5 cup ovenproof dish.

3 Blend the yeast extract with the water and stir in with the thyme and some salt and pepper.

4 Spoon the mashed potato over the top and sprinkle with the cheese. Bake in the oven for about 35 minutes until golden and piping hot.

Rice and Vegetable Stir-fry

This is delicious on its own or as an accompaniment to any Chinese-style meat or poultry dishes.

SERVES 4

175 g/6 oz/¾ cup long-grain rice

45 ml/3 tbsp sunflower oil

4 spring onions (scallions), cut into
short lengths

1 carrot, cut into thin matchsticks

5 cm/2 in piece of cucumber, cut into
thin matchsticks

100 g/4 oz mangetout (snow peas)

100 g/4 oz baby corn cobs

1 red (bell) pepper, cut into thin strips

100 g/4 oz button mushrooms, sliced

1 piece of stem finger in syrup, finely
chopped

1 garlic clove, crushed

30 ml/2 tbsp soy sauce

Salt and freshly ground black pepper

1 Cook the rice according to the packet directions (or see page 294). Drain, rinse with boiling water and drain again.

2 Meanwhile, heat the oil in a wok or large frying pan (skillet). Add all the remaining ingredients except the soy sauce and seasoning and cook, stirring, for 5 minutes.

3 Add the rice and stir gently until well mixed and hot through. Sprinkle in the soy sauce, season to taste (be very sparing, as it will not need much), then stir again and serve.

Savoury Egg Pasta

For a delicious variation, use a 425 g/15 oz/large can of chickpeas (garbanzos), drained, instead of the eggs.

SERVES 4

225 g/8 oz pasta shapes

3 eggs, scrubbed under cold running water

50 g/2 oz/¼ cup butter or margarine

1 large onion, finely chopped

1 garlic clove, crushed

225 g/8 oz spring (collard) greens, shredded

400 g/14 oz/1 large can of chopped tomatoes

5 ml/1 tsp caster (superfine) sugar

A good pinch of dried basil

Salt and freshly ground black pepper

1 quantity of Quick White Sauce (see page 328)

25 g/1 oz/1 small packet of cheese and onion crisps (chips)

1 Cook the pasta according to the packet directions (or see page 293), adding the eggs to the water at the same time. When cooked, lift the eggs out of the pan and place in a bowl of cold water. Drain the pasta in a colander.

2 Melt 40 g/1½ oz/3 tbsp of the butter or margarine in the pasta saucepan and cook the onion and garlic over a fairly high heat for 2 minutes, stirring.

3 Add the greens, tomatoes, sugar, basil and a little salt and pepper. Cover, turn down the heat to moderate and cook for 5 minutes, stirring occasionally. Stir in the drained pasta.

4 Use a little of the remaining butter or margarine to grease a 1.2 litre/2 pt/ 5 cup ovenproof dish.

5 Spoon half the pasta into the dish. Shell the eggs, slice and put in a layer over the pasta. Add the remaining pasta. Preheat the oven to 190°C/ 375°F/gas mark 5.

6 Make the white sauce and spoon over.

7 Sprinkle with the crushed crisps. Bake in the oven for about 25 minutes until hot through and turning golden on top.

Neapolitan Tortellini

SERVES 2–4

250 g/9 oz/1 packet of dried tortellini, stuffed with cheese or mushrooms

500 ml/17 fl oz/2¼ cups passata (sieved tomatoes)

5 ml/1 tsp dried basil

Salt and freshly ground black pepper

Grated Parmesan cheese, to garnish

A Mixed Salad (see page 308), to serve

1 Cook the tortellini according to the packet directions (or see page 293). Drain in a colander and return to the pan.

2 Add the passata and basil and a good grinding of pepper. Heat through, stirring, until bubbling and the tortellini is bathed in the sauce. Meanwhile, make the salad.

3 Spoon the pasta and sauce into warm bowls, sprinkle with Parmesan cheese and serve with the salad.

Spaghetti with Exotic Mushrooms and Herbs

You can buy mixed packs of exotic mushrooms in most supermarkets. If not, use oyster or chestnut mushrooms instead.

SERVES 4

100 g/4 oz/½ cup unsalted (sweet) butter, softened
50 g/2 oz/½ cup ground almonds
30 ml/2 tbsp grated Parmesan cheese
30 ml/2 tbsp chopped fresh parsley
15 ml/1 tbsp snipped fresh chives
15 ml/1 tbsp chopped fresh sage
Salt and freshly ground black pepper
175 g/6 oz mixed exotic mushrooms, sliced
60 ml/4 tbsp water
350 g/12 oz spaghetti
A Tomato and Onion Salad (see page 309), to serve

1 Mash the butter with the almonds, Parmesan, herbs, a little salt and a good grinding of pepper.
2 Put the mushrooms in a saucepan with the water. Heat rapidly until boiling, then turn down the heat to low, cover and cook gently for 6 minutes until tender.
3 Cook the spaghetti according to the packet directions (or see page 293). Drain and return to the saucepan. Make the salad.
4 Add the flavoured butter and the mushrooms to the pasta and lift and stir over a gentle heat until the butter has melted and every strand is bathed in the fragrant mixture.
5 Pile into warm bowls and serve with the salad.

Spaghetti Quolognese

SERVES 4

15 ml/1 tbsp olive oil
1 onion, chopped
1 garlic clove, crushed
2 carrots, coarsely grated
175 g/6 oz minced (ground) quorn
100 g/4 oz mushrooms, sliced
400 g/14 oz/1 large can of chopped tomatoes
30 ml/2 tbsp tomato purée (paste)
30 ml/2 tbsp red wine
15 ml/1 tbsp yeast extract
60 ml/4 tbsp water
2.5 ml/½ tsp caster (superfine) sugar
1 bay leaf
Salt and freshly ground black pepper
350 g/12 oz spaghetti
Grated Parmesan cheese, to serve

1 Heat the oil in a saucepan. Add the onion, garlic and carrots and cook, stirring, for 2 minutes.
2 Add all the remaining ingredients except the spaghetti. When the mixture bubbles, turn down the heat and let it cook gently, bubbling round the edges for 20 minutes, stirring occasionally. Discard the bay leaf, taste and add more salt and pepper, if necessary.
3 Cook the spaghetti according to the packet directions (or see page 293).
4 Spoon the cooked spaghetti into warm, shallow bowls. Spoon the quorn mixture over and sprinkle with cheese before serving.

Spaghettini with Herby Lentil and Tomato Sauce

Put the ingredients in a saucepan early in the morning, then it's ready to cook quickly at lunchtime or in the evening.

SERVES 4

225 g/8 oz/1⅓ cups green lentils
400 g/14 oz/1 large can of chopped tomatoes
600 ml/1 pt/2½ cups vegetable stock, made with 2 stock cubes
1 onion, chopped
1 green (bell) pepper, chopped
5 ml/1 tsp dried basil
Salt and freshly ground black pepper
15 ml/1 tbsp chopped fresh parsley
350 g/12 oz spaghettini
60 ml/4 tbsp grated Parmesan cheese

1 Put all the ingredients except the spaghettini and cheese in a saucepan and leave to stand for several hours.
2 Heat rapidly, stirring occasionally, until the mixture is boiling, then turn down the heat so it is bubbling gently round the edges. Cover and cook for 30 minutes, stirring occasionally. Taste and add more seasoning if necessary.
3 Meanwhile, cook the spaghettini according to the packet directions (or see page 293) – it will usually take about 6 minutes. Drain and return to the pan. Add the lentil sauce and lift and stir well with a spoon and fork until every strand is coated in the sauce.
4 Pile on warm plates and sprinkle with cheese before serving.

Bean and Ratatouille Lasagne

SERVES 4

2 quantities of Cheese Sauce (see page 329)
8 sheets of no-need-to-precook lasagne
425 g/15 oz/1 large can of ratatouille
425 g/15 oz/1 large can of cannellini beans, drained
5 ml/1 tsp dried oregano
Freshly ground black pepper
25 g/1 oz/¼ cup Parmesan cheese, grated

1 Preheat the oven to 190°C/375°F/gas mark 5.
2 Spoon a little of the sauce in the base of a shallow, rectangular, 1.5 litre/2½ pt/6 cup ovenproof dish.
3 Top with two lasagne sheets.
4 Mix the ratatouille with the beans, oregano and a good grinding of pepper.
5 Spread a layer of one-third of this mixture over the lasagne. Repeat the layers, finishing with a layer of lasagne.
6 Spoon the cheese sauce over and sprinkle with the Parmesan. Bake in the oven for about 35 minutes until the top is golden and the lasagne feels tender when a knife is inserted down through the centre.

Broad Bean and Pine Nut Pasta

You can buy shaved Parmesan, but it's best to buy it in a block (it keeps for ages in the fridge). Hold it firmly in one hand and shave off strips with a potato peeler.

SERVES 4

60 ml/4 tbsp pine nuts

225 g/8 oz conchiglie (pasta shells)

225 g/8 oz fresh shelled or frozen baby broad (fava) beans

50 g/2 oz/¼ cup unsalted (sweet) butter

150 ml/¼ pt/⅔ cup single (light) cream

30 ml/2 tbsp chopped fresh parsley

A good pinch of grated nutmeg

Salt and freshly ground black pepper

30 ml/2 tbsp shaved Parmesan cheese

1 Put the pine nuts in a saucepan and cook, stirring over a high heat, until golden. Tip out of the pan straight away to prevent over-browning.

2 Pour water into the pan to a level 5 cm/2 in from the top and add a good pinch of salt. Heat rapidly until boiling. Add the pasta, stir and cook for 5 minutes. Add the broad beans and continue cooking for 5 minutes until the beans and pasta are just tender. Drain in a colander, then return to the saucepan.

3 Cut the butter into small pieces, add to the pan and stir gently until melted.

4 Stir in the cream, parsley, nutmeg, a little salt and lots of pepper. Cook, stirring over a very gentle heat, until piping hot. Do not allow to boil.

5 Spoon the pasta on to plates, sprinkle with the pine nuts and the shavings of Parmesan.

Pasta con Salsa Alfredo

Ideally use fresh pasta for this dish – the Italians always do! Follow it with a crisp green salad, made in advance.

SERVES 4

350 g/12 oz any fresh pasta

450 ml/¾ pt/2 cups double (heavy) cream

50 g/2 oz/¼ cup butter

175 g/6 oz/1½ cups Parmesan cheese, grated

Freshly ground black pepper

Ciabatta bread and a dish of green olives, to serve

1 Cook the fresh pasta according to the packet directions (or see page 293). It will take about 4 minutes only. Drain in a colander and return to the pan.

2 Meanwhile, bring the cream and butter to the boil in a saucepan over a high heat. Reduce the heat until just bubbling very gently and cook for 1 minute.

3 Add half the cheese and some pepper and whisk with a wire whisk until smooth.

4 Add to the cooked pasta with the remaining cheese and lift and stir gently over a fairly low heat.

5 Pile on to warm plates, add a good grinding of pepper and serve with ciabatta bread and a dish of green olives.

Tagliatelle with Aubergines

SERVES 4

2 small aubergines (eggplants)
30 ml/2 tbsp plain (all-purpose) flour
Salt and freshly ground black pepper
5 ml/1 tsp dried oregano
350 g/12 oz tagliatelle
90 ml/6 tbsp olive oil
1 garlic clove, crushed
100 g/4 oz/1 cup Mozzarella cheese, grated

1 Slice the aubergines and then cut each slice into matchsticks. Put in a bowl.

2 Mix the flour with a little salt and pepper and the oregano. Sprinkle over the aubergines and mix with your hands to coat completely.

3 Cook the tagliatelle according to the packet directions (or see page 293). Drain in a colander and return to the saucepan.

4 Meanwhile, heat 60 ml/4 tbsp of the oil in a large frying pan (skillet) until hot, but not smoking. Add the aubergines and garlic and fry (sauté), stirring, for about 5 minutes until golden and tender.

5 Tip the aubergine and the remaining oil into the pasta and, lifting and stirring with a spoon and fork, heat gently until it is all piping hot.

6 Spoon on to warm plates and scatter the cheese over before serving.

Veggie Satay

SERVES 4

1 small swede (rutabaga), cut into chunks
2 large carrots, cut into chunks
1 large parsnip, cut into chunks
2 courgettes (zucchini), cut into chunks
15 g/½ oz/1 tbsp butter or margarine
15 ml/1 tbsp clear honey
Salt and freshly ground black pepper
150 ml/¼ pt/⅔ cup milk
75 ml/5 tbsp smooth peanut butter
1.5 ml/¼ tsp chilli powder
Caribbean Rice and Peas (see page 314), to serve

1 Soak eight wooden kebab skewers in cold water for 1 hour.

2 Heat a large saucepan of lightly salted water until boiling, then add the vegetables and cook for 4 minutes until almost tender. Drain.

3 When cool enough to handle, thread the vegetables on the skewers and lay them on foil on the grill (broiler) rack. Preheat the grill.

4 Melt the butter or margarine with the honey and seasoning and brush all over the kebabs.

5 Cook under the grill, turning once or twice and brushing with more honey mixture, until golden.

6 Meanwhile, put the milk, peanut butter and chilli powder in a saucepan and heat gently, stirring, until the mixture forms a thick sauce.

7 Put the kebabs on warm plates and spoon the sauce over. Serve with Caribbean Rice and Peas.

Gingered Mushroom and Courgette Kebabs with Cheesy Corn Mash

SERVES 4

700 g/1½ lb potatoes, peeled and cut into chunks

100 g/4 oz/½ cup butter or margarine

200 g/7 oz/1 small can of sweetcorn (corn)

75 g/3 oz/¾ cup Cheddar cheese, grated

Salt and freshly ground black pepper

3 courgettes (zucchini), trimmed and cut into 8 pieces

24 button mushrooms

2 garlic cloves, crushed

5 ml/1 tsp grated fresh root ginger

15 ml/1 tbsp chopped fresh parsley

1 Soak eight wooden skewers in cold water for 1 hour.

2 Boil the potatoes for 10–15 minutes. While they are cooking, bring a separate saucepan of water to the boil. Drop in the courgettes and mushrooms and boil for 2 minutes to soften slightly. Drain in a colander.

3 Drain the potatoes and return to the pan. Mash with half the butter or margarine.

4 Briskly stir in the sweetcorn, cheese and some salt and pepper.

5 Melt the remaining butter in a saucepan with the garlic, ginger and a little salt and pepper.

6 Thread the mushrooms and courgettes alternately on the soaked skewers. Preheat the grill (broiler).

7 Lay them on foil on the grill rack and brush all over with the garlic and ginger butter.

8 Grill (broil) for about 6 minutes until golden, turning and brushing with more of the butter during cooking.

9 Pile the mash on four warm plates and top with the kebabs. Pour any remaining garlic butter over and sprinkle with the parsley.

Cashew Nut Paella

SERVES 4

30 ml/2 tbsp olive oil

1 leek, well-washed and thinly sliced

1 green (bell) pepper, diced

1 red pepper, diced

225 g/8 oz/1 cup long-grain rice

5 ml/1 tsp saffron powder

100 g/4 oz oyster mushrooms, sliced

100 g/4 oz/1 cup raw cashew nuts

600 ml/1 pt/2½ cups vegetable stock, made with 1 stock cube

Salt and freshly ground black pepper

5 ml/1 tsp dried oregano

15 ml/1 tbsp chopped fresh parsley

1 Heat the oil in a large frying pan (skillet). Add the leek and peppers and cook, stirring, for 2 minutes.

2 Stir in the rice and cook for 1 minute until every grain is glistening.

3 Add all the remaining ingredients except the parsley. Cook, stirring gently over a high heat, until bubbling.

4 Turn down the heat as low as possible. Cover with a lid and cook very gently for 20 minutes. Remove the lid and stir well. The rice should have absorbed all the liquid and be just tender. Spoon on to warm plates and top with the parsley.

Sweet and Sour Tofu

Cook the Egg Fried Rice before starting on the tofu. You can reheat it for a few minutes just before serving.

SERVES 4

15 ml/1 tbsp sunflower oil
1 carrot, cut into matchsticks
1 onion, thinly sliced
5 cm/2 in piece of cucumber, cut into matchsticks
320 g/12 oz/1 medium can of pineapple pieces
2.5 ml/½ tsp ground ginger
15 ml/1 tbsp light brown sugar
30 ml/2 tbsp soy sauce
15 ml/1 tbsp red wine vinegar
15 ml/1 tbsp tomato ketchup (catsup)
15 ml/1 tbsp cornflour (cornstarch)
30 ml/2 tbsp water
250 g/9 oz/1 block of firm tofu, cubed
Egg Fried Rice (see page 315), to serve

1 Heat the oil in a wok or large frying pan (skillet). Add the carrot and onion and cook, stirring, for 3 minutes.

2 Add all the remaining ingredients except the cornflour, water and tofu. Heat, stirring, until bubbling, then cook for 1 minute.

3 Mix the cornflour with the water and stir into the pan. Heat, stirring, until bubbling, then continue to cook and stir for 1 minute.

4 Add the tofu and simmer for 3 minutes. Serve with the Egg Fried Rice.

Potato and Tofu Sauté

SERVES 4

700 g/1½ lb new potatoes, scraped and cut into bite-sized pieces
50 g/2 oz/¼ cup butter or margarine
30 ml/2 tbsp olive oil
1 bunch of spring onions (scallions), chopped
1 green (bell) pepper, sliced
1 red pepper, sliced
320 g/12 oz/1 medium can of sweetcorn (corn) with peppers, drained
250 g/9 oz/1 block of smoked tofu, cubed
15 ml/1 tbsp paprika
5 ml/1 tsp dried thyme
Salt and freshly ground black pepper

1 Put the potatoes in a pan, cover with cold water and add a pinch of salt. Cover with a lid and boil for 5 minutes or until just tender. Drain well.

2 Heat the butter and oil in a large frying pan (skillet) or wok. Add the spring onions and peppers and fry (sauté), stirring, over a high heat for 2 minutes.

3 Add the potatoes and continue to fry, stirring and turning, for 5 minutes until turning golden.

4 Add the remaining ingredients to the pan, season to taste with salt and pepper and continue to cook, stirring and turning, for 3 minutes until everything is piping hot. Serve straight from the pan.

Smoked Tofu with Asparagus Stir-fry

SERVES 4

225 g/8 oz/1 cup long-grain rice
15 ml/1 tbsp sunflower oil
15 ml/1 tbsp sesame oil
225 g/8 oz thin asparagus, trimmed and cut into short lengths
1 red (bell) pepper, cut into thin strips
225 g/8 oz smoked tofu, cubed
15 ml/1 tbsp light brown sugar
15 ml/1 tbsp white wine vinegar
15 ml/1 tbsp soy sauce
1.5 ml/¼ tsp cayenne
150 ml/¼ pt/⅔ cup vegetable stock, made with ½ stock cube
10 ml/2 tsp sesame seeds

1 Cook the rice according to the packet directions (or see page 294). Drain in a colander. Put some water in the saucepan and sit the colander on top. Cover the rice with the saucepan lid and keep warm over a very gentle heat until ready to serve.

2 Heat the oils in a wok or large frying pan (skillet).

3 Add the asparagus and pepper and cook, stirring, for 5 minutes.

4 Add the tofu and all the remaining ingredients except the sesame seeds and rice. Bring to the boil and cook for 7 minutes, stirring occasionally. Sprinkle with the sesame seeds.

5 Serve straight away with the rice.

Smoked Tofu Kedgeree

SERVES 4

225 g/8 oz/1 cup long-grain rice
2 eggs, scrubbed under cold running water
100 g/4 oz/1 cup frozen peas
15 g/½ oz/1 tbsp butter or margarine
1 bunch of spring onions (scallions), chopped
250 g/9 oz/1 block of smoked tofu, cubed
A good pinch of grated nutmeg
Salt and freshly ground black pepper
30 ml/2 tbsp single (light) cream
30 ml/2 tbsp chopped fresh parsley

1 Cook the rice according to the packet directions (or see page 294), adding the eggs with the rice. Add the peas after 5 minutes' cooking time.

2 When cooked, lift out the eggs and put immediately into a bowl of cold water. Drain the rice and peas in a colander.

3 Shell the eggs and cut into wedges.

4 Heat the butter or margarine in the rice saucepan. Add the spring onions and cook for 2 minutes, stirring. Stir in the rice and peas, the tofu, nutmeg and some salt and pepper. Cook over a moderate heat, stirring all the time, until the tofu is piping hot. Stir in the cream and heat for a further 1 minute, stirring.

5 Spoon on to warm plates, top with the egg wedges and sprinkle with the parsley.

Quorn Chilli

This is quite a hot chilli, so for a milder version halve the quantity of chilli powder.

SERVES 4

15 ml/1 tbsp olive oil

2 garlic clove, crushed

1 large onion, chopped

5 ml/1 tsp chilli powder

175 g/6 oz minced (ground) quorn

2 x 425 g/15 oz/large cans of red kidney beans

10 ml/2 tsp yeast extract

30 ml/2 tbsp boiling water

450 ml/¾ pt/2 cups passata (sieved tomatoes)

15 ml/1 tbsp tomato purée (paste)

5 ml/1 tsp caster (superfine) sugar

Salt and freshly ground black pepper

225 g/8 oz/1 cup long-grain rice

100 g/4 oz/1 cup Cheddar cheese, grated

½ small iceberg lettuce, shredded

1 Heat the oil in a large saucepan. Add the onion and garlic and cook, stirring, for 2 minutes. Add the chilli powder and cook for a further 1 minute.

2 Add the quorn. Drain one of the cans of kidney beans and add this to the pan with the entire contents of the second can.

3 Dissolve the yeast extract with the water and add to the pasta with the passata, tomato purée, sugar and some salt and pepper. When boiling, turn down the heat until just bubbling round the edges and cook for 20 minutes, stirring occasionally, until thick and rich.

4 Meanwhile, cook the rice according to the packet directions (or see page 294). Spoon the rice into warm bowls. Top with the chilli and serve with the grated cheese and shredded lettuce.

Quorn Hash

This is also good topped with fried (sautéed) eggs (see page 76).

SERVES 4

50 g/2 oz/¼ cup butter or margarine

4 potatoes, peeled and cut into small pieces

1 large onion, chopped

175 g/6 oz quorn pieces

400 g/14 oz/1 large can of baked beans

10 ml/2 tsp brown table sauce

Salt and freshly ground black pepper

15 ml/1 tbsp chopped fresh parsley

Crusty bread, to serve

1 Heat the butter or margarine in a large frying pan (skillet). Add the potatoes and onion and fry (sauté), stirring, over a fairly high heat for 2 minutes.

2 Cover with a lid, turn down the heat to low and cook for 10 minutes, stirring once or twice until the potatoes are soft.

3 Stir the quorn into the pan and cook for 1 minute. Add the beans, sauce and some salt and pepper and cook, stirring, for 2–3 minutes.

4 Spoon into warm bowls, sprinkle with parsley and serve with crusty bread.

Flageolet and Cashew Nut Burgers

Start to cook the chips (fries) before you fry (sauté) the burgers.

SERVES 4

425 g/15 oz/1 large can of flageolet beans, drained

2 courgettes (zucchini), grated

50 g/2 oz/½ cup raw cashew nuts, chopped

50 g/2 oz/1 cup fresh white breadcrumbs

5 ml/1 tsp soy sauce

2.5 ml/½ tsp yeast extract

Freshly ground black pepper

15 ml/1 tbsp chopped fresh parsley

1 egg, beaten

A little flour, for dusting

Oil, for shallow-frying

4 burger buns

45 ml/3 tbsp mayonnaise

Shredded lettuce and slices of tomato, to garnish

Chips (see page 296), to serve

1 Mash the beans in a bowl with a potato masher or fork. Mix with the courgettes, nuts, breadcrumbs, soy sauce, yeast extract, some pepper and the parsley. Add the beaten egg and mix well to bind.

2 Using floured hands, shape the mixture into four flat cakes.

3 Heat a little oil in a large frying pan (skillet). Fry the burgers for about 3 minutes on each side until golden brown and cooked through.

4 Drain on kitchen paper (paper towels), then put in the burger buns, top with a little mayonnaise, lettuce and tomato, and serve with the chips.

Quoston Baked Beans

SERVES 4

1 large onion, chopped

15 ml/1 tbsp olive oil

2 x 425 g/15 oz/large cans of haricot (navy) beans, drained

1 garlic clove, crushed

1 bouquet garni sachet

5 cm/2 in piece of cinnamon stick

30 ml/2 tbsp black treacle (molasses)

300 ml/½ pt/1¼ cups vegetable stock, made with 1 stock cube

225 g/8 oz/1 small can of chopped tomatoes

175 g/6 oz quorn pieces

Salt and freshly ground black pepper

Crusty bread, to serve

1 Put the onion and oil and a flameproof casserole (Dutch oven). Cook over a high heat for 2 minutes, stirring, until turning lightly golden. Add the remaining ingredients and cook until boiling, stirring all the time.

2 Turn down the heat until just bubbling gently round the edges, stir again and cook gently for about 40 minutes, stirring occasionally, until the liquid is reduced and the beans and quorn are bathed in a rich sauce.

3 Discard the bouquet garni and cinnamon stick. Taste and add more salt and pepper if necessary.

4 Spoon into bowls and serve with crusty bread.

Nutty Stuffed Peppers

SERVES 4

4 red (bell) peppers, halved
225 g/8 oz frozen mixed vegetables
5 ml/1 tsp dried minced onion
25 g/1 oz/½ cup fresh wholemeal breadcrumbs
25 g/1 oz/¼ cup pine nuts
50 g/2 oz/½ cup Cheddar cheese, grated
15 ml/1 tbsp soy sauce
1 egg
Salt and freshly ground black pepper
120 ml/4 fl oz/½ cup water

1 Preheat the oven to 190°C/375°F/ gas mark 5.
2 Heat a large saucepan of water with a good pinch of salt until boiling. Add the peppers and mixed vegetables, bring back to the boil and cook for 5 minutes.
3 Tip into a colander to drain. Rinse under cold water, then drain again. Place the peppers in a baking tin (pan). Tip the mixed vegetables into a bowl.
4 Add the dried minced onion, breadcrumbs, pine nuts and cheese to the mixed vegetables.
5 Whisk the soy sauce and egg together in a small bowl with a wire whisk and season very lightly (it won't need much as the soy sauce is very salty). Stir into the mixture to bind.
6 Spoon the mixture into the peppers and pour the measured water around.
7 Bake in the oven for 15–20 minutes until golden and cooked through. Serve hot.

Pine Nut and Cashew Tabbouleh

SERVES 4

225 g/8 oz/2 cups bulghar (cracked wheat)
600 ml/1 pt/2½ cups boiling water
Salt and freshly ground black pepper
1 bunch of spring onions (scallions), trimmed and finely chopped, reserving the trimmings
60 ml/4 tbsp chopped fresh parsley
30 ml/2 tbsp chopped fresh mint
60 ml/4 tbsp olive oil
Finely grated rind and juice of ½ lemon
30 ml/2 tbsp white wine vinegar
1 garlic clove, crushed
5 cm/2 in piece of cucumber, chopped
100 g/4 oz cherry tomatoes, halved
100 g/4 oz/1 cup roasted cashew nuts
50 g/2 oz/½ cup pine nuts

1 Put the bulghar in a large bowl. Add the boiling water, stir and leave to stand for 30 minutes or until swollen, soft and the water has been absorbed. Leave to cool.
2 Tip the bulghar into a large salad bowl. Stir in the remaining ingredients. Season to taste. Cover and chill for at least 2 hours before serving.

Sweet and Sour Cashew Nut Stir-fry

If your noodles have cooled before your stir-fry is ready, put the colander of noodles in the sink and pour a little boiling water over them to reheat. Drain thoroughly again, then serve.

SERVES 4

250 g/9 oz/1 packet of Chinese egg noodles

15 ml/1 tbsp sunflower oil

1 red (bell) pepper, thinly sliced

1 bunch of spring onions (scallions), cut into short lengths

225 g/8 oz mushrooms, sliced

225 g/8 oz/1 small can of pineapple pieces

30 ml/2 tbsp tomato purée (paste)

30 ml/2 tbsp soy sauce

30 ml/2 tbsp white wine vinegar

30 ml/2 tbsp clear honey

Salt and freshly ground black pepper

60 ml/4 tbsp water

15 ml/1 tbsp cornflour (cornstarch)

175 g/6 oz/3 cups beansprouts

100 g/4 oz/1 cup raw cashew nuts

1 Cook the noodles according to the packet directions. Drain in a colander.

2 Meanwhile, heat the oil in a wok or large frying pan (skillet).

3 Add the pepper, spring onions and mushrooms and cook, stirring, for 3–4 minutes.

4 Add the pineapple and its juice, the tomato purée, soy sauce, vinegar, honey and a little seasoning (it will not need much as the soy sauce is very salty).

5 Mix the water and cornflour together in a cup and stir in. Bring to the boil and cook for 1 minute, stirring.

6 Add the beansprouts and nuts and stir in carefully. Cook for a further 2–3 minutes. Spoon the noodles into four bowls and spoon the stir-fry over.

Basic Nut Roast

SERVES 4

25 g/1 oz/2 tbsp butter or margarine, plus a little for greasing

150 g/5 oz/1¼ cups chopped mixed nuts

75 g/3 oz/1½ cups fresh wholemeal breadcrumbs

1 small onion, finely chopped

15 ml/1 tbsp soy sauce

2.5 ml/½ tsp dried oregano

5 ml/1 tsp lemon juice

5 ml/1 tsp yeast extract

150 ml/¼ pt/⅔ cup hot water

Mashed Potatoes (see page 298), a green vegetable and Vegetable Gravy (see page 324), to serve

1 Preheat the oven to 190°C/375°F/ gas mark 5. Lightly grease a 1.2 litre/ 2 pt/5 cup ovenproof dish with a little butter or margarine.

2 Mix together everything except the yeast extract and water.

3 Blend the yeast extract and water together and stir thoroughly into the mixture. Spoon into the prepared dish.

4 Bake in the oven for 30–40 minutes until golden brown and hot through.

5 Meanwhile, cook and mash the potatoes and prepare and cook a green vegetable and the gravy. Serve with the nut roast.

Spinach and Peanut Loaf

SERVES 4

225 g/8 oz frozen spinach, thawed
1 large onion, quartered
1 garlic clove
175 g/6 oz/1½ cups roasted peanuts
4 slices of wholemeal bread, torn into
   pieces
1 egg
5 ml/1 tsp yeast extract
5 ml/1 tsp dried thyme
Salt and freshly ground black pepper
A little sunflower oil, for greasing
450 ml/¾ pt/2 cups passata (sieved
   tomatoes)
Plain potatoes and sweetcorn (corn),
   to serve

1 Preheat the oven to 180°C/350°F/
gas mark 4.
2 Squeeze out the spinach to remove
as much moisture as possible. Place in a
blender or food processor, run the
machine and drop in the onion, garlic,
peanuts and bread. Alternatively, pass
the ingredients through a coarse mincer
(grinder), mincing the bread last.
3 Using a fork, stir the egg briskly with
the yeast extract in a small bowl until
well blended, then stir into the spinach
mixture with the thyme and a little salt
and pepper.
4 Turn into a greased 450 g/1 lb loaf tin
(pan) and cover with foil.
5 Bake in the oven for 1 hour or until
firm to the touch. Meanwhile, cook the
potatoes.
6 Leave the loaf to cool for
3–4 minutes while you warm the
passata with plenty of pepper and
heat the sweetcorn in a pan.

7 Turn out the loaf on to a warm
serving dish and serve sliced with the
passata, potatoes and sweetcorn.

Herby Baked Mushroom and Cheese Omelette

SERVES 2

4 eggs, beaten
225 g/8 oz/1 cup cottage cheese
100 g/4 oz button mushrooms, sliced
15 ml/1 tbsp chopped fresh parsley
15 ml/1 tbsp snipped fresh chives
1 small garlic clove, crushed
Salt and freshly ground black pepper
A good knob of butter or margarine,
   for greasing

1 Preheat the oven to 200°C/400°F/
gas mark 6.
2 Place all the ingredients except the
butter or margarine in a bowl and mix
well.
3 Grease a 1.2 litre/2 pt/5 cup shallow
ovenproof dish. Pour in the egg mixture
and bake in the oven for about
20–25 minutes until set and golden.
4 Serve cut into pieces.

Chestnut and Mushroom Pie

SERVES 4

700 g/1½ lb potatoes, cut into small pieces

30 ml/2 tbsp milk

65 g/2½ oz/scant ⅓ cup butter or margarine

1 onion, chopped

225 g/8 oz chestnut mushrooms, quartered

25 g/1 oz/¼ cup plain (all-purpose) flour

250 ml/8 fl oz/1 cup vegetable stock, made with 1 stock cube

30 ml/2 tbsp dried milk powder (non-fat dry milk)

430 g/15½ oz/1 large can of chestnuts, quartered

Salt and freshly ground black pepper

30 ml/2 tbsp chopped fresh parsley

5 ml/1 tsp dried thyme

50 g/2 oz/½ cup Cheddar cheese, grated

Baked Tomatoes with Basil (see page 306), to serve

1 Boil and mash the potatoes with the milk and 15 g/½ oz/1 tbsp of the butter or margarine. Preheat the oven to 190°C/375°F/gas mark 5.

2 Melt the remaining butter or margarine in a saucepan. Add the onion and mushrooms and fry (sauté) for 3 minutes, stirring.

3 Add the flour and cook for 1 minute.

4 Remove from the heat and blend in the stock and milk powder. Return to the heat, bring to the boil and cook for 2 minutes, stirring.

5 Add the chestnuts and season to taste. Stir in the herbs.

6 Turn into an ovenproof serving dish. Top with the potato, decorate with the prongs of a fork and sprinkle with the cheese.

7 Bake in the oven for about 30 minutes until golden brown. Meanwhile, prepare and cook the tomatoes. Serve hot with the pie.

Rice and Corn Cakes

Put the tomatoes to cook before you fry (sauté) the corn cakes.

SERVES 4

100 g/4 oz/½ cup long-grain rice

5 ml/1 tsp ground turmeric

200 g/7 oz/1 small can of sweetcorn (corn), drained

4 eggs, beaten

Salt and freshly ground black pepper

A good pinch of chilli powder

Oil, for shallow-frying

Pan-roasted Vine Tomatoes (see page 305), to serve

1 Cook the rice according to the packet directions (or see page 294), adding the turmeric to the cooking water. Drain and return to the pan.

2 Stir in the sweetcorn, eggs, some salt and pepper and the chilli powder.

3 Heat about 5 mm/¼ in oil in a large frying pan (skillet) until hot, but not smoking. Drop in spoonfuls of the mixture and fry for about 2 minutes on each side until golden brown and set.

4 Drain each batch on kitchen paper (paper towels) and keep warm while cooking the remainder.

5 Transfer to warm plates and serve with the Pan-roasted Vine Tomatoes.

Curried Eggs

SERVES 4

25 g/1 oz/2 tbsp butter or margarine
1 onion, chopped
15 ml/1 tbsp plain (all-purpose) flour
15 ml/1 tbsp curry powder
450 ml/¾ pt/2 cups vegetable stock, made with 1 stock cube
15 ml/1 tbsp mango chutney
50 g/2 oz creamed coconut, cut into pieces
A squeeze of lemon juice
Salt and freshly ground black pepper
225 g/8 oz/1 cup long-grain rice
8 eggs, scrubbed under cold running water

1 Heat the butter or margarine in a saucepan. Add the onion and cook, stirring, over a moderate heat for 3 minutes until lightly golden.
2 Add the flour and curry powder and cook, stirring, for 1 minute.
3 Remove from the heat. Blend in the stock and add the chutney and coconut. Cook, stirring, until thickened and the coconut has melted.
4 Turn down the heat until gently bubbling and cook for a further 15 minutes. Add lemon juice, salt and pepper to taste.
5 Cook the rice according to the packet directions (or see page 294), adding the eggs to the water at the same time as the rice. Lift the eggs out of the pan and put immediately into a bowl of cold water. Drain the rice.
6 Shell the eggs and cut into halves.
7 Spoon the rice on warm plates. Top with the egg halves, then spoon the curry sauce over.

Nutty Cottage Cheese and Celery Loaf

SERVES 4

A knob of butter or margarine, for greasing
225 g/8 oz/1 cup cottage cheese with chives
2 celery sticks, chopped
50 g/2 oz/½ cup chopped mixed nuts
2.5 ml/½ tsp dried oregano
A few drops of Tabasco sauce
100 g/4 oz/2 cups fresh wholemeal breadcrumbs
Salt and freshly ground black pepper
2 eggs, beaten
New potatoes and a Tomato and Onion Salad (see page 309), to serve

1 Grease a 450 g/1 lb loaf tin (pan) and line the base with an oblong of non-stick baking parchment. Preheat the oven to 180°C/350°F/gas mark 4.
2 Mix all the ingredients together, turn into the tin and level the surface.
3 Bake in the oven for about 40 minutes until set. Meanwhile, cook the potatoes and prepare the Tomato and Onion Salad.
4 Cool the loaf for 5 minutes, then turn out on to a warm plate, remove the paper, then cut into slices and serve with the new potatoes and salad.

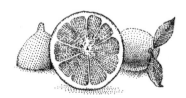

Egg and Chestnut Mushroom Pie

SERVES 4

1 kg/2¼ lb potatoes, peeled and cut into chunks

4 eggs, scrubbed under cold running water

30 ml/2 tbsp milk

25 g/1 oz/2 tbsp butter or margarine

1 onion, chopped

175 g/6 oz chestnut mushrooms, sliced

295 g/10½ oz/1 medium can of condensed mushroom soup

30 ml/2 tbsp chopped fresh parsley

Salt and freshly ground black pepper

50 g/2 oz/½ cup Cheddar cheese, grated

A Green Salad (see page 308), to serve

1 Put the potatoes and eggs in a pan and cover with water. Add a good pinch of salt and heat rapidly until the water boils. Cook for 10 minutes, then remove the eggs and put immediately into a bowl of cold water.

2 Test the potatoes and cook a little longer if not quite tender. Drain and return to the pan.

3 Preheat the oven to 200°C/400°F/ gas mark 6. Mash the potatoes with the milk and half the butter or margarine.

4 Melt the remaining butter or margarine in a flameproof casserole (Dutch oven). Add the onion and mushrooms and cook, stirring, over a moderate heat for 3 minutes.

5 Remove from the heat. Shell the eggs, slice and add to the casserole. Pour the soup over and add the parsley and a good grinding of pepper.

6 Top with the potato and sprinkle with the cheese. Cook in the oven for about 20 minutes until golden and piping hot. Meanwhile, make the salad.

7 Serve the pie hot with the salad.

Tortilla

This is a traditional Spanish omelette. For a tasty variation, add one red and one green (bell) pepper, thinly sliced, to the potatoes before cooking.

SERVES 4

60 ml/4 tbsp olive oil

2 onions, thinly sliced

2 large potatoes, thinly sliced

6 eggs

Salt and freshly ground black pepper

1 Heat the oil in a large frying pan (skillet).

2 Add the onions and potatoes and cook over a moderate heat, stirring, for 2 minutes. Turn down the heat to low, cover with a lid and cook gently for about 8 minutes, stirring occasionally, until softened but not browned. Spread out evenly.

3 Break the eggs into a bowl and whisk gently with a wire whisk or fork, adding a little salt and pepper. Pour over the vegetables in the pan.

4 Cook, lifting and stirring, until the egg is golden brown underneath and just set. Slide out of the pan on to a plate. Invert back into the pan to cook the other side. Serve hot or cold.

West Indian Bean and Fruit Salad

SERVES 4

100 g/4 oz/½ cup long-grain rice
2 satsumas, peeled, all pith removed, and segmented
425 g/15 oz/1 large can of red kidney beans, drained
100 g/4 oz/1 cup Monterey Jack cheese, cubed
15 ml/1 tbsp chilli relish
75 ml/5 tbsp plain yoghurt
Salt and freshly ground black pepper
Lettuce leaves

1 Cook the rice according to the packet directions (or see page 294). Drain in a colander, rinse with cold water and drain again.
2 Place in a bowl and add the fruit, beans and cheese.
3 Whisk the relish with the yoghurt, a little salt and a good grinding of pepper in a small bowl with a wire whisk. Add to the bowl and mix gently.
4 Pile on to a bed of lettuce leaves and serve.

Stuffed Tomato Salad

Make the Warm Potato Salad with Fragrant Herbs in advance or, alternatively, while the tomatoes are chilling.

SERVES 4

4 eggs
4 beefsteak tomatoes
1 Weetabix, crumbled
Salt and freshly ground black pepper
15 ml/1 tbsp olive oil
15 ml/1 tbsp mayonnaise
15 ml/1 tbsp snipped fresh chives
50 g/2 oz/1 cup beansprouts
10 ml/2 tsp soy sauce
Warm Potato Salad with Fragrant Herbs, (see page 310) to serve

1 Hard boil (hard-cook) the eggs (see page 76) and put straight away in cold water. Leave to stand while preparing the tomatoes.
2 Cut the tops off the tomatoes and scoop out the seeds into a bowl.
3 Add the Weetabix, a little salt and pepper, the oil, mayonnaise and chives.
4 Shell the eggs and chop. Add to the bowl and mix everything together thoroughly. Pack into the tomatoes and replace the tops.
5 Put the beansprouts on four plates and sprinkle with the soy sauce. Put a tomato in the centre of each and chill until ready to serve with the potato salad.

Photograph opposite: Pine Nut and Cashew Tabbouleh (see page 282)

Hot Mushroom and Cannellini Bean Salad

SERVES 4

8 field mushrooms

120 ml/4 fl oz/½ cup olive oil

2 garlic cloves, chopped

5 ml/1 tsp dried thyme

30 ml/2 tbsp chopped fresh parsley

Salt and freshly ground black pepper

4 slices of wholemeal bread, cut into cubes

425 g/15 oz/1 large can of cannellini beans

10 ml/2 tsp lemon juice

Lettuce leaves

1 Peel the mushrooms by gently pulling off the outer layer, starting from the edge all round. Remove any stalks and chop. Slice the caps.

2 Heat 60 ml/4 tbsp of the oil in a frying pan (skillet). Add the mushrooms and cook, stirring gently, for 2 minutes. Cover with a lid, turn down the heat to low and cook for a further 5 minutes, stirring occasionally.

3 Sprinkle with the garlic, thyme, parsley and a little salt and pepper.

4 Heat 75 ml/3 tbsp of the remaining oil in a separate pan and fry (sauté) the bread cubes, stirring until golden brown all over. Drain on kitchen paper (paper towels).

5 Heat the beans in a saucepan, then drain and tip into a salad bowl. Add the remaining oil, the lemon juice and the contents of the mushroom pan.

6 Put lettuce leaves on four plates. Mix the croûtons into the salad, spoon on to the lettuce and serve straight away.

Egg, Pea and Potato Salad

SERVES 4

700 g/1½ lb new potatoes, scrubbed and cut into bite-sized pieces

4 eggs, scrubbed under cold running water

30 ml/2 tbsp mayonnaise

10 ml/2 tsp white wine vinegar

5 ml/1 tsp made English mustard

Salt and freshly ground black pepper

15 ml/1 tbsp chopped fresh mint

275 g/10 oz/1 medium can of minted garden peas, drained

1 Put the potatoes in a saucepan and cover with cold water. Add a good pinch of salt and the eggs. Bring to the boil and cook for 10 minutes.

2 Lift out the eggs with a draining spoon and place immediately in a bowl of cold water.

3 Test the potatoes and cook a little longer if necessary until just tender, then drain.

4 Mix the mayonnaise with the vinegar, mustard, a little salt and pepper and half the mint in a salad bowl.

5 Shell the eggs and cut into chunks.

6 Add the potatoes to the mayonnaise mixture and stir gently until completely coated. Add the peas and eggs and stir in very gently.

7 Spoon into bowls and sprinkle with the remaining mint. Serve warm or cold.

Photograph opposite: **Perfect Potato Wedges (see page 295) and Middle Eastern Coleslaw (see page 311)**

Vegetables, Salads and Other Accompaniments

Plain cooked meat and two veg is fine, but can be a bit boring. And you may have thought that salads are rather dull, too. If your idea of a salad is a bowl of lettuce leaves with a few slices of tomato and cucumber, then I tend to agree. But with very little effort, you can do much better than that!

This first part of this chapter contains step-by-step instructions on how to prepare and cook all kinds of vegetables, pasta and rice to accompany any main course. These are followed by a huge range of colourful and tasty hot and cold dishes.

To prepare and cook vegetables

It is worth learning these basic techniques, so that your preparation is quick and easy and you don't end up cooking your lovely fresh veggies to a tasteless mush.

Potatoes and root vegetables

This method is suitable for parsnips, carrots, etc.

1 Peel thinly with a potato peeler or sharp vegetable knife, or scrape or scrub, as necessary.
2 Cut into even-sized pieces (for instance, large chunks for potatoes, slices or sticks for carrots, chunky wedges for parsnips). Leave baby vegetables and new potatoes whole.
3 Place in a pan with just enough cold water to cover and add a very little salt.
4 Cover with a lid and bring up to the boil over a high heat. When the water is boiling, turn the heat down to moderate, so that it is still bubbling gently and let the vegetables cook until they feel tender when a knife is inserted in them. This could be 5–15 minutes, depending on the size of the pieces, so keep testing at intervals until they are cooked to your liking.
5 Tip into a colander in the sink to drain. (If you want the cooking water for making gravy, then put the colander over a bowl.)

Green leafy vegetables

Use this method for cabbage, spring (collard) greens, etc.

1 Pull or cut off any outer, damaged leaves.
2 Separate into leaves, discarding any thick stalks. Cut cabbage in half and cut out the central stump. Rinse in cold water and drain.
3 Cut the leaves into pieces or thin shreds as appropriate.
4 Put about 2.5 cm/1 in water in a saucepan with a good pinch of salt. Put the pan over a high heat until it is boiling rapidly. Add the greens and push down well as they begin to soften. Boil over a high heat for 3–5 minutes until they are just tender but still with some texture.
5 Drain in a colander in the sink or over a bowl if you want the cooking water for gravy.

Note: To cook spinach, wash well (it can be gritty). Place in a pan with just the drops still clinging to it, and a sprinkling of salt. Do not add extra water. Cover and cook over a moderate heat for about 5 minutes until just tender. Drain thoroughly in a colander. Snip with scissors, if liked, before serving.

Green beans, shelled peas and beans

This includes runner beans, mangetout (snow peas), sugar snap peas, etc. and baby corn cobs.

1   Top and tail the vegetables if they are to be cooked whole (for instance, mangetout, sugar snap peas, French (green) beans and baby corn cobs), i.e. snap off the stalk and the point where the flower was. For fresh peas, broad (fava) beans, etc., remove from the pods. For runner beans, cut off the string all round the edge. Slice runner and flat beans into thin diagonal slices or 2.5 cm/1 in chunks.

2   Put about 5 cm/2 in water and a good pinch of salt in a saucepan. Bring to the boil over a high heat.

3   Add the vegetable and boil until they are just tender but still have a little 'bite' – this may take as little as 2–3 minutes for mangetout and up to 6 minutes for some thicker green beans. Keep testing until cooked to your liking.

4   Drain the vegetable in a colander in the sink or over a bowl if you want the cooking water for gravy.

To cook pasta

Pasta comes in all shapes and sizes, but the cooking method is more or less the same for all. The only difference is the length of time they each take – usually 10–15 minutes. Allow 50–75 g/2–3 oz of dried pasta per person.

Note: If you buy fresh pasta, it cooks much more quickly than dried – about 4–7 minutes.

Plain spaghetti

1   Fill a large pan with water up to about 5 cm/2 in from the top, and add a small teaspoonful of salt and a tablespoon of oil (this will help to stop it boiling over). Put over a high heat, cover with a lid and leave it until boiling, then remove the lid.

2   Hold the saucepan handle with one hand and the spaghetti with the other. Stand the ends of the spaghetti in the water, on the base of the pan.

3   Gently push the strands down, keeping a firm hold on the pan so that it does not move. They will gradually curl round as they soften. Do not push too hard or they will snap. Once submerged, stir gently to separate the strands. Cook for the time directed on the packet. This is usually 8–10 minutes. Do not cover the pan.

4   Test to see if the spaghetti is cooked by lifting a strand out of the pan (be careful not to burn yourself) and biting it. It should feel just soft but still with a little bit of chewiness to it. (You can also test it by throwing it at the wall – it will stick if it is cooked!)

5   Put a colander in the sink. Pour the contents of the saucepan into the colander and allow to drain well. Lift up the colander of spaghetti and place on top of the saucepan to finish draining while you prepare to serve the rest of the meal.

Pasta shapes

Cook pasta shapes, such as tagliatelle, macaroni, pappardelle and conchiglie, and stuffed pasta in exactly the same way but simply add (carefully) to the boiling water, rather than feeding them in gradually. Stir well to separate before cooking.

To cook rice

There are lots of different rices available, but the most common is long-grain rice. I particularly like Basmati rice, but you can use any other type of long-grain in the same way. Allow about 50 g/2 oz rice per person.

Plain long-grain rice

1   Fill a large pan with water up to 5 cm/2 in from the top, and add a small teaspoonful of salt. Put over a high heat, cover with a lid and leave until it is boiling.
2   Remove the pan lid. Pour the rice in a thin stream into the boiling water and stir well to separate the grains. Do not cover the pan again.
3   Boil for the time directed on the packet. Meanwhile, boil a kettle of water.
4   To test if it is cooked, lift out a few grains with a draining spoon and either taste or pinch a grain between your thumb and index finger. It should feel almost soft but still have some texture, or 'bite'.
5   Place a colander in the sink and pour in the contents of the pan. Pour boiling water all over the grains to rinse off any excess starch, then lift up the colander and place on top of the saucepan to finish draining. Stir gently with a fork to loosen (fluff up) the grains, then serve.

Note: To cook Thai fragrant rice, wash it well first, then cook as above. It will be stickier than other long-grain varieties.

Roast Potatoes

If your oven is slightly hotter (when cooking game birds, for instance), don't worry, simply cook the potatoes for slightly less time. Keep an eye on them though, to make sure they don't over-brown. Floury-textured potatoes are better than waxy ones for roasting.

SERVES 4

4 good-sized potatoes
30 ml/2 tbsp sunflower or olive oil

1 Preheat the oven to 190°C/375°F/ gas mark 5.

2 Peel the potatoes and cut each into three or four even-sized pieces.

3 Put the potatoes in a saucepan and cover with water. Add a good pinch of salt.

4 Cover and bring to the boil over a high heat. Cook for 3 minutes to part-cook (this is called par-boiling). Drain, reserving the water for making gravy, if liked.

5 Holding the lid on the pan, shake the pan vigorously to roughen the edges of the potatoes.

6 Meanwhile, heat the oil in a roasting tin (pan) towards the top of the oven. When sizzling, tip in the potatoes and turn over in the hot oil. Roast for 1–1½ hours until golden brown, turning once.

Roast Parsnips

SERVES 4

Prepare and cook roast parsnips and other root vegetables as for roast potatoes but there is no need to shake the pan after draining off the cooking water.

Perfect Potato Wedges

SERVES 4

4 large potatoes
30 ml/2 tbsp sunflower or olive oil
10 ml/2 tsp barbecue seasoning

1 Preheat the oven to 220°C/425°F/ gas mark 7.

2 Prick the potatoes and either boil in water for about 20 minutes or cook in the microwave according to the manufacturer's instructions until almost tender. Drain, if necessary.

3 When cool enough to handle, cut the potatoes in halves, then each half into wedges. Lay the wedges in a roasting tin (pan) and trickle the oil over. Sprinkle with half the barbecue seasoning.

4 Cook at the top of the oven for 10–15 minutes until golden on top. Turn the wedges over, sprinkle with the remaining barbecue seasoning and cook for a further 10–15 minutes until crisp and golden.

Garlic Potato Wedges

SERVES 4

Prepare and cook as for Perfect Potato Wedges, but add 5 ml/1 tsp garlic powder to the barbecue seasoning.

Sauté Potatoes

SERVES 4

4 medium potatoes, diced
25 g/1 oz/2 tbsp butter or margarine
30 ml/2 tbsp sunflower oil

1 Put the potatoes in a saucepan with enough water to cover. Bring to the boil over a high heat and cook for about 3 minutes until almost tender.
2 Drain and tip them on to kitchen paper (paper towels) and pat dry.
3 Heat the butter or margarine and oil in a large frying pan (skillet). Add the potatoes and fry (sauté) over a moderate heat, turning gently occasionally, until golden brown and cooked through.
4 Drain on kitchen paper, then serve.

Sauté Potatoes with Garlic

SERVES 4

Prepare as for Sauté Potatoes but add two halved garlic cloves to the butter or margarine and oil. Discard the garlic before serving.

Chips

SERVES 4

4 large potatoes
Oil, for deep-frying

1 Wash or scrub the potatoes (you don't have to peel them unless you want to). Cut each one into four thick slices, then cut the slices into fingers to make chips (fries). Wrap in a clean tea towel (dish cloth) to dry.
2 Pour about 2.5 cm/1 in oil into a frying pan (skillet) and heat until your

hand feels hot when held 5 cm/2 in above the surface.
3 Slide the chips down the fish slice into the pan (this helps to prevent splashing the hot oil) and allow to cook until golden, gently turning them occasionally.
Note: If you have a deep-fat fryer, follow the manufacturer's instructions.

Jacket-baked Potatoes

The potatoes can be cooked at any temperature along with a casserole or other baked or roast dish. They will take slightly longer in a lower oven, or slightly less in a hotter one (and the skins will become more crispy). To shorten cooking times, thread the potatoes on metal skewers.

SERVES 4

4 large potatoes, scrubbed
A little sunflower or olive oil
Salt
25 g/1 oz/2 tbsp butter or margarine

1 Preheat the oven to 180°C/350°F/ gas mark 4.
2 Prick the potatoes all over and rub with a little oil and salt.
3 Place directly on the oven shelf and cook for about 1½ hours or until tender when squeezed (use an oven glove!). If they are ready before the rest of the meal, put them nearer the bottom of the oven and cover loosely with foil.
4 Make a cross cut in the top of each potatoes, squeeze gently, then add a knob of butter or margarine to each before serving.

Croquette Potatoes

SERVES 4

450 g/1 lb potatoes, peeled and cut into even-sized chunks

A good knob of butter or margarine

30 ml/2 tbsp plain (all-purpose) flour

Salt and freshly ground black pepper

1 egg, beaten

75 g/3 oz/¾ cup dried breadcrumbs

Oil, for shallow-frying

1 Place the potatoes in a saucepan and cover with cold water. Add a good pinch of salt.

2 Cover the pan and cook over a high heat until the water boils, then lower the heat a little and continue to cook for 10–15 minutes (depending on their size) until the potatoes are really tender.

3 Drain in a colander, return to the pan and mash well with the butter or margarine, using a fork or potato masher.

4 Briskly stir in the flour and salt and pepper to taste, using a wooden spoon.

5 Shape into small sausage shapes, then brush with beaten egg and roll in the breadcrumbs. Chill until ready to cook.

6 Heat about 5 mm/¼ in oil in a frying pan (skillet) until hot, but not smoking, and shallow-fry the croquettes for 3–4 minutes over a moderate heat, turning them occasionally, until golden brown all over. Drain on kitchen paper (paper towels) and serve hot.

Duchesse Potatoes

Do not use a food processor for these or the potato will go gluey and will not hold its shape.

SERVES 4

450 g/1 lb potatoes, peeled and cut into even-sized chunks

50 g/2 oz/¼ cup butter or margarine

1 large egg yolk

Salt and freshly ground black pepper

1 Place the potatoes in a saucepan with enough cold water to cover. Add a good pinch of salt.

2 Cover with a lid and cook over a high heat until the water boils, then turn down the heat a little and continue to cook for 10–15 minutes until the potatoes are really tender. Drain in a colander, then tip the potatoes into a sieve (strainer) over a bowl. Press them through with a wooden spoon. Briskly stir in the butter or margarine, then the egg yolk.

3 Preheat the oven to 180°C/350°F/gas mark 4.

4 For a professional look, put the potato mixture in a piping (pastry) bag, fitted with a large star tube (tip). Pipe into whirls on a greased baking (cookie) sheet. Alternatively – and more simply – pile spoonfuls of the mixture on the sheet and decorate with the prongs of a fork.

5 Bake in the oven for about 20 minutes until golden.

Scalloped Potatoes

SERVES 4

450 g/1 lb potatoes, thinly sliced
50 g/2 oz/¼ cup butter or margarine,
   plus extra for greasing
Salt and freshly ground black pepper
300 ml/½ pt/1¼ cups milk

1 Preheat the oven to 190°C/375°F/
gas mark 5.
2 Grease an ovenproof dish with butter
or margarine, and layer the potatoes
with a little salt and pepper, adding
flakes of butter or margarine between
each layer.
3 Pour the milk over. Cover with foil
and bake in the oven for 1½ hours until
really tender.

Super Creamed Potatoes

SERVES 4

1 kg/2¼ lb potatoes, peeled and cut
   into even-sized chunks
25 g/1 oz/2 tbsp butter or margarine
30 ml/2 tbsp single (light) cream
Freshly ground black pepper

1 Put the potatoes in a saucepan and
cover with cold water. Add a good
pinch of salt.
2 Cover and bring to the boil over a
high heat. Cook for 10–15 minutes until
really tender. Drain in a colander and
return to the pan over a moderate
heat. Shake the pan for 1 minute to dry
out the potatoes.
3 Mash the potatoes well with a
potato masher or fork, then briskly stir
in the butter or margarine and the
cream, until soft and fluffy. Season to
taste.

Mashed Potatoes

SERVES 4

Prepare as for Super Creamed
Potatoes, but use milk instead of
cream and omit the pepper.

Cheese Potatoes

SERVES 4

Prepare as for Super Creamed
Potatoes, but add 75 g/3 oz/¾ cup
Cheddar cheese, grated, with the
butter or margarine and continue as
before.

Potato and Celeriac Mash

SERVES 4

Prepare as for Super Creamed
Potatoes but use only 700 g/1½ lb
potatoes and add a small celeriac,
peeled and cut into smallish chunks,
with the potatoes.

Potato and Leek Mash

SERVES 4

Prepare as for Super Creamed
Potatoes but use only 700 g/1½ lb
potatoes and add 2 leeks, well-washed
and cut into chunks, with the potatoes.

Potato and Parsnip Mash

SERVES 4

Prepare as for Super Creamed
Potatoes but use only 700 g/1½ lb
potatoes and add two parsnips, peeled
and cut into chunks, with the potatoes.
Add a good pinch of grated nutmeg
with the seasoning at the end.

Puréed Potatoes

These are particularly good with plain grilled (broiled) or fried (sautéed) meat or poultry.

SERVES 4

700 g/1½ lb potatoes, peeled and cut
into neat pieces
A large knob of butter
Freshly ground black pepper

1 Put the potatoes in a saucepan and cover with cold water. Add a good pinch of salt.

2 Cover with a lid and bring to the boil over a high heat, continue to boil, for about 10–15 minutes until really tender. Drain thoroughly in a colander.

3 Tip the potatoes into a blender or food processor and add the butter. Run the machine until the mixture is smooth. Serve straight away.

Bombay Puréed Potatoes

SERVES 4

Prepare as for Puréed Potatoes, but add 5 ml/1 tsp garam masala with the butter or margarine. Top the potato with a crumbled, grilled (broiled) piece of Bombay duck (it's not a duck – it's a sort of dried fish!). Serve with any curry, as a change from rice.

Dauphine Potatoes

SERVES 4

700 g/1½ lb potatoes, thinly sliced
A knob of butter or margarine
225 g/8 oz/2 cups Gruyère or
Emmental (Swiss) cheese, grated
Salt and freshly ground black pepper
2 eggs
150 ml/¼ pt/⅔ cup single (light) cream
150 ml/¼ pt/⅔ cup milk
1 garlic clove, crushed
A sprig of parsley, to garnish

1 Put the sliced potatoes in a saucepan of cold water. Cook over a high heat until the water boils, then cook for 2 minutes. Tip into a colander in the sink to drain, then rinse with cold water to cool them quickly.

2 Preheat the oven to 180°C/350°F/ gas mark 4. Use the butter or margarine to grease a 1.2 litre/2 pt/ 5 cup ovenproof serving dish.

3 Put a layer of potato slices in the base. Cover with a little of the cheese and a little salt and pepper. Repeat the layers until all the potatoes and cheese are used, finishing with a layer of cheese.

4 Whisk the eggs, cream and milk together with the garlic in a small bowl with a wire whisk and pour over the potatoes.

5 Bake in the oven for about 1–1¼ hours until the potatoes are tender and the top is golden brown. Serve hot.

Golden Seeded Potatoes

You can cook these for a slightly shorter time in a hotter oven if that suits the other dishes you are cooking.

SERVES 4

700 g/1½ lb potatoes, scrubbed and halved or quartered

50 g/2 oz/¼ cup butter or margarine

30 ml/2 tbsp black mustard, sesame or caraway seeds

1 Preheat the oven to 180°C/350°F/ gas mark 4.

2 Put the potatoes in a saucepan and cover with cold water. Cover and bring to the boil over a high heat. Turn down the heat and cook, still bubbling, for 3 minutes. Drain in a colander.

3 Tip the potatoes in a roasting tin (pan). Add the butter or margarine and stir and turn them gently to coat completely.

4 Sprinkle with the seeds. Roast towards the top of the oven, turning once during cooking, for 1½ hours or until golden brown and tender.

Oven-sautéed Potatoes with Garlic

SERVES 4

700 g/1½ lb potatoes, scrubbed and diced

45 ml/3 tbsp olive oil

40 g/1½ oz/3 tbsp butter or margarine

1–2 garlic cloves, finely chopped

Salt

1 Preheat the oven to 200°C/400°F/ gas mark 6. Put the diced potatoes in a bowl of cold water until ready to cook. Drain and dry on kitchen paper (paper towels).

2 Heat the oil and butter or margarine in a baking tin (pan) over a moderate heat. Add the potatoes and stir and turn to coat completely.

3 Add the garlic and a little salt and toss again.

4 Cook on a shelf near the top of the oven for about 45 minutes, turning two or three times, until golden brown and cooked through. Drain on kitchen paper and serve hot.

Potato Pudding

SERVES 4

A little butter or margarine, for greasing

4 large potatoes, peeled and grated

1 egg, beaten

Salt and freshly ground black pepper

30 ml/2 tbsp snipped fresh chives

1 Preheat the oven to 190°C/375°F/ gas mark 5.

2 Grease a 1.2 litre/2 pt/5 cup ovenproof dish.

3 Mix all the ingredients together and spoon into the dish.

4 Bake in the oven for about 1 hour until the potatoes are cooked and the top is golden brown.

Pan Haggerty

If you have a mandolin slicer or a food processor with a slicing attachment, it's ideal for cutting wafer-thin slices of potato. If not, use a sharp knife.

SERVES 4

60 ml/4 tbsp sunflower oil
1 kg/2¼ lb potatoes, very thinly sliced
2 large onions, very thinly sliced
150 g/5 oz/1¼ cups Cheddar cheese, grated
Salt and freshly ground black pepper

1 Heat the oil in a heavy-based frying pan (skillet).

2 Layer the potatoes, onions and cheese in the pan, seasoning each layer of potatoes with salt and pepper and finishing with a layer of cheese.

3 Cover the pan with a lid or foil and cook over a low heat for about 35 minutes until golden and the potatoes are tender. Preheat the grill (broiler).

4 Put the pan under the grill and continue to cook for about 5 minutes until golden brown on top. Serve cut into wedges, straight from the pan.

Clapshot

This is also good made with turnips instead of swede (rutabaga).

SERVES 4

450 g/1 lb potatoes, diced
1 small swede, diced
50 g/2 oz/¼ cup butter or margarine
Salt and freshly ground black pepper
15 ml/1 tbsp chopped fresh parsley

1 Put the potatoes and swede in a pan and cover with water. Add a good pinch of salt.

2 Heat rapidly until the water boils, then turn down to moderate and cook for about 15 minutes until really tender.

3 Drain the vegetables in a colander and return to the pan. Mash well with a potato masher, then, still using the masher, beat in the butter or margarine and salt and pepper to taste.

4 Serve sprinkled with the parsley.

Spicy Caramelised Onions

SERVES 4

450 g/1 lb onions
50 g/2 oz/¼ cup butter or margarine
45 ml/3 tbsp boiling water
30 ml/2 tbsp balsamic vinegar
30 ml/2 tbsp red wine vinegar
45 ml/3 tbsp light brown sugar
1.5 ml/¼ tsp chilli powder
Salt and freshly ground black pepper

1 Preheat the oven to 190°C/375°F/ gas mark 5.

2 Peel and slice the onions and put them in an even layer a casserole dish (Dutch oven).

3 Cut the butter or margarine into small pieces and place in a bowl. Add the boiling water and stir to melt.

4 Stir in the remaining ingredients, adding salt and pepper to taste. Pour over the onions.

5 Cover with the lid and cook in the oven for 50 minutes. Remove the lid, stir well and cook for a further 5–10 minutes to evaporate any liquid.

Curried Cabbage

SERVES 4

1 small cabbage
1 vegetable or chicken stock cube
50 g/2 oz/¼ cup butter or margarine
10 ml/2 tsp mango chutney, chopped if
    lumpy
5 ml/1 tsp curry paste
15 ml/1 tbsp lemon juice
Salt and freshly ground black pepper
45 ml/3 tbsp desiccated (shredded)
    coconut

1 Prepare the cabbage and cut into shreds.
2 Cook the cabbage in 2.5 cm/1 in boiling water to which the stock cube has been added in a large flameproof casserole dish (Dutch oven) for 3–5 minutes until just tender. Drain in a colander over a bowl (use the stock for soup or gravy) and return the cabbage to the pan.
3 Add all the remaining ingredients except the coconut and stir over a low heat until well blended.
4 Put the coconut in a non-stick frying pan (skillet) and heat, stirring all the time, until the coconut turns a golden brown. Sprinkle over the cooked cabbage and serve.

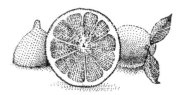

Sweet and Sour Red Cabbage

This is really good left to get cold,
then reheated the next day. It can
also be cooked in a saucepan over a
fairly low heat, stirring occasionally.
You can use the same method for
white cabbage for a change.

SERVES 6

450 g/1 lb red cabbage, shredded,
    discarding the thick stump
1 onion, thinly sliced
1 cooking (tart) apple, peeled and
    chopped
50 g/2 oz/⅓ cup raisins
30 ml/2 tbsp red or white wine vinegar
30 ml/2 tbsp water
30 ml/2 tbsp light brown sugar
Salt and freshly ground black pepper
25 g/1 oz/2 tbsp butter or margarine
30 ml/2 tbsp snipped fresh chives, to
    garnish

1 Preheat the oven to 160°C/325°F/ gas mark 3.
2 Layer the cabbage, onion, apple and raisins in a casserole dish (Dutch oven).
3 Mix all the remaining ingredients except the butter or margarine together and pour over. Cut the butter or margarine into small flakes and scatter over the surface.
4 Cover and cook in the oven for 1¼ hours until tender. Stir well, then sprinkle with snipped chives before serving.

French-style Peas

SERVES 4

1 onion, finely chopped
50 g/2 oz/¼ cup butter or margarine
225 g/8 oz/2 cups frozen peas
5 ml/1 tsp dried mint
Salt and freshly ground black pepper
½ small round lettuce, shredded

1 Put the onion and butter or margarine in a saucepan. Cover and cook over a moderate heat for 3 minutes, stirring once or twice.
2 Add the remaining ingredients, stir gently, cover and cook for about 8 minutes until tender, stirring gently from time to time. Serve hot.

Dutch Roast Onions

These are particularly good with roast chicken or pork, and can also be served on their own with crusty bread for a light meal.

SERVES 4

4 Spanish onions, unpeeled
Salt and freshly ground black pepper
50 g/2 oz/¼ cup butter or margarine
10 ml/2 tsp chopped fresh sage
75 g/3 oz/¾ cup Gouda cheese, grated

1 Preheat the oven to 180°C/350°F/ gas mark 4.
2 Cut the root end off each unpeeled onion. Cut a slice off each top, sprinkle the onions with salt and pepper, then put the tops back in position. Line a small roasting tin (pan) with foil and spread with a little of the butter or margarine. Stand the onions in the tin.

3 Roast in the oven for 2 hours until the onions feel tender when a knife is inserted in them.
4 Discard the 'lids' and, using a knife and fork, carefully peel off the skins. Top with the butter, sage and cheese. Return to the oven for 5 minutes or until the cheese melts.
5 Transfer to warm plates and spoon the juices over.

Crisp Onion Rings

SERVES 4

50 g/2 oz/½ cup plain (all-purpose) flour
Salt and freshly ground black pepper
2 large onions, thinly sliced and separated into rings
Oil, for deep-frying

1 Season the flour with salt and pepper. Add the onions and turn the rings until well coated.
2 Heat the oil in a saucepan or deep-fat fryer to 190°C/375°F or until a cube of day-old bread browns in 30 seconds. Add about a quarter of the onion rings and deep-fry for about 4 minutes until crisp and golden. Drain on kitchen paper (paper towels) and keep warm.
3 Reheat the oil and continue until all the onion rings are cooked. Serve hot with fried (sautéed) and grilled (broiled) meat or poultry dishes.

Parsnip Cream

SERVES 4

450 g/1 lb parsnips
A knob of butter or margarine
Salt and freshly ground black pepper
A good pinch of grated nutmeg
300 ml/½ pt/1¼ cups single (light)
    cream

1 Preheat the oven to 190°C/375°F/ gas mark 5.
2 Peel and thinly slice the parsnips.
3 Grease a shallow ovenproof dish with the butter or margarine.
4 Layer the parsnips in the dish, sprinkling each layer with salt, pepper and nutmeg.
5 Pour over the cream. Cover the dish with foil.
6 Bake in the oven for 1 hour. Remove the foil and cook for a further 15 minutes to brown the top.

Baked Spiced Carrots

SERVES 4

25 g/1 oz/2 tbsp butter or margarine
4 large carrots, thinly sliced
Grated rind and juice of 1 orange
1.5 ml/¼ tsp ground cumin
A good pinch of ground ginger
Salt and freshly ground black pepper
30 ml/2 tbsp water
15 ml/1 tbsp snipped fresh chives

1 Preheat the oven to 190°C/375°F/ gas mark 5.
2 Melt the butter or margarine in a small, flameproof casserole (Dutch oven).
3 Add the remaining ingredients and mix well.

4 Cover with a lid and cook in the oven for about 1 hour until the carrots are tender.
5 Stir well, sprinkle with the chives and serve.

Carrots Vichy

This is a famous way of serving carrots, which retains their full, sweet flavour.

SERVES 4

450 g/1 lb carrots
450 ml/¾ pt/2 cups water
A pinch of salt
5 ml/1 tsp clear honey
15 g/½ oz/1 tbsp butter or margarine
Freshly ground black pepper
30 ml/2 tbsp chopped fresh parsley

1 Peel or scrape the carrots and cut into dice, slices or matchsticks.
2 Place in a flameproof casserole (Dutch oven) with the water, salt, honey and half the butter or margarine.
3 Heat rapidly until the water boils.
4 Turn down the heat, so that the water is gently bubbling round the edges. Cook for 30–40 minutes, stirring occasionally, until the carrots are tender and all the liquid has evaporated.
5 Cut the remaining butter or margarine in small pieces and stir gently into the carrots. Add a good grinding of pepper and sprinkle with the parsley before serving.

Broad Beans with Oyster Mushrooms

SERVES 4

100 g/4 oz oyster mushrooms, sliced

225 g/8 oz shelled fresh or frozen broad (fava) beans

15 g/½ oz/1 tbsp butter or margarine

15 ml/1 tbsp chopped fresh parsley

1 bouquet garni sachet

5 ml/1 tsp lemon juice

Salt and freshly ground black pepper

150 ml/¼ pt/⅔ cup vegetable or chicken stock, made with ½ stock cube

15 ml/1 tbsp cornflour (cornstarch)

15 ml/1 tbsp water

30 ml/2 tbsp double (heavy) cream (optional)

1 Preheat the oven to 180°C/350°F/ gas mark 4.

2 Put the mushrooms and broad beans in a flameproof casserole (Dutch oven).

3 Cut the butter or margarine into small pieces and scatter over, then add the parsley, bouquet garni and lemon juice and season lightly.

4 Pour on the stock and bring to the boil. Cover and cook in the oven for 45 minutes to 1 hour or until tender. Discard the bouquet garni sachet.

5 Mix the cornflour with the water in a cup and stir in. Bring to the boil over a high heat and cook for 1 minute, stirring.

6 Stir in the cream, if using. Taste and re-season if necessary before serving.

Pan-roasted Vine Tomatoes

Vine tomatoes, which are sold still attached to their stalk, have a particularly good flavour.

SERVES 4

16 small tomatoes on the vine

30 ml/2 tbsp olive oil

15 ml/1 tbsp balsamic vinegar

Freshly ground black pepper

5 ml/1 tsp rock salt

1 Snip the tomato vine into four pieces with four tomatoes on each.

2 Heat the oil in a large frying pan (skillet). Add the tomatoes and cook over a moderate heat for 2 minutes. Turn over and cook for a further 2 minutes until just cooked but still holding their shape.

3 Pour over the balsamic vinegar and a good grinding of pepper and cook for 1 minute more.

4 Transfer to warm plates, spoon any juices over and sprinkle with the salt.

Baked Tomatoes with Basil

SERVES 4

8 firm tomatoes
25 g/1 oz/2 tbsp butter or margarine
15 ml/1 tbsp chopped fresh basil
Salt and freshly ground black pepper
A good pinch of caster (superfine)
    sugar

1 Preheat the oven to 190°C/375°F/gas mark 5.
2 Put the tomatoes in an ovenproof dish just large enough to hold them comfortably in a single layer.
3 Cut the butter or margarine into small flakes and scatter over the tomatoes.
4 Sprinkle with the basil, salt and pepper and the sugar. Cover with a lid or foil and bake in the oven for 20 minutes until the tomatoes are tender but still hold their shape.

Fried Bananas

You can cook plantains in the same way, but they need cooking for slightly longer as they are much firmer.

SERVES 4

4 small bananas
40 g/1½ oz/3 tbsp butter or margarine
15 ml/1 tbsp sunflower oil

1 Peel and halve the bananas lengthways.
2 Melt the butter or margarine in a frying pan (skillet) with the oil over a fairly high heat and fry (sauté) the banana halves for about 2 minutes on each side until golden but still holding their shape.

3 Drain on kitchen paper (paper towels) and serve hot with fried or grilled (broiled) chicken or turkey dishes.

Ratatouille

SERVES 4

1 aubergine (eggplant), sliced
1 red onion, sliced
1 green (bell) pepper, sliced
1 red pepper, sliced
1 yellow pepper, sliced
1 large courgette (zucchini), sliced
4 ripe tomatoes, quartered
30 ml/2 tbsp olive oil
15 ml/1 tbsp tomato purée (paste)
30 ml/2 tbsp red wine or water
2.5 ml/½ tsp dried mixed herbs
A pinch of caster (superfine) sugar
Salt and freshly ground black pepper

1 Place the aubergine in a colander and sprinkle with salt. Leave to stand for 30 minutes. Rinse thoroughly and drain.
2 Place in a large saucepan with the remaining sliced vegetables and the oil.
3 Cook over a moderate heat, stirring, until the vegetables are beginning to soften slightly.
4 Add the tomato purée, wine or water, herbs, sugar and a little salt and pepper. Bring to the boil, cover, turn the heat down and cook gently for 20 minutes until tender, stirring occasionally. Serve hot or leave until cold, then chill before serving.

Bubble and Squeak

SERVES 4

450 g/1 lb cooked potatoes, mashed
 with a fork
225 g/8 oz cooked cabbage, chopped
Salt and freshly ground black pepper
25 g/1 oz/2 tbsp butter or margarine
30 ml/2 tbsp sunflower oil

1 Mix the potatoes and cabbage
together and season well.

2 Heat half the butter or margarine
and the oil in a large non-stick frying
pan (skillet). Add the potato mixture
and press down well. Fry (sauté) for
about 10 minutes until richly brown
and crisp underneath.

3 Carefully slide out of the pan on to a
plate, then invert into the pan, so the
brown side is up, and continue to fry
for about 5–10 minutes until the other
side is well browned. Serve cut into
wedges.

Colcannon

*This is an Irish version of Bubble and
Squeak, which is traditionally cooked
in beef or pork dripping. If you
haven't any, use butter or margarine
instead.*

SERVES 4

50 g/2 oz/¼ cup dripping
1 onion, finely chopped
6 rashers (slices) of streaky bacon,
 rinded and diced
450 g/1 lb cooked potatoes, mashed
 with a fork
225 g/8 oz cooked cabbage, chopped
Salt and freshly ground black pepper
A little flour, for dusting

1 Heat half the dripping in a heavy-
based frying pan (skillet). Add the
onion and bacon and cook for about
3 minutes over a fairly high heat,
stirring, until softened and lightly
golden.

2 Remove from the pan with a
draining spoon and place in a bowl
with the potatoes and cabbage.
Season well and mix together with a
wooden spoon.

3 With floured hands, shape the
mixture into four cakes and flatten to
about 1 cm/½ in thick.

4 Heat the remaining dripping in the
same frying pan. Add the cakes and
fry (sauté) for 3–4 minutes on each side
over a fairly high heat until golden
brown. Serve hot.

Corn Fritters

These are the perfect accompaniment to fried (sautéed) chicken but are also delicious served with Aioli (see page 341) as a starter.

SERVES 4–6

100 g/4 oz/1 cup plain (all-purpose) flour
1 small onion, grated
1 egg
150 ml/¼ pt/⅔ cup milk
320 g/12 oz/1 medium can of sweetcorn (corn), drained
Salt and freshly ground black pepper
45 ml/3 tbsp sunflower oil

1 Mix the flour and the onion together in a bowl.
2 Make a well in the centre and add the egg. Gradually stir in the milk to form a thick batter, using a wire whisk or wooden spoon, and once blended, stir briskly until smooth.
3 Stir in the sweetcorn and some salt and pepper.
4 Heat the oil in a frying pan (skillet). Add spoonfuls of the corn mixture and fry over a fairly high heat for about 2 minutes on each side until golden brown. Drain on kitchen paper (paper towels) and keep each batch warm while cooking the remainder. Serve hot.

Mixed Salad

Use whatever salad stuffs you like to get a variety of colours and textures.

SERVES 4

1 small round lettuce
¼ cucumber
2 tomatoes
1 small onion
1 (bell) pepper, any colour
30–45 ml/2–3 tbsp French dressing (see page 337)

1 Prepare the lettuce and other leaves. Cut off any root and separate into leaves. Wash, pat dry on kitchen paper (paper towels), then tear into pieces.
2 Cut the cucumber into slices.
3 Halve the tomatoes, then cut into wedges.
4 Prepare the onion and cut into rings.
5 Prepare the pepper and cut into rings.
6 Put all the ingredients in a salad bowl. Add the French Dressing, then gently turn the vegetables over in the dressing until it is all glistening, using salad servers or a large spoon and fork. Don't be rough or you'll bruise everything.

Green Salad

SERVES 4

Prepare as for mixed salad (above) but use all green salad stuffs. There are lots of different kinds of lettuce, and you can include cucumber, green (bell) pepper, baby spinach leaves, salad cress, rocket, watercress and spring onions (scallions). You could even add some drained, canned artichoke hearts.

Tomato and Onion Salad

SERVES 4

4–6 tomatoes, sliced
1 small onion, finely chopped
30 ml/2 tbsp olive oil
10 ml/2 tsp balsamic vinegar
Salt and freshly ground black pepper

1 Put the tomatoes in a shallow dish and scatter the onion over the surface.
2 Whisk together the oil, vinegar a pinch of salt and a good grinding of pepper in a bowl with a wire whisk. Pour over the salad and leave to stand for 30 minutes before serving, if possible, to allow the flavours to develop.

Tomato and Cucumber Salad

SERVES 4

4 tomatoes, sliced
¼ cucumber, thinly sliced
5 ml/1 tsp dried dill (dill weed)
30 ml/2 tbsp olive oil
10 ml/2 tsp white wine vinegar
Freshly ground black pepper
5 ml/1 tsp clear honey

1 Arrange the tomatoes and cucumber slices attractively in a shallow dish.
2 Whisk the remaining ingredients together in a small bowl with a wire whisk and trickle over the salad. Chill until ready to serve.

Hot Potato Salad

Season with pepper only, as the anchovies are very salty.

SERVES 6–8

1 kg/2¼ lb potatoes, scrubbed and halved if large
50 g/2 oz/1 small can of anchovies, drained
250 ml/8 fl oz/1 cup crème fraîche
5 ml/1 tsp lemon juice
A pinch of caster (superfine) sugar
Freshly ground black pepper
Paprika, to garnish

1 Put the potatoes in a saucepan with enough cold water to cover. Add a good pinch of salt.
2 Cover and bring to the boil over a high heat. Turn down the heat to moderate so that they continue to bubble and cook for 10–15 minutes until really tender. Drain in a colander. When cool enough to handle, peel off the skins.
3 Cut into chunks and return to the pan. Reserve four anchovies for decoration. Finely chop the remainder. Mix with the crème fraîche, lemon juice, sugar and a little pepper. Add to the potatoes and lift and stir lightly over a low heat.
4 Spoon into a warm serving dish. Cut the reserved anchovies into halves, lengthways. Arrange attractively on top, sprinkle with paprika and serve hot.

Warm Potato Salad with Fragrant Herbs

SERVES 4

450 g/1 lb waxy baby potatoes, scrubbed
75 ml/5 tbsp plain yoghurt
75 ml/5 tbsp mayonnaise
2.5 ml/½ tsp finely grated lemon rind
15 ml/1 tbsp chopped fresh parsley
15 ml/1 tbsp chopped fresh basil
15 ml/1 tbsp snipped fresh chives
Salt and freshly ground black pepper

1 Cook the potatoes, drain in a colander and leave to cool.
2 Mix the remaining ingredients together in a salad bowl. Add the potatoes and lift and stir gently until coated in the dressing. Serve warm.

Village Salad

SERVES 4

¼ small white cabbage, shredded
¼ iceberg lettuce, shredded
2 beefsteak tomatoes, quartered and sliced
10 cm/4 in piece of cucumber, diced
12 black olives
1 small onion, sliced and separated into rings
100 g/4 oz Feta cheese, cut into small pieces
2.5 ml/½ tsp dried oregano
15 ml/1 tbsp chopped fresh parsley or coriander (cilantro)
Salt and freshly ground black pepper
45 ml/3 tbsp olive oil
15 ml/1 tbsp red wine vinegar

1 Put the cabbage and lettuce on a shallow serving platter.
2 Scatter the tomatoes, cucumber, olives, onion and cheese over.
3 Sprinkle with the oregano, parsley and some salt and pepper.
4 Trickle the oil and vinegar all over the surface and leave to stand for 30 minutes before serving.

Beansprout Salad

SERVES 4

225 g/8 oz/1 small can of pineapple rings, drained, reserving the juice
1 green (bell) pepper, diced
1 red pepper, diced
2 spring onions (scallions), chopped
175 g/6 oz/3 cups beansprouts
15 ml/1 tbsp soy sauce
15 ml/1 tbsp sunflower oil
A pinch of Chinese five spice powder

1 Cut the pineapple into small pieces and mix with the peppers, spring onions and beansprouts in a salad bowl.
2 Put all the remaining ingredients in a small bowl and add 15 ml/1 tbsp of the pineapple juice. Whisk with a wire whisk until well blended.
3 Pour over the salad, lift and stir gently until coated in the dressing and serve.

English Coleslaw

SERVES 4

½ small white cabbage

2 carrots

½ small onion

45 ml/3 tbsp mayonnaise

15 ml/1 tbsp olive oil

15 ml/1 tbsp white wine vinegar

A pinch each of caster (superfine)
   sugar, salt and pepper

1 Cut out the thick core from the cabbage and discard any damaged outer leaves. Peel the carrots and onion, discarding the ends.

2 Coarsely grate all the vegetables into a salad bowl.

3 Mix the remaining ingredients together and add to the bowl. Stir gently until well mixed. Chill, if time allows, before serving.

Middle Eastern Coleslaw

SERVES 4

½ small white cabbage

2 carrots

30 ml/2 tbsp raisins

30 ml/2 tbsp sliced green olives

Salt and freshly ground black pepper

45 ml/3 tbsp olive oil

30 ml/2 tbsp black mustard seeds

15 ml/1 tbsp lemon juice

1 Cut out the thick core from the cabbage and discard any damaged outer leaves.

2 Coarsely grate the cabbage into a salad bowl. Peel the carrots and coarsely grate into the bowl, discarding the ends.

3 Add the raisins and olives. Season lightly.

4 Heat the oil in a frying pan (skillet). Add the mustard seeds and fry (sauté) over a high heat until they start to 'pop'.

5 Add the lemon juice, stir, pour over the salad, lift and stir until well mixed and serve.

Italian Coleslaw

Use a food processor, if you have one, to shred the vegetables.

SERVES 4

½ small white cabbage,

½ small celeriac (celery root)

1 small garlic clove, crushed

60 ml/4 tbsp olive oil

20 ml/1½ tbsp white wine vinegar

A good pinch of dried oregano

1.5 ml/¼ tsp celery salt

Salt and freshly ground black pepper

1 Cut out the thick core from the cabbage and discard any damaged outer leaves. Thickly peel the celeriac to remove any knobbly bits.

2 Finely shred the vegetables and place in a salad bowl.

3 Put the remaining ingredients in a small bowl and whisk together with a wire whisk. Pour over the salad and lift and stir to combine. Leave to stand for at least 30 minutes before serving, if possible.

Tabbouleh

SERVES 4

225 g/8 oz/2 cups bulghar (cracked
wheat)

600 ml/1 pt/2½ cups boiling water

4 spring onions (scallions), chopped

1 garlic clove, crushed

60 ml/4 tbsp chopped fresh parsley

30 ml/2 tbsp chopped fresh mint

30 ml/2 tbsp lemon juice

60 ml/4 tbsp olive oil

Salt and freshly ground black pepper

¼ cucumber, finely chopped

4 ripe tomatoes, cut into small pieces

1 Put the bulghar in a large bowl.
Cover with the boiling water and leave
to stand for 30 minutes. Stir with a fork
to fluff up.

2 Add the spring onions, garlic, herbs,
lemon juice and olive oil. Lift and stir
until thoroughly mixed and leave until
cold.

3 Stir in the cucumber and tomatoes
and serve.

Tomato, Sweetcorn and Onion Salad

SERVES 4

6 tomatoes, cut into small wedges

200 g/7 oz/1 small can of sweetcorn
(corn), drained

4 spring onions (scallions), cut into
short lengths

15 ml/1 tbsp apple juice

10 ml/2 tsp lemon juice

45 ml/3 tbsp olive oil

Salt and freshly ground black pepper

Lettuce leaves

1 Mix the tomatoes, sweetcorn and
spring onions together.

2 Whisk the apple juice, lemon juice
and oil together with a little salt and
pepper in a small bowl with a wire
whisk.

3 Pour over the salad and lift and stir
until well blended.

4 Line four individual salad bowls with
lettuce leaves and add the salad.

Celeriac and Carrot Salad

SERVES 4

1 small celeriac (celery root)

2 large carrots

30 ml/2 tbsp olive oil

15 ml/1 tbsp white wine vinegar

5 ml/1 tsp caster (superfine) sugar

1.5 ml/¼ tsp salt

Freshly ground black pepper

30 ml/2 tbsp snipped fresh chives

1 Thickly peel the celeriac to remove all
the knobbly bits. Cut into quarters,
then coarsely grate.

2 Peel and coarsely grate the carrots.

3 Mix the vegetables together in a
salad bowl.

4 Add the oil, vinegar, sugar, salt and a
good grinding of pepper. Turn the
mixture over, using a spoon and fork
until well coated in the dressing. Add
the chives and mix gently again. Leave
to stand for at least 30 minutes to
allow the flavours to develop.

Mixed Bean Salad

SERVES 4

425 g/15 oz/1 large can of mixed pulses
1 onion, chopped
200 g/7 oz/1 small can of pimiento caps, drained and sliced
4 gherkins (cornichons), chopped
30 ml/2 tbsp olive oil
15 ml/1 tbsp red wine vinegar
A pinch of caster (superfine) sugar
Salt and freshly ground black pepper
5 ml/1 tsp dried chives

1 Drain the can of pulses, rinse and drain again. Mix with the onion, pimientos and gherkins in a salad bowl.

2 Whisk the remaining ingredients together in a small bowl with a wire whisk and pour over the salad. Lift and stir gently until well blended, then chill for at least 1 hour to develop the flavours.

Fasoulia

This cold bean dish is delicious as a side dish or on its own with French bread for a light lunch. It's worth using extra virgin olive oil if you have it, for its wonderful, mellow flavour.

SERVES 4

150 ml/¼ pt/⅔ cup olive oil
1 large onion, finely chopped
1 large garlic clove, crushed
1 bay leaf
2.5 ml/½ tsp dried oregano
1 large tomato, chopped
15 ml/1 tbsp tomato purée (paste)
Juice of ½ large lemon
2 x 425 g/15 oz/large cans of haricot (navy) beans, drained
Salt and freshly ground black pepper
15 ml/1 tbsp chopped fresh parsley

1 Heat the oil in a saucepan. Add the onion and cook for 2–3 minutes over a moderate heat until softened but not browned.

2 Add the remaining ingredients, stir well and cook over a moderate heat for 10 minutes, stirring gently.

3 Leave to cool, then remove the bay leaf. Taste and re-season if necessary. Spoon into bowls, sprinkle with chopped parsley and serve cold.

Curried Rice Salad

SERVES 4

225 g/8 oz/1 cup long-grain rice
50 g/2 oz/½ cup frozen peas
30 ml/2 tbsp flaked (slivered) almonds
10 ml/2 tsp mild curry paste
30 ml/2 tbsp mayonnaise
30 ml/2 tbsp currants
Salt and freshly ground black pepper
15 ml/1 tbsp chopped fresh coriander (cilantro)

1 Cook the rice according to the packet directions (or see page 294), adding the peas after 5 minutes' cooking time. Drain in a colander, rinse with cold water and drain again.

2 Meanwhile, put the almonds in a frying pan (skillet) and cook, stirring, over a fairly high heat until they begin to brown. Tip them out of the pan immediately so they don't burn.

3 Mix the curry paste with the mayonnaise. Stir in the rice, currants and nuts.

4 Season to taste with salt and pepper and serve sprinkled with the coriander.

Russian Salad

For speed you can use canned mixed vegetables – drain them very well first – but the flavour isn't quite as good.

SERVES 4

350 g/12 oz frozen diced mixed
  vegetables
45 ml/3 tbsp mayonnaise
15 ml/1 tbsp olive oil
15 ml/1 tbsp cider vinegar
30 ml/2 tbsp caraway seeds

1 Bring a saucepan of water to the boil and add a good pinch of salt. Cook the vegetables for 5–6 minutes until they are just tender but still have some 'bite'.
2 Drain in a colander, rinse with cold water and drain again.
3 Meanwhile, mix the mayonnaise with the oil and vinegar in a salad bowl. Add half the caraway seeds. Stir in the vegetables until well coated.
4 Sprinkle the salad with the remaining caraway seeds and chill until ready to serve.

Caribbean Rice and Peas

The 'peas' are actually beans in this recipe!

SERVES 4

300 ml/½ pt/1¼ cups canned coconut
  milk
300 ml/½ pt/1¼ cups water
225 g/8 oz/1 cup long-grain rice
425 g/15 oz/1 large can of red kidney
  beans, drained
Salt and freshly ground black pepper
5 ml/1 tsp paprika
A few drops of Tabasco sauce
1 spring onion (scallion), chopped

1 Put the coconut milk and water in a saucepan over a high heat.
2 When boiling, add the rice, beans, some salt and pepper and the paprika and stir well.
3 Bring back to the boil once more, turn down the heat as low as possible, cover with a lid and cook for about 20 minutes until the rice is tender and has absorbed all the liquid.
4 Stir with a fork, add Tabasco sauce to taste, sprinkle with the spring onion and serve.

Quick Pilau Rice

SERVES 4

175 g/6 oz/¾ cup basmati rice
5 ml/1 tsp ground turmeric
4–6 split cardamom pods
2.5 cm/1 in piece of cinnamon stick
15 ml/1 tbsp sunflower oil
1 onion, finely chopped
Salt and freshly ground black pepper

1 Cook the rice according to the packet directions (or see page 294), adding the spices to the water. Drain in a colander.
2 Meanwhile, heat the oil in a frying pan (skillet) and fry (sauté) the onion over a high heat for 3–4 minutes until golden brown and soft.
3 Use a fork to mix the onion into the rice, then season to taste. Remove the spices if you wish before serving.

Egg Fried Rice

SERVES 4

175 g/6 oz/¾ cup long-grain rice
50 g/2 oz/½ cup frozen peas
30 ml/2 tbsp sunflower oil
1–2 eggs, beaten
A pinch of Chinese five spice powder
5 ml/1 tsp soy sauce
Salt and freshly ground black pepper

1 Cook the rice according to the packet directions (or see page 294). Add the peas halfway through cooking. Drain in a colander, rinse with cold water and drain again thoroughly.
2 Heat the oil in a frying pan (skillet).
3 Add the rice and peas and cook over a fairly high heat, stirring and turning, for 2 minutes.
4 Push the mixture to one side and tilt the pan. Pour in the beaten egg.
5 Cook the egg, stirring, then gradually draw in the rice until it is filled with tiny strands of egg. Add a pinch of Chinese five spice powder and a sprinkling of soy sauce. Taste and adjust the seasoning if necessary, remembering that the soy sauce is very salty. Toss and serve.

Oven Pilaf

This is particularly good with roast pork or lamb.

SERVES 4–6

100 g/4 oz/⅔ cup dried fruit salad, soaked overnight in cold water
25 g/1 oz/2 tbsp butter or margarine
1 onion, finely chopped
225 g/8 oz/1 cup long-grain rice, well-washed and drained
600 ml/1 pt/2½ cups chicken stock, made with 1 stock cube
Salt and freshly ground black pepper

1 Put the fruit and its soaking water in saucepan, bring to the boil over a high heat, then turn down the heat until just bubbling round the edges and cook gently for 10 minutes or until tender. Leave to cool. Drain, then roughly chop the fruit, discarding any stones (pits).
2 Preheat the oven to 200°C/400°F/ gas mark 6.
3 Melt the butter or margarine in a flameproof casserole (Dutch oven) over a fairly high heat and fry (sauté) the onion for 2 minutes.
4 Stir in the rice until coated in the butter. Pour in the stock and add a little seasoning. Bring to the boil, cover with the lid and transfer to a low shelf in the oven. Cook for 10 minutes.
5 Add the chopped fruit and stir in with a fork. Cover with foil and then the lid (to give a tight seal) and return to the lowest shelf in the oven for a further 10 minutes until the rice is cooked and has absorbed all the liquid. Stir with a fork to fluff up and serve.

Crispy Noodle Cake

SERVES 4

250 g/9 oz/1 packet of Chinese egg
noodles
45 ml/3 tbsp sunflower oil

1 Cook the noodles according to the packet directions. Drain and dry thoroughly on kitchen paper (paper towels).

2 Heat 30 ml/2 tbsp of the oil in a frying pan (skillet).

3 Add the noodles and spread out in the pan to an even layer. Fry (sauté) over a high heat until golden brown underneath. Tip out of the pan on to a plate. Add the remaining oil to the pan and heat again.

4 Slide the noodle cake back into the pan, browned side up. Continue to fry until crisp and golden. Serve whole with any Chinese-style dish spooned over, or cut it into wedges and serve as an accompaniment.

Crisp Fried Noodles

If you can't find short ribbon noodles, use tagliatelle and break them into short lengths. If you don't have a wire basket, fish the noodles out of the hot oil with a draining spoon.

SERVES 4

175 g/6 oz short ribbon noodles
Oil, for deep-frying
Coarse sea salt

1 Cook the pasta according to the packet directions (or see page 293). Drain, rinse with cold water and drain again, then dry thoroughly on kitchen paper (paper towels). Make sure the

pasta is completely dry and that the strands are separate.

2 Heat the oil in a large saucepan or deep-fat fryer to 190°C/375°F or until a cube of day-old bread browns in 30 seconds. Deep-fry the noodles in small batches until crisp and golden brown.

3 Drain on kitchen paper, then sprinkle with coarse sea salt.

Note: Other cooked pasta shapes can also be deep-fried. They make a good garnish for oriental dishes and soups and also a tasty nibble to serve with drinks.

Fettuccine with Cream

This is delicious served with plain grilled (broiled) meat or poultry.

SERVES 4–6

450 g/1 lb fresh fettuccine
100 g/4 oz/½ cup unsalted (sweet)
butter
300 ml/½ pt/1¼ cups double (heavy)
cream
Salt and freshly ground black pepper

1 Cook the fettuccine according to the packet directions (or see page 293). It will take only about 4 minutes. Drain in a colander and return to the saucepan.

2 Cut the butter into flakes and add to the pan with the cream. Stir over a gentle heat until well coated. Season the pasta thoroughly with a little salt and lots of black pepper.

Onion Bhajis

If you aren't sure how to seed chillies, see Fiery Mussel Spaghettini, page 134.

SERVES 4

75 g/3 oz/¾ cup gram (besan) or plain (all-purpose) flour

2.5 ml/½ tsp salt

A good pinch of ground turmeric

1 green chilli, seeded and chopped

15 ml/1 tbsp chopped fresh coriander (cilantro)

About 120 ml/4 fl oz/½ cup water

2 onions, chopped

Oil, for deep-frying

1 Mix the flour, salt and turmeric into a bowl. Stir in the chilli and coriander.

2 Using a wire whisk, mix with the water, a little at a time, to form a thick batter (you may need slightly more or less than I have suggested, depending on the flour you use). Leave to stand for 30 minutes.

3 Stir in the onions.

4 Heat the oil in a saucepan or deep-fat fryer to 190°C/375°F or until a cube of day-old bread browns in 30 seconds. Drop spoonfuls of the batter into the pan and cook until golden brown. Drain on kitchen paper (paper towels) and keep each batch warm while cooking the remainder. Serve hot with any curries or as a starter with lime pickle.

Mushroom Bhajis

SERVES 4

Prepare as for Onion Bhajis but omit the onions. When the batter has been standing, stir in 5 ml/1 tsp bicarbonate of soda (baking soda) and 100 g/4 oz button mushrooms. Drop individual coated mushrooms in the hot oil and cook as before.

Potato Bhajis

SERVES 4

Prepare as for Onion Bhajis but omit the onion. Cut a large potato into thin slices, then dry on kitchen paper (paper towels). Dip into the batter and deep-fry individual slices as for the onion balls.

Poppadoms

MAKE AS MANY AS YOU LIKE

You can buy packets of ready-made poppadoms in any supermarket. The best way to cook them is in the microwave. You do not need to add any oil. Place one at a time on a plate. Microwave on Full Power for about 20–30 seconds until beginning to puff up. Turn over and microwave again until puffy all over. Repeat with as many as you like. Alternatively, grill (broil) them, turning once, but take care, they burn very easily (usually the minute you look away!).

Dhal

Serve this with any curry. It's particularly good if you're using up a small amount of leftover meat or chicken in the main curry as lentils are high in protein.

SERVES 4

175 g/6 oz/1 cup red lentils
1 onion, chopped
1 large garlic clove, crushed
15 ml/1 tbsp ground turmeric
15 ml/1 tbsp ground cumin
15 ml/1 tbsp ground coriander (cilantro)
10 ml/2 tsp paprika
600 ml/1 pt/2½ cups vegetable stock, made with 1 stock cube

1 Put all the ingredients in a saucepan and cook over a high heat until boiling, stirring occasionally.
2 Skim off any scum from the surface with a draining spoon, then turn down the heat until gently bubbling round the edges.
3 Cook for 20–30 minutes until pulpy, stirring frequently to prevent the mixture sticking. If becoming too dry after about 15 minutes, add a little more water.

Brinjals

Serve this with any curry or spiced dish for an extra-tasty accompaniment. If you aren't sure how to seed chillies, see Fiery Mussel Spaghettini, page 134.

SERVES 4–6

1 large aubergine (eggplant)
1 onion
1 green chilli, seeded and chopped
A pinch of salt
Caster (superfine) sugar, to taste
Juice of 1 small lemon

1 Cut the stalk off the aubergine. Bring a saucepan of water to the boil, add the aubergine and cook for about 10 minutes or until tender.
2 Drain in a colander, rinse with cold water and drain again. Cut in half and scoop out the softened pulp into a bowl. Discard the skin.
3 Cut a few thin rings off the onion and reserve for garnish, then finely chop the remainder. Stir briskly into the aubergine pulp with the chilli. Season to taste with salt, sugar and lemon juice.
4 Spoon into a small serving dish and arrange the onion rings on top to garnish. Chill until ready to serve.

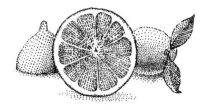

Polenta

Purists will tell you that precooked polenta doesn't give a very good result. I disagree – and it's much quicker. Serve it as a side dish with braised meats, poultry or fish or serve with a tomato sauce (see page 335), sprinkled with grated Parmesan cheese.

SERVES 6

2 litres/3½ pts/8½ cups water
Salt
375 g/13 oz/1 large packet of precooked polenta (cornmeal)

1 Bring the water to the boil with a good pinch of salt added.
2 Once boiling rapidly, gradually pour in the polenta in a thin stream, stirring all the time until the mixture is thick and smooth. Cook for a further 1 minute, then serve.

Polenta Fritta

SERVES 6

1 quantity of Polenta
15 g/½ oz/1 tbsp butter
45 ml/3 tbsp olive oil
Grated Parmesan cheese, to serve

1 Cook the polenta as above, then add the butter and stir briskly with a wooden spoon until blended.
2 Brush a roasting tin (pan) with a little of the oil and spoon in the polenta. Spread out, leave to cool and then chill for at least an hour to set.
3 Cut the polenta into slices.
4 Heat the oil in a frying pan (skillet) and fry (sauté) the pieces over a fairly high heat for about 2 minutes on each side until golden. Serve hot, sprinkled with Parmesan cheese.

Polenta Concia

SERVES 6

1 quantity of Polenta
30 ml/2 tbsp milk
100 g/4 oz Italian cheese (Gorgonzola, Dolcelatte, Fontina, etc.), cut into small pieces
15 g/½ oz/1 tbsp butter or margarine, for greasing
60 ml/4 tbsp grated Parmesan cheese

1 Cook the polenta (see left).
2 Put the milk and cheese in a separate pan and cook over a moderate heat, stirring until melted.
3 Stir thoroughly into the polenta.
4 Preheat the oven to 200°C/400°F/ gas mark 6.
5 Grease a fairly shallow, large ovenproof dish and add the polenta. Spread out.
6 Sprinkle the polenta with the Parmesan and bake in the oven for 15–20 minutes until golden. Serve hot.

Savoury Sauces and Sundries

This chapter contains everything you need to add those finishing touches to your meal. In the first section, you'll find stuffings of all kinds to add flavour and texture to meat, fish and poultry, plus other traditional accompaniments for roast dishes. Later in the chapter, you'll find sauces to complement all kinds of savoury dishes. And finally there are delicious dressings for salads, dips and flavoured butters to accompany plain grills and fries (sautés), and marinades and rubs for grills and barbecues.

Stuffings

Stuffings can be cooked in either of two ways. They can be cooked inside the meat – rolled inside boned joints of meat, or tucked into fish, game or the neck end of poultry. Alternatively, they can be cooked in a separate greased dish, usually placed on the shelf below a roast for the last part of the cooking time. When using any of the following recipes to stuff a turkey, double the quantities of all the ingredients.

A good tip is to keep a packet of stuffing mix in the cupboard. Make up as directed on the packet, then enhance it by adding a freshly chopped onion, a handful of fresh chopped herbs or a handful of chopped nuts and use as required.

If you have a food processor, you can make any of the bread-based stuffings in it. Add the bread in pieces first to make the crumbs, then add the remaining dry ingredients. Once everything is blended, add the egg, water, etc. to bind.

Sage and Onion Stuffing

SERVES 4–6

50 g/2 oz/1 cup fresh white
    breadcrumbs
1 small onion, finely chopped
8 fresh sage leaves, finely chopped
Salt and freshly ground black pepper
15 ml/1 tbsp melted butter or
    margarine
1 egg yolk
15 ml/1 tbsp milk

1 Mix the breadcrumbs with the onion, sage and some salt and pepper.
2 Stir in the melted butter, egg yolk and milk.

Parsley and Thyme Stuffing

If using to stuff a turkey, double the quantities but use one whole egg to bind instead of two egg yolks.

SERVES 4–6

50 g/2 oz/1 cup fresh white
    breadcrumbs
30 ml/2 tbsp chopped fresh parsley
15 ml/1 tbsp chopped fresh thyme
Salt and freshly ground black pepper
1 egg yolk
15 ml/1 tbsp boiling water

Mix all the ingredients together and use as required.

Nutty Rice Stuffing

If you don't have any leftover cooked rice, boil 25 g/1 oz/2 tbsp long-grain rice (see page 294).

SERVES 4–6

100 g/4 oz/1 cup cooked long-grain rice
30 ml/2 tbsp raisins
25 g/1 oz/¼ cup walnuts, chopped
15 ml/1 tbsp snipped fresh chives
15 g/½ oz/1 tbsp butter or margarine, softened
Salt and freshly ground black pepper

1 Mash the rice, raisins, walnuts and chives into the softened butter or margarine with a fork or the back of a spoon in a bowl.
2 Season to taste with salt and pepper. Use as required.

Caraway Sausage Stuffing

SERVES 4–6

15 g/½ oz/1 tbsp butter or margarine
50 g/2 oz button mushrooms, sliced
100 g/4 oz pork sausagemeat
5 ml/1 tsp caraway seeds
Freshly ground black pepper

1 Melt the butter or margarine in a saucepan. Add the mushrooms and fry (sauté) over a moderate heat, stirring, for 3 minutes. Remove from the heat.
2 Mash in the sausagemeat, caraway seeds and a little pepper, using the back of a spoon. Use as required.

Liver and Garlic Stuffing

If using to stuff a turkey, use the one liver and double the quantity of the remaining ingredients. If your bird has no giblets, use 50 g/2 oz smooth liver pâté.

SERVES 4–6

15 g/½ oz/1 tbsp butter or margarine
The liver from the giblets of the bird, trimmed and chopped
1 garlic clove, crushed
50 g/2 oz/1 cup fresh white or wholemeal breadcrumbs
15 ml/1 tbsp chopped fresh parsley
Finely grated rind and juice of ½ small lemon
Salt and freshly ground black pepper

1 Melt the butter or margarine in a frying pan (skillet). Add the liver and fry (sauté) over a moderate heat for 2 minutes. Tip into a bowl.
2 Stir in the remaining ingredients. Use as required.

Herby Bacon Stuffing

SERVES 4–6

50 g/2 oz/1 cup fresh wholemeal breadcrumbs
1 small onion, finely chopped
2 rashers (slices) of streaky bacon, rinded and finely diced
2.5 ml/½ tsp dried mixed herbs
Salt and freshly ground black pepper
1 small egg, beaten

Mix all the ingredients together and use as required.

Prune and Walnut Stuffing

If using to stuff a turkey, double the quantities but use one whole egg to bind instead of doubling up the egg yolks.

SERVES 4–6

50 g/2 oz/⅓ cup no-need-to-soak prunes, chopped
25 g/1 oz/¼ cup walnut halves, roughly chopped
50 g/2 oz/1 cup fresh white breadcrumbs
15 ml/1 tbsp chopped fresh mint
Salt and freshly ground black pepper
1 egg yolk

1 Mix the dry ingredients thoroughly together in a bowl.
2 Mix with the egg yolk to bind. Use as required.

Accompaniments for traditional roasts

As well as the stuffing, it is worth making the right sauces and accompaniments to finish off your roast dinner. Gravy can be made with stock cubes, but the flavour is much better if you use either giblet stock (for poultry) or vegetable water and the juices from the joint or bird, to give what I call Real Gravy. If you are a vegetarian, use my Vegetable Gravy (see page 324) instead.

Giblet Stock

MAKES ABOUT 450 ML/¾ PT/2 CUPS

Giblets from any poultry or game bird
600 ml/1 pt/2½ cups water

1 Put the giblets in a saucepan. Pour on the water.
2 Bring to the boil over a high heat, turn down the heat until just bubbling, cover and cook gently for 1 hour.
3 Strain and use for the gravy for poultry or game.

Real Gravy

When you remove a joint or bird from the roasting tin (pan), always keep the roasting juices left in the pan to make gravy. For thinner gravy, increase the liquid to 600 ml/1 pt/2½ cups or use only 30 ml/2 tbsp flour.

MAKES 450 ML/¾ PT/2 CUPS

Juices from roasting a joint or bird
45 ml/3 tbsp plain (all-purpose) flour
450 ml/¾ pt/2 cups vegetable water, giblet stock (above) or stock, made with a stock cube
Gravy block or browning
Salt and freshly ground black pepper

1 Tilt the roasting tin and spoon off all but 30 ml/2 tbsp of the fat, but leave all the juices that lie underneath. Put the roasting tin on top of the stove.
2 Stir in the flour and cook over a fairly high heat, stirring, for 1 minute.
3 Remove from the heat and gradually blend in the stock or water.
4 Return to the heat, turn it up to high, bring to the boil and cook for 2 minutes, stirring. Add gravy block or browning and seasoning to taste.

Vegetable Gravy

SERVES 4

50 g/2 oz/¼ cup butter or margarine
2 onions, chopped
30 ml/2 tbsp plain (all-purpose) flour
300 ml/½ pt/1¼ cups vegetable water
    or stock made with a vegetable
    stock cube
5 ml/1 tsp Worcestershire sauce
5 ml/1 tsp yeast extract
Salt and freshly ground black pepper

1 Melt the butter or margarine in a saucepan. Add the onions and cook over a fairly high heat, stirring, for 5 minutes until soft and golden brown. Remove from the heat.
2 Stir the flour into the pan with a wooden spoon, stirring well until smooth, then add the Worcestershire sauce and yeast extract.
3 Return to the heat, bring to the boil over a high heat and cook for 2 minutes, stirring. Season to taste. Strain, if liked.

Extra Tasty Gravy

When you've no meat juices, this makes a good gravy that is delicious with all grilled (broiled), fried (sautéed) or roasted meat or poultry. Use a stock cube appropriate to the meat you are cooking.

SERVES 4

15 ml/1 tbsp sunflower or olive oil
1 onion, chopped
5 ml/1 tsp caster (superfine) sugar
45 ml/3 tbsp plain (all-purpose) flour
300 ml/½ pt/1¼ cups stock, made with
    1 stock cube
2.5 ml/½ tsp dried mixed herbs
A little gravy block or browning
    (optional)
Salt and freshly ground black pepper

1 Heat the oil in a saucepan. Add the onion and sugar and fry (sauté), stirring, over a fairly high heat for about 4 minutes until well browned.
2 Remove from the heat and stir in the flour. Then, using a wire whisk, gradually stir in the stock until smooth. Add the herbs.
3 Return to a high heat, bring to the boil and cook for 2 minutes, stirring all the time with the whisk until thickened and smooth.
4 Stir in a little gravy block or browning, if liked, and season to taste. Serve as it is or strain through a sieve (strainer) into a jug or small bowl, to remove the onion.

Yorkshire Puddings

These are the traditional accompaniment for roast beef. You can make either one large or 12 small puddings with this quantity of batter.

SERVES 4

100 g/4 oz/1 cup plain (all-purpose) flour

A pinch of salt

2 eggs

300 ml/½ pt/1¼ cups milk and water, mixed

Oil, for greasing

1 Mix the flour and salt in a bowl.

2 Make a well in the centre and break in the eggs. Add half the milk and water.

3 Gradually work in the flour, then beat with a wooden spoon or wire whisk until the mixture is smooth.

4 Stir in the remaining milk and water. Leave to stand for 30 minutes, if possible.

5 Pour about 5 ml/1 tsp oil into 12 sections of a tartlet tin (patty pan) or 60 ml/4 tbsp into an 18 x 28 cm/ 7 x 11 in shallow baking tin (pan). Heat in the oven at 220°C/425°F/gas mark 7 until sizzling.

6 Pour in the batter and bake on a shelf near the top of the oven for about 15–20 minutes for small ones, 25–30 minutes for a large one, until puffy, crisp and golden.

Buttered Crumbs

These are traditionally served with roast game. They also make a nice change from bread sauce with roast chicken or turkey.

SERVES 4

25 g/1 oz/2 tbsp butter

100 g/4 oz/2 cups fresh white breadcrumbs

1 Melt the butter in a frying pan (skillet) over a moderate heat.

2 Add the crumbs and stir gently until evenly coated in the butter, golden and crisp. Serve hot.

Forcemeat Balls

Serve these with any roast joint or poultry.

SERVES 4

50 g/2 oz/1 cup fresh white breadcrumbs

25 g/1 oz/2 tbsp shredded (chopped) vegetable suet

30 ml/2 tbsp chopped fresh parsley

5 ml/1 tsp dried mixed herbs

Salt and freshly ground black pepper

1 egg, beaten

Oil, for greasing

1 Mix the dry ingredients together and stir in enough of the beaten egg to bind the mixture together without being too wet.

2 Shape the stuffing into small balls and place in a lightly oiled, shallow baking dish. Roast for about 30–40 minutes until golden.

Game Chips

These are traditionally served with roast game but they are good with any roast or grilled (broiled) meat or poultry.

ALLOW 1 MEDIUM POTATO PER PERSON

1 Peel as many potatoes as you need.
2 Cut into very thin slices, using either a sharp knife, a mandolin or the slicing attachment of a food processor.
3 Soak in cold water for at least 10 minutes. Drain and dry well on kitchen paper (paper towels).
4 Heat oil for deep-frying in a large saucepan or deep-fat fryer until a cube of day-old bread browns in 30 seconds.
5 Cook the potatoes a small batch at a time for about 3 minutes until crisp and golden. Drain on kitchen paper.
6 Keep the cooked chips warm in the oven while cooking the remainder. Sprinkle with salt before serving.

Cheat's Game Chips

SERVES 4

150 g/5 oz/1 large bag of salted kettle chips

Tip the chips on to a baking (cookie) sheet and heat in the oven, after removing the roast bird or joint, for 2–3 minutes before serving.

Bread Sauce

This sauce is a traditional accompaniment to roast poultry. You can, if you prefer, cook it in a small, covered ovenproof dish near the bottom of the oven while roasting your bird. Remove the onion and clove and stir well with a fork before serving.

SERVES 4

50 g/2 oz/1 cup fresh white breadcrumbs
1 small onion
1 whole clove
A good pinch of grated nutmeg
Salt and freshly ground black pepper
300 ml/½ pt/1¼ cups milk

1 Put the breadcrumbs in a non-stick saucepan.
2 Press the clove into the onion and place in the saucepan with the nutmeg, a little salt and pepper and the milk.
3 Bring to the boil, stirring, over a high heat. Turn down the heat to moderate and cook gently for 5 minutes, stirring all the time.
4 Cover with a circle of wetted greaseproof (waxed) paper (this will prevent a skin from forming) and leave to cool.
5 To serve, remove the paper, bring back to the boil, stirring, discard the onion and clove and spoon into a small serving bowl.

Cranberry Sauce

This is a traditional accompaniment for roast turkey.

SERVES 6

100 g/4 oz/½ cup granulated sugar
Finely grated rind and juice of 1 orange
225 g/8 oz cranberries

1 Put the sugar in a saucepan.
2 Measure the orange juice and make up to 150 ml/¼ pt/⅔ cup with water, if necessary. Add to the sugar and cook over a gentle heat, stirring, until the sugar dissolves.
3 Turn up the heat and bring to the boil, then turn the heat down again and cook gently for about 5 minutes until the cranberries 'pop'. Stir in the orange rind.
4 Spoon into a small bowl and leave to cool.

Mint Sauce

This is traditionally served with roast lamb. You can use 15 ml/1 tbsp dried mint instead of the fresh but the flavour is not so good.

SERVES 4

60 ml/4 tbsp chopped fresh mint
15 ml/1 tbsp caster (superfine) sugar
30 ml/2 tbsp boiling water
Malt vinegar

1 Put the mint in a small bowl.
2 Add the sugar and stir in the boiling water until the sugar dissolves.
3 Leave to stand for at least 30 minutes, preferably longer, to allow the flavour to develop.
4 Just before serving, stir in some vinegar, a little at a time, to taste.

Cumberland Sauce

This is particularly good served as an accompaniment to roast gammon and game.

SERVES 4–6

1 orange
1 lemon
5 ml/1 tsp grated onion
60 ml/4 tbsp redcurrant jelly (clear conserve)
120 ml/4 fl oz/½ cup port
5 ml/1 tsp Dijon mustard
A pinch of ground ginger
Salt and freshly ground black pepper

1 Cut off the rind from the orange and lemon very thinly, being careful not to remove any white pith. Cut into very thin strips.
2 Bring a small saucepan of water to the boil over a high heat. Drop in the rinds and boil for 3 minutes. Drain in a sieve (strainer), rinse with cold water and drain again.
3 Squeeze the juice from the orange and lemon. Put the onion, redcurrant jelly and port in the same saucepan and heat over a moderate heat, stirring all the time, until the jelly melts.
4 Add the juices, rinds, mustard and ginger and season to taste. Continue to cook for 4 minutes, then pour into a sauceboat and serve either hot or cold.

Apple Sauce

Serve with roast pork.

SERVES 4–6

450 g/1 lb cooking (tart) apples,
   peeled, cored and sliced
15 ml/1 tbsp caster (superfine) sugar
30 ml/2 tbsp water
25 g/1 oz/2 tbsp butter or margarine

1 Put the apples in a saucepan with
the sugar and water. Bring to the boil
over a fairly high heat.
2 Turn down the heat to low, cover
and cook gently for about 5 minutes,
stirring occasionally, until the fruit is
pulpy. Stir in the butter vigorously with
a wooden spoon.
3 Spoon into a sauceboat and serve
warm.

Savoury sauces

Sauces may be used as accompaniments,
to contrast and complement the flavour
of dishes, or they may form the basis of
the dish in which the meat, poultry, etc.
are cooked.

Quick White Sauce

*This is a simple, foolproof white
sauce, which can be used as the
basis of many flavoured sauces.*

SERVES 4

45 ml/3 tbsp plain (all-purpose) flour
300 ml/½ pt/1¼ cups milk
A knob of butter or margarine
Salt and freshly ground black pepper

1 Put the flour in a small saucepan.
2 Using a balloon whisk and stirring all
the time, gradually add the milk until

the mixture is smooth.
3 Add the butter or margarine and a
sprinkling of salt and pepper.
4 Cook over a fairly high heat, stirring
with the whisk all the time, until the
mixture is thick and bubbling. Continue
to cook the sauce for 2 minutes. Use as
required.

Parsley Sauce

*Serve with fish, chicken or
vegetables.*

SERVES 4

1 quantity of Quick White Sauce
30 ml/2 tbsp chopped fresh parsley

1 Prepare the sauce.
2 Add the parsley to the sauce once
cooked.

Mushroom Sauce

*Serve with chicken, fish, vegetables,
pork or pasta.*

SERVES 4

1 quantity of Quick White Sauce
4–5 button mushrooms, finely chopped
30 ml/2 tbsp water
Lemon juice, to taste (optional)

1 Prepare the sauce.
2 Cook the mushrooms in the water in
a covered pan for 3 minutes.
3 Remove the lid and boil rapidly, if
necessary, to evaporate any remaining
liquid.
4 Stir into the cooked white sauce and
add a squeeze of lemon juice, if liked.

Cheese Sauce

Serve with fish, pasta or vegetables.

SERVES 4

1 quantity of Quick White Sauce
50 g/2 oz/½ cup Cheddar cheese, grated

1 Prepare the sauce.
2 Add the cheese and cook, stirring, for about 2 minutes.

Caper Sauce

Serve with lamb or fish.

SERVES 4

1 quantity of Quick White Sauce
30 ml/2 tbsp capers, chopped

1 Prepare the sauce.
2 Add the capers with the seasoning.

Mustard Sauce

Serve with boiled beef, boiled ham or oily fish, such as mackerel.

SERVES 4

1 quantity of Quick White Sauce
10 ml/2 tsp made English mustard
15 ml/1 tbsp light brown sugar
Malt vinegar, to taste

1 Prepare the sauce.
2 Stir in the mustard and sugar.
3 Add malt vinegar, a very little at a time, tasting as you go, until sweet but sharp.

Cucumber and Dill Sauce

Serve with fish or chicken.

SERVES 4

1 quantity of Quick White Sauce
¼ cucumber, finely chopped
5 ml/1 tsp dried dill (dill weed)

1 Prepare the sauce.
2 Stir in the cucumber and dill.

Green Cress Sauce

Serve with fish or chicken.

SERVES 4

1 quantity of Quick White Sauce
1 bunch of watercress, finely chopped
A pinch of cayenne

1 Prepare the sauce.
2 Stir in the watercress and add a pinch of cayenne.

Onion Sauce

Serve with lamb, pork or chicken or vegetables.

SERVES 4

1 quantity of Quick White Sauce
2 onions, finely chopped
30 ml/2 tbsp water

1 Prepare the sauce.
2 While it is cooking, cook the chopped onions gently in a saucepan with the water for 10 minutes until really soft.
3 Stir into the white sauce and re-season if liked.

Béchamel Sauce

Use this classic, delicately flavoured sauce in any recipe that calls for a savoury white sauce. It is also delicious with cooked vegetables.

SERVES 4

300 ml/½ pt/1¼ cups milk
1 slice of onion
1 bouquet garni sachet
A few black peppercorns
A good knob of butter or margarine
20 g/¾ oz/3 tbsp plain (all-purpose) flour
Salt

1 Put the milk, onion, bouquet garni and peppercorns in a saucepan over a high heat.
2 As soon as it comes to the boil, remove from the heat (be quick, or it will boil over).
3 Cover with a lid and leave for 15 minutes to allow the flavours to infuse. Pour through a sieve (strainer) into a jug and throw away the flavourings.
4 Melt the butter or margarine in the rinsed-out pan.
5 Stir in the flour and cook over a high heat for 1 minute, stirring. This is called making a roux.
6 Remove from the heat and gradually blend in the infused milk using a wire whisk to prevent lumps.
7 Return to the heat, bring to the boil and cook for 2 minutes, stirring thoroughly with the whisk all the time. Season to taste.

Fast Hollandaise Sauce

Hollandaise makes a delicious, creamy accompaniment for any plain grilled (broiled) or poached fish. This is a quick and easy version.

SERVES 4

2 eggs
30 ml/2 tbsp lemon juice
100 g/4 oz/½ cup butter, melted
A pinch of cayenne

1 Whisk the eggs in a saucepan with the lemon juice, using a wire whisk.
2 Gradually whisk the melted butter into the egg mixture, a trickle at a time.
3 Whisk over a low heat until thickened. Do not boil or it will curdle.
4 Whisk in the cayenne.

Curried Hollandaise

SERVES 4

Prepare as for Fast Hollandaise Sauce, whisking in 15 ml/1 tbsp mild curry paste with the egg yolks and lemon juice.

Green Hollandaise

SERVES 4

1 quantity of Fast Hollandaise Sauce
1 bunch of watercress
4 sprigs of parsley
8 fresh marjoram or tarragon leaves

1 Prepare the sauce.
2 Chop the watercress, parsley and marjoram or tarragon leaves.
3 Add to the finished sauce.

Curry Sauce

This simple sauce is wonderfully versatile. Try it as an accompaniment for grilled (broiled) chicken or hard-boiled (hard-cooked) eggs. Alternatively, add diced, cooked chicken or turkey to the sauce, heat through until piping hot and serve with rice. You can also add leftover diced roast lamb, pork or beef but you will have to cook the meat in the sauce over a very gentle heat for at least 20 minutes to tenderise it, stirring frequently to prevent sticking.

SERVES 4–6

295 g/10½ oz/1 medium can of condensed celery or mushroom soup

90 ml/6 tbsp water

30 ml/2 tbsp tomato purée (paste)

1 garlic clove, crushed

5 ml/1 tsp dried onion granules

15 ml/1 tbsp curry paste

5 ml/1 tsp garam masala

5 ml/1 tsp ground turmeric

30 ml/2 tbsp mango chutney

50 g/2 oz piece of creamed coconut

Salt and freshly ground black pepper

1 Put all the ingredients in a saucepan. Heat, stirring, over a moderate heat until the coconut is melted and the mixture is bubbling.

2 Thin with a little more water if necessary and adjust the seasoning to taste.

Espagnole Sauce

Serve this sauce as an accompaniment to any grilled (broiled) or roast meat. It can also be used as the base for a braised meat dish.

SERVES 4

1 onion, roughly chopped

1 celery stick, chopped

1 carrot, chopped

1 rasher (slice) of bacon, rinded and diced

15 g/½ oz/1 tbsp butter or margarine

10 ml/2 tsp sunflower oil

25 g/1 oz/¼ cup plain (all-purpose) flour

450 ml/¾ pt/2 cups beef stock, made with 1 stock cube

10 ml/2 tsp tomato purée (paste)

1 bouquet garni sachet

A little gravy block or browning

Salt and freshly ground black pepper

1 Put the onion, celery, carrot and bacon in a saucepan with the butter or margarine and oil. Cook over a moderate heat for about 8 minutes, stirring, until well browned. Remove from the heat.

2 Stir in the flour and then the stock.

3 Return to a high heat and bring to the boil, stirring until thickened.

4 Stir in the tomato purée and add the bouquet garni sachet. Cover, turn down the heat to low and cook gently for 30 minutes.

5 Strain the sauce through a sieve (strainer) into a clean saucepan. Add a little gravy block or browning if necessary to give a good, rich colour, then season to taste and reheat.

Bigarde Sauce

This makes a good accompaniment for roast or grilled (broiled) duck, game, pork or venison. Any sweet orange will do if Seville oranges are out of season.

SERVES 4–6

1 quantity of Espagnole Sauce (see page 331)

Thinly pared rind and juice of 1 Seville orange

15 ml/1 tbsp lemon juice

30 ml/2 tbsp port

1 Prepare and strain the Espagnole Sauce into the saucepan.

2 Cut the orange rind into very thin strips and boil in a small saucepan of water for 5 minutes. Drain in a sieve (strainer).

3 Add to the sauce with the strained orange juice, the lemon juice and port. Reheat, stirring until bubbling.

Gooseberry Sauce

Use this as an accompaniment for grilled (broiled) or fried (sautéed) mackerel, herring, pork chops or duck breasts.

SERVES 4–6

Prepare as for Apple Sauce (see page 328), but substitute gooseberries, topped and tailed, for the apples and add a pinch of grated nutmeg to the mixture.

Sweet and Sour Sauce

Use this as the basis to cook Chinese pork, fish and poultry dishes. For Chunky Sweet and Sour Sauce, use a 225 g/8 oz/small can of pineapple chunks in natural juice instead of the pineapple juice and add a 2.5 cm/1 in piece of finely chopped cucumber and a coarsely grated carrot.

SERVES 4

30 ml/2 tbsp cornflour (cornstarch)

30 ml/2 tbsp water

30 ml/2 tbsp soy sauce

45 ml/3 tbsp tomato ketchup (catsup)

90 ml/6 tbsp clear honey

60 ml/4 tbsp malt vinegar

60 ml/4 tbsp pineapple juice

60 ml/4 tbsp orange juice

1 Mix the cornflour with the water in a small saucepan with a wooden spoon or wire whisk.

2 Add all the remaining ingredients.

3 Bring to the boil over a high heat and cook for 1 minute until thickened and clear, stirring all the time. Serve hot.

Pizzaiola Sauce

This is ideal with Spiced Chicken Burgers (see page 220), any grilled (broiled) or fried (sautéed) pork, poultry or game or with pasta.

SERVES 4–6

2 onions, finely chopped
2 garlic cloves, crushed
1 green (bell) pepper, diced
1 red pepper, diced
15 ml/1 tbsp olive oil
50 g/2 oz button mushrooms, chopped
400 g/14 oz/1 large can of chopped tomatoes
15 ml/1 tbsp tomato purée (paste)
Tabasco sauce, to taste
5 ml/1 tsp dried oregano
Salt and freshly ground black pepper

1 Put the onions, garlic, peppers and oil in a saucepan and cook, stirring, over a moderate heat for 5–10 minutes.
2 Add the mushrooms and stir for 1 minute.
3 Add the tomatoes and tomato purée. Cook over a high heat until bubbling, then turn down the heat to fairly low and cook for 10 minutes until pulpy and the vegetables are tender.
4 Season to taste with a good dash of Tabasco sauce, the oregano and a little salt and pepper.

Barbecue Sauce

If you are having a barbecue, make this in advance in a saucepan that you can stand on the barbecue rack to reheat while you cook the meats.

SERVES 4–6

1 garlic clove, crushed
1 small onion, very finely chopped
10 ml/2 tsp sunflower oil
100 g/4 oz tomato purée (paste)
300 ml/½ pt/1¼ cups fruity dry white wine
10 ml/2 tsp soy sauce
30 ml/2 tbsp clear honey
30 ml/2 tbsp white wine vinegar
A few drops of Tabasco sauce
Salt and freshly ground black pepper

1 Put the garlic, onion and oil in a small saucepan. Cook for 2 minutes over a high heat, stirring, until the onion is softened.
2 Add the remaining ingredients, bring to the boil, reduce the heat to fairly low and cook gently, stirring frequently, for about 20 minutes until thick.
3 Taste and re-season if necessary. Serve with any barbecued or grilled (broiled) meats, fish or vegetables.

Fast Barbecue Sauce

This tasty sauce has lots of uses: brush it on food while grilling (broiling) or frying (sautéing) or serve as a dip or side sauce for plain cooked meats, poultry, fish or quorn steaks.

SERVES 4

30 ml/2 tbsp wine or malt vinegar
30 ml/2 tbsp tomato ketchup (catsup)
30 ml/2 tbsp golden (light corn) syrup
15 ml/1 tbsp Worcestershire sauce
Salt and freshly ground black pepper
2.5 ml/½ tsp garlic granules (optional)

Whisk all the ingredients together in a bowl using a wire whisk.

Peanut Sauce

SERVES 4

100 ml/3½ fl oz/scant ½ cup water
3 spring onions (scallions), finely chopped
225 g/8 oz/1 cup crunchy peanut butter
15 ml/1 tbsp clear honey
30 ml/2 tbsp light soy sauce
A few drops of Tabasco sauce

1 Put the water in a small saucepan with two of the spring onions.
2 Bring to the boil over a high heat, turn down to fairly low and cook for 1 minute.
3 Stir in the peanut butter, honey, soy sauce and Tabasco sauce to taste. Stir until smooth and thin with a little more water, if necessary.
4 Heat until bubbling, then spoon into a small bowl and sprinkle with the remaining spring onion.

Orange and Mango Salsa

If you're not sure about seeding a chilli, see Fiery Mussel Spaghettini, page 134.

SERVES 4–6

1 large just-ripe mango
4–6 spring onions (scallions), finely chopped
2 oranges
1 small red chilli, seeded and chopped
15 ml/1 tbsp chopped fresh mint
2.5 ml/½ tsp grated fresh root ginger
A pinch of salt
Freshly ground black pepper
5 ml/1 tsp lemon juice

1 Peel the mango and cut all the fruit off the stone (pit). Cut into small dice and place in a bowl. Add the spring onions.
2 Finely grate the rind from one of the oranges, then cut off all the peel and pith from both. Slice the fruit and cut into small pieces. Add to the mango and onion.
3 Add the remaining ingredients and mix well. Cover and chill for at least 1 hour to allow the flavours to develop.

Orange and Pineapple Salsa

Serve this with grilled (broiled) fish, meat or poultry.

SERVES 4

Prepare as for Orange and Mango Salsa but use a 250 g/9 oz/medium can of crushed pineapple, well-drained, instead of the mango.

Brown Onion Salsa

This is delicious with grilled (broiled) steaks or burgers.

SERVES 4–6

25 g/1 oz/2 tbsp butter or margarine
450 g/1 lb onions, chopped
30 ml/2 tbsp light brown sugar
Salt and freshly ground black pepper
15 ml/1 tbsp chopped fresh parsley

1 Melt the butter or margarine in a saucepan over a moderate heat. Add the onions and cook, stirring, for 5 minutes until softened.
2 Add the sugar, turn up the heat and continue cooking for about a further 5 minutes or until a rich golden brown.
3 Purée in a blender or food processor and season to taste. Stir in the parsley. Reheat gently, if liked.

Quick Tomato Sauce

Serve this hot with any grilled (broiled) meat, fish or poultry, or with pasta.

SERVES 4

1 onion, finely chopped
1 garlic clove, crushed (optional)
15 ml/1 tbsp sunflower or olive oil
400 g/14 oz/1 large can of chopped
    tomatoes
15 ml/1 tbsp tomato purée (paste)
2.5 ml/½ tsp caster (superfine) sugar
Salt and freshly ground black pepper

1 Place the onion and garlic, if using, in a saucepan with the oil and fry (sauté) for 2 minutes, stirring.
2 Add the tomatoes, tomato purée and sugar.

3 Bring to the boil over a high heat and boil rapidly for about 5 minutes until pulpy.
4 Season to taste.

Tomato Sauce with Fresh Basil

SERVES 4

Prepare as for Quick Tomato Sauce but omit the dried basil or oregano. Stir in 6–8 chopped fresh basil leaves after cooking.

Provençal Sauce

Serve with grilled (broiled) fish, chicken, pork or continental sausages.

SERVES 4

1 onion, finely chopped
1–2 garlic cloves, crushed
1 chopped green (bell) pepper
15 ml/1 tbsp sunflower or olive oil
400 g/14 oz/1 large can of chopped
    tomatoes
15 ml/1 tbsp tomato purée (paste)
12 stuffed green olives, halved
2.5 ml/½ tsp caster (superfine) sugar
Salt and freshly ground black pepper

1 Place the onion, garlic and pepper in a saucepan with the oil and fry (sauté) for 2 minutes, stirring.
2 Add the tomatoes, tomato purée, olives and sugar.
3 Bring to the boil over a high heat and boil rapidly for about 5 minutes until pulpy. Season to taste.

Simple Pesto Sauce

This can be used in many ways. Add it to cooked pasta and lift and stir over a gentle heat before serving; spread on slices of ciabatta bread and grill (broil) until melted or use as a stuffing for chicken breasts or fish.

SERVES 4

20 fresh basil leaves
1 large sprig of parsley
50 g/2 oz/½ cup pine nuts
1 large garlic clove, halved
90 ml/6 tbsp olive oil
30 ml/2 tbsp grated Parmesan cheese
A pinch of salt
Freshly ground black pepper
15 ml/1 tbsp hot water

1 Put the herbs, nuts and garlic in a blender or food processor. Run the machine briefly to chop.
2 With the machine running, gradually add the oil in a thin trickle to form a thick paste. Stop the machine and scrape down the sides from time to time.
3 Add the cheese, salt and some pepper and run the machine again, adding the water, to form a glistening paste.
4 Store in a screw-topped jar in the fridge. It will keep for up to 2 weeks.

Goulash Sauce

Serve this sauce, topped with a spoonful of crème fraîche and a sprinkling of caraway seeds, with grilled (broiled) meat, chicken, fish or (bell) peppers.

SERVES 4

1 onion, finely chopped
1 garlic clove, crushed
15 ml/1 tbsp paprika
15 ml/1 tbsp sunflower or olive oil
400 g/14 oz/1 large can of chopped tomatoes
15 ml/1 tbsp tomato purée (paste)
2.5 ml/½ tsp caster (superfine) sugar
Salt and freshly ground black pepper

1 Place the onion, garlic and paprika in a saucepan with the oil and fry (sauté) for 2 minutes, stirring, until softened.
2 Add the tomatoes, tomato purée and sugar.
3 Bring to the boil over a high heat and boil rapidly for about 5 minutes until pulpy.
4 Season to taste.

Tartare Sauce

Serve with grilled (broiled), fried (sautéed) or poached fish or chicken. Add more mayonnaise if you like.

SERVES 4

45 ml/3 tbsp mayonnaise
15 ml/1 tbsp double (heavy) cream
15 ml/1 tbsp capers, chopped
2 gherkins (cornichons), chopped
10 ml/2 tsp snipped fresh chives

1 Mix all the ingredients together in a small bowl.
2 Chill until ready to serve.

Rouille

Serve this glistening, spicy sauce with plain cooked chicken or fish or as a dip. It is also traditionally served with fish soup, stirred in to taste at the table. To seed chillies, see Fiery Mussel Spaghettini, page 134.

SERVES 4–6

1 red chilli, seeded and chopped
1 red (bell) pepper, chopped
2 large garlic cloves, crushed
1 slice of white bread, crusts removed
1 egg yolk
Salt and white pepper
75 ml/5 tbsp sunflower oil
75 ml/5 tbsp olive oil

1 Put the chilli, red pepper, garlic, bread and egg yolk in a blender. Add a sprinkling of salt and pepper. Run the machine until smooth, stopping and scraping down the sides as necessary.
2 With the machine running, add the oil in a thin trickle until the mixture is thick and glossy. The trick is not to add it too fast.
3 Spoon the mixture into a small bowl and cover in clingfilm (plastic wrap). Chill until required.

Dressings

Whatever kind of salad you make, it will almost always be improved by a suitable dressing. Tangy, smooth, crunchy, creamy, sweet – the choice is yours.

French Dressing

For added flavour, add a squeeze of garlic purée, or a small teaspoonful of Dijon mustard or a good pinch of dried mixed herbs, tarragon or oregano to the basic mixture.

MAKES 120 ML/3¹/₂ FL OZ/SCANT ¹/₂ CUP

90 ml/6 tbsp olive oil
30 ml/2 tbsp red or white wine vinegar
A good pinch of caster (superfine) sugar
Salt and freshly ground black pepper

1 Pour the oil into a clear screw-topped jar.
2 Add the vinegar, sugar and a good pinch each of salt and pepper.
3 Screw on the lid and shake thoroughly. Store in the fridge and use as required. Shake well before use.

Honey Nut Dressing

This gives texture as well as flavour to leafy salads.

SERVES 4

30 ml/2 tbsp clear honey
30 ml/2 tbsp sunflower oil
15 ml/1 tbsp lemon juice
30 ml/2 tbsp finely chopped nuts
15 ml/1 tbsp chopped fresh parsley
Salt and freshly ground black pepper

Put all the ingredients in a screw-topped jar and shake vigorously until well blended.

Sweet Creamy Dressing

This is delicious served with a plain lettuce salad, or with cold meat and a mixed salad.

SERVES 4

15 ml/1 tbsp light brown sugar
60 ml/4 tbsp crème fraîche
2.5 ml/½ tsp made English mustard
A pinch of salt
Freshly ground black pepper
Malt vinegar, to taste

1 Whisk the sugar, crème fraîche, mustard, salt and lots of pepper together in a small bowl or jug using a wire whisk.
2 Whisk in vinegar to taste.

Cheese Dressing

SERVES 4

60 ml/4 tbsp medium-fat soft cheese
10 ml/2 tsp snipped fresh chives
10 ml/2 tsp chopped fresh parsley
30 ml/2 tbsp milk
5 ml/1 tsp dried onion granules
Salt and freshly ground black pepper

1 Put all the ingredients except the salt and pepper in a small bowl. Whisk using a wire whisk until well blended.
2 Thin with a little more milk if necessary and season with salt and pepper to taste.

Creamy Garlic Dressing

SERVES 4–6

15 ml/1 tbsp olive oil
75 ml/5 tbsp crème fraîche
15 ml/1 tbsp lemon juice
1 garlic clove, crushed
15 ml/1 tbsp chopped fresh parsley
A pinch of salt
Freshly ground black pepper
5 ml/1 tsp clear honey
A little cold milk

1 Whisk all the ingredients together in a small bowl.
2 Chill until ready to serve.

Vinaigrette

SERVES 4

30 ml/2 tbsp white wine vinegar
30 ml/2 tbsp olive oil
1 shallot, very finely chopped
2.5 ml/½ tsp Dijon mustard
10 ml/2 tsp chopped fresh parsley
5 ml/1 tsp caster (superfine) sugar
Salt and freshly ground black pepper

1 Put all the ingredients in a screw-topped jar and shake until well blended.
2 Store in the fridge until ready to use.

Oriental Soy Dressing

SERVES 4

30 ml/2 tbsp light soy sauce
45 ml/3 tbsp sunflower oil
15 ml/1 tbsp sesame oil
15 ml/1 tbsp medium-dry sherry
10 ml/2 tsp light brown sugar
5 ml/1 tsp grated fresh root ginger
Freshly ground black pepper

Whisk all the ingredients together in a small bowl with a wire whisk.

Yoghurt Mayonnaise

SERVES 4

30 ml/2 tbsp mayonnaise
30 ml/2 tbsp plain yoghurt
2.5 ml/½ tsp lemon juice
A pinch of salt, caster sugar and freshly ground black pepper

Mix all the ingredients together in a small bowl and chill until ready to serve.

Simple Cocktail Dressing

Use this with any salad item – prawns (shrimp), mushrooms, avocado, chicken – as a starter, spooned on a bed of shredded lettuce in small dishes, or in a sandwich filling.

SERVES 4

60 ml/4 tbsp mayonnaise
15 ml/1 tbsp tomato ketchup (catsup)
2.5 ml/½ tsp Worcestershire sauce
Freshly ground black pepper
A few drops of Tabasco sauce

Mix all the ingredients together with a wooden spoon in a small bowl.

Blue Cheese Mayonnaise

This lovely, creamy dressing is ideal for a plain green salad but also makes an excellent dip.

SERVES 4

100 g/4 oz/1 cup Danish Blue cheese, crumbled
60 ml/4 tbsp mayonnaise
45 ml/3 tbsp crème fraîche
5 ml/1 tsp lemon juice
Salt and freshly ground black pepper

1 Using a fork, mash the cheese with 15 ml/1 tbsp of the mayonnaise until fairly smooth.
2 Briskly stir in the remaining mayonnaise, the crème fraîche, lemon juice, salt and pepper to taste.

Curried Mayonnaise

Another dressing that can double as a dip!

SERVES 4

60 ml/4 tbsp mayonnaise
15 ml/1 tbsp curry paste
15 ml/1 tbsp sultanas (golden raisins)
15 ml/1 tbsp chopped fresh coriander (cilantro), optional
A little milk

1 Mix the mayonnaise with the curry paste and stir in the sultanas.
2 Add the coriander, if liked. Thin with a little milk if necessary.

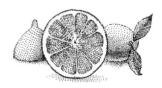

Dips and dipping sauces

Dips are amazingly versatile – they make an ideal, quick snack or starter, served with chunks of fresh vegetables and other nibbles (see Starters, pages 33–58, and Nibbles, pages 418–30). They can also be used to accompany cooked dishes, such as grills and curries.

Chilli Dipping Sauce

This is an Oriental chilli sauce, and makes a perfect accompaniment for deep-fried crumb- or batter-coated pieces of chicken, turkey, seafood or vegetables. For a hotter sauce, add more chilli powder or a few drops of Tabasco sauce.

SERVES 4

75 ml/5 tbsp water

10 ml/2 tsp cornflour (cornstarch)

2 spring onions (scallions), finely chopped

10 ml/2 tsp grated fresh root ginger

1 garlic clove, crushed

60 ml/4 tbsp medium-dry sherry

20 ml/4 tsp caster (superfine) sugar

30 ml/2 tbsp tomato purée (paste)

2.5 ml/½ tsp chilli powder

A good pinch of Chinese five spice powder

A pinch of salt

A good grinding of black pepper

1 Mix the water and cornflour in a saucepan.

2 With a wooden spoon or wire whisk, stir in all the remaining ingredients .

3 Bring to the boil over a high heat and cook for 1 minute, stirring. Use hot or cold.

Piquant Dip

This is particularly good with chicken or oily fish, such as mackerel. It's also great with raw vegetable dippers as a starter.

SERVES 4–6

6 stuffed green olives, finely chopped

1 spring onion (scallion), finely chopped

75 ml/5 tbsp mayonnaise

30 ml/2 tbsp tomato ketchup (catsup)

A few drops of Tabasco sauce

Salt and freshly ground black pepper

Mix all the ingredients together in a small bowl and chill until ready to serve.

Minted Yoghurt and Cucumber

Use this to top jacket-baked potatoes or to serve with curries. It also makes a delicious starter or snack, served with warm pitta breads.

SERVES 4

5 cm/2 in piece of cucumber, grated

5 ml/1 tsp dried mint

1 small garlic clove, crushed (optional)

150 ml/¼ pt/⅔ cup thick plain yoghurt

Salt and freshly ground black pepper

1 Squeeze the grated cucumber to remove excess moisture. Place in a bowl.

2 Add the remaining ingredients and mix thoroughly.

3 Chill until ready to serve.

Aioli

This makes a wonderful, tangy dip to serve with anything from deep-fried mushrooms and chicken pieces to prawns and chilled sticks of vegetables.

SERVES 4–6

300 ml/½ pt/1¼ cups mayonnaise
2 garlic cloves, crushed
2.5 ml/½ tsp lemon juice
A few drops of Tabasco sauce
Salt and freshly ground black pepper

Mix all the ingredients together in a small bowl and chill until ready to serve.

Ginger Dipping Sauce

Serve this with fried (sautéed) seafood, chicken, beef or pork.

SERVES 4

20 ml/4 tsp grated fresh root ginger
45 ml/3 tbsp medium-dry sherry
30 ml/2 tbsp soy sauce
45 ml/3 tbsp hot water

1 Mix all the ingredients together.
2 Pour into individual small bowls to serve.

Flavoured butters

Use any of the following butters to brighten up plain grilled (broiled) meat, fish, poultry, game, quorn or firm tofu. It will appear that you've taken an enormous amount of time and trouble but, in fact, they are amazingly simple! Don't try to use a soft margarine instead of butter – it won't harden in the fridge so you won't be able to slice it.

Parsley Butter

SERVES 4

50 g/2 oz/¼ cup butter, softened
10 ml/2 tsp lemon juice
15 ml/1 tbsp chopped fresh parsley
Freshly ground black pepper

1 Stir the butter in a small bowl with a wooden spoon until soft.
2 Stir in the parsley and lemon juice vigorously and add a good grinding of pepper.
3 Roll into a sausage shape on a piece of greaseproof (waxed) paper. Wrap and chill.
4 Cut into slices for serving.

Lemon Butter

SERVES 4

Prepare as for Parsley Butter but omit the parsley and add the finely grated rind of half a lemon.

Curry Butter

SERVES 4

Prepare as for Parsley Butter but add 5 ml/1 tsp curry powder and 1.5 ml/¼ tsp ground turmeric to the mixture.

Chive Butter

SERVES 4

Prepare as for Parsley Butter, but substitute snipped fresh chives for the parsley.

Garlic Butter

SERVES 4

Prepare as for Parsley Butter, adding a large crushed garlic clove to the mixture.

Devilled Butter

SERVES 4

50 g/2 oz/¼ cup butter, softened
5 ml/1 tsp lemon juice
2.5 ml/½ tsp made English mustard
5 ml/1 tsp tomato purée (paste)
5 ml/1 tsp Worcestershire sauce
1.5 ml/¼ tsp chilli powder
Freshly ground black pepper

1 Stir the butter in a small bowl with a wooden spoon until soft.
2 Stir all the remaining ingredients vigorously, until well blended.
3 Roll into a sausage shape on a piece of greaseproof (waxed) paper. Wrap and chill.
4 Cut into slices for serving.

Green Herb Butter

SERVES 4

50 g/2 oz/¼ cup butter, softened
10 ml/2 tsp lemon juice
5 ml/1 tsp chopped fresh parsley
5 ml/1 tsp chopped fresh tarragon
5 ml/1 tsp chopped fresh thyme
1 large sprig of watercress, finely chopped
1.5 ml/¼ tsp onion powder
Freshly ground black pepper

1 Stir the butter in a small bowl with a wooden spoon until soft.
2 Stir in all the remaining ingredients vigorously until well blended.
3 Roll into a sausage shape on a piece of greaseproof (waxed) paper. Wrap and chill.
4 Cut into slices for serving.

Tomato Butter

SERVES 4

50 g/2 oz/¼ cup butter, softened
5 ml/1 tsp tomato purée (paste)
1 sun-dried tomato in oil, drained and finely chopped
5 ml/1 tsp oil from the sun-dried tomatoes
2.5 ml/½ tsp icing (confectioners') sugar
2.5 ml/½ tsp Worcestershire sauce
Freshly ground black pepper

1 Stir the butter in a small bowl with a wooden spoon until soft.
2 Stir in the remaining ingredients vigorously and add a good grinding of pepper.
3 Roll into a sausage shape on a piece of greaseproof (waxed) paper. Wrap and chill.
4 Cut into slices for serving.

Mustard Butter

SERVES 4

50 g/2 oz/¼ cup butter, softened
5 ml/1 tsp lemon juice
15 ml/1 tbsp snipped fresh chives
10 ml/2 tsp Dijon mustard
A pinch of icing (confectioners') sugar
Freshly ground black pepper

1 Stir the butter in a small bowl with a wooden spoon until soft.
2 Stir in the remaining ingredients vigorously and add a good grinding of pepper.
3 Roll into a sausage shape on a piece of greaseproof (waxed) paper. Wrap and chill.
4 Cut into slices for serving.

Marinades and rubs

Any of these can be used to flavour and tenderise any meat, poultry or game before grilling (broiling) or roasting. Simply lay the meat in a shallow dish, pour over the marinade, turn it over to coat completely, cover and leave in a cool place – 30 minutes is the minimum, really, but even a few minutes to let the flavours penetrate is better than nothing. As a guide, red wine and strong-flavoured ones go best with red meats and game, the white wine and lighter-flavoured ones complement poultry and fish. Don't marinade fish for more than 2 hours or it will become too soft. All these marinades can be stored in an airtight container in the fridge for up to a week. Use any leftover marinade to brush the food while cooking.

Chinese-style Marinade

Use to marinate pork or chicken. I don't recommend this for game.

MAKES ABOUT 450 ML/¾ PT/2 CUPS

Finely grated rind and juice of 1 lime
45 ml/3 tbsp rice wine or white wine vinegar
30 ml/2 tbsp soy sauce
15 ml/1 tbsp dry sherry
15 ml/1 tbsp sesame oil
60 ml/4 tbsp sunflower oil
15 ml/1 tbsp clear honey
2.5 ml/½ tsp Chinese five spice powder
15 ml/1 tbsp chopped fresh coriander (cilantro)

Whisk all the ingredients together.

White Wine Marinade

Use this to marinate any white meat or fish.

MAKES ABOUT 450 ML/¾ PT/2 CUPS

1 onion, chopped
A sprig of parsley
A sprig of thyme
1 small bay leaf
300 ml/½ pt /1¼ cups dry white wine
30 ml/2 tbsp white wine vinegar or lemon juice
15 ml/1 tbsp clear honey
20 ml/2 tbsp olive oil
5 ml/1 tsp juniper berries, crushed (optional)
1.5 ml/¼ tsp salt
Freshly ground black pepper

Whisk all the ingredients together.

Red Wine Marinade

Use to marinate any red meat or game.

MAKES ABOUT 450 ML/¾ PT/2 CUPS

1 onion, chopped
1 garlic clove, crushed
A sprig of parsley
A sprig of rosemary
300 ml/½ pt/1¼ cups red wine
30 ml/2 tbsp red wine vinegar
15 ml/1 tbsp light brown sugar
30 ml/2 tbsp olive oil
5 ml/1 tsp ground cumin (optional)
1.5 ml/¼ tsp salt
Freshly ground black pepper

Whisk all the ingredients together.

Taiwanese Marinade

Use to marinate pork, beef or chicken. I don't recommend this for game.

MAKES ABOUT 450 ML/¾ PT/2 CUPS

Finely grated rind and juice of 2 limes
45 ml/3 tbsp Thai fish sauce
75 ml/5 tbsp sesame oil
75 ml/5 tbsp sunflower oil
2 large garlic cloves, crushed
45 ml/3 tbsp roasted salted peanuts, finely chopped
1 stalk of lemon grass, crushed
1 green chilli, seeded and chopped
30 ml/2 tbsp chopped fresh coriander (cilantro)

Whisk all the ingredients together.

Curried Yoghurt Marinade

Use to marinate any meat, poultry or game for at least 1 hour.

MAKES ABOUT 450 ML/¾ PT/2 CUPS

300 ml/½ pt/1¼ cups plain yoghurt
30 ml/2 tbsp chopped fresh coriander (cilantro)
30 ml/2 tbsp mild curry paste
30 ml/2 tbsp red wine vinegar
45 ml/3 tbsp sunflower oil
15 ml/1 tbsp light brown sugar

Whisk the ingredients together until thoroughly blended.

Sesame Citrus Marinade

Use to marinate any white fish or meat for at least 1 hour.

MAKES ABOUT 450 ML/¾ PT/2 CUPS

Finely grated rind and juice of 1 lemon
Finely grated rind of ½ orange
Juice of the whole orange
150 ml/¼ pt/⅔ cup sunflower oil
30 ml/2 tbsp sesame oil
2 garlic cloves, crushed
5 ml/1 tsp ground cumin
5 ml/1 tsp dried mixed herbs
45 ml/3 tbsp chopped fresh parsley
30 ml/2 tbsp sesame seeds, toasted and lightly crushed
A pinch of salt
Freshly ground black pepper

Whisk all the ingredients together.

Garlic and Parsley Marinade

Use to marinate any white meat or fish.

MAKES ABOUT 450 ML/¾ PT/2 CUPS

300 ml/½ pt/1¼ cups dry white wine
120 ml/4 fl oz/½ cup olive oil
1 large bay leaf, split in half
2 large garlic cloves, crushed
5 ml/1 tsp caster (superfine) sugar
Salt and freshly ground black pepper
30 ml/2 tbsp chopped fresh parsley

Whisk the ingredients together.

Italian-style Marinade

Use to marinate any poultry or game for at least 2 hours.

MAKES ABOUT 450 ML/¾ PT/2 CUPS

Finely grated rind and juice of 1 lemon
60 ml/4 tbsp balsamic vinegar
30 ml/2 tbsp red wine vinegar
200 ml/7 fl oz/scant 1 cup olive oil
2 garlic cloves, crushed
2 canned anchovies, mashed
10 ml/2 tsp capers, chopped
45 ml/3 tbsp chopped fresh basil
Freshly ground black pepper

Whisk the ingredients all together.

Tropical Marinade

Use to marinate any poultry or game for at least 2 hours.

MAKES ABOUT 450 ML/¾ PT/2 CUPS

120 ml/4 fl oz/1 cup mixed tropical fruit
  juice with no added sugar
2 garlic cloves, crushed
30 ml/2 tbsp white rum
60 ml/4 tbsp sunflower oil
30 ml/2 tbsp light brown sugar
Finely grated rind and juice of 1 lime
5 ml/1 tsp Tabasco sauce
5 ml/1 tsp ground cumin
5 ml/1 tsp dried oregano
15 ml/1 tbsp chopped fresh coriander
  (cilantro)
Salt and freshly ground black pepper

Whisk all the ingredients together.

Cranberry Marinade

Use to marinate turkey, duck and game for at least 2 hours.

MAKES ABOUT 450 ML/¾ PT/2 CUPS

350 g/12 oz jar of ready-made
  cranberry sauce
60 ml/4 tbsp red wine vinegar
45 ml/3 tbsp pure orange juice
1 onion, chopped
1 garlic clove, crushed
60 ml/4 tbsp sunflower oil
5 ml/1 tsp dried thyme
Salt and freshly ground black pepper

Whisk all the ingredients together.

Peking-style Marinade

Use to marinate any pork, poultry or game for at least 3 hours.

MAKES ABOUT 300 ML/½PT/1¼ CUPS

15 ml/1 tbsp hoisin sauce
90 ml/6 tbsp plum jam (conserve)
30 ml/2 tbsp soy sauce
2 garlic cloves, crushed
10 ml/2 tsp grated fresh root ginger
5 ml/1 tsp sesame oil
45 ml/3 tbsp sunflower oil
5 ml/1 tsp lemon juice
30 ml/2 tbsp dry sherry

Whisk all the ingredients together until smooth (or place in a blender or food processor).

Chilli Rub

Use for meat, fish or poultry.

SERVES 4–6

1 garlic clove, crushed
1 small onion, grated
5 ml/1 tsp chilli powder
1.5 ml/¼ tsp salt
1.5 ml/¼ tsp coarsely ground black
  pepper
Sunflower oil, for brushing

1 Mix the ingredients together and use
to rub all over the meat, fish or poultry.
2 Leave to stand for at least 2 hours
before cooking.
3 Brush with oil before grilling (broiling)
or roasting.

Rosemary and Garlic Rub

Use for lamb or poultry.

SERVES 4–6

2 garlic cloves, crushed
60 ml/4 tbsp finely chopped fresh
  rosemary
5 ml/1 tsp dry mustard powder
5 ml/1 tsp dried oregano
A pinch of cayenne
Salt and freshly ground black pepper
Olive oil, for brushing

1 Mix together the ingredients.
2 Rub all over the lamb or poultry and
leave to stand for at least 3 hours.
3 Brush with oil before grilling (broiling)
or roasting.

Cajun Rub

Use for any meat or poultry.

SERVES 4–6

2 garlic cloves, crushed
1 small onion, grated
45 ml/3 tbsp paprika
15 ml/1 tbsp cayenne
10 ml/2 tsp dried thyme
10 ml/2 tsp dried oregano
15 ml/1 tbsp light brown sugar
Salt and freshly ground black pepper
Sunflower oil, for brushing

1 Mix the ingredients together until well
blended.
2 Rub all over the meat or poultry and
leave to stand for at least 3 hours.
3 Brush with oil before grilling (broiling)
or roasting.

Totally Dry Onion Rub

*Use for any meat, fish, poultry or
game.*

SERVES 4–6

10 ml/2 tsp dried onion granules
5 ml/1 tsp garlic salt
5 ml/1 tsp celery salt
15 ml/1 tbsp coarsely ground black
  pepper
10 ml/2 tsp dried basil
5 ml/1 tsp paprika or pimenton
Sunflower oil, for brushing

1 Mix together the ingredients and rub
all over the meat, fish, poultry or game.
2 Leave to stand for at least 2 hours.
3 Brush with oil before grilling (broiling)
or roasting.

Desserts and Sweet Sauces

Puddings are many people's favourite foods but lots of novice cooks are a little nervous of trying to make their own. This section contains a whole range of really simple but delicious hot and cold puds for both everyday meals and special occasions. You will also find a selection of sauces for pouring over everything from fresh fruit and ice cream to hot, steamed puds. Heaven!

Traditional Apple Pie

If you want to try making your own shortcrust pastry (basic pie crust), see the recipe on page 391.

SERVES 6

350 g/12 oz ready-made shortcrust pastry, thawed if frozen
A little flour, for dusting
10 ml/2 tsp cornflour (cornstarch)
4 large cooking (tart) apples
45 ml/3 tbsp granulated sugar
2 whole cloves (optional)
A little milk, for glazing
Caster (superfine) sugar, for dusting
Cream or custard, to serve

1 Make the pastry (paste) first if you are using home-made. Preheat the oven to 200°C/400°F/gas mark 6.

2 Cut the dough in half. Dust a board or surface with a little flour and roll out one half to the size of a pie plate. Gently fold the pastry into three and lift over the plate. Unfold and press gently in place. Sprinkle with the cornflour (this will thicken the juices as the fruit cooks and stop the pastry base becoming soggy). Roll out the other half of the pastry in the same way and put aside.

3 Peel the apples, cut into quarters, cut out the cores and cut the apples into slices. Place in the centre of the pastry-lined plate, leaving a rim all round. Sprinkle with the granulated sugar and add the cloves, if liked.

4 Brush the edge of the pastry with water.

5 Fold the remaining rolled pastry as before and lift on top of the pie. Unfold and press the edges well together to seal. Trim the edge all round with a sharp knife, then press the edges to seal and decorate with the prongs of a fork. If the fork sticks to the pastry, dip it in flour first.

6 Make a hole in the centre to allow steam to escape. Make leaves or other shapes out of pastry trimmings and use to decorate the pie.

7 Brush with milk and sprinkle with a little caster sugar. Place on a baking (cookie) sheet. Bake in the oven for about 40 minutes until golden and cooked through. Sprinkle with a little more caster sugar and serve warm or cold with cream or custard.

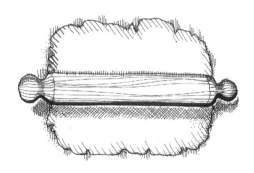

Cherry and Almond Pie

If you want to make your own pastry (paste), see the recipe for Sweet Shortcrust Pastry on page 391.

SERVES 6

275 g/10 oz ready-made sweet shortcrust pastry (basic pie crust), thawed if frozen

A little flour, for dusting

400 g/14 oz/1 large can of cherry pie filling

A little milk, for glazing

A little caster (superfine sugar), for dusting

30 ml/2 tbsp flaked (slivered) almonds

1 Preheat the oven to 200°C/400°F/ gas mark 6. If you are using home-made pastry, make it now. Cut the dough in half. Roll out one half on a floured surface to a round large enough to line a shallow 18 cm/7 in pie dish. Carefully slide the rolling pin under the pastry, then lift into the dish. Press gently into place all round.

2 Spoon in the cherry pie filling.

3 Roll out the remaining pastry in the same way and lift it into position. Press the edges together all round with your thumb to seal, then trim with a sharp knife. Make a small hole in the centre with a sharp knife to allow steam to escape.

4 Brush the surface with a little milk, sprinkle with caster sugar and the almonds. Bake in the oven for about 35 minutes until golden brown. Serve warm or cold.

Classic Syrup Tart

If you want to use your own shortcrust pastry (basic pie crust), make three-quarters of the quantity in the recipe on page 391.

SERVES 6

225 g/8 oz ready-made shortcrust pastry, thawed if frozen

50 g/2 oz/1 cup soft white breadcrumbs

90 ml/6 tbsp golden (light corn) syrup

Finely grated rind and juice of ½ small lemon

Cream or ice cream, to serve

1 Preheat the oven to 220°C/425°F/ gas mark 7. If using home-made pastry (paste), make it now.

2 Roll out the dough and use to line a 23 cm/9 in deep pie plate. Trim the edges.

3 Spread the breadcrumbs in the plate. Spoon the syrup over and sprinkle with the lemon rind and juice.

4 Press the prongs of a fork all round the edge of the pastry to decorate attractively. Roll out the pastry trimmings and cut into thin strips. Arrange in a lattice pattern over the top of the pie.

5 Bake for about 30 minutes until golden. Serve warm or cold with cream or ice cream.

Blackberry and Apple Pie

If you want to make your own pastry (paste), see the recipe for Sweet Shortcrust Pastry on page 391.

SERVES 6

275 g/10 oz ready-made sweet shortcrust pastry (basic pie crust), thawed if frozen

A little flour, for dusting

10 ml/2 tsp cornflour (cornstarch)

2 large cooking (tart) apples

225 g/8 oz fresh blackberries

45 ml/3 tbsp granulated sugar

A little milk, for glazing

Caster (superfine) sugar, for dusting

Cream or custard, to serve

1 Make the pastry now if using home-made. Preheat the oven to 200°C/400°F/gas mark 6.

2 Dust a board or the surface with a little flour. Cut the dough in half. Roll out one half to the size of a pie plate. Gently fold the pastry into three and lift over the plate. Unfold and press gently in place. Sprinkle with the cornflour (this will thicken the juices as the fruit cooks and stop the pastry base becoming soggy). Roll out the other half of the pastry in the same way and put aside.

3 Peel, quarter and core the apples, then cut into slices. Mix with the blackberries and place in the centre of the pastry-lined plate, leaving a rim all round. Sprinkle with the granulated sugar.

4 Brush the edge of the pastry with water.

5 Fold the remaining rolled pastry as before and lift on top of the pie. Unfold and press the edges well together to seal. Trim the edge with a sharp knife all round, then press the edges to seal and decorate with the prongs of a fork. If the fork sticks to the pastry, dip it in flour first.

6 Make a hole in the centre to allow steam to escape. Roll out the pastry trimmings and cut out a few 'leaves' or other shapes. Use to decorate the pie.

7 Brush the surface with milk and sprinkle with a little caster sugar. Place on a baking (cookie) sheet. Bake in the oven for 40 minutes until golden and cooked through. Sprinkle with a little more caster sugar and serve warm or cold with cream or custard.

Maple, Pecan and Apple Flan

If you want to make your own shortcrust pastry (basic pie crust), see the recipe on page 391. You wil need three-quarters of the quantity.

SERVES 6

225 g/8 oz ready-made shortcrust pastry, thawed if frozen
A little flour, for dusting
90 ml/6 tbsp maple syrup
2 large cooking (tart) apples
50 g/2 oz/½ cup pecan halves
15 g/½ oz/1 tbsp butter or margarine
Whipped cream, to serve

1 Preheat the oven to 200°C/400°F/ gas mark 6. Make the pastry (paste) if using home-made.

2 Roll out the dough on a lightly floured surface and use to line a 23 cm/9 in flan dish (pie pan). Trim the edges with a sharp knife.

3 Spoon half the syrup on to the pastry case (pie shell).

4 Peel, quarter and core the apples, then cut into slices. Arrange over the syrup.

5 Top with the pecan halves, arranged attractively. Spoon over the remaining syrup.

6 Cut the butter or margarine into small pieces and place all over the surface.

7 Bake in the oven for about 40 minutes until the apples are tender.

8 Serve warm or cold with whipped cream.

Sticky Toffee Banana Pudding

SERVES 4

50 g/2 oz/¼ cup butter or margarine
225 g/8 oz/1 cup light brown sugar
15 ml/1 tbsp lemon juice
4 thick slices of wholemeal bread, crusts removed and cubed
4 slightly unripe bananas, cut into chunks
Crème fraîche, to serve

1 Melt the butter or margarine in a large frying pan (skillet) over a moderate heat.

2 Add the sugar and lemon juice and stir until the sugar has melted. Turn down the heat to fairly low.

3 Stir the bread gently through the toffee mixture until evenly coated.

4 Add the bananas, stir gently, then cover and cook for about 4 minutes until the bananas are soft but still hold their shape.

5 Serve hot, or cool and then chill before serving with crème fraîche.

Sticky Toffee Plum Pudding

SERVES 4

Prepare as for Sticky Toffee Banana Pudding but use 450 g/1 lb plums, halved and stoned (pitted) instead of the bananas. Add a small handful of slivered (flaked) almonds to the mixture too, if liked.

Pear and Mincemeat Parcels

The number of parcels depends on the number of pear halves in the can, which tends to vary slightly!

MAKES ABOUT 6

About 6 sheets of filo pastry (paste), thawed if frozen

75 g/3 oz/⅓ cup butter or margarine, melted

410 g/14½ oz/1 large can of pear halves, drained, reserving the juice

450 g/1 lb/1 jar of mincemeat

1 Preheat the oven to 200°C/400°F/ gas mark 6. For each parcel, brush a filo pastry sheet with a little butter or margarine. Fold in half widthways and brush again.

2 Place a pear half in the centre and add a spoonful of mincemeat. Draw the pastry up over the fruit to form a parcel.

3 Transfer to a buttered baking (cookie) sheet. Brush with a little more butter or margarine. Repeat with the remaining pear halves.

4 Bake in the oven for about 15 minutes until golden brown. Serve hot or cold with a little of the reserved juice spooned over.

Peach Filo Tarts

SERVES 4

6 large sheets of filo pastry (paste), thawed if frozen

25 g/1 oz/2 tbsp butter or margarine

4 peaches, halved, stoned (pitted) and thinly sliced

30 ml/2 tbsp demerara sugar

2.5 ml/½ tsp ground cinnamon

1 Preheat the oven to 200°C/400°F/ gas mark 6.

2 Put one sheet of pastry on a work surface, brush with a little of the butter or margarine. Add another sheet of pastry on top. Continue to brush and layer the sheets.

3 Using a saucer as a guide, cut out four rounds from the stack of filo.

4 Transfer to a lightly greased baking (cookie) sheet and brush with any remaining butter or margarine.

5 Arrange the peach slices in a starburst pattern on the pastry rounds. Sprinkle with the sugar and cinnamon.

6 Bake in the oven for about 20 minutes until golden. Serve warm.

Photograph opposite: **Maple, Pecan and Apple Flan** (see page 351)

Creamy Rice Pudding

The exact time and temperature aren't vital – you can always leave rice pudding cooking for a little longer time, if necessary (but not shorter). If you are cooking a casserole at 160°C/325°F/gas mark 3, put this in the oven at the same time and cook for about 2½ hours.

SERVES 4

50 g/2 oz/¼ cup pudding rice
25 g/1 oz/2 tbsp caster (superfine)
   sugar
400 g/14 oz/1 large can of
   unsweetened condensed milk
A little grated nutmeg
A knob of butter or margarine

1 Preheat the oven to 180°C/350°F/ gas mark 4. Put the rice and sugar in a 1.2 litre/2 pt/5 cup ovenproof serving dish.

2 Stir in the can of milk, then fill the can with water and stir into the milk and rice until completely blended.

3 Dust the top with grated nutmeg. Cut the knob of butter or margarine into tiny pieces and scatter over the surface.

4 Bake in the oven for about 1½ hours until golden on top and the rice is tender and creamy.

Syrup Baked Apples

SERVES 4

4 even-sized cooking (tart) apples
60 ml/4 tbsp golden (light corn) syrup
Cream or custard, to serve

1 Preheat the oven to 180°C/350°F/ gas mark 4.

2 Cut the cores out of the apples but leave them whole. Using a sharp knife, cut a line around the middle of the apples, just cutting through the skin (this will help to prevent them bursting during cooking).

3 Place them in a baking tin (pan) and add about 5 mm/¼ in water to the tin.

4 Spoon the syrup into the centres. Bake in the oven for about 50 minutes to 1 hour until just tender. Transfer to warm dishes and spoon the juices over.

Fruit-stuffed Baked Apples

SERVES 4

Prepare as for Syrup Baked Apples, but fill the centres with mixed dried fruit (fruit cake mix) instead of syrup and sprinkle each apple with 5 ml/1 tsp demerara sugar.

Photograph opposite: **Peach and Ginger Upside-down Pudding (see page 361)**

Rhubarb Charlotte

SERVES 4–5

450 g/1 lb rhubarb, cut into short
   lengths
100 g/4 oz/½ cup demerara or light
   brown sugar
5 slices of bread
75 g/3 oz/⅓ cup butter or margarine,
   melted

1 Preheat the oven to 180°C/350°F/
gas mark 4. Mix the rhubarb with
three-quarters of the sugar.

2 Cut four of the slices of bread into
triangles and dip in the melted butter
or margarine.

3 Use to line a 1 litre/1¾ pt/4¼ cup
ovenproof dish.

4 Fill with the rhubarb and sugar. Dice
the remaining bread and stir into the
remaining butter. Scatter over the top
and sprinkle with the remaining sugar.

5 Cook in the oven for about
40 minutes until golden brown and
cooked through.

Apple Charlotte

SERVES 4

Prepare as for Rhubarb Charlotte but
use cooking (tart) apples, peeled, cored
and sliced, instead of the rhubarb. Add
a pinch of ground cloves or cinnamon
to the apple with the sugar.

Christmas Pudding

SERVES 6

100 g/4 oz/1 cup plain (all-purpose)
   flour
100 g/4 oz/2 cups fresh white
   breadcrumbs
A pinch of salt
5 ml/1 tsp mixed (apple-pie) spice
100 g/4 oz/1 cup shredded (chopped)
   suet
150 g/5 oz/⅔ cup dark brown sugar
500 g/18 oz/3 cups dried mixed fruit
   (fruit cake mix)
1 large egg, beaten
120 ml/4 fl oz/½ cup brown ale or stout
Butter, margarine or oil, for greasing

1 Mix everything except the egg and
ale in a large bowl, then stir the egg
and ale into the mixture. Cover with a
cloth and leave to stand for 24 hours.

2 Grease a 900 ml/1½ pt/3¾ cup
pudding basin and line the base with a
circle of non-stick baking parchment.

3 Stir the pudding again and turn into
the basin. Cover with a circle of
greaseproof (waxed paper), then an
old saucer, then a double thickness of
foil, twisting and folding it under the rim
of the basin to secure.

4 Place in a steamer over a pan of
boiling water or put on an old saucer
in the saucepan with enough boiling
water to come halfway up the sides of
the basin. Cover with a lid and steam
for 6 hours, topping up with boiling
water as necessary. Leave to cool.

5 Re-cover and store in a cool dark
place. Steam for a further 2½ hours
before serving.

Steamed Jam Pudding

Use any flavour of jam (conserve) you like.

SERVES 4-6

75 g/3 oz/⅓ cup butter or margarine,
  softened, plus extra for greasing
75 g/3 oz/⅓ cup caster (superfine)
  sugar
2 eggs
100 g/4 oz/1 cup self-raising (self-rising)
  flour
5 ml/1 tsp baking powder
15 ml/1 tbsp milk
2.5 ml/½ tsp vanilla essence (extract)
30–45 ml/2–3 tbsp jam
Jam Sauce (see page 385) and cream,
  to serve

1 Grease a 900 ml/1½ pt/3¾ cup
pudding basin.

2 Put all the remaining ingredients
except the jam in a bowl and stir
briskly with a wooden spoon or beat
with an electric beater until smooth
and fluffy.

3 Spoon the jam into the base of the
basin, then the cake mixture.

4 Cover with a double thickness of
well-greased foil, twisting and folding it
under the rim of the basin to seal well.

5 Place in a steamer over a pan of
boiling water or stand the basin on an
old saucer in the saucepan with
enough boiling water to come halfway
up the sides of the basin. Cover with a
lid and steam for 1½ hours, topping up
with boiling water as necessary.

6 Remove the foil, loosen the edge of
the pudding all round. Put a shallow
serving dish over the top. Hold firmly
with oven gloves and invert. Give a
good shake and remove the basin.
Serve hot with Jam Sauce and cream.

Steamed Chocolate Pudding

SERVES 4-6

Prepare as for Steamed Jam Pudding
but substitute 15 g/½ oz/2 tbsp of the
flour with cocoa (unsweetened
chocolate) powder and use chocolate
spread instead of jam (conserve) in the
base of the pudding. Serve with
Peppermint Custard (see page 384).

Steamed Syrup Pudding

SERVES 4-6

Prepare as for Steamed Jam Pudding
but omit the vanilla essence (extract)
and add the grated rind of half a
lemon in the sponge mixture. Use
golden (light corn) syrup instead of the
jam (conserve) and serve with Syrup
Sauce (see page 385) and custard.

Steamed Spiced Raisin Sponge

SERVES 4–6

75 g/3 oz/⅓ cup butter or margarine, softened, plus extra for greasing

75 g/3 oz/⅓ cup caster (superfine) sugar

2 eggs

100 g/4 oz/1 cup self-raising (self-rising) flour

5 ml/1 tsp baking powder

175 g/6 oz/1 cup raisins (preferably the large stoned variety)

5 ml/1 tsp mixed (apple-pie) spice

Cream or custard, to serve

1 Grease a 900 ml/1½ pt/3¾ cup pudding basin.

2 Put all the remaining ingredients in a bowl and stir briskly with a wooden spoon or beat with an electric beater until smooth and fluffy.

3 Spoon the cake mixture into the basin.

4 Cover with a double thickness of well-greased foil, twisting and folding it under the rim of the basin to seal well.

5 Place in a steamer over a pan of boiling water or stand the basin on an old saucer in the saucepan with enough boiling water to come halfway up the sides of the basin. Cover with a lid and steam for 1½ hours, topping up with boiling water as necessary.

6 Remove the foil, loosen the edge of the pudding all round. Put a shallow serving dish over the top. Hold firmly with oven gloves and invert. Give a good shake and remove the basin. Serve hot with cream or custard.

Rich Bread Pudding

This is also delicious served cold.

SERVES 6–8

100 g/4 oz bread, cubed

150 ml/¼ pt/⅔ cup milk

3 eggs

50 g/2 oz/¼ cup dark brown sugar

5 ml/1 tsp ground cinnamon

5 ml/1 tsp grated nutmeg

5 ml/1 tsp ground mace

175 g/6 oz/1 cup mixed dried fruit (fruit cake mix)

20 g/¾ oz/1½ tbsp butter or margarine, melted

Caster (superfine) sugar, for dusting

Cream or custard, to serve

1 Put the bread in a bowl.

2 Add the milk and leave to soak for 30 minutes. Stir briskly with a fork until well broken up.

3 Preheat the oven to 180°C/350°F/gas mark 4.

4 Lightly beat the eggs and mix in with the sugar, spices and fruit. Brush a 1.5 litre/2½ pt/6 cup ovenproof dish with some of the butter or margarine.

5 Turn the mixture into the dish and level the surface. Trickle the remaining butter or margarine over the surface.

6 Bake in the oven for about 1 hour or until golden brown and set.

7 Cool slightly, dust with caster sugar and serve cut into pieces with cream or custard.

Sussex Pond Pudding

There are many variations of this traditional recipe. This is my favourite.

SERVES 6

225 g/8 oz/2 cups self-raising (self-rising) flour

A pinch of salt

100 g/4 oz/1 cup shredded (chopped) vegetable suet

100 g/4 oz/⅔ cup currants

150 g/5 oz/⅔ cup light brown sugar

Grated rind and juice of 1 lemon

About 60 ml/4 tbsp cold water, to mix

100 g/4 oz/½ cup butter, softened plus a little for greasing

Single (light) cream, to serve

1 Sift the flour and salt into a bowl.

2 Add the suet, currants and 25 g/1 oz/ 2 tbsp of the sugar.

3 Mix with the lemon juice and add the measured water, a spoonful at a time, mixing until you have a soft but not sticky dough.

4 Grease a 900 ml/1½ pt/3¾ cup pudding basin with a little butter.

5 Squeeze the dough gently on a lightly floured surface to form a ball. Cut off a quarter and roll out to a round the size of the top of the basin to use as a 'lid'. Roll out the remaining dough and use to line the basin, pressing it gently but firmly against the sides.

6 Put the remaining sugar, the lemon rind and the butter in a separate bowl and stir briskly with a wooden spoon until smooth.

7 Place inside the dough in the basin, brush the edges of the dough with water and cover with the 'lid'. Press the edges well together to seal.

8 Cover with a double thickness of greased greaseproof (waxed) paper or foil, pleated in the middle to allow for rising. Twist and fold under the rim of the basin to secure.

9 Place in a steamer over a pan of boiling water or on an old saucer in the saucepan with enough water to come halfway up the sides of the basin. Cover with a lid and steam for 2½ hours, topping up with boiling water as necessary.

10 Remove the paper, loosen the edge all round with a knife. Put a shallow serving dish on top. Hold firmly (wear an oven glove as the steam will scald your hands), invert, give it a good shake, then remove the basin. Serve with cream.

Apple Crumble

SERVES 4

3 large cooking (tart) apples
75 g/3 oz/⅓ cup caster (superfine)
  sugar
30 ml/2 tbsp water
A good pinch of ground cloves
  (optional)
100 g/4 oz/1 cup plain (all-purpose)
  flour
50 g/2 oz/¼ cup butter or margarine,
  cut into small pieces

1 Preheat the oven to 190°C/375°F/
gas mark 5.
2 Peel and core the apples, then slice
and put in a 1.2 litre/2 pt/5 cup
ovenproof serving dish.
3 Sprinkle with 25 g/1 oz/2 tbsp of the
sugar and add the water. Sprinkle with
the cloves, if using.
4 Put the flour in a bowl. Add the
butter or margarine and, lifting a little
flour with the fat, rub it between your
thumbs and fingertips, letting it fall
back into the bowl. Repeat until the
mixture resembles breadcrumbs and all
the fat is rubbed in.
5 Stir in the remaining sugar. Spoon
over the apples and press down lightly.
6 Bake in the oven for about
45 minutes or until golden and the
apple is cooked through.

Apple and Raisin Crumble

SERVES 4

Prepare as for Apple Crumble, but add
45 ml/3 tbsp raisins to the apples and
use ground cinnamon instead of cloves.

Apple and Blackberry Crumble

SERVES 4

Prepare as for Apple Crumble but use
only two apples and add 225 g/8 oz
blackberries to the mixture. Omit the
ground cloves.

Rhubarb Crumble

SERVES 4

Prepare as for Apple Crumble but use
450 g/1 lb rhubarb, cut into short
lengths, instead of the apple. Add an
extra 15 g/½ oz/1 tbsp caster (superfine)
sugar to sweeten the rhubarb, and use
ground ginger instead of cloves.

Blueberry Almond Crumble

SERVES 4

350 g/12 oz blueberries

175 g/6 oz/¾ cup caster (superfine) sugar

10 ml/2 tsp lemon juice

75 g/3 oz/¾ cup ground almonds

75 g/3 oz/1½ cups plain cake crumbs

2.5 ml/½ tsp ground cinnamon

50 g/2 oz/¼ cup unsalted (sweet) butter, melted

30 ml/3 tbsp flaked (slivered) almonds

Crème fraîche, to serve

1 Preheat the oven to 180°C/350°F/ gas mark 4.

2 Place the blueberries in a shallow, ovenproof dish with 75 g/3 oz/⅓ cup of the sugar and the lemon juice.

3 Mix together the remaining sugar, the ground almonds, cake crumbs and cinnamon. Stir in the melted butter.

4 Sprinkle the crumble mixture over the blueberries and press down lightly. Bake in the oven for 20 minutes.

5 Sprinkle the flaked almonds over the top and bake for a further 15–20 minutes until golden brown on top. Serve hot with crème fraîche.

Fresh Apricot and Crunchy Almond Crumble

SERVES 4

700 g/1½ lb fresh apricots, halved and stoned (pitted)

15 g/½ oz/1 tbsp caster (superfine) sugar

45 ml/3 tbsp water

Finely grated rind of ½ lemon

75 g/3 oz/¾ cup plain (all-purpose) flour

50 g/2 oz/¼ cup butter or margarine, softened

25 g/1 oz/¼ cup chopped almonds

50 g/2 oz/¼ cup demerara sugar

1 Preheat the oven to 190°C/375°F/ gas mark 5.

2 Put the apricots in a 1.2 litre/2 pt/ 5 cup ovenproof dish.

3 Sprinkle with caster sugar, water and lemon rind.

4 Put the flour in a bowl and mash in the butter or margarine with a fork until crumbly.

5 Mix in the nuts and demerara sugar. Spoon over the apricots and press down gently.

6 Bake in the oven for about 35 minutes or until the fruit is tender and the top is golden brown.

Apple Strudel

SERVES 4–6

2 cooking (tart) apples
40 g/1½ oz/3 tbsp granulated sugar
2.5 ml/½ tsp ground cinnamon
45 ml/3 tbsp sultanas (golden raisins)
4 sheets of filo pastry (paste), thawed
  if frozen
25 g/1 oz/2 tbsp butter or margarine,
  melted
15 ml/1 tbsp icing (confectioners') sugar

1 Peel, core and thinly slice the apples
and mix with the sugar, cinnamon and
sultanas.
2 Lay a sheet of filo on a clean cloth or
piece of greaseproof (waxed) paper
and brush very lightly with butter or
margarine. Lay a second sheet on top
and brush again. Repeat with the
remaining two sheets, so you have a
stack of four.
3 Spoon the apple mixture along the
length of the pastry, just in from the edge.
4 Using the cloth or paper to help, roll
the pastry over the filling to form a
sausage shape.
5 Preheat the oven to 190°C/375°F/
gas mark 5.
6 Brush a baking (cookie) sheet with
some of the remaining butter or
margarine. Carefully lift the strudel and
place on the sheet in a horseshoe
shape.
7 Brush with any remaining butter or
margarine. Bake in the oven for about
20–25 minutes or until the pastry is
golden and the apple is cooked.
8 Put the icing sugar in a sieve
(strainer) and sprinkle it over the
surface. Serve warm.

Cherry Almond Strudel

SERVES 4–6

225 g/8 oz ripe cherries, stoned (pitted)
40 g/1½ oz/3 tbsp granulated sugar
50 g/2 oz/½ cup ground almonds
25 g/1 oz/¼ cup flaked (slivered)
  almonds
4 sheets of filo pastry (paste), thawed
  if frozen
25 g/1 oz/2 tbsp butter or margarine,
  melted
15 ml/1 tbsp icing (confectioners') sugar

Mix the cherries with the sugar and the
ground and flaked almonds, then
continue as for Apple Strudel, steps 2–8,
using the cherry filling instead of apples.

Pineapple Upside-down Pudding

Reserve any unused juice, if liked, to serve with the pudding.

SERVES 4–6

120 g/4½ oz/generous ½ cup butter or margarine

30 ml/2 tbsp light brown sugar

225 g/8 oz/1 small can of pineapple slices

4 glacé (candied) cherries, halved

A few angelica 'leaves', cut from a piece of angelica, or green jelly diamond cake decorations

100 g/4 oz/½ cup caster (superfine) sugar

100 g/4 oz/1 cup self-raising (self-rising) flour

5 ml/1 tsp baking powder

2 eggs

1 Preheat the oven to 190°C/375°F/ gas mark 5.

2 Grease the sides and base of a 20 cm/8 in flan dish (pie pan) with 15 g/½ oz/1 tbsp of the butter or margarine, spreading it thickly on the base.

3 Sprinkle with the brown sugar, then add 15 ml/1 tbsp of the juice from the can of pineapple.

4 Lay the pineapple slices in the base. Place the cherries, cut sides up, in the centres of the rings, adding the angelica or jelly diamonds to decorate.

5 Put the remaining butter or margarine, the caster sugar, flour, baking powder and eggs in a large bowl and beat until smooth with a wooden spoon or electric beater.

6 Spread over the pineapple.

7 Bake in the oven for about 20 minutes until the mixture is risen and golden and the centre springs back when lightly pressed. Cool slightly, loosen the edge, then turn out on to serving dish and serve warm or cold.

Pear and Walnut Chocolate Upside-down Pudding

SERVES 4–6

Prepare as for Pineapple Upside-down Pudding but use a 410 g/14½ oz/large can of pear halves instead of the pineapple, and a few walnut halves instead of the cherries and angelica. Substitute 15 g/½ oz/2 tbsp of the flour with cocoa (unsweetened chocolate) powder to make a chocolate sponge, then continue as before.

Peach and Ginger Upside-down Pudding

SERVES 4–6

Prepare as for Pineapple Upside-down Pudding but use a 410 g/14½ oz/large can of peach halves instead of the pineapple. Make the sponge with light brown sugar instead of caster (superfine) sugar and add 7.5 ml/1½ tsp ground ginger to the mixture.

Queen of Puddings

SERVES 4

75 g/3 oz/1½ cups fresh white
  breadcrumbs
600 ml/1 pt/2½ cups milk
15 g/½ oz/1 tbsp butter or margarine
75 g/3 oz/⅓ cup caster (superfine)
  sugar
2 eggs, separated
45 ml/3 tbsp raspberry jam (conserve)

1 Put the breadcrumbs in a 1.2 litre/
2 pt/5 cup ovenproof dish.
2 Put the milk in a saucepan with the
butter or margarine and bring to the
boil. Pour over the breadcrumbs and
stir well. Leave to soak for 15 minutes.
3 Preheat the oven to 180°C/350°F/
gas mark 4.
4 Using a fork, beat 25 g/1 oz/2 tbsp of
the sugar and the egg yolks into the
bread mixture.
5 Bake in the oven for about 45
minutes until the mixture is set and no
longer wet in the middle.
6 Whisk the egg whites until stiff in a
clean bowl with an electric or balloon
whisk. Whisk in the remaining sugar.
7 Spread the jam over the surface of
the set pudding. Pile the meringue on
top, spreading out to the edges. Return
to the oven for about 15 minutes until
the peaks of the meringue are turning
lightly golden. Serve hot.

Chocolate Queen of Puddings

SERVES 4

Prepare as for Queen of Puddings but
add 60 ml/4 tbsp drinking (sweetened)
chocolate powder to the breadcrumbs
before adding the milk, and spread the
top of the set pudding with 45 ml/
3 tbsp chocolate hazelnut spread
before adding the meringue.

Banana Queen of Puddings

SERVES 4

Prepare as for Queen of Puddings but
blend the hot milk with a ripe banana
before stirring into the breadcrumbs.
Spread the top of the pudding with
strawberry jam (conserve) instead of
raspberry and top with a second, sliced
banana before adding the meringue.

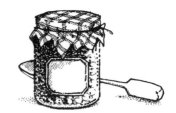

Swiss Baked Alaska

SERVES 4–6

1 small Swiss (jelly) roll, filled with raspberry jam (conserve)

3 egg whites

175 g/6 oz/¾ cup caster (superfine) sugar

8 scoops of vanilla or raspberry ripple ice cream

3 glacé (candied) cherries, halved

6 angelica 'leaves'

1 Preheat the oven to 230°C/450°F/ gas mark 8.

2 Slice the Swiss roll and place in a single layer on an ovenproof plate.

3 Put the egg whites in a large, clean bowl. Whisk until stiff with an electric or balloon whisk.

4 Add half the sugar and continue whisking until stiff and glossy. Gently stir in the remaining sugar, with a metal spoon, until just mixed.

5 Pile the ice cream up in the centre of the Swiss roll. Cover completely with the meringue and decorate with the cherries and angelica 'leaves'.

6 Bake immediately in the oven for 2 minutes until the meringue is turning pale golden. Serve immediately.

Bread and Butter Pudding

You'll get the best result if you leave the mixture to stand for 30 minutes before baking.

SERVES 4

4–6 thin slices of white bread

50 g/2 oz/¼ cup butter or margarine

60 ml/4 tbsp sultanas (golden raisins)

50 g/2 oz/¼ cup granulated sugar

600 ml/1 pt/2½ cups milk

2 eggs

A few drops of vanilla essence (extract)

1 Preheat the oven to 180°C/350°F/ gas mark 4.

2 Spread the bread with the butter or margarine. Cut each slice into four triangles.

3 Line a 1.2 litre/2 pt/5 cup ovenproof dish with half the bread. Sprinkle with half the sugar and half the fruit.

4 Top with the remaining bread triangles arranged attractively on top. Scatter the remaining fruit over.

5 Whisk the milk and eggs together with a few drops of vanilla essence in a bowl with a whisk or a fork. Pour over the bread and sprinkle with the remaining sugar.

6 Bake for about 1 hour until golden and set.

Jalousie

SERVES 6–8

225 g/8 oz puff pastry (paste), thawed if fozen

About 75 ml/5 tbsp jam (conserve), any flavour

A little milk, for glazing

15 ml/1 tbsp icing (confectioners') sugar

1 Preheat the oven to 220°C/425°F/ gas mark 7.

2 Cut the pastry in half and roll out each half to a rectangle about 20 x 25 cm/8 x 10 in.

3 Rinse a baking (cookie) sheet with water and leave it damp. Transfer one rectangle to this and spread with jam to within 2.5 cm/1 in of the edge all round. Brush all round the edges with milk.

4 Fold the second rectangle of pastry in half lengthways. Make a series of cuts into the pastry along the fold to within 2.5 cm/1 in of the open edges (like making a child's paper lantern).

5 Open out the rectangle and place over the jam, pressing the edges together all round.

6 Pinch the edges together all the way round to seal. Brush the surface with milk.

7 Bake in a preheated oven at 220°C/425°F/gas mark 7 for 15–20 minutes until golden and puffy.

8 Put the icing sugar in a sieve (strainer) – I use a tea strainer – and sprinkle it all over the surface. Serve warm.

Yuletide Jalousie

SERVES 6–8

Prepare as for Jalousie but substitute mincemeat for the jam (conserve). Serve with Brandy Sauce (see page 389).

Bread, Butter and Jam Pudding

SERVES 4

4–6 thin slices of white bread

50 g/2 oz/¼ cup butter or margarine

45 ml/3 tbsp raspberry jam (conserve)

50 g/2 oz/¼ cup granulated sugar

600 ml/1 pt/2½ cups milk

2 eggs

A few drops of almond essence (extract)

1 Preheat the oven to 180°C/350°F/ gas mark 4.

2 Spread the bread with the butter or margarine and jam. Cut each slice into four triangles.

3 Line a 1.2 litre/2 pt/5 cup ovenproof dish with half the bread. Sprinkle with half the sugar.

4 Arrange the remaining bread triangles attractively on top.

5 Beat the milk and eggs together with a few drops of almond essence. Pour over the bread and sprinkle with the remaining sugar.

6 Bake in the oven for about 1 hour until golden and set.

Doughnut Bites

*This is a great way of using a loaf
that has been reduced in price
because it is near its sell-by date!*

SERVES 4–6

1 small white unsliced loaf
300 ml/½ pt/1¼ cups apple juice
2 eggs, beaten
Oil, for deep-frying
60 ml/4 tbsp caster (superfine) sugar
2.5 ml/½ tsp ground cinnamon
Jam Sauce (see page 385), to serve

1 Cut the crusts off the loaf, then cut it
into large cubes.
2 Dip first in apple juice, then in beaten
egg to coat completely.
3 Heat the oil in a large saucepan or
deep-fat fryer to 190°C/375°F or until a
piece of the crust from the loaf browns
in 30 seconds. Deep-fry the bread
cubes for about 3 minutes until crisp
and golden brown, turning occasionally
if necessary. Drain on kitchen paper
(paper towels).
4 Mix the sugar and cinnamon
together in a bowl. Add the bread
cubes and turn them over in the
mixture to coat. Pile on to plates and
trickle the sauce over. Serve straight
away.

Crêpes Suzette

SERVES 4

1 quantity of Simple Pancakes (see
    page 392)
25 g/1 oz/2 tbsp butter or margarine
45 ml/3 tbsp light brown sugar
Grated rind and juice of 1 large orange
Grated rind and juice of ½ lemon
45 ml/3 tbsp brandy or orange liqueur

1 Make the pancakes.
2 Melt the butter or margarine in the
frying pan (skillet) and add the sugar.
Stir until the sugar dissolves.
3 Stir in the fruit rinds and juices.
Simmer for 3–4 minutes, stirring, until
the caramel dissolves and a smooth
sauce is formed.
4 Fold the pancakes in quarters and
add to the pan one at a time, bathing
in the sauce and pushing to one side
before adding the next.
5 Pour over the brandy or liqueur.
Ignite and shake the pan gently until
the flames subside. Serve straight away.

Norwegian Cream

SERVES 6

6 eggs, separated
100 g/4 oz/½ cup caster (superfine) sugar
15 ml/1 tbsp powdered gelatine
20 ml/4 tsp orange juice
30 ml/2 tbsp raspberry jam (conserve)
150 ml/¼ pt/⅔ cup whipping cream, whipped
Grated chocolate or a crumbled chocolate Flake, to decorate

1 Put the egg whites in a large, clean bowl. Whisk with an electric or balloon whisk until stiff. Add the sugar and whisk again until standing in peaks.
2 Whisk the yolks in a separate bowl and stir gently into the meringue with a metal spoon using a figure-of-eight movement.
3 Mix the gelatine into the orange juice in a small bowl. Stand the bowl over a pan of hot water, stirring until the gelatine has dissolved completely or heat briefly in the microwave. Stir gently into the egg mixture.
4 Spoon into an 18 cm/7 in soufflé dish and chill until set.
5 When set, spread the top with jam, then whipped cream and cover with grated chocolate or crumbled Flake.

Fresh Orange Jelly

SERVES 4

Finely grated rind and juice of 1 orange
15 ml/1 tbsp powdered gelatine
About 450 ml/¾ pt/2 cups pure orange juice

1 Put the orange rind and juice in a measuring jug and sprinkle the gelatine over. Leave to soften for 5 minutes.
2 Stand the jug in a pan of hot water and stir until the gelatine has dissolved completely or heat briefly in the microwave.
3 Make up to 600 ml/1 pt/2½ cups with pure orange juice.
4 Pour into a 600 ml/1 pt/2½ cup jelly (jello) mould. Chill until set.
5 To turn out the jelly, dip the mould briefly in hot water, then put a plate over the top. Hold firmly, invert, give the jelly a good shake, then lift off the mould.

Fresh Lemon Jelly

SERVES 4

Prepare as for Fresh Orange Jelly but use the finely grated rind and juice of two lemons and make up with pure pineapple juice instead of orange juice.

Pears in Spiced Red Wine

SERVES 4

15 ml/1 tbsp light brown sugar
5 ml/1 tsp lemon juice
5 cm/2 in piece of cinnamon stick
300 ml/½ pt/1¼ cups red wine
4 pears, peeled

1 Preheat the oven to 160°C/325°F/
gas mark 3.
2 Put the sugar, lemon juice, cinnamon
and wine in a saucepan and heat until
the sugar dissolves, stirring occasionally.
3 Cut a thin slice off the bottom of
each pear so it will stand upright and
gently cut out the cores with a sharp,
pointed knife.
4 Lay the pears in an ovenproof dish
and pour over the wine. Cover with foil
and bake in the oven for 30 minutes,
turning once. Remove the cinnamon
stick and stand the pears on end. Serve
hot with the wine spooned over or
cool, then chill.

Peaches in Spiced White Wine

SERVES 4

Prepare as for Pears in Spiced Red
Wine but use peaches instead of pears.
Either leave them whole or cut into
halves and remove the stones (pits).
Flavour with two whole cloves instead
of the cinnamon and use a fruity white
wine instead of red.

Tropical Compôte

SERVES 6

100 g/4 oz/½ cup granulated sugar
150 ml/¼ pt/⅔ cup water
2 pomegranates
1 passion fruit
2 oranges
1 mango
2 kiwi fruit
1 small pineapple

1 Put the sugar and water in a
saucepan and heat gently, stirring, until
the sugar has dissolved. Bring to the
boil and boil for 3 minutes.
2 Meanwhile, halve the pomegranates
and passion fruit and squeeze as you
would a lemon, then strain the juice
through a sieve (strainer) into the
syrup.
3 Hold the oranges over the saucepan
to catch the juice and cut off all the
rind and pith, then slice and halve the
slices. Add to the syrup.
4 Peel the mango and cut all the flesh
off the stone (pit) in long strips. Halve if
very big and add to the syrup.
5 Peel and slice the kiwi fruit and add
to the syrup. Cut all the skin off the
pineapple, slice the fruit, then cut into
chunks, discarding any thick, central
core. Add to the syrup.
6 Mix all together and leave until cold.
Transfer to a glass serving dish and chill
for at least 2 hours to allow the
flavours to develop.

Fresh Fruit Salad

Make the fruit salad at least 1 hour in advance so that the flavours have time to develop. Allow about 3 good tablespoonfuls of prepared fruit per person and leave on any edible peel (such as on apples, peaches, nectarines or plums) for colour and texture.

SERVES 4–6

300 g/11 oz/1 medium can of mandarin oranges in natural juice

150 ml/¼ pt/⅔ cup pure apple or orange juice

5 ml/1 tsp lemon juice

A selection of fresh fruits, chopped, sliced or left whole as necessary, discarding any stones (pits)

1 Put the mandarins and juice in a glass bowl. Stir in the fruit juices.

2 Add the prepared fruits (but if adding juicy berries such as raspberries or blueberries, add at the last moment so the colour does not run too much).

3 Chill until ready to serve.

Fruit Platter

You can prepare all the fruits and the sauce in advance, and then assemble everything at the last moment.

SERVES 4–6

1 papaya

1 star fruit

2 kiwi fruit

6 large strawberries

1 small pineapple

1 quantity of Fresh Raspberry Sauce (see page 386)

1 Cut the papaya in half and scoop out the seeds. Peel off the skin, then cut the flesh into slices.

2 Cut the star fruit into thin slices.

3 Peel the kiwi fruit and cut into slices.

4 Slice the strawberries, removing the green calyxes.

5 Cut off the top and base of the pineapple, then stand the pineapple up and cut off all the skin in strips from the top to the base. Cut the fruit into slices and cut out the thick, central core.

6 Make the sauce and spoon a pool over the base of each of four plates. Arrange the fruits attractively on top and serve.

Pineapple Flambé

SERVES 4

1 ripe pineapple

50 g/2 oz/¼ cup butter or margarine

45 ml/3 tbsp kirsch

30 ml/2 tbsp caster (superfine) sugar

45 ml/3 tbsp brandy

Whipped cream, to serve

1 Cut the top and bottom off the pineapple, then cut off all the rind in strips from the top to the base all round. Cut the fruit into eight thin slices and cut out the hard central core of each slice.

2 Melt the butter or margarine in a large frying pan (skillet).

3 Add the fruit and sprinkle with the kirsch and sugar. Cook for 2 minutes, then turn over.

4 Add the brandy, ignite and shake the pan until the flames subside.

5 Serve straight away from the pan with whipped cream.

Banana Flambé

SERVES 4

Prepare as for Pineapple Flambé but use four large bananas. Cut each one in half widthways and then split each half lengthways. Use orange juice instead of the kirsch and rum instead of the brandy, if you prefer.

Lemon Sorbet

If the sugar starts to colour, take it off the heat immediately and plunge the base of the pan in cold water to stop it cooking any further.

SERVES 6–8

600 ml/1 pt/2½ cups water
225 g/8 oz/1 cup granulated sugar
Thinly pared rind and juice of 2 large
    lemons
About 400 ml/14 fl oz/1¾ cups bottled
    lemon juice
2 egg whites

1 Put the water and sugar in a saucepan. Heat over a fairly low heat, stirring, until the sugar has dissolved.
2 Bring to the boil over a high heat and boil for 10 minutes until thick but not coloured. Remove from the heat, add the lemon rind and leave until cold.
3 Make the freshly squeezed lemon juice up to 450 ml/¾ pt/2 cups with bottled lemon juice. Stir into the syrup.
4 Pour through a sieve (strainer) into a freezer-proof container and freeze for about 1½ hours until frozen round the edges. Whisk with a fork to break up the ice crystals.

5 Put the egg whites in a large, clean bowl. Whisk until stiff with an electric or wire whisk and stir into the lemon mixture gently with a metal spoon until just mixed.
6 Return to the freezer and freeze until firm.

Orange Sorbet

SERVES 8

Prepare as for Lemon Sorbet but use the thinly pared rind and juice of two oranges instead of lemons, pure orange juice instead of bottled lemon juice and sharpen to taste with lemon juice if liked.

Mango Fool

SERVES 4

1 ripe mango
45 ml/3 tbsp lemon juice
15 ml/1 tbsp caster (superfine) sugar
425 g/15 oz/1 large can of custard
150 ml/¼ pt/⅔ cup double (heavy)
    cream, whipped
A few angelica 'leaves' or green jelly
    diamond cake decorations

1 Peel the mango and cut all the flesh off the stone (pit).
2 Purée in a blender or processor with the lemon juice and sugar.
3 Gently stir in the custard and half the whipped cream.
4 Spoon into four wine goblets. Decorate each with a swirl of the remaining cream and an angelica 'leaf' or jelly diamond. Eat within 2 hours.

Vanilla Ice Cream

SERVES 6

30 ml/2 tbsp custard powder
100 g/4 oz/½ cup caster (superfine)
  sugar
300 ml/½ pt/1¼ cups milk
5 ml/1 tsp vanilla essence (extract)
1 egg, separated
250 ml/8 fl oz/1 cup double (heavy) or
  whipping cream, chilled

1 Using a wire whisk, mix the custard powder with the sugar and 30 ml/ 2 tbsp of the milk in a saucepan. Stir in the remaining milk.

2 Bring to the boil over a high heat, stirring all the time, and then cook for 2 minutes, still stirring, until thick and smooth. Whisk in the egg yolk and the vanilla essence.

3 Remove from the heat, cover with a circle of wet greaseproof (waxed) paper (to stop a skin from forming) and leave to cool.

4 Whip the cream in a bowl with an electric or balloon whisk until thick and standing in soft peaks. Stir gently into the custard and spoon into a freezer-proof container. Cover and freeze for 2 hours until frozen around the edges.

5 Whisk with a fork to break up all the ice crystals.

6 Whisk the egg white until stiff in a bowl with an electric or balloon whisk and stir gently into the mixture with a metal spoon. Return to the container and freeze until firm. Remove from the freezer 10 minutes before serving to soften slightly.

Chocolate Ice Cream

SERVES 6

Prepare as for Vanilla Ice Cream but blend 20 ml/4 tsp cocoa (unsweetened chocolate) powder with 30 ml/2 tbsp boiling water and whisk into the milk before blending into the custard powder mixture.

Coffee Ice Cream

SERVES 6

Prepare as for Vanilla Ice Cream but add 15 ml/1 tbsp of coffee granules to the milk.

Fruit Ice Cream

SERVES 6

Prepare as for Vanilla Ice Cream but add one quantity of any fruit purée (see page 377) to the partially frozen ice cream when whisking until smooth, before stirring in the egg white.

Raspberry Ripple Ice Cream

SERVES 6

Prepare as for Vanilla Ice Cream but after breaking up the ice crystals (step 5), stir in the egg white gently, then stir in one quantity of Fresh Raspberry Sauce (see page 386) just until rippled with colour. Don't over-mix. Freeze until firm.

Vanilla Yoghurt Ice

SERVES 6–8

4 eggs, separated

175 g/6 oz/¾ cup caster (superfine) sugar

300 ml/½ pt/1¼ cups thick vanilla yoghurt

300 ml/½ pt/1¼ cups crème fraîche

2.5 ml/½ tsp vanilla essence (extract)

1 Whisk the egg yolks and sugar together until thick and pale with an electric or balloon whisk.

2 Stir in the yoghurt, crème fraîche and vanilla essence gently.

3 Spoon into a freezer-proof container and freeze for 2 hours.

4 Stir well with a fork to break up the ice crystals.

5 Put the egg whites in a large, clean bowl. Whisk with an electric or balloon whisk until stiff, then stir gently into the yoghurt mixture.

6 Return to the freezer container and freeze until firm.

Strawberry Sparkle

SERVES 4

225 g/8 oz strawberries, hulled and sliced

20 ml/4 tsp caster (superfine) sugar

½ lime

½ bottle sparkling rosé wine, chilled

1 Divide the strawberries between four champagne cups.

2 Sprinkle with the sugar and add a squeeze of lime juice to each.

3 Chill for at least 30 minutes.

4 When ready to serve, top up with the sparkling wine and serve at once.

Honeyed Nectarine Bubble

SERVES 4

4 ripe nectarines

20 ml/4 tsp clear honey

½ bottle sparkling dry white wine

Amaretti biscuits, to serve

1 Halve the nectarines, remove the stones (pits) and cut the fruit into slices.

2 Put the fruit in four wine glasses and trickle a teaspoonful of honey over each.

3 When ready to serve, pour over the sparkling wine and serve with amaretti biscuits.

Melon Glacé

Trickle Fresh Raspberry Sauce (see page 386) instead of ginger wine over the ice cream, if liked. Use bought ice cream if you prefer.

SERVES 4

2 small round melons

4 scoops of Vanilla Ice Cream (see page 370)

30 ml/2 tbsp ginger wine

1 Cut each melon in half, scoop out the seeds and place the melon halves in four serving dishes.

2 Add a scoop of ice cream to the cavity in each and spoon the ginger wine over. Serve straight away.

Italian-style Cassata

SERVES 6

1 litre/1¾ pts/4¼ cups soft-scoop vanilla
ice cream

200 g/7 oz/1 small jar of Maraschino
cherries, drained and roughly
chopped, reserving one half cherry
for decoration

50 g/2 oz/½ cup chocolate chips

25 g/1 oz angelica, chopped, reserving
a small piece as a 'leaf' for
decoration

1 Put the ice cream in a bowl.
2 Working quickly, mash in the cherries,
chocolate chips and angelica until just
blended. Don't over-mix or the ice
cream will melt.
3 Pack into a 1 litre/1¾ pt/4¼ cup
pudding basin, cover with foil and
freeze until firm.
4 To serve, loosen the edge with a knife
warmed in hot water. Put a plate over
the bowl. Hold firmly, invert, give it a
good shake and remove the bowl.
5 Put the half cherry on top with the
angelica 'leaf'. Serve straight away, cut
into slices.

Gooseberry Fool

*Try this with other fruits like rhubarb,
apples or greengages.*

SERVES 4

450 g/1 lb gooseberries, topped and
tailed

45 ml/3 tbsp water

100 g/4 oz/½ cup granulated sugar

300 ml/½ pt/1¼ cups double (heavy)
cream

1 Put the gooseberries in a saucepan
with the water and sugar.
2 Heat gently, stirring until the sugar
has all dissolved, then turn up the heat
and bring to the boil. Turn down the
heat to fairly low, cover and cook
gently until the gooseberries are very
soft.
3 Purée in a blender or food processor.
Leave until cold.
4 Whip the cream until standing in
peaks, using an electric or balloon
whisk. Stir gently into the puréed
gooseberries.
5 Spoon into glasses and chill for
1–2 hours before serving.

Less Rich Fruit Fool

SERVES 4

Prepare the fruit purée as for
Gooseberry Fool but mix it gently with
a 400 g/14 oz/large can of custard
instead of the whipped cream. It looks
pretty if you fold it in only briefly, to
leave a marbled effect. Spoon into
glasses and chill.

Creamy Apricot Fool

SERVES 4

410 g/14½ oz/1 large can of apricot
  halves, drained
150 ml/¼ pt/⅔ cup double (heavy)
  cream
15 ml/1 tbsp caster (superfine) sugar
Finely grated rind of ½ orange
Toasted flaked (slivered) almonds, to
  decorate

1 Purée the apricots in a blender or
food processor.
2 In a bowl, whip the cream with the
sugar until standing in peaks, using an
electric or balloon whisk.
3 Stir it gently into the apricot purée
with the orange rind.
4 Spoon into four glass dishes and serve
decorated with a few toasted almonds.

Greek Figs

*This is also delicious with drained,
canned figs instead of fresh ones.*

SERVES 4

4 fresh figs, trimmed and cut into bite-
  sized pieces
30 ml/2 tbsp brandy (preferably Greek
  or Spanish) or orange juice
450 ml/¾ pt/2 cups Greek-style
  yoghurt with honey
4 small sprigs of mint

1 Put the figs in the base of four glass
dishes and spoon the brandy or orange
juice over.
2 Spoon the yoghurt on top and
decorate each with a small sprig of
mint. Chill, if time allows, before serving.

Anytime Blackcurrant Mousse

*Try this with other canned fruits with
matching or contrasting jellies.*

SERVES 4

1 packet of blackcurrant-flavoured
  jelly (jello)
300 g/11 oz/1 medum can of
  blackcurrants
170 g/6 oz/1 small can of unsweetened
  condensed milk, chilled
170 g/6 oz/1 small of can cream

1 Dissolve the tablet of jelly in 150 ml/
¼ pt/⅔ cup boiling water in a large
measuring jug.
2 Stir in the juice from the can of
blackcurrants and chill until on the
point of setting.
3 Meanwhile, whisk the chilled milk
until thick and fluffy.
4 When the jelly is the consistency of
egg white, whisk it into the fluffy milk.
5 Spoon it into four glasses and chill
until set.
6 Spread the cream over and top with
the blackcurrants.

Baked Pear Brûlée

SERVES 4

425 g/15 oz/1 large can of pear
  quarters, drained, reserving the
  juice
10 ml/2 tsp cornflour (cornstarch)
5 ml/1 tsp lemon juice
150 ml/¼ pt/⅔ cup plain yoghurt
1 large egg
2.5 ml/½ tsp ground cinnamon
45 ml/3 tbsp light brown sugar

1 Preheat the oven to 180°C/350°F/
gas mark 4.

2 Put the pear quarters in a 900 ml/
1½ pt/3¾ cup ovenproof dish.

3 Using a wire whisk, mix the cornflour
with a little of the reserved juice in a
saucepan. Stir in the remaining pear
juice and the lemon juice. Bring to the
boil, stirring until thickened and clear.
Allow to bubble for 1 minute. Pour over
the pears.

4 Use the same whisk to blend the
yoghurt with the egg and cinnamon.
Pour over the pears.

5 Bake in the oven for about
20 minutes until the custard is set.

6 Preheat the grill (broiler). Sprinkle the
top of the pudding liberally with the
sugar and place under the grill until the
sugar melts and bubbles. Serve hot.

Crème Brûlée

SERVES 4

4 egg yolks
5 ml/1 tsp cornflour (cornstarch)
500 ml/17 fl oz/2¼ cups single (light)
  cream
2.5 ml/½ tsp vanilla essence (extract)
30 ml/2 tbsp icing (confectioners')
  sugar
About 100 g/4 oz/½ cup caster
  (superfine) sugar

1 Whisk the egg yolks, cornflour, cream
and vanilla essence together with the
icing sugar.

2 Place the bowl over a pan of hot
water and continue whisking until the
mixture thickens slightly. To test if it's
ready, dip in a wooden spoon and lift
out of the mixture, rounded side up.
The mixture should coat it so that
when you draw your finger through it,
it leaves a trail.

3 Pour into four individual flameproof
dishes (or one large one) and leave to
cool, then chill until set.

4 Preheat the grill (broiler). Cover the
pudding with a thick layer of caster
sugar and place under the hot grill until
the sugar melts and caramelises. Chill
again before serving.

Zabaglione

SERVES 4

2 eggs
25 g/1 oz/2 tbsp caster (superfine)
sugar
45 ml/3 tbsp Marsala, medium-dry or
sweet sherry
Sponge (lady) fingers, to serve

1 Heat a saucepan of water until boiling, then turn down the heat until bubbles are rising round the edges.
2 Put the eggs, sugar and Marsala or sherry in a bowl and stand it over the pan. Whisk with an electric or balloon whisk until thick and voluminous. (This may take up to 20 minutes by hand.)
3 Spoon into wine goblets. Serve straight away with sponge fingers.

Peach Zabaglione

Substitute kirsch or orange liqueur for the Archers liqueur, if you prefer.

SERVES 4

4 ripe peaches, halved, stoned (pitted)
and cut into small dice
2 eggs
25 g/1 oz/2 tbsp caster (superfine)
sugar
45 ml/3 tbsp Archers or other peach
liqueur

1 Put the fruit into four sundae glasses.
2 Bring a large pan of water to the boil, then turn down the heat until small bubbles are rising round the edges.
3 Put the eggs, sugar and peach liqueur in a bowl and stand it over the pan of water. Whisk with an electric beater or balloon whisk until thick, creamy and voluminous.

4 Spoon on top of the peaches. Serve while still warm.

Flora's Flummery

SERVES 4

15 ml/1 tbsp medium oatmeal
150 ml/¼ pt/⅔ cup double (heavy)
cream
150 ml/¼ pt/⅔ cup crème fraîche
45 ml/3 tbsp clear honey
45 ml/3 tbsp whisky
15 ml/1 tbsp lemon juice

1 Put the oatmeal in a frying pan (skillet). Cook over a moderate heat, stirring until it turns golden brown, then immediately tip it out of the pan.
2 Put the two creams in a bowl and whisk with an electric beater or balloon whisk until softly peaking but not stiff.
3 Put the honey, whisky and lemon in a saucepan and heat gently until little bubbles rise to the surface but the mixture is not boiling.
4 Pour in a trickle into the cream, whisking all the time until all the honey mixture is blended in.
5 Spoon into wine goblets and sprinkle with the toasted oatmeal. Serve straight away.

Strawberry Meringue Surprise

Make the chocolate shavings by paring them off a bar of chocolate with a potato peeler.

SERVES 4

4 meringue nests
60 ml/4 tbsp chocolate hazelnut
  spread
15 ml/1 tbsp brandy or orange juice
150 ml/¼ pt/⅔ cup double (heavy) or
  whipping cream
45 ml/3 tbsp icing (confectioners')
  sugar
175 g/6 oz small strawberries
Shavings of plain (semi-sweet)
  chocolate, to decorate

1 Put the nests on a board. Mix the chocolate spread with the brandy or orange juice in a small bowl.
2 Spread the chocolate mixture in the centre of the nests.
3 Pour the cream into a bowl and add half the icing sugar. Whip with an electric or wire whisk until standing in peaks.
4 Save four of the best strawberries for decoration. Slice the remainder, discarding the green calyxes. Add to the cream and stir in gently with a metal spoon.
5 Put a meringue nest on each of four plates. Pile the cream and strawberries on top. Put a reserved strawberry on the top of each.
6 Sprinkle a few chocolate shavings over each nest and serve.

Brandied Chocolate Cups

This is a complete cheat but looks so impressive that everyone will think you've slaved away for ages!

SERVES 6

150 ml/¼ pt/⅔ cup whipping cream
30 ml/2 tbsp chocolate hazelnut
  spread
15 ml/1 tbsp brandy
6 ready-made chocolate cases
6 toasted hazelnuts (filberts), to
  decorate
2–3 kiwi fruit, peeled and sliced

1 Put the cream in a bowl and whip with an electric or balloon whisk until standing in soft peaks.
2 Add the chocolate spread and brandy and whip gently again until blended.
3 Spoon into the chocolate cases and top each with a hazelnut. Chill until firm.
4 To serve, put a chocolate case on each of six plates and lay two or three slices of kiwi fruit to one side of each case.

Fruit Purée

You can, of course, make a larger quantity if you prefer – it can be frozen for later use. It is a good way of preserving soft fruits when you've gone mad at a pick-your-own farm or have a glut in the garden.

SERVES 4

225 g/8 oz any fresh soft fruit (raspberries, strawberries, blackcurrants, etc.)

15 ml/1 tbsp water

15 ml/1 tbsp sugar, plus extra to taste

Ice cream, yoghurt or custard, to serve

1 Rinse the fruit. Remove any stalks. Slice strawberries.

2 Place in a saucepan with the water. Add the sugar and heat gently until the juice runs.

3 Cover with a lid and cook over the gentlest heat until the fruit is pulpy.

4 Purée in a blender or food processor, then tip into a sieve (strainer) over a bowl and stir, pressing the fruit against the sides until the pulp passes through, leaving any pips behind. (If you don't have a blender or processor, you can just rub the mixture through the sieve, but it's harder work!)

5 Taste and stir in more sugar, a little at a time, until it is as sweet as you like. Serve with ice cream, yoghurt or custard.

Banana Condé

SERVES 4

50 g/2 oz/¼ cup round-grain (pudding) rice

30 ml/2 tbsp custard powder

600 ml/1 pt/2½ cups milk

30 ml/2 tbsp caster (superfine) sugar

4 small ripe bananas

30 ml/2 tbsp apricot jam (conserve)

10 ml/2 tsp lemon juice

2 glacé (candied) cherries

1 Put the rice in a pan and cover with water. Bring to the boil, stirring, reduce the heat until gently bubbling round the edges and cook for 15–20 minutes until tender, stirring occasionally. Drain in a colander.

2 Mix the custard powder with a little of the milk in a saucepan with the sugar.

3 Stir in the remaining milk and add the rice. Bring to the boil over a high heat and cook for 2 minutes, stirring all the time, until thickened and smooth. Remove from the heat. Cover with a circle of wet greaseproof (waxed) paper, to prevent a skin forming, and leave to cool.

4 When cold, spoon half the rice mixture into four sundae glasses. Slice the bananas and put half on top of the rice. Top with the remaining rice and bananas.

5 Heat the jam and lemon juice together and brush over the surface of the bananas. Top each with half a glacé cherry and serve.

Chocolate Ginger Cake Mousse

SERVES 6

175 g/6 oz/1½ cups plain (semi-sweet) chocolate

3 eggs, separated

150 ml/¼ pt/⅔ cup double (heavy) cream

75 g/3 oz/⅓ cup light brown sugar

2 thick slices of ginger cake, crumbled

30 ml/2 tbsp orange juice

1 Break up half the chocolate into pieces and place in a bowl.

2 Put half a pan of water over a high heat until gently bubbling. Stand the bowl of chocolate over the pan and stir until melted. Alternatively, put in the microwave and heat on High for 1–2 minutes until melted. Stir well.

3 Meanwhile, put the egg whites in a clean bowl and whisk with an electric or balloon whisk until stiff. Using the same beater, whip the cream until softly peaking, then whisk the egg yolks with the sugar until thick and pale.

4 Stir the chocolate into the eggs and sugar, then the cake and orange juice. Lightly stir in the cream, followed by the egg whites using a figure-of-eight movement.

5 Spoon the mixture into six individual dishes. Grate the remaining chocolate and sprinkle over the surfaces. Chill before serving.

Banoffee Brûlée

SERVES 4

4 bananas

450 ml/¾ pt/2 cups toffee yoghurt

100 g/4 oz/½ cup light brown sugar

1 Preheat the grill (boiler).

2 Slice the bananas and place in four individual flameproof dishes.

3 Spoon the yoghurt over.

4 Sprinkle liberally with the sugar to cover the tops completely.

5 Remove the grill rack and place the dishes in the pan. Grill (broil) until the sugar melts and bubbles.

6 Serve straight away or leave to cool, then chill before serving.

Sherry Trifle

SERVES 4

4 trifle sponges

300 g/11 oz/1 small can of strawberries

30 ml/2 tbsp medium-dry sherry

425 g/15 oz/1 large can of custard

300 ml/½ pt/1¼ cups whipping cream, whipped until softly peaking

15 ml/1 tbsp toasted flaked (slivered) almonds

1 Crumble the sponges into the base of a glass serving dish.

2 Empty the can of strawberries over and gently mash into the sponges.

3 Sprinkle the sherry over, then cover with the custard. Gently spread the cream over.

4 Sprinkle the surface with toasted almonds and chill until ready to serve.

Chocolate Éclairs

Choux pastry (paste) really isn't complicated. The only bit of effort is beating in the eggs. The mixture goes slippery before they blend in, which is why you should only add a little egg at a time.

MAKES 9

1 quantity of Choux Pastry (see page 392)

A little oil, for greasing

150 ml/¼ pt/⅔ cup double (heavy) cream

10 ml/2 tsp caster superfine) sugar

15 ml/1 tbsp cocoa (unsweetened chocolate) powder

100 g/4 oz/⅔ cup icing (confectioners') sugar

20 ml/4 tsp water

1 Make the choux pastry. Preheat the oven to 220°C/425°F/gas mark 7.

2. Spoon nine short sausage shapes on to a greased baking (cookie) sheet. Use lightly oiled fingers if necessary, to mould the pastry into shape.

3 Cook in the oven for 15 minutes, then reduce the heat to 180°C/350°F/gas mark 4 and cook for a further 10 minutes or until crisp and golden.

4 Transfer to a wire rack, make a slit in the side of each one to allow steam to escape and leave to cool.

5 Whip the cream and sugar until standing in peaks and use to fill the éclairs. Sift the icing sugar and cocoa together and mix with enough of the cold water to form a smooth paste. Spread the icing (frosting) over each éclair and leave until set.

Chocolate Profiteroles

SERVES 4

Make as for Chocolate Éclairs but spoon the mixture into about 16 small balls on the baking (cookie) sheet. When cool, fill with the sweetened cream, then put in glass dishes and top with Hot Chocolate Caramel Sauce (see page 385) instead of the icing (frosting).

Summer Pudding

Slice or quarter larger fruit.

SERVES 6

900 g/2 lb soft fruit such as raspberries, blackberries, blackcurrants, strawberries

Finely grated rind of ½ orange (optional)

45 ml/3 tbsp water

100–175 g/4–6 oz/½–¾ cup granulated sugar

8 slices of white bread, crusts removed

1 Put the fruit in a saucepan with the orange rind, if using, the water and 100 g/4 oz/½ cup of the sugar.

2 Heat gently until the juices run and the fruit is soft but still holding its shape. Taste and add more sugar if necessary.

3 Line a large pudding basin with some of the bread, cutting it to fit.

4 Spoon in the fruit and juice and cover with the remaining bread, again trimming it to fit and filling in any gaps.

5 Put the basin on a small plate and cover with a saucer. Stand weights or a couple of cans on top. Chill overnight. The pudding is ready when all the juice has soaked through the bread.

6 Loosen the edge with a palette knife. Turn out on to a serving dish.

Tiramisu

SERVES 6

250 g/9 oz/good 1 cup Mascarpone cheese

2 eggs, separated

60 ml/4 tbsp caster (superfine) sugar

10 ml/2 tsp strong black coffee

120 ml/4 fl oz/½ cup weak coffee

90 ml/6 tbsp Amaretto or coffee liqueur

20 sponge (lady) fingers

Drinking (sweetened) chocolate powder, for dusting

1 Briskly stir the cheese and egg yolks together with a wooden spoon and gradually add the sugar.

2 Pour in the strong coffee and mix thoroughly. Whisk the egg whites until stiff in a clean bowl with an electric or balloon whisk and gently stir into the cheese mixture using a figure-of-eight movement.

3 Mix the weak coffee with the liqueur and dip half the sponge fingers in it. Use to line the base of a shallow serving dish. Pour in half the cheese mixture.

4 Dip the remaining sponge fingers in the coffee mixture and lay on top. Top with the remaining cheese mixture.

5 Tap the dish on the work surface gently to settle the contents. Chill for at least 2 hours and sprinkle with chocolate powder before serving.

Banoffee Pie

SERVES 6

350 g/12 oz/1 large can of sweetened condensed milk

200 g/7 oz/1¾ cups plain biscuits (cookies), crushed

50 g/2 oz/¼ cup butter or margarine, melted

2 bananas

300 ml/½ pt/1¼ cups double (heavy) cream

30 ml/2 tbsp caster (superfine) sugar

15 ml/1 tbsp instant coffee powder

Drinking (sweetened chocolate) powder or grated chocolate, to decorate

1 Put the can of condensed milk, unopened, in a saucepan of water. Bring to the boil, turn down the heat, part-cover with a lid and leave to bubble gently for 3 hours, topping up with boiling water as necessary to keep the can covered. Pour off the boiling water and fill the pan with cold water. Leave to cool.

2 Mix the biscuit crumbs with the butter or margarine and press into the base and sides of a 20 cm/8 in flan tin (pie pan). Chill until firm.

3 Tip out the milk from the can – it will be golden brown and thick – and spread the cold caramelised milk in the flan. Slice the bananas and arrange on the top.

4 Whip the cream, sugar and coffee powder together in a clean bowl with an electric or balloon whisk and spread over the bananas.

5 Sprinkle with chocolate powder or grated chocolate and chill until ready to serve.

Simple Lemon Cheesecake

SERVES 4

1 packet of lemon jelly (jello)

Boiling water

175 g/6 oz/1½ cups digestive biscuits (graham crackers), crushed

75 g/3 oz/⅓ cup butter or margarine, melted

25 g/1 oz/2 tbsp light brown sugar

200 g/7 oz/scant 1 cup medium-fat soft cheese

50 g/2 oz/¼ cup caster (superfine) sugar

Finely grated rind and juice of 1 small lemon

150 ml/¼ pt/⅔ cup double (heavy) cream

Ground cinnamon, for dusting

1 Break up the jelly tablet in a measuring jug and make up to 300 ml/½ pt/1¼ cups with boiling water. Stir until dissolved and leave to cool.

2 Meanwhile, mix the biscuits (cookies) with the melted butter or margarine and brown sugar. Turn into a 20 cm/ 8 in flan tin (pie pan) and press down well.

3 Mix the cheese and caster sugar together with the lemon rind and juice with a balloon whisk. Whisk in the cold jelly and leave to set.

4 When on the point of setting, whip the cream in a bowl with the same whisk and fold in.

5 Turn into the flan case (pie shell) and chill until set. Decorate with a dusting of ground cinnamon.

Rich Vanilla Cheesecake

SERVES 8–10

200 g/7 oz/1¾ cups digestive biscuits (graham crackers), crushed

75 g/3 oz/⅓ cup unsalted (sweet) butter, melted, plus a little for greasing

700 g/1½ lb/3 cups medium-fat soft cheese

225 g/8 oz/1 cup caster (superfine) sugar

2 eggs

5 ml/1 tsp vanilla essence (extract)

150 ml/¼ pt/⅔ cup soured (dairy sour) cream

Grated nutmeg, to decorate

1 Preheat the oven to 150°C/300°F/ gas mark 2. Mix the crushed biscuits (cookies) into the butter or margarine. Press into the base and a little way up the sides of a 20 cm/8 in deep, round, loose-bottomed cake tin (pan).

2 Mix the cheese with the sugar, eggs and vanilla until smooth, using a wooden spoon. Turn into the prepared tin and smooth the surface.

3 Bake in the oven for 1–1¼ hours or until just set. Turn off the oven and leave to cool in the oven.

4 Chill for at least 2 hours or overnight. Decorate the top with the soured cream, swirling it over the surface, and sprinkle with grated nutmeg.

Processor Chocolate Mousse

SERVES 6

4 eggs, separated

200 g/7 oz/1¾ cups plain (semi-sweet) chocolate

75 ml/5 tbsp strong hot coffee

2.5 ml/½ tsp vanilla essence (extract)

300 ml/½ pt/1¼ cups double (heavy) or whipping cream, whipped

15 ml/1 tbsp grated chocolate, to decorate

1 Put the egg whites in a large clean bowl and whisk until stiff, using an electric or balloon whisk.

2 Break the chocolate up and place in a food processor or blender. Run the machine until the chocolate is completely crushed.

3 Add the hot coffee and continue running the machine until the mixture is smooth.

4 Add the egg yolks and vanilla essence and blend for a further 1 minute.

5 Pour the chocolate mixture slowly over the egg whites and very gently mix it in with a metal spoon, using a figure-of-eight movement.

6 Spoon into individual dishes or one large serving dish and chill until set. Top with a little whipped cream and a sprinkling of grated chocolate.

Strawberry Cheesecake

SERVES 6

23 cm/9 in sponge flan case (pie shell)

200 g/7 oz/scant 1 cup medium-fat soft cheese

50 g/2 oz/¼ cup caster (superfine) sugar

2.5 ml/½ tsp vanilla essence (extract)

150 ml/¼ pt/⅔ cup whipping cream, whipped

410 g/14½ oz/1 large can of strawberry pie filling

1 Put the flan case on a serving plate.

2 Mix the cheese with the sugar and vanilla essence until well blended, using a wooden spoon. Stir in the whipped cream gently, using a metal spoon.

3 Spoon into the flan case and chill until fairly firm. Spread the strawberry pie filling over before serving.

Hazelnut Pavlova with Raspberries

SERVES 6

4 egg whites

225 g/8 oz/1 cup caster (superfine) sugar

50 g/2 oz/½ cup ground hazelnuts (filberts)

5 ml/1 tsp vanilla essence (extract)

1.5 ml/¼ tsp cream of tartar

15 ml/1 tbsp white wine vinegar

150 ml/¼ pt/⅔ cup double (heavy) or whipping cream, whipped

350 g/12 oz raspberries

A little icing (confectioners') sugar, for dusting

A few toasted chopped hazelnuts

1 Preheat the oven to 150°C/300°F/ gas mark 2.

2 Put the egg whites in a clean bowl and whisk until stiff, using an electric or balloon whisk. Gradually whisk in the sugar until the mixture forms shiny peaks.

3 Whisk in the ground hazelnuts, vanilla essence, cream of tartar and vinegar.

4 Place a sheet of non-stick baking parchment on a baking (cookie) sheet. Spoon the mixture into a round about 20 cm/8 in in diameter. Make a slight well in the centre.

5 Bake in the oven for about 1–1½ hours until a pale golden colour on the outside. Remove from the oven and leave to cool.

6 Carefully loosen with a fish slice and transfer to a serving plate.

7 Fill the centre with the cream and top with the raspberries. Dust with icing sugar and sprinkle with a few toasted, chopped hazelnuts.

Strawberry Pavlova

Substitute other fresh fruit of your choice, if you prefer.

SERVES 8

4 egg whites

225 g/8 oz/1 cup caster (superfine) sugar

15 ml/1 tbsp cornflour (cornstarch)

1.5 ml/¼ tsp vanilla essence (extract)

10 ml/2 tsp vinegar

150 ml/¼ pt/⅔ cup double (heavy) or whipping cream, whipped

225 g/8 oz small strawberries, halved

1 Preheat the oven to 150°C/300°F/ gas mark 2.

2 Put the egg whites in a large clean bowl and whisk using an electric or balloon whisk until stiff. Gradually whisk in the sugar, then the cornflour, vanilla and vinegar.

3 Spoon in a large circle on non-stick baking parchment on a baking (cookie) sheet, making a slight hollow in the centre.

4 Bake in the oven for 1½ hours until a pale gold colour, crisp on the outside and slightly fluffy in the middle. Leave to cool.

5 Loosen with a fish slice, then carefully transfer to a serving plate, fill the centre with whipped cream and top with strawberries.

Sweet Vanilla Sauce

Serve this with any hot puddings.

SERVES 4

45 ml/3 tbsp cornflour (cornstarch)
300 ml/½ pt/1¼ cups milk
1.5 ml/¼ tsp vanilla essence (extract)
15 ml/1 tbsp caster (superfine) sugar

1 Mix the cornflour with a little of the milk in a saucepan with a wooden spoon or wire whisk.
2 Stir in the remaining milk, the vanilla and sugar.
3 Bring to the boil over a high heat and cook for 1 minute, stirring, until thickened and smooth.

Cheat's Custard

I usually use canned or carton custard, but if you haven't any (and don't have any custard powder), make this instead.

SERVES 4

Prepare as for Sweet Vanilla Sauce but add a few drops of yellow food colouring when mixing the milk and cornflour.

Peppermint Custard

This is great with Steamed Chocolate Pudding (see page 355).

SERVES 4

Prepare as for Sweet Vanilla Sauce but add a few drops of peppermint essence (extract) and green food colouring. Omit the vanilla essence.

Photograph opposite: **Banana and Cinnamon Muffins (see page 410)**

Velvet Chocolate Sauce

For a dark chocolate sauce, substitute cocoa (unsweetened chocolate) powder for the drinking (sweetened) chocolate powder and add 15 ml/1 tbsp caster (superfine) sugar or more, to taste.

SERVES 4

30 ml/2 tbsp cornflour (cornstarch)
30 ml/2 tbsp drinking chocolate powder
300 ml/½ pt/1¼ cups milk

1 Mix the cornflour and chocolate with a little of the milk in a saucepan with a wooden spoon or wire whisk.
2 Stir in the remaining milk.
3 Bring to the boil over a high heat and cook for 2 minutes, stirring all the time, until thickened and smooth.

Instant Chocolate Sauce

Serve over ice cream or fruit. It's particularly good with bananas and pears. Make sure you use the kind of drinking (sweetened) chocolate powder with the milk powder added, that makes an instant hot chocolate drink.

SERVES 1

45 ml/3 tbsp instant drinking chocolate powder
Boiling water

1 Put the instant chocolate powder in a small jug or cup.
2 Using a wire whisk, whisk in boiling water, 5 ml/1 tsp at a time, to form a smooth paste. Stop when you have a thick, pouring consistency.

Hot Chocolate Caramel Sauce

Try this with ice cream and fruit. Also use it to top profiteroles (see the recipe on page 379).

SERVES 2–4

1 chocolate caramel bar
90 ml/6 tbsp milk
15 g/½ oz/1 tbsp butter or margarine
15 ml/1 tbsp drinking (sweetened)
    chocolate powder

1 Cut the bar into pieces and place in a saucepan.
2 Add the remaining ingredients and heat gently, stirring all the time with a wooden spoon, until smooth and thickened. Serve hot.

Hot Lemon Sauce

Serve this with steamed puddings, pancakes or apple pie.

SERVES 4–6

15 g/½ oz/2 tbsp cornflour (cornstarch)
25 g/1 oz/2 tbsp caster (superfine)
    sugar
300 ml/½ pt/1¼ cups water
Juice of 2 lemons

1 Mix the cornflour and sugar with a little of the water in a saucepan. Add the remaining water and the lemon juice.
2 Bring to the boil over a high heat and cook for 2 minutes, stirring, until thickened and clear. Serve hot.

Hot Orange Sauce

SERVES 4

Prepare as Hot Lemon Sauce, using oranges instead of lemons. Add a dash of lemon juice if liked, to sharpen.

Syrup Sauce

Pour this over steamed puddings or pancakes.

SERVES 4

90 ml/6 tbsp golden (light corn) syrup
30 ml/2 tbsp lemon juice

Heat the syrup and lemon juice in a saucepan over a moderate heat, stirring all the time until hot but not boiling. Serve hot.

Maple Syrup Sauce

This is good with pancakes or ice cream.

SERVES 4

Prepare as for Syrup Sauce but use maple syrup instead of golden (light corn) syrup.

Jam Sauce

Use any flavour of jam (conserve) you like. Serve it with sweet omelettes, steamed puddings or milk puddings.

SERVES 4–6

60 ml/4 tbsp jam
30 ml/2 tbsp caster (superfine) sugar
Finely grated rind and juice of ½ lemon
75 ml/5 tbsp water

1 Finely chop any fruit in the jam.
2 Mix all the ingredients in a saucepan and cook over a moderate heat, stirring, until the sugar has dissolved.
3 Continue to bubble gently for 3 minutes. Serve hot.

Photograph opposite: **Duck Mandarin Whirls (see page 422) and Peach and Ginger Sizzler (see page 433)**

Marmalade Sauce

SERVES 4-6

60 ml/4 tbsp marmalade
30 ml/2 tbsp caster (superfine) sugar
Finely grated rind of ½ lemon
Finely grated rind of ½ orange
60 ml/4 tbsp water

1 Heat all the ingredients in a saucepan over a gentle heat, stirring until the sugar dissolves.
2 Bring to the boil and bubble for 2 minutes. Serve hot.

Hot Honey Sauce

SERVES 4

15 g/½ oz/2 tbsp cornflour (cornstarch)
300 ml/½ pt/1¼ cups milk
15–30 ml/1–2 tbsp clear honey

1 Mix the cornflour with a little of the milk in a saucepan. Stir in the remaining milk.
2 Add half the honey and bring to the boil over a high heat, stirring all the time, and cook for 2 minutes.
3 Taste and add more honey if liked. Serve hot.

Fresh Raspberry Sauce

SERVES 4-6

225 g/8 oz raspberries
25 g/1 oz/3 tbsp icing (confectioners') sugar
15 ml/1 tbsp lemon juice

1 Purée the raspberries with the sugar and lemon juice in a blender or food processor.
2 Tip into a sieve (strainer) over a bowl and stir with a wooden spoon to rub the fruit through. Discard the seeds.

Raspberry Jelly Sauce

SERVES 6

1 packet of raspberry-flavoured jelly (jello)
30 ml/2 tbsp redcurrant jelly (clear conserve)
200 ml/7 fl oz/scant 1 cup water
5 ml/1 tsp arrowroot or cornflour (cornstarch)

1 Break up the jelly tablet and place in a saucepan with the redcurrant jelly and most of the water. Heat gently, stirring until dissolved.
2 Mix the arrowroot or cornflour with the remaining water and stir into the mixture. Bring to the boil, stirring until slightly thickened and clear. Serve hot.

All-year Raspberry Sauce

SERVES 4-6

390 g/13½ oz/1 large can of raspberries
10 ml/2 tsp cornflour (cornstarch)

1 Purée the raspberries and their juice in a blender or food processor.
2 Tip into a sieve (strainer) over a bowl and rub with a wooden spoon to press the fruit through, leaving the seeds behind.
3 Mix a little of the raspberry purée with the cornflour in a saucepan until smooth. Stir in the remaining purée. Bring to the boil over a high heat and cook for 2 minutes, stirring all the time, until thickened and clear. Serve hot or cover with a circle of wetted greaseproof (waxed) paper (this prevents a skin from forming) and leave to cool.

Brandied Loganberry Sauce

SERVES 4-6

225 g/8 oz fresh or frozen loganberries
45 ml/3 tbsp brandy
15 ml/1 tbsp water
Icing (confectioners') sugar, to taste

1 Gently stew the loganberries in the brandy and water for about 8 minutes.
2 Purée in a blender or food processor, then tip into a sieve (strainer) over a bowl and rub through with a wooden spoon to remove the seeds.
3 Sweeten the purée to taste with sifted icing sugar and serve cold.

Apple and Strawberry Sauce

SERVES 6

450 g/1 lb cooking (tart) apples, peeled, cored and sliced
60 ml/4 tbsp strawberry jam (conserve)
15 ml/1 tbsp water
5 ml/1 tsp lemon juice
Caster (superfine) sugar, to taste

1 Put all the ingredients except the sugar in a saucepan. Bring to the boil over a high heat, turn down the heat to fairly low, cover and cook until the apple is pulpy.
2 Tip into a sieve (strainer) over a bowl and rub through with a wooden spoon. Alternatively, purée in a blender or food processor.
3 Return to the pan and sweeten to taste. Reheat and serve hot.

Smooth Strawberry Sauce

SERVES 4-6

225 g/8 oz strawberries, quartered
15 ml/1 tbsp crème de cassis or blackcurrant cordial
15 ml/1 tbsp icing (confectioners') sugar
A few drops of vanilla essence (extract)

1 Put all the ingredients in a blender or food processor and purée until smooth.
2 Chill until ready to serve.

Fresh Apricot Sauce

SERVES 4

450 g/1 lb apricots, halved and stoned (pitted)
150 ml/¼ pt/⅔ cup sweet white wine
50 g/2 oz/¼ cup granulated sugar
Finely grated rind of ½ lemon
30 ml/2 tbsp kirsch

1 Put the apricots in a saucepan with the wine, sugar and lemon rind. Heat over a moderate heat until the sugar melts, then turn up the heat and boil for 4 minutes.
2 Purée in a blender or food processor with in the kirsch. Serve warm or cold.

Greengage Sauce

SERVES 4

Prepare as for Apricot Sauce but use greengages instead of apricots and sweeten with honey instead of sugar, if preferred.

Red Plum Sauce

SERVES 4

Prepare as for Apricot Sauce but use ripe red plums instead of apricots.

Smooth Cherry Sauce

SERVES 4

Prepare as for Fresh Apricot Sauce (page 387), using ripe cherries instead of apricots, and add port instead of sweet white wine.

Rainbow Pineapple Sauce for Ice Cream

Add this to vanilla ice cream for an Italian Cassata with a difference!

SERVES 4–6

250 g/9 oz/1 medium can of crushed pineapple
25 g/1 oz/2 tbsp caster (superfine) sugar
25 g/1 oz/¼ cup glacé (candied) cherries, chopped
15 ml/1 tbsp chopped angelica
15 ml/1 tbsp currants
10 ml/2 tsp cornflour (cornstarch)
60 ml/4 tbsp water
Finely grated rind and juice of 1 lemon or lime

1 Put the pineapple in a saucepan and add the sugar, cherries, angelica and currants.
2 Mix the cornflour with the water in a cup, then add to the pan with the lemon or lime rind and juice.
3 Bring to the boil over a high heat, stirring all the time, and cook, stirring for 1 minute.
4 Serve hot over ice cream.

Pineapple and Orange Sauce

SERVES 6

250 g/9 oz/1 medium can of crushed pineapple
10 ml/2 tsp arrowroot or cornflour (cornstarch)
150 ml/¼ pt/⅔ cup pure orange juice

1 Put the crushed pineapple in a saucepan. Mix the arrowroot or cornflour with a little of the orange juice in a cup and add to the pan with the remaining orange juice.
2 Bring to the boil over a high heat and cook for 2 minutes, stirring all the time, until thickened and clear. Serve hot.

White Rum Sauce

SERVES 4–6

25 g/1 oz/2 tbsp granulated sugar
120 ml/4 fl oz/½ cup water
Grated rind of ½ lemon
25 g/1 oz/2 tbsp unsalted (sweet) butter
5 ml/1 tsp cornflour (cornstarch)
120 ml/4 fl oz/½ cup white rum

1 Put the sugar, water and lemon rind in a saucepan. Heat gently, stirring, until the sugar dissolves.
2 Whisk in the butter with a wire whisk.
3 Mix the cornflour with the rum in a small cup and stir into the sauce. Heat rapidly until boiling, then cook for 2 minutes, stirring all the time. Serve hot.

Red Wine Sauce

Serve this with steamed sponge pudding or plain poached fruit.

SERVES 4

15 ml/1 tbsp caster (superfine) sugar
150 ml/¼ pt/⅔ cup water
30 ml/2 tbsp redcurrant jelly (clear
    conserve)
Thinly pared rind of ½ lemon
5 ml/1 tsp arrowroot or cornflour
    (cornstarch)
45 ml/3 tbsp red wine

1 Put the sugar, water, redcurrant jelly and lemon rind in a saucepan. Cook over a gentle heat, stirring, for about 5 minutes.
2 Mix the arrowroot or cornflour with the wine in a small cup and stir in.
3 Turn up the heat, bring to the boil and cook for 1 minute, stirring all the time. Serve hot.

Dark Rum Sauce

SERVES 4–6

30 ml/2 tbsp cornflour (cornstarch)
30 ml/2 tbsp dark brown sugar
300 ml/½ pt/1¼ cups milk
30 ml/2 tbsp dark rum

1 Mix the cornflour with the sugar and a little of the milk in a saucepan. Stir in the remainder.
2 Bring to the boil over a high heat and cook for 2 minutes, stirring all the time.
3 Stir in the rum. Pour into a warm sauce boat and serve.

Brandy Sauce

SERVES 4–6

Prepare as for Dark Rum Sauce but use caster (superfine) sugar instead of dark brown sugar and brandy instead of rum.

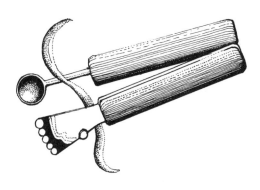

Home Baking

Cooking breads, biscuits (cookies) and cakes is very satisfying. The aroma of freshly baked bread is wonderful and a pile of newly cooked biscuits or a moist chocolate cake, cooling on a rack, is a treat to behold. With the recipes in this chapter, you will be able to produce near perfection every time as all are very easy to make and the results are sure to make everyone's mouth water. I've also included standard recipes for all kinds of pastry (paste) and other basics that are called for throughout the book.

Traditional Shortcrust Pastry

If you are making a double-crust pie, this will be enough for a 18–20 cm/ 7–8 in dish.

MAKES 1 x 23 CM/9 IN FLAN CASE (PIE SHELL)

225 g/8 oz/2 cups plain (all-purpose) flour

A pinch of salt

50 g/2 oz/¼ cup hard block margarine, cut into small pieces

50 g/2 oz/¼ cup white vegetable fat or lard (shortening), cut into small pieces

About 75 ml/5 tbsp water, to mix

1 Sift the flour and salt into a bowl.

2 Add the margarine, fat or lard.

3 Lifting some of the mixture with your hands, rub it between your thumbs and fingertips, letting it fall back in the bowl. Repeat until all the fat is rubbed into the flour and the mixture looks like breadcrumbs.

4 Using a round-bladed knife, gradually mix in the water, adding a fraction more if necessary, until the mixture forms a firm dough.

5 Squeeze it gently between your hands to form a ball. Use as required.

Fork Shortcrust Pastry

If you are making a double-crust pie, this will be enough for a 18–20 cm/ 7–8 in dish.

MAKES 1 x 23 CM/9 IN FLAN CASE (PIE SHELL)

150 g/5 oz/generous ⅔ cup butter or hard block margarine, softened

30 ml/2 tbsp water

225 g/8 oz/2 cups plain (all-purpose) flour

A pinch of salt

1 Put the butter or margarine in a bowl. Add the water and 50 g/2 oz/ ½ cup of the flour.

2 Mash to a smooth paste with a fork.

3 Work in the remaining flour and salt to form a soft dough.

4 Wrap and chill for 30 minutes before using.

Sweet Shortcrust Pastry

This quantity will also make one 18 cm/7 in double-crust pie.

MAKES 1 x 23 CM/9 IN FLAN CASE (PIE SHELL)

175 g/6 oz/1½ cups plain (all-purpose) flour

45 ml/3 tbsp icing (confectioners') sugar

100 g/4 oz/½ cup butter or hard block margarine, cut into small pieces

1 egg, separated

About 30 ml/2 tbsp cold water, to mix

1 Sift the flour and icing sugar into a bowl.

2 Add the butter or margarine and, lifting some of the mixture with your hands, rub it between your thumbs and fingertips, then let it fall back into the bowl. Repeat until all the fat is rubbed into the flour and the mixture looks like breadcrumbs.

3 Use a round-bladed knife to mix in the egg yolk and a little cold water, adding it gradually, to form a soft but not sticky dough. Draw the dough together with your hands, then tip out on to a lightly floured board.

4 Squeeze the pastry (paste) very gently until it is almost free of cracks. Wrap in foil or a plastic bag and chill for 30 minutes before using.

Choux Pastry

This quantity will also make nine éclairs or enough profiteroles for four people.

MAKES 1 GOUGÈRE

65 g/2½ oz/scant ¾ cup plain (all-purpose) flour
A pinch of salt
150 ml/¼ pt/⅔ cup water
50 g/2 oz/¼ cup butter or margarine
2 eggs, beaten

1 Sift the flour and salt on to a sheet of kitchen paper (paper towel).
2 Put the water and butter or margarine in a saucepan and heat until the fat melts.
3 Add the sifted flour all in one go and stir briskly with a wooden spoon until the mixture leaves the sides of the pan clean.
4 Remove from the heat and gradually add the eggs, a little at a time, stirring briskly after each addition, until the mixture is smooth and glossy but still holds its shape. Use immediately.

Biscuit Crumb Flan Case

MAKES 1 x 20 CM/8 IN CASE

175 g/6 oz digestive biscuits (graham crackers)
15 g/½ oz/1 tbsp caster (superfine) sugar
75 g/3 oz/⅓ cup butter or margarine, melted

1 Crush the biscuits in a bag with a rolling pin or in a food processor. Mix with the sugar and butter or margarine.
2 Press into the base and sides of a 20 cm/8 in flan dish (pie pan). Chill until firm. Fill as required.

Simple Pancakes

These can be served filled, with any sweet or savoury fillings, or plain, sprinkled with sugar and lemon juice. They freeze well, each separated with a sheet of non-stick baking parchment, then sealed in a plastic bag.

MAKES ABOUT 8

100 g/4 oz/1 cup plain (all-purpose) flour
A pinch of salt
1 egg
300 ml/½ pt/1¼ cups milk (or milk and water mixed)
15 g/½ oz/1 tbsp butter or margarine, melted (optional)
A little oil, for cooking

1 Mix the flour and salt in a bowl.
2 Make a well in the centre and add the egg and half the milk or milk and water.
3 Use a wire whisk to whisk vigorously until thick and smooth.
4 Stir in the melted butter or margarine, if using, and the remaining milk or milk and water. Leave to stand, if possible, for 30 minutes before use.
5 Heat a little oil in a frying pan (skillet) and pour off the excess into a small bowl to use for the next pancake.
6 When very hot, pour in just enough batter to coat the base of the pan when it is tipped and swirled gently.
7 Cook until set and the base of the pancake is golden brown.
8 Toss or flip over with a palette knife. Cook the other side.
9 Slide out and keep warm on a plate over a pan of hot water while cooking the remainder. Use as required.

Basic Yeast Bread Dough

This bread dough is easy to make – and very therapeutic! If you have a food processor, mix the dough in it, then let the machine run for 1 minute more to 'knead' it. Continue from step 5.

MAKES 1 x 900 G/2 LB LOAF

450 g/1 lb strong white (bread) flour
5 ml/1 tsp salt
10 ml/2 tsp easy-blend dried yeast
15 ml/1 tbsp sunflower or olive oil, plus a little for greasing
250 ml/8 fl oz/1 cup hand-hot water

1 Preheat the oven to 220°C/425°F/ gas mark 7.

2 Sift the flour and salt into a bowl. Stir in the yeast and oil.

3 Mix with the water to form a soft but not sticky dough, adding a little more water if necessary.

4 Knead gently on a lightly floured surface by pushing down and stretching the dough away from you with the heel of one hand, holding it steady with the other hand. Fold the dough back over and push away with the heel of your hand again. Repeat for about 5 minutes until smooth and elastic.

5 Wrap in a lightly oiled plastic bag and leave in a warm place for about 45 minutes until doubled in bulk.

6 Knock back (punch down) the dough to return it to its original size and shape into a roll to fit a lightly oiled 900 g/2 lb loaf tin (pan).

7 Place in the tin and leave in a warm place until the bread reaches the top. Brush with beaten egg or milk to glaze.

8 Bake in the oven for about 25 minutes until risen and golden and the base sounds hollow when the loaf is tipped out of the tin and is tapped with your knuckles.

9 Cool on a wire rack.

Cheese and Sesame Rolls

MAKES 8

375 g/13 oz/3¼ cups strong plain (bread) flour
1 vitamin C tablet, crushed
2.5 ml/½ tsp salt
30 ml/2 tbsp olive oil
25 g/1 oz/2 tbsp sesame seeds
100 g/4 oz/1 cup Cheddar cheese, grated
A good pinch of mustard powder
10 ml/2 tsp easy-blend dried yeast
5 ml/1 tsp caster (superfine) sugar
250 ml/8 fl oz/1 cup hand-hot water
A little plain milk, to glaze

1 Preheat the oven to 200°C/400°F/ gas mark 7.

2 Mix the flour with the salt in a large bowl. Stir in the remaining ingredients except half the cheese and the water.

3 Gradually add enough water to form a soft but not sticky dough.

4 Knead gently on a lightly floured surface for 5 minutes until smooth and elastic (see step 4, Basic Yeast Bread Dough, left).

5 Shape into eight rolls and place well apart on a lightly oiled baking (cookie) sheet. Brush with milk to glaze and sprinkle with the remaining cheese.

6 Bake for 20 minutes until risen, and golden and the bases sound hollow when tapped.

Milk Bread

MAKES 1 x 900 G/2 LB LOAF

450 g/1 lb/4 cups strong plain (bread) flour
5 ml/1 tsp salt
10 ml/2 tsp easy-blend dried yeast
20 g/³⁄₄ oz/1½ tbsp butter or margarine
300 ml/½ pt/1¼ cups milk, hand-hot
1 small egg, beaten
A little extra milk, to glaze
A little sunflower oil, for greasing

1 Preheat the oven to 230°C/450°F/ gas mark 8.
2 Sift the flour and salt into a bowl. Stir in the yeast. Make a well in the centre.
3 Melt the fat in a saucepan. Add the milk and heat until it feels bearably hot to the touch but not boiling. Add to the bowl with the egg. Mix with a wooden spoon to form a dough, then beat with your hand, using a clawing movement, until smooth and elastic.
4 Cover with lightly greased clingfilm (plastic wrap) and leave in a warm place for about 45 minutes until doubled in bulk.
5 Knock back (punch down) and knead briefly on a lightly floured surface. Shape into an oval and place in a lightly greased 900 g/2 lb loaf tin (pan) and leave in a warm place until the dough reaches the top of the tin.
6 Brush with a little milk, to glaze and bake for 20–25 minutes until golden brown and the base sounds hollow when the loaf is tipped out and tapped. Cool on a wire rack.

Quick Sun-dried Tomato and Olive Rolls

MAKES 8

375 g/13 oz/3¼ cups strong plain (bread) flour
2.5 ml/½ tsp salt
1 vitamin C tablet, crushed
30 ml/2 tbsp olive oil
10 ml/2 tsp easy-blend dried yeast
5 ml/1 tsp caster (superfine) sugar
5 sun-dried tomatoes, chopped
30 ml/2 tbsp sliced stoned (pitted) black olives
250 ml/8 fl oz/1 cup hand-hot water
A little plain yoghurt, to glaze

1 Preheat the oven to 200°C/400°F/ gas mark 6.
2 Mix the flour and salt in a large bowl. Stir in all the remaining ingredients except the water.
3 Gradually add enough water to form a soft but not sticky dough.
4 Knead gently on a lightly floured surface for 5 minutes until smooth and elastic (see step 4, Basic Yeast Bread Dough, page 393).
5 Shape into eight rolls and place well apart on a lightly oiled baking (cookie) sheet. Brush with yoghurt to glaze.
6 Bake for 20 minutes until risen and golden and the bases sound hollow when tapped.

Quick Walnut Rolls

MAKES 8

Prepare as for Quick Sun-dried Tomato and Olive Rolls but substitute 50 g/2 oz/½ cup chopped walnuts for the tomatoes and olives and add 15 ml/1 tbsp snipped fresh chives.

Garlic and Herb Bread

SERVES 6

1 small baguette
50 g/2 oz/¼ cup butter or margarine
1–2 garlic cloves, crushed
15 ml/1 tbsp chopped fresh parsley
15 ml/1 tbsp chopped fresh tarragon

1 Preheat the oven to 200°C/400°F/ gas mark 6.
2 Cut the bread into 12 slices, not quite through the base crust.
3 Mash the butter or margarine with the garlic and herbs, using a fork.
4 Spread between each slice and spread any remainder over the top.
5 Wrap in foil and bake in the oven for about 15 minutes until the crust feels crisp and the centre soft when squeezed.

Garlic Bread

SERVES 4–6

Prepare as for Garlic and Herb Bread but omit the herbs.

Fresh Herb Baguette

SERVES 4–6

Prepare as for Garlic and Herb Bread but omit the garlic and add 15 ml/1 tbsp chopped fresh thyme with the other herbs.

Herb and Sunflower Seed Bread

SERVES 4

1 small wholemeal French stick
75 g/3 oz/⅓ cup butter or margarine
15 ml/1 tbsp chopped fresh parsley
15 ml/1 tsp chopped fresh marjoram
30 ml/2 tbsp sunflower seeds
2.5 ml/½ tsp celery salt
Freshly ground black pepper

1 Preheat the oven to 200°C/400°F/ gas mark 6.
2 Cut the bread into 12 slices, not quite through the bottom crust.
3 Mash the butter or margarine with the herbs, seeds, celery salt and a good grinding of pepper.
4 Spread between the slices and spread any remainder over the top.
5 Wrap in foil, sealing the edges well, and bake for about 15 minutes until the crust feels crisp when gently squeezed with an oven-gloved hand.

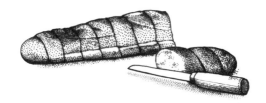

Rosemary Teacup Loaf

This is also delicious made with mint instead of rosemary. Use the same teacup to measure all the ingredients.

MAKES 1 x 900 G/2 LB LOAF

1 teacup raisins

1 teacup sultanas (golden raisins)

½ teacup currants

½ teacup light brown sugar

½ teacup pure apple juice

½ teacup cold black tea

5 ml/1 tsp dried rosemary, crushed

¼ teacup butter or margarine

2 teacups self-raising (self-rising) flour

1 Put all the ingredients except the flour in a saucepan and heat over a fairly low heat until the butter or margarine melts, then turn up the heat, bring to the boil and boil for 2 minutes. Remove from the heat.

2 Leave until lukewarm, then stir in the flour.

3 Preheat the oven to 180°C/350°F/ gas mark 4. Grease a 900 g/2 lb loaf tin (pan). Cut a piece of non-stick baking parchment to fit the base of the tin and put it in.

4 Spoon the mixture into the tin. Bake in the oven for 1¼ hours or until risen and golden and a skewer inserted in the centre comes out clean.

5 Leave to cool in the tin for a few minutes, then turn out on to a wire rack, remove the paper and leave to cool.

Malted Milk Loaf

MAKES 1 x 450 G/1 LB LOAF

A little oil, for greasing

225 g/8 oz/2 cups self-raising (self-rising) flour

50 g/2 oz/½ cup malted milk drink granules

50 g/2 oz/¼ cup dark brown sugar

75 g/3 oz/½ cup raisins

30 ml/2 tbsp golden (light corn) syrup

About 200 ml/7 fl oz/scant 1 cup milk

Butter or margarine, to serve

1 Grease a 450 g/1 lb loaf tin. Cut a piece of non-stick baking parchment to fit in the base of the tin. Put it in. Preheat the oven to 160°C/325°F/ gas mark 3.

2 Mix the flour with the malt drink granules and sugar in a bowl. Add the raisins.

3 Warm the syrup with 150 ml/¼ pt/ ⅔ cup of the milk, in a small saucepan, stirring until blended. Stir into the flour mixture and mix well. Add more milk, a little at a time, until the mixture is soft and will drop off the spoon but is not runny.

4 Spoon the mixture into the tin and bake straight away for 1½ hours until risen, golden and a skewer inserted in the centre comes out clean.

5 Leave to cool for 10 minutes, then loosen the edge and turn out on to a wire rack, remove the paper and leave to cool. Serve sliced and buttered.

Plain Yoghurt Scones

MAKES 6–8

225 g/8 oz/2 cups self-raising (self-rising) flour

A pinch of salt

50 g/2 oz/¼ cup butter or margarine, plus extra for spreading

75 ml/5 tbsp plain yoghurt

About 45 ml/3 tbsp milk, plus extra for glazing

1 Preheat the oven to 230°C/450°F/gas mark 8.

2 Sift the flour and salt into a bowl.

3 Add the measured butter or margarine and rub in with your thumbs and fingertips until the mixture resembles breadcrumbs.

4 Stir in the yoghurt and enough milk to form a soft but not sticky dough.

5 Squeeze gently into a round and pat out to about 2 cm/¾ in thick. Cut into six to eight scones (biscuits) using a biscuit (cookie) cutter, reshaping and cutting the trimmings as required.

6 Transfer to a non-stick baking (cookie) sheet and brush with milk.

7 Bake for about 12 minutes until well risen and golden and the bases sound hollow when tapped. Serve warm, split and buttered.

Sweet Yoghurt Scones

MAKES 6–8

Prepare as for Plain Yoghurt Scones, but add 30 ml/2 tbsp caster (superfine) sugar to the mixture.

Banana Bread

MAKES 1 x 900 G/2 LB LOAF

A little oil, for greasing

2–3 ripe bananas

5 ml/1 tsp bicarbonate of soda

50 g/2 oz/¼ cup butter or margarine, plus extra for spreading

100 g/4 oz/½ cup caster (superfine) sugar

275 g/10 oz/2½ cups self-raising (self-rising) flour

2.5 ml/½ tsp ground cinnamon or mixed (apple-pie) spice

1 egg

1 Grease a 900 g/2 lb loaf tin (pan). Cut a piece of non-stick baking parchment to fit the base of the tin and place it in the bottom. Preheat the oven to 180°C/350°F/gas mark 4.

2 Put the bananas in a food processor and run the machine until smooth.

3 Add the remaining ingredients and run the machine until well blended.

4 Turn into the prepared loaf tin.

5 Bake in the oven for about 50 minutes until risen and golden and a skewer inserted in the centre comes out clean.

6 Cool slightly. Remove from the tin, take off the paper and leave to cool on a wire rack. Serve sliced and buttered.

Fruit Yoghurt Scones

MAKES 6–8

Prepare as for Plain or Sweet Yoghurt Scones but add 30 ml/2 tbsp sultanas (golden raisins) to the dry mixture before adding the yoghurt and milk.

Plain Oven-fresh Scones

MAKES 8

225 g/8 oz/2 cups self-raising (self-rising) flour
A pinch of salt
10 ml/2 tsp baking powder
25 g/1 oz/2 tbsp butter or margarine, softened, plus extra for greasing
About 150 ml/¼ pt/⅔ cup milk to mix, plus a little extra to glaze

1 Preheat the oven to 230°C/450°F/gas mark 8.
2 Sift the flour, salt and baking powder in a bowl.
3 Mash the butter or margarine into the flour with a fork until crumbly.
4 Mix with enough milk to form a soft but not sticky dough.
5 Draw the mixture into a ball on a lightly floured surface, squeezing it very gently to remove most of the cracks. Handle as little as possible. Pat out to about 1 cm/½ in thickness and cut into eight scones, using a 5 cm/2 in biscuit (cookie) cutter. Reshape and cut the trimmings as necessary.
6 Transfer to a lightly greased baking (cookie) sheet and brush the tops with a little milk. Bake immediately for about 10 minutes until risen and golden and the bases sound hollow when lifted (wear an oven glove) and tapped with your fingers. Transfer to a wire rack to cool slightly. Best served warm.

Sweet Oven-fresh Scones

MAKES 8

Prepare as for Plain Oven-fresh Scones but add 30 ml/2 tbsp caster (superfine) sugar to the flour mixture.

Cheese and Chive Scones

MAKES 8

Prepare as for Plain Oven-fresh Scones but add 50 g/2 oz/½ cup strong Cheddar cheese, grated, 1.5 ml/¼ tsp cayenne and 15 ml/1 tbsp snipped, fresh chives to the dry ingredients before adding the milk.

Sultana Scones

MAKES 8

Prepare as for Plain Oven-fresh Scones but add 15 g/½ oz/1 tbsp light brown sugar and 50 g/2 oz/⅓ cup sultanas (golden raisins) to the dry ingredients before adding the milk.

Plain Drop Scones

These are delicious spread with butter, cheese, yeast extract or other savoury spreads. Alternatively, serve them as blinis with smoked salmon or lumpfish roe as a starter (see page 47), in which case make them larger, using two spoonfuls of batter per pancake, or American-style, with maple syrup.

MAKES ABOUT 24

100 g/4 oz/1 cup plain (all-purpose) flour
A pinch of salt
2 eggs, separated
300 ml/½ pt/1¼ cups milk
Oil, for shallow-frying

1 Sift the flour and salt in a bowl.
2 Add the egg yolks and half the milk and mix thoroughly with a wooden spoon or wire whisk until smooth.
3 Stir in the remaining milk.
4 Whisk the egg whites until stiff in a clean bowl with an electric or balloon whisk and gently mix in, using a metal spoon and a figure-of-eight movement.
5 Heat a little oil in a large frying pan (skillet) and pour off the excess. Drop spoonfuls of the mixture into the pan and cook until golden brown underneath and bubbles are appearing on the surface.
6 Flip over with a palette knife and cook the other sides briefly. Keep each batch warm, wrapped in a clean cloth on a plate over a pan of hot water, while cooking the remainder. Serve warm.

Sweet Drop Scones

MAKES ABOUT 24

Prepare exactly as for Plain Drop Scones but add 15 g/½ oz/1 tbsp caster (superfine) sugar to the mixture.

Rye Drop Scones

These have a delicious 'nutty' flavour.

MAKES 24

Prepare as for either of the Drop Scone recipes but use rye flour instead of plain (all-purpose) flour.

Baking Powder Bread

MAKES 2 x 450 G/1 LB LOAVES

450 g/1 lb plain (all-purpose) flour
20 ml/4 tsp baking powder
25 g/1 oz/2 tbsp butter or margarine, plus extra for greasing
300 ml/½ pt/1¼ cups milk

1 Preheat the oven to 230°C/450°F/ gas mark 8.
2 Sift the flour and baking powder into a bowl. Mash the butter or margarine into the flour with a fork until crumbly.
3 Mix with enough of the milk to form a soft but not sticky dough.
4 Divide the dough in half. Shape each into a loaf and place in two greased 450 g/1 lb loaf tins (pans). Bake in the oven for 20–25 minutes until risen and golden and the bases sound hollow when tipped out of the tins and tapped with your knuckles.
5 Place on a wire rack to cool.

Soda Bread

MAKES 1 x 450 G/1 LB LOAF

450 g/1 lb/4 cups plain (all-purpose) flour

10 ml/2 tsp bicarbonate of soda (baking soda)

10 ml/2 tsp cream of tartar

5 ml/1 tsp salt

25 g/1 oz/2 tbsp butter or margarine, softened, plus a little extra for greasing and serving

300 ml/½ pt/1¼ cups milk

1 Preheat the oven to 220°C/425°F/ gas mark 7. Lightly grease a baking (cookie) sheet.

2 Sift the flour, soda, cream of tartar and salt into a bowl.

3 Add the butter or margarine and mash into the flour with a fork until crumbly.

4 Stir in the milk to form a soft but not sticky dough.

5 Dust your hands with flour and draw the dough together, then shape into a ball.

6 Place the ball on the baking sheet, flatten slightly and cut a cross in the top of the dough to mark it in quarters.

7 Bake in the oven for 20–25 minutes until golden and risen and the base sounds hollow when the loaf is lifted (wear an oven glove) and tapped with your knuckles. Cool on a wire rack.

8 To serve, break into quarters, then thickly slice and spread with butter or margarine.

Cheese Soda Bread

MAKES 1 x 450 G/1 LB LOAF

Make as for Soda Bread but add 100 g/4 oz/1 cup Cheddar cheese, grated, and 5 ml/1 tsp mustard powder to the dry ingredients before mixing in the milk.

Brown Seeded Soda Bread

MAKES 1 x 450 G/1 LB LOAF

Make as for Soda Bread but use half wholemeal and half plain (all-purpose) flour. Add 30 ml/2 tbsp sunflower seeds and 15 ml/1 tbsp caraway seeds to the dry ingredients before adding the milk.

Oatmeal Bannocks

MAKES 6

175 g/6 oz/1½ cups wholemeal flour
15 ml/1 tbsp baking powder
2.5 ml/½ tsp salt
50 g/2 oz/½ cup medium oatmeal
15 g/½ oz/1 tbsp light brown sugar
25 g/1 oz/2 tbsp butter or margarine,
    softened, plus extra for serving
150 ml/¼ pt/⅔ cup water

1 Mix the flour, baking powder, salt,
oatmeal and sugar together.
2 Mash in the butter or margarine with
a fork until crumbly.
3 Stir in the water to form a soft but
not sticky dough.
4 Draw the dough together with your
hands to form a ball and divide into six
pieces.
5 With lightly floured hands, shape
each piece into a round, flat cake,
about 1 cm/½ in thick.
6 Heat a griddle or heavy-based
frying pan (skillet). When hot, add
the bannocks and cook for about
5 minutes on each side until golden
brown, well risen and cooked through.
Serve straight from the pan, split and
buttered.

Oatcakes

*These are delicious with cheese or
for breakfast with butter and jam
(conserve) or honey.*

MAKES 8

75 g/3 oz/¾ cup medium oatmeal, plus
    extra for dusting
A good pinch of salt
1.5 ml/¼ tsp bicarbonate of soda
    (baking soda)
15 g/½ oz/1 tbsp butter or margarine
60 ml/4 tbsp water
Oil, for greasing

1 Mix the oatmeal with the salt and
bicarbonate of soda in a bowl.
2 Heat the butter or margarine and
water together until the fat melts. Pour
into the oat mixture and mix to a
dough with a knife.
3 Draw the mixture together into a
ball.
4 Dust the work surface with a little
oatmeal and roll out the dough as
thinly as possible to a 25 cm/10 in
round, using a dinner plate as a guide.
5 Cut into eight wedges.
6 Brush a large frying pan (skillet) with
oil and heat gently. Add the oatcakes
a few at a time and cook for
2–3 minutes until firm. Carefully turn
them over, using a fish slice so they
don't break, and cook the other sides
for a further 2–3 minutes. Cool on a
wire rack. Store in an airtight tin.

Fat-free Jam Sponge

You can also make a Swiss (jelly) roll with this mixture. Cook in a lined Swiss roll tin (jelly roll pan), turn out, trim the edges with a knife, spread with the jam (conserve) and roll up.

MAKES 1 x 18 CM/7 IN CAKE

2 eggs

50 g/2 oz/¼ cup caster (superfine) sugar

A few drops of vanilla essence (extract)

50 g/2 oz/½ cup self-raising (self-rising) flour

40 ml/2½ tbsp raspberry jam

5 ml/1 tsp icing (confectioners') sugar

1 Preheat the oven to 200°C/400°F/ gas mark 6. Cut two circles of non-stick baking parchment, using the tins (pans) as a guide, and place in the base of two 18 cm/7 in sandwich tins.

2 Put the eggs, sugar and vanilla in a bowl.

3 Whisk with an electric whisk until thick and pale and the whisk leaves a trail when lifted out of the mixture.

4 Sift the flour through a sieve (strainer) over the surface and stir in gently with a metal spoon using a figure-of-eight movement. Do not over-mix.

5 Spoon into the tins and level the tops. Bake in the oven for about 8–10 minutes until risen and golden and the centres spring back when lightly pressed.

6 Cool slightly, then loosen the edges all round and turn out on to a wire rack. Remove the paper and leave to cool.

7 Sandwich the cakes together with the jam, transfer to a serving plate and sift the icing sugar over the surface.

All-in-one Victoria Sandwich

MAKES 1 x 18 CM/7 IN CAKE

A little oil, for greasing

175 g/6 oz/¾ cup caster (superfine) sugar

175 g/6 oz/¾ cup soft tub margarine

175 g/6 oz/1½ cups self-raising (self-rising) flour

5 ml/1 tsp baking powder

3 eggs

About 45 ml/3 tbsp jam (conserve)

A little icing (confectioners') sugar or extra caster sugar, to decorate

1 Preheat the oven to 190°C/375°F/ gas mark 5. Grease two 18 cm/7 in sandwich tins (pans). Cut two circles the same size as the tins and place in the bases.

2 Put all the ingredients except the jam in a bowl and stir briskly with a wooden spoon or use an electric whisk until smooth and fluffy. Alternatively, blend in a food processor until just mixed.

3 Spoon into the prepared tins and level the surfaces.

4 Bake in the oven for about 20 minutes until risen, golden and the centres spring back when lightly pressed.

5 Cool slightly, then loosen the edges with a round-bladed knife, turn out on to a wire rack, remove the paper and leave to cool.

6 Sandwich together with jam. Dust with icing or caster sugar, if liked.

Chocolate Sandwich

MAKES 1 x 18 CM/7 IN CAKE

Prepare as All-in-one Victoria
Sandwich but substitute 15 g/½ oz/
2 tbsp of the flour with cocoa
(unsweetened chocolate) powder and
add an extra 2.5 ml/½ tsp baking
powder. Sandwich together with
whipped cream instead of jam
(conserve).

Jam and 'Cream' Sponge

MAKES 1 x 18 CM/7 IN CAKE

**225 g/8 oz/1 cup butter or margarine,
plus extra for greasing**

**175 g/6 oz/¾ cup caster (superfine)
sugar**

**175 g/6 oz/1½ cups self-raising (self-
rising) flour**

5 ml/1 tsp baking powder

2.5 ml/½ tsp vanilla essence (extract)

3 eggs

**100 g/4 oz/⅔ cup icing (confectioners')
sugar, plus extra for dusting**

45 ml/3 tbsp raspberry jam (conserve)

1 Grease two 18 cm/7 in round
sandwich tins (pans). Cut circles of non-
stick baking parchment to fit the bases

and place in the bases of the tins.
Preheat the oven to 190°C/375°F/
gas mark 5.

2 Put 175 g/6 oz/¾ cup of the butter or
margarine in a food processor with the
sugar, flour, baking powder, vanilla and
eggs and run the machine just until
smooth. Do not over-mix. Alternatively,
place in a bowl and beat with a
wooden spoon until smooth.

3 Divide between the tins and smooth
the surfaces. Bake in the oven for
20 minutes until risen, golden and the
centres spring back when lightly
pressed.

4 Cool slightly, then loosen the edges
with a round-bladed knife, turn out on
to a wire rack, remove the paper and
leave to cool completely.

5 Put the remaining butter or
margarine in a bowl. Sift the icing sugar
into the bowl through a sieve (strainer).
Stir briskly with a wooden spoon until
smooth and fluffy.

6 Sandwich the cakes together with
the jam and 'cream'. Place on a serving
plate. Sift a little icing sugar over the
surface.

Black Forest Gâteau

MAKES 1 x 18 CM/7 IN CAKE

225 g/8 oz/1 cup butter or margarine, plus extra for greasing

175 g/6 oz/¾ cup caster (superfine) sugar

160 g/5½ oz/scant 1½ cups self-raising (self-rising) flour

20 g/¾ oz/3 tbsp cocoa (unsweetened chocolate) powder

10 ml/2 tsp baking powder

3 eggs

100 g/4 oz/⅔ cup icing (confectioners') sugar, plus extra for dusting

45 ml/3 tbsp black cherry jam (conserve)

1 Grease two 18 cm/7 in sandwich tins (pans). Cut two circles of non-stick baking parchment the same size as the bases. Put in the bottom of the tins. Preheat the oven to 190°C/375°F/ gas mark 5.

2 Put 175 g/6 oz/¾ cup of the butter or margarine in a food processor with the sugar.

3 Sift the flour, 15 g/½ oz/2 tbsp of the cocoa powder and the baking powder over the surface through a sieve (strainer). Add the eggs.

4 Run the machine until the mixture is just smooth. Do not over-mix. Alternatively, put the ingredients in a bowl and stir briskly with a wooden spoon until smooth.

5 Divide between the tins and smooth the surfaces.

6 Bake in the oven for 20 minutes until risen and the centres spring back when lightly pressed.

7 Cool slightly, then loosen the edges with a round-bladed knife, turn out on to a wire rack, remove the paper and leave to cool.

8 Put the remaining butter or margarine in a bowl. Sift the icing sugar and remaining cocoa over the surface. Stir briskly with a wooden spoon until smooth and fluffy.

9 Sandwich the cakes together with the jam and chocolate 'cream' and place on a serving plate. Dust the top with a little icing sugar and serve.

Almond Macaroons

MAKES 12

2 egg whites

150 g/5 oz/⅔ cup caster (superfine) sugar

A few drops of almond essence (extract)

150 g/5 oz/1¼ cups ground almonds

Rice paper

12 whole blanched almonds, to decorate

1 Preheat the oven to 190°C/375°F/ gas mark 5.

2 Lightly whisk the egg whites with a balloon whisk until frothy.

3 Add the sugar, almond essence and almonds. Mix to a paste. Roll into balls and place well apart on a baking (cookie) sheet lined with rice paper.

4 Top each with an almond. Bake in the oven for about 20 minutes until pale biscuit-coloured.

5 Leave to cool for 10 minutes, then cut or tear the rice paper round each macaroon and transfer to a wire rack to cool. Store in an airtight container.

Boiled Fruit Salad Cake

MAKES 1 x 18 CM/7 IN CAKE

100 g/4 oz/½ cup butter or margarine, plus extra for greasing

175 g/6 oz/¾ cup dark brown sugar

120 ml/4 fl oz/½ cup pure orange juice

75 ml/5 tbsp water

250 g/9 oz/1 small packet of dried fruit salad, chopped, discarding any stones (pits)

5 ml/1 tsp bicarbonate of soda (baking soda)

10 ml/2 tsp mixed (apple-pie) spice

225 g/8 oz/2 cups self-raising (self-rising) flour

5 ml/1 tsp baking powder

1 large egg, beaten

30 ml/2 tbsp milk

1 Grease an 18 cm/7 in square cake tin (pan). Cut a piece of non-stick baking parchment to fit in the base and a strip as wide as the sides of the tin to line the sides. Place in the tin.

2 Put everything except the flour, baking powder, egg and milk in a saucepan.

3 Bring to the boil over a high heat and boil for 1 minute. Remove from the heat and leave to cool for 5 minutes.

4 Preheat the oven to 180°C/350°F/ gas mark 4.

5 Stir the flour, baking powder, egg and milk into the fruit mixture. Spoon it into the prepared tin.

6 Cook in the oven for about 1 hour 10 minutes or until a skewer inserted in the centre comes out clean.

7 Cool for 10 minutes, then turn out on to a wire rack, remove the paper and leave to cool.

Everyday Fruit Cake

MAKES 1 x 18 CM/7 IN CAKE

175 g/6 oz/¾ cup butter or margarine, plus extra for greasing

175 g/6 oz/¾ cup caster (superfine) sugar

3 eggs

225 g/8 oz/2 cups plain (all-purpose) flour

5 ml/1 tsp mixed (apple-pie) spice

225 g/8 oz/1⅓ cups dried mixed fruit (fruit cake mix)

15–30 ml/1–2 tbsp milk

1 Preheat the oven to 160°C/325°F/ gas mark 3.

2 Grease an 18 cm/7 in deep, round cake tin (pan) and line with greased greaseproof (waxed) paper (see step 1, Boiled Fruit Salad Cake, left).

3 Stir the butter or margarine and sugar briskly together until light and fluffy.

4 Add the eggs, one at a time, stirring vigorously after each addition. If the mixture curdles, stir in 30 ml/2 tbsp of the flour.

5 Sift the flour and spice over the surface. Stir in gently with a metal spoon.

6 Stir in the fruit and add the milk if necessary, to give a soft, dropping consistency, but don't make it too wet.

7 Spoon into the prepared tin and level the surface. Bake for about 1¼ hours until golden brown and a skewer inserted in the centre comes out clean.

8 Cool slightly, then turn out on to a wire rack, remove the paper and leave to cool. Store in an airtight container.

Coffee Walnut Sandwich

Make this cake in a food processor, if you prefer.

MAKES 1 x 18 CM/7 IN CAKE

175 g/6 oz/¾ cup soft margarine, plus extra for greasing

175 g/6 oz/1½ cups self-raising (self-rising) flour

175 g/6 oz/¾ cup caster (superfine) sugar

3 eggs

30 ml/2 tbsp instant coffee granules or powder

20 ml/4 tsp hot water

150 ml/¼ pt/⅔ cup double (heavy) or whipping cream

45 ml/3 tbsp icing (confectioners') sugar

50 g/2 oz/½ cup chopped walnuts

Walnut halves, to decorate

1 Preheat the oven to 190°C/375°F/ gas mark 5. Grease two 18 cm/7 in sandwich tins (pans). Cut two circles of non-stick baking parchment, the same size as the base, and place in the bottom of each tin.

2 Put the margarine, flour, caster sugar and eggs in a large mixing bowl. Mix half the coffee with half the water and add to the bowl.

3 Hold the bowl firmly with one hand and stir very briskly with a wooden spoon until smooth and fluffy. Alternatively, blend in a food processor until just mixed.

4 Divide the mixture between the two prepared tins and level the surfaces with a palette knife or the back of a spoon.

5 Bake in the oven for about 20 minutes until risen and golden and the centres spring back when lightly pressed.

6 Cool slightly, then turn out on to a wire rack, remove the paper and leave to cool.

7 Pour the cream into a bowl and add the icing sugar. Whip with an electric or balloon whisk until standing in soft peaks. Dissolve the remaining coffee in the remaining water. Add to the cream and whisk in briefly until the cream stands in soft peaks again. Add the chopped nuts and stir in gently with a metal spoon.

8 Put one of the cakes, upside-down, on a serving plate. Spoon half the cream mixture over and top with the second cake, the right way up (so the two flat undersides are sandwiched together).

9 Spoon the remaining cream on top and spread out evenly. Pat the top gently with a knife or the spoon to make the cream stand in little peaks. Decorate with the walnut halves and chill until ready to serve.

Carrot Cake

MAKES 1 x 900 G/2 LB CAKE

A little oil, for greasing

2 large carrots, grated

225 g/8 oz/2 cups self-raising (self-rising) flour

10 ml/2 tsp baking powder

5 ml/1 tsp mixed (apple-pie) spice

100 g/4 oz/½ cup light brown sugar

150 g/5 oz/⅔ cup butter or margarine, plus extra for greasing

1 egg, beaten

1 Preheat the oven to 180°C/350°F/ gas mark 4/fan oven 160°C and grease a 900 g/2 lb loaf tin (pan). Cut a piece of non-stick baking parchment the same size as the base and put in the bottom of the tin.

2 Grate the carrots into a large bowl.

3 Add the flour, baking powder and spice.

4 Put the sugar and butter or margarine in a saucepan and heat, stirring, until the fat melts.

5 Pour into the dry ingredients and mix well.

6 Mix in the beaten egg completely.

7 Turn into the prepared tin and bake in the oven for about 40 minutes until risen, golden and a skewer inserted in the centre comes out clean.

8 Leave to cool in the tin for about 10 minutes, then turn out, remove the paper and leave to cool.

Carrot and Walnut Cake

MAKES 1 x 900 G/2 LB CAKE

Prepare as for Carrot Cake, but add 40 g/1½ oz/⅓ cup chopped walnut halves to the dry ingredients before warming the butter or margarine and the sugar.

Carrot and Orange Cake

MAKES 1 x 900 G/2 LB CAKE

Prepare as for Carrot Cake but add the grated rind of half an orange to the mixture. Once cooked, make some orange butter cream: stir 50 g/2 oz/ ¼ cup butter briskly until soft. Work in 150 g/5 oz/scant 1 cup sifted icing (confectioners') sugar and the grated rind and juice of half an orange. Spread this over the top of the cooled cake and leave to set.

Fast Sultana Cake

Use mixed dried fruit (fruit cake mix), currants or raisins if you prefer.

MAKES 1 x 18 CM/7 IN CAKE

A little oil, for greasing

225 g/8 oz/2 cups self-raising (self-rising) flour

175 g/6 oz/¾ cup soft tub margarine

175 g/6 oz/¾ cup caster (superfine) sugar

3 eggs

5 ml/1 tsp mixed (apple-pie) spice

50 g/2 oz/⅓ cup sultanas (golden raisins)

15 ml/1 tbsp milk

1 Preheat the oven to 160°C/325°F/gas mark 3. Grease an 18 cm/7 in loose-bottomed cake tin (pan). Cut a circle of non-stick baking parchment the same size as the base and put in the bottom of the tin. Cut a strip the width of the sides and long enough to go all round the tin. Use to line the inside of the tin.

2 Put the flour, margarine, sugar, eggs and spice in a food processor. Run the machine until just blended. Alternatively, put in a bowl and stir briskly with a wooden spoon until smooth.

3 Stir in the fruit and add the milk, to give a soft, dropping consistency.

4 Spoon into the tin and level the top.

5 Bake in the oven for about 1½ hours until golden, risen and a skewer inserted in the centre comes out clean.

6 Leave to cool in the tin for 10 minutes, then turn out on to a wire rack, remove the paper and leave to cool completely.

Date and Walnut Cake

For a nuttier texture, substitute half the flour with self-raising (self-rising) wholemeal flour.

MAKES 1 x 450 G/1 LB CAKE

A little oil, for greasing

225 g/8 oz/2 cups self-raising (self-rising) flour

5 ml/1 tsp mixed (apple-pie) spice

100 g/4 oz/½ cup butter or margarine, softened

100 g/4 oz/½ cup caster (superfine) sugar

75 g/3 oz/½ cup chopped cooking dates

30 ml/2 tbsp chopped walnut halves

1 egg, beaten

75 ml/5 tbsp milk

1 Grease a 450 g/1 lb loaf tin (pan). Cut a rectangle on non-stick baking parchment to fit the base and place in the bottom of the tin. Preheat the oven to 180°C/350°F/gas mark 4.

2 Sift the flour and spice into a bowl through a sieve (strainer).

3 Add the butter or margarine and mash with a fork until crumbly.

4 Stir in the sugar, dates and walnuts.

5 Stir in the egg and enough of the milk to form a soft consistency that will drop off the spoon easily.

6 Turn into the tin and level the surface.

7 Bake in the oven for about 1¼ hours until risen and golden and a skewer inserted in the centre comes out clean.

8 Cool slightly, then loosen the edges with a round-bladed knife. Turn out on to a wire rack, remove the paper and leave to cool.

Shortbread Triangles

Don't try to use margarine for this recipe – butter gives a far better flavour.

MAKES 8

75 g/3 oz/¾ cup plain (all-purpose) flour

A pinch of salt

25 g/1 oz/2 tbsp rice flour or cornflour (cornstarch)

65 g/2½ oz/scant ⅓ cup caster (superfine) sugar

100 g/4 oz/½ cup butter

1 Preheat the oven to 150°C/300°F/ gas mark 2.

2 Sift the flour, salt and rice flour or cornflour into a bowl.

3 Add 50 g/2 oz/¼ cup of the sugar and the butter, cut into small pieces, and mash with a fork until the mixture resembles fine breadcrumbs.

4 Press into an 18 cm/7 in sandwich tin (pan). Prick all over with a fork and mark into eight equal triangles. Chill for 1 hour.

5 Bake in the oven for about 1 hour until a very pale golden brown.

6 Sprinkle with the reserved caster sugar. Leave to cool in the tin, then transfer to a wire rack and break or cut into triangles before serving.

Fork Cookies

MAKES ABOUT 20

A little oil, for greasing

65 g/2½ oz/scant ⅓ cup soft tub margarine

50 g/2 oz/¼ cup caster (superfine) sugar

5 ml/1 tsp vanilla essence (extract)

100 g/4 oz/1 cup self-raising (self-rising) flour

Glacé (candied) cherries, halved, to decorate

1 Preheat the oven to 190°C/375°F/ gas mark 5. Grease two baking (cookie) sheets.

2 Put all the ingredients except the cherries in a bowl and mix with a fork until the mixture forms a dough.

3 Shape the dough into walnut-sized balls and place on the baking sheets.

4 Flatten with a fork dipped in cold water.

5 Bake one above the other in the oven for about 15 minutes until pale golden brown, swapping the sheets over halfway through cooking.

6 Top each with a halved cherry and leave until firm, then transfer to a wire rack to cool completely.

Banana and Cinnamon Muffins

MAKES ABOUT 16

3 ripe bananas
75 g/3 oz/⅓ cup light brown sugar
5 ml/1 tsp ground cinnamon
90 ml/6 tbsp sunflower oil
10 ml/2 tsp baking powder
1 egg
350 g/12 oz/3 cups self-raising (self-rising) flour
150 ml/¼ pt/⅔ cup milk
50 g/2 oz/⅓ cup raisins

1 Place paper cake cases (cupcake papers) in the sections of a tartlet tin. Preheat the oven to 190°C/375°F/ gas mark 5.
2 Reserve a small piece of banana, slice it, then cut it into wedges.
3 Purée the remaining bananas with the sugar until smooth.
4 Add the cinnamon, oil, baking powder and egg, stirring briskly.
5 Add the flour and mix again.
6 Mix in the milk to form a thick batter and stir in the raisins.
7 Spoon the mixture into the paper cases, almost to the top. Top with the banana wedges.
8 Bake in the oven for about 20 minutes until risen and golden and the centres spring back when lightly pressed. Cool on a wire rack.

Double Chocolate Muffins

MAKES ABOUT 12

190 g/6½ oz/ generous 1½ cups self-raising (self-rising) flour
40 g/1½ oz/3 tbsp cocoa (unsweetened chocolate) powder
10 ml/2 tsp baking powder
50 g/2 oz/¼ cup caster (superfine) sugar
1 egg
250 ml/8 fl oz/1 cup milk
90 ml/6 tbsp sunflower oil
50 g/2 oz/½ cup chocolate chips

1 Place paper cake cases (cupcake papers) in 12 sections of a tartlet tin (patty pan). Preheat the oven to 190°C/375°F/gas mark 5.
2 Sift the flour, cocoa and baking powder into a bowl. Stir in the sugar.
3 Whisk the egg, milk and oil together in a small bowl with a fork until the egg is well blended.
4 Pour into the flour mixture and mix with a wooden spoon until smooth.
5 Stir in the chocolate chips.
6 Spoon the mixture into the paper cases, almost to the top.
7 Bake in the oven for 20 minutes until risen and the centres spring back when lightly pressed. Cool on a wire rack.

Blueberry Muffins

MAKES ABOUT 15

100 g/4 oz/⅔ cup dried blueberries

45 ml/3 tbsp boiling water

225 g/8 oz/2 cups self raising (self-rising) flour

10 ml/2 tsp baking powder

65 g/2½ oz/generous ¼ cup caster (superfine) sugar

200 ml/7 fl oz/scant 1 cup milk

1 egg

90 ml/6 tbsp sunflower oil

1 Put the blueberries in a bowl and add the boiling water. Stir and leave to stand for 1 hour until they have soaked up the water.

2 Place paper cake cases (cupcake papers) in the sections of tartlet tins (patty pans). Preheat the oven to 190°C/375°F/gas mark 5.

3 Sift the flour and baking powder into a bowl. Stir in the sugar.

4 Whisk the milk, egg and oil together with a fork until the egg is well blended.

5 Add this to the flour mixture, and mix with a wooden spoon until smooth.

6 Stir in the soaked blueberries. Spoon into the cake cases, almost to the top.

7 Bake in the oven for 20 minutes or until risen, golden and the centres spring back when lightly pressed.

Chocolate Walnut Brownies

MAKES 12

50 g/2 oz/½ cup plain (all-purpose) flour

15 ml/1 tbsp bran

1.5 ml/¼ tsp baking powder

50 g/2 oz/½ cup walnuts, chopped

65 g/2½ oz/good ¼ cup butter or margarine

50 g/2 oz/½ cup plain (semi-sweet) chocolate, broken into pieces

175 g/6 oz/¾ cup dark brown sugar

2 eggs, beaten

2.5 ml/½ tsp vanilla essence (extract)

1 Grease a 28 cm × 18 cm/11 × 7 in shallow baking tin (pan). Cut a piece of non-stick baking parchment long enough to fit right round the tin with about 5 cm/2 in overlap. Press round the inside of the tin, cutting down into each corner so you can fold the paper round to fit.

2 Preheat the oven to 180°C/350°F/gas mark 4.

3 Mix together the flour, bran, baking powder and nuts. Melt the butter or margarine with the chocolate and sugar in a small saucepan.

4 Cool slightly, then whisk in the eggs and vanilla essence with a fork. Pour into the flour mixture and mix well. Turn into the prepared tin and bake in the oven for 35 minutes until risen and the centre springs back when lightly pressed.

5 Leave to cool in the tin, then cut into squares.

Rum and Raisin Truffle Cakes

If you haven't any stale, plain cake lying in the cupboard, use crumbled trifle sponges. Omit the raisins if you prefer smooth truffles. Petit fours cases are just like tiny paper cake cases (cupcake papers).

MAKES 12

25 g/1 oz/2 tbsp butter or margarine

30 ml/2 tbsp golden (light corn) syrup

30 ml/2 tbsp cocoa (unsweetened chocolate) powder, plus extra for dusting

15 ml/1 tbsp icing (confectioners') sugar

30 ml/2 tbsp raisins

100 g/4 oz/2 cups plain cake crumbs

2.5 ml/½ tsp rum essence (extract)

1 Put the butter or margarine with the syrup, cocoa and icing sugar in a saucepan, and cook over a gentle heat, stirring, until melted and blended. Remove from the heat.

2 Put the raisins in a cup and snip with scissors to chop. Tip into the chocolate mixture.

3 Add the cake crumbs and mix until thoroughly blended. Flavour with rum essence, to taste.

4 Roll into 12 small balls and place on a plate. Chill for 30 minutes, then roll in cocoa powder to coat completely. Place in paper petits fours cases and chill until ready to serve.

Maids of Honour

MAKES 10

175 g/6 oz ready-made puff pastry (paste), thawed if frozen

A little flour, for dusting

75 g/3 oz/⅓ cup medium-fat soft cheese

20 g/¾ oz/2 tbsp dried mixed fruit (fruit cake mix)

15 g/½ oz/1 tbsp butter or margarine, softened

25 g/1 oz/2 tbsp caster (superfine) sugar

Finely grated rind of ½ lemon

15 g/½ oz/2 tbsp ground almonds

1 egg, beaten

A little sifted icing (confectioners') sugar, to decorate.

1 Roll out the pastry on a lightly floured surface and cut into 10 rounds using a 7.5 cm/3 in biscuit (cookie) cutter. Use to line 10 sections of a tartlet tin (patty pan).

2 Preheat the oven to 190°C/375°F/ gas mark 5.

3 Mix all the remaining ingredients together thoroughly with a wooden spoon and use to fill the pastry cases (pie shells).

4 Bake in the oven for 35 minutes until risen and golden brown.

5 Transfer to a wire rack to cool, then dust with sifted icing sugar before serving.

Traditional Flapjacks

MAKES 9

50 g/2 oz/¼ cup butter or margarine,
plus a little for greasing
25 g/1 oz/2 tbsp light brown sugar
30 ml/2 tbsp golden (light corn) syrup
100 g/4 oz/1 cup rolled oats

1 Preheat the oven to 190°C/375°F/
gas mark 5. Grease an 18 cm/7 in
square, shallow baking tin (pan).
2 Put the margarine, sugar and syrup
in a saucepan and heat gently until the
fat melts.
3 Stir in the oats.
4 Tip the mixture into the tin and press
out to the corners. Bake in the oven for
about 20 minutes until golden brown.
5 Mark into nine pieces, then leave to
cool in the tin.

Chocolate Chip Flapjacks

MAKES 9

Prepare as for Traditional Flapjacks but
stir in 50 g/2 oz/½ cup chocolate chips
with the oats.

Cranberry Flapjacks

MAKES 9

Prepare as for Traditional Flapjacks but
add 50 g/2 oz/⅓ cup dried cranberries
and an extra 15 g/½ oz/1 tbsp light
brown sugar to the mixture.

Extra Crunchy Flapjacks

MAKES 18

75 g/3 oz/⅓ cup butter or margarine
25 g/1 oz/2 tbsp light brown sugar
30 ml/2 tbsp golden (light corn) syrup
175 g/6 oz/1½ cups Original Oat Crunch
cereal
50 g/2 oz/½ cup plain (all-purpose)
flour

1 Preheat the oven to 190°C/375°F/
gas mark 5.
2 Melt the butter or margarine, sugar
and syrup in a saucepan.
3 Stir in the remaining ingredients until
well mixed.
4 Turn into a non-stick 18 cm/7 in
square baking tin (pan) and press
down well.
5 Bake in the oven for 12 minutes or
until golden.
6 Cool slightly, then mark into 18 fingers.
Leave until completely cold before
removing from the tin. Store in an
airtight container.

Eccles Cakes

MAKES ABOUT 9

225 g/8 oz ready-made puff pastry (paste), thawed if frozen

A little flour, for dusting

15 g/½ oz/1 tbsp butter or margarine, melted

25 g/1 oz/2 tbsp granulated sugar

50 g/2 oz/⅓ cup currants

15 g/½ oz/2 tbsp mixed chopped (candied) peel

1.5 ml/¼ tsp ground cinnamon

1.5 ml/¼ tsp ground mace

1 Preheat the oven to 230°C/450°F/ gas mark 8.

2 On a lightly floured surface, roll out the pastry thinly and cut into rounds using a 10 cm/4 in cutter, re-rolling the trimmings to make the last few if necessary.

3 Brush a baking (cookie) sheet with a little of the butter or margarine.

4 Mix the remainder with the remaining ingredients.

5 Put a spoonful of the mixture on to the centre of each round. Brush the edges with water.

6 Draw the pastry up over the filling, pressing the edges well together to seal.

7 Turn the cakes over and roll gently with a rolling pin until you can see the currants through the pastry. Transfer to the baking sheet. Cut three slits in the top of each to decorate.

8 Bake in the oven for 15 minutes or until crisp and lightly golden. Serve warm or cold.

Vanilla Cut-and-bake Biscuits

Make the full quantity of mixture and store it in the fridge. The mixture will keep for up to 10 days before baking. You can then cook a batch as you wish for fresh, gorgeous snacks.

MAKES ABOUT 60

200 g/7 oz/1¾ cups plain (all-purpose) flour

25 g/1 oz/¼ cup cornflour (cornstarch)

5 ml/1 tsp baking powder

100 g/4 oz/½ cup butter or margarine, softened, plus extra for greasing

175 g/6 oz/¾ cup caster (superfine) sugar

5 ml/1 tsp vanilla essence (extract)

1 egg, beaten

1 Put the flour, cornflour and baking powder into a sieve (strainer) over a bowl and rub through using a wooden spoon.

2 Add the softened butter or margarine and work in with a fork until the mixture is crumbly.

3 Stir in the sugar, vanilla and egg to form a dough.

4 Draw together with your hands and shape into a long sausage. Wrap in foil and chill overnight.

5 To bake, preheat the oven to 190°C/ 375°F/gas mark 5. Cut thin slices off the roll and lay a little apart on a greased baking (cookie) sheet.

6 Bake in the oven for 12 minutes until a pale golden brown. Cool slightly, then transfer to a wire rack to cool. Store in an airtight container.

Almond Cut-and-bake Biscuits

MAKES ABOUT 60

Prepare as for Vanilla Cut-and-bake Biscuits (cookies), but use almond essence (extract) instead of vanilla and add 50 g/2 oz/½ cup chopped almonds to the mixture.

Date and Walnut Bars

MAKES 16

A little oil, for greasing
150 ml/¼ pt/⅔ cup sweetened condensed milk
50 g/2 oz/½ cup plain (all-purpose) flour
2.5 ml/½ tsp baking powder
A pinch of salt
100 g/4 oz/⅔ cup chopped cooking dates
40 g/1½ oz/⅓ cup walnut halves, chopped
A pinch of grated nutmeg

1 Grease an 18 cm × 28 cm/7 × 11 in shallow baking tin (pan). Preheat the oven to 190°C/375°F/gas mark 5.
2 Mix all the ingredients together in a bowl.
3 Tip the mixture into the tin and spread out.
4 Bake in the oven for about 30 minutes until golden brown. Mark into fingers while still hot, then leave to cool, remove from the tin and store in an airtight container.

Chocolate Bran Flake Cakes

You can, of course, make these with cornflakes, but I prefer the texture of branflakes.

MAKES 12

50 g/2 oz/¼ cup butter or margarine
45 ml/3 tbsp golden (light corn) syrup
50 g/2 oz/¼ cup light brown sugar
30 ml/2 tbsp cocoa (unsweetened chocolate) powder
A few drops of vanilla essence (extract)
100 g/4 oz/2 cups bran flakes

1 Put everything except the bran flakes in a saucepan and cook over a gentle heat, stirring until melted.
2 Stir in the bran flakes until thoroughly coated.
3 Spoon the mixture into paper cake cases (cupcake papers) and chill until firm.

Chocolate Banana Bran Flake Cakes

MAKES 12

Prepare exactly as for Chocolate Bran Flake Cakes but add 30 ml/2 tbsp dried banana slices, broken into pieces, with the bran flakes.

Chocolate Almond Bran Flake Cakes

MAKES 12

Prepare as for Chocolate Bran Flake Cakes but use almond essence (extract) instead of vanilla and add 30 ml/2 tbsp chopped almonds with the bran flakes.

No-bake Cherry and Walnut Cookies

MAKES 12

A little oil, for greasing
50 g/2 oz/¼ cup butter or margarine
45 ml/3 tbsp golden (light corn) syrup
50 g/2 oz/¼ cup caster (superfine) sugar
100 g/4 oz/1 cup rolled oats
75 g/3 oz/¾ cup glacé (candied) cherries, chopped
75 g/3 oz/¾ cup walnut halves, chopped

1 Lightly oil an 18 cm/7 in shallow, square baking tin (pan).
2 Put the butter or margarine, syrup and sugar in a saucepan and cook over a fairly low heat, stirring until melted. Remove from the heat.
3 Stir in the remaining ingredients.
4 Press into the prepared tin, leave to cool, then chill until firm and cut into fingers.

Strawberry Mallows

MAKES 12

50 g/2 oz/¼ cup butter or margarine
45 ml/3 tbsp strawberry jam (conserve)
50 g/2 oz pink marshmallows
100 g/4 oz/2 cups puffed rice cereal

1 Put the butter or margarine, jam and marshmallows in a saucepan. Cook over a fairly low heat, stirring until melted. Remove from the heat.
2 Stir in the puffed rice cereal and spoon into paper cake cases (cupcake papers). Leave to cool, then chill until firm.

Chocolate Biscuit Bars

This no-bake cake is always popular. You can buy broken biscuits very cheaply in supermarkets.

MAKES 15

100 g/4 oz/½ cup butter or margarine, plus extra for greasing
15 ml/1 tbsp caster (superfine) sugar
15 ml/1 tbsp golden (light corn) syrup
30 ml/2 tbsp cocoa (unsweetened chocolate) powder
225 g/8 oz/2 cups broken plain biscuits (cookies), roughly crushed
75 g/3 oz/⅓ cup sultanas (golden raisins)

1 Grease a 28 × 18 cm/11 × 7 in shallow baking tin (pan) with a little butter or margarine.
2 Put the butter or margarine, sugar, syrup and cocoa in a saucepan. Cook over a moderate heat, stirring until the fat melts and the mixture is well blended. Do not boil. Remove from the heat.
3 Add the biscuits and sultanas and mix with a wooden spoon until thoroughly blended.
4 Tip the mixture into the prepared tin and spread out evenly. Press down well with the back of a spoon. Leave until cool, then chill until firm. Cut into fingers before serving. Store any remainder in an airtight container.

Marbled Chocolate Biscuit Bars

MAKES 15

Prepare exactly as for Chocolate Biscuit Bars and leave to set. Break up 100 g/4 oz/1 cup each of plain (semi-sweet) chocolate and white chocolate and place in separate bowls. Stand the bowls in a large container of hot water, and stir until the chocolate melts (or microwave briefly on High). Spoon both lots on top of the biscuit slab, then spread out, swirling them together with a palette knife to give a marbled effect. Let the chocolate set before cutting into bars.

Muesli Cookies

MAKES ABOUT 30

75 g/3 oz/⅓ cup butter or margarine
75 g/3 oz/⅓ cup light brown sugar
25 ml/1½ tbsp golden (light corn) syrup
5 ml/1 tsp bicarbonate of soda (baking soda)
75 g/3 oz/¾ cup plain (all-purpose) flour
150 g/5 oz/1¼ cups muesli

1 Preheat the oven to 190°C/375°F/gas mark 5. Melt the butter or margarine, sugar and syrup in a saucepan.
2 Add the soda (it will froth). Stir in the flour and muesli.
3 Shape into walnut-sized balls and place a little way apart on two greased baking (cookie) sheets.
4 Flatten slightly with a fork. Bake in the oven for about 10 minutes until golden. Leave to cool for a few minutes, then transfer to a wire rack until cold. Store in an airtight container

Ginger Cracks

MAKES ABOUT 16

150 g/5 oz/generous ½ cup butter or margarine
100 g/4 oz/½ cup caster (superfine) sugar
225 g/8 oz/2 cups plain (all-purpose) flour
30 ml/2 tbsp ground ginger
5 ml/1 tsp baking powder
1 small egg, beaten
Pieces of crystallised (candied) ginger, to decorate

1 Put all the ingredients in a food processor and run the machine until the mixture forms a ball.
2 Shape into a roll about 5 cm/2 in in diameter and wrap in greaseproof (waxed) paper. Chill in the fridge for up to 2 weeks before use.
3 Cut into slices about 5 mm/¼ in thick and place on greased baking (cookie) sheet. Top each with a piece of candied ginger. Bake in a preheated oven at 190°C/375°F/gas mark 5 for 10–12 minutes until golden. Transfer to a wire rack to cool. Store in an airtight container.

Nibbles

This chapter contains recipes for all sorts of simple finger foods that you can enjoy as a quick snack or to serve as part of a buffet or with drinks. Use these as basic recipes and then ring the changes and try different variations as you become more adventurous.

Quick Cheese Straws

MAKES 30

175 g/6 oz puff pastry (paste), thawed
   if frozen
100 g/4 oz/1 cup strong Cheddar
   cheese, finely grated
A good pinch of cayenne
Beaten egg, to glaze

1 Preheat the oven to 190°C/375°F/
gas mark 5. Rinse a baking (cookie)
sheet with water and leave damp.
2 Roll out the pastry thinly to a
rectangle.
3 Sprinkle half the cheese over half the
pastry.
4 Fold the uncovered pastry over the
top and roll again with the rolling pin.
5 Cover half with the remaining cheese
and sprinkle with cayenne. Fold over,
roll out and brush with beaten egg.
6 Cut into thin strips, then, holding both
ends of each strip, twist gently. Place on
the baking (cookie) sheet.
7 Bake in the oven for 15–20 minutes
until crisp and golden brown. Serve
warm.

Twisted Savoury Sticks

MAKES 60

250 g/9 oz puff pastry (paste), thawed
   if frozen
15 ml/1 tbsp yeast extract
50 g/2 oz/½ cup Cheddar cheese, finely
   grated
1 egg, beaten, to glaze

1 Preheat the oven to 200°C/400°F/
gas mark 6. Rinse a baking (cookie)
sheet with water and leave damp.

2 Roll out the pastry to a 30 cm/12 in
square and trim the edges.
3 Spread with the yeast extract, then
sprinkle half the square with the cheese.
4 Fold the pastry in half over the
cheese and press together well.
5 Roll gently with the rolling pin to
flatten, then brush with beaten egg.
6 Cut into thin strips, widthways.
7 Hold each end of each strip and twist
it gently. Place on the baking sheet.
8 Bake in the oven for 10–15 minutes
until golden. Cool on a wire rack.

Bacon-wrapped Chipolatas

*These are also the perfect
accompaniment to roast chicken or
turkey. Make as many as you need.
Simply allow 1–2 chipolata sausages,
and 1–2 rashers (slices) of streaky
bacon per person.*

ALLOW 2–4 PER PERSON

1 Preheat the oven to 190°C/375°F/
gas mark 5.
2 Cut the sausages in half. Cut the rind
off the bacon if necessary. Stretch the
rashers by scraping the length of them
gently with the back of a knife, then
cut into half.
3 Wrap half a rasher of bacon round
each half sausage. Place in a small
roasting tin (pan) with the bacon ends
underneath.
4 Cook towards the top of the oven
for about 30 minutes until richly
browned, turning once. Drain on
kitchen paper (paper towels) before
serving, skewered on cocktail sticks
(toothpicks).

Cherubs on Horseback

MAKES 24

24 no-need-to-soak prunes
8 rashers (slices) of streaky bacon, rinded

1 Preheat the oven to 190°C/375°F/ gas mark 5.
2 Discard any stones (pits) in the prunes. Stretch the bacon rashers by scraping gently along them with the back of a knife, then cut each rasher into three pieces.
3 Wrap a piece of bacon round each prune. Place in a small roasting tin (pan), with the end of the bacon underneath, and cook towards the top of the oven for about 20 minutes until the bacon is crisp and brown. Spear on cocktail sticks (toothpicks) for serving.

Devils on Horseback

MAKES 24

Prepare as for Cherubs on Horseback but substitute a small button mushroom for each prune.

Angels on Horseback

MAKES ABOUT 24

250 g/9 oz/1 can of mussels in brine, drained
8–10 rashers (slices) of streaky bacon, rinded

Prepare and cook as for Cherubs on Horseback.

Crisp Crab Pinwheels

MAKES ABOUT 40

100 g/4 oz/½ cup Cheddar cheese spread
25 g/1 oz/2 tbsp butter or margarine, softened, plus extra for spreading
170 g/6 oz/1 small can of white crabmeat, drained
5 ml/1 tsp anchovy essence (extract)
Freshly ground black pepper
10 slices of white bread from a large sliced loaf

1 Preheat the oven to 180°C/350°F/ gas mark 4.
2 Mash the cheese spread with the butter or margarine, crabmeat, and anchovy essence. Season with pepper.
3 Cut the crusts off the bread and spread the slices on one side with butter or margarine.
4 Spread the unbuttered sides with the cheese and crab mixture and roll up.
5 Cut each roll into four or five slices and place on two baking (cookie) sheets.
6 Bake in the oven, one above the other, for 10–15 minutes until golden brown, swapping the sheets over halfway through cooking. Serve warm or cold.

Herby Hazelnut Bites

MAKES ABOUT 15

225 g/8 oz/1 cup medium-fat soft
cheese
90 ml/6 tbsp ground hazelnuts
(filberts)
15 ml/1 tbsp chopped fresh parsley
15 ml/1 tbsp snipped fresh chives
Salt and freshly ground black pepper

1 Mix the cheese with 60 ml/4 tbsp of
the nuts, the parsley, chives and salt
and pepper to taste.
2 Shape into bite-sized balls, then roll in
the remaining hazelnuts. Chill until
ready to serve.

Smoked Salmon Morswiches

MAKES 36

8 thin slices of brown bread
100 g/4 oz/½ cup medium-fat soft
cheese
4 thin slices of smoked salmon
A little lemon juice
Freshly ground black pepper
60 ml/4 tbsp salad cress

1 Spread one side of each slice of bread
with the cheese.
2 Top four slices with smoked salmon,
trimming to fit.
3 Sprinkle with a little lemon juice, a
good grinding of pepper and the cress.
4 Sandwich together with the
remaining bread.
5 Cut off the crusts, then cut each
sandwich into nine squares (by making
two cuts in each direction). Arrange on
a serving plate.

Asparagus and Pesto Pinwheels

*You can make your own pesto, using
the recipe for Simple Pesto Sauce on
page 336.*

MAKES 30

5 medium slices of white bread
Butter or margarine, for spreading
45 ml/3 tbsp ready-made pesto
295 g/10½ oz/1 medium can of
asparagus spears, drained

1 Roll the bread gently with a rolling
pin to flatten slightly.
2 Spread very thinly with butter or
margarine on one side and cut off the
crusts.
3 Spread the pesto thinly over.
4 Dry the asparagus on kitchen paper
(paper towels), then lay one or two
spears along one edge of each slice. Roll
up gently and wrap in clingfilm (plastic
wrap). Chill in the fridge until ready to
serve.
5 Cut each roll into five slices and
arrange the pinwheels on a serving
plate.

Duck Mandarin Whirls

MAKES 30

5 medium slices of wholemeal bread
Butter or margarine, for spreading
100 g/4 oz duck pâté
15 ml/1 tbsp mayonnaise
300 g/11 oz/1 medium can of mandarin
   orange segments, drained

1 Gently roll the bread with a rolling pin to flatten slightly.
2 Spread one side of each with a little butter or margarine. Cut off the crusts.
3 Mash the pâté with the mayonnaise until smooth and spreadable. Spread over the buttered slices.
4 Drain the mandarin oranges well on kitchen paper (paper towels). Put a line of the fruit down one edge of each slice. Roll up and wrap in clingfilm (plastic wrap). Chill in the fridge until ready to serve.
5 Cut each roll into five slices and arrange the whirls on a serving plate.

Hot Mushroom Bakes

MAKES ABOUT 40

8 slices of bread, crusts removed
Butter or margarine, for spreading
170 g/6 oz/1 small can of creamed
   mushrooms
5 ml/1 tsp dried oregano

1 Preheat the oven to 190°C/375°F/ gas mark 5.
2 Spread the bread on one side only with butter or margarine. Place buttered sides down on a baking (cookie) sheet.
3 Spread with the creamed mushrooms and sprinkle with oregano. Roll up, making sure the sealed edge is underneath. Cut each into five pinwheels, and arrange on the sheet.
4 Bake in the oven for about 10 minutes or until crisp and golden. Serve hot.

Hot Chilli Ham Bakes

MAKES ABOUT 40

8 slices of bread, crusts removed
Butter or margarine, for spreading
8 slices of ham
Chilli relish

1 Preheat the oven to 190°C/375°F/ gas mark 5. Spread the bread on one side with butter or margarine.
2 Place buttered sides down on a baking (cookie) sheet and top each with a slice of ham. Spread with chilli relish to taste.
3 Roll up and cut each into five pinwheels. Arrange on the sheet.
4 Bake in the oven for about 10 minutes or until crisp and golden. Serve hot.

'Caviar' on Toast

MAKES 45

5 medium slices of white bread
Butter or margarine, for spreading
50 g/2 oz/1 small jar of Danish lumpfish
  roe
½ small lemon, thinly sliced

1 Toast the bread on both sides and
butter while still hot.
2 Cut off the crusts and make two cuts
in each direction to cut each slice into
nine bite-sized squares.
3 Top each with a little lumpfish roe.
4 Cut the lemon slices into tiny wedges
and put a piece on top of each pile of
'caviar'. Arrange on a serving plate.

Sardine Cucumber Bites

MAKES ABOUT 24

120 g/4½ oz/1 small can of sardines,
  drained
175 g/6 oz/¾ cup medium-fat soft
  cheese
10 ml/2 tsp soy sauce
5 ml/1 tsp horseradish relish
Freshly ground black pepper
1 large cucumber
Cayenne, to garnish

1 Mash the sardines well with the
cheese, soy sauce, horseradish and
pepper to taste. Chill.
2 Cut the cucumber into 1 cm/½ in thick
slices. Scoop out some of the seeds to
form a shallow bowl in the centre of
each slice. Pat dry on kitchen paper
(paper towels).
3 Spoon the sardine mixture into the
centres and sprinkle with cayenne.
Arrange on a serving plate.

Celery and Cheese Boats with Caraway

MAKES ABOUT 24

2 celery sticks
175 g/6 oz/¾ cup cheese spread
30 ml/2 tbsp caraway seeds

1 Trim the celery and cut each stick into
short lengths.
2 Spread the cheese in the groove in
each piece and sprinkle with caraway
seeds. Arrange on a serving plate.

Smoked Mussel Pâté Canapés

MAKES ABOUT 30

100 g/4 oz/1 small can of smoked
  mussels, drained
150 ml/¼ pt/⅔ cup crème fraîche
100 g/4 oz/½ cup medium-fat soft
  cheese
5 ml/1 tsp Dijon mustard
15 ml/1 tbsp soy sauce
Grated rind of ½ lemon
1 packet of party-sized rice cakes or
  small, round crackers
Butter or margarine, for spreading
30 ml/2 tbsp snipped fresh chives, to
  garnish

1 Put all the ingredients except the rice
cakes, butter or margarine and chives
in a blender or food processor and run
the machine until smooth. Turn into a
small container, cover and chill.
2 Spread the rice cakes or crackers
with butter or margarine, then top
with the mussel mixture. Sprinkle with
chives to garnish.

Prawn Toasts

These are a bit more adventurous but worth trying out for a tasty snack or supper dish. Keep warm in a low oven at 140°C/275°F/gas mark 1, covered loosely with foil, until ready to serve.

MAKES 32

10 raw peeled tiger prawns (jumbo shrimp)

½ small garlic clove, crushed

5 ml/1 tsp soy sauce, plus extra for serving

5 ml/1 tsp lemon juice

A few drops of Tabasco sauce

50 g/2 oz/½ cup sesame seeds

8 slices of white bread, crusts removed

Oil, for deep-frying

1 Purée the prawns, garlic, soy sauce, lemon juice, Tabasco sauce and half the sesame seeds in a blender or food processor, stopping and scraping down the sides as necessary.

2 Spread over one side of each slice of bread, sprinkle with the remaining sesame seeds, then press down well and cut into triangles.

3 Heat the oil for deep-frying in a saucepan or deep-fat fryer to 190°C/375°F or until a cube of day-old bread browns in 30 seconds. Cook the toasts a few at a time for about 3 minutes until golden brown and crisp. Drain on kitchen paper (paper towels) and keep warm while cooking the remainder.

4 Put a small bowl of soy sauce for dipping in the centre of a large plate and arrange the toasts around.

Nacho Nibbles

MAKES ABOUT 30

425 g/15 oz/1 large can of red kidney beans, drained

2 spring onions (scallions), finely chopped

15 ml/1 tbsp sunflower oil

1 large tomato, finely chopped

5 ml/1 tsp chilli powder

200 g/7 oz/1 large packet of tortilla chips

100 g/4 oz/1 cup Mozzarella cheese, grated

100 g/4 oz/1 cup Cheddar cheese, grated

1 Preheat the oven to 200°C/400°F/ gas mark 6.

2 Put the beans in bowl. Mash thoroughly with a potato masher, then work in the spring onions, oil, tomato and chilli powder with a wooden spoon.

3 Spread thinly on the tortilla chips. Place on a baking (cookie) sheet.

4 Mix the two cheeses together and sprinkle a little on top of each tortilla.

5 Bake in the oven for about 8 minutes until the cheese melts and bubbles. Serve straight away.

Cheese and Pecan Bites

MAKES ABOUT 24

225 g/8 oz ready-made puff pastry (paste), thawed if frozen
100 g/4 oz/½ cup cottage cheese with chives
30 ml/2 tbsp tomato relish
A few drops of Tabasco sauce
Salt and freshly ground black pepper
24 pecan halves

1 Preheat the oven to 230°C/450°F/ gas mark 8.
2 Roll out the pastry thinly and cut into 24 rounds, using a 2.5 cm/1 in biscuit (cookie) cutter or bottle top as a guide, re-rolling the trimmings as necessary to make the final few.
3 Place on a baking (cookie) sheet and bake in the oven for 8–10 minutes until golden and crisp. Cool on a wire rack.
4 Mix all the remaining ingredients except the nuts and pile on the pastry rounds. Top each with a pecan half and arrange on a serving plate.

Spiced Almonds

SERVES ABOUT 6

25 g/1 oz/2 tbsp unsalted (sweet) butter
175 g/6 oz/1½ cups whole blanched almonds
5 ml/1 tsp chilli powder
5 ml/1 tsp mixed (apple-pie) spice
2.5 ml/½ tsp salt
A good grinding of black pepper

1 Melt the butter in a frying pan (skillet).
2 Add the almonds and cook, stirring until golden. Remove from the heat.

3 Sprinkle over the chilli and mixed spice. Stir well to mix.
Drain on kitchen paper (paper towels). Tip into a bowl, add the salt and pepper and stir again. Leave to cool.

Stuffed Cherry Tomatoes

If you think filling the tomatoes is too fiddly, spoon the mixture on slices of buttered toast, then cut the crusts off and cut into small squares.

MAKES ABOUT 20

About 20 good-sized cherry tomatoes
225 g/8 oz/1 cup cottage cheese with prawns
15 ml/1 tbsp mayonnaise
15 ml/1 tbsp snipped fresh chives
About 20 cooked peeled prawns (shrimp)

1 Cut a slice off the rounded end of each tomato.
2 Scoop out the seeds and discard. Stand the tomatoes upside-down on kitchen paper (paper towels) to drain.
3 Mix the cheese and mayonnaise together. Using a teaspoon, spoon the mixture into each tomato.
4 Sprinkle with a few snipped chives and top each with a prawn. Arrange, standing on their stalk ends, on a serving plate and chill until ready to serve.

Toasted Red Dills

MAKES 24

6 slice of granary bread, crusts
removed

24 slices of dill-pickled cucumber,
drained on kitchen paper (paper
towels)

175 g/6 oz/1½ cups red Leicester cheese,
grated

15 g/½ oz/1 tbsp butter or margarine

A good pinch of cayenne

2.5 ml/½ tsp tomato ketchup (catsup)

2.5 ml/½ tsp dried dill (dill weed)

1 Preheat the oven to 220°C/425°F/
gas mark 7.

2 Toast the bread on both sides and
cut into quarters.

3 Top each with a slice of dill pickle and
place on a baking (cookie) sheet.

4 Mash the cheese with the butter or
margarine, cayenne, tomato ketchup
and dill. Spoon over the top of the dill
pickles.

5 Bake in the oven for 5 minutes until
golden and bubbling. Serve hot.

Pizza Bites with Anchovies

MAKES 24

1 small French stick

4 tomatoes, each cut into 6 slices

100 g/4 oz/1 cup Mozzarella cheese,
grated

5 ml/1 tsp dried oregano

50 g/2 oz/1 small can of anchovies,
drained

1 Preheat the oven to 220°C/425°F/
gas mark 7.

2 Cut the French stick into 24 thin slices.

3 Toast on both sides.

4 Top each with a slice of tomato, a
little Mozzarella and a sprinkling of
oregano.

5 Cut each anchovy fillet into three
pieces, roll into a curl and place on top
of each bread slice.

6 Bake in the oven for about 5 minutes
or until the cheese melts and bubbles.
Serve hot.

Greek Pitta Bites

*These are fiddly but delicious! If you
can't find the tiny pitta breads, fill
large pittas fairly thinly with the dips,
then cut them into bite-sized pieces.*

MAKES ABOUT 30

1 packet of party (bite-sized) pitta
breads

100 g/4 oz/1 small tub of taramasalata

100 g/4 oz/1 small tub of hummus

100 g/4 oz/1 small tub of tzatziki

100 g/4 oz black olives, to serve

1 Warm the pittas briefly in a hot oven
at 200°C/400°F/gas mark 6 for
2 minutes to puff up.

2 Carefully spit along one edge of each
and spoon in one of the fillings, using a
small teaspoon.

3 Put a pile of olives in the centre of a
large dish and arrange the pittas
around.

Prosciutto Porcupine

Quantities are not important for this party dish. Simply make as many as you like of the following and skewer each on a cocktail stick (toothpick).

ALLOW 2–3 STICKS PER PERSON

Stuffed olives wrapped in strips of Milano salami

Cubes or balls of melon wrapped in strips of Parma ham

Cubes of fried (sautéed) pancetta with pieces of sun-dried tomato in oil

Cubes of Mozzarella cheese wrapped in strips of bresaola

1 Place a large grapefruit or orange, stalk-side down, in a shallow bowl, to prevent it from rolling around.
2 Push the cocktail sticks firmly in all over the fruit.

Cheesy Porcupine

Make your porcupine as above and use different varieties of cheese for colour and flavour. Make up as many cocktail sticks (toothpicks) as you like.

ALLOW 2–3 STICKS PER PERSON

Cubes of Cheddar cheese with canned or fresh pineapple cubes

Cubes of a creamy blue cheese such as Dolcelatte with cocktail (pearl) onions

Cubes of Mozzarella with half a cherry tomato and a fresh basil leaf

Cubes of Gruyère (Swiss) cheese with green or black stoned (pitted) olives

Almond-stuffed Dates

MAKES 24

24 fresh dates
100 g/4 oz white almond paste
24 whole blanched almonds

1 Using a sharp knife, make a slit in the side of each date and remove the stone (pit).
2 Cut the almond paste into 24 equal pieces. Roll each into a small sausage shape and push inside a date.
3 Push a whole, blanched almond into the top of the paste. Arrange on a serving plate.

Garlic Potato Bites

MAKES 24

24 waxy baby new potatoes, scrubbed
25 g/1 oz/2 tbsp butter or margarine
30 ml/2 tbsp olive oil
1 large garlic clove, quartered
150 ml/¼ pt/⅔ cup mayonnaise
15 ml/1 tbsp snipped fresh chives

1 Put the potatoes in a pan and cover with water. Add a good pinch of salt.
2 Bring to the boil and boil for about 10 minutes until the potatoes are tender. Drain.
3 Melt the butter or margarine with the oil in a frying pan (skillet). Add the potatoes and garlic. Fry (sauté) for about 10 minutes, stirring, until golden brown all over. Drain on kitchen paper (paper towels) and discard the garlic. Spear on cocktail sticks (toothpicks).
4 Spoon the mayonnaise into a small pot and sprinkle with the chives. Serve with the hot potatoes.

Stuffed Quail's Eggs with Avocado

MAKES 24

12 quail's eggs
1 small ripe avocado
2.5 ml/½ tsp lemon juice
5 ml/1 tsp olive oil
2.5 ml/½ tsp Worcestershire sauce
Salt and freshly ground black pepper
A few lettuce leaves
A little paprika, for dusting

1 Put the eggs in a saucepan and cover with water. Bring to the boil and boil for 3 minutes. Pour off the boiling water, fill the pan with cold water and leave the eggs to cool.
2 Roll them gently on the work surface to break the shells, then carefully peel.
3 Cut the avocado in half, remove the stone (pit), then scoop the flesh into a bowl.
4 Mash with the lemon juice, olive oil and Worcestershire sauce until fairly smooth.
5 Cut the eggs in halves and gently scoop the yolks into the avocado. Mash well, then stir briskly with a wooden spoon until smooth. Season with salt and pepper.
6 Pile the mixture back into the eggs. Arrange on a bed of lettuce and sprinkle each with a little paprika.

Stuffed Hen's Eggs with Avocado

MAKES 8

Prepare as for Stuffed Quail's Eggs, but use four hen's eggs and boil them for 10 minutes.

Ham and Pepper Roll-ups

MAKES 16

175 g/6 oz/¾ cup medium-fat soft cheese
1 small red (bell) pepper, finely chopped
2 spring onions (scallions), finely chopped
1 celery stick, finely chopped
Salt and freshly ground black pepper
8 thin slices of ham

1 Mash the cheese with the pepper, onion, celery and some salt and pepper to taste.
2 Cut the slices of ham in half and spread each half with the cheese mixture. Roll up and arrange on a serving plate, with the ends tucked underneath. Chill until ready to serve.

Artichoke and Prawn Snacks

MAKES ABOUT 24

425 g/15 oz/1 large can of artichoke hearts, drained
About 24 cooked peeled tiger prawns (jumbo shrimp)
1 quantity of Aioli (see page 341)

1 Dry the artichoke hearts well on kitchen paper (paper towels) and cut into quarters or halves, if not very large.
2 Thread a piece of artichoke and a prawn on cocktail sticks (toothpicks).
3 Make the Aioli and spoon into a small pot. Put in the centre of a serving plate and arrange the artichoke and prawn snacks around to dip in.

Canapés at the Ritz

*The number you make will depend
how many broken biscuits there are
in the box! Ring the changes with
ham, salami, tuna – anything you
have in the storecupboard and
fridge. Don't forget to butter the
crackers first so they don't go soggy.*

MAKES ABOUT 30

1 box of Ritz crackers

Butter or margarine, for spreading

2 hard-boiled (hard-cooked) eggs,
sliced

50 g/2 oz/1 very small jar of Danish
lumpfish roe

2 thin slices of Cheddar cheese, cut into
2.5 cm/1 in squares

A little sweet pickle

50 g/2 oz cooked peeled prawns
(shrimp)

50 g/2 oz/¼ cup medium-fat soft
cheese

A few drops of Tabasco sauce

50 g/2 oz smooth liver pâté

¼ red (bell) pepper, cut into small
diamond shapes

Sprigs of parsley, to garnish

1 Butter the crackers.

2 Top some crackers with a slice of
hard-boiled egg and a tiny spoonful of
Danish lumpfish roe.

3 On others, arrange a square of
Cheddar cheese and a tiny blob of
sweet pickle.

4 Chop all but eight of the prawns. Mix
with the cheese and a few drops of
Tabasco sauce. Spoon on crackers and
top with the reserved prawns.

5 Top the remaining crackers with
smooth liver pâté and add a piece of
red pepper to garnish.

6 Arrange attractively on a large
platter, garnished with sprigs of parsley.

Scallops and Parma Ham with Orange Mayo

MAKES 24

15 ml/1 tbsp olive oil

24 queen scallops

Finely grated rind and juice of
1 orange

Freshly ground black pepper

6 slices of Parma ham

150 ml/¼ pt/⅔ cup mayonnaise

45 ml/3 tbsp snipped fresh chives

1 Heat the oil in a small saucepan. Add
the scallops and stir gently over a high
heat, turning them over in the oil, for
2 minutes. Add half the orange juice
and a good grinding of pepper. Stir
well, remove from the heat and leave
to cool.

2 Cut each piece of Parma ham into
four strips. Roll a cooled scallop in each
piece of ham and secure with a
cocktail stick. Chill.

3 Mix the mayonnaise with the juices
from the pan, the orange rind and
remaining orange juice. Season with
pepper and stir in the chives. Tip into a
small bowl and chill until ready to
serve.

4 Put the bowl in the centre of a large
serving plate and arrange the scallops
around.

Turkey Bites with Cranberry Dip

MAKES ABOUT 24

150 ml/¼ pt/⅔ cup crème fraîche
2 spring onions (scallions), finely chopped
45 ml/3 tbsp cranberry sauce
Salt and freshly ground black pepper
3 turkey breast steaks
1 egg
85 g/3½ oz/1 small packet of sage and onion stuffing mix
Oil, for shallow-frying

1 Mix the crème fraîche with the spring onions, cranberry sauce and salt and pepper to taste. Spoon the mixture into a small bowl and chill until ready to serve.
2 Cut the turkey steaks into bite-sized pieces (they should make about eight each).
3 Beat the egg on one plate and empty the stuffing mix on to another.
4 Dip the turkey pieces first in the egg, then the stuffing mix, to coat completely.
5 Heat about 5 mm/¼ in oil in a large frying pan (skillet). Fry (sauté) the turkey for about 3 minutes on each side until golden and cooked through. Drain on kitchen paper (paper towels).
6 Spear on cocktail sticks (toothpicks) and arrange around the dish of dip on a large serving plate. Serve warm or cold.

Croquet Squares

MAKES 36

8 medium slices of white bread, crusts removed
Butter or margarine, for spreading
175 g/6 oz/1½ cups Cheddar cheese, grated
1 onion, finely chopped
8 sage leaves, finely chopped
Freshly ground black pepper
2 eggs
30 ml/2 tbsp milk
Oil, for shallow-frying

1 Spread one side of each bread slice with butter or margarine.
2 Make into sandwiches with the cheese, onion, sage and pepper.
3 Beat the eggs and milk together.
4 Cut the sandwiches into nine small squares by making two cuts in each direction. Dip in the egg and milk to coat completely.
5 Heat about 5 mm/¼ in oil in a large frying pan (skillet). Add the mini sandwiches and fry (sauté) for about 2 minutes on each side until golden brown. Drain on kitchen paper (paper towels) and serve hot.

Drinks

This section contains recipes for hot and cold drinks suitable for every occasion, whether you're having a big party, a small celebration or just a quiet evening in the garden. They include long, refreshing coolers, smooth, creamy shakes, hot and cold punches and after-dinner coffees. There is also a range of non-alcoholic recipes for children, teetotallers and drivers. And don't forget, you can find the perfect accompaniments in the Nibbles chapter on pages 418–30.

Minted Cider Cup

SERVES 6-8

100 g/4 oz/½ cup granulated sugar
150 ml/¼ pt/⅔ cup boiling water
1 large sprig of mint
45 ml/3 tbsp lemon juice
150 ml/¼ pt/⅔ cup gin
Ice cubes
5 cm/2 in piece of cucumber, cut into very thin slices
1 litre/1¾ pts/4¼ cups dry cider

1 Put the sugar in a bowl and stir in the boiling water until dissolved. Add the mint sprig and leave until cold.

2 Remove the mint and stir in the lemon juice and gin.

3 Put ice cubes and slices of cucumber in tall glasses. Mix the cider into the gin mixture and pour over the ice. Serve.

Planters' Punch

SERVES 6-8

250 ml/8 fl oz/1 cup dark rum
60 ml/4 tbsp grenadine syrup
450 ml/¾ pt/2 cups pure orange juice
300 ml/½ pt/1¼ cups pure pineapple juice
Juice of 1 lime
1 orange, sliced
1 lemon sliced
Ice cubes

1 Mix all the ingredients except the ice cubes together in a large jug. Chill until ready to serve.

2 Fill tumblers with ice and pour the punch over.

Sparkling Melon Punch

Use a pack of thawed, frozen melon balls, if you prefer

SERVES 12-15

1 small honeydew melon
1 bottle of medium-dry white wine
30 ml/2 tbsp clear honey
30 ml/2 tbsp brandy
20 fresh mint leaves
2-3 handfuls of ice cubes
1 bottle of sparkling medium or dry white wine

1 Cut the melon in half and discard the seeds. Scoop out the flesh with a melon baller or cut off all the skin and dice the flesh.

2 Put in a large bowl and stir in the still wine, the honey, brandy and mint. Leave to soak for 1 hour in the fridge.

3 When ready to serve, add the ice cubes and sparkling wine and ladle into glasses.

Sangria

SERVES 6-8

300 ml/½ pt/1¼ cups water
45 ml/3 tbsp caster (superfine) sugar
1 bottle of red wine
30 ml/2 tbsp lemon juice
1 orange, sliced
1 lemon, sliced
30 ml/2 tbsp brandy
300 ml/½ pt/1¼ cups lemonade, chilled

1 Mix all the ingredients except the lemonade in a large jug. Chill.

2 When ready to serve, add the lemonade, stir and serve.

DRINKS

Pimms

SERVES 6

5 cm/2 in piece of cucumber, thinly
sliced
A handful of fresh borage or mint
leaves
1 lemon, halved and sliced
½ bottle Pimms No. 1 Cup
Ice cubes
Lemonade

1 Put the cucumber, borage or mint
and lemon in a large jug and add the
Pimms. Chill until ready to serve.
2 Top up the jug with lemonade to
taste, stir and serve over ice in tall
glasses.

Peach and Ginger Sizzler

SERVES 6

300 ml/½ pt/1¼ cups Archers peach
liqueur
1 lemon, halved and sliced
1 fresh peach, thinly sliced
Ice cubes
600 ml/1 pt/2½ cups ginger ale, chilled
A few fresh mint leaves

1 Put the peach liqueur in a jug with
the slices of lemon and peach. Chill until
ready to serve.
2 Fill tall glasses with ice cubes. Stir the
ginger ale into the jug, then pour over
the ice cubes, top with the mint leaves
and serve.

Papaya Sling

SERVES 4

1 ripe papaya
50 g/2 oz/¼ cup caster (superfine)
sugar
2 limes
45 ml/3 tbsp single (light) cream
150 ml/¼ pt/⅔ cup milk
Crushed ice

1 Peel the papaya, cut in half and
remove the black seeds. Cut into pieces
and place in a blender or food
processor with the sugar.
2 Squeeze the juice of one of the limes
and add with the cream and milk.
3 Run the machine until the mixture is
thick and smooth.
4 Pour over crushed ice in glasses. Cut
four slices off the remaining lime. Make
a small cut into each from the centre
to the edge and hang over the rim of
each glass.

Daiquiri

SERVES 4

Juice of 3 limes
15 ml/1 tbsp icing (confectioners') sugar
175 ml/6 fl oz/¾ cup white rum
Cracked ice

1 Mix the lime juice and sugar together
until dissolved.
2 Pour into four cocktail glasses.
3 Stir in the rum and fill the glasses with
cracked ice. Serve straight away.

Banana Daiquiri

SERVES 4

1 ripe banana, broken into pieces
250 ml/8 fl oz/1 cup white rum
30 ml/2 tbsp banana liqueur or orange
  liqueur
Juice of 2 limes
15 ml/1 tbsp caster (superfine) sugar
Cracked ice

1 Put the banana in a blender or food processor with all the ingredients except the ice. Run the machine until smooth and thick.
2 Fill four tumblers with cracked ice and pour in the cocktail. Serve at once.

Pineapple Daiquiri

SERVES 4

250 ml/9 oz/1 medium can of crushed
  pineapple
Juice of 2 limes
150 ml/¼ pt/⅔ cup white rum
15 ml/1 tbsp brandy
Crushed ice

1 Put the pineapple in a blender with the remaining ingredients. Run the machine briefly until almost smooth but still with some 'bits'.
2 Put lots of crushed ice in four cocktail glasses, pour over and serve.

Strawberry Daiquiri

SERVES 4

225 g/8 oz ripe strawberries, hulled
Juice of 2 limes
200 ml/7 fl oz/scant 1 cup white rum
30 ml/2 tbsp icing (confectioners')
  sugar
15 ml/1 tbsp orange liqueur
Crushed ice

1 Put all the ingredients except the ice in a blender or food processor. Run the machine until smooth.
2 Fill four cocktail glasses with crushed ice and pour the cocktail over. Serve straight away.

Caribbean Sunrise

SERVES 2

6 ice cubes
150 ml/¼ pt/⅔ cup dark rum
50 ml/2 fl oz/¼ cup sweet red
  vermouth

1 Put the ice in two tumblers.
2 Pour in the rum.
3 Tilt the glasses and gently pour in the vermouth but don't mix completely into the rum. Serve.

Sloe Gin

If you are lucky enough to have sloes growing nearby, do try making this famous and delicious alcoholic drink. The sloes, once soaked, can be stoned (pitted) and used as part of a fruit salad or served with ice cream.

MAKES 600 ML/1 PT/2¼ CUPS

225 g/8 oz/1 cup sloes
175 g/6 oz/¾ cup granulated sugar
4 drops of almond essence (extract)
4 juniper berries, crushed
450 ml/¾ pt/2 cups gin

1 Wash the sloes and prick them two or three times with a large, clean needle or fine skewer.

2 Put them in an empty gin bottle.

3 Add the sugar, almond essence and juniper berries. Pour on the gin and screw the cap on tightly. Shake gently until the sugar dissolves.

4 Leave in a dark place for at least 3 months, shaking occasionally. Strain through a sieve (strainer) into a jug, then pour back into the bottle and screw back the cap. Use as required.

Tequila Sunrise

SERVES 2

Crushed ice
250 ml/8 fl oz/1 cup pure orange juice
100 ml/3½ fl oz/scant ½ cup tequila
30 ml/2 tbsp grenadine syrup

1 Fill two tumblers with crushed ice. Add the orange juice, then the tequila. Stir well.

2 Hold the spoon over the top of the drink and gently pour the grenadine over, to float on the top. Serve at once.

Margaritas

SERVES 2

Juice of 2 limes
Sea salt
90 ml/6 tbsp tequila
30 ml/2 tbsp orange liqueur
10 ml/2 tsp caster (superfine) sugar
Crushed ice

1 Dip the rim of two cocktail glasses in the lime juice, then in sea salt to give a frosted rim.

2 Whisk the remaining lime juice with the tequila, orange liqueur and sugar (or put in a cocktail shaker).

3 Fill the cocktail glasses with crushed ice and pour the cocktail over. Serve straight away.

Vinka 1812

I created this cocktail a long time ago. It's very potent but very delicious and very dry.

SERVES 8

150 ml/¼ pt/⅔ cup vodka
1 lemon
1 bottle of dry white wine, chilled

1 Put the vodka in a screw-topped jar or other sealable container. Cut off all the lemon rind and add to the vodka. Cover tightly and chill in the fridge for at least 6 hours, preferably 24 hours.

2 When ready to serve, discard the lemon rind, pour the vodka into a large jug and stir in the chilled wine. Pour into cocktail glasses and serve.

Brandy Sour

SERVES 6

175 ml/6 fl oz/¾ cup brandy
Juice of 3 lemons
Ice cubes
Sparkling mineral water
1 lemon, sliced, to decorate

1 Put the brandy and lemon juice in a cocktail shaker full of ice. Shake well, then pour into tall glasses.
2 Top up with sparkling water to taste and stir. Add a slice of lemon and serve.

Whisky Sour

SERVES 2

120 ml/4 fl oz/½ cup whisky
30 ml/2 tbsp pure orange juice
30 ml/2 tbsp lemon juice
15 ml/1 tbsp caster (superfine) sugar
2 Maraschino cherries

1 Mix all the ingredients except the cherries together.
2 Pour into cocktail glasses and add a Maraschino cherry to each.

Champagne Cocktail

SERVES 6

6 small sugar cubes
12 dashes of Angostura bitters
1 bottle of champagne, chilled

1 Put a sugar cube in the base of each champagne glass. Add two drops of bitters to each.
2 Top up with champagne but do not stir.

Champagne Kicker

SERVES 6

Prepare as for Champagne Cocktail but add 15 ml/1 tbsp brandy to each glass before adding the champagne.

Brandy Alexander

SERVES 2

60 ml/4 tbsp brandy
60 ml/4 tbsp double (heavy) cream
60 ml/4 tbsp Crème de Cacao
Ice cubes

Whisk the brandy, cream and Crème de Cacao together and pour over ice cubes in two small glasses.

Manhattan

SERVES 2

100 ml/3½ fl oz/scant ½ cup whisky
 45 ml/3 tbsp sweet red vermouth
A few drops of Angostura bitters
2 Maraschino cherries (optional)

Mix the whisky, vermouth and Angostura bitters together and pour into two cocktail glasses. Add a cherry . to each, if liked.

Martini

SERVES 2

90 ml/6 tbsp gin
90 ml/6 tbsp dry vermouth
2 green olives or 2 thin shavings of
    lemon peel

Mix the gin and vermouth together in cocktail glasses and add an olive or shaving of lemon peel to each.

Gibson

SERVES 2

Prepare as for Martini but add a white pearl cocktail onion to each glass instead of the olive or lemon peel.

Sidecar

They say if you can make a good one of these, you're a great barman!

SERVES 2

120 ml/4 fl oz/½ cup brandy
60 ml/4 tbsp Cointreau
1 large lemon
Cracked ice

1 Mix the brandy with the Cointreau.
2 Pare off two strips of lemon rind and reserve. Cut the fruit in half, squeeze the juice and pour through a sieve (strainer) into the alcohol.
3 Fill two narrow tumblers with cracked ice. Add a strip of lemon rind to each. Pour in the alcohol and lemon mixture, stir with a swizzle stick and serve.

Rusty Nail

SERVES 2

Cracked ice
150 ml/¼ pt/⅔ cup whisky
50 ml/2 fl oz/¼ cup Drambuie
Ice cubes

1 Put lots of cracked ice in a cocktail shaker or jug.
2 Add the alcohol and shake or stir well.
3 Fill two narrow tumblers with ice cubes. Strain the cocktail over and serve.

Black Velvet

For those with a sweeter tooth, choose Mackeson or other milk stout rather than Guinness.

SERVES 8

2 bottles of Guinness, chilled
1 bottle of champagne, chilled

1 Divide the Guinness between eight tall glasses.
2 Top with champagne and serve.

Banana Egg Nog

SERVES 2

1 ripe banana, broken into pieces
10 ml/2 tsp light brown sugar
1 egg
300 ml/½ pt/1¼ cups ice-cold milk
15 ml/1 tbsp brandy

1 Put the banana and sugar in a blender or food processor and run the machine until smooth.
2 Add the remaining ingredients and blend again until thick and frothy. Pour into two small glasses and serve.

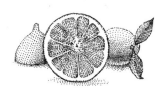

Blackcurrant and Orange Mull

SERVES 6

2 oranges
150 ml/¼ pt/⅔ cup blackcurrant
  cordial, undiluted
5 cm/2 in piece of cinnamon stick
1 bottle of German medium-dry white
  wine
150 ml/¼ pt/⅔ cup water

1 Cut all the rind off the oranges and place in a saucepan. Squeeze the juice and pour through a fine sieve (strainer) into the pan.
2 Add the remaining ingredients. Heat gently, stirring, until very hot but not boiling.
3 Remove the orange rind and cinnamon stick and serve in glass mugs or thick glasses.

The Bishop

SERVES 10

1 lemon
6 whole cloves
300 ml/½ pt/1¼ cups water
25 g/1 oz/2 tbsp light brown sugar
600 ml/1 pt/2½ cups ruby port

1 Cut the lemon in half and stud each half with 3 cloves. Place in a saucepan with the water and sugar. Heat gently, stirring, until the sugar dissolves, then cover and cook over a very low heat for 10 minutes.
2 Add the port and heat gently until almost boiling. Remove the lemon and cloves, pressing well against the sides of the pan with the back of a spoon to remove most of the juice.
3 Stir and serve in small glasses.

Warming Rum Mull

SERVES 6

1 orange
8 whole cloves
300 ml/½ pt/1¼ cups water
45 ml/3 tbsp light brown sugar
1 bottle of red wine
60 ml/4 tbsp dark rum

1 Stud the orange with the cloves and place in a large saucepan with the water and sugar.
2 Heat gently, stirring until the sugar dissolves. Cover and cook over a gentle heat for 5 minutes.
3 Add the wine and rum and continue to heat, stirring for 5 minutes but do not allow to boil.
4 Remove the orange and serve hot in small, thick glasses.

Dr Johnson's Choice

SERVES 8

1 orange, halved
4 whole cloves
1 bottle of red wine
60 ml/4 tbsp orange liqueur
300 ml/½ pt/1¼ cups water
40 g/1½ oz/3 tbsp granulated sugar
Freshly grated nutmeg

1 Stud the orange halves with the cloves. Put them in a large saucepan with all the remaining ingredients except the nutmeg.
2 Cook over a gentle heat until almost boiling, then turn down the heat as low as possible, and heat for 5 minutes.
3 Ladle into small glasses and sprinkle each with a little nutmeg.

Brandied Milk Punch

SERVES 4–6

600 ml/1 pt/2½ cups milk
45 ml/3 tbsp clear honey
30 ml/2 tbsp single (light) cream
30 ml/2 tbsp brandy
Freshly grated nutmeg

1 Put all the ingredients except the nutmeg in a saucepan and heat gently, stirring until almost boiling, when small bubbles are rising to the surface round the edge.
2 Add a good grating of nutmeg over the surface, stir and pour into small glasses.

Glühwein

SERVES 6

1 bottle of red wine
½ orange, sliced
½ lemon, sliced
1 whole clove
5 cm/2 in piece of cinnamon stick
30 ml/2 tbsp granulated sugar

1 Put all the ingredients in a saucepan and heat gently, stirring, until almost boiling.
2 Ladle the liquid into small mugs or thick glasses and serve.

Swedish Christmas Spirit

SERVES 12

300 ml/½ pt/1¼ cups aquavit or kirsch
1 bottle of red wine
50 g/2 oz/⅓ cup large stoned (pitted) raisins
40 g/1½ oz/3 tbsp light brown sugar
6 cardamom pods
2 whole cloves
5 cm/2 in piece of cinnamon stick
1 lemon, sliced

1 Put half the aquavit or kirsch in a saucepan with the remaining ingredients.
2 Heat gently, stirring, until almost boiling. Turn down the heat as low as possible and leave the mixture to heat for 20 minutes. Remove from the heat.
3 Pour the remaining aquavit or kirsch into a soup ladle. Ignite and pour into the pan. Stir until the flames subside, then spoon the liquid into small glasses and serve.

Gaelic Coffee

SERVES 4

20 ml/4 tsp light brown sugar
150 ml/¼ pt/⅔ cup Scotch whisky
450 ml/¾ pt/2 cups hot black coffee
150 ml/¼ pt/⅔ cup double (heavy)
    cream, chilled

1 Spoon the sugar into four wine goblets or glass mugs and add the whisky. Stir until dissolved.
2 Put a spoon in the glass, then pour on the hot coffee. Stir again.
3 Hold a cold teaspoon, rounded side up, over the top of the coffee, almost touching the surface, and slowly pour the cream over the back of the spoon, so that it floats in a layer on top of the coffee.

Calypso Coffee

SERVES 4

Prepare as for Gaelic Coffee but use dark rum instead of Scotch whisky.

Caribbean Coffee

SERVES 4

Prepare as for Gaelic Coffee but use white rum instead of Scotch whisky.

French Coffee

SERVES 4

Prepare as for Gaelic Coffee but use cognac instead of Scotch whisky.

Irish Coffee

SERVES 4

Prepare as for Gaelic Coffee but use Irish whisky instead of Scotch.

Italian Coffee

SERVES 4

Prepare as for Gaelic Coffee but use Amaretto instead of whisky.

Mocha Liqueur Coffee

SERVES 4

Prepare as for Gaelic Coffee but use chocolate liqueur instead of Scotch whisky.

Russian Coffee

SERVES 4

Prepare as for Gaelic Coffee but use vodka instead of Scotch whisky.

Non-alcoholic Drinks

Caribbean Pineapple Pleasure

SERVES 6–8

250 g/9 oz/1 medium can of crushed
  pineapple
300 ml/½ pt/1¼ cups apple juice
300 ml/½ pt/1¼ cups pure orange juice
300 ml/½ pt/1¼ cups canned coconut
  milk
30 ml/2 tbsp lemon juice
Ice cubes
300 ml/½ pt/1¼ cups sparkling mineral
  water
150 ml/¼ pt/⅔ cup double (heavy)
  cream

1 Mix the pineapple, apple juice, orange
juice, coconut and lemon juice together
and chill.
2 Fill tumblers with ice cubes. Mix the
mineral water into the juices and pour
over the ice.
3 Float a little cream on top of each
and put a straw in each.

Dawning Day

SERVES 2

Cracked ice
250 ml/8 fl oz pure orange juice
60 ml/4 tbsp grenadine syrup

1 Fill two tall glasses with cracked ice
and add the orange juice.
2 Hold a spoon over the top and
gently pour on the grenadine. Do not
mix.

Summer Refresher

SERVES 6

225 g/8 oz raspberries
2 peaches, stoned (pitted) and
  quartered
300 ml/½ pt/1¼ cups pure orange juice
Juice of 1 lime
Crushed ice
600 ml/1 pt/2½ cups traditional
  lemonade

1 Put the raspberries, peaches, orange
and lime juices in a blender or food
processor and run the machine until
smooth.
2 Tip the purée in a sieve (strainer)
over a bowl and rub the mixture
through with a wooden spoon to
remove the seeds and skins.
3 Fill six glasses with crushed ice. Add
the purée. Top with lemonade and stir
before serving.

Quick Tropical Sparkler

SERVES 10–12

1 litre/1¾ pts/4¼ cups tropical fruit juice
  drink
150 ml/¼ pt/⅔ cup lime juice cordial
60 ml/4 tbsp lemon juice
1 litre/1¾ pts/4¼ cups sparkling bitter
  lemon
Ice cubes
Maraschino cherries

1 Mix the tropical juice drink with the
lime juice cordial and lemon juice. Chill.
2 When ready to serve, add the bitter
lemon. Pour over ice cubes in tall
glasses and add a Maraschino cherry to
each glass.

441

Iced Orange Cream

SERVES 2

300 ml/½ pt/1¼ cups pure orange juice
A pinch of ground cinnamon
5 ml/1 tsp lemon juice
4 scoops of vanilla ice cream
4 ice cubes

1 Put the ingredients in a blender or food processor and run the machine until smooth and frothy.
2 Put 2 ice cubes in each tumbler and pour the orange cream over. Serve straight away.

Apricot Ambrosia

SERVES 4

375 ml/13 fl oz/1½ cups apricot nectar
15 ml/1 tbsp icing (confectioners') sugar
300 ml/½ pt/1¼ cups ice-cold milk
4 scoops of vanilla ice cream
8 ice cubes
600 ml/1 pt/2½ cups American dry
   ginger ale

1 Put all the ingredients except the ginger ale in a blender or food processor and run the machine until frothy and smooth.
2 Put two ice cubes in each tall glass and pour the thick apricot mixture over. Top up with ginger ale and stir well before serving.

Spiced Peach Soda

SERVES 4

Prepare as for Apricot Ambrosia but use peach nectar instead of apricot and add 1.5 ml/¼ tsp mixed (apple-pie) spice to the mixture.

Fresh Banana Milkshake

SERVES 1

1 large ripe banana, broken into pieces
5 ml/1 tsp clear honey
250 ml/8 fl oz/1 cup ice-cold milk

1 Put the ingredients in a blender or food processor and run the machine until smooth, thick and frothy.
2 Pour into a tall glass and serve.

Chocolate Caramel Velvet

SERVES 2–3

1 chocolate caramel bar
15 ml/1 tbsp light brown sugar
600 ml/1 pt/2½ cups milk
150 ml/¼ pt/⅔ cup double (heavy)
   cream, chilled

1 Break up the caramel bar in a saucepan and add the sugar and milk.
2 Cook over a gentle heat, stirring all the time, until the bar and sugar have melted. Bring almost to the boil, just until bubbling gently round the edges.
3 Pour into mugs. Hold a spoon, rounded side up, over the top and carefully pour a little chilled double cream over the surface of each. Drink through the cream.

Chocolate Pear Soda

SERVES 4

410 g/14 oz/1 large can of pear quarters
300 ml/½ pt/1¼ cups apple juice
30 ml/2 tbsp drinking (sweetened)
   chocolate powder
4 scoops of chocolate ice cream
8 ice cubes
300 ml/½ pt/1¼ cups cream soda

1 Put the pears and their juice, the apple juice and chocolate powder in a blender or food processor and run the machine until smooth.
2 Add the ice cream and run the machine until smooth and frothy.
3 Put the ice cubes in glasses. Pour over the pear mixture and top up with cream soda. Stir again and serve.

Strawberry Yoghurt Cooler

SERVES 4

225 g/8 oz strawberries
300 ml/½ pt/1¼ cups strawberry
   yoghurt
300 ml/½ pt/1¼ cups ice-cold milk
15 ml/1 tbsp clear honey
Finely grated rind and juice of ½ lime
Crushed ice

1 Put the strawberries and yoghurt in a blender or food processor and run the machine until smooth, gradually adding the milk.
2 Add the honey and lime rind and juice and blend again.
3 Fill four tall glasses with crushed ice. Pour in the strawberry mixture and serve.

Brazilian Bedtime Mocha

For those with a very sweet tooth, add 15 ml/1 tbsp caster (superfine) sugar with the coffee.

SERVES 4

100 g/4 oz/1 cup plain (semi-sweet)
   chocolate, chopped
150 ml/¼ pt/⅔ cup strong black coffee
600 ml/1 pt/2½ cups milk

1 Put the chocolate and coffee in a saucepan and cook over a moderate heat, stirring all the time until the chocolate melts.
2 Whisk in the milk with a balloon whisk and continue to heat, whisking all the time until almost boiling and frothy.
3 Pour into mugs and serve.

Index